Beyond the Canyon

Beyond the Canyon

Inside Epic California Homes

Roger Davies

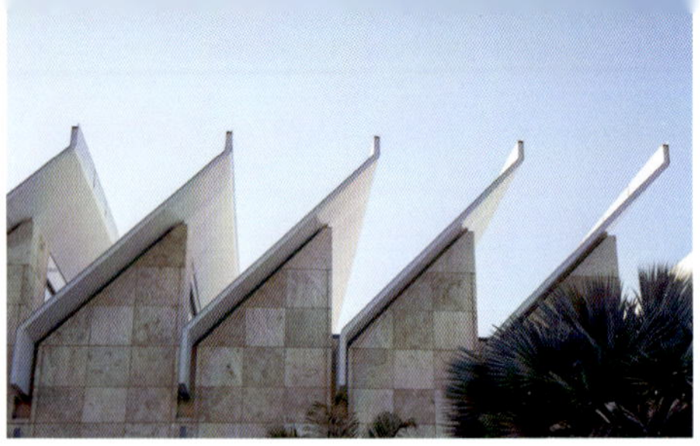

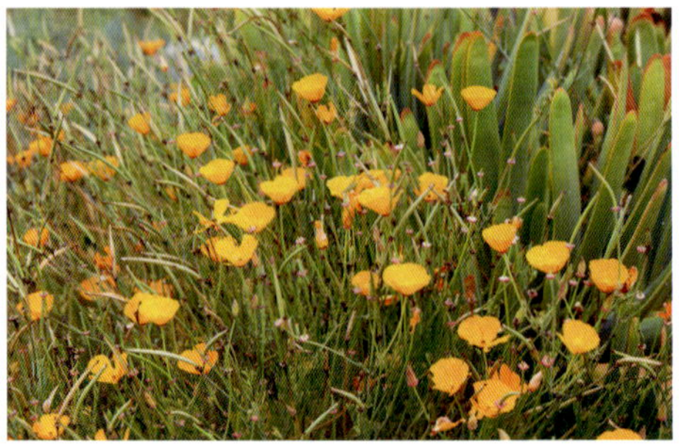

Foreword

Drew Barrymore

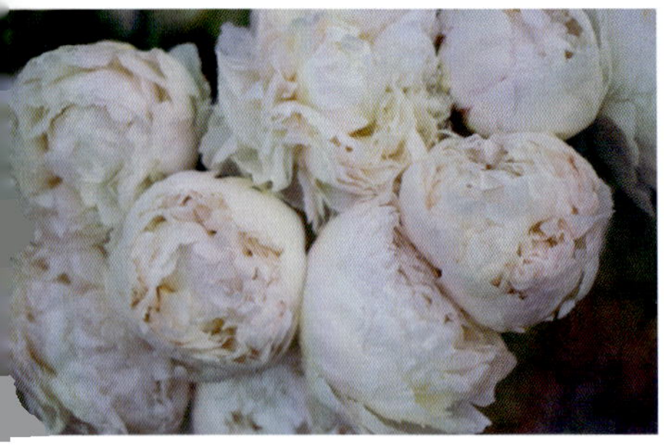

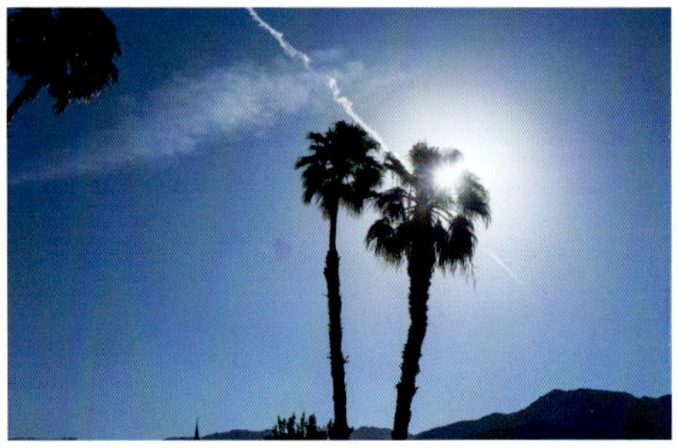

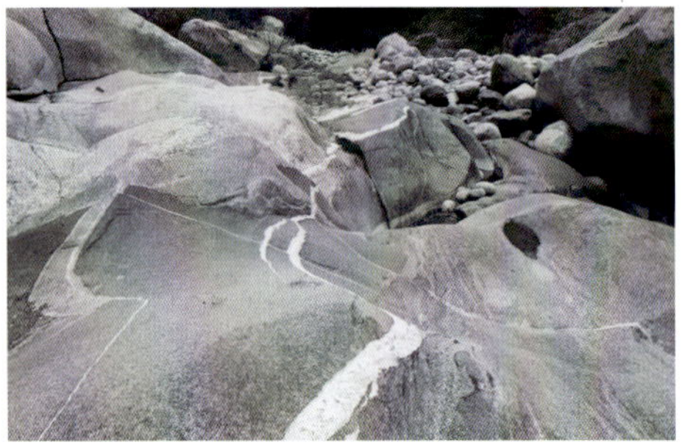

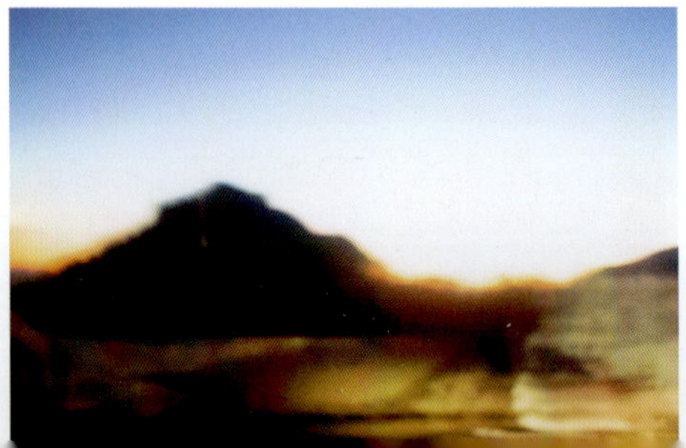

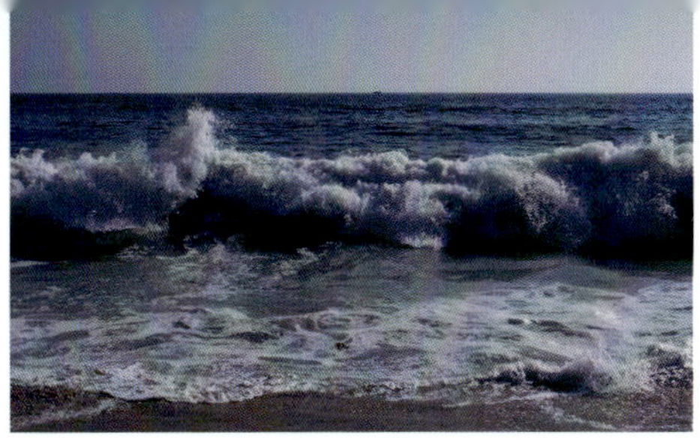

There's really nothing Roger Davies cannot do with a camera. His lens takes us into a hybrid of reality and fantasy in these extraordinary homes, details, and curiosities. Through his eyes we see everything from grand exteriors to intimate interior moments, and every little corner in between.

Roger's photography transports us to fairy-tale spaces and at the same time reveals the remarkable work and creativity of others—his unselfish way of bringing architect, decorator, and homeowner together while luring the viewer. He embodies artistry and generously shares his work with us to marvel at. I believe he is the masterful conduit. (I also think that he is a kind and lovely human being who, you realize from the moment you meet him, has a wonderful energy.)

Roger pays compliment to his subjects by showing them at their very best and at their most intimate, and the skill to be able to achieve both is so rare. When Roger shoots people, they look like who they are in the best way possible; I feel like the greatest version of myself when I'm in his hands. Likewise, when he shoots homes, they become portraits of their inhabitants.

One of my favorite activities in life is to pore over every captured moment of architecture and decor so that I may keep learning what is possible and see what someone else did that I would never have thought of: a window treatment, an unexpected paint color, an ingenious gathering of collectibles, a perfectly composed salon art wall, a sparse kitchen that makes me wish I could be a minimalist. Thanks to Roger, these images last in your mind. After looking at them, you feel like you have been gifted the opportunity to be transported by, and even live inside, these moments long after your eyes have left the page.

I love what Roger brings to the world.

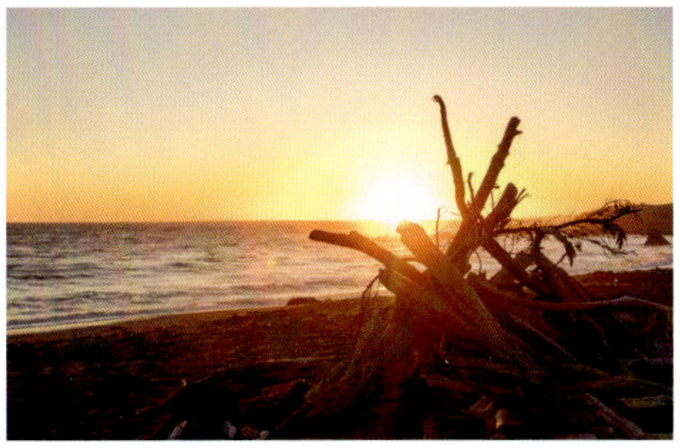

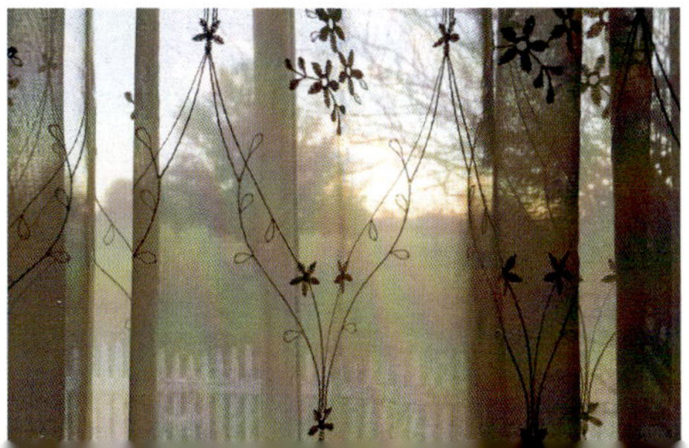

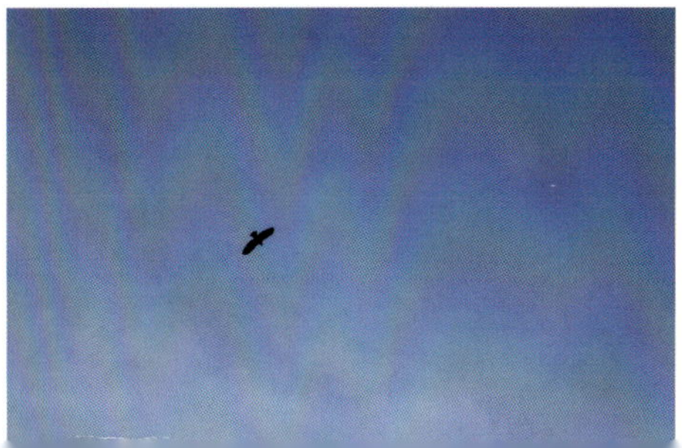

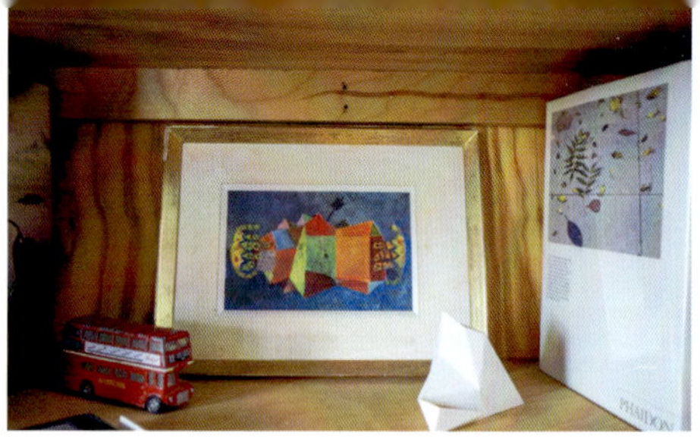

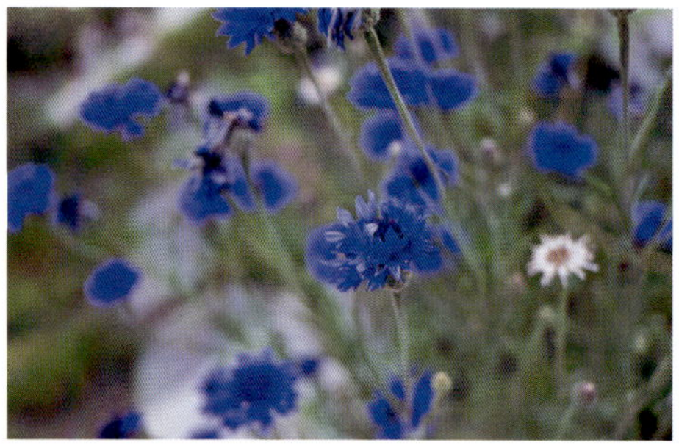

Introduction

Roger Davies

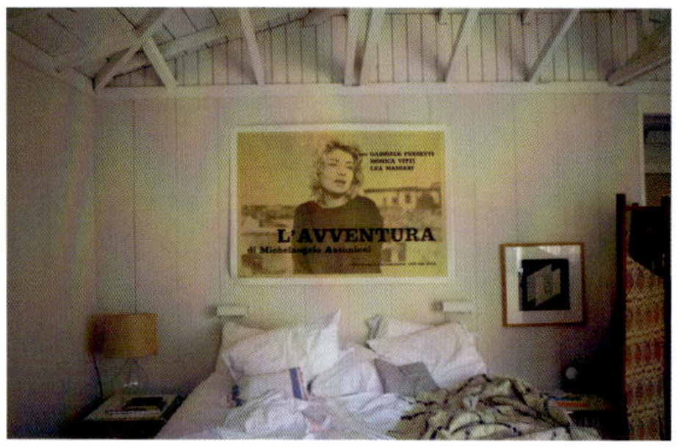

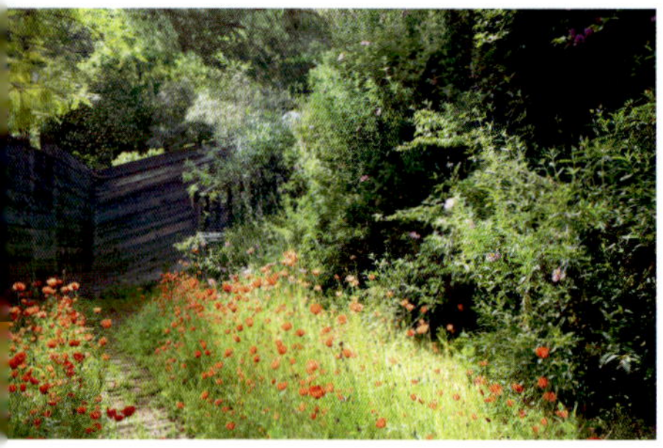

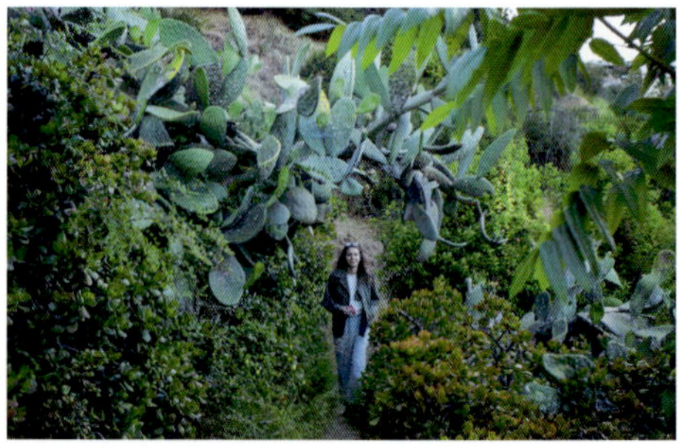

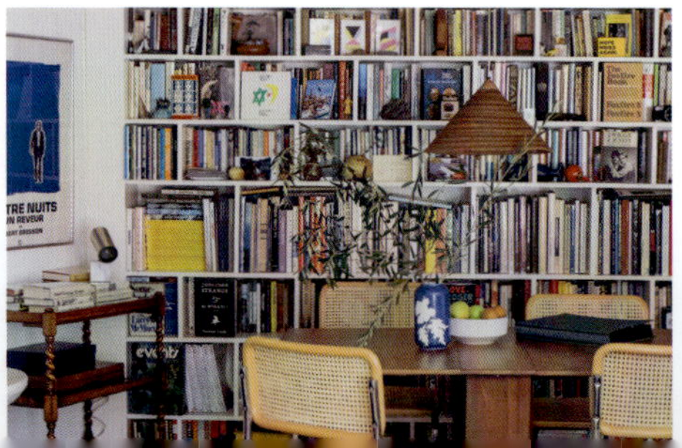

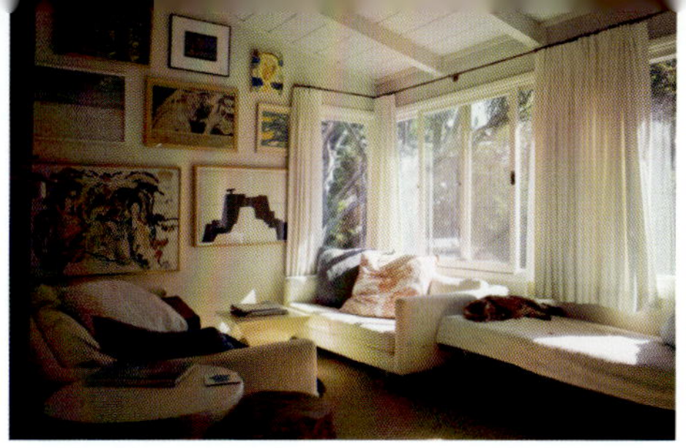

In a land of earthquakes, fires, and mudslides, it's dangerous to fall in love with a house, but houses can cast a spell on you. This is California, and of course there are surfers and sunsets and sports cars, but there is also a concentration of raw creative ambition and a passion for design unlike anywhere else. The homes in this book were created by artists of all kinds striving to push the limits, to live in extremes—of both architecture and landscape—and to experiment with ways of living in search of an idyll.

Long before I had found my own personal paradise in Laurel Canyon—this sleepy, creative community in the hills of Hollywood known for the music folklore of its hippie heyday—like many others, I had come from colder, grayer climes. In a quiet village in beautiful Derbyshire, England, in the washhouse of our family home, my dad taught my brother and me how to develop and print black-and-white photographs. Dad spent his life working for British Rail, but somehow he had always had this skill. My mum was also used to developing film, from the X-rays she produced as a radiographer at the hospital. The chemicals from the developer, stop, and fixer gently perfumed our clothes for years, and my brother and I both went on to become photographers.

A little while later, in 1992, I was in the United States. Fresh out of college, I walked the streets of New York, just a few days after arriving, looking for a job without much success. Finding myself lost, I asked a stylish young woman for directions to the East Village, and it happened to be the same way she was walking. After a couple of blocks of chitchat, I told her I was a photographer. "Are you any good?" she asked, and proceeded to change my life. I had caught a lucky break: I was talking to an editor at *Interview* magazine. It was through the kindness of this complete stranger that I was introduced to the photography world in America.

What ensued were years on the road photographing other people's lives, before finally making a California home of my own with my wife and son in a wobbly 1928 hunter's cabin in Laurel Canyon, our improbable city neighbors the hummingbirds, coyotes, and deer. It's from here that I leave before

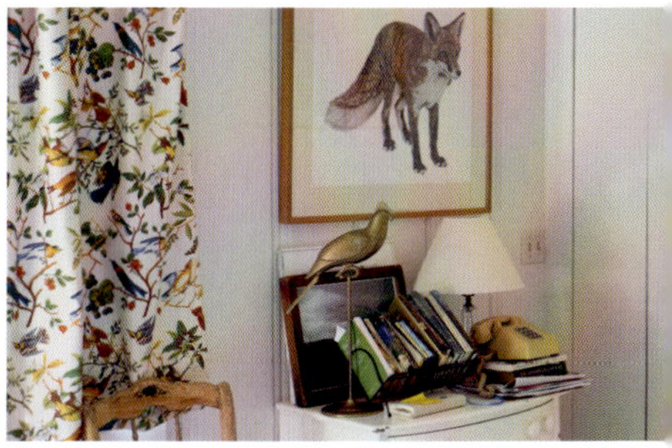

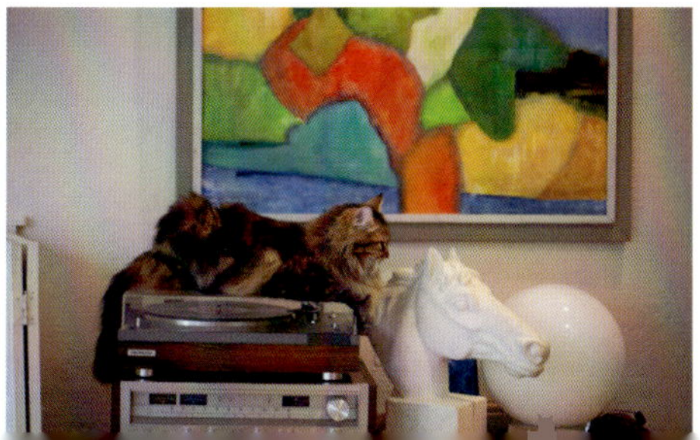

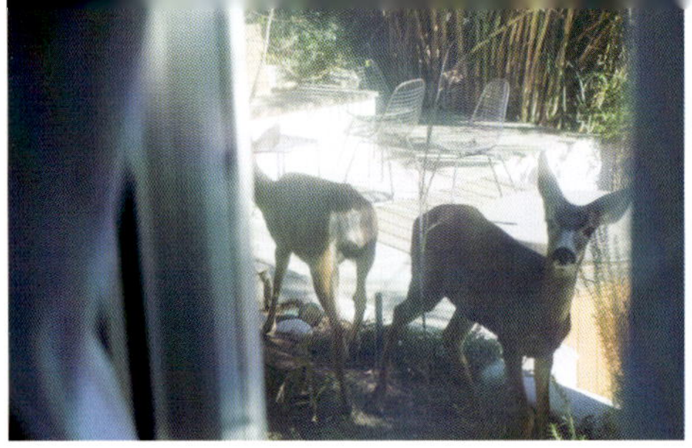

dawn and return in the dark. But the images that I shoot on the journey to and from the assignments are as much a part of me as the commissioned images ; the desire to take pictures is inherent in every photographer. (The snapshots that open and close this book were all taken in California, which I never grow tired of photographing, in Big Sur, Laguna Beach, Three Rivers, Malibu, and, of course, where it all starts and ends: my little cabin in the Canyon.)

Over time the rhythms of the Golden State have become familiar, closely recorded through my camera. I've learned how to anticipate whether the ocean's morning marine layer will burn off; how to account for May Gray and June Gloom; that the best light in the harsh Palm Desert arrives, as if by the flick of a switch, just after the sun falls behind the mountains, and the gorgeous glow of the dusk lasts forever; and that the winds on the cliffs above Santa Barbara will whisk a drone right into the Pacific. Though it's fair to say that the weather near the Golden Gate Bridge is a mystery to all.

For photographers in any line of work, the focus is the conscious act of looking, as opposed to the unconscious act of seeing. We search for angles and vistas and sunlight. Arriving at a house for the first time, we may delight in things that the person living there no longer sees. As one of my heroes of photography, Robert Frank, once said, "I'm a hunter; I hunt for pictures. I'm not a verbal man. I have nothing to reveal. It's all in the work, I hope." Well, unfortunately I'm no Robert Frank, so here's how a typical shoot day goes for me.

It all starts with the homeowner, who has invited us into their private world, knowing it will soon become public. When I show up on set, all the heavy lifting has been done, sometimes years and years of collaborations between homeowners, architects, interior designers, and landscape architects. I've shot monthlong projects in China and one-day jobs in Uruguay, and while the fundamentals of every photo shoot are the same, each house has its secrets to unlock. The interior designer has already shaped the space, but I work with a crew to make the images of that space as good as they can be:

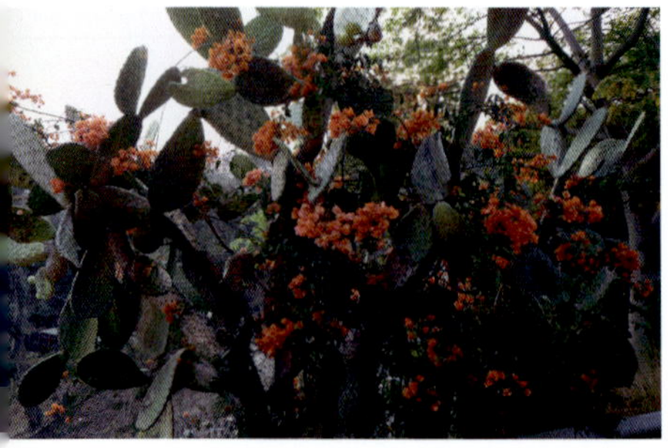

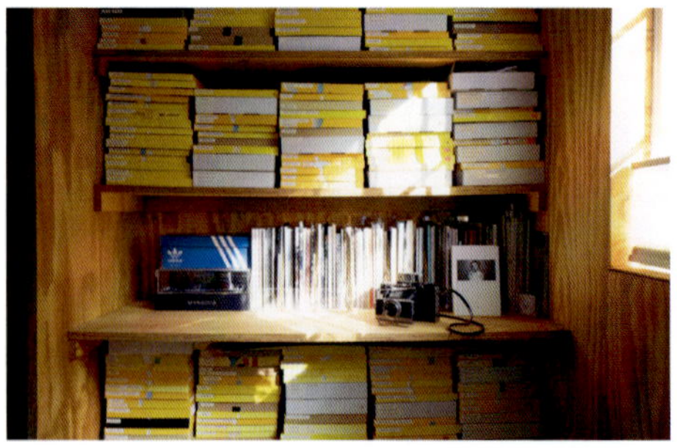

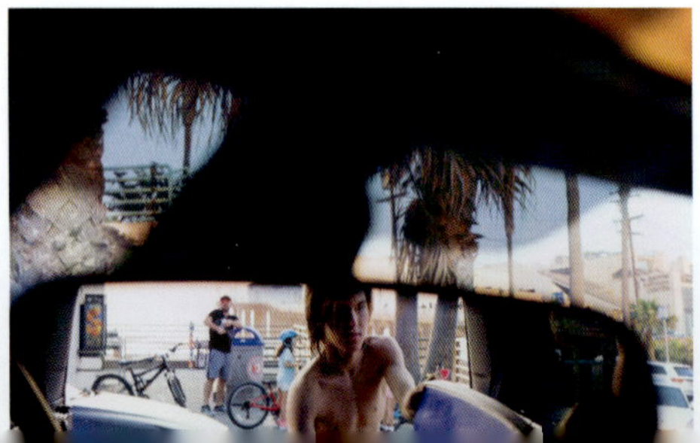

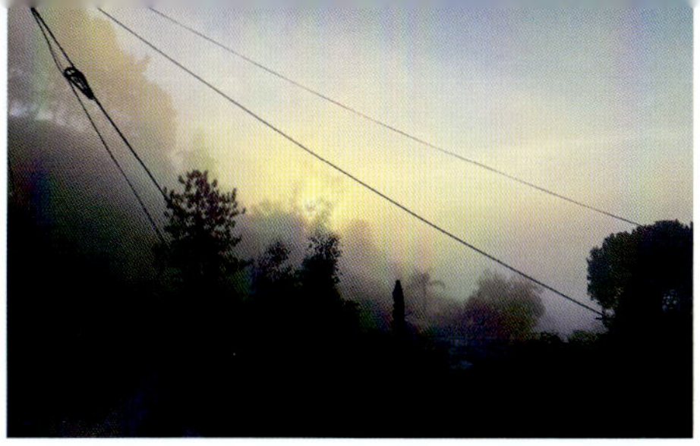

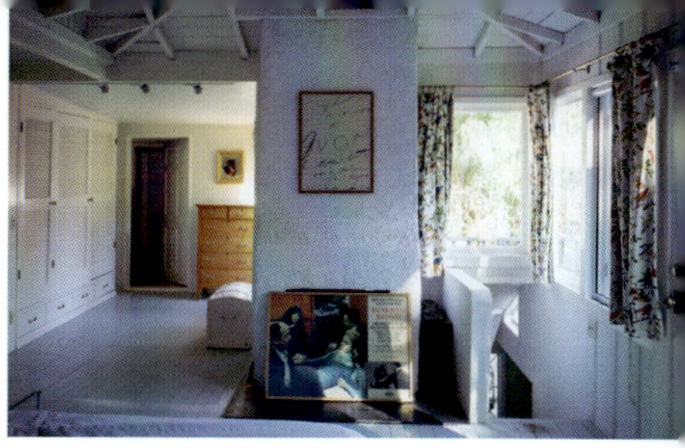

editors, prop stylists, digital techs, assistants, drone pilots, lighting gurus, and retouchers. Every photograph is the result of teamwork, and while those teams may change from day to day, nothing is ever achieved alone.

I take any number of test shots, checking the lighting and styling and more. When everything is just right, I put my hand in front of the camera and snap a picture. My palm on the monitor can draw nervous looks and plenty of side-eye, but this is my marker for the editing stage, a quirk that tells me in a week or a year, *This is where the good ones start.*

Of course, everyone's best-laid plans don't always go smoothly. I've lost camera bags in Marrakech, gotten paint on my clothes in a house in Bel Air after the homeowners had it repainted through the night, and shot a house at the height of the wildfires and never been able to successfully color-correct out the orange hue from the images. I've been asked to "clean" the pool and "cut" the hedges in Photoshop, and struggled with the tripod while on crutches after a skiing accident. Once, an assistant disappeared into the world of Zurich's nightlife, narrowly making the flight home. Another time a shoot was canceled after an all-night row between the husband and the wife, with the end result being that if we stepped over the threshold, a divorce would ensue. And once, a homeowner's pit bull took a dislike to me and bit me in the arse—thank tetanus for thick APC denim jeans.

Sometimes the technology of a house can slow you down. The button to open the cover on the Olympic-size swimming pool can't be found; it's probably in the same place as the remote for the motorized window shades. The TV controller turns out to be more complicated than a NASA launch station, and the fireplace is gas or maybe electric or the flue can't be opened.

Even after more than twenty years as a working photographer, things never get dull. I see all sorts of things—pictures with presidents, any number of Oscars (and even an EGOT), and once, sex toys left out in the bedroom. Art on opposing sides of a toilet door: a Frank Stella on one side and a de Kooning

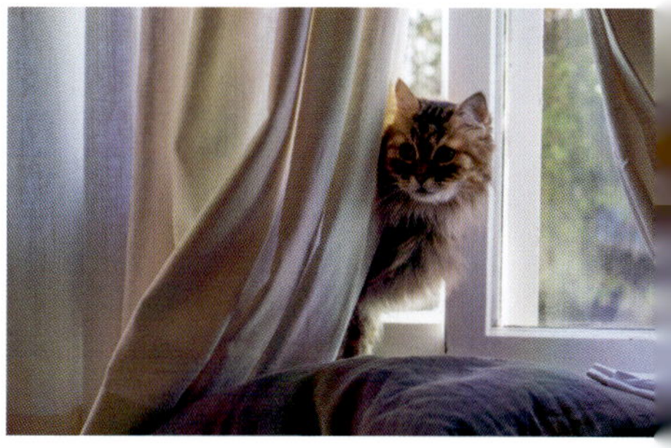

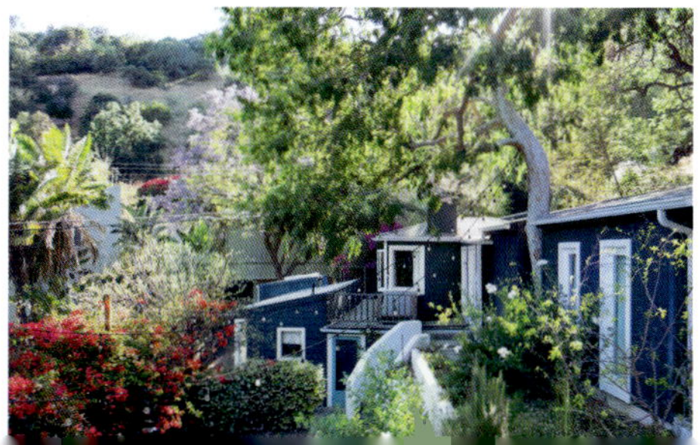

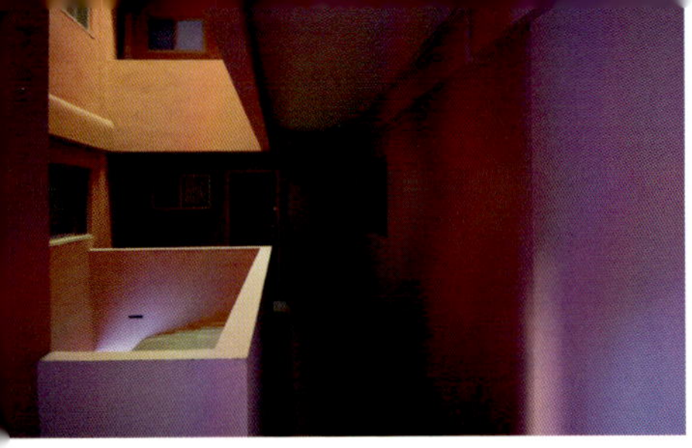

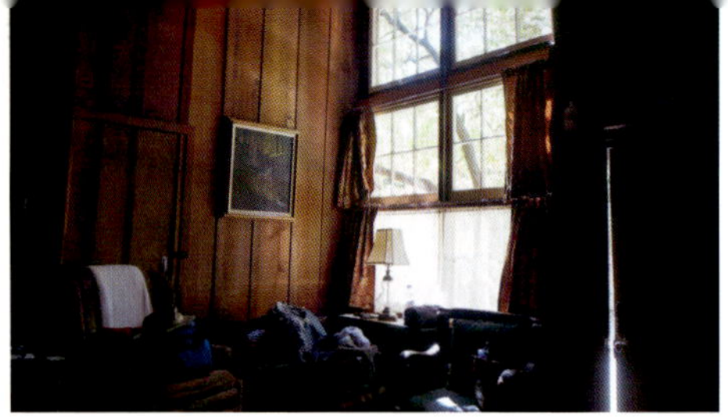

on the other. I've seen ex-Navy SEALs who are now private security guards suddenly emerge from the bushes. I've seen the Maltese Falcon, sniper rifles, live rattlesnakes, dinosaur skulls, doomsday bunkers, and safe rooms but never enough cats—no one ever has cats. I've seen bulletproof cars, a Second World War Nazi Enigma cypher machine, and a steel briefcase with foam lining cradling a 1976 BASF cassette tape containing the original Apple operating system, with the handwritten inscription, "Good Luck."

When I photograph homes in California, more than anywhere else, every day is different, and no two houses are alike. A midcentury modern might be nestled next to a Craftsman's bungalow, a Spanish colonial, or a Tuscarranean (my wife's name for the unfortunate hybrid that pops up far too often). You see homes that are loved, homes with history, passion projects, and follies, often in extremes. There are houses suspended on stilts and tranquil wooden masterpieces nestled into the hillsides, expansive glass windows cut into rock, columns of Mayan Revival carvings—designs that embrace very specific landscapes, microclimates, and lifestyles. Often architecture, interior design, sculpture, art, and environment merge in different ways, and the dreamy California weather blurs the boundary between inside and out even further. I'm in awe of the design-loving addicts whose devotion to interiors and architecture has led to them living in—and serving as custodians of—these masterpieces.

My job is to document a brief moment in the life of a home. In time the houses will evolve into something different from what they were in the instant I caught them. They will be redecorated and relandscaped, Grandma's knickknacks will move in, and the teenager will paint their room black. They will be sold, torn down, and, as in the case of one house in this book, lost to a wildfire, but for the blink of an eye that I get to spend in these astonishing homes, they are glorious.

So this is where the good ones start.

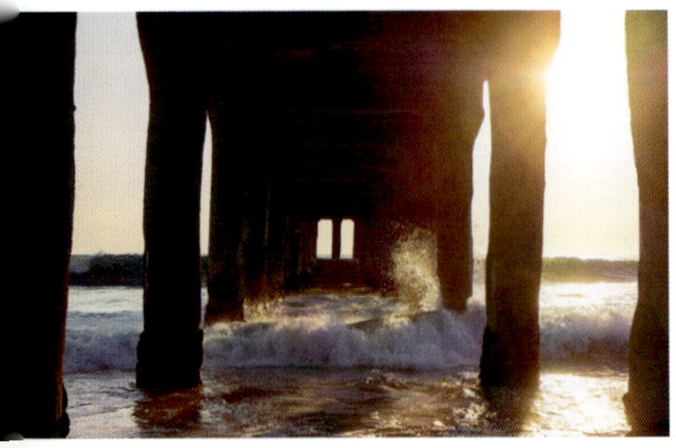

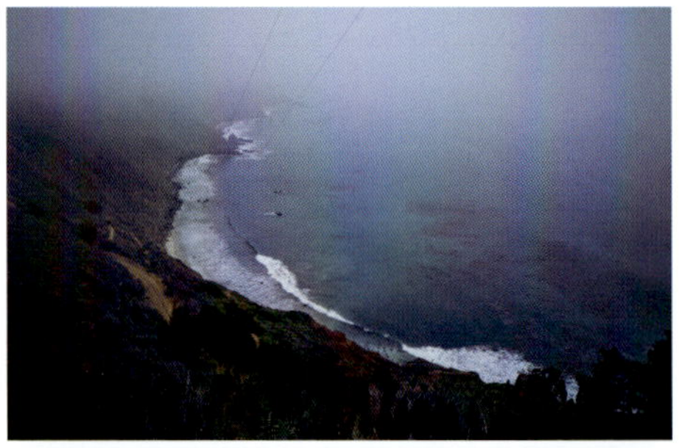

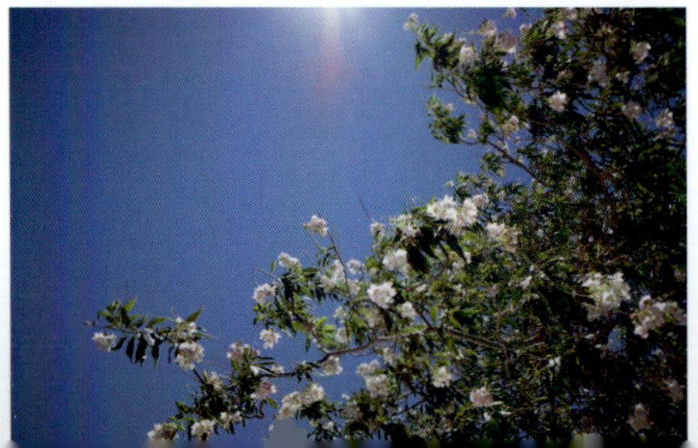

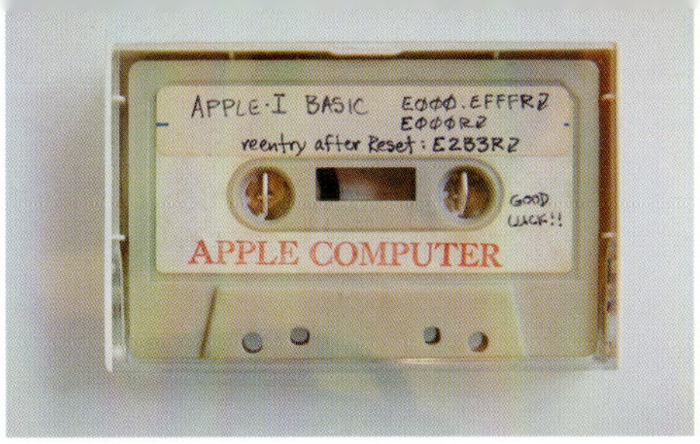
APPLE-I BASIC
reentry after Reset: E2B3R
GOOD LUCK!!
APPLE COMPUTER

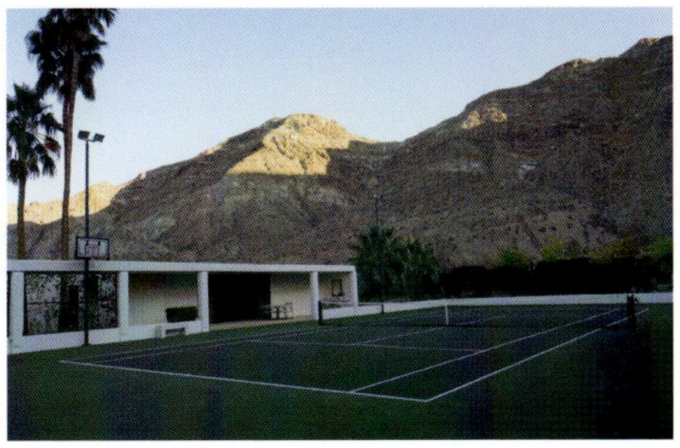

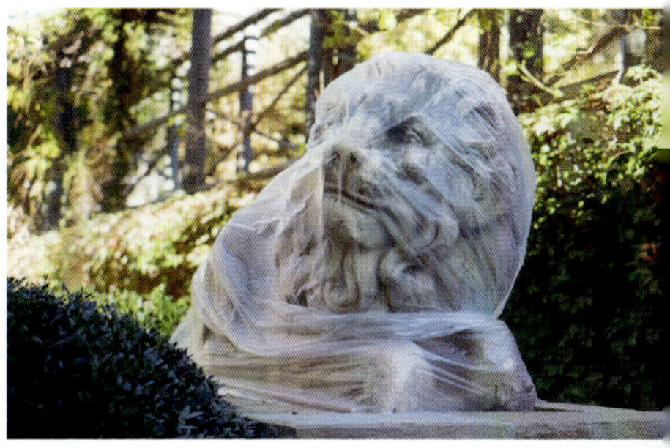

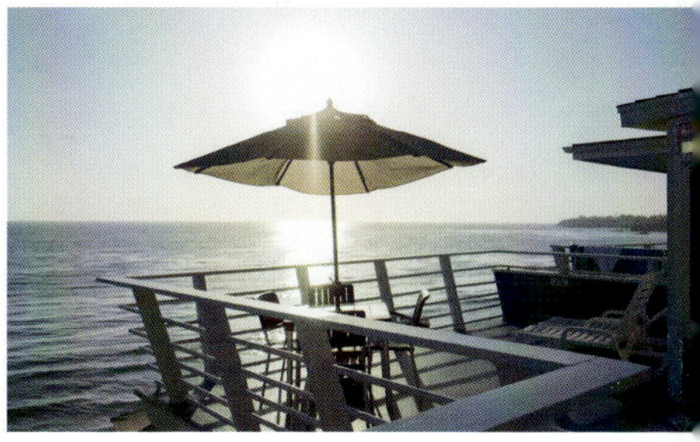

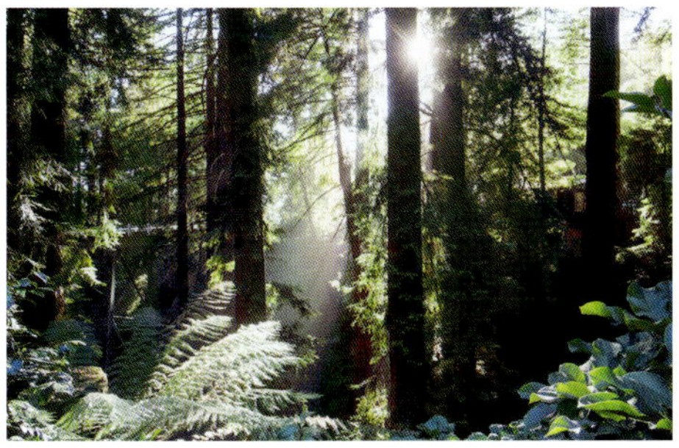

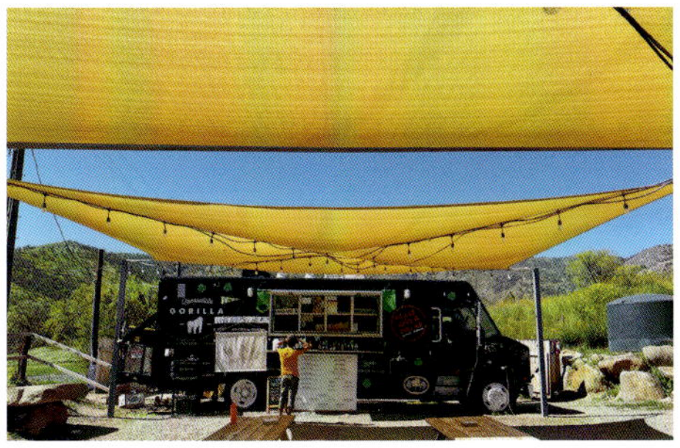

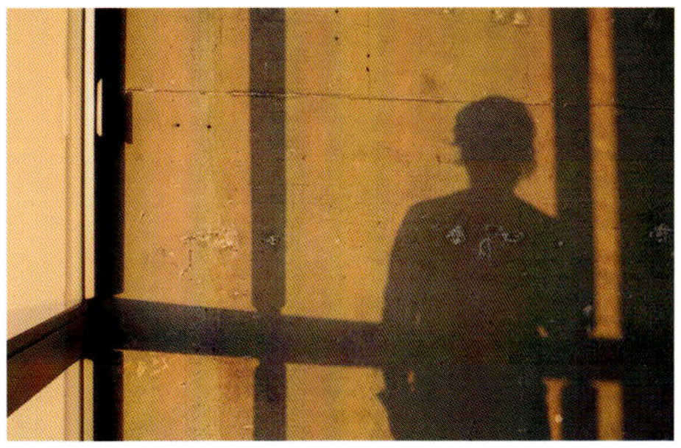

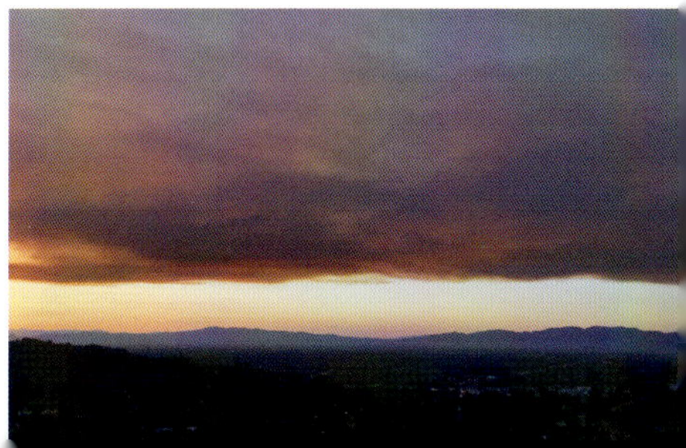

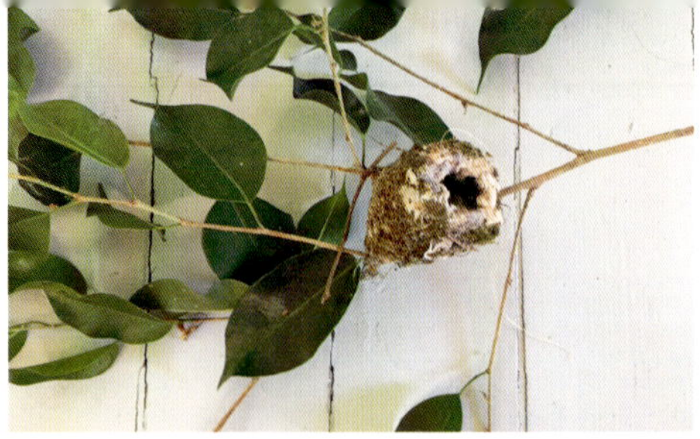

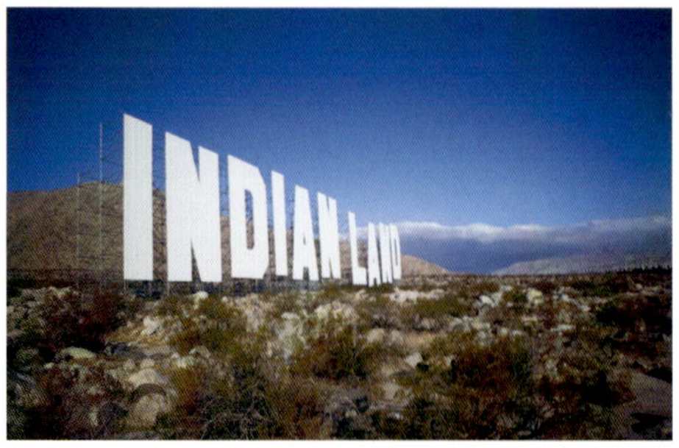
INDIAN LAND

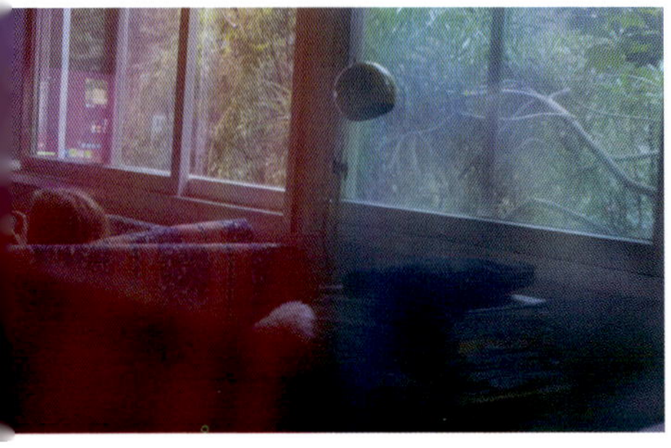

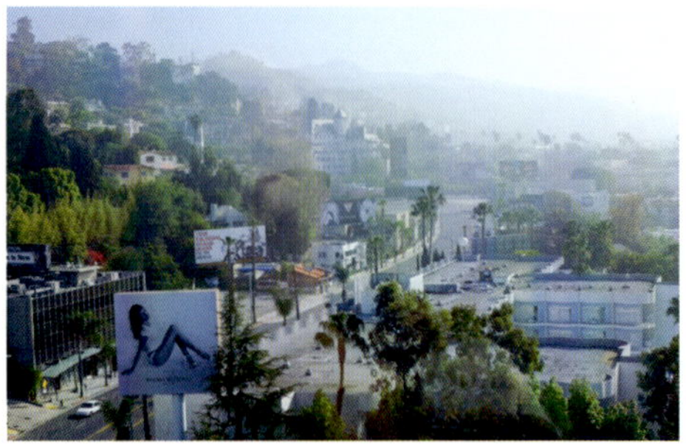

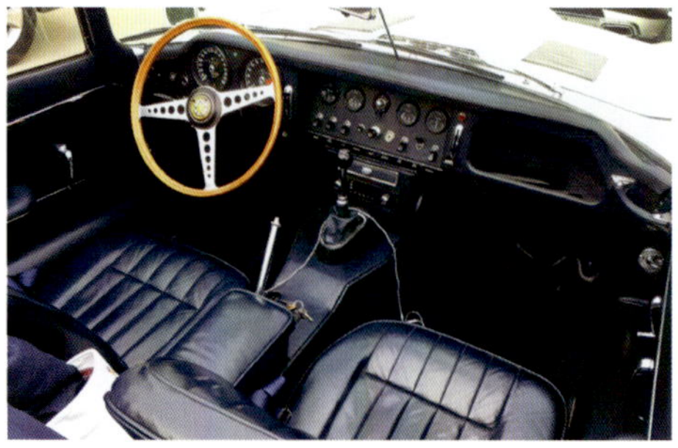

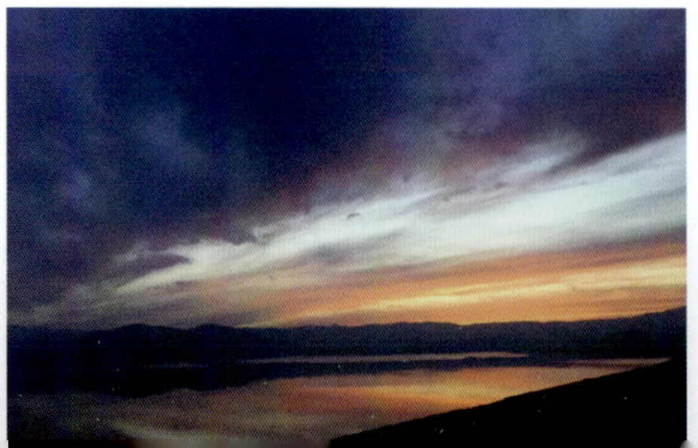

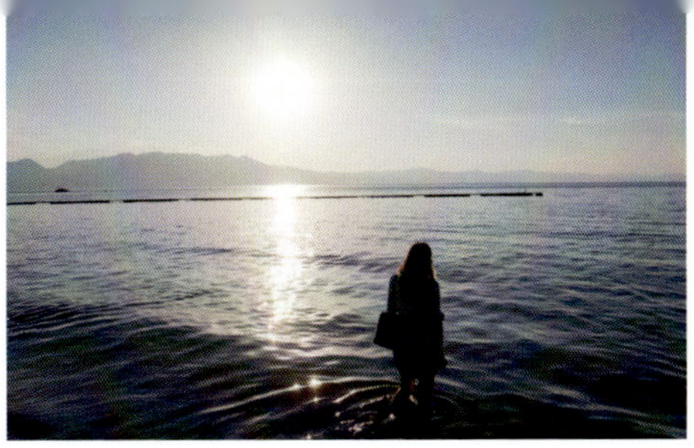

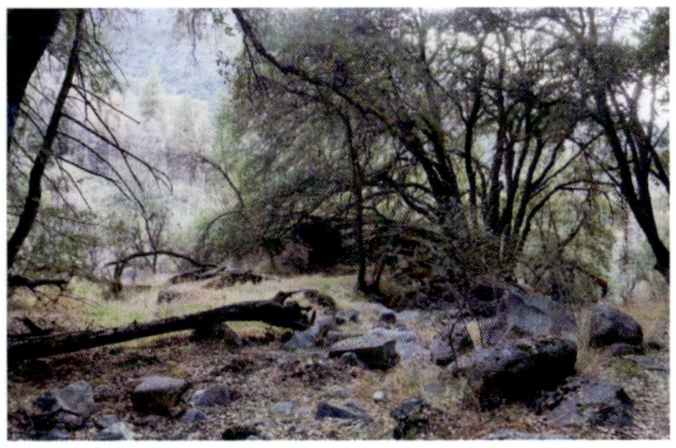

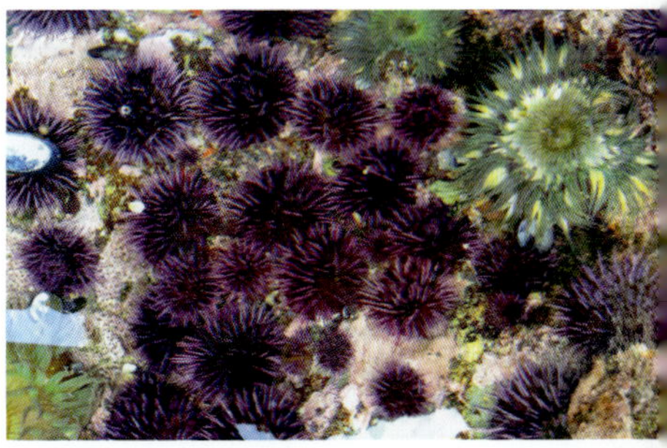

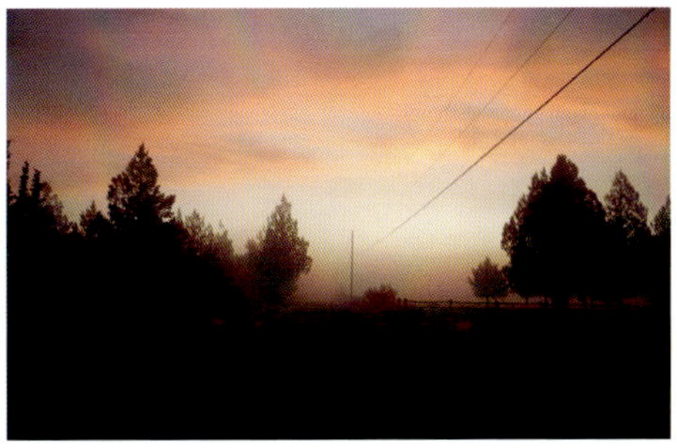

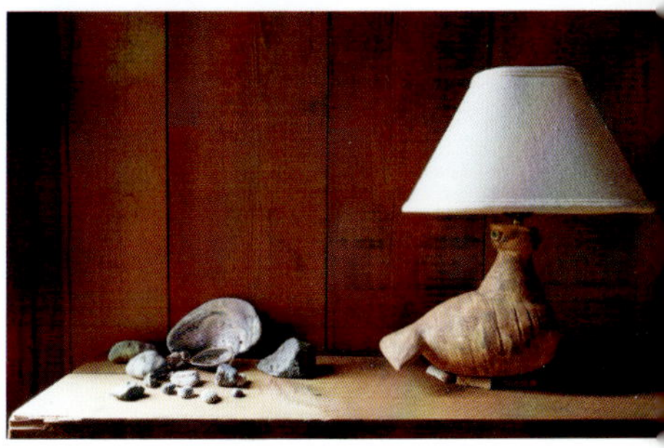

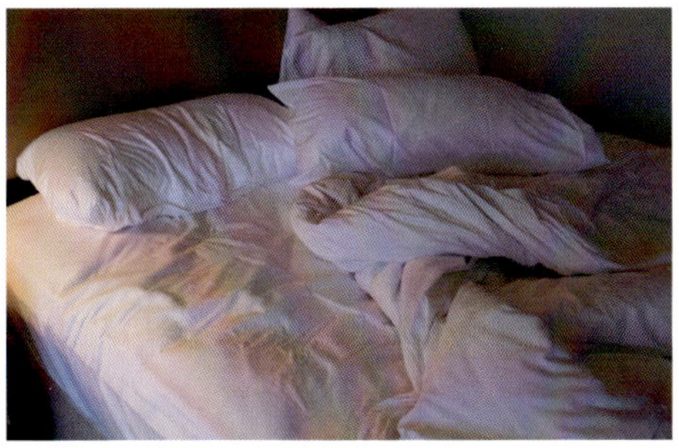

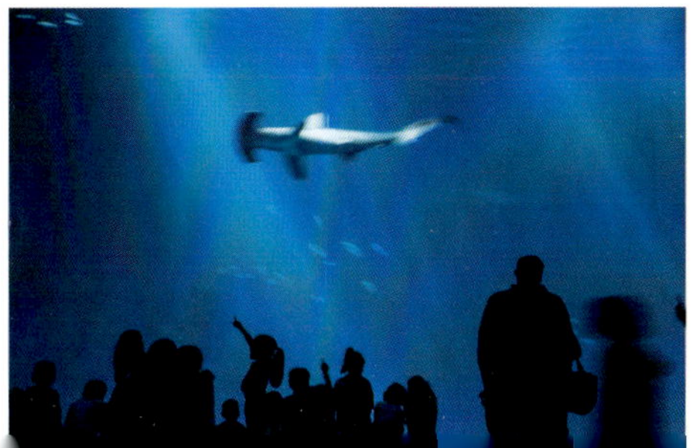

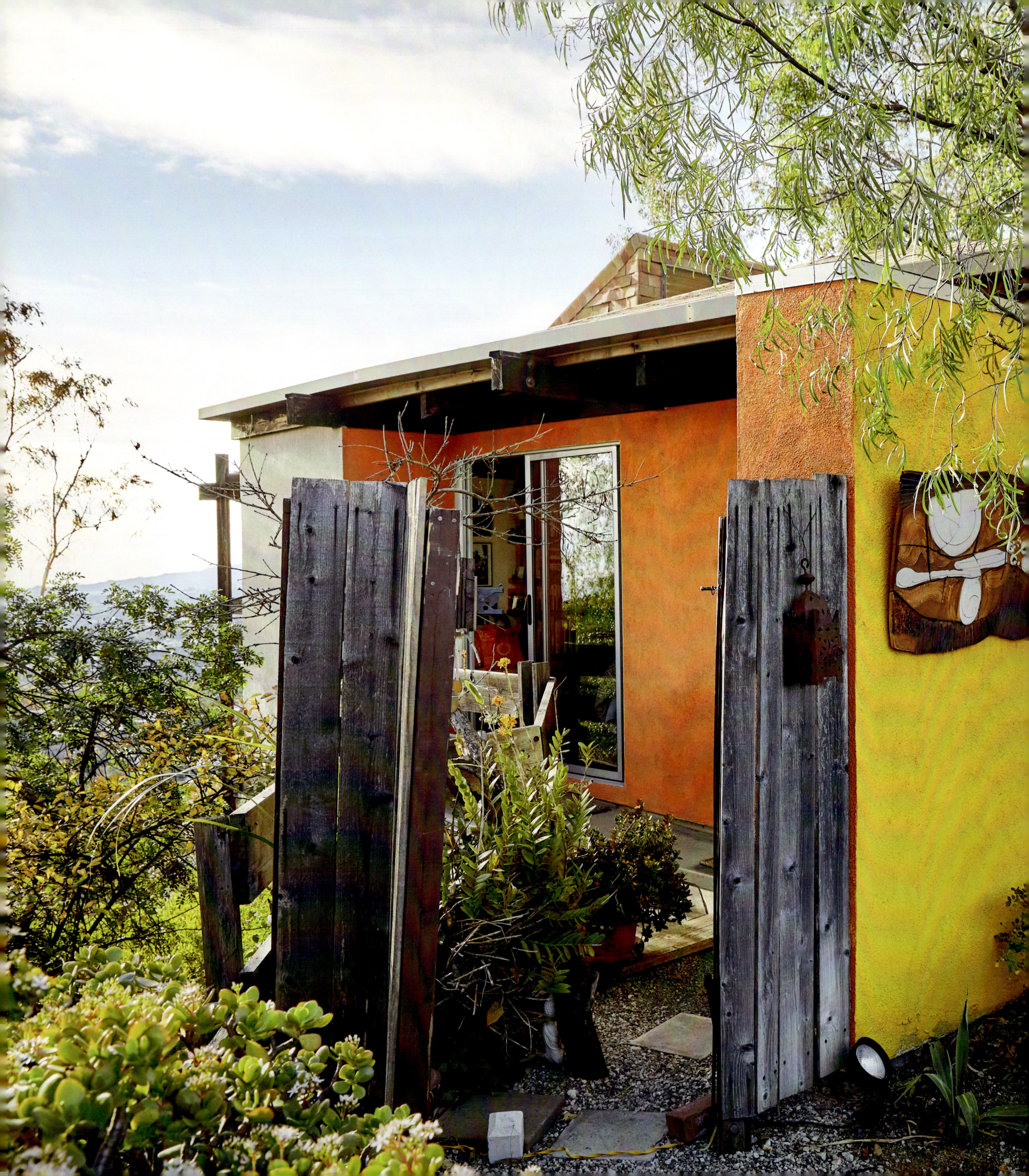

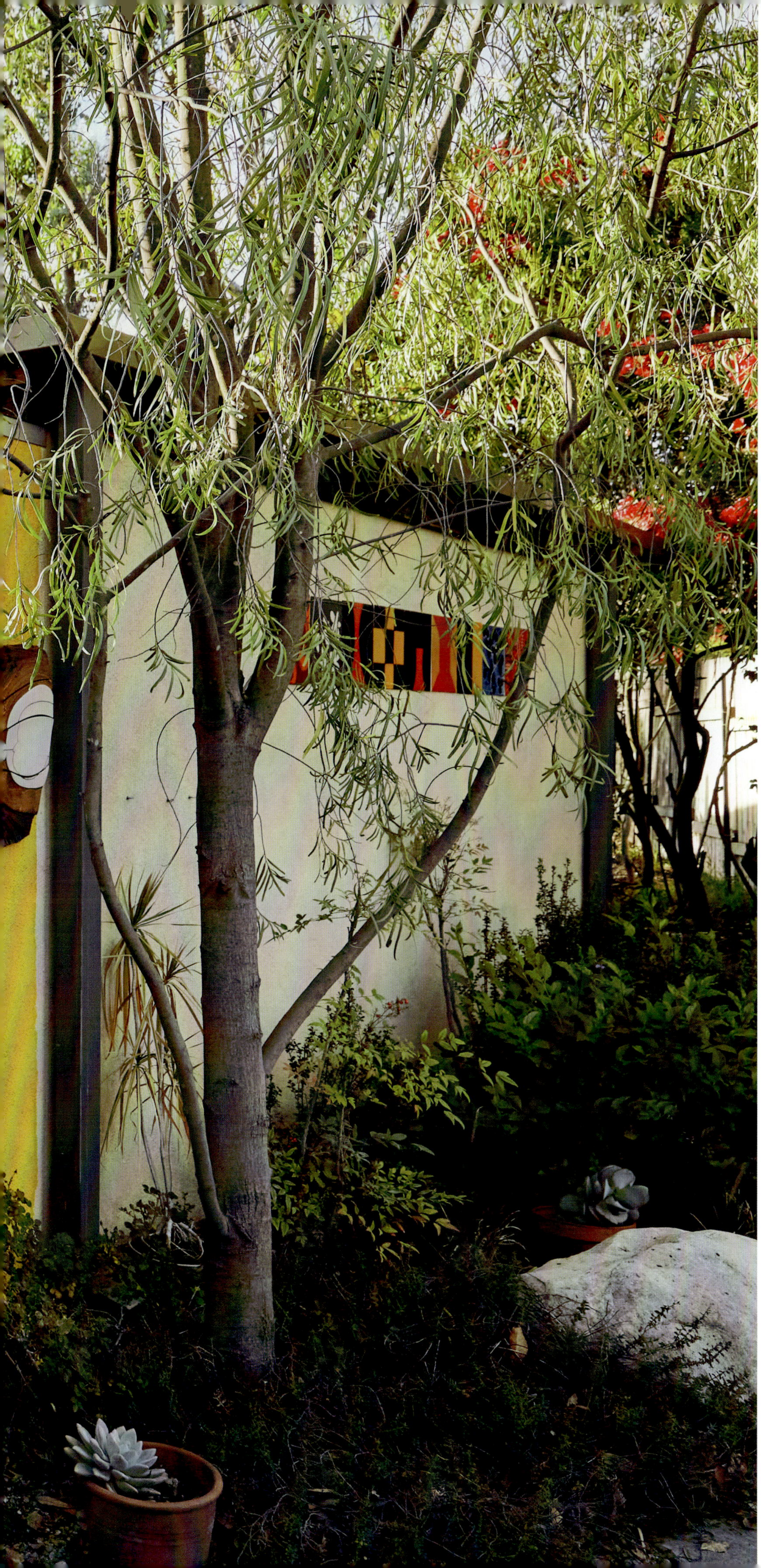

The Tree House
Laurel Canyon

Architect
Bernard Judge

Residents
Bernard Judge and Blaine Mallory

Had you known Bernard Judge—the globe-trotting experimental architect—he would likely have been the most interesting person you had ever met. Judge told stories with quiet humility but a dangerous twinkle in his eyes—stories of a life well lived.

Judge served in a mobile construction battalion in the U.S. Navy for four years after high school and then lived in Paris for a year, studying architecture at the École des Beaux-Arts. He then returned to the States to finish his architectural studies at the University of Southern California. Judge's daring architectural inclinations were evident from the beginning. In 1959, while still at USC, he began construction on his first project, the Triponent House, a dwelling within a fifty-foot-diameter geodesic dome that he had received from a friend, a former student of Buckminster Fuller. Not only was the dome the largest ever erected at the time, but it was embedded in a steeply inclined hillside in Los Angeles's Beachwood Canyon. Photographs of the futuristic house shot for the *Los Angeles Times* by the master of architectural photography Julius Shulman are (predictably) stunning and reveal Judge's innovative approach.

A decade later, after visiting the famous Treetops Hotel while traveling in Kenya, Judge designed and built the house we see in these pages, the home he would share with his wife, Blaine Mallory, and their family. Relying on a highly innovative structural system that minimizes the building's footprint, the Tree House is essentially a modest two-story residence suspended from four steel piers driven into the earth. Judge's ingenious design can be applied to almost any site and take on almost any environmental challenge: in the event of an earthquake, the house sways from its columns, and floodwaters or sliding mud would sweep right under the living space. The Tree House perfectly encapsulates Judge's conviction that housing should be affordable and tread lightly on the land.

But while he was building this quiet masterpiece in the Hollywood Hills, Judge was also overseeing a much more glamorous project: a compound for his client and friend Marlon Brando on the Tahitian island of Tetiaroa. I can't begin to do his stories justice, so I'll just suggest that you pick up a copy of Judge's memoir of this period, *Waltzing with Brando*.

This was a house I shot for myself and not a commission. Set high in the hills of Laurel Canyon, with an unmatched view of Los Angeles and filled with treasures from a lifetime of travel and friendship, Judge's place has more character and love in it than most any I have had the good fortune to photograph, and I will miss him.

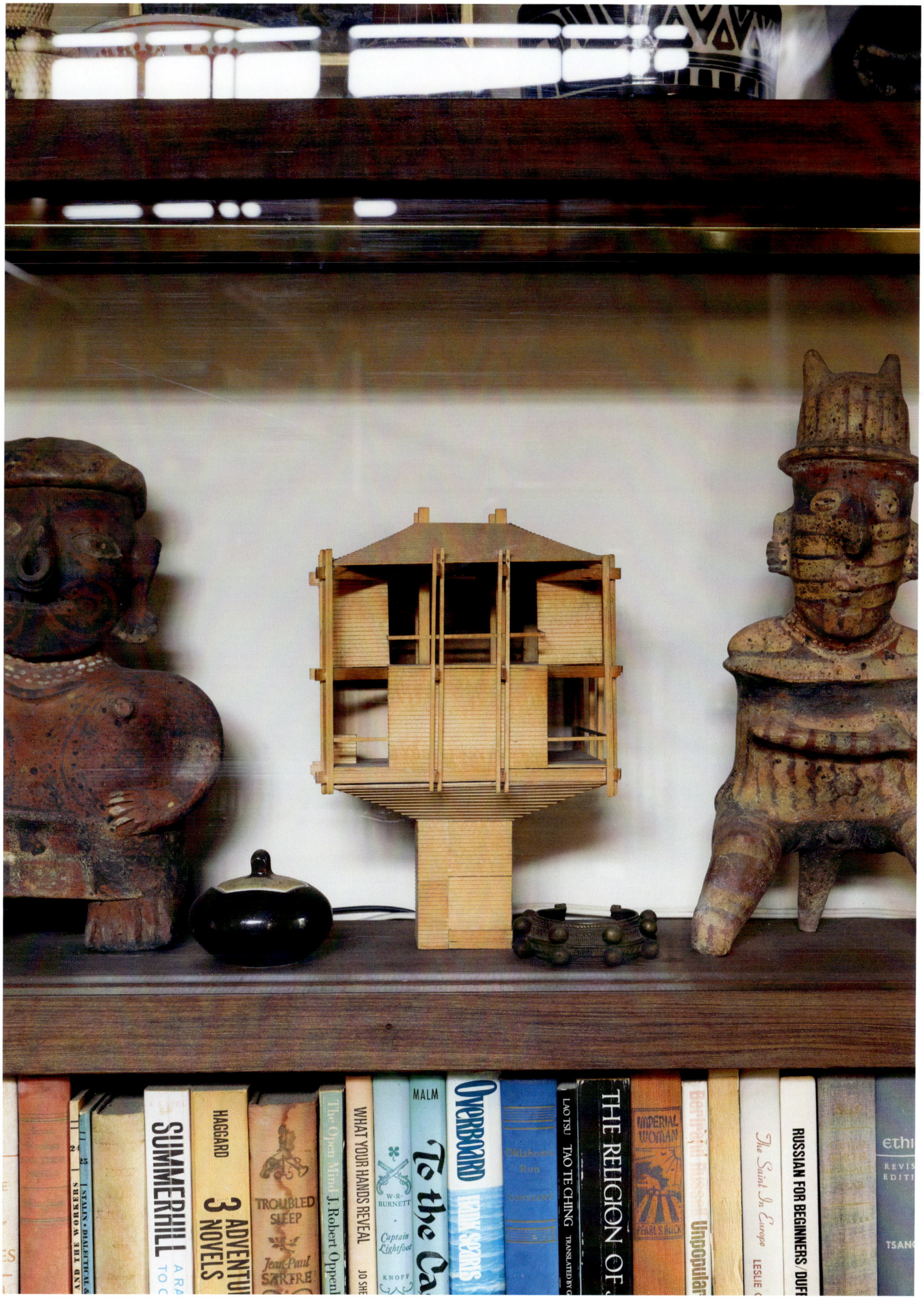
SUMMERHILL
HAGGARD
3 NOVELS
TROUBLED SLEEP
Jean-Paul SARTRE
J. Robert Oppenheimer
WHAT YOUR HANDS REVEAL
MALM
W.R. BURNETT
Captain Lightfoot
KNOPF
OVERBOARD
LAO TSU
TAO TE CHING
IMPERIAL WOMAN
PEARL S. BUCK
Unpopular
The Saint In Europe
RUSSIAN FOR BEGINNERS

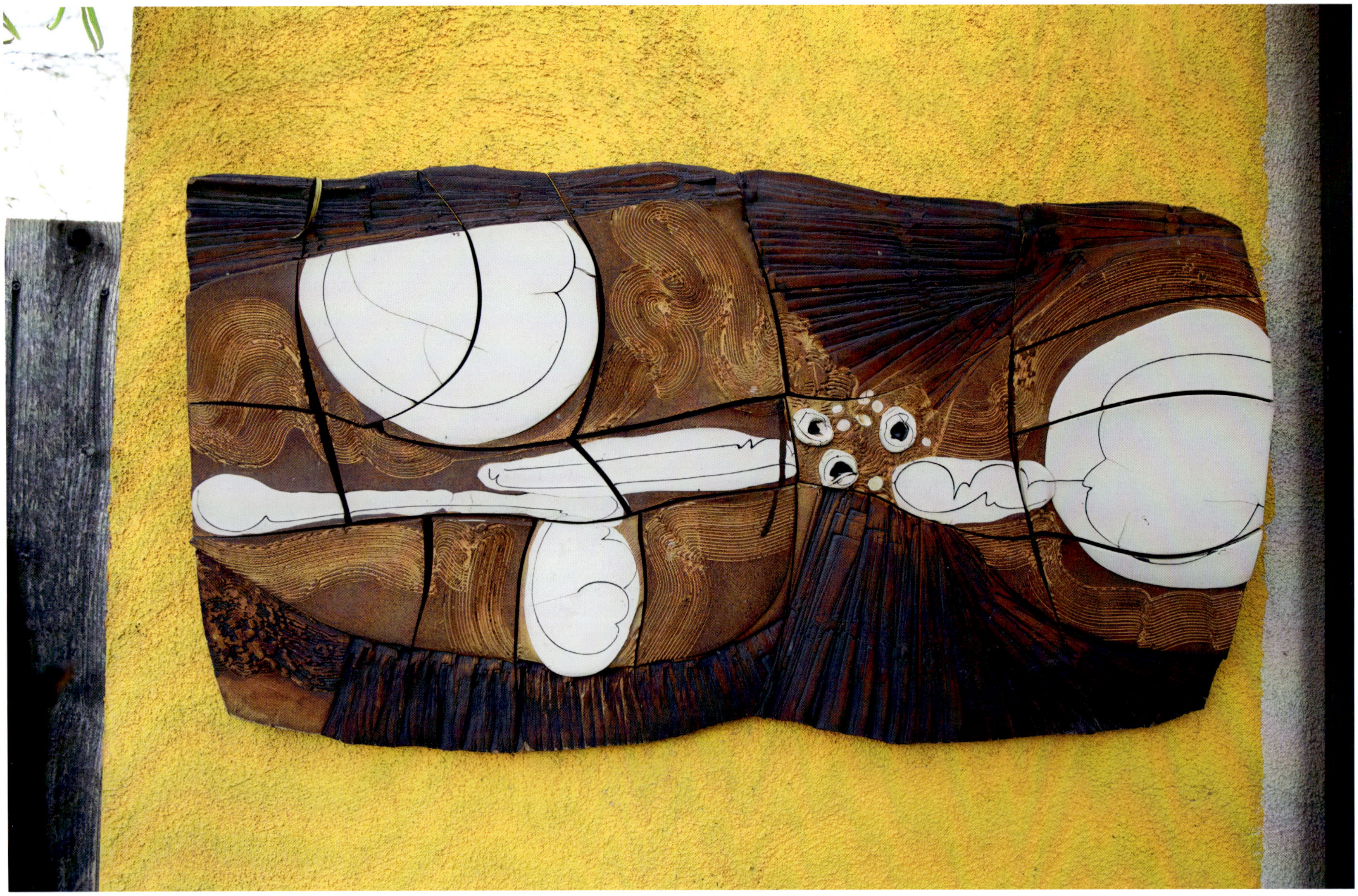

A wood relief and the hand-painted tiles on the home's exterior and lining the shower were made by the artist Dora de Larios, Judge's first wife.

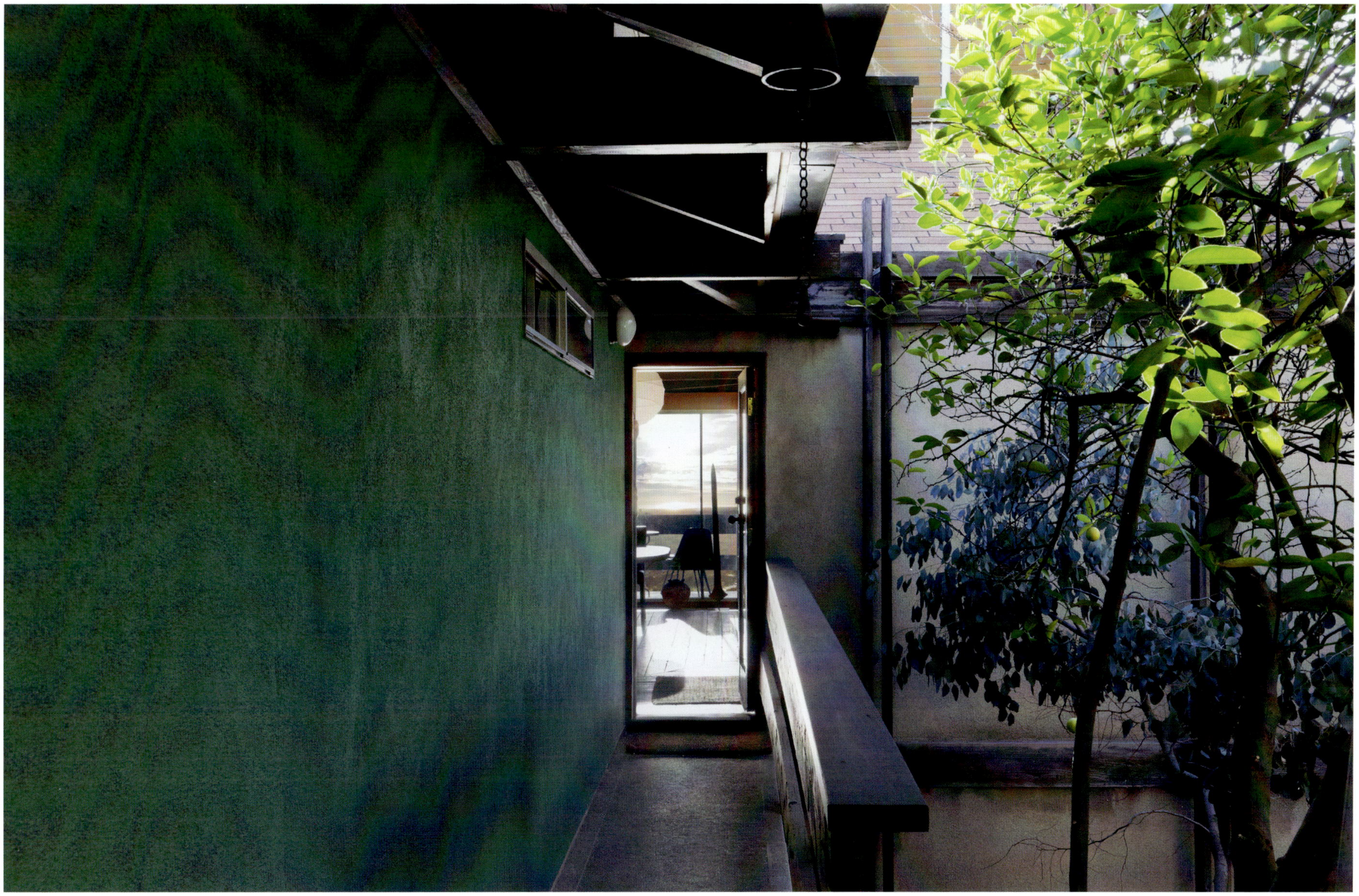

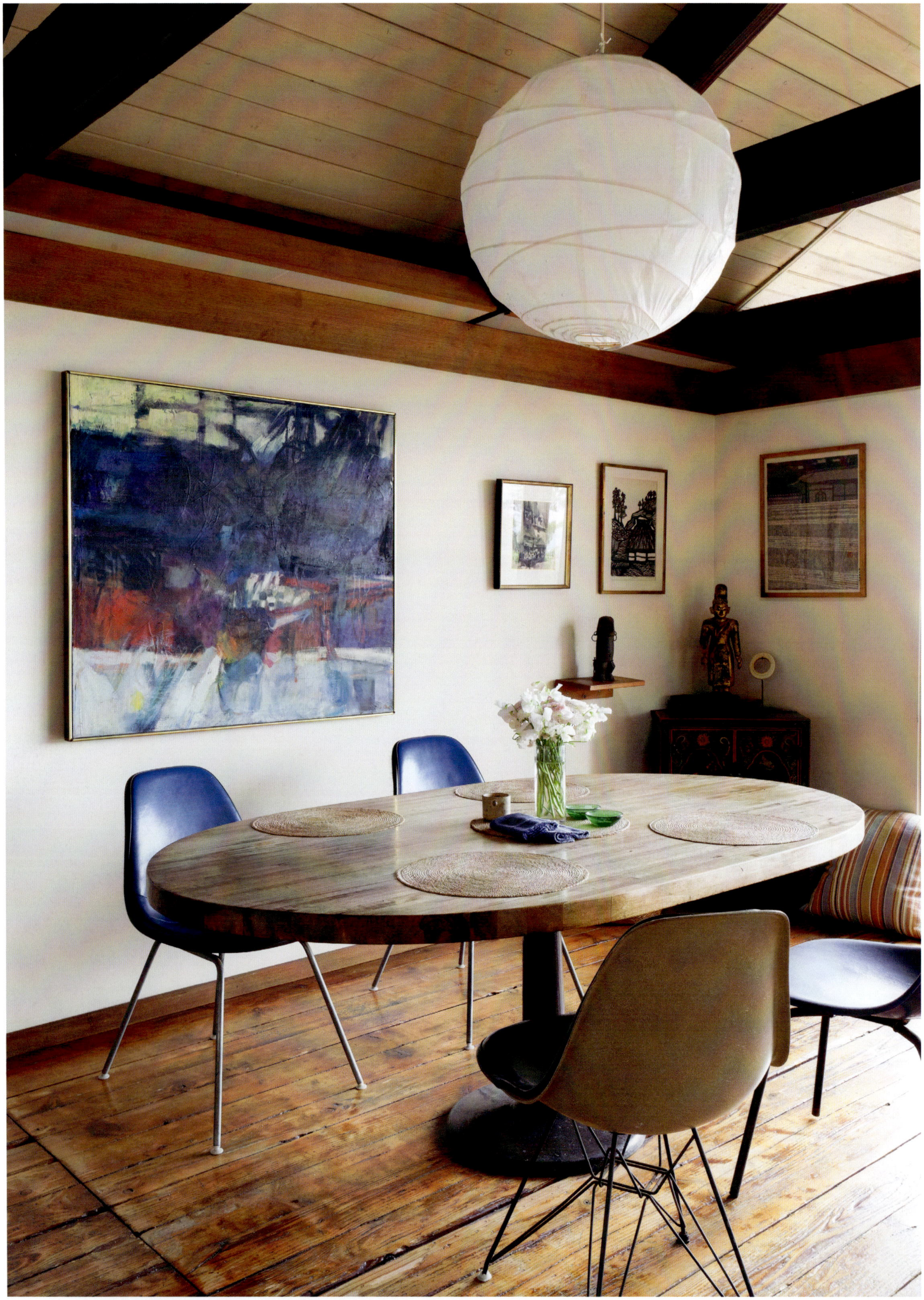

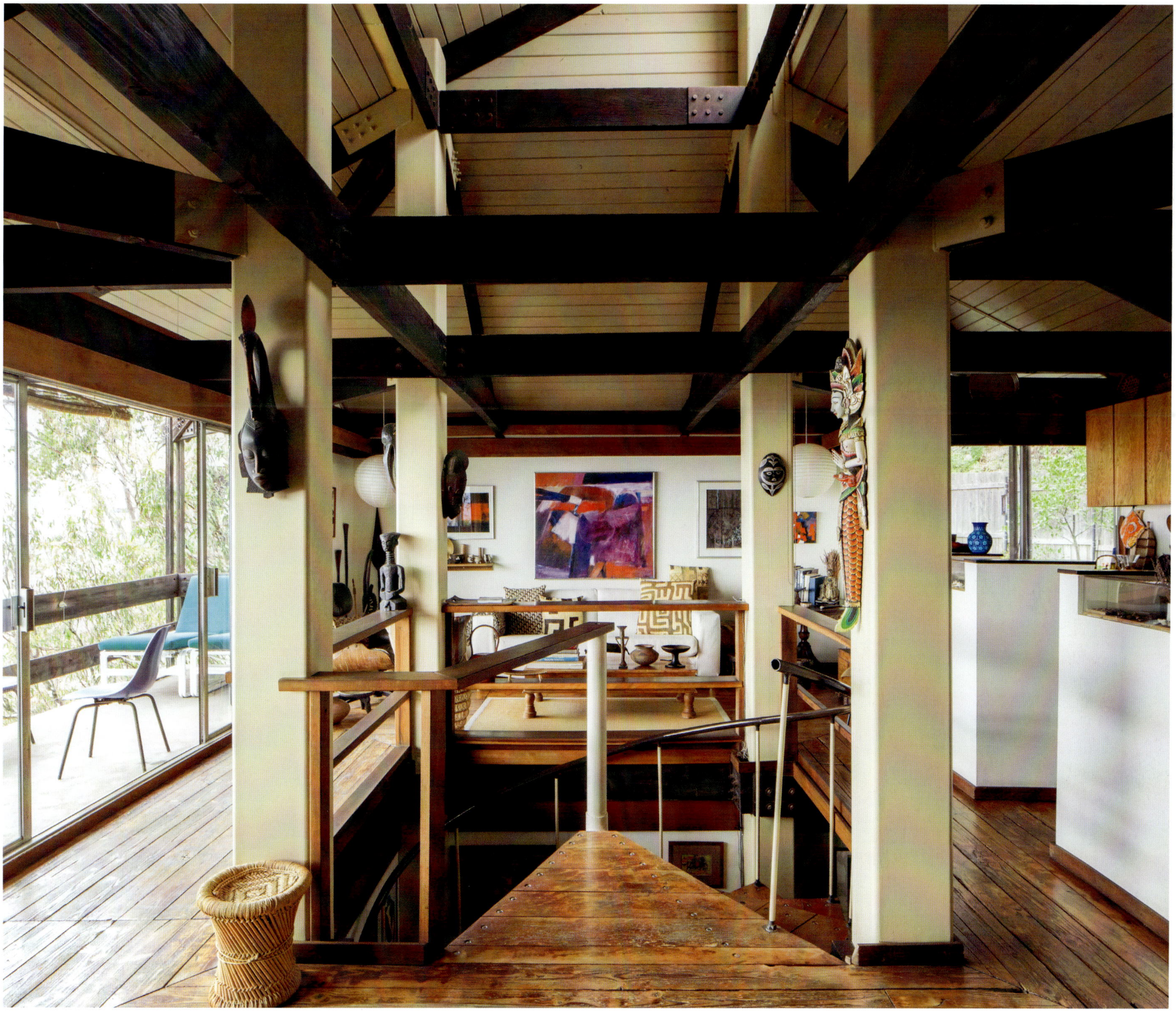

Marlon Brando, whose Tahiti compound Judge was designing as he built the Tree House, joined small dinner parties at Judge's home.

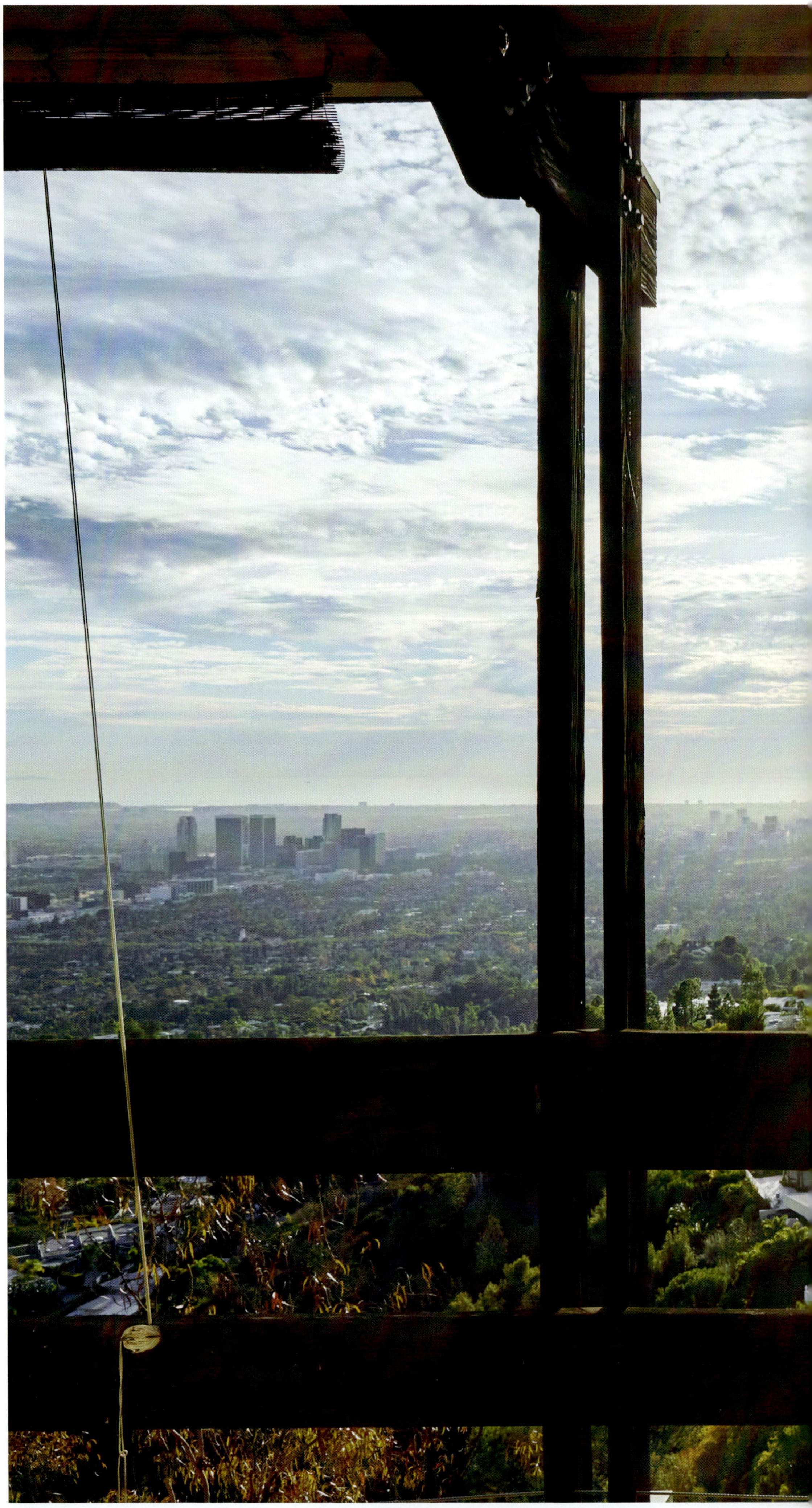

The balcony of this modest home
offers a spectacular view of the city,
right to the ocean.

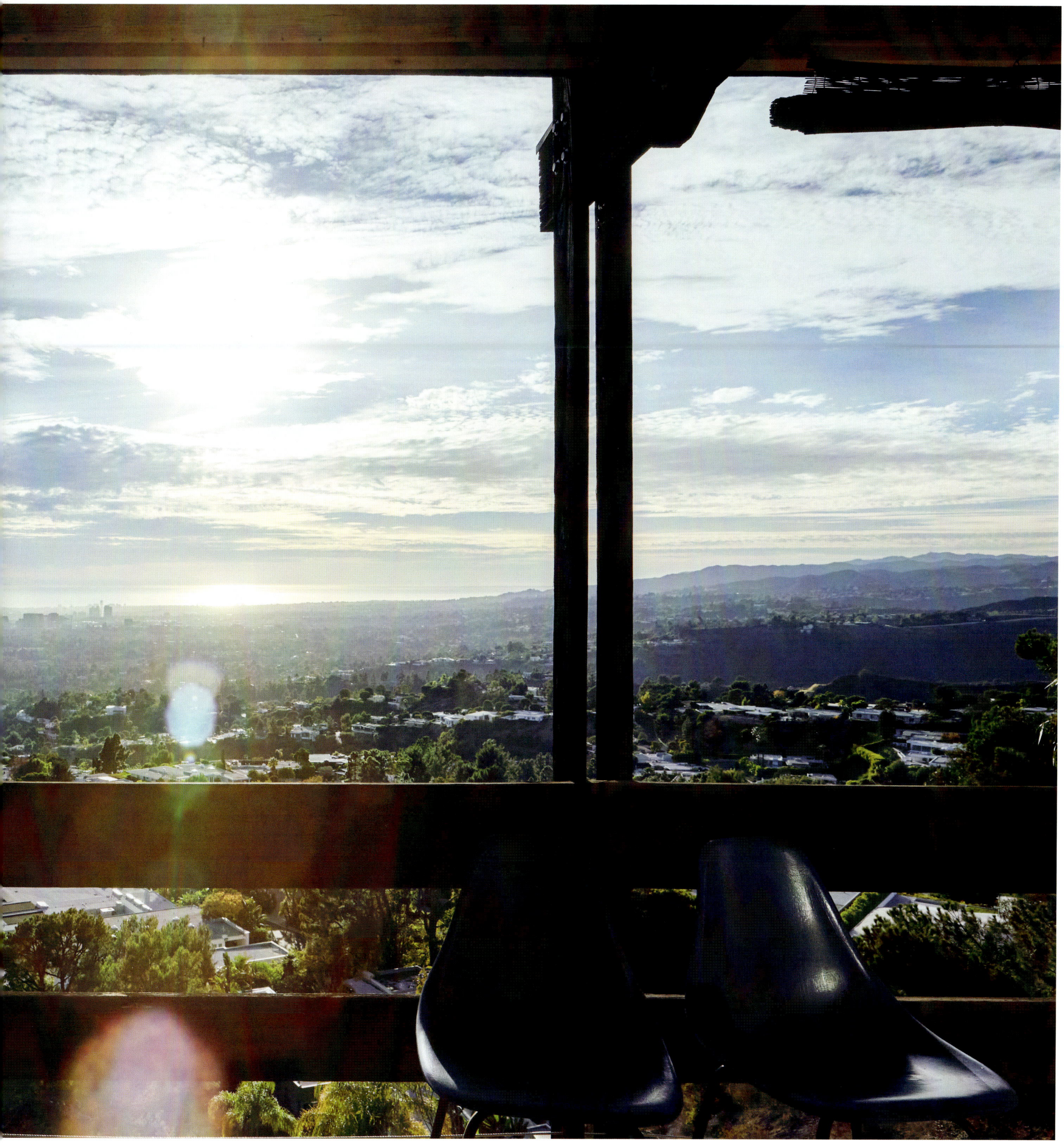

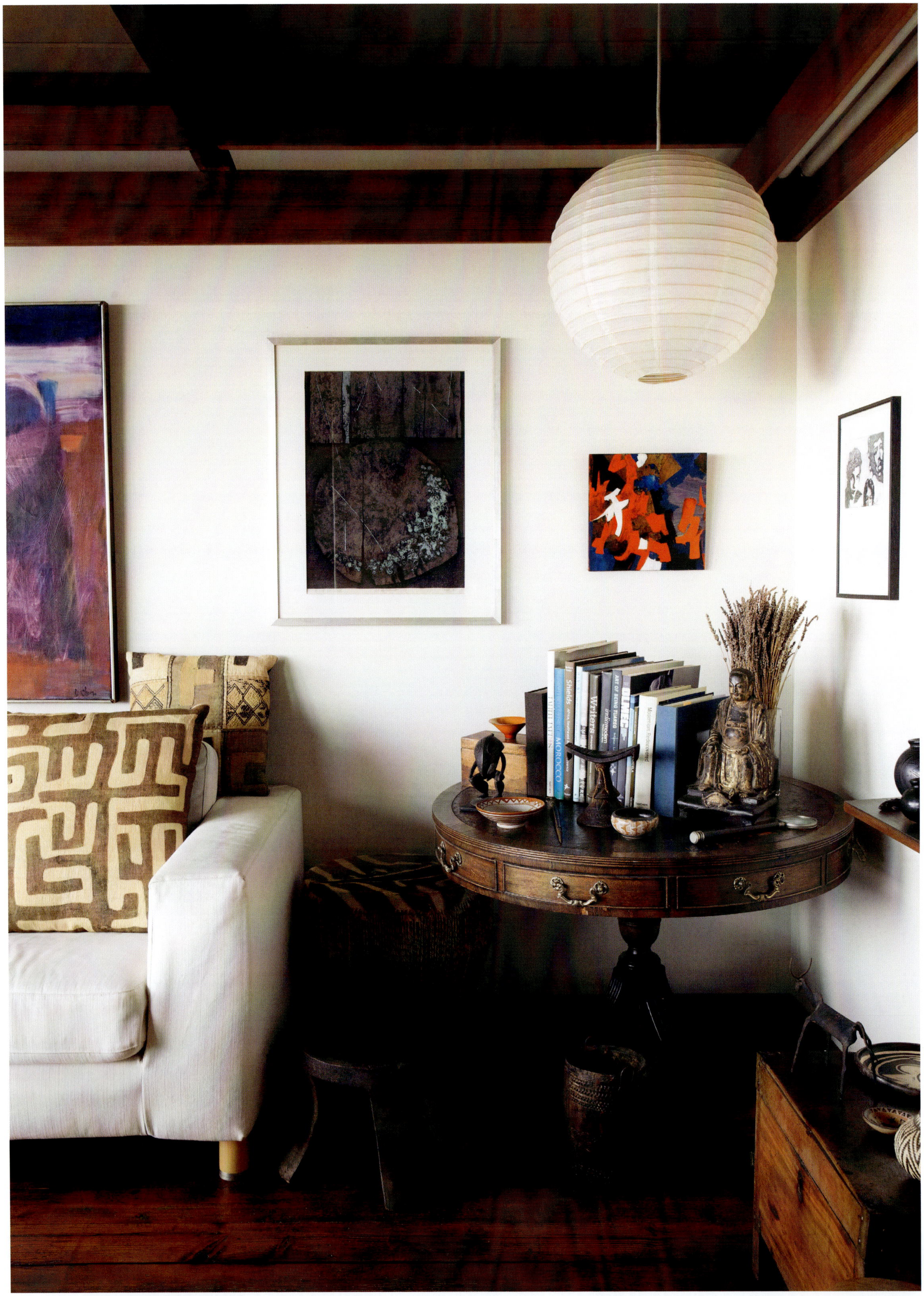
MOROCCO
Shields
Writers
ART OF BEING TUAREG
indiamodern
OLMEC
Modernism Rediscovered
TASCHEN

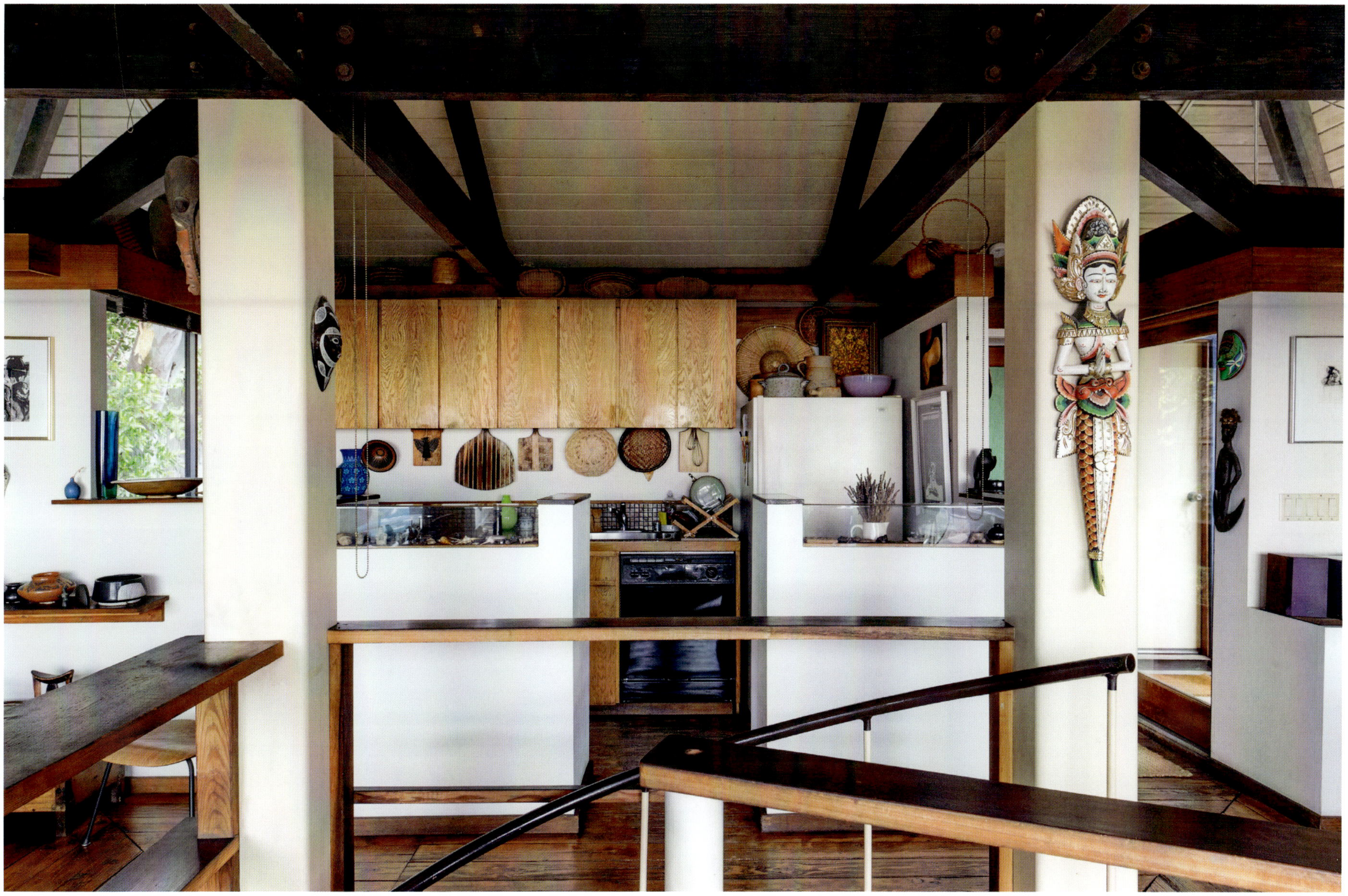

Most of the art in the house was made by friends of Judge. Other pieces he purchased in Japan in the 1960s.

Overleaf: The Tree House's spiral staircase was repurposed from Judge's Triponent House.

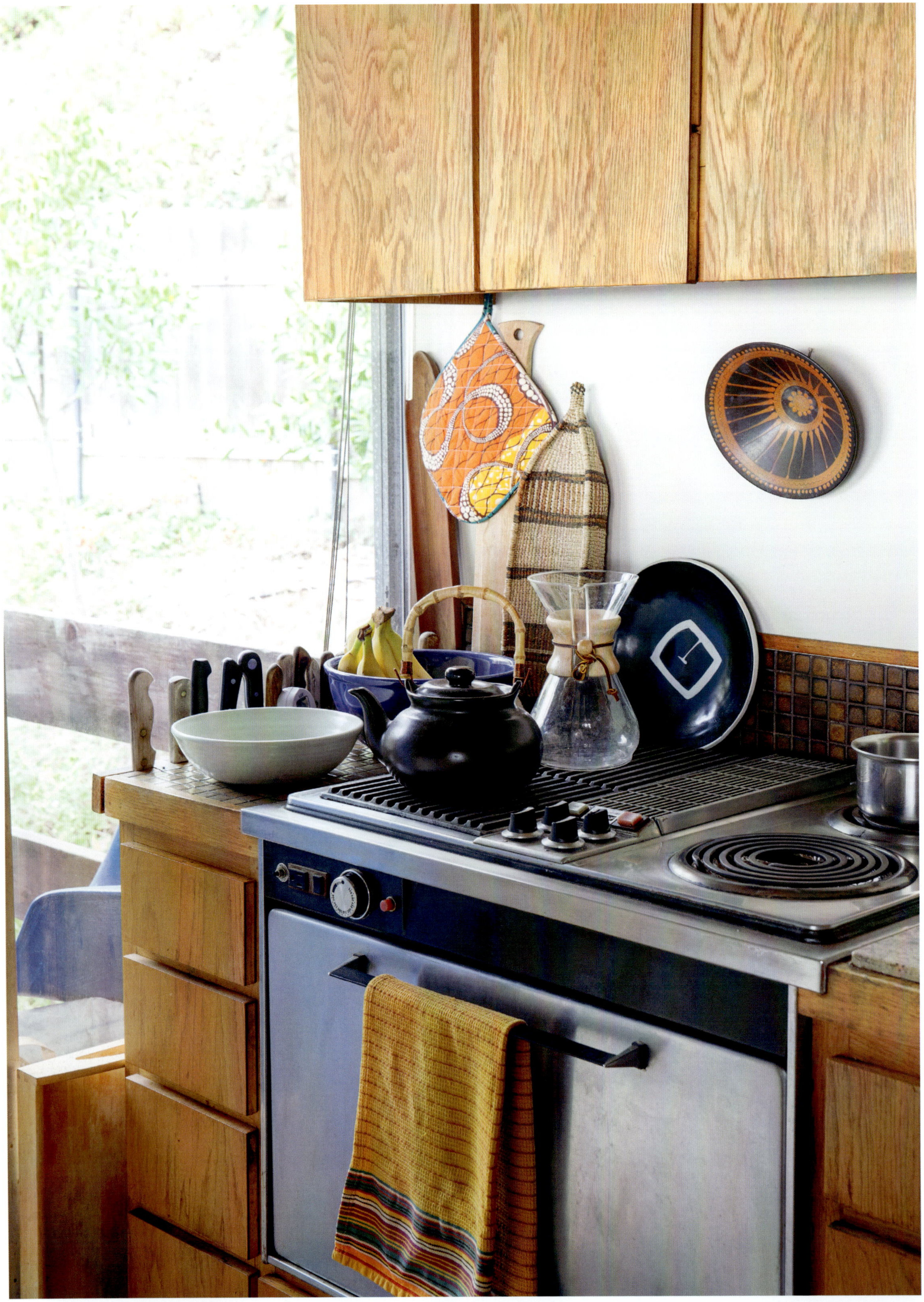

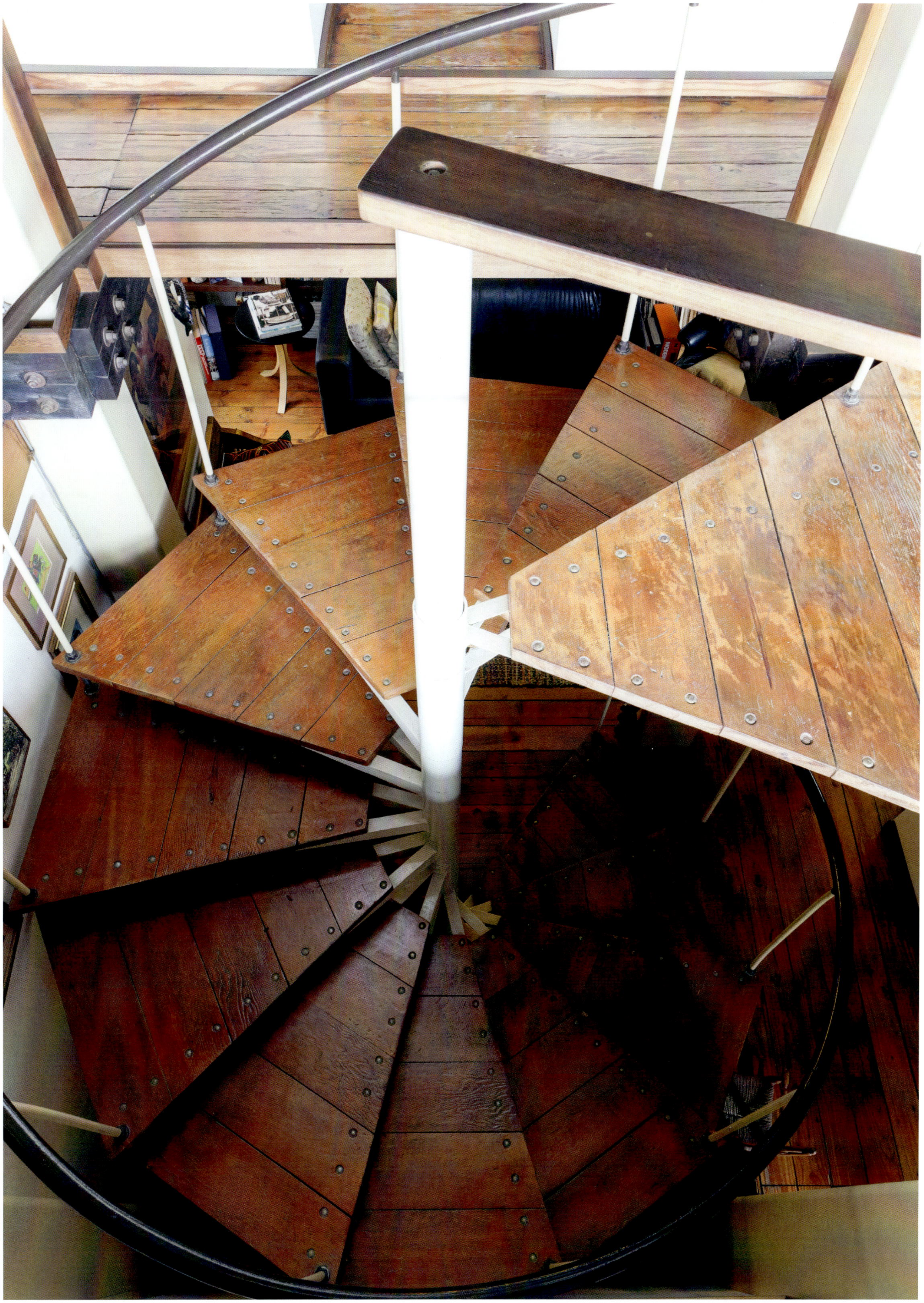

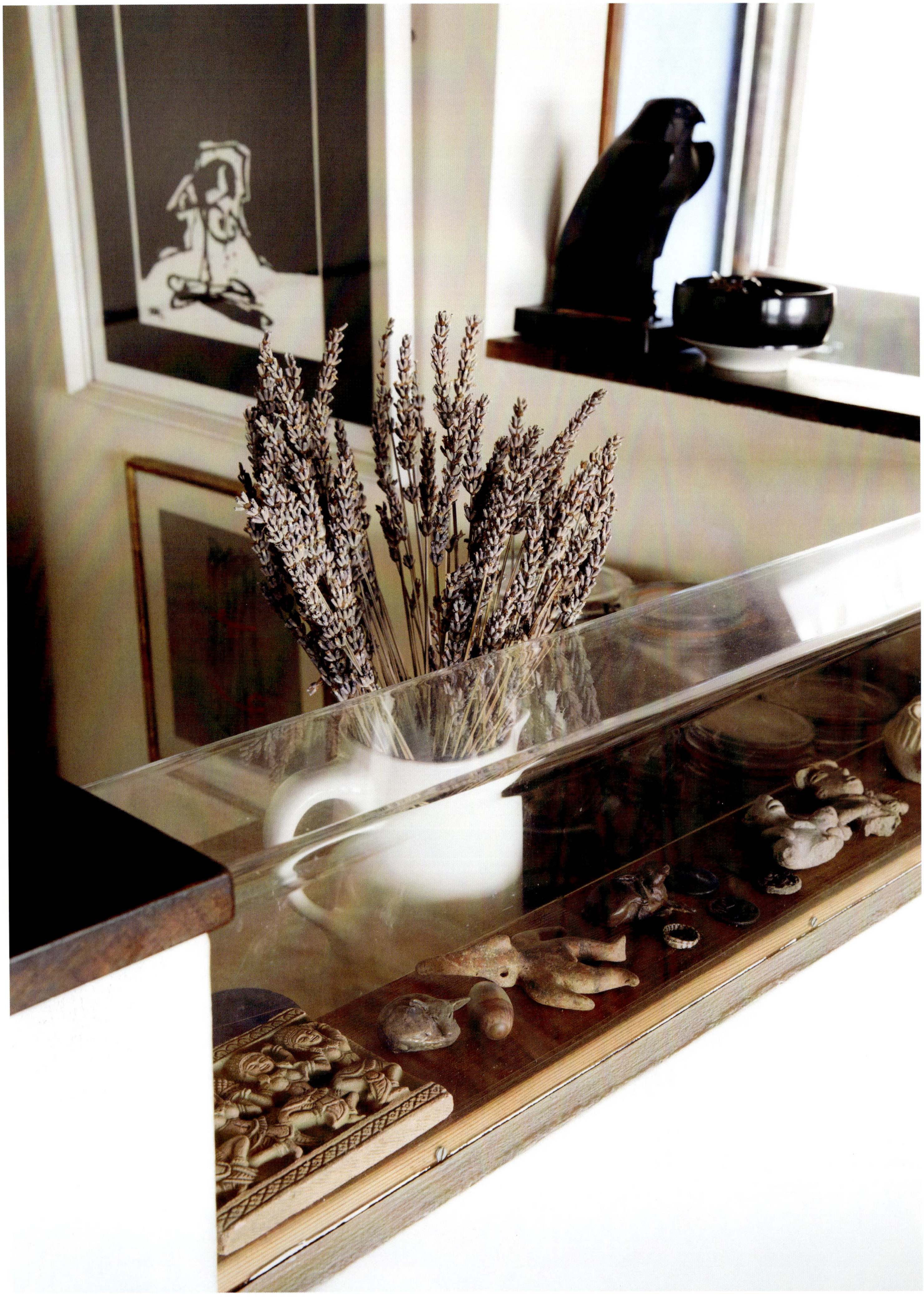

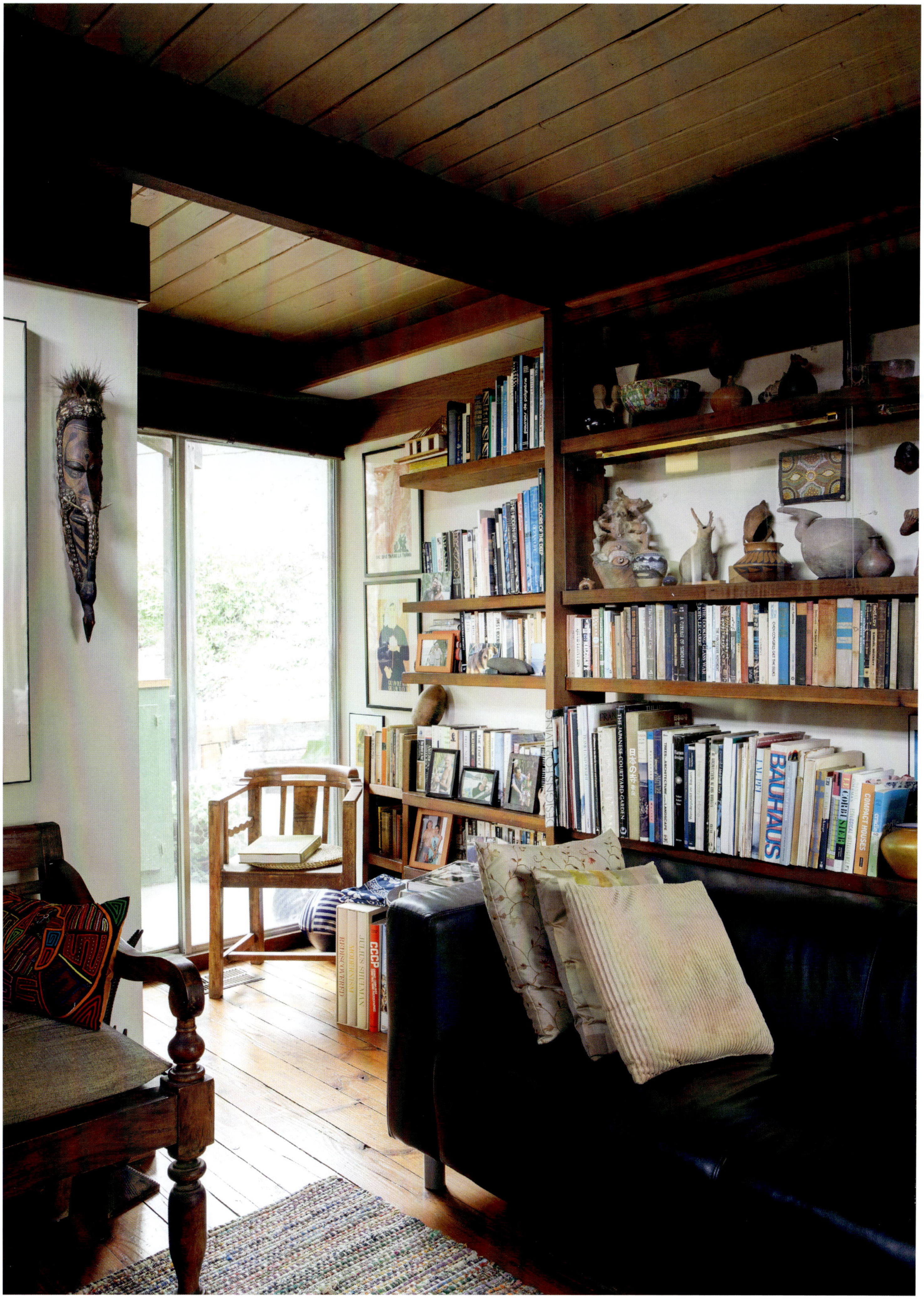
BAUHAUS
THE JAPANESE COURTYARD GARDEN
JULIUS SHULMAN
CCCP
COMPACT HOUSES

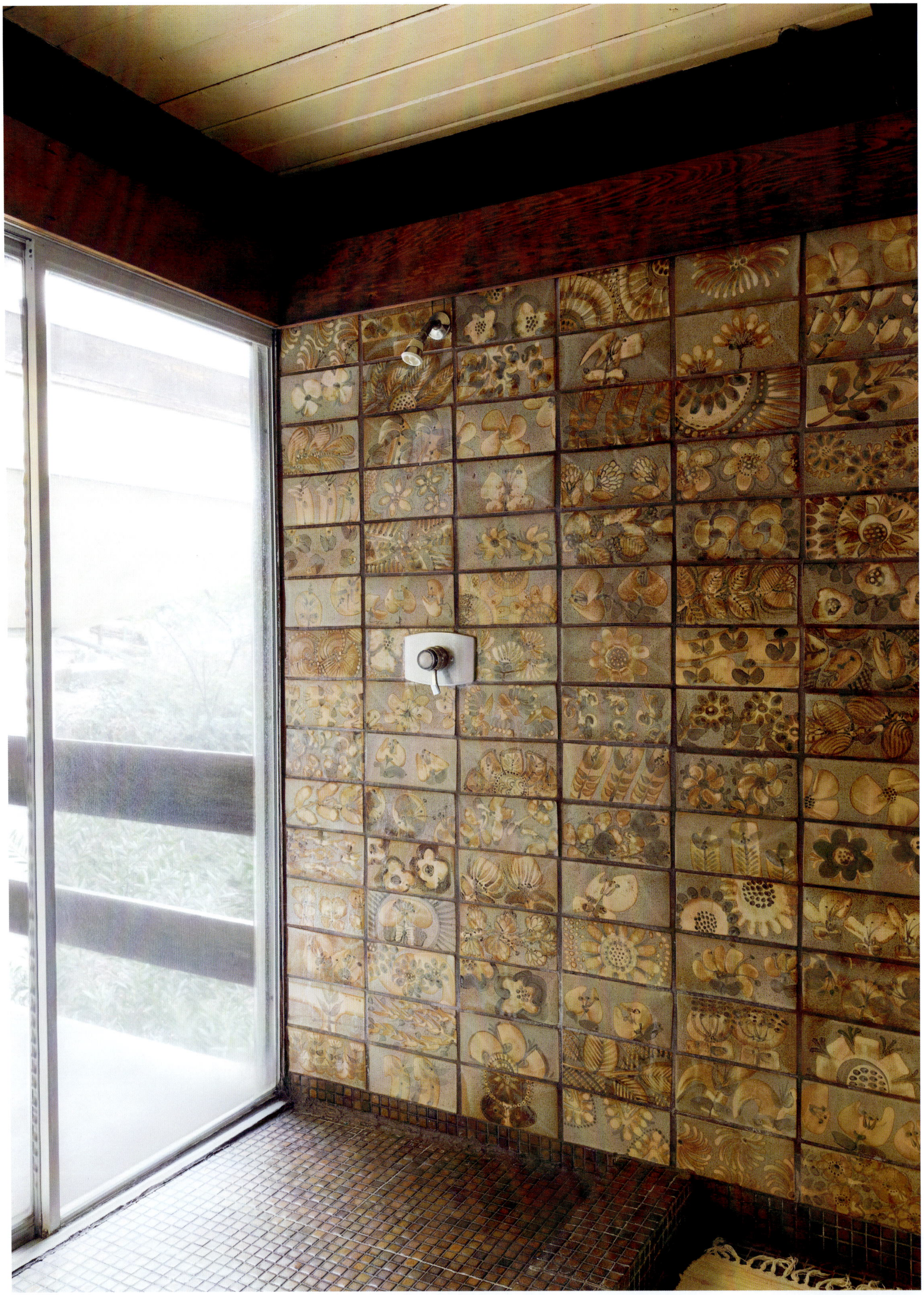

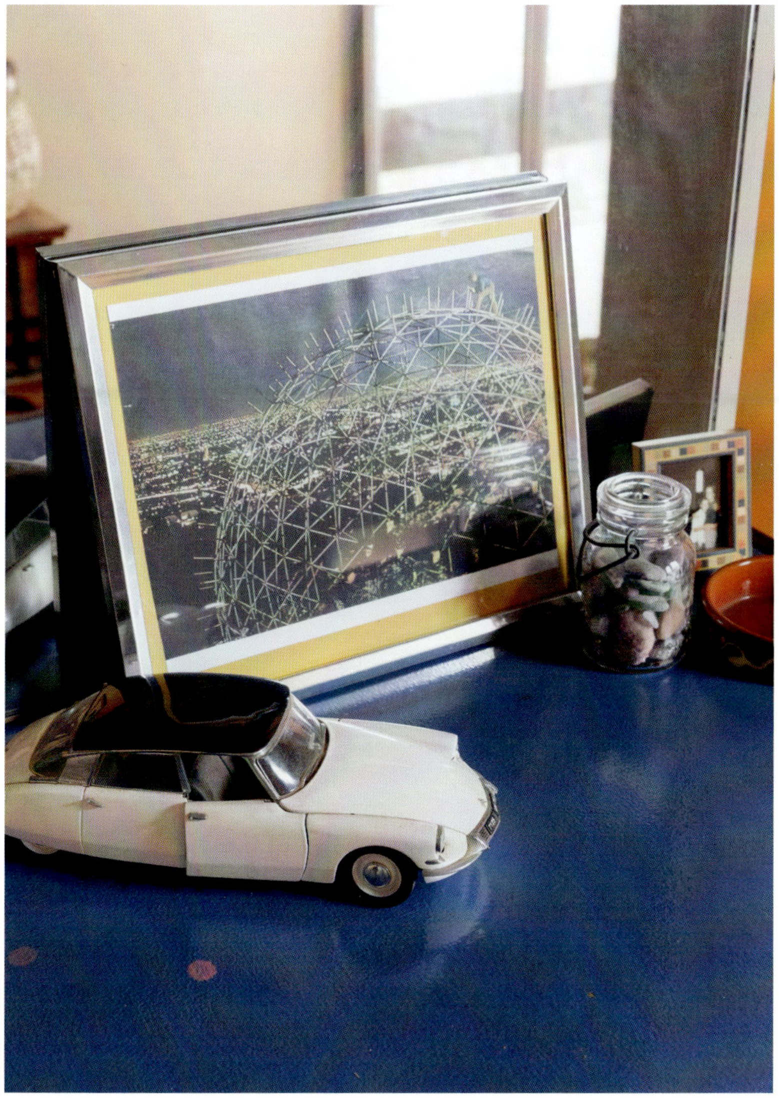

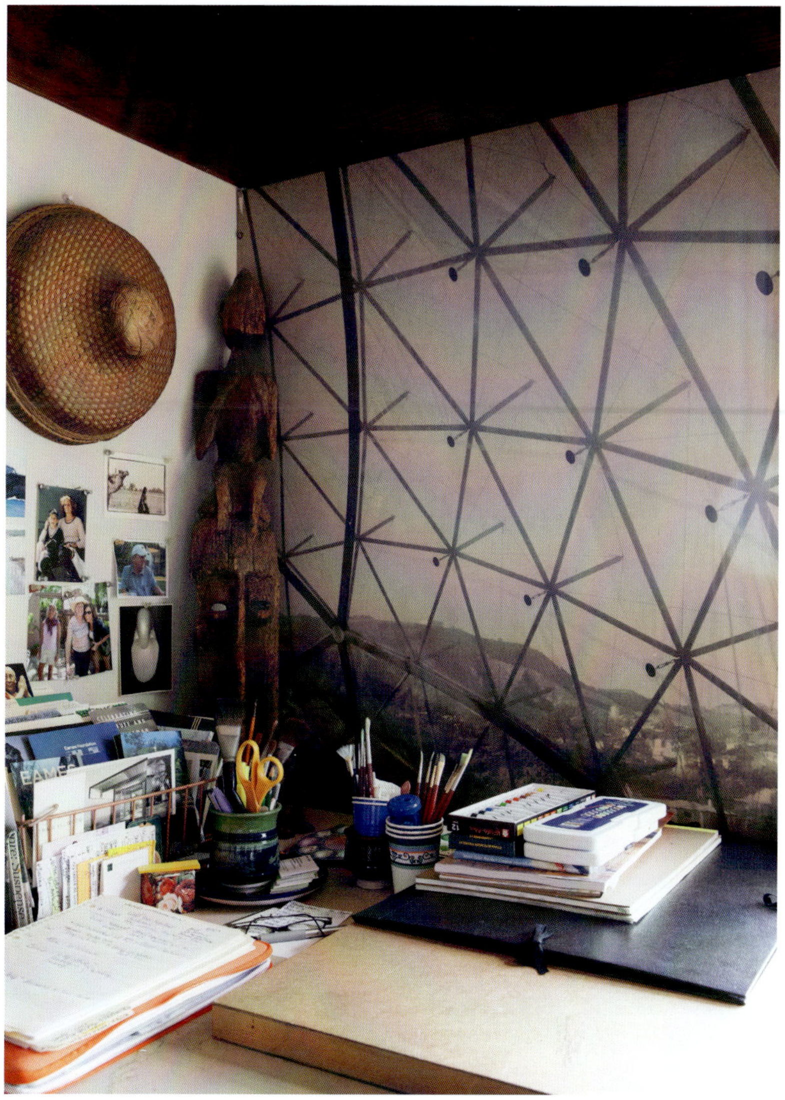

Previous: Bernard Judge and Blaine Mallory collected the masks and objects on display in built-in vitrines and throughout the house during their travels in Africa, New Guinea, and Indonesia.

On the desk in Judge's office is a picture that appeared in the June 20, 1960, issue of *Life* magazine: the architect as a young man scaling the Triponent House's geodesic dome.

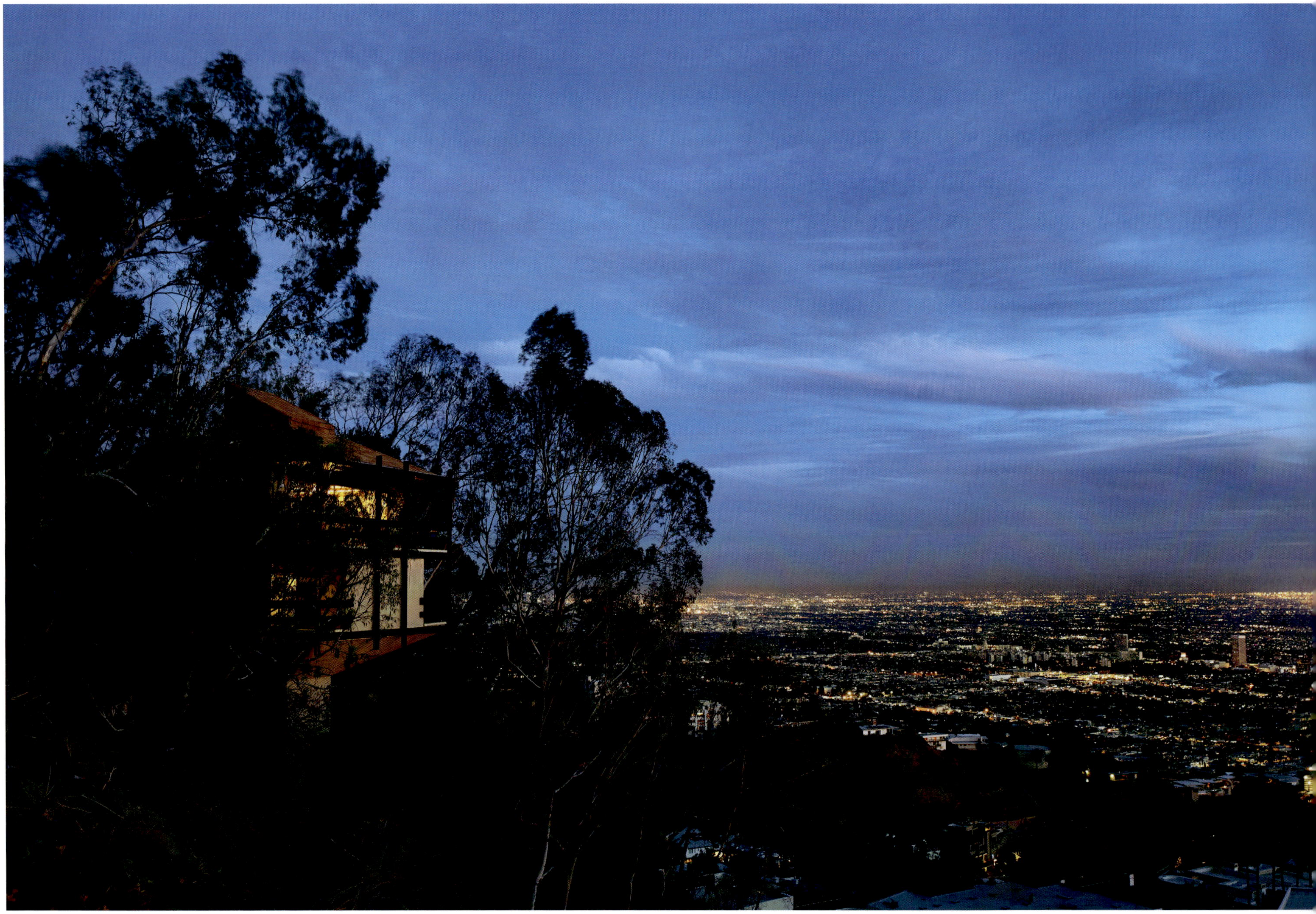

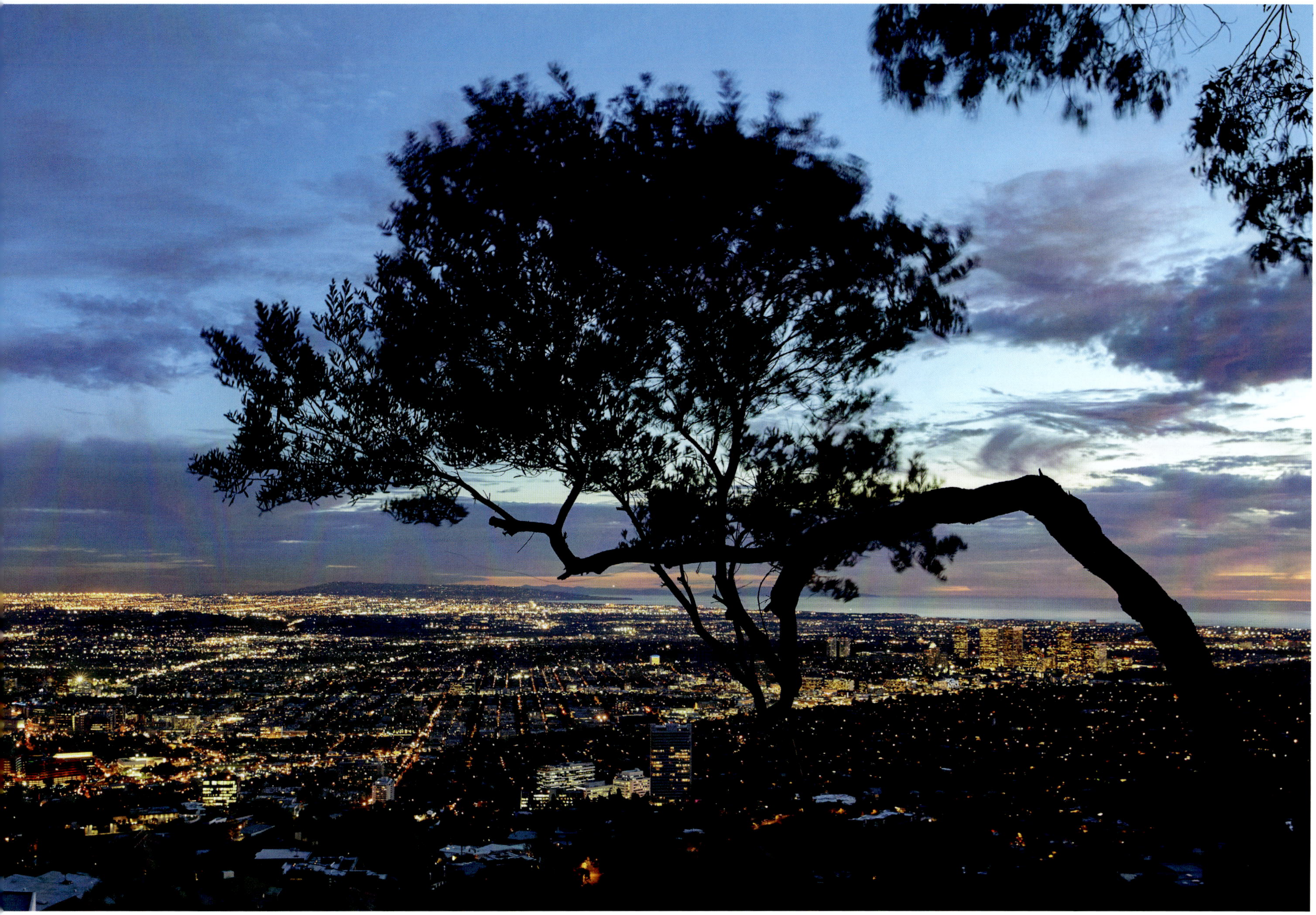

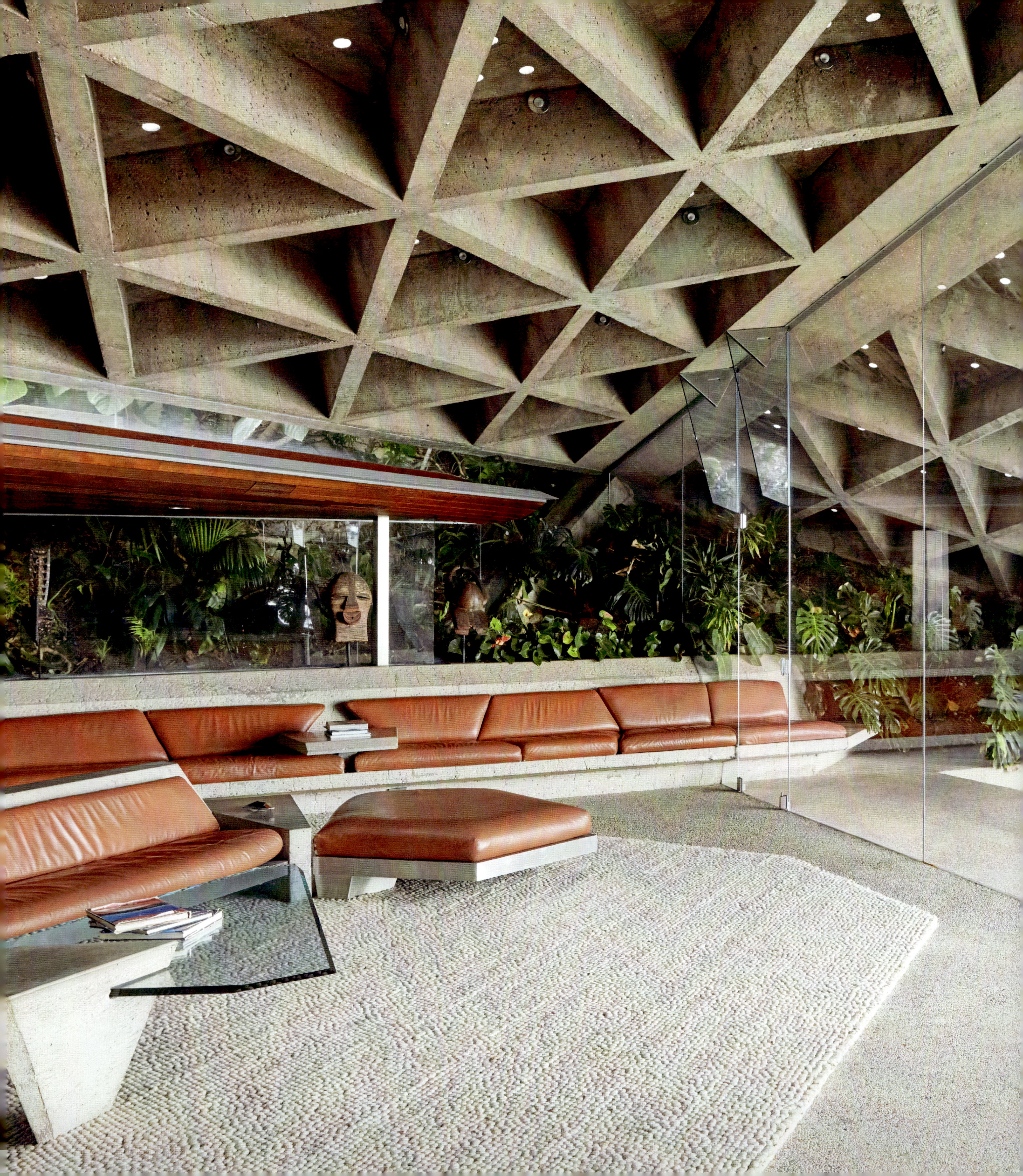

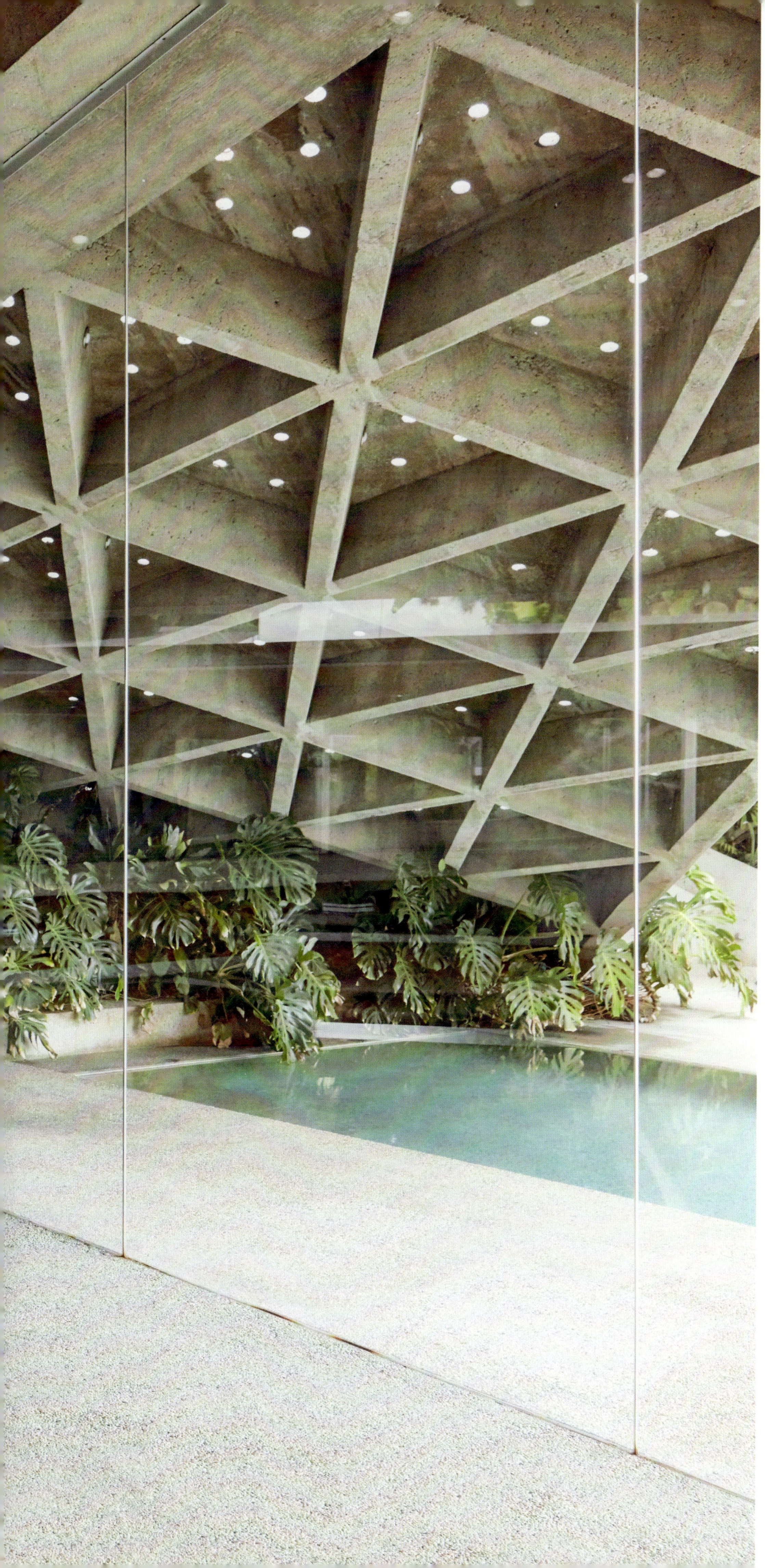

Sheats-Goldstein Residence

Beverly Hills

Architect

John Lautner

Resident

James Goldstein

If you've seen the Coen brothers film *The Big Lebowski*, you know this house. This space-age concrete-and-glass bachelor pad is one of the most architecturally significant houses in California.

Designed by architect John Lautner in 1963, the Sheats-Goldstein Residence is hidden in the hillsides above Beverly Hills, enveloped in a jungle spanning some four acres. But this isn't the story of an architectural gem concealed from public view; rather, it has been thoroughly shared and enjoyed.

Fashion, architecture, and basketball fanatic James Goldstein bought the house in 1972 and has been nurturing it ever since. For twenty-two years, Lautner worked with Goldstein on the main house and an adjacent property until the architect's death in 1994, after which Goldstein continued with Lautner protégé Duncan Nicholson.

Over five decades, Goldstein extensively landscaped the property and added a tennis court, a lap pool, a wing with offices, and a private nightclub—Club James. The house is constantly abuzz with film and photo shoots, architectural tours, and parties. It's come a long way from the family home designed and built for Helen and Paul Sheats in the early 1960s.

The first time I visited, as the evening drew in, Mr. Goldstein—dressed in his signature snakeskin hat and leather suit—asked if we wanted to experience the James Turrell Skyspace, another stellar addition to the property. After we trekked down through the winding paths of the wilds below the house, the keypad on the door wouldn't work, and we were locked out. It turned out some chancers had been sneaking in at night, claiming the art as their playground, and new security measures had been put in place. Tortured by the missed opportunity, on a later visit Goldstein's friend and house manager, Roberta, kindly let my brother-in-law and me experience the intensely sensory installation.

In 2016 Goldstein donated the entire house and property to the Los Angeles County Museum of Art, including the artworks by James Turrell, Ed Ruscha, De Wain Valentine, and Kenny Scharf; his extensive collection of couture clothing; and his 1961 Rolls-Royce Silver Cloud, along with a $17 million preservation fund. Through Goldstein's gift of the architectural masterpiece to LACMA, the property and artworks will be enjoyed by the public for years to come.

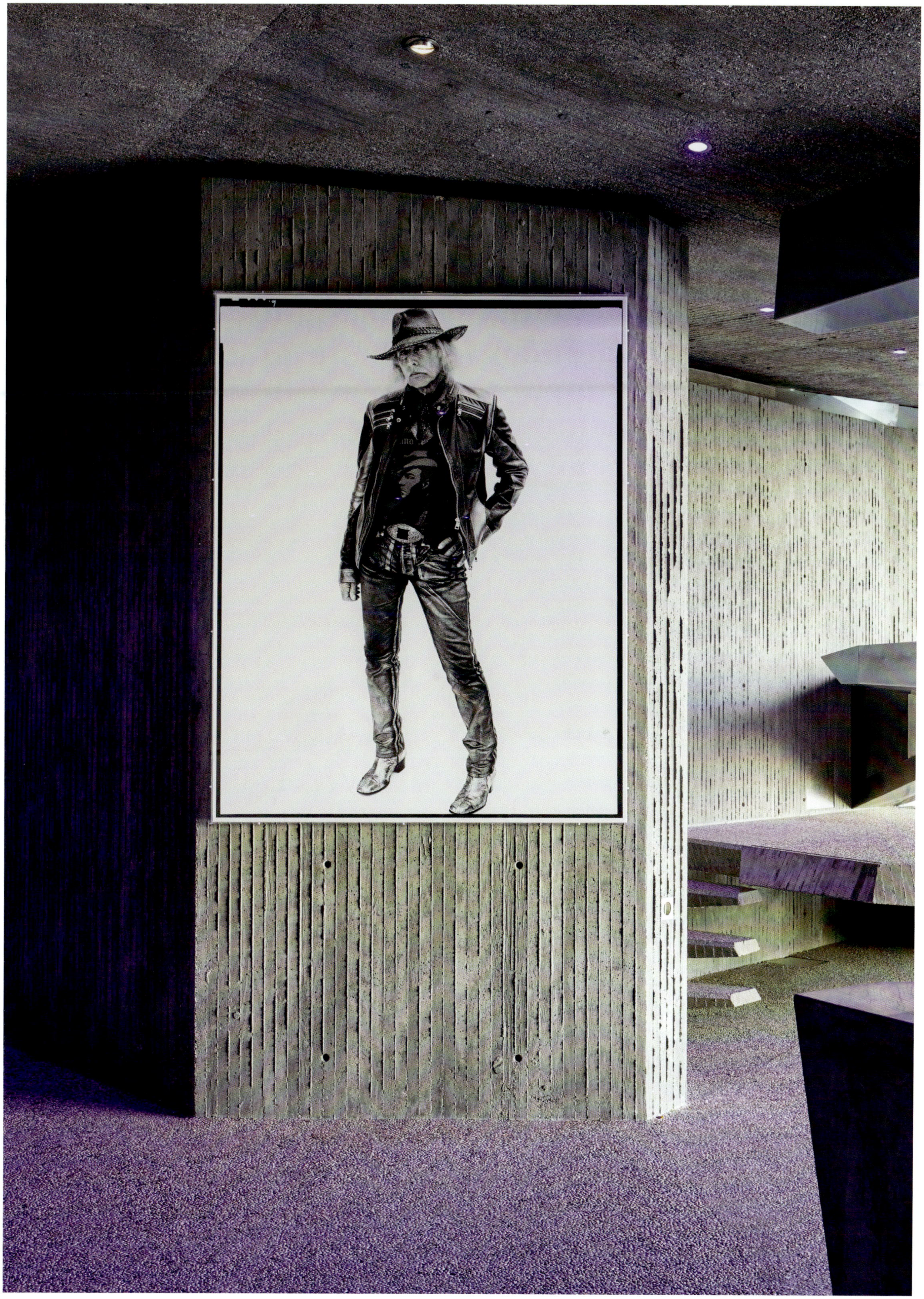

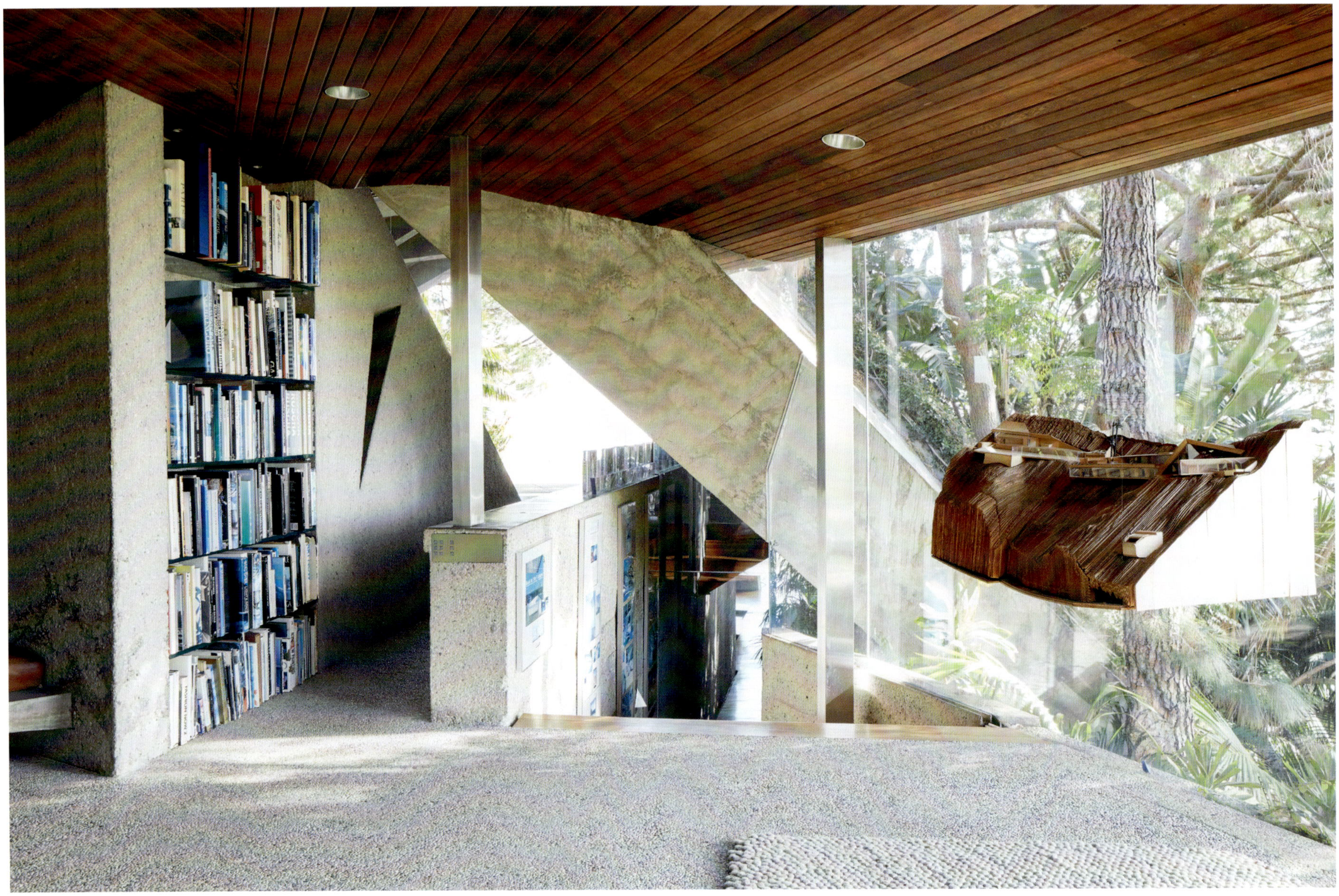

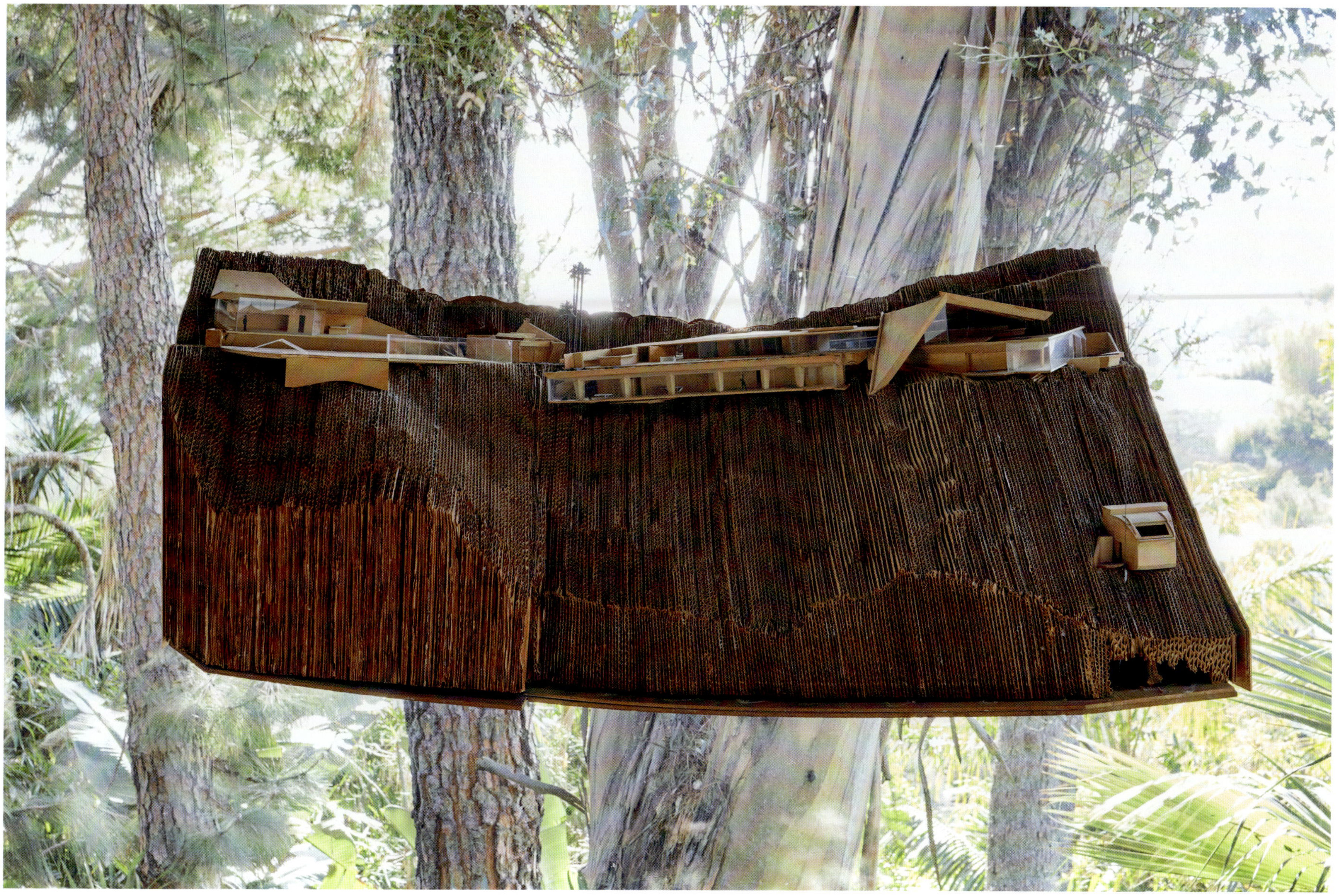

The story goes that Helen Sheats watched as architect John Lautner arrived at the idea for her house by folding a sheet of paper. This model shows how the residence and night-club nestle into the hillside. The small building at the bottom right of the property is a James Turrell Skyspace.

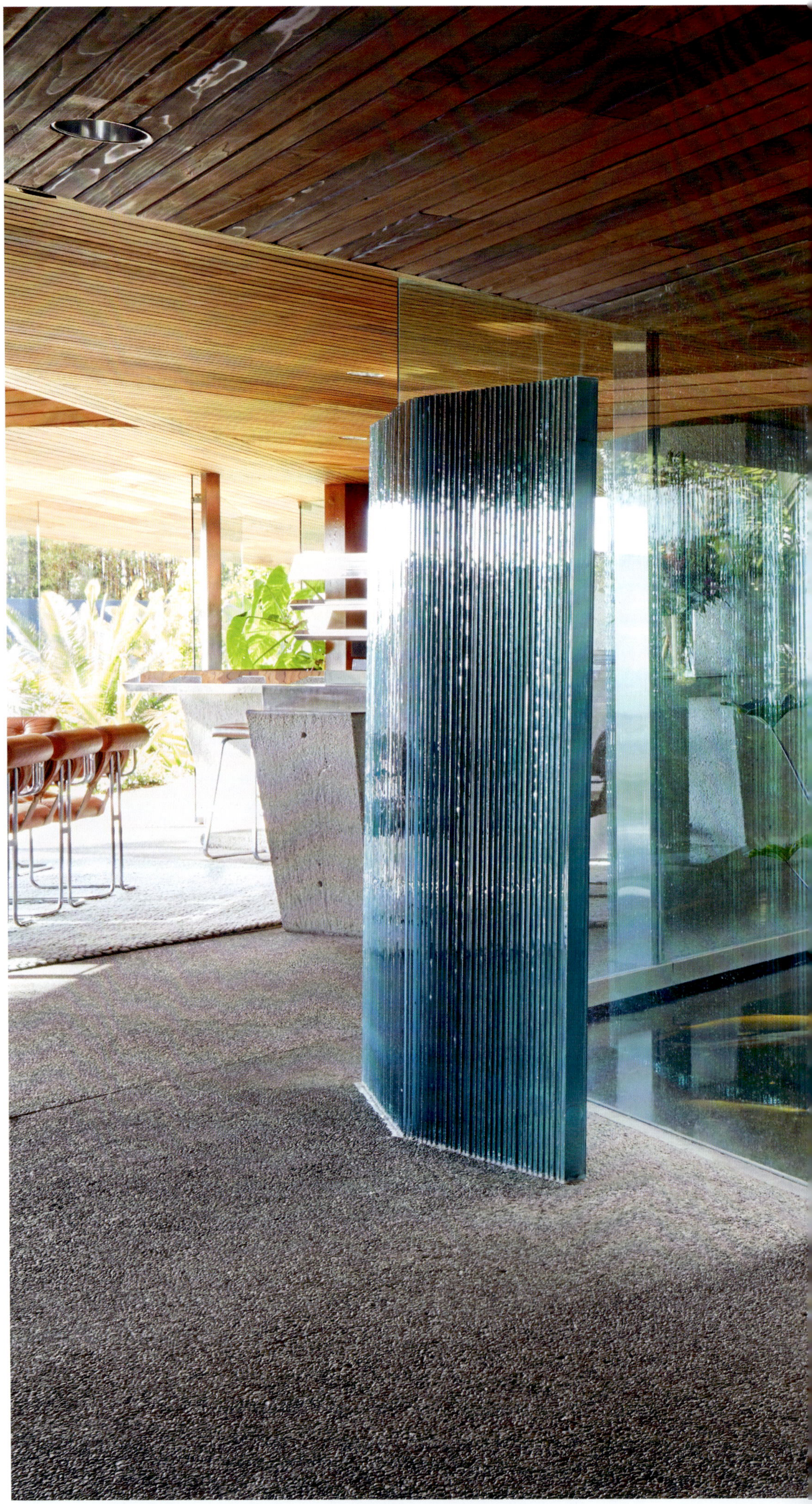

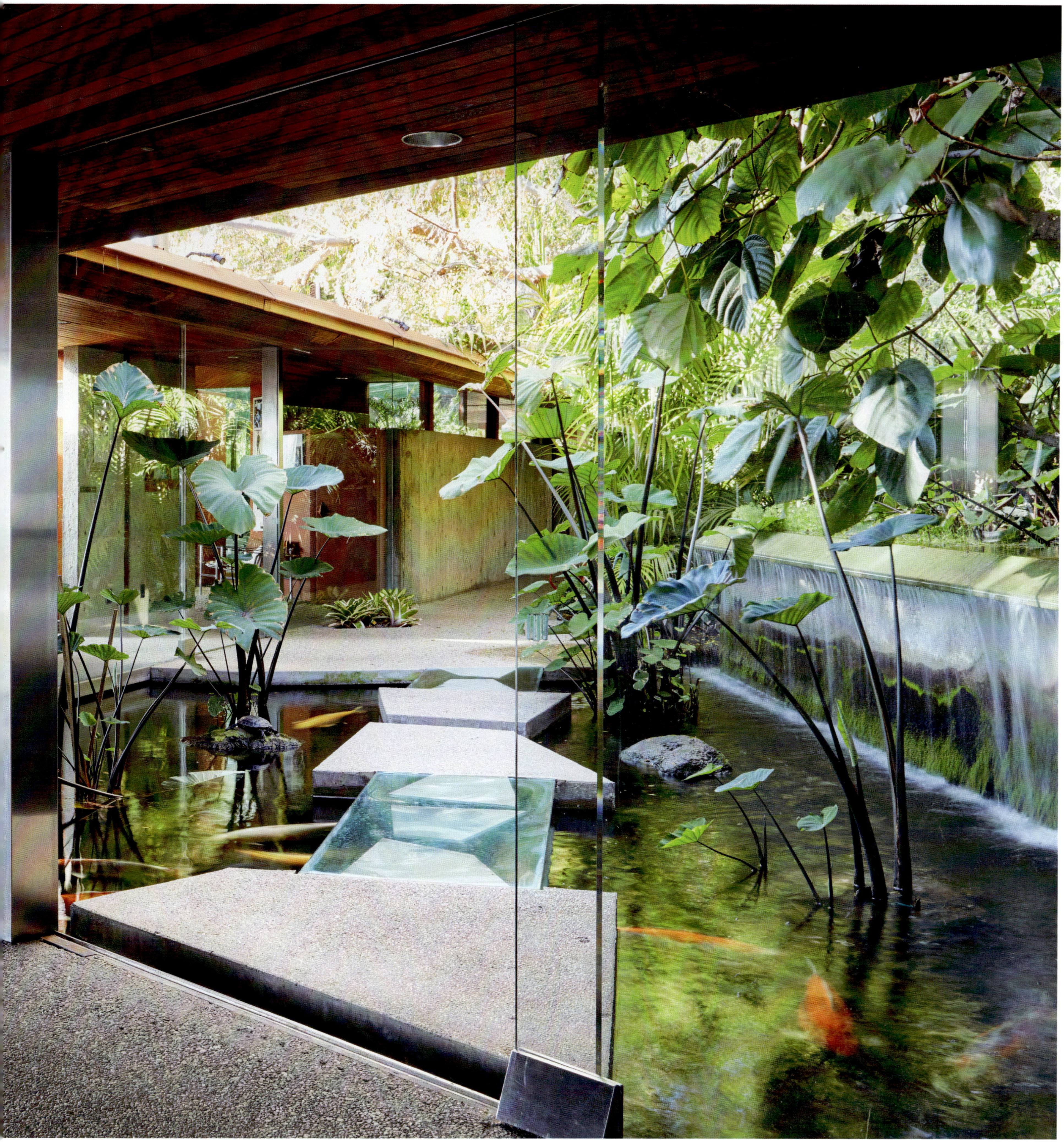

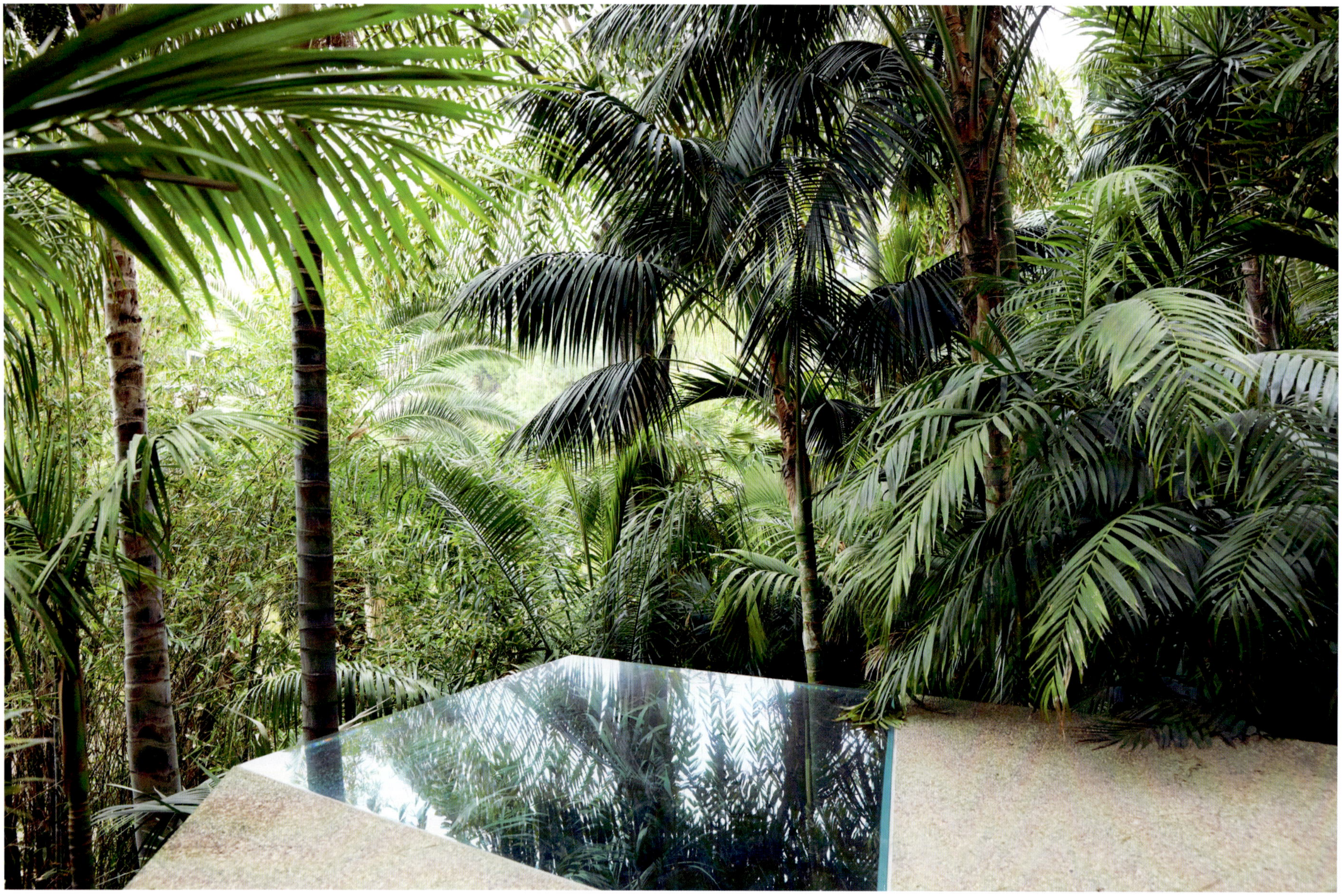

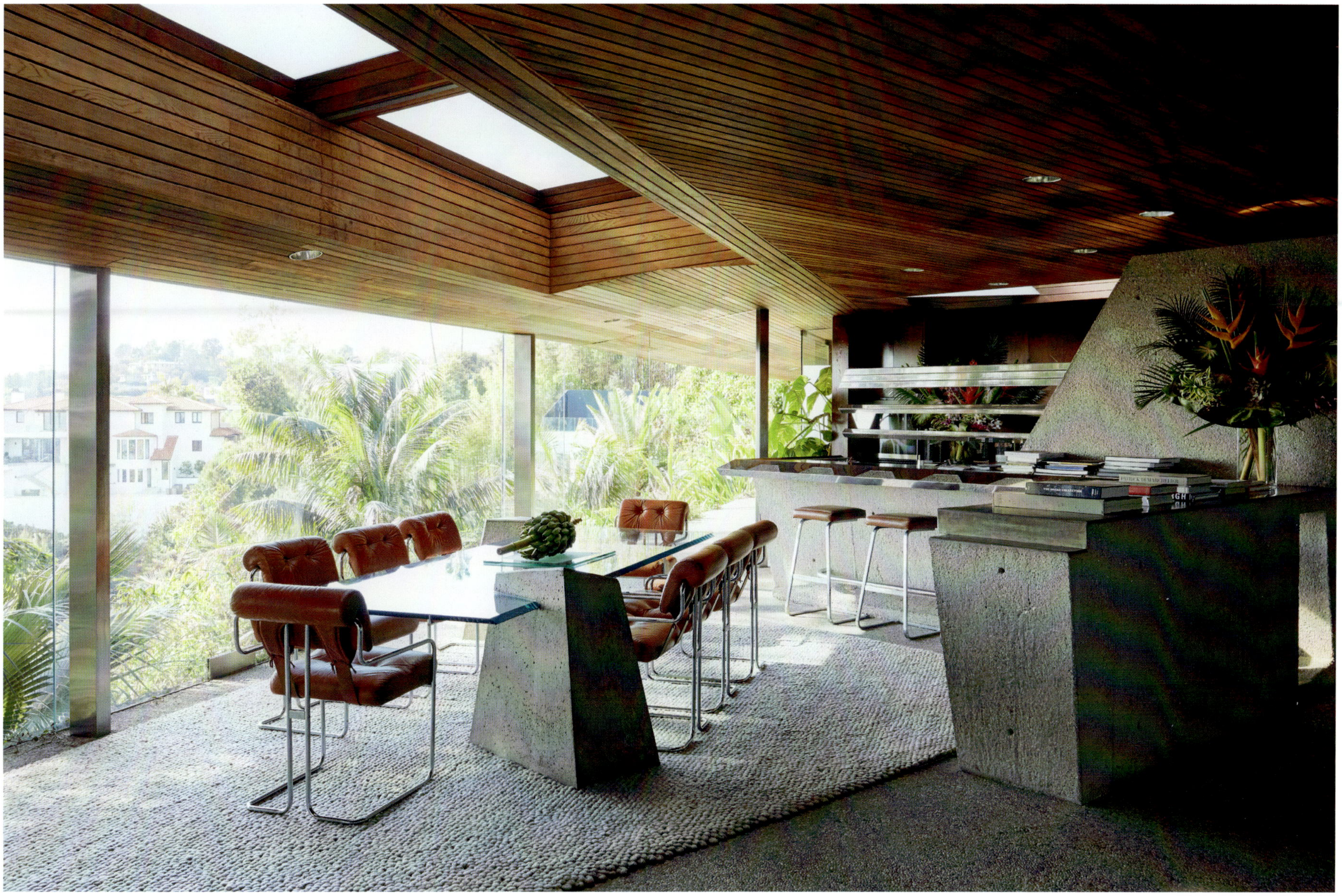

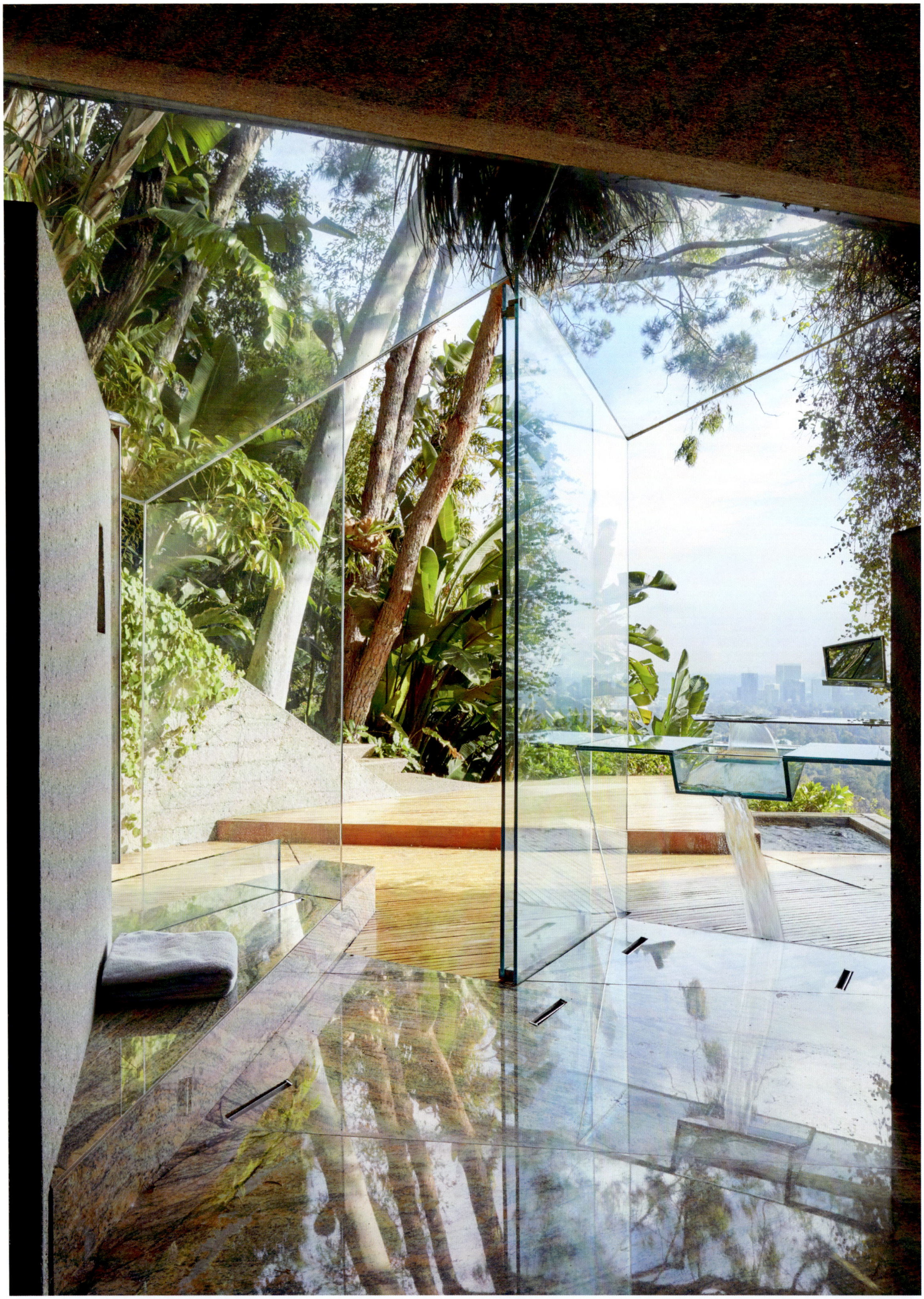

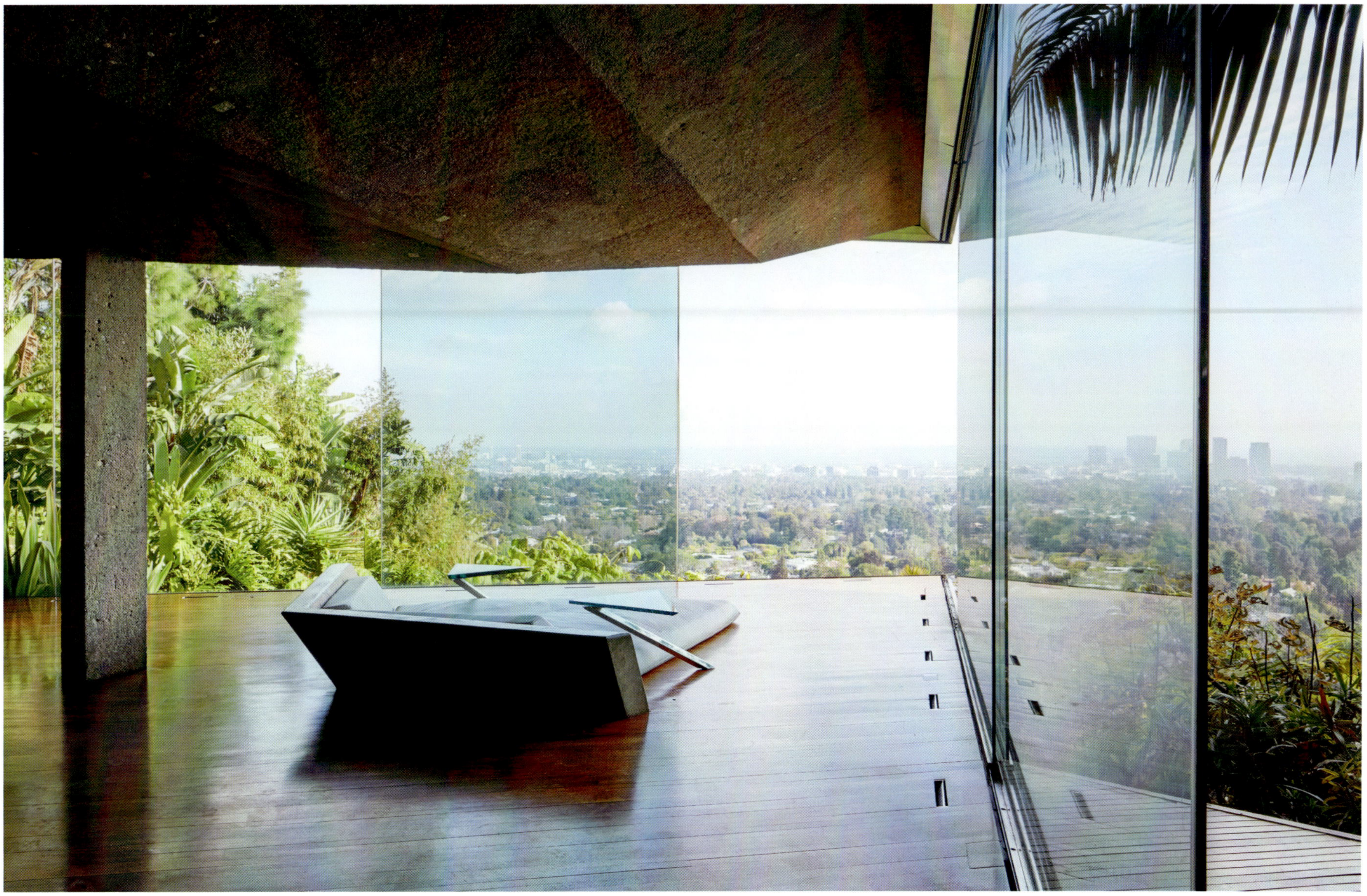

The Sheats-Goldstein residence is to *The Big Lebowski* as Casa Malaparte is to Jean-Luc Godard's *Contempt* (only with more Jackie Treehorn and less Brigitte Bardot).

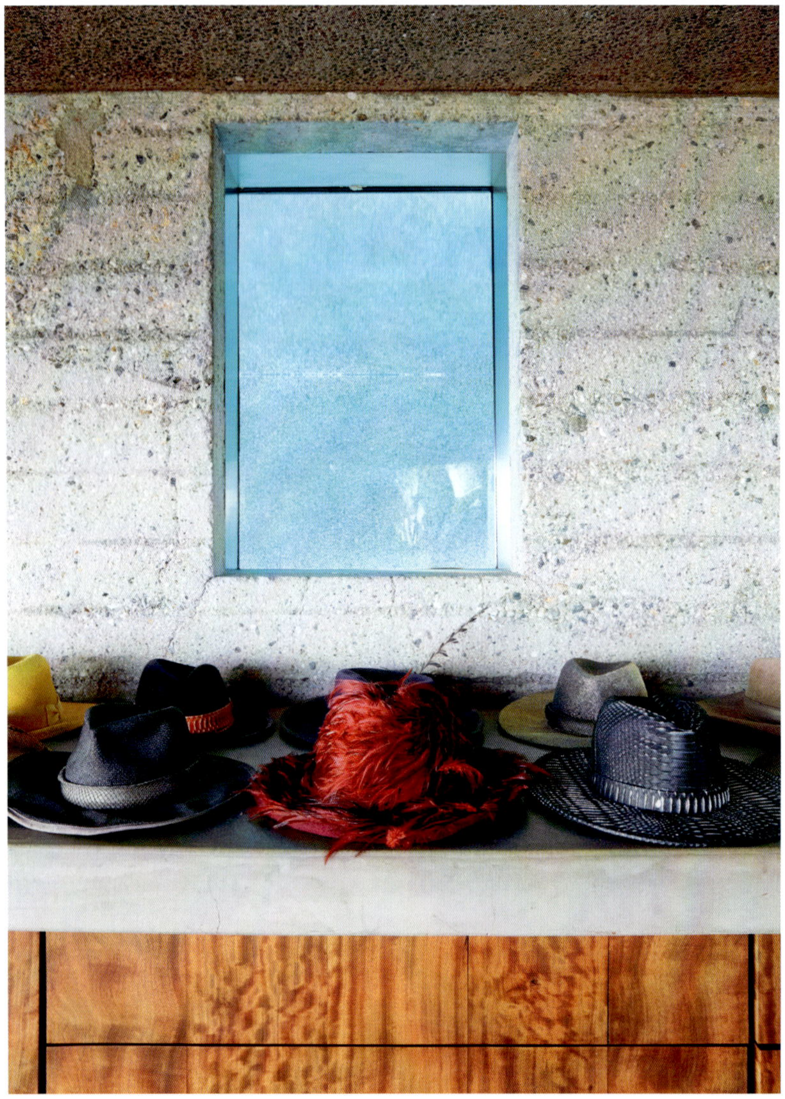

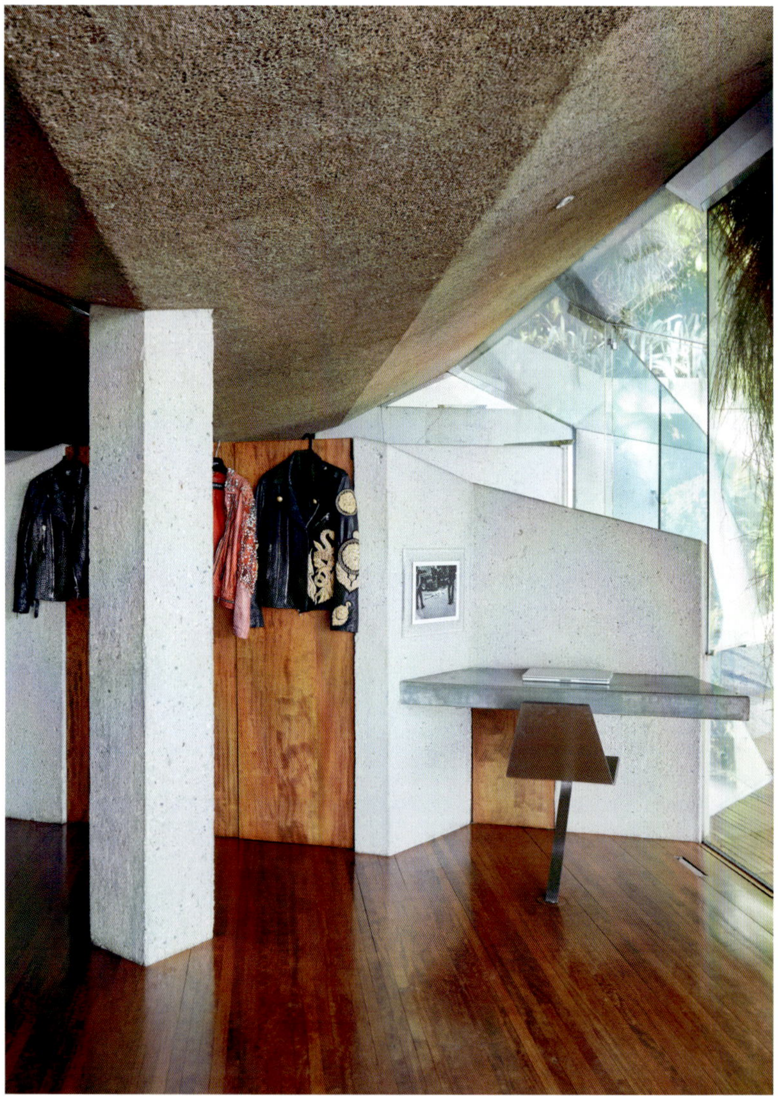

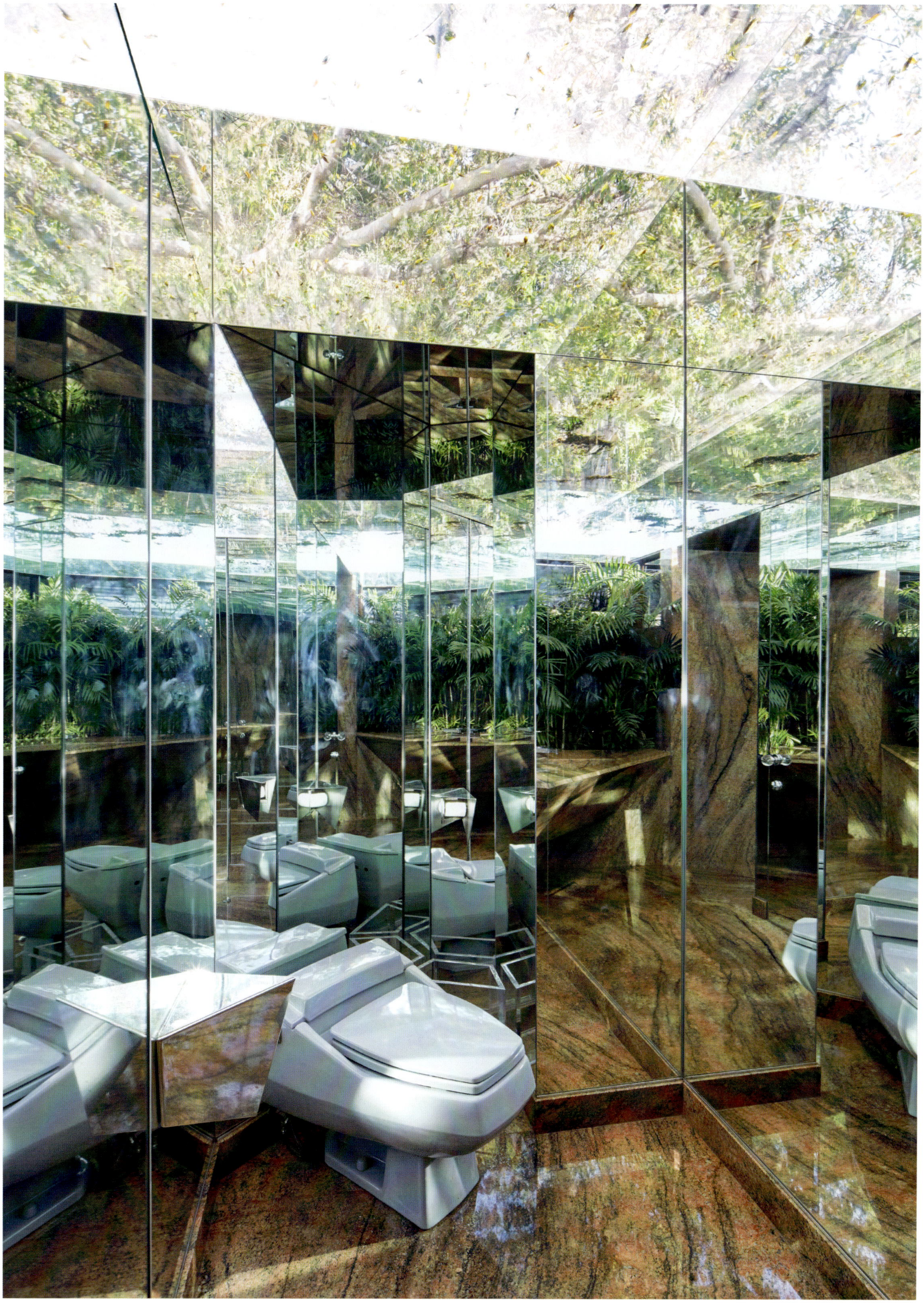

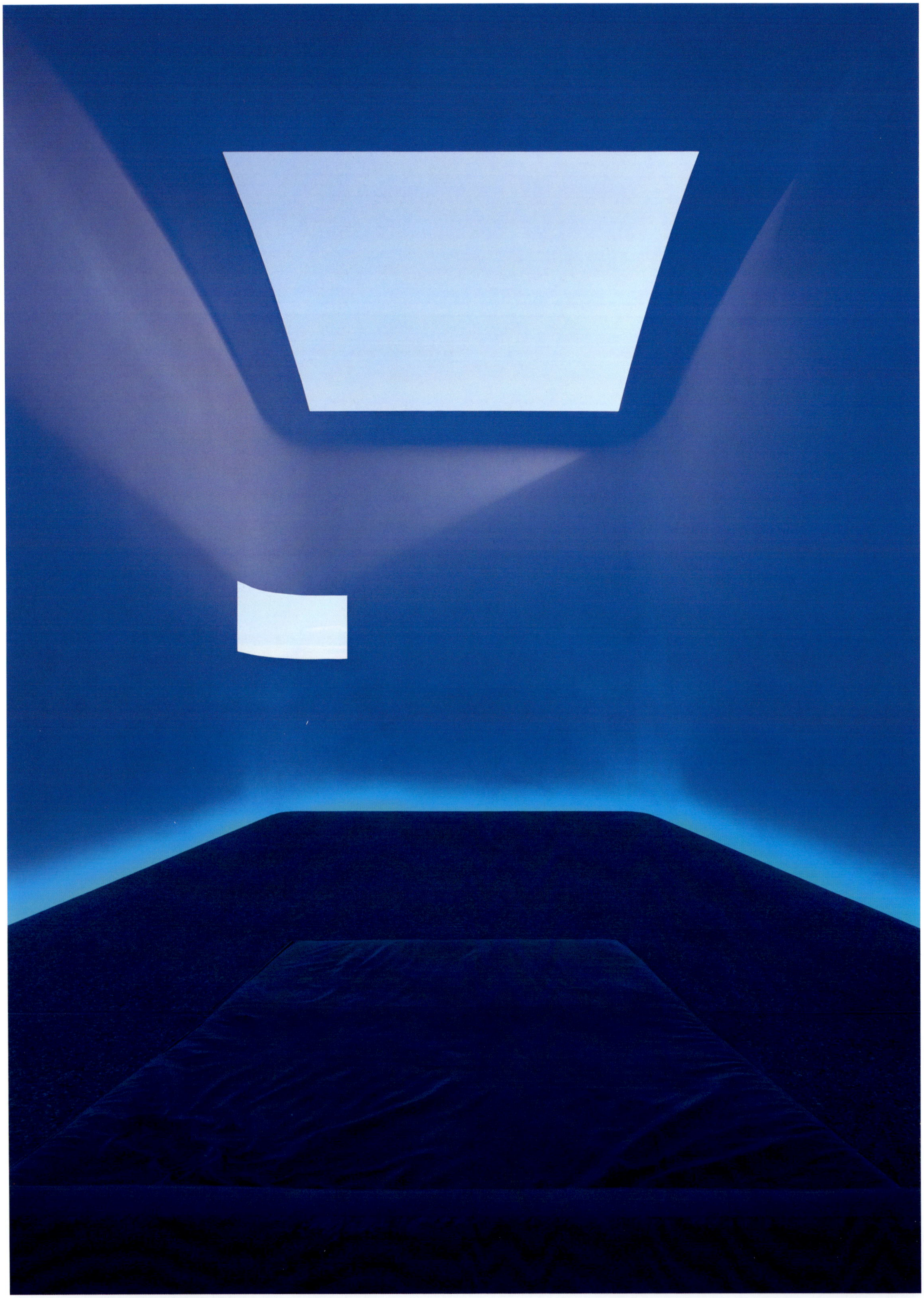

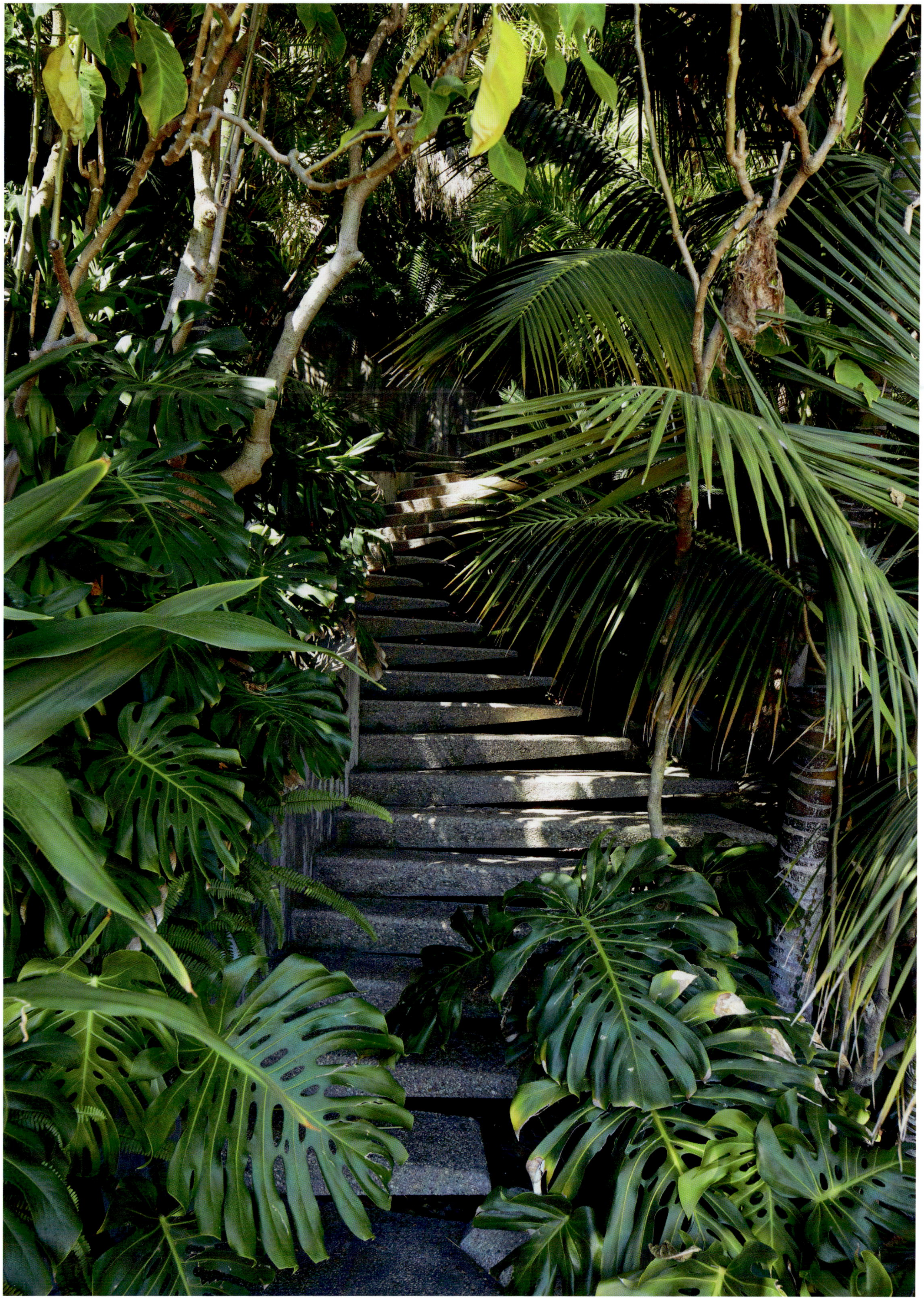

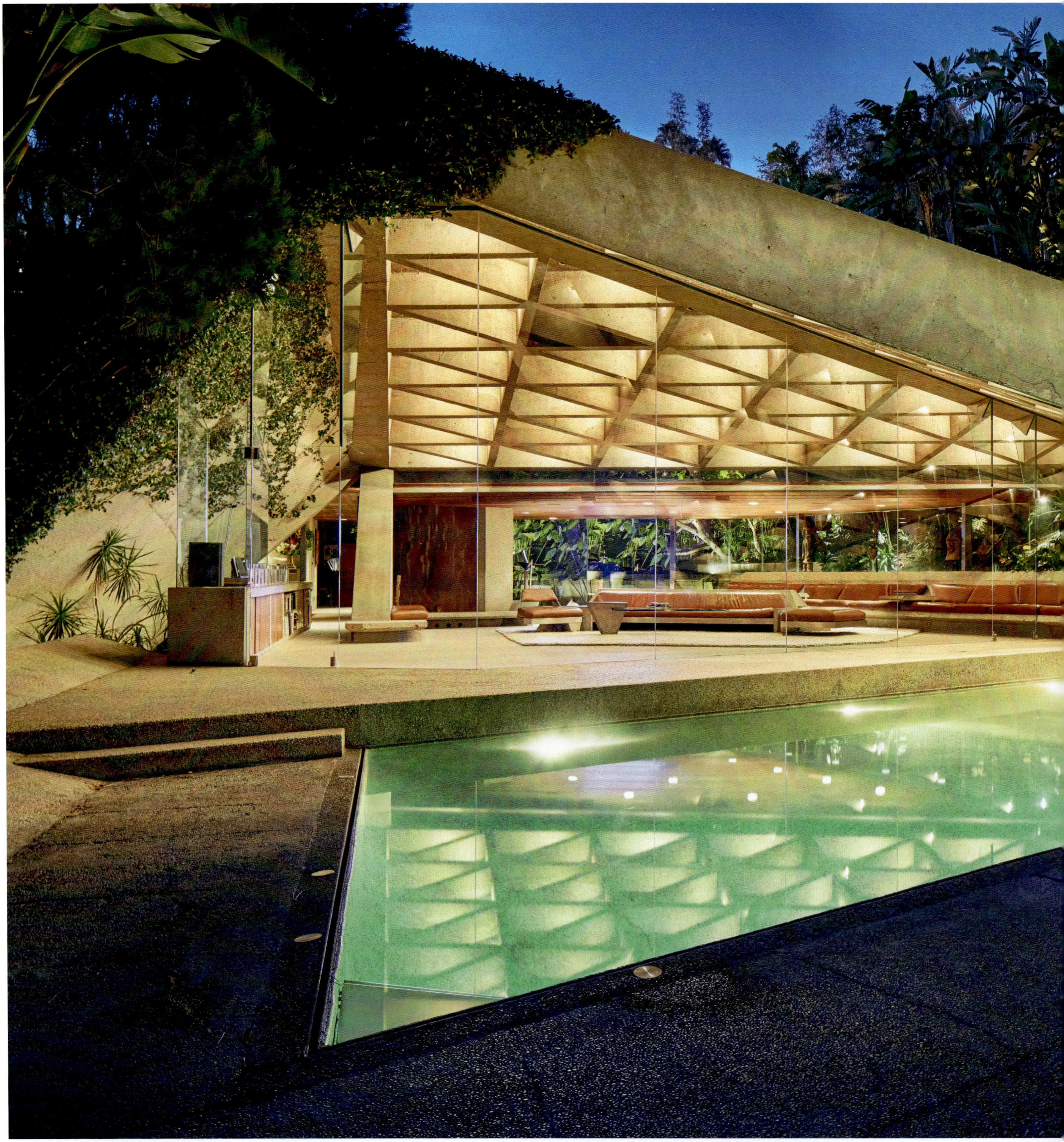

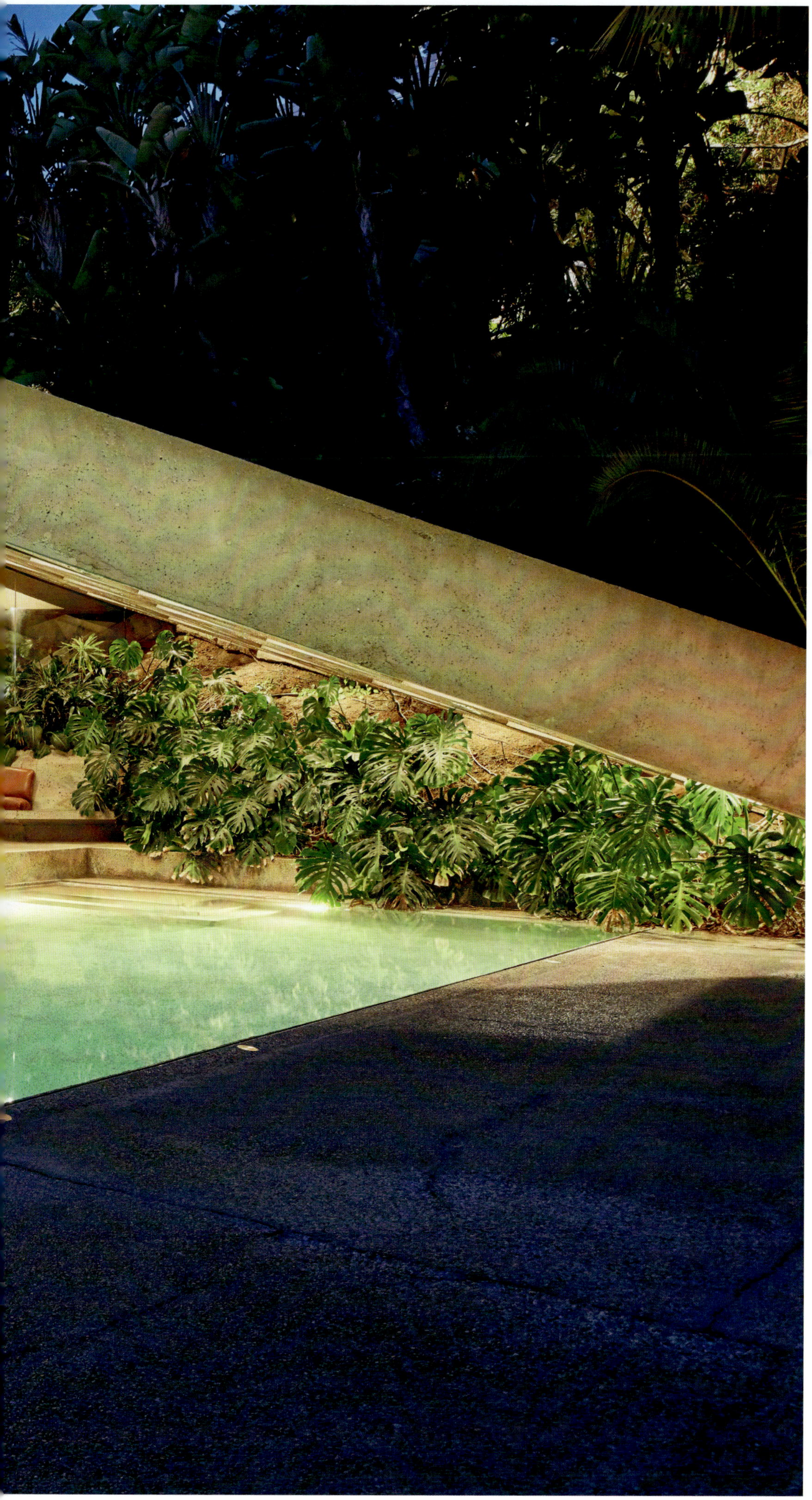

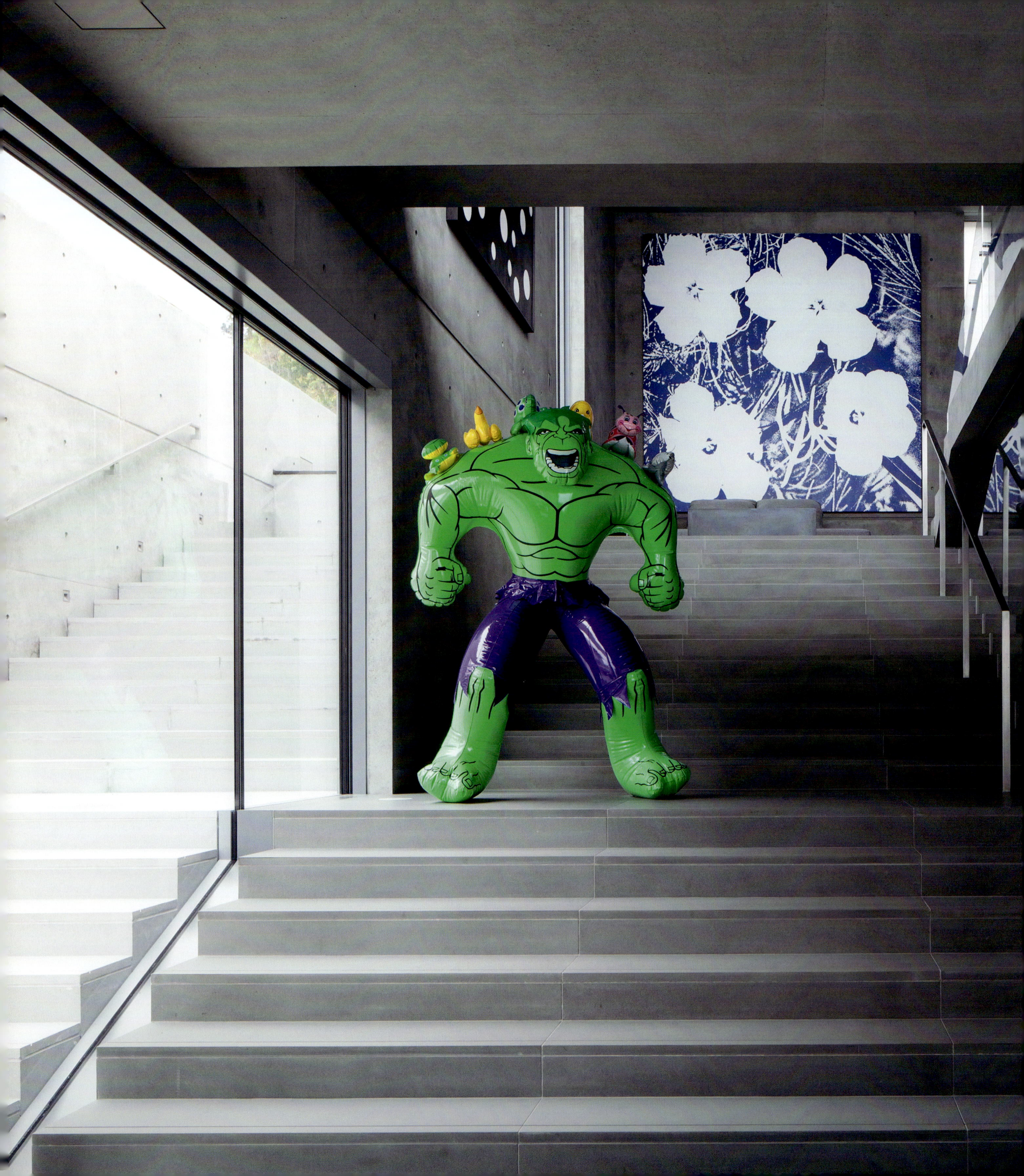

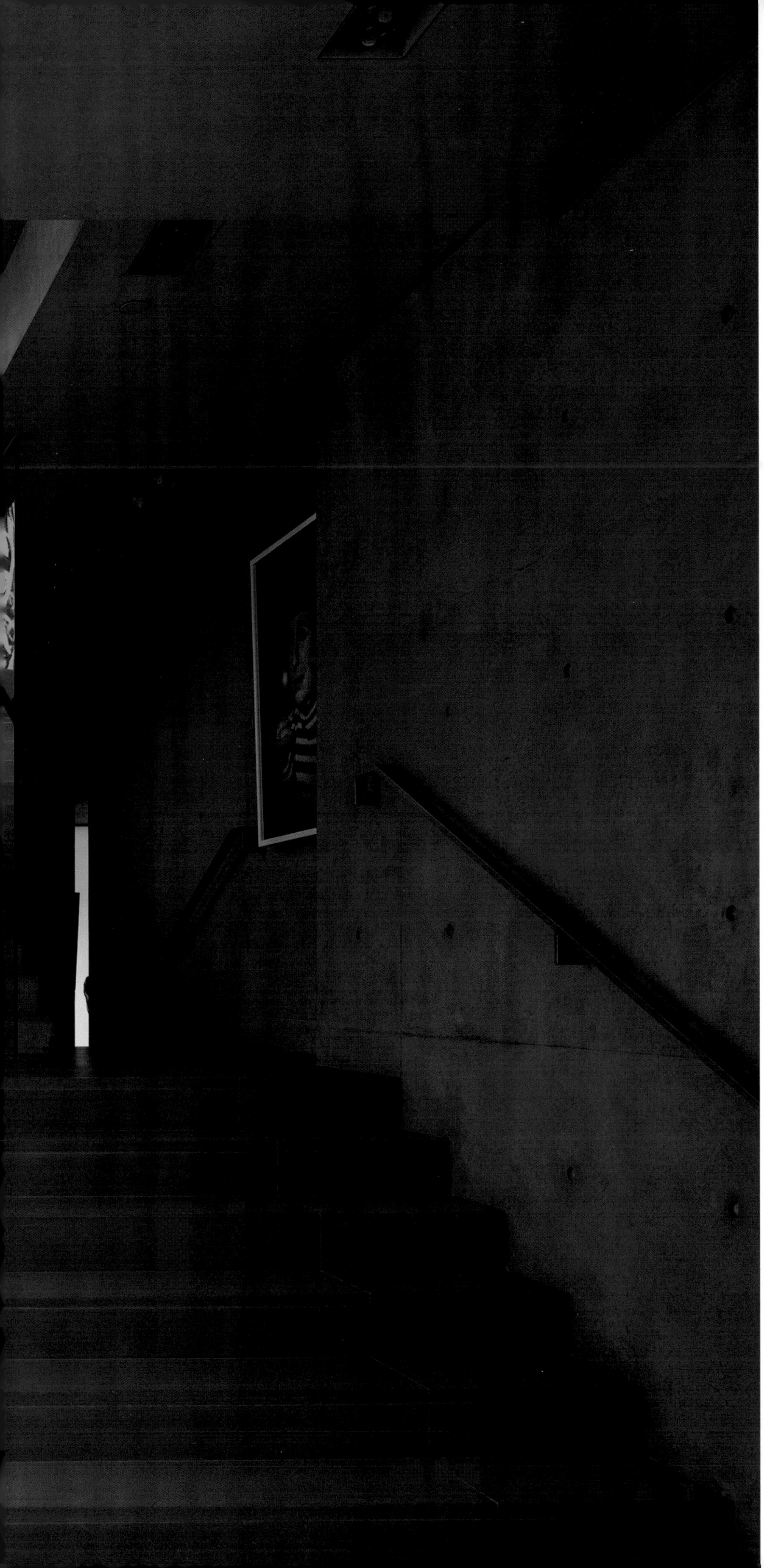

A House in Malibu

Malibu

Architect

Tadao Ando

There are very few residences designed by Pritzker Prize–winning architect Tadao Ando in America, so photographing this beach house in Malibu was both an honor and a huge learning experience.

Not everything about living on the water is as relaxed as it sounds. The house, which was realized by Los Angeles architects Marmol Radziner, is a technical marvel, innovative in its use of space and respectful of its site. After years of planning and with careful navigation of its small lot—which closely abuts neighboring beachfront properties—its construction involved sinking concrete pylons sixty feet into the earth to prevent the concrete house from sinking. But when I arrived, it was complete, and it was perfect.

As soon as you step inside, there is overwhelming calm, and the view through the floor-to-ceiling windows is distilled to the sky and the Pacific. The house comprises three floors with distinct purposes: the lower level welcomes guests, the ground floor features an outdoor lounge area for entertaining, and the top floor includes the primary bedroom suite and a deck set back to provide privacy from the beach. The residence—which combines Ando's clean, minimalist aesthetic with artwork by Cindy Sherman, Richard Prince, Kenny Scharf, George Condo, and Jeff Koons, among many others—is as much an art gallery suitable for such an extraordinary collection as a living space. And as with Ando's transcendent work on the island of Naoshima and his many museums around the world, the architecture itself becomes art.

I've shot houses every which way, and the exterior photographs aren't always the easiest to figure out. To find the right angle in varying locations, I've shot from a neighboring mountain with a long lens, while snowshoeing across a frozen lake, while standing atop rental cars, using drones, in boats, and hanging out of helicopters with the doors removed. I wanted a dusk shot of the Ando house, but the water was high and there wasn't much beach. So after studying the tide charts, my assistant and I were in wetsuits in the ocean, balancing on a twelve-foot ladder while trying to get long exposures between the waves. Apparently from the house we looked crazy. Whatever it takes, I guess!

I photographed this house four times, both before and after it was furnished, giving me a rare opportunity to experience Ando's work in different states; I especially loved the play of shadows and light in the empty building. Several months after moving in completely, the homeowner threw a small but star-studded gathering at the house in honor of the enigmatic architect. Ando, accompanied by his colleague and translator for the evening Masataka Yano, held court quietly from a corner, greeting the guests who hovered around in appreciation.

Previous: The central staircase is half the width of the house and continues from the interior out, providing a space for gathering and entertaining as well as a gallery to showcase works by Jeff Koons and Cindy Sherman, among others.

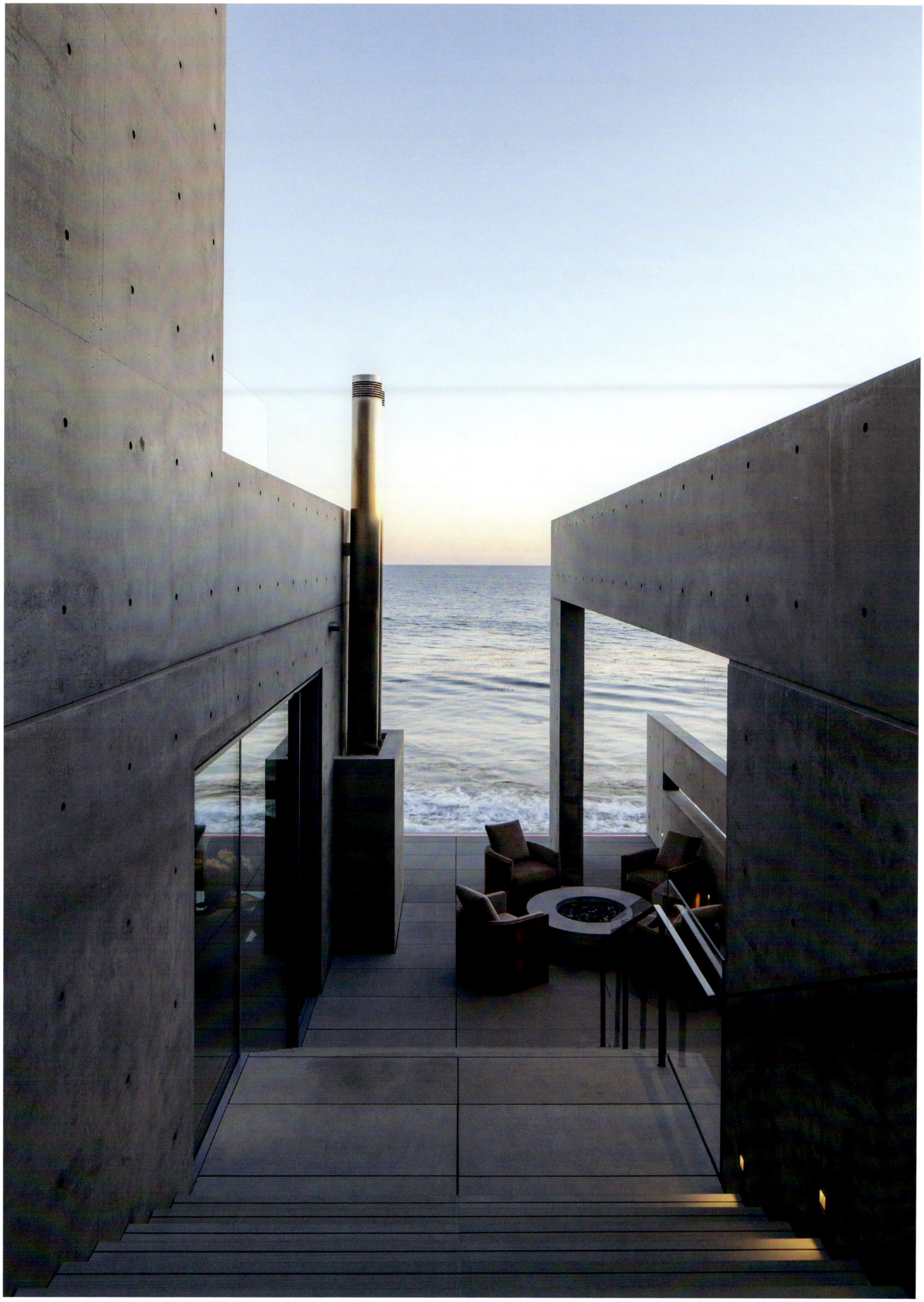

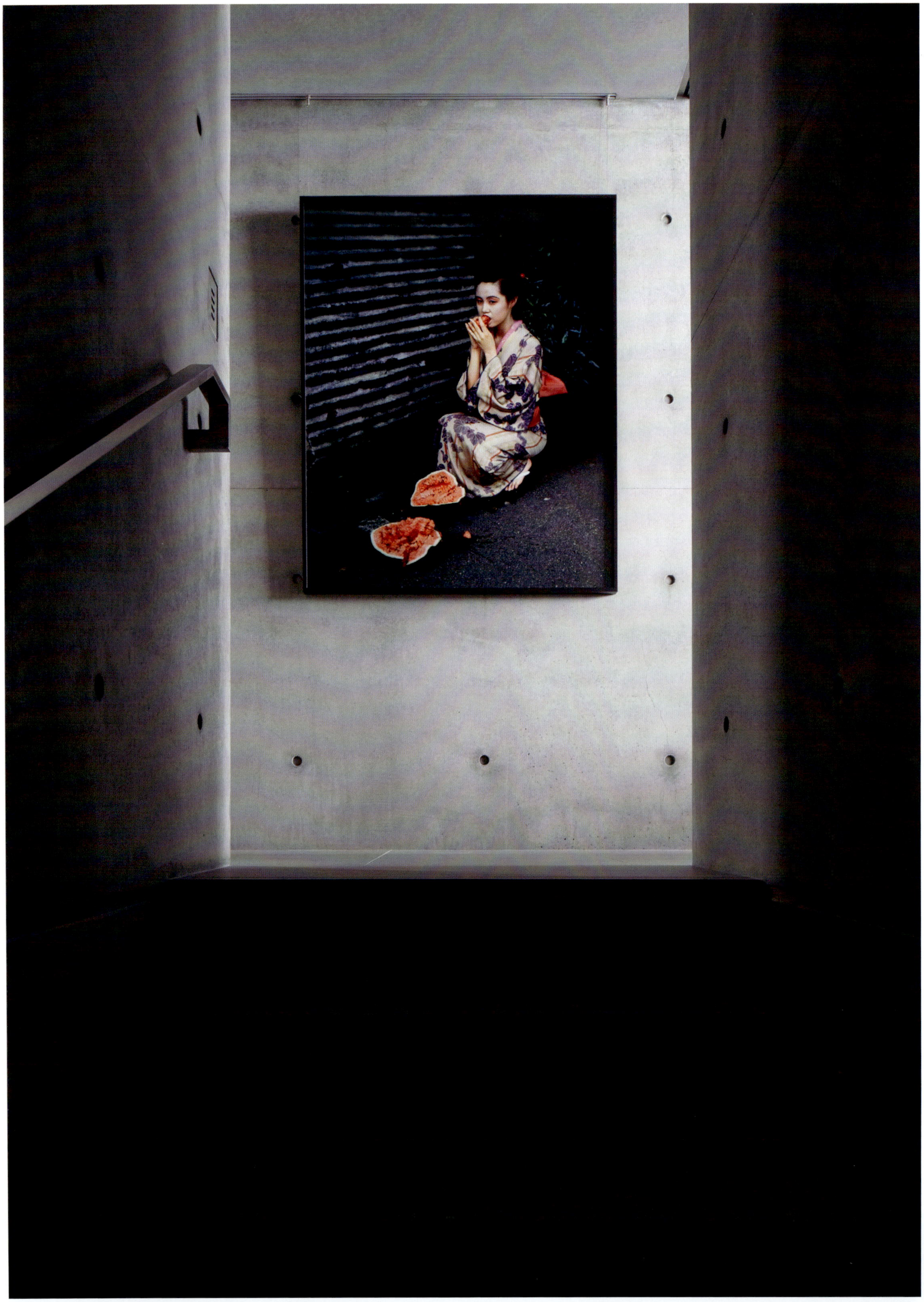

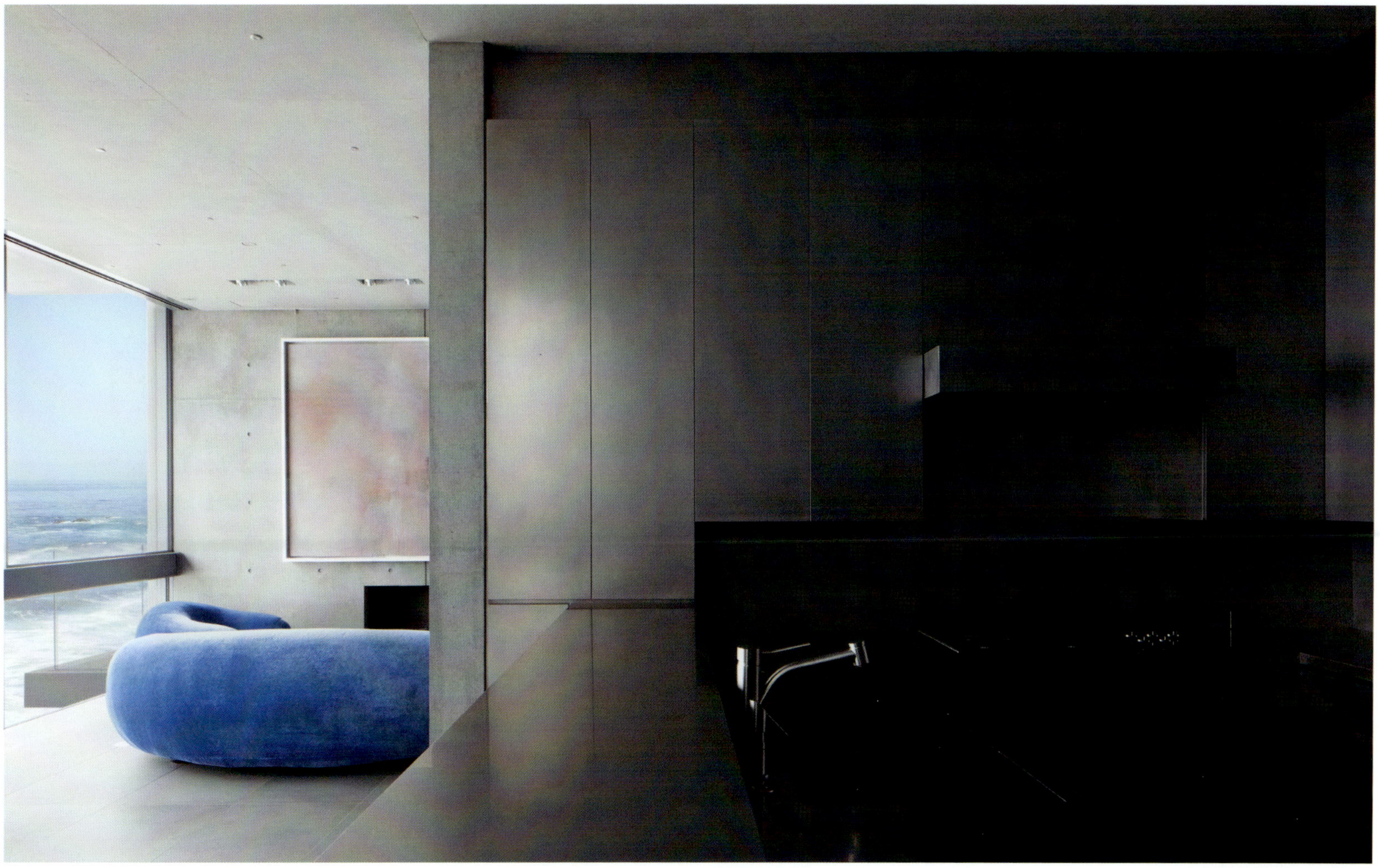

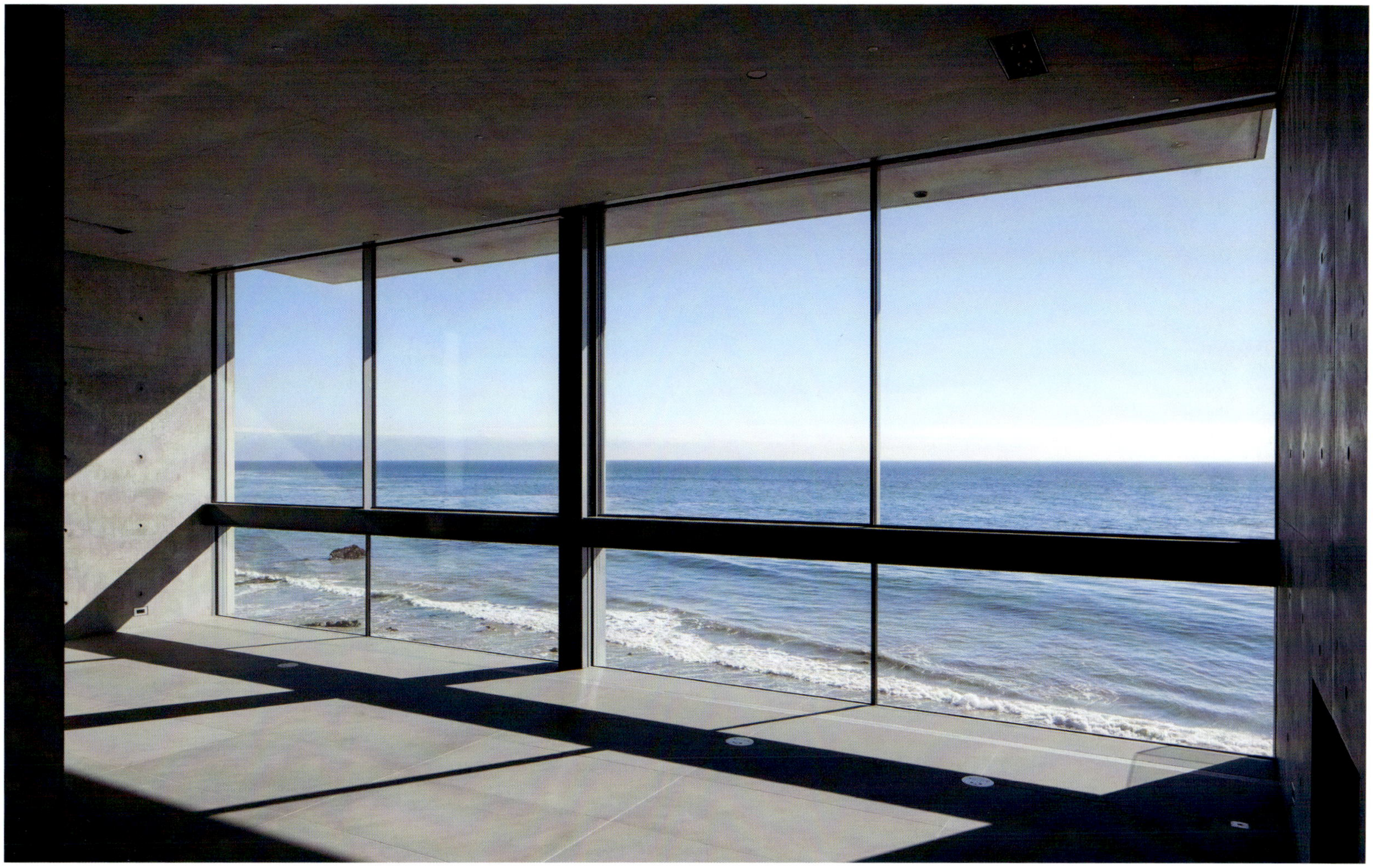

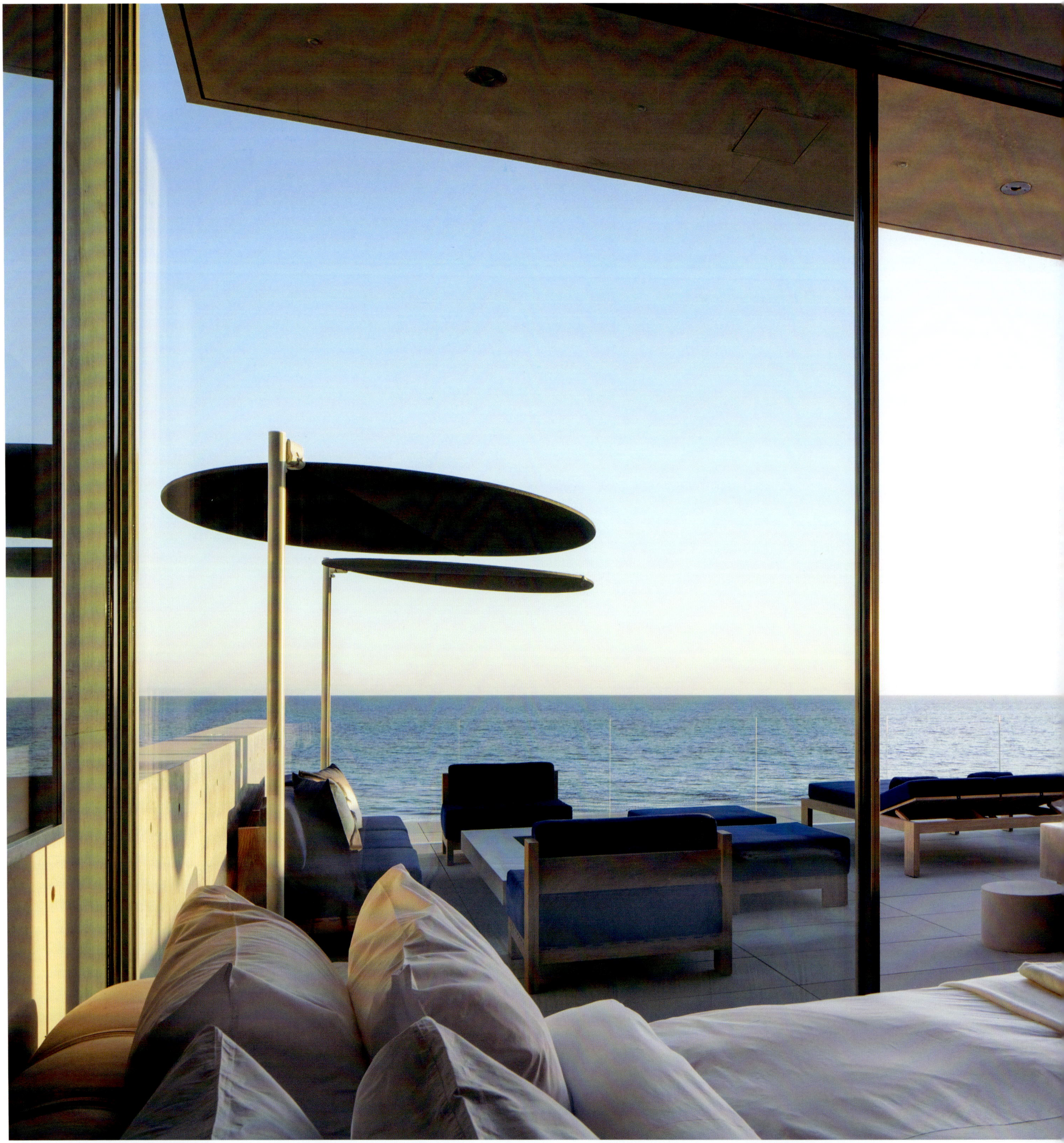

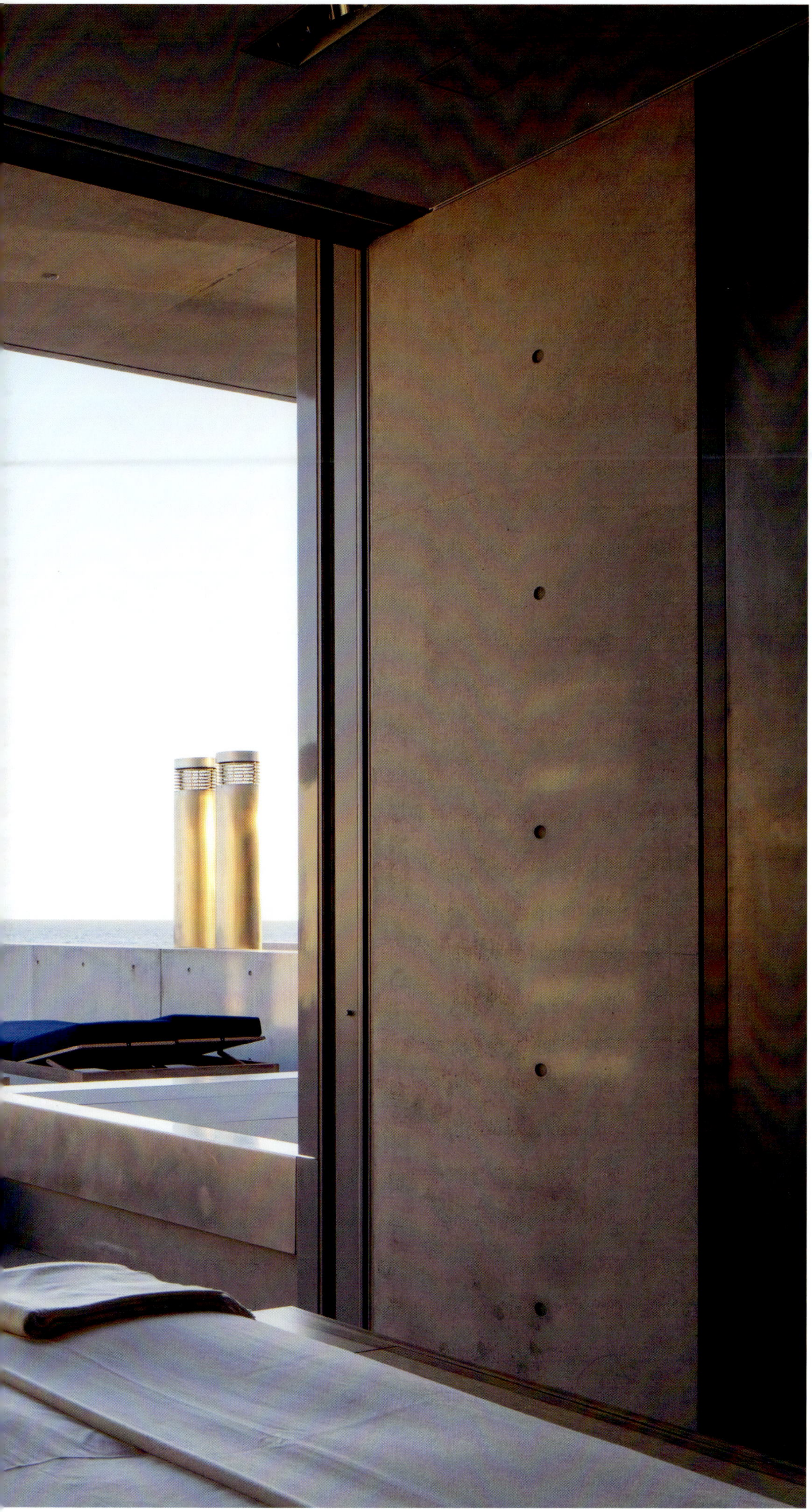

A patio off the primary bedroom suite overlooks the ocean and is set back into the house to provide privacy from the beach.

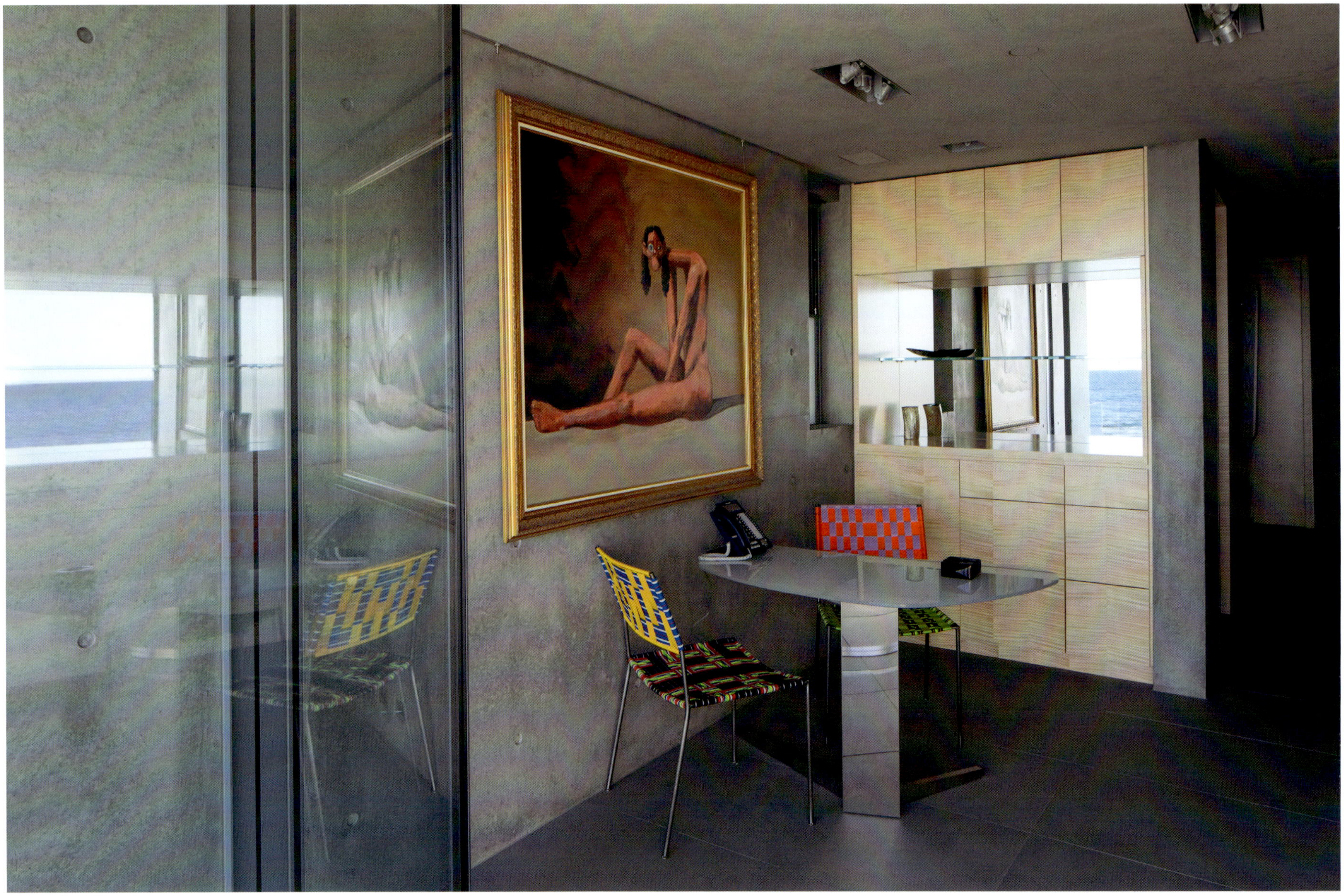

Tucked neatly between its neighbors, the house's unassuming street-facing facade belies the elegant, sculptural, and almost monastic building beyond, from which all attention is directed toward the water.

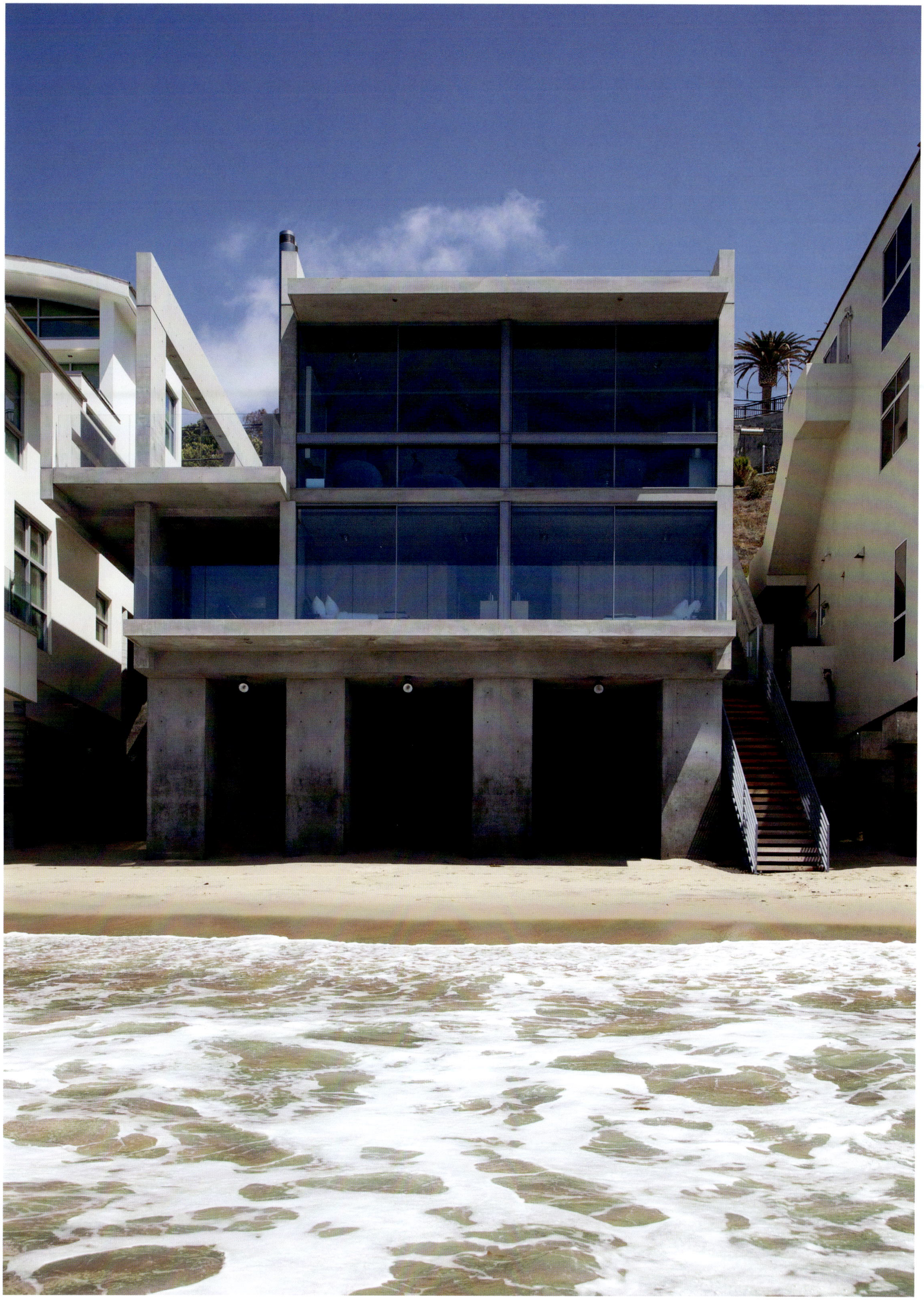

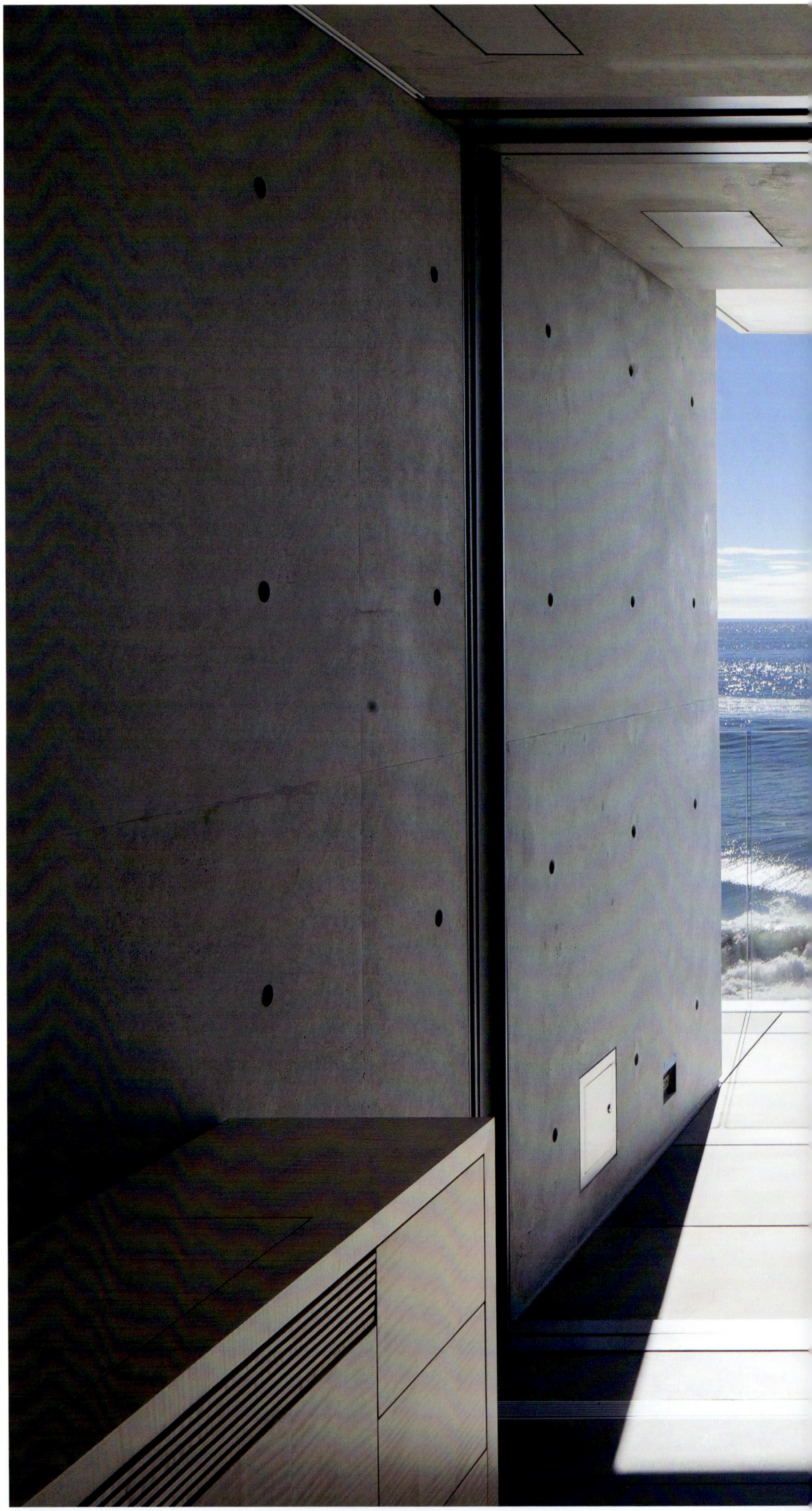

Through the house's floor-to-ceiling windows, the building seems to hover directly over the ocean.

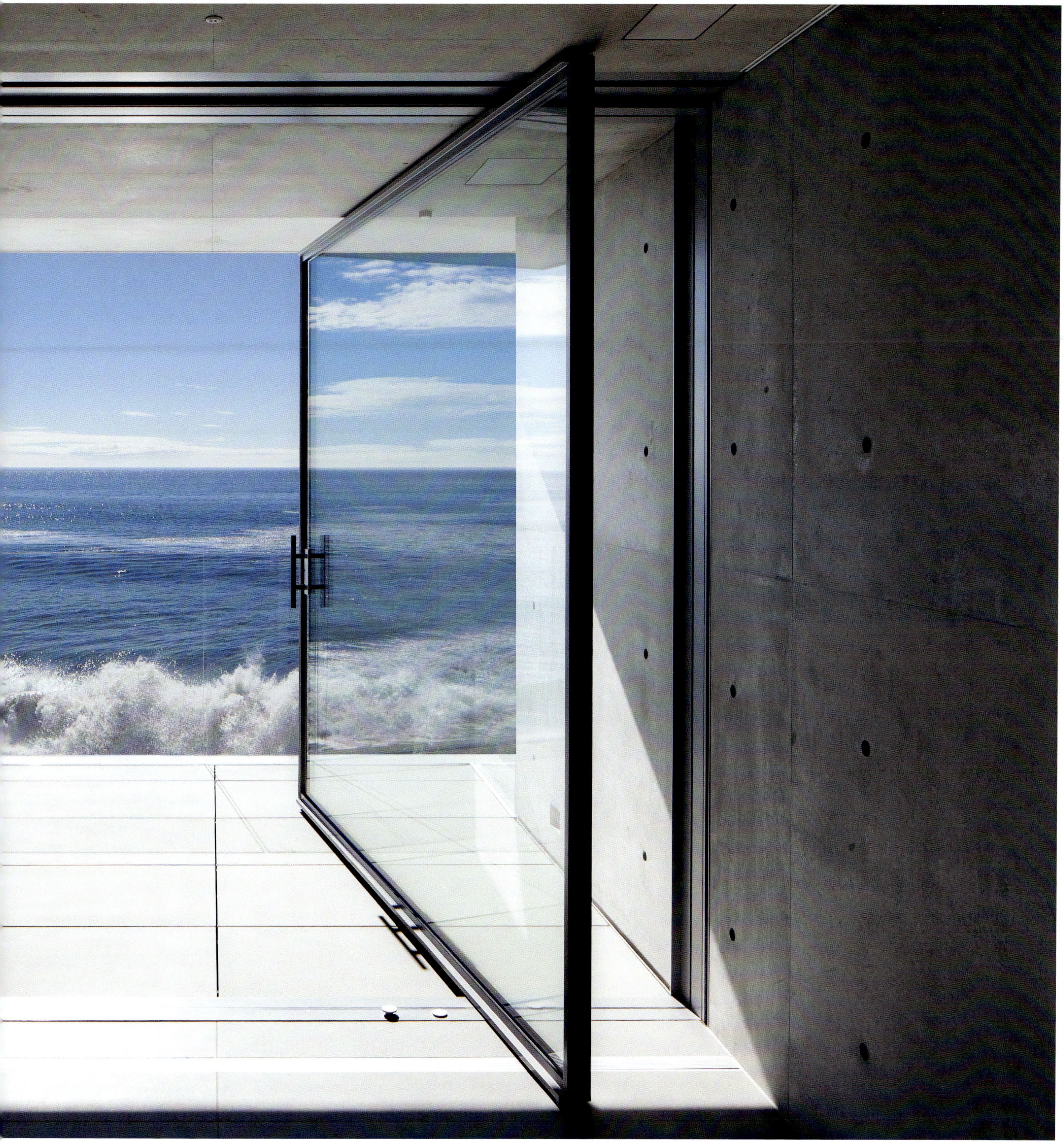

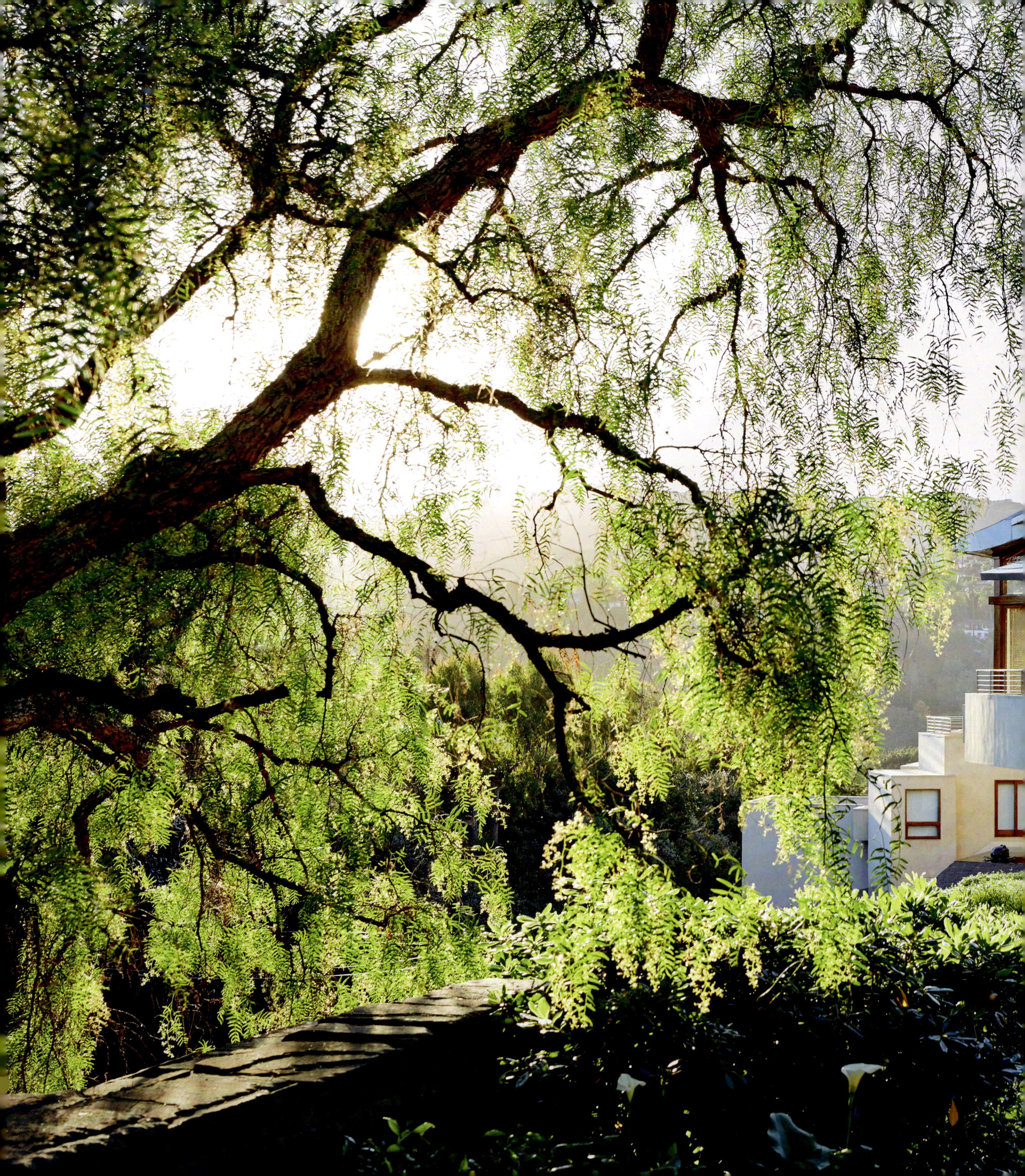

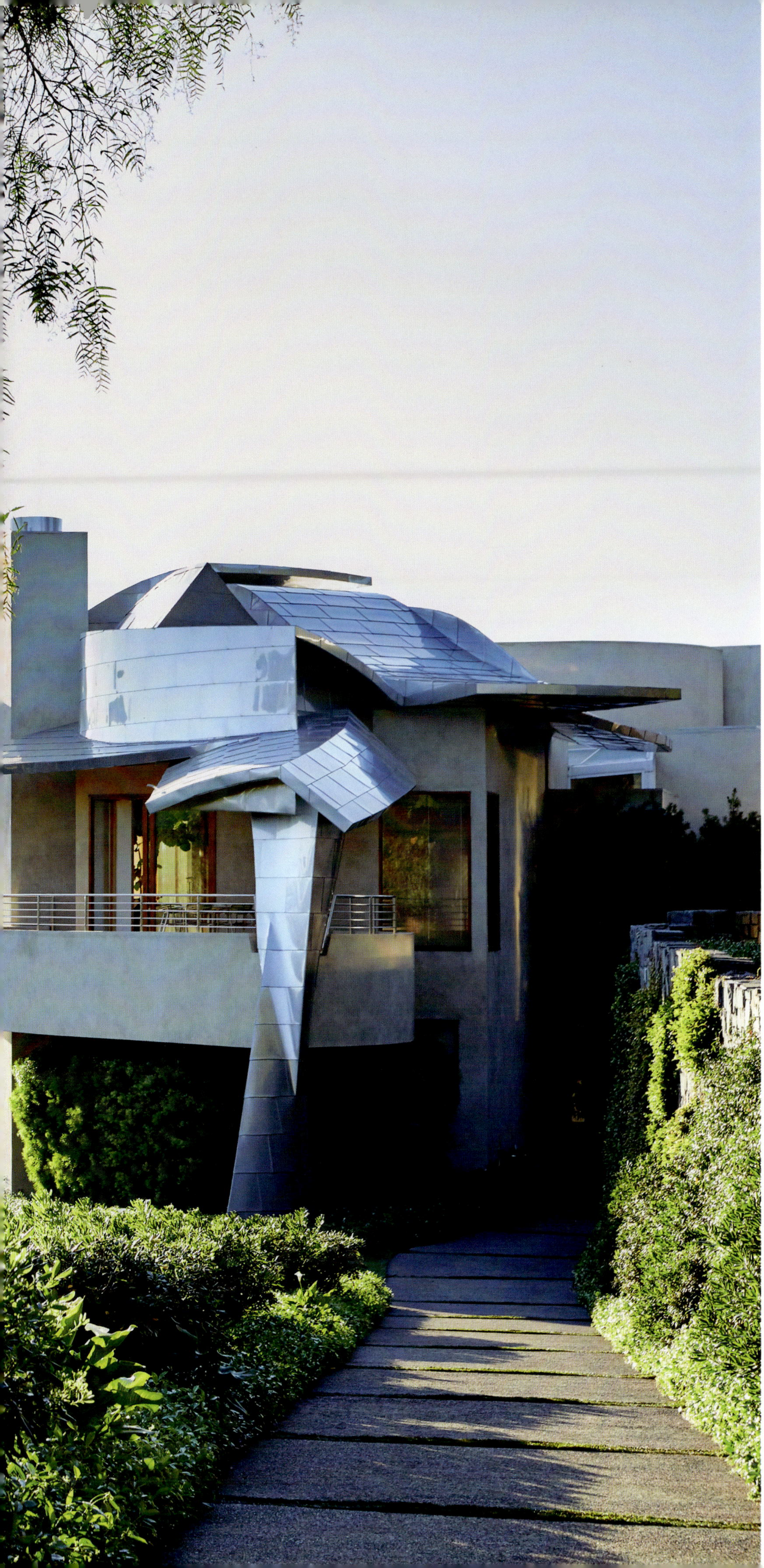

Broad Residence

Brentwood

Architect

Frank Gehry

Residents

Eli and Edythe Broad

One rather special perk of spending time in these remarkable homes is being up close and personal with some of the most exceptional art in the world, if only for a fleeting moment. It was perhaps at the home of Eli and Edythe Broad that I experienced the height of this privilege.

It was clear that the Broads lived and breathed art; it permeated the residence, inside and out, from the private galleries on the lower level to the living and powder rooms to the garden. The house itself is arguably a work of art. Designed by Frank Gehry and completed in 1994, it features the stainless-steel-clad swoops and complex curves that would swiftly become the architect's signature.

The time that photographers are given to shoot a home is limited—typically two days, though sometimes only one. Years of learning the craft and working in the field gives us a certain muscle memory: when we enter a room, it's often readily apparent which are the hero angles and, in order to give the space more shape, where to add light or, more often, take it away. All of this experience is utterly upended when walking into a building designed by Gehry. His rooms and their light do not follow any established conventions. Nor do they even fit comfortably into the image ratio of the camera most photographers have been looking through for the last twenty years. Gehry's buildings are immersive experiences that defy photography. Just like the best art, his work challenges us to think anew.

Already renowned for their philanthropy, in 2017 the Broads opened the Broad, a 120,000-square-foot contemporary art museum in downtown Los Angeles with free admission for all. In the space of a year, I was fortunate to photograph some of the stunning artworks first in the Broads' Brentwood home, then later in the newly opened museum, which showcases nearly two thousand works from their collection. It is fascinating to experience art in both public and private settings—responding, for example, to heavenly Twomblys in a living room and viewing the same paintings hung in a museum that welcomes more than nine hundred thousand visitors per year. Sadly, Mr. Broad passed away in 2021, but his incomparable legacy as a patron of the arts endures.

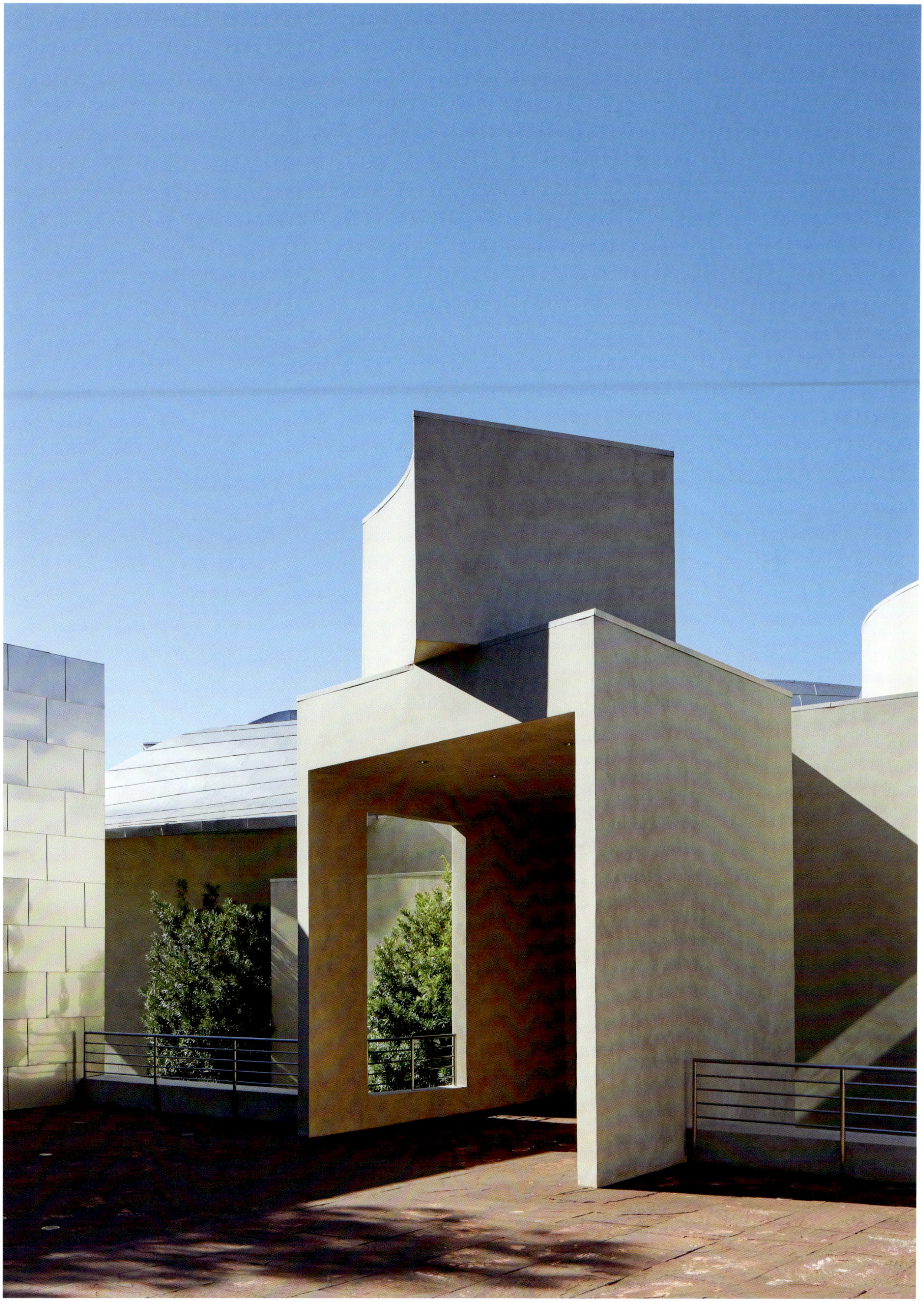

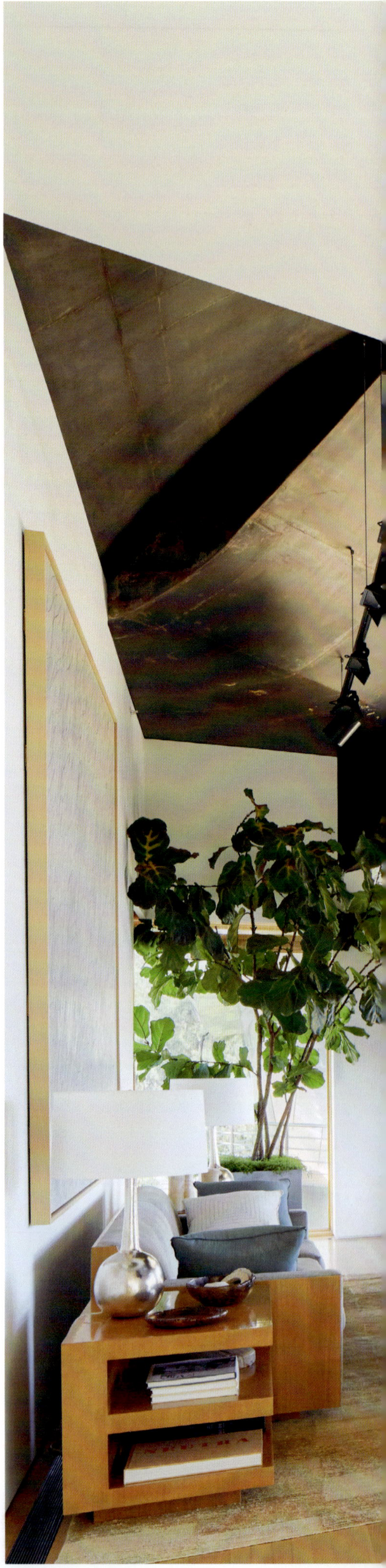

Art and architecture merge in the living room, in which the dynamic swooping forms of Frank Gehry's design are visible above work by such artists as Robert Rauschenberg, Jasper Johns, Cy Twombly, and Henry Moore. Much of the Broads' incomparable collection is now accessible to the public at their namesake museum.

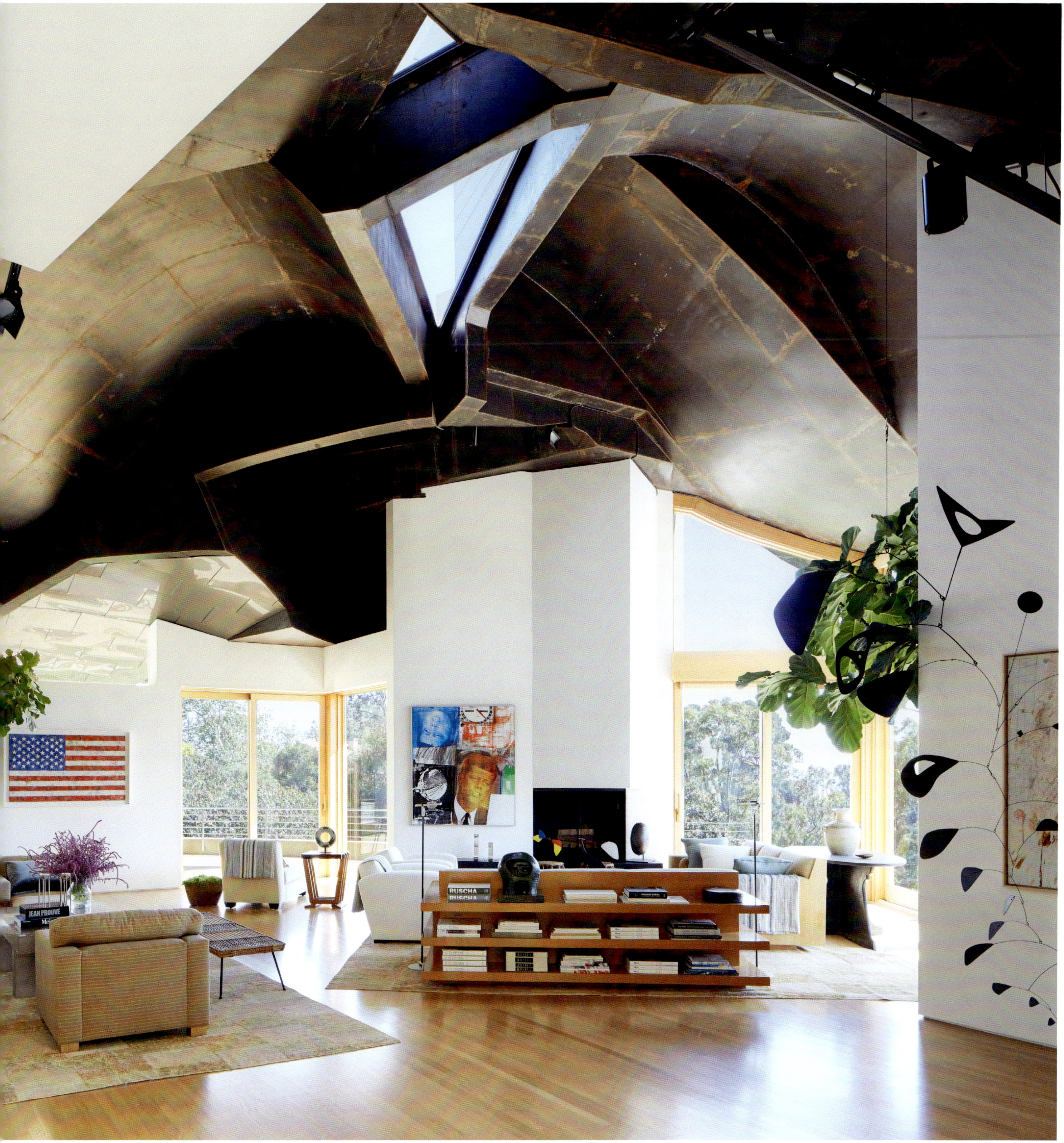
RUSCHA
RUSCHA
JEAN PROUVÉ

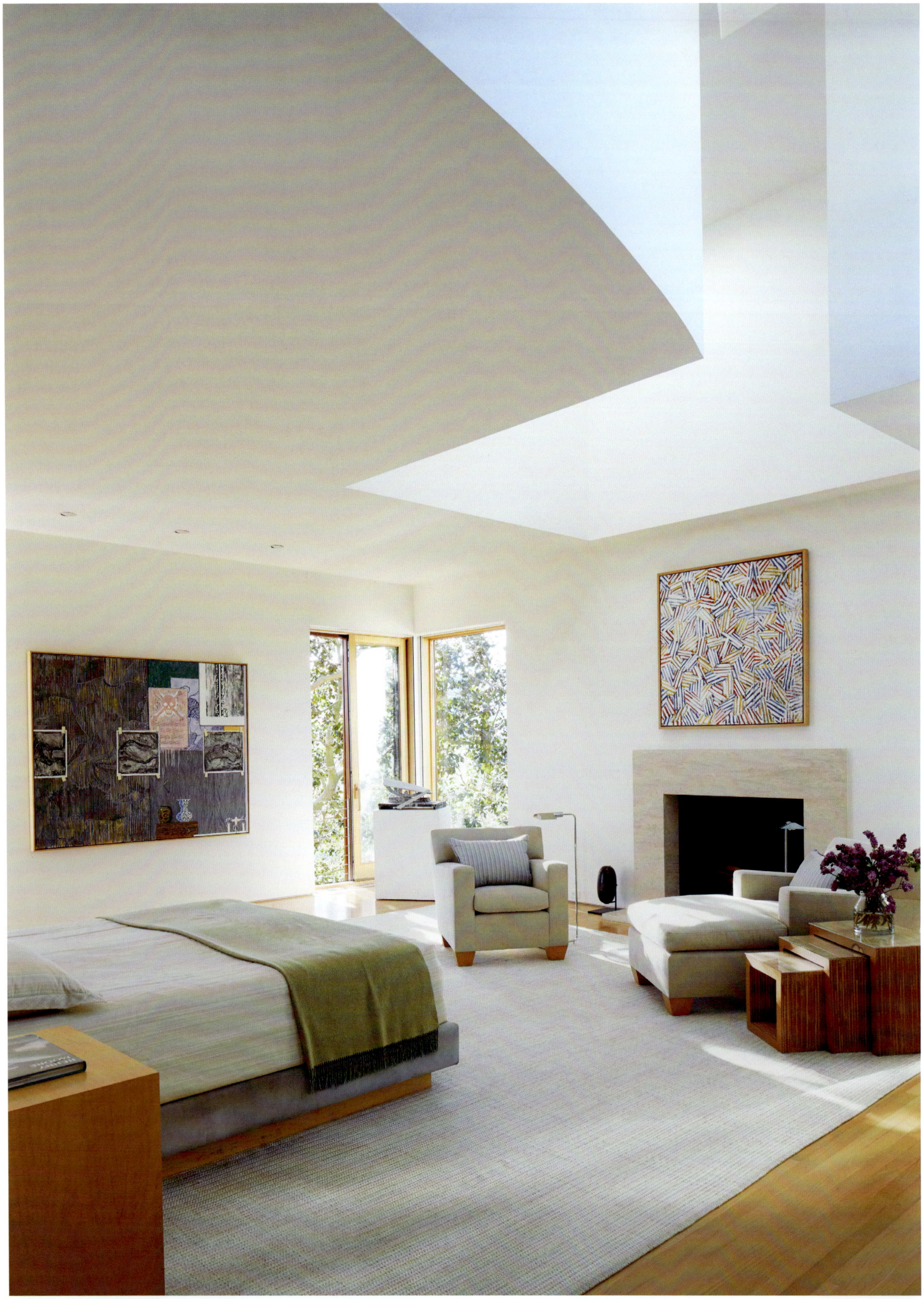

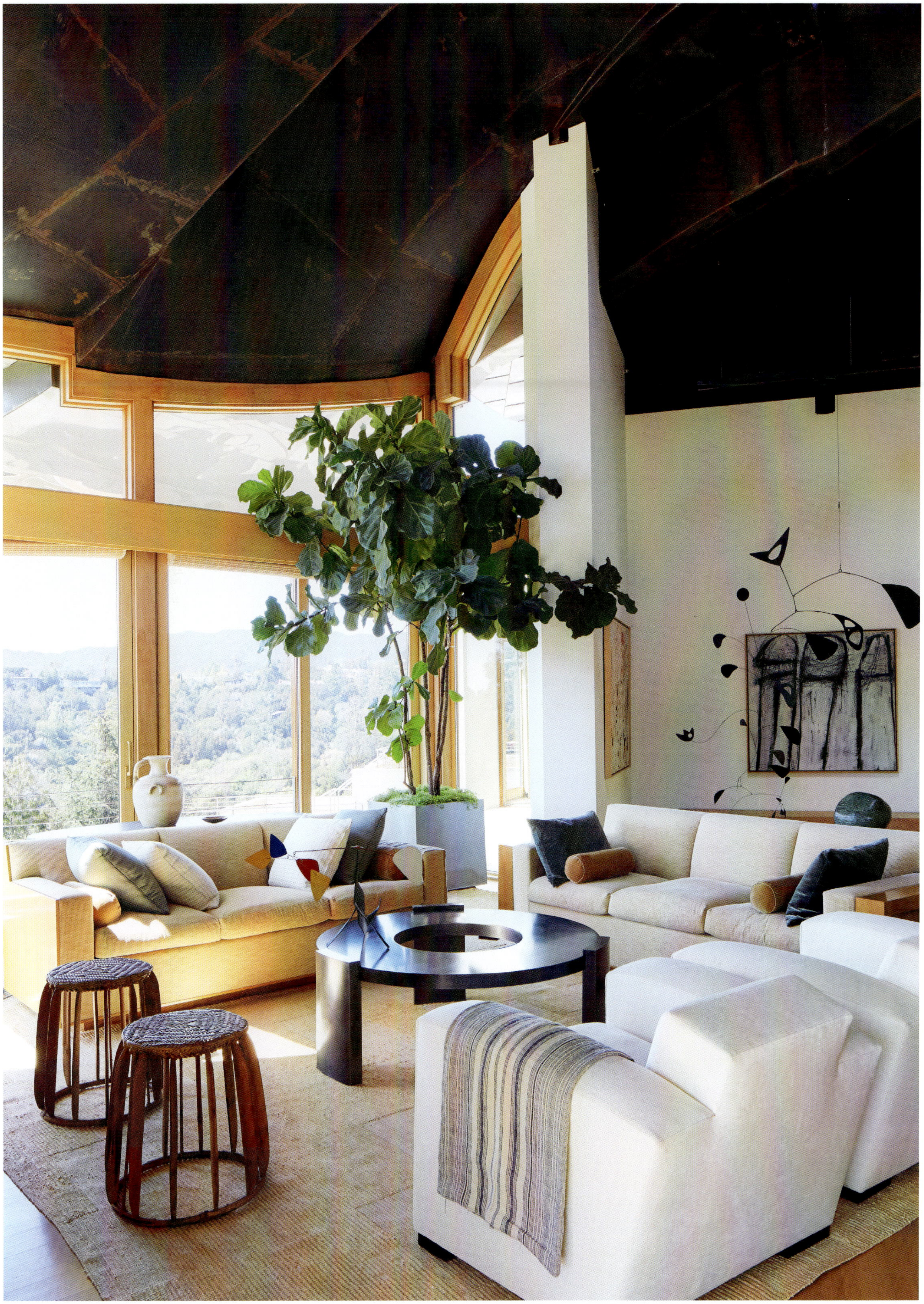

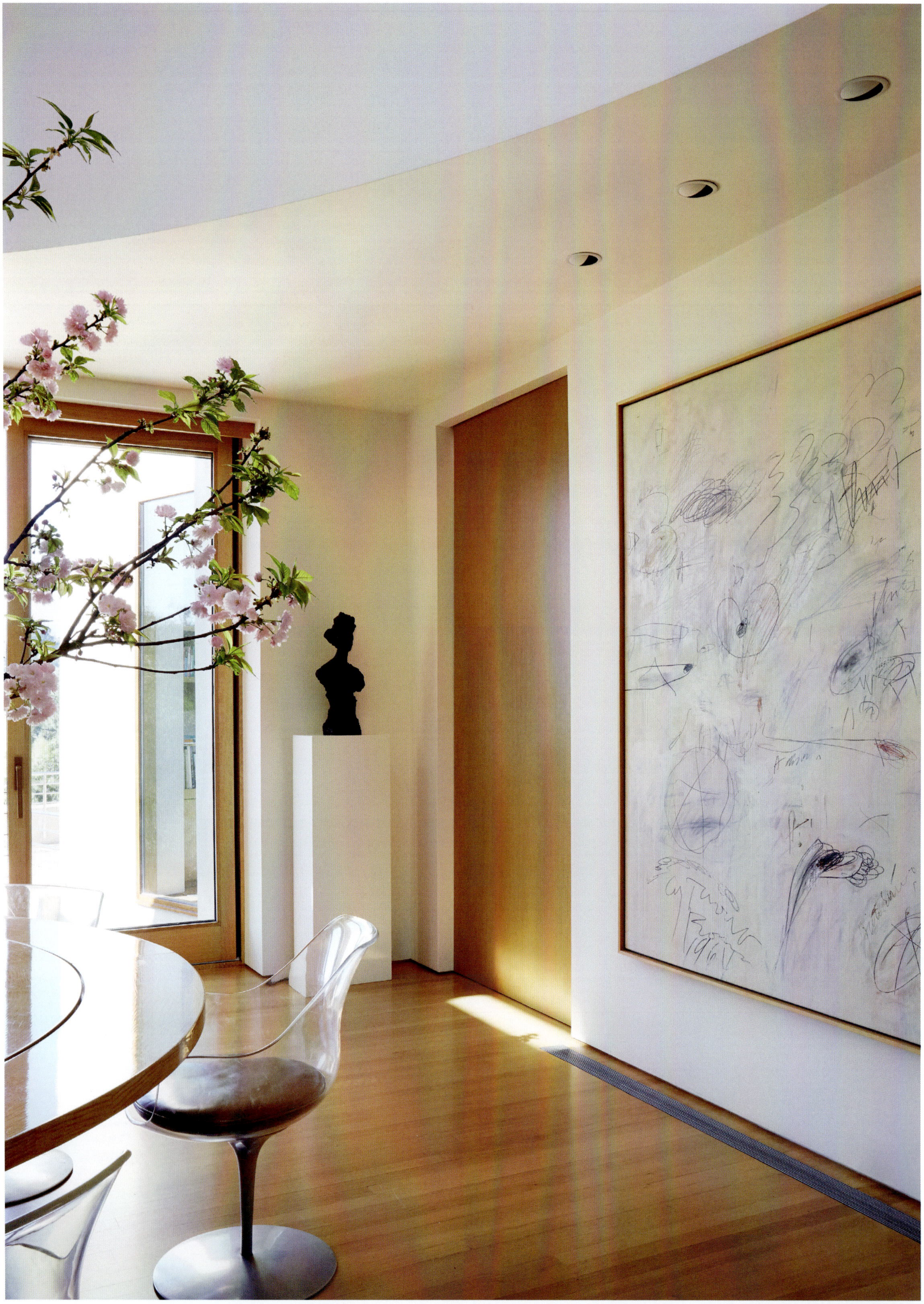

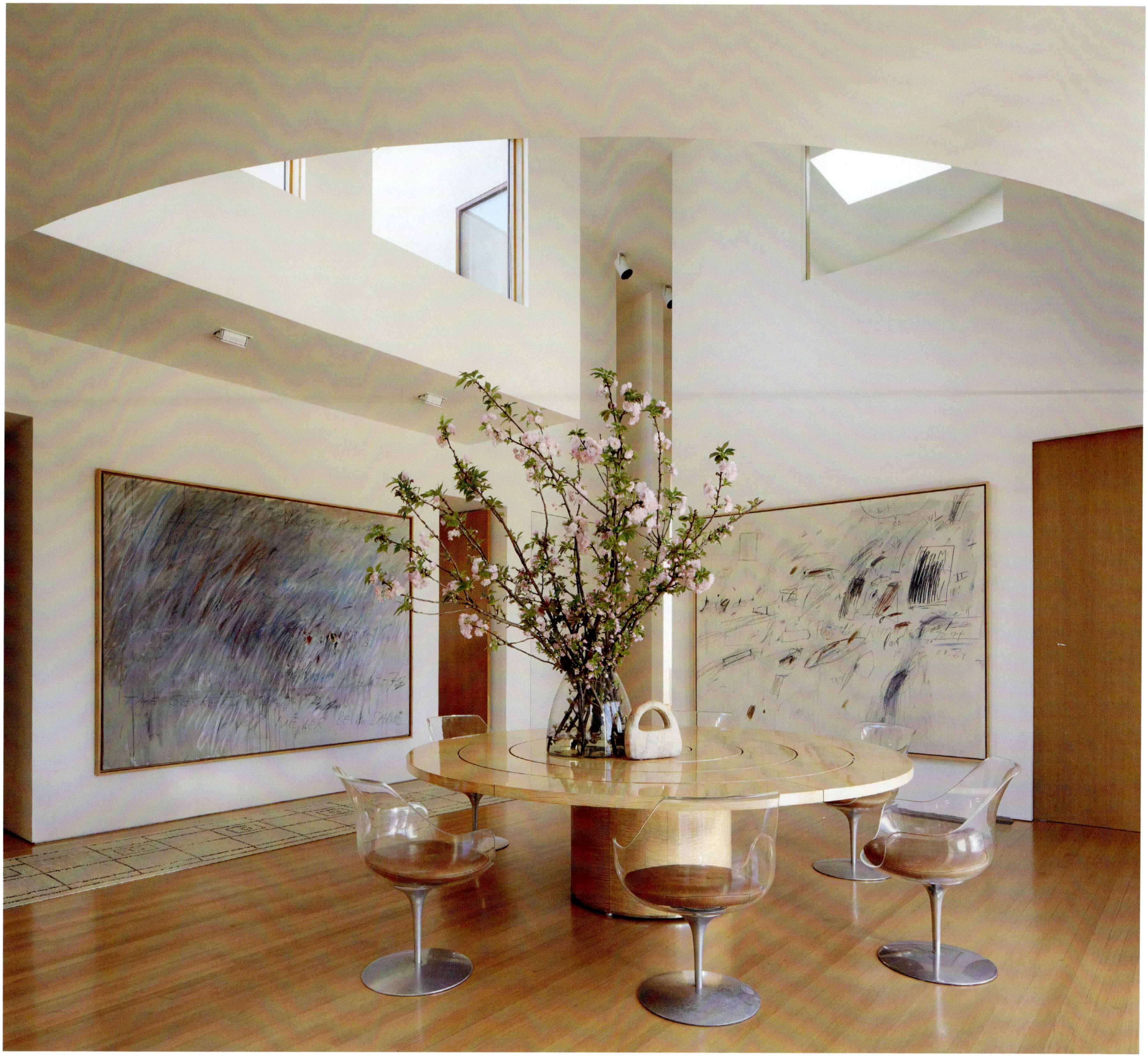

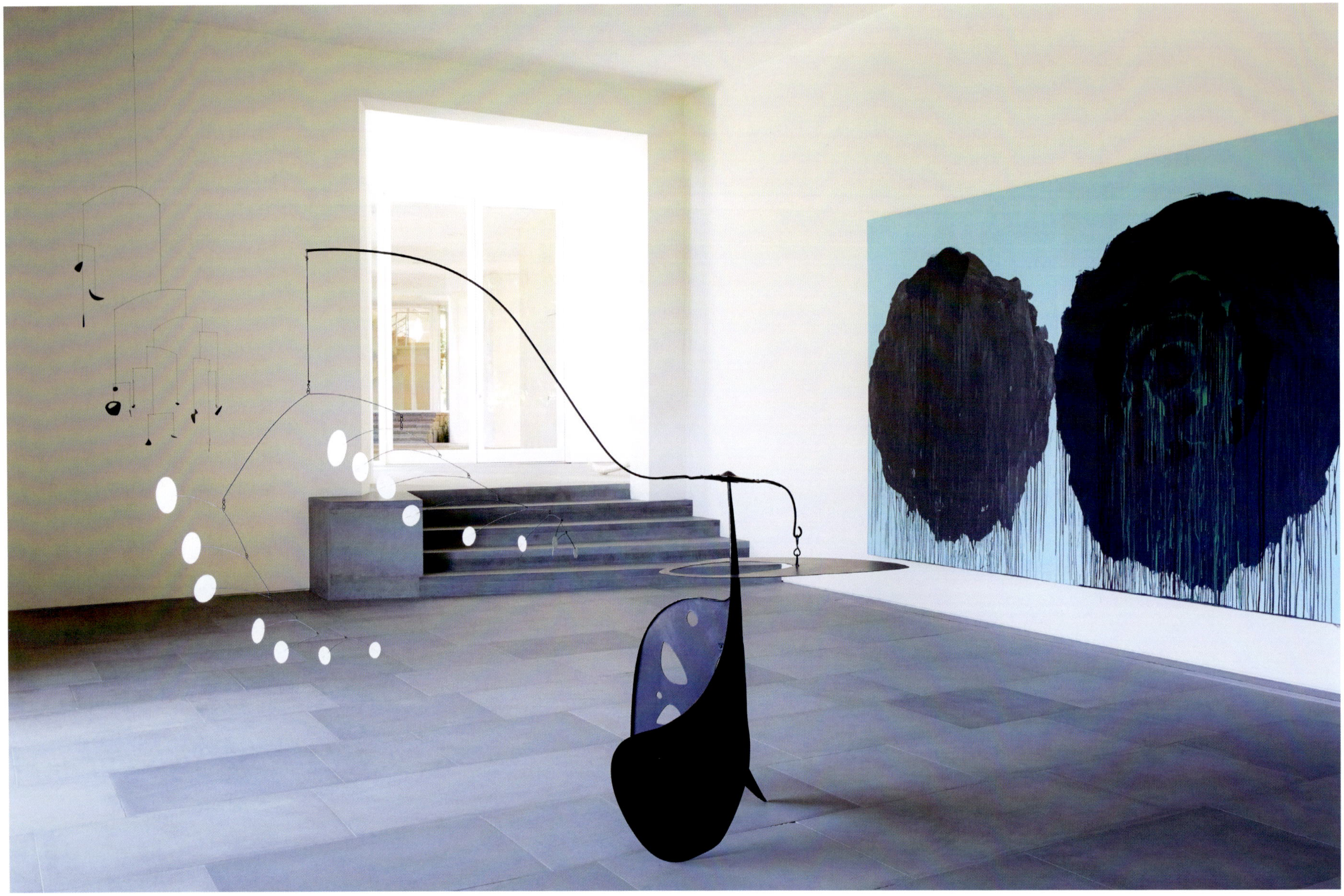

Art pervades the entire thirteen-thousand-square-foot residence, but a private gallery space on the lower level (where guest rooms are also located) is accessed by a coiling staircase that ends at Jenny Holzer's white granite *The Living Series: It takes a while before you.*

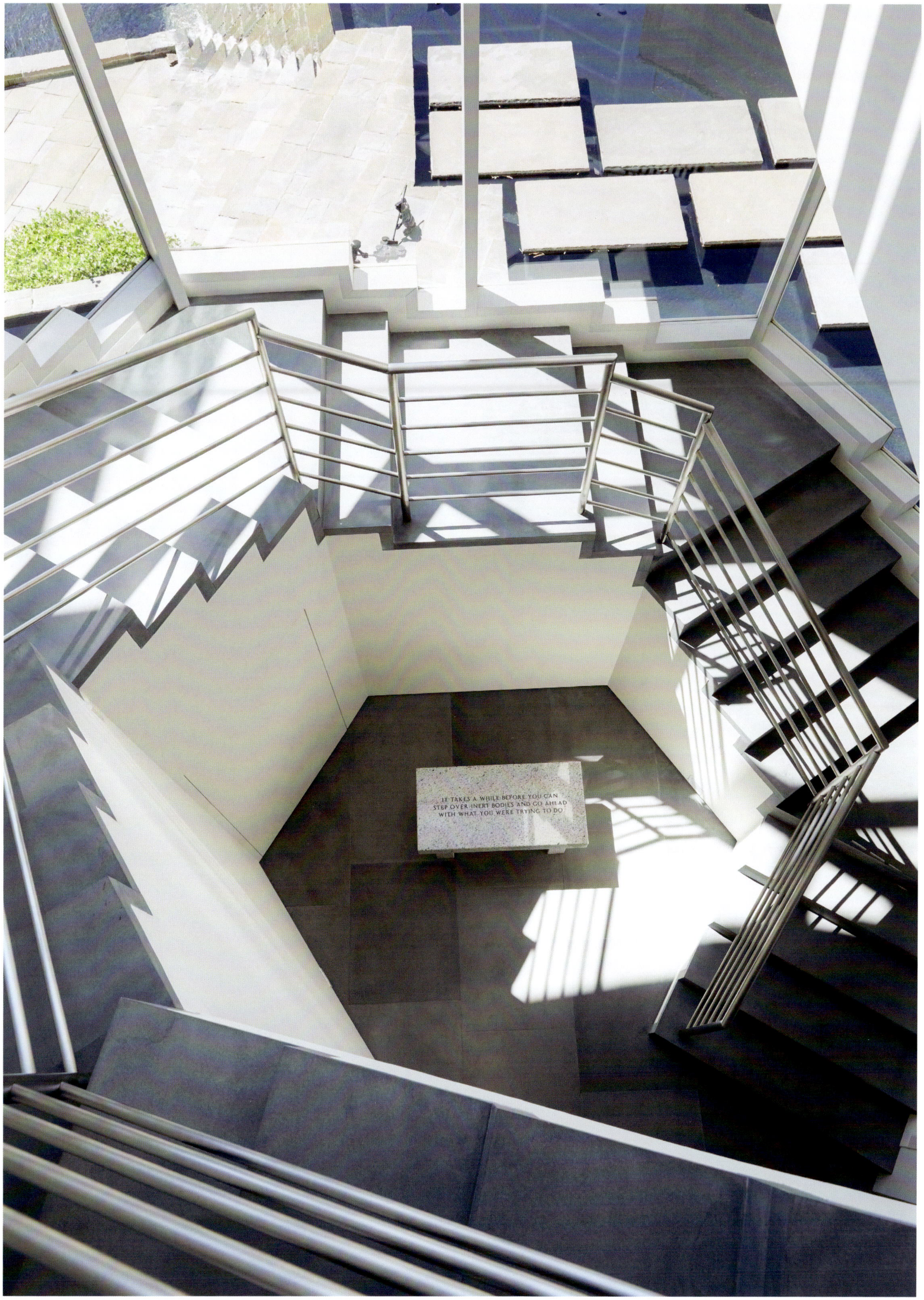
IT TAKES A WHILE BEFORE YOU CAN
STEP OVER INERT BODIES AND GO AHEAD
WITH WHAT YOU WERE TRYING TO DO

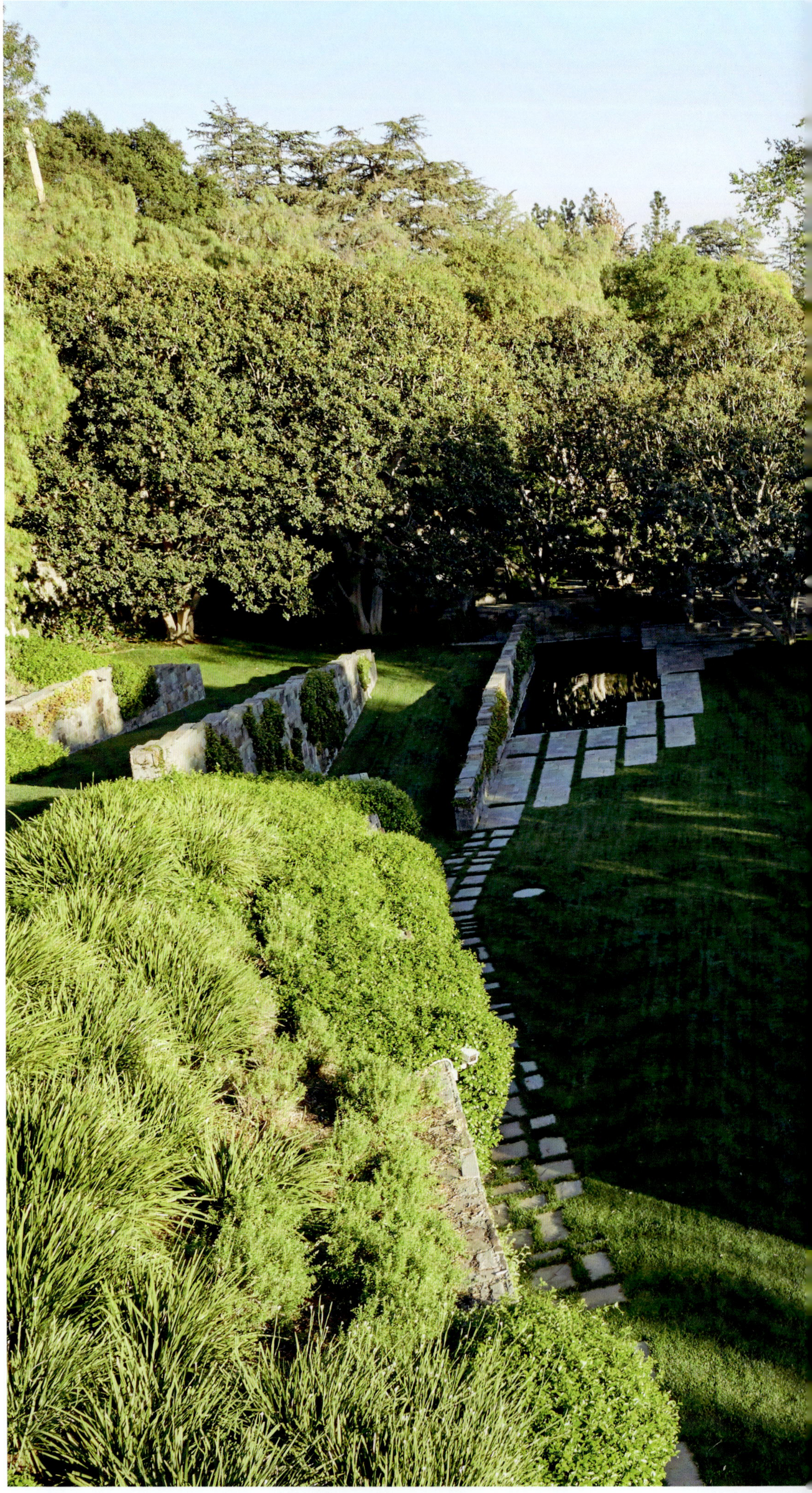

The three-acre property is like a sculpture garden, with large-scale art by Joan Miró and David Smith, and this work by Richard Serra, *No Problem*, 1995.

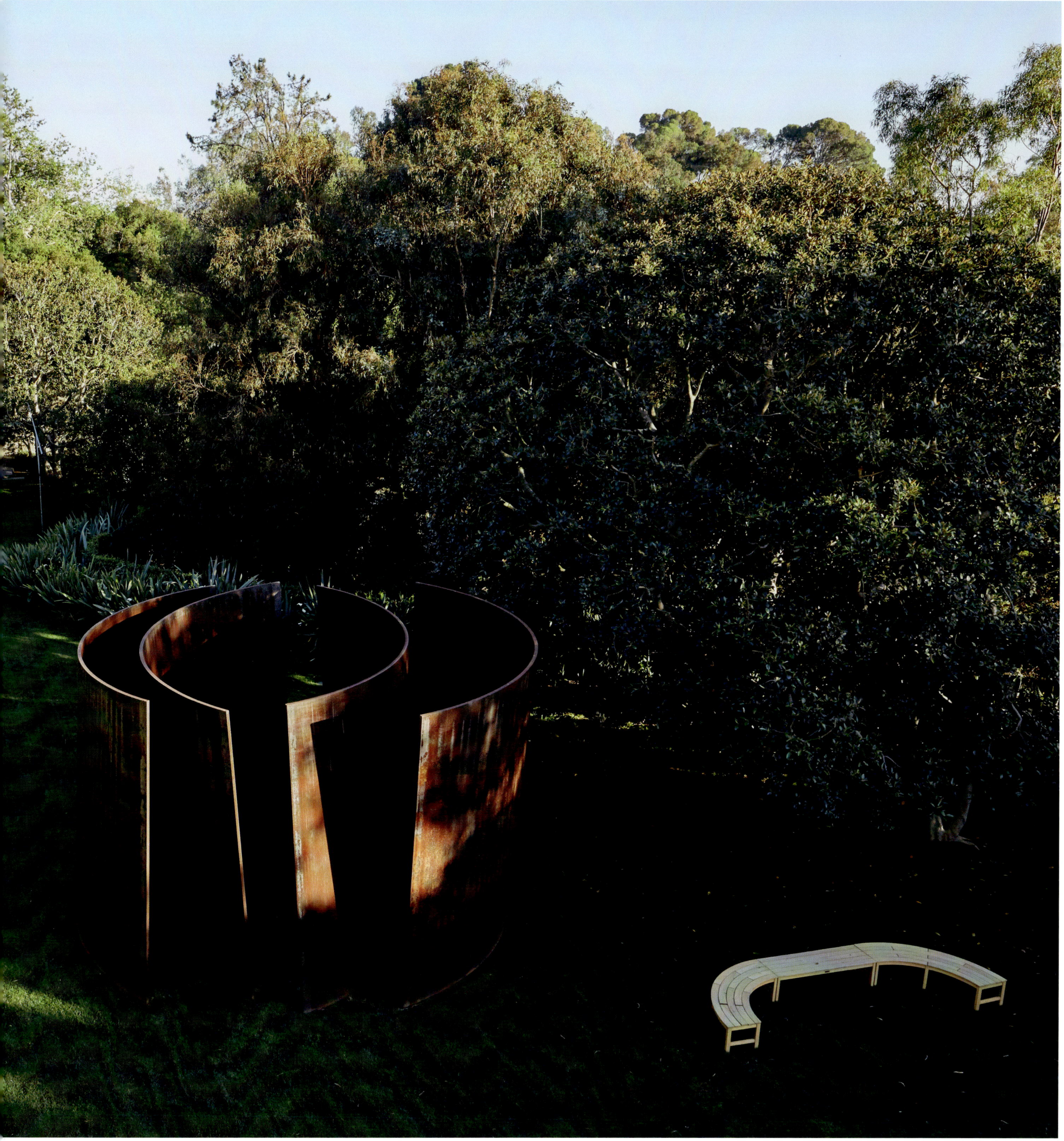

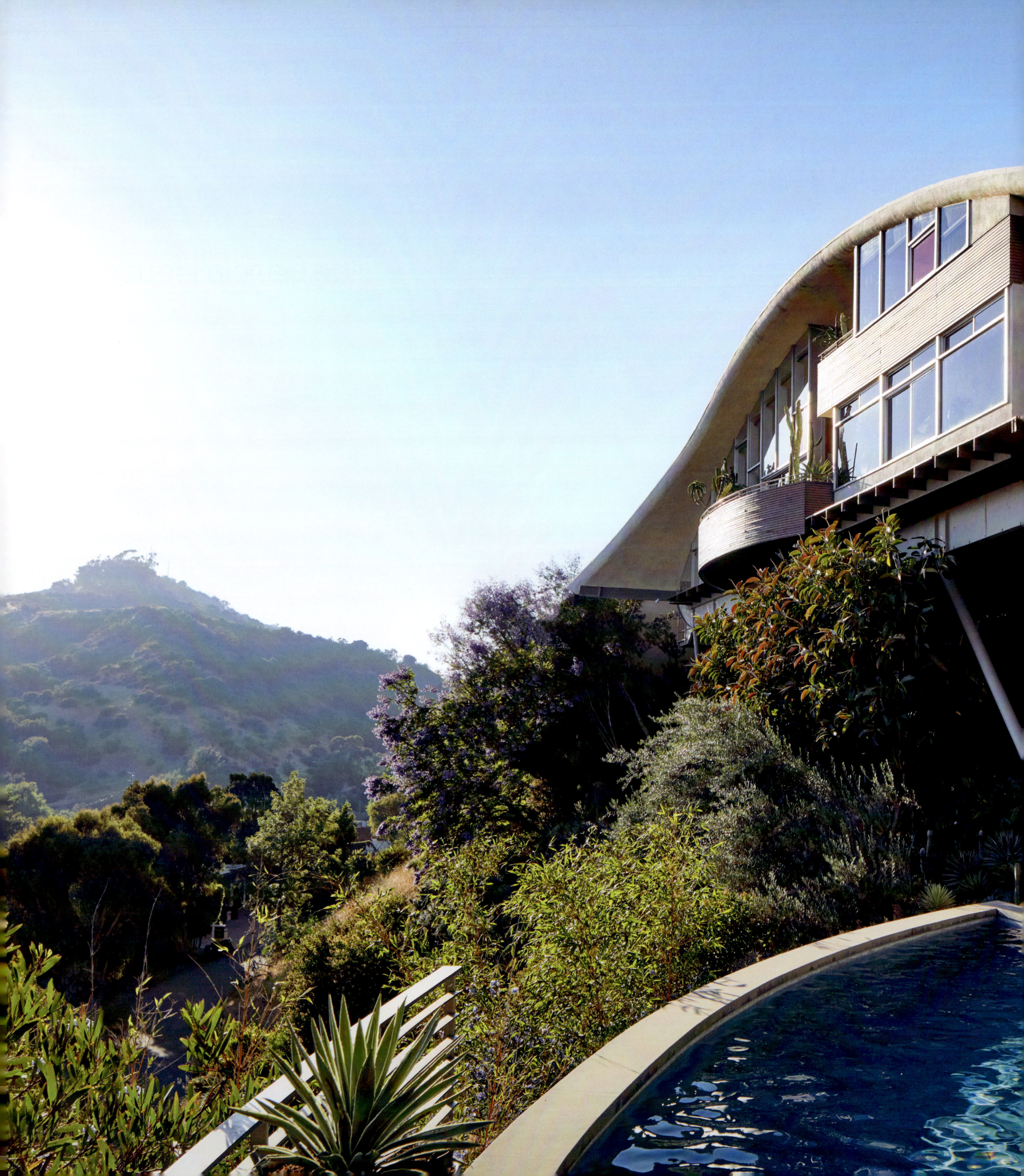

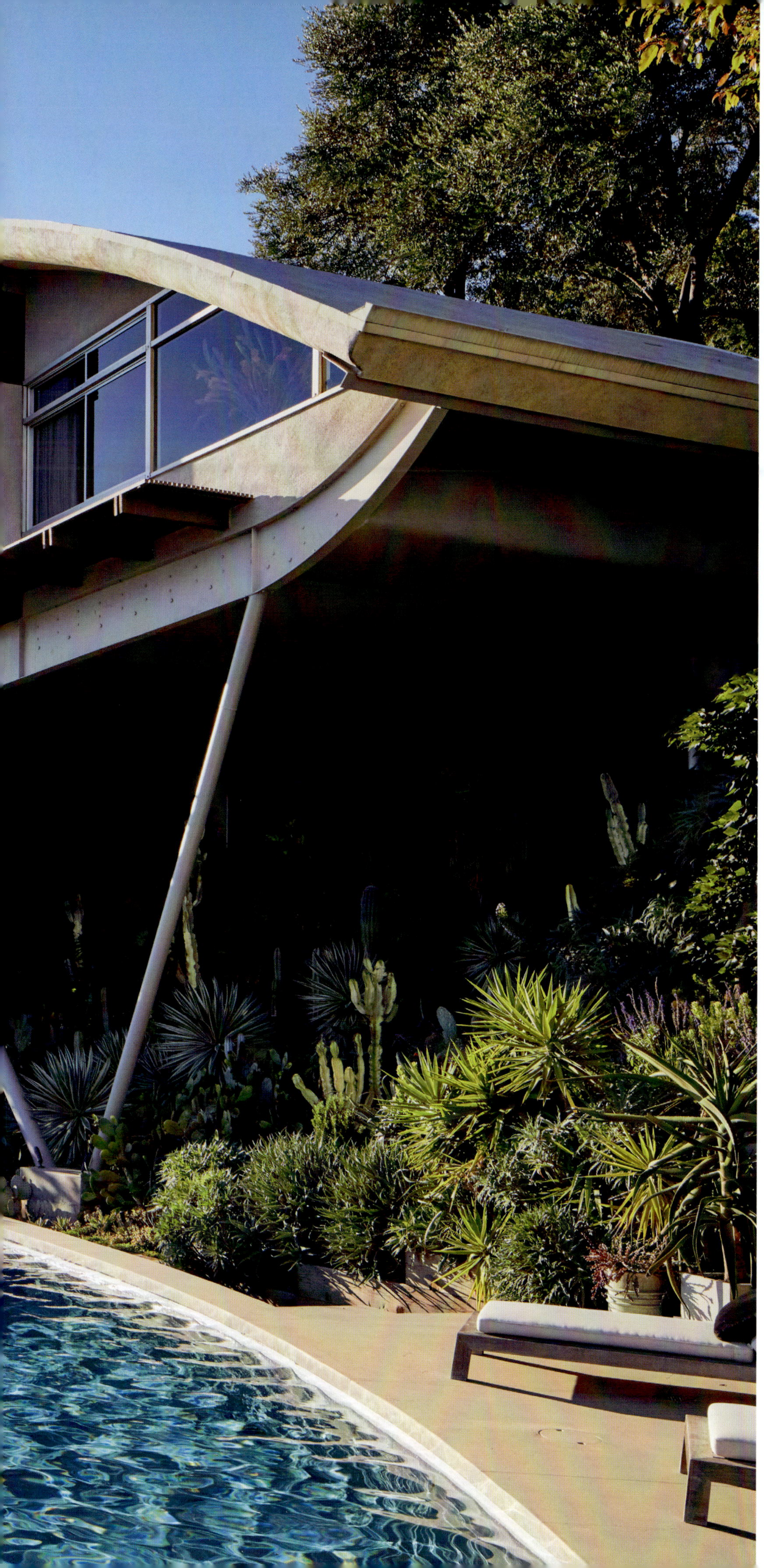

The Garcia House

Hollywood Hills

Architect

John Lautner

Residents

John McIlwee
and Bill Damaschke

Designed in 1962 by architect John Lautner and located on Los Angeles's legendary Mulholland Drive, the Garcia House (also known as the Rainbow House for its color-blocked stained-glass windows) is an architectural icon, practically a Hollywood star in its own right, that floats sixty feet above Nichols Canyon on V-shaped steel struts.

The house was originally designed and built for Russell and Gina Garcia. Mr. Garcia was a jazz arranger and composer and needed a quiet environment in which to work, while Mrs. Garcia was social and liked to throw lavish parties for a hundred guests or more. To accommodate the Garcias' different needs, the house was divided into two discrete sections—private and public. A sweeping stairway descends from the entrance on Mulholland, separating the two halves of the house, which are united under its iconic arched roof.

The Garcias moved out toward the end of the 1960s, and since then the house has had five or six owners. In 1989 the then owners allowed the Garcia House to gain the dubious distinction of being the base for the gang of drug dealers in the 1989 film *Lethal Weapon 2* (a reason this is my son's favorite house).

Every significant architectural gem needs stewards like current owners John McIlwee and Bill Damaschke. Since purchasing the Garcia House in 2002 from actor and director Vincent Gallo, they have dedicated themselves to its preservation, not least by hiring expert architectural firm Marmol Radziner to manage an extensive renovation. They also went further, adding the Lautner-designed, but previously unbuilt, ellipse-shaped pool. Once swinging with music and parties, the house feels dynamic and alive again.

Since restoring the Garcia House to Lautner's original design, McIlwee and Damaschke have continued to explore the home's potential, collaborating with interior designer Darren Brown to create a fresh 1980s Italian–meets–Studio 54 feel by way of bold textures and patterns, thick shag carpeting, and Saporiti furniture. Enriching the interior is their ever-growing collection of artworks by Diane Arbus, Terry Richardson, Cindy Sherman, Raymond Pettibon, Ed Paschke, and Alex Prager. Brought in to reimagine the house's relationship to the ground it floats above, landscape designer John Sharp planted a riot of Australian ferns, agave, and cacti.

During the shoot, an open-top Hollywood tour bus pulled up to show the eager visitors the house from *Lethal Weapon 2*, and after an awkward wave between parties, the bus slowly pulled away as they realized that my assistant and I were nobodies. But they had seen what they had truly come for: the ultimate celebrity of Hollywood architecture.

Previous: The Garcia House looks like a spaceship that landed in the Hollywood Hills.

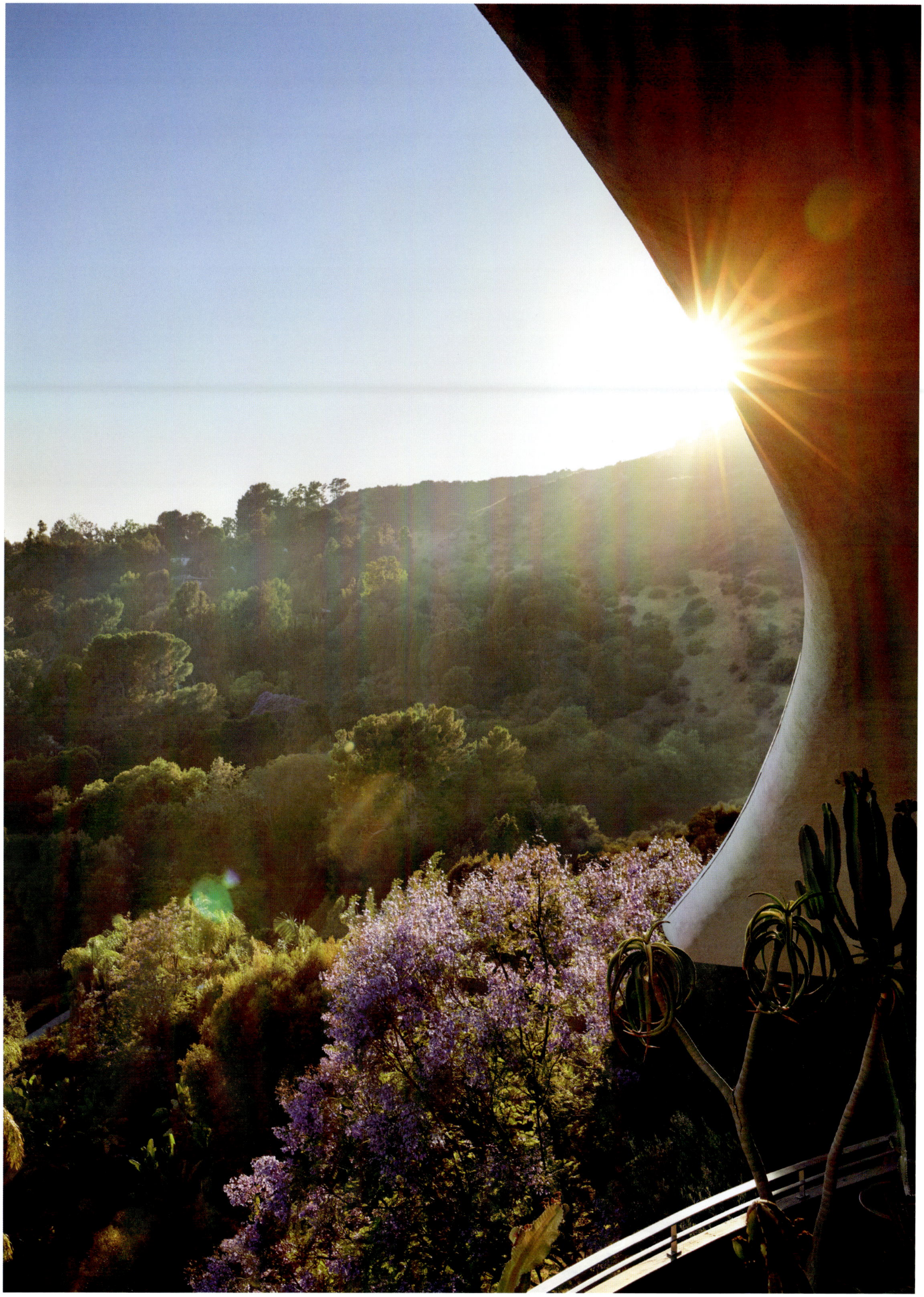

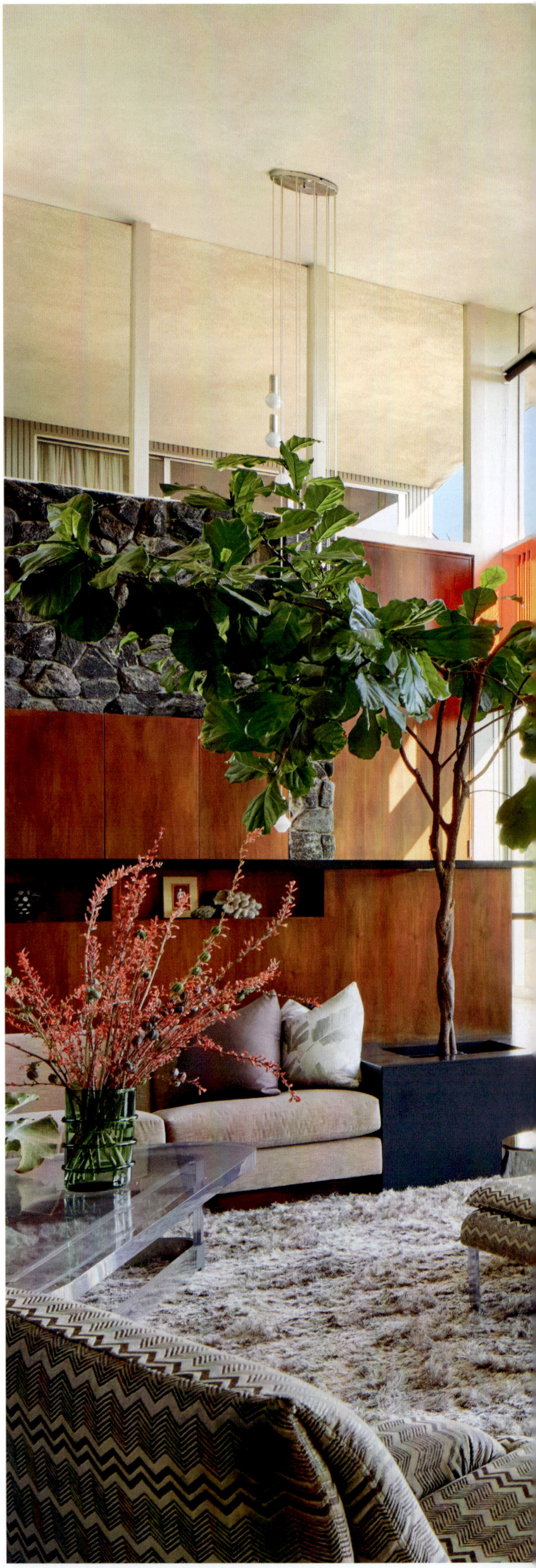

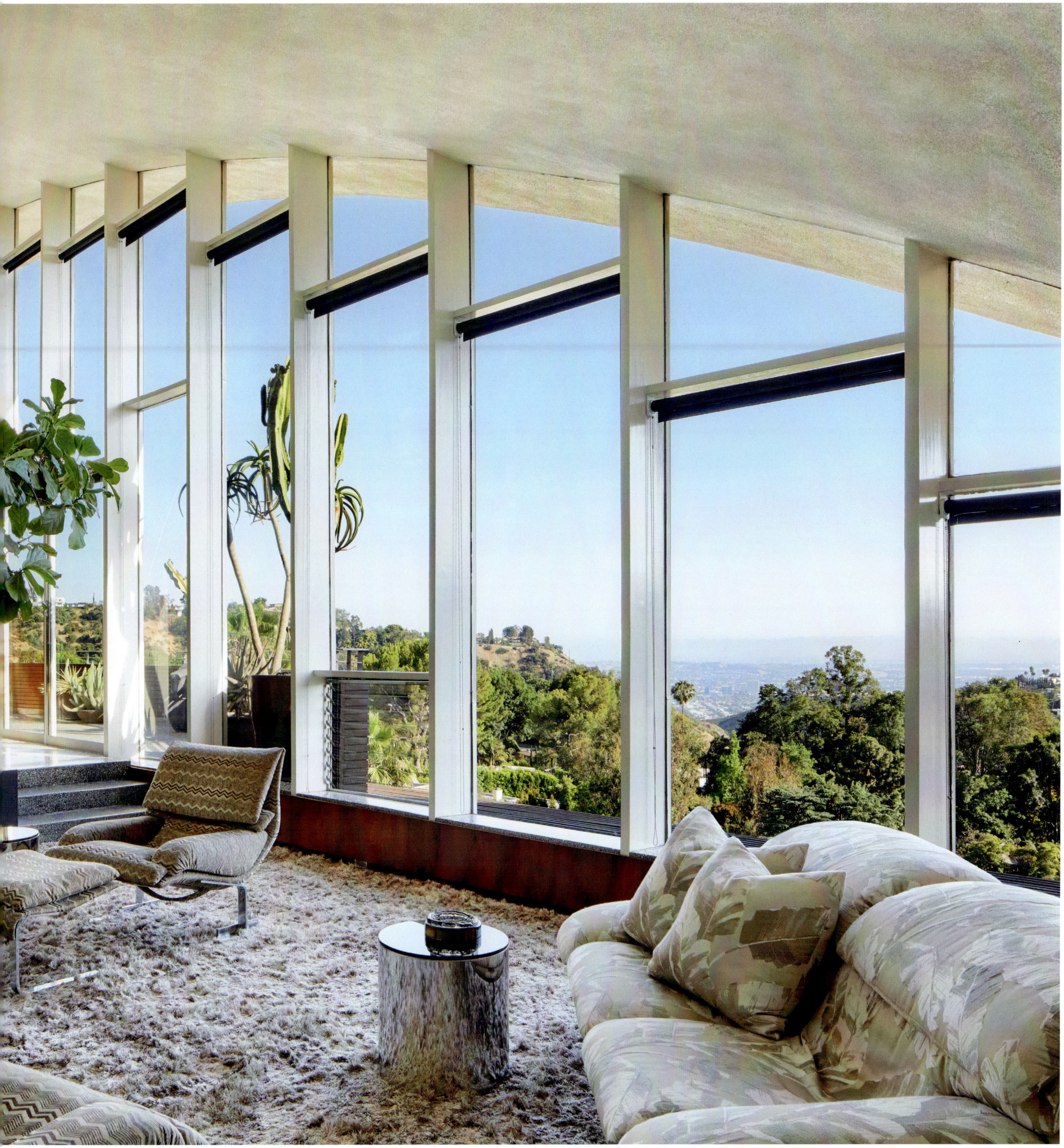

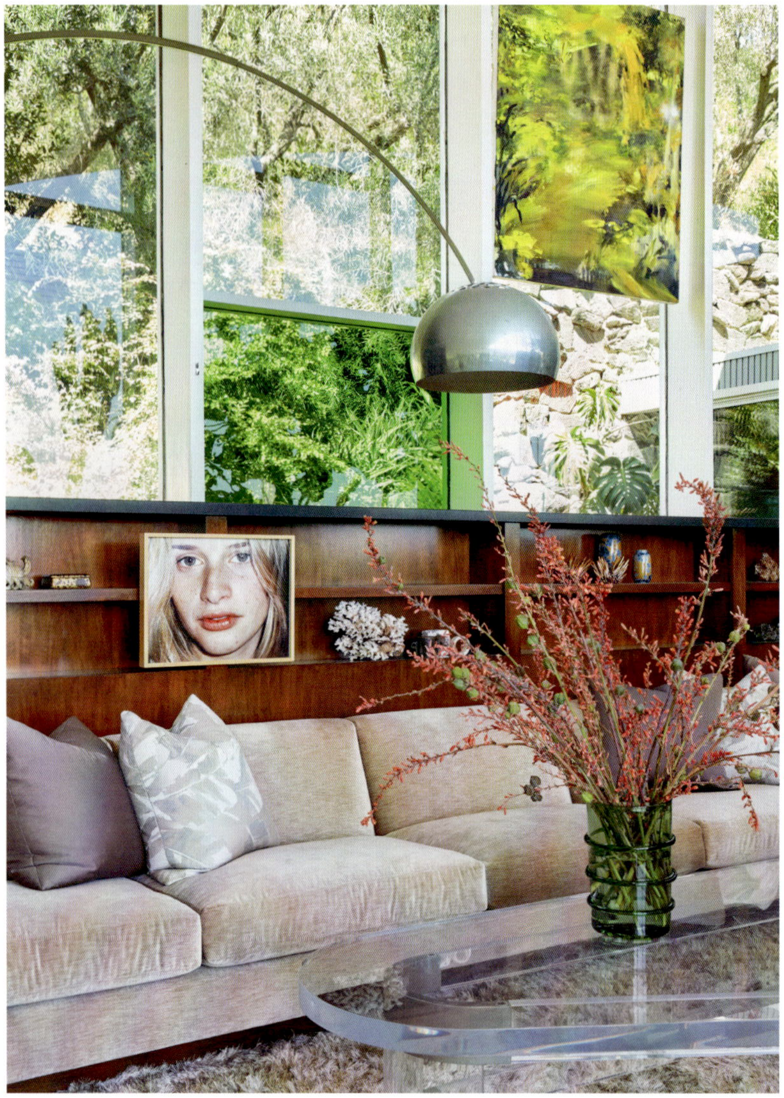

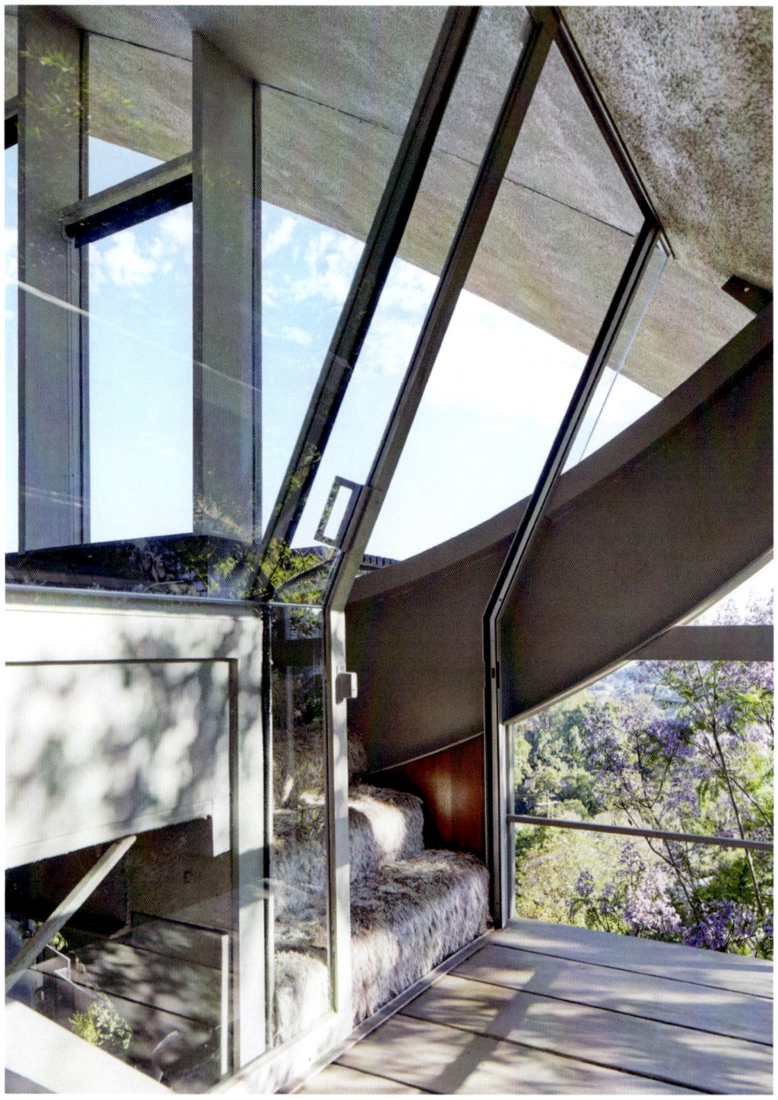

The pointed oval or almond shape is a visual thread that runs through the house, from the overall form of the architecture to the swimming pool (a feature of John Lautner's original design that was added by the present homeowners) to the handle on the front door.

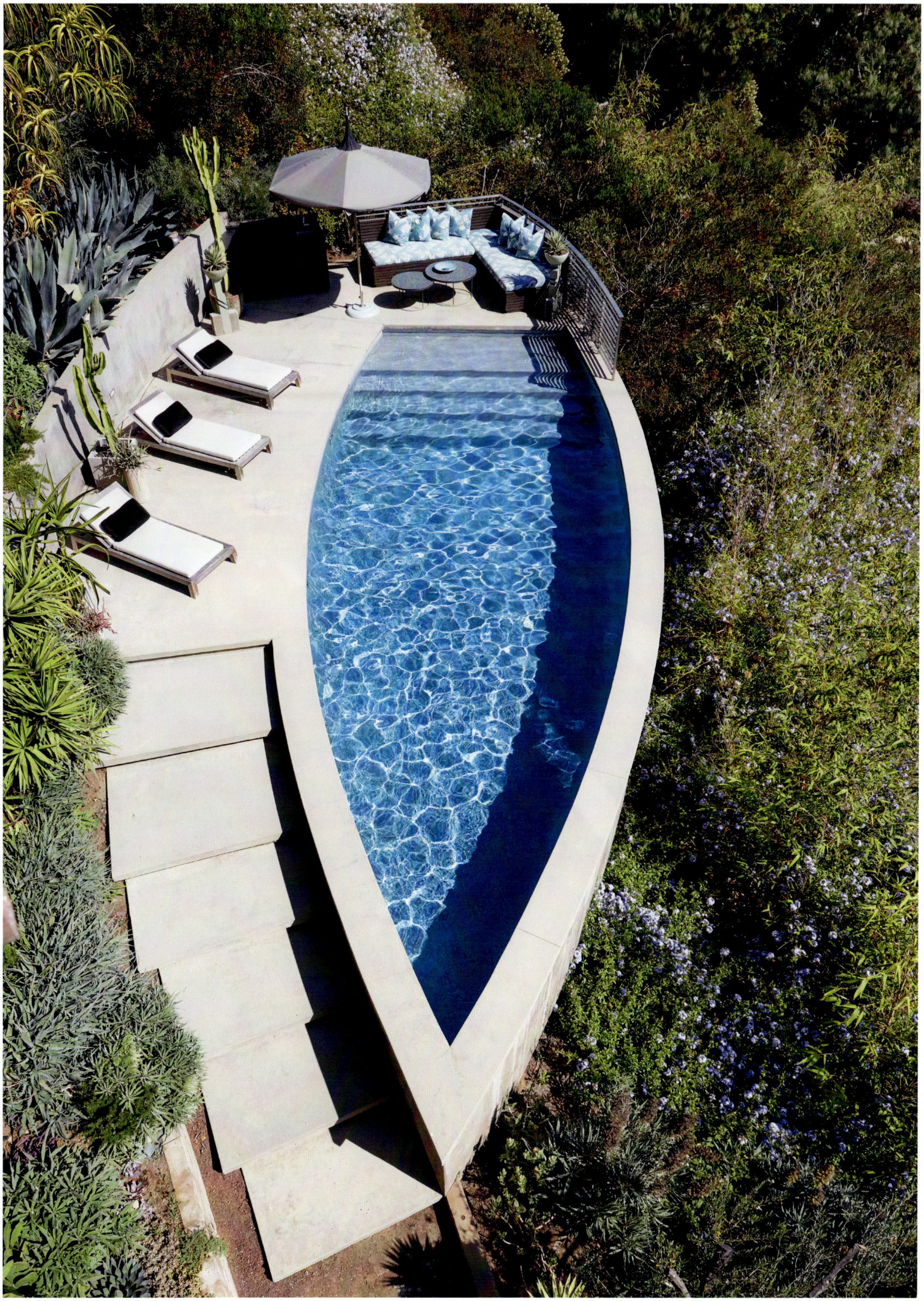

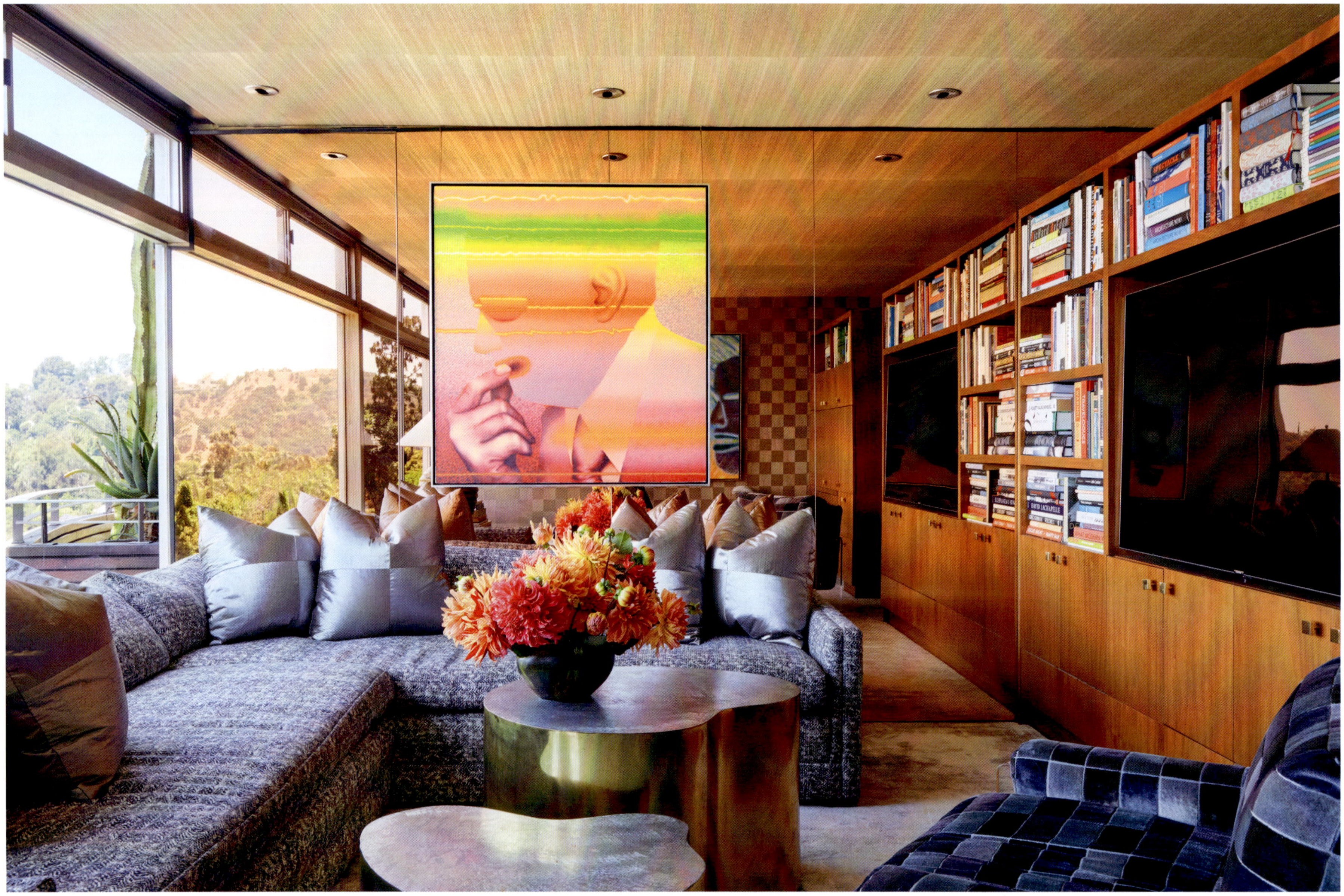

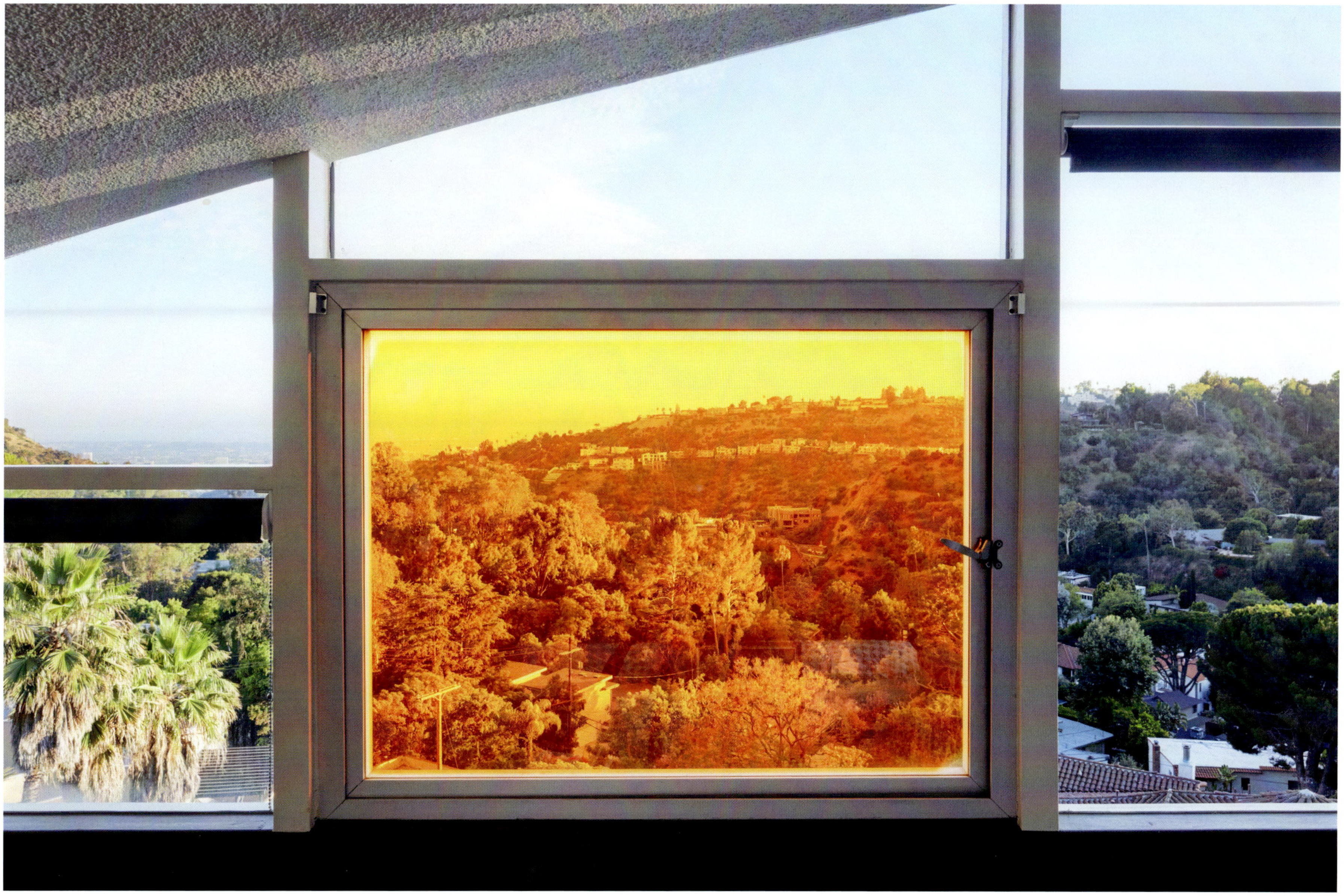

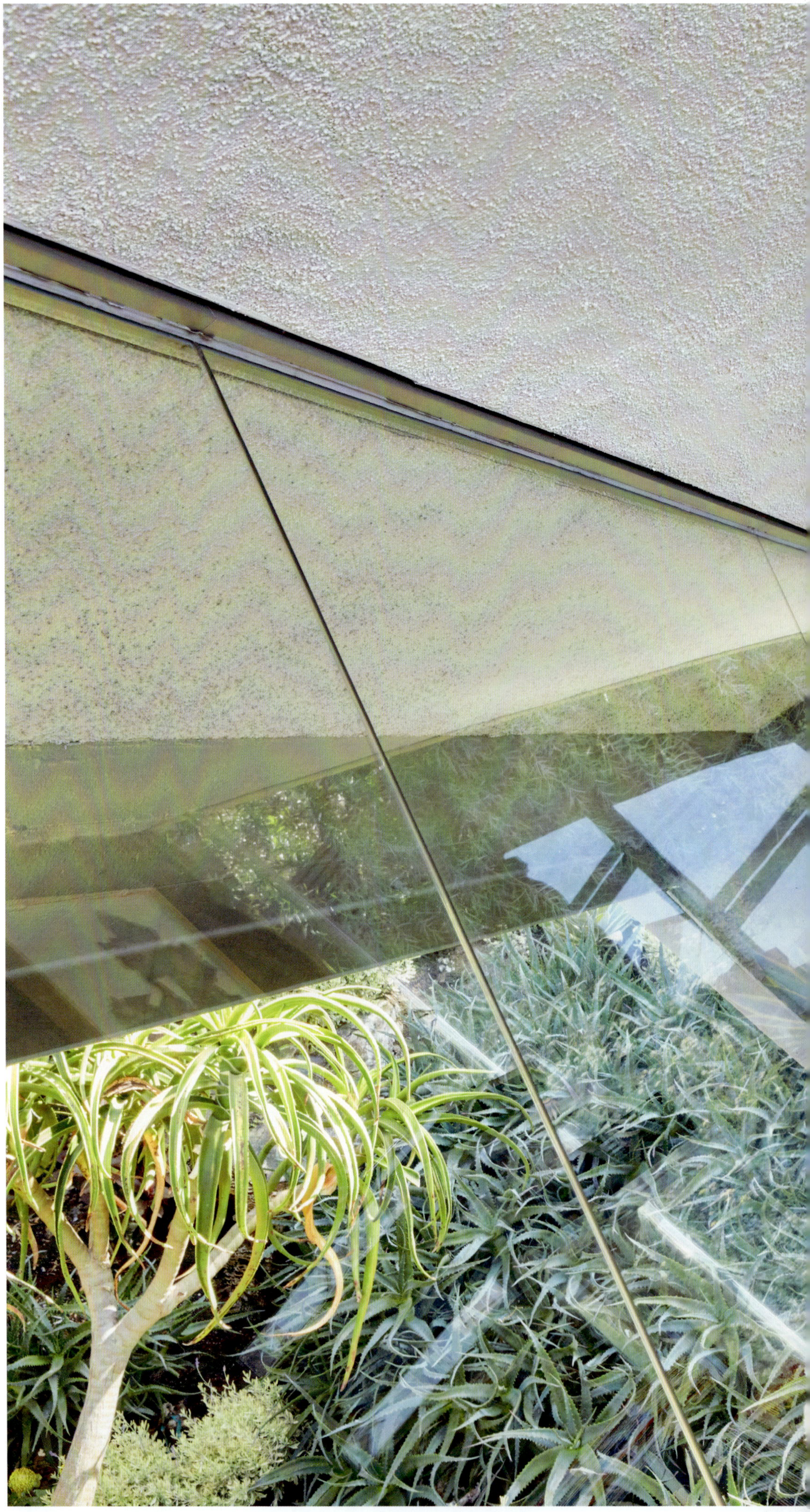

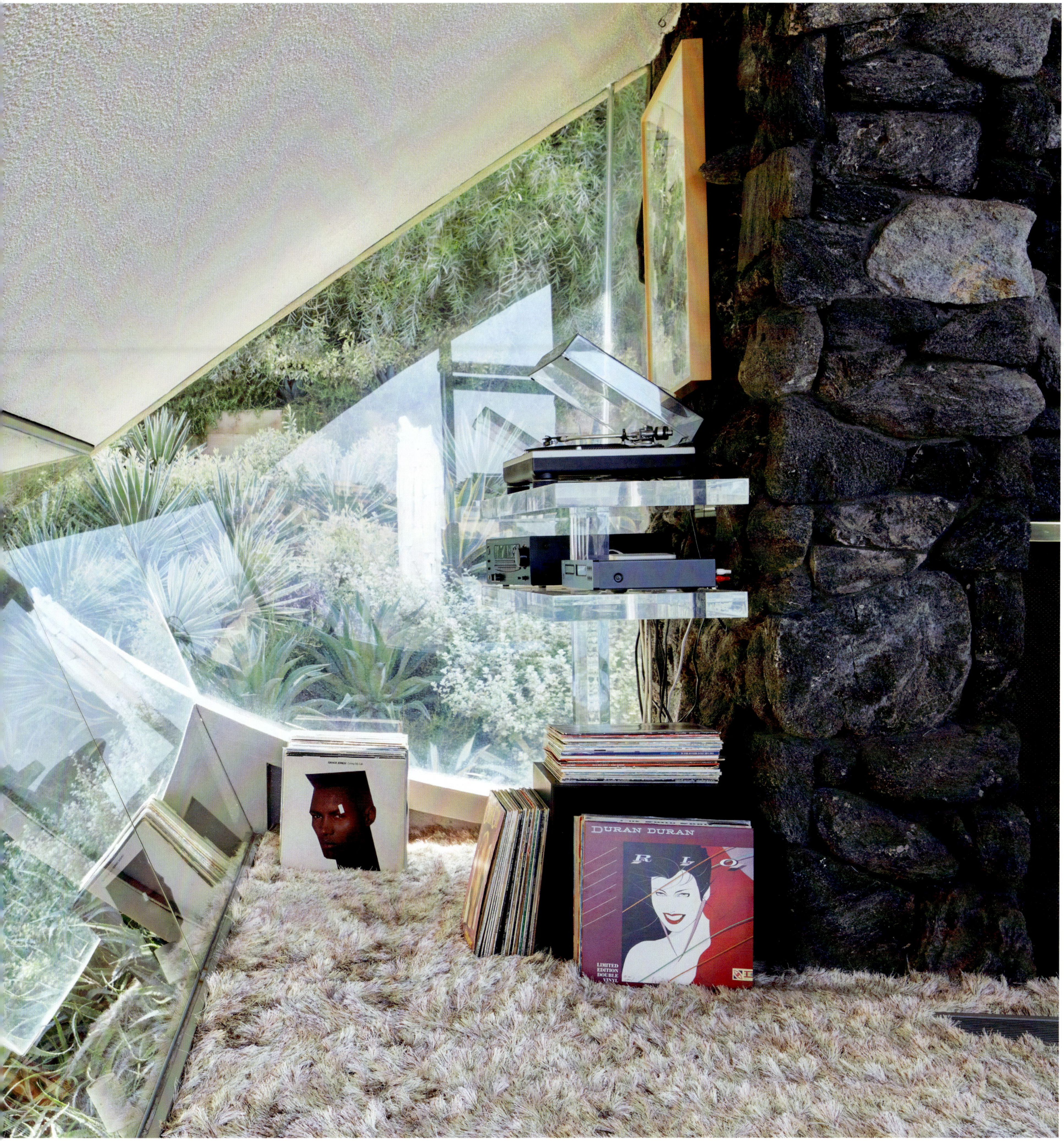
DURAN DURAN
LIMITED
EDITION
DOUBLE
VINYL

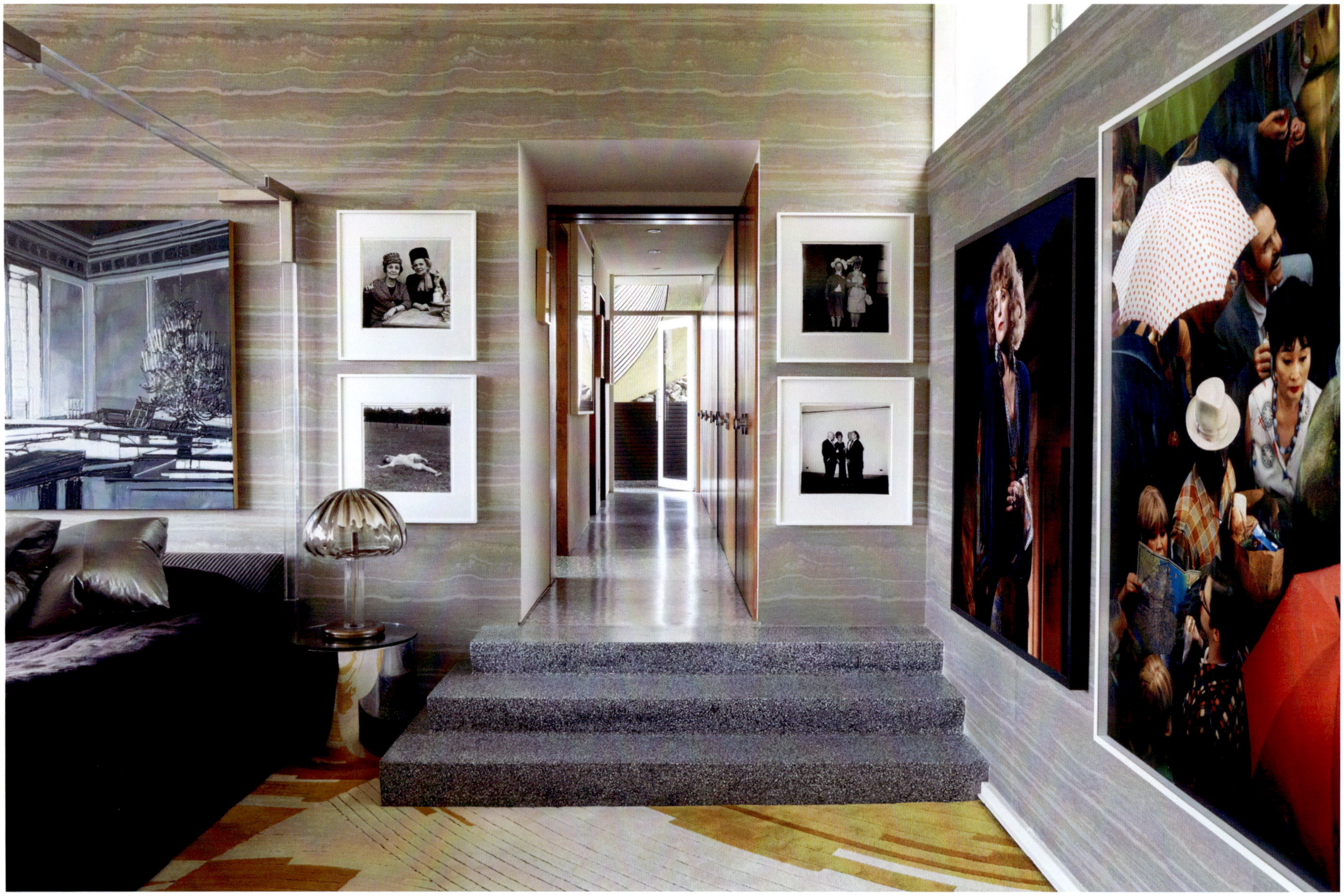

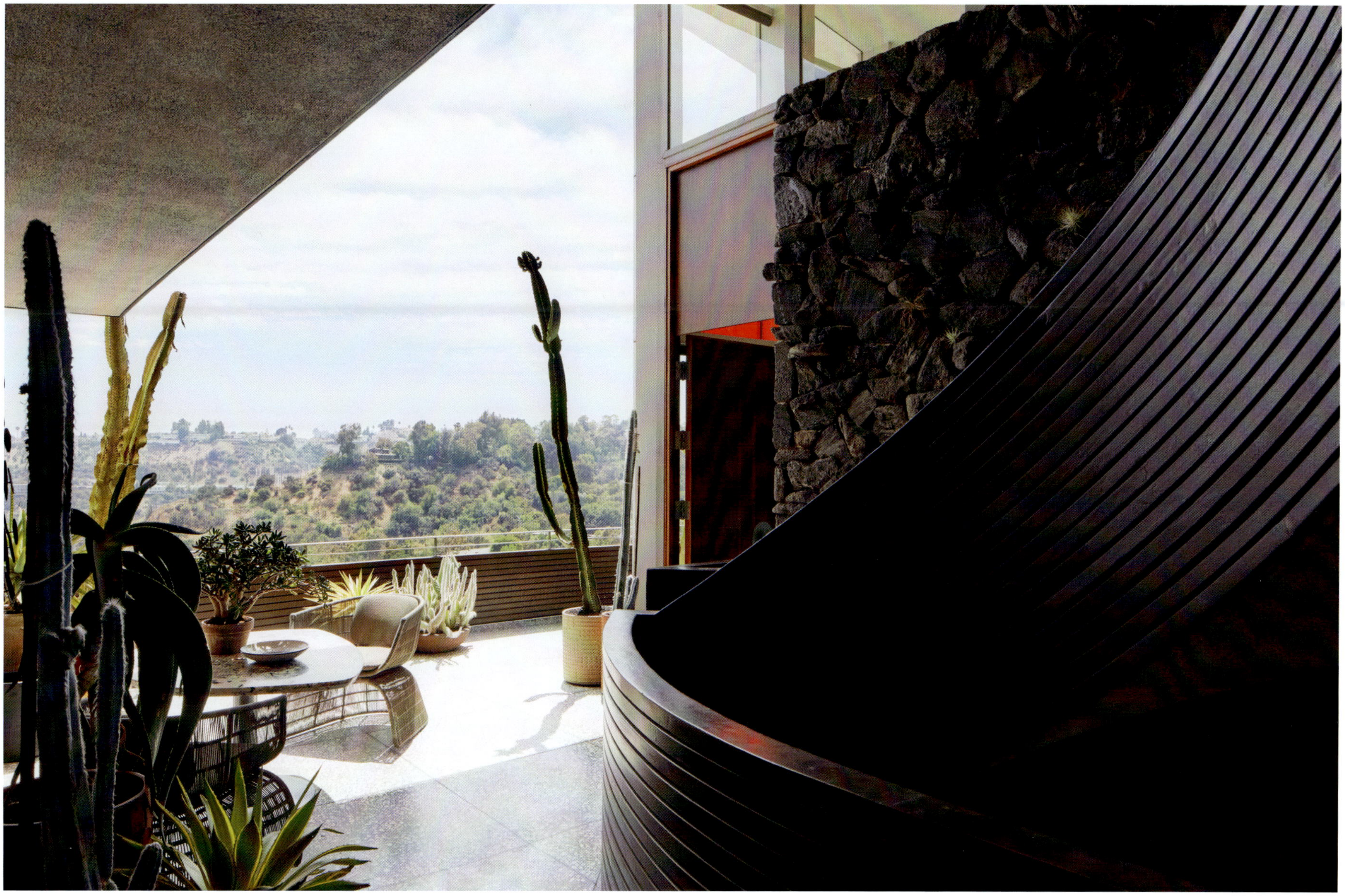

Once through the street-level front entry on Mulholland Drive, you descend a curved staircase between the two sides of the house—the private side and the more public side.

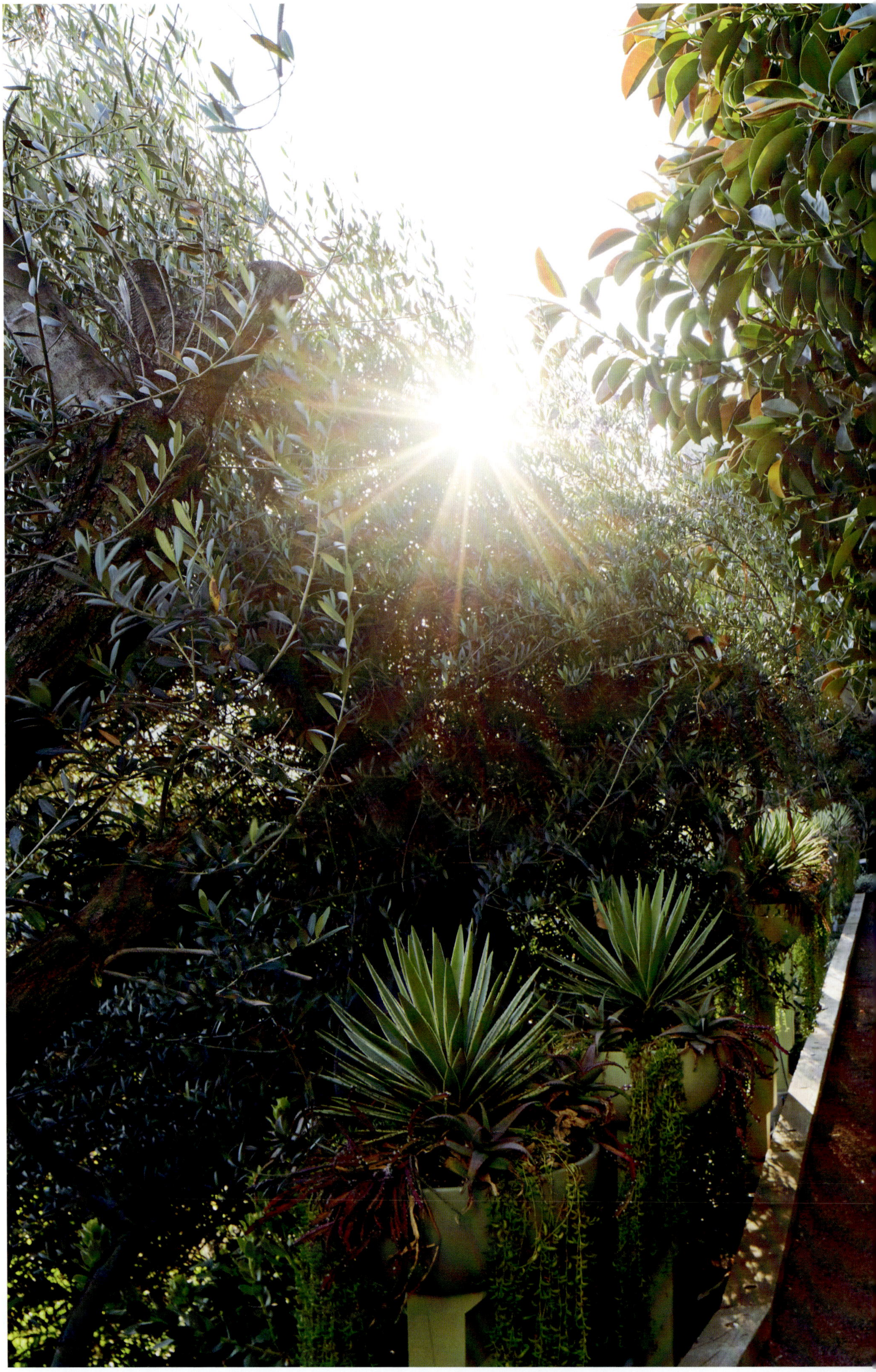

Landscape designer John Sharp reimagined the property, extending the plantings beneath the house as never before.

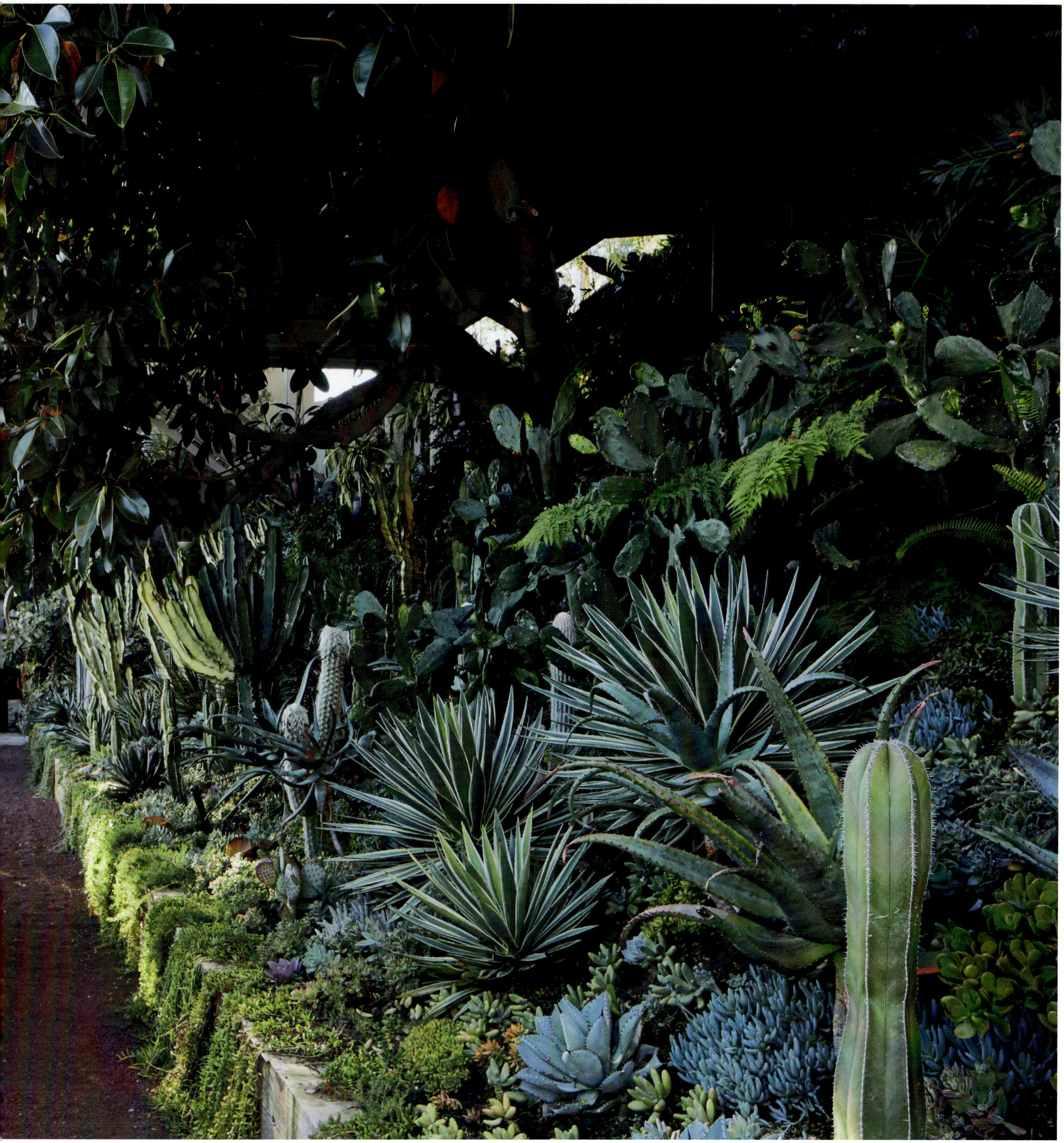

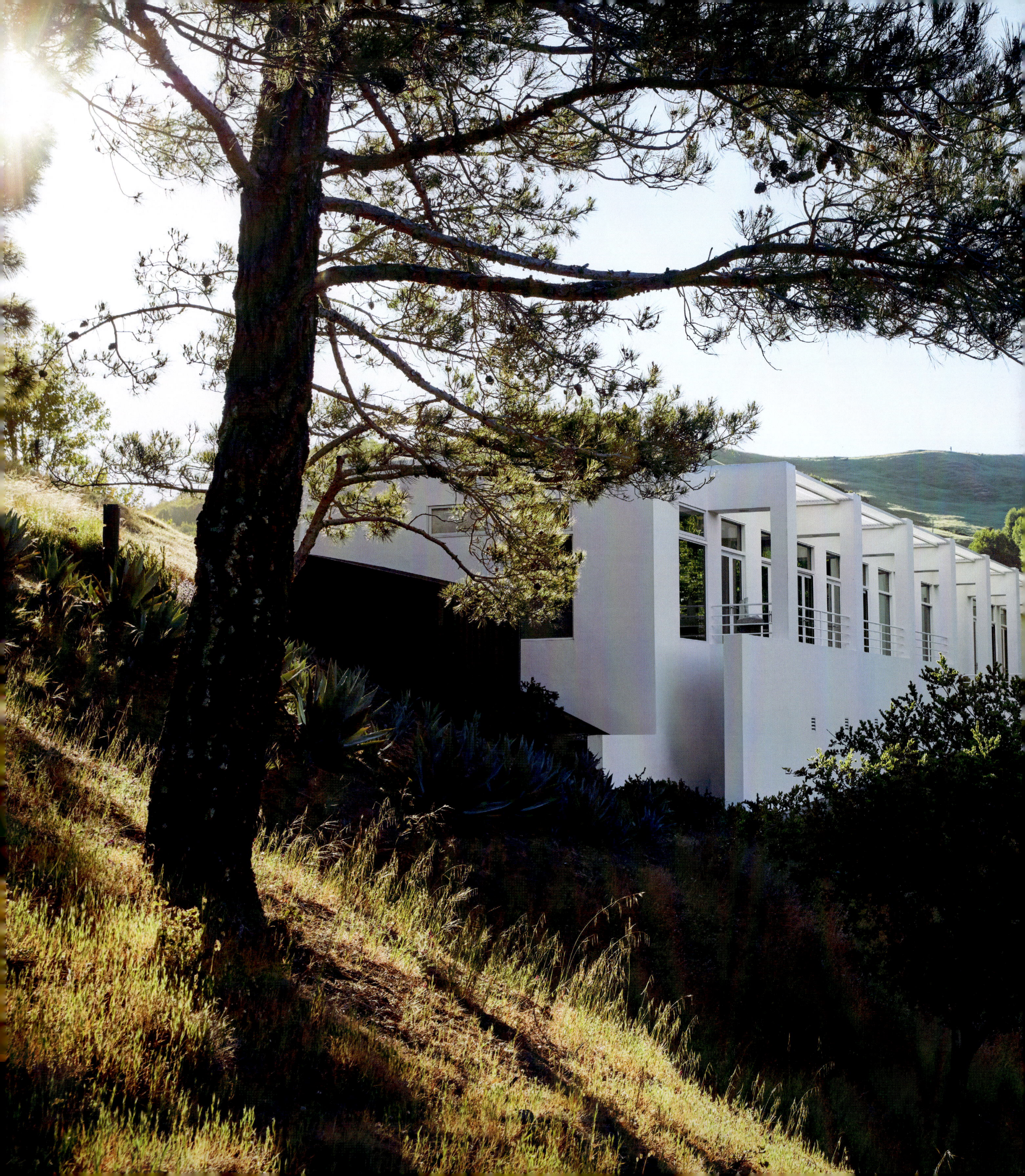

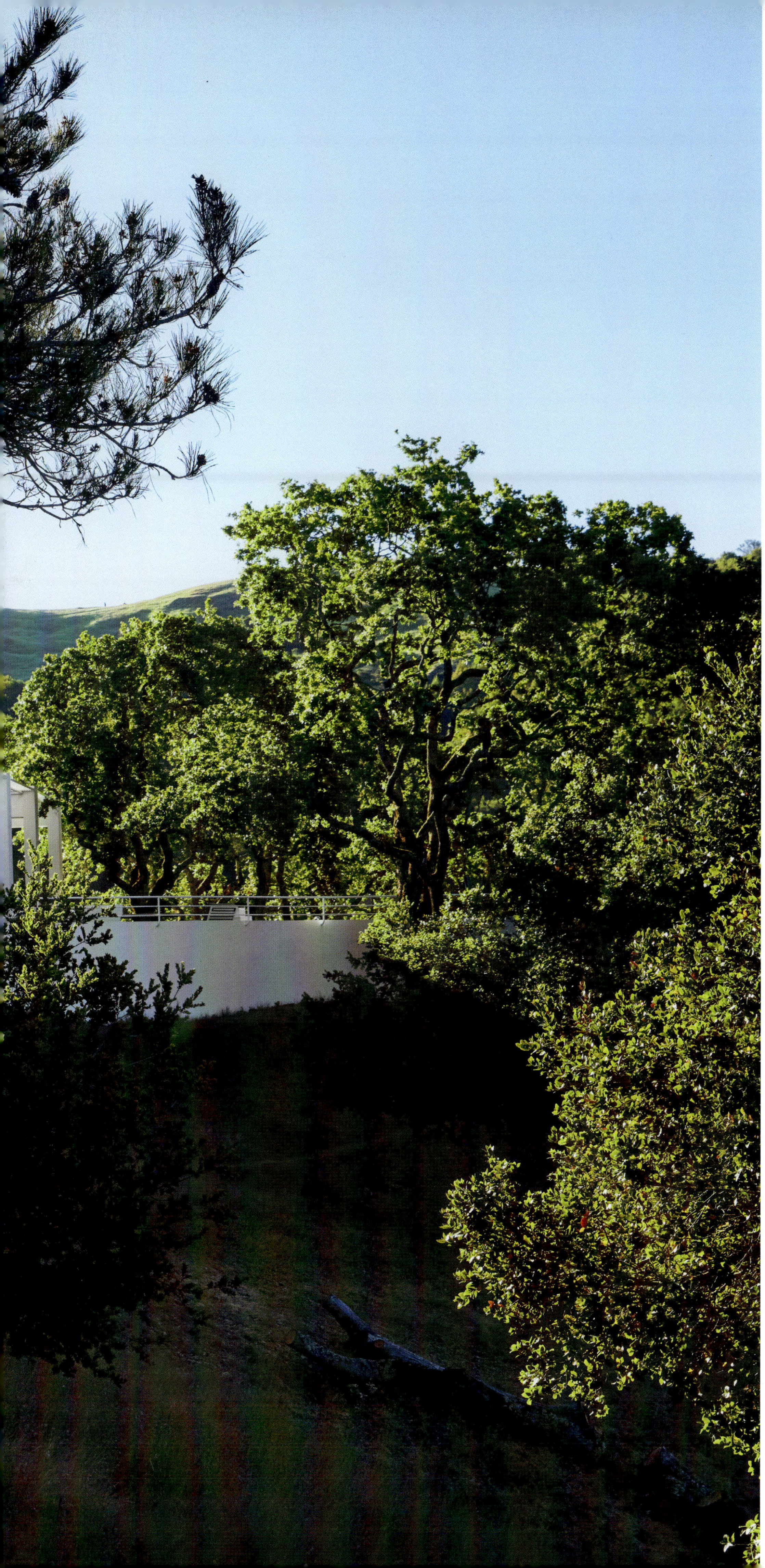

Ca Tana

Marin County

Architect
Daniel Solomon

Residents
Roger Thomas and Art Libera

For nearly fifteen years interior designer Roger Thomas and his partner, Art Libera, have called this quiet escape in the hillsides of Northern California home, their closest neighbors the mountain lions and bobcats that roam the hills. While the house is a stone's throw from San Francisco, it has the feel of a secluded treasury containing the riches of a lifetime of collecting, friendships, and travel.

Thomas and Libera now split their time between a retreat on a canal in Venice, Italy, and this house near a tiny, Marin County time-warp of a town where mom-and-pop stores still rule. But Thomas has spent his career designing residences, hotels, casinos, and restaurants around the world, so in 2008, when he and Libera purchased the house by Bay Area architect Daniel Solomon, they renovated the building to fit their lifestyle and passions. Most significantly, they replaced an indoor pool (the previous owner was photographer Howard Schatz, who shot his signature underwater photographs there) with a library to accommodate their extraordinary collection of books, art, and mementos.

Wedged into a bookcase in the library is a picture of Andy Warhol taking a study photo of Thomas with his favored Polaroid Big Shot camera for the 1981 double portrait that hangs nearby. Thomas counted Warhol as a friend and was a frequent visitor to the Factory, spending many a night out with him at Studio 54. Before starting his portrait, Warhol promised Thomas that he would give him eyes bluer than Paul Newman's, and he did. Thomas's only regret is not picking up the many discarded Polaroids from the floor.

While I was drooling over the 1975 Warhol print of Mick Jagger that hangs in Thomas and Libera's bedroom, Thomas pointed out that while Jagger's signature is visible on the bottom left, Warhol's has faded from the bottom right, which he thought would have amused Andy.

Blessed with openhearted intellectual and creative curiosity, Thomas and Libera know how to live with art. In their home, 1930s French furniture by André Arbus, Jean-Michel Frank, and Jaques Adnet sits with ease alongside depictions of San Sebastian from the sixteenth to the twentieth centuries, Giorgio Morandi still lifes, a wall-mounted Donald Judd, and artwork by Chuck Close, Joseph Cornell, and too many others to mention. I'll often play a game with myself on set: "If I could have just one thing . . ." In this house there was too much to choose from. One of the little Morandi paintings? A Warhol silkscreen? Or maybe it would be a straw marquetry box by Jean-Michel Frank. As a parting gift, Thomas very generously gave me a book on Frank featuring one of the very boxes on its cover.

I've worked on numerous projects with Thomas all over the globe, and I've never seen him without a smile and a kind word for those around him. The time I spent listening to Thomas and Libera's stories over supper after the shoot ranks up there with the best I've spent. Sometimes the highlights of a project are not just the travel and the spaces I'm lucky enough to witness but the quiet moments with good people.

At the front entry, Roger Thomas created a sculptural installation of stacked white cast-concrete forms, with stones found on the property and driftwood gathered from a nearby beach.

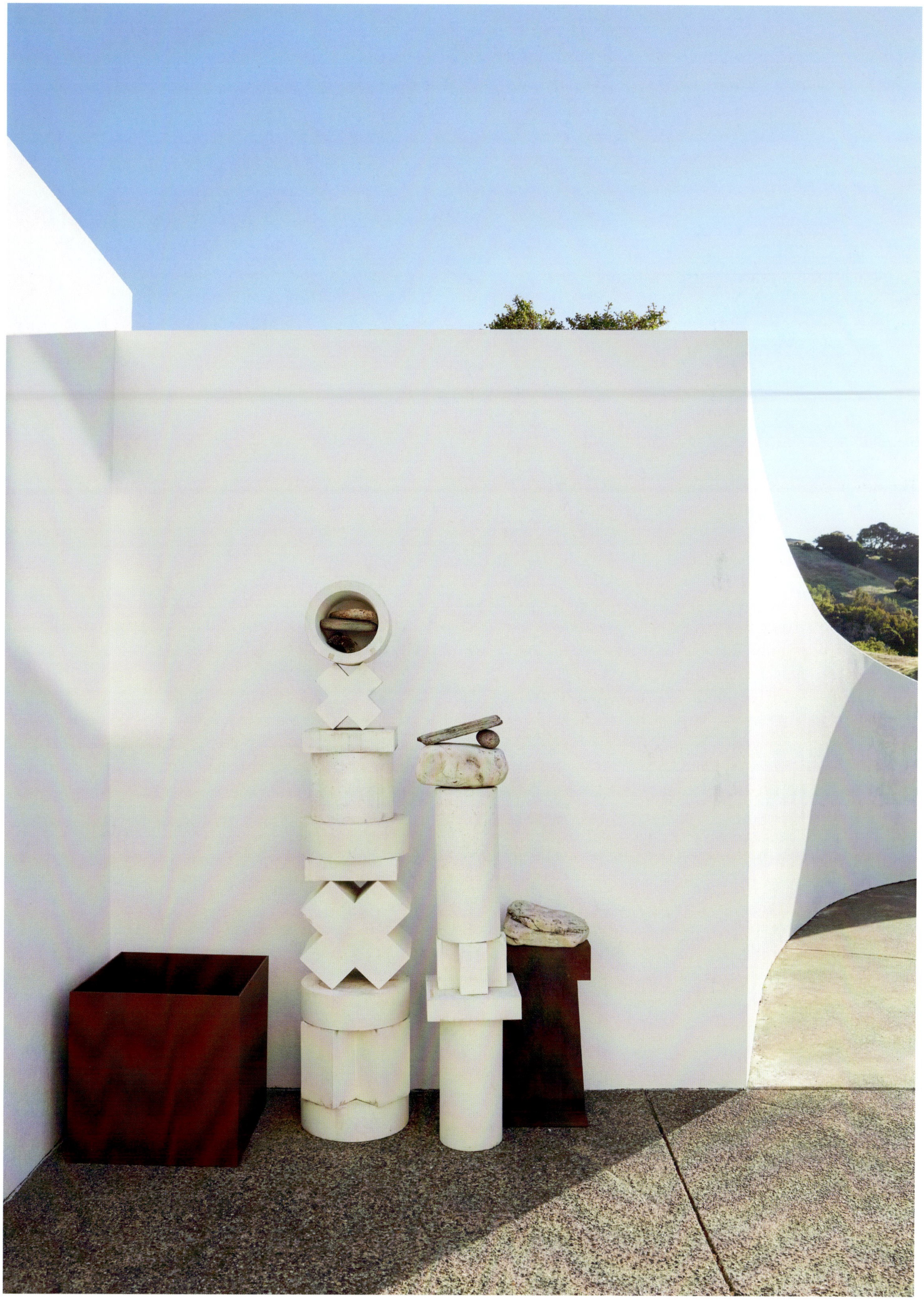

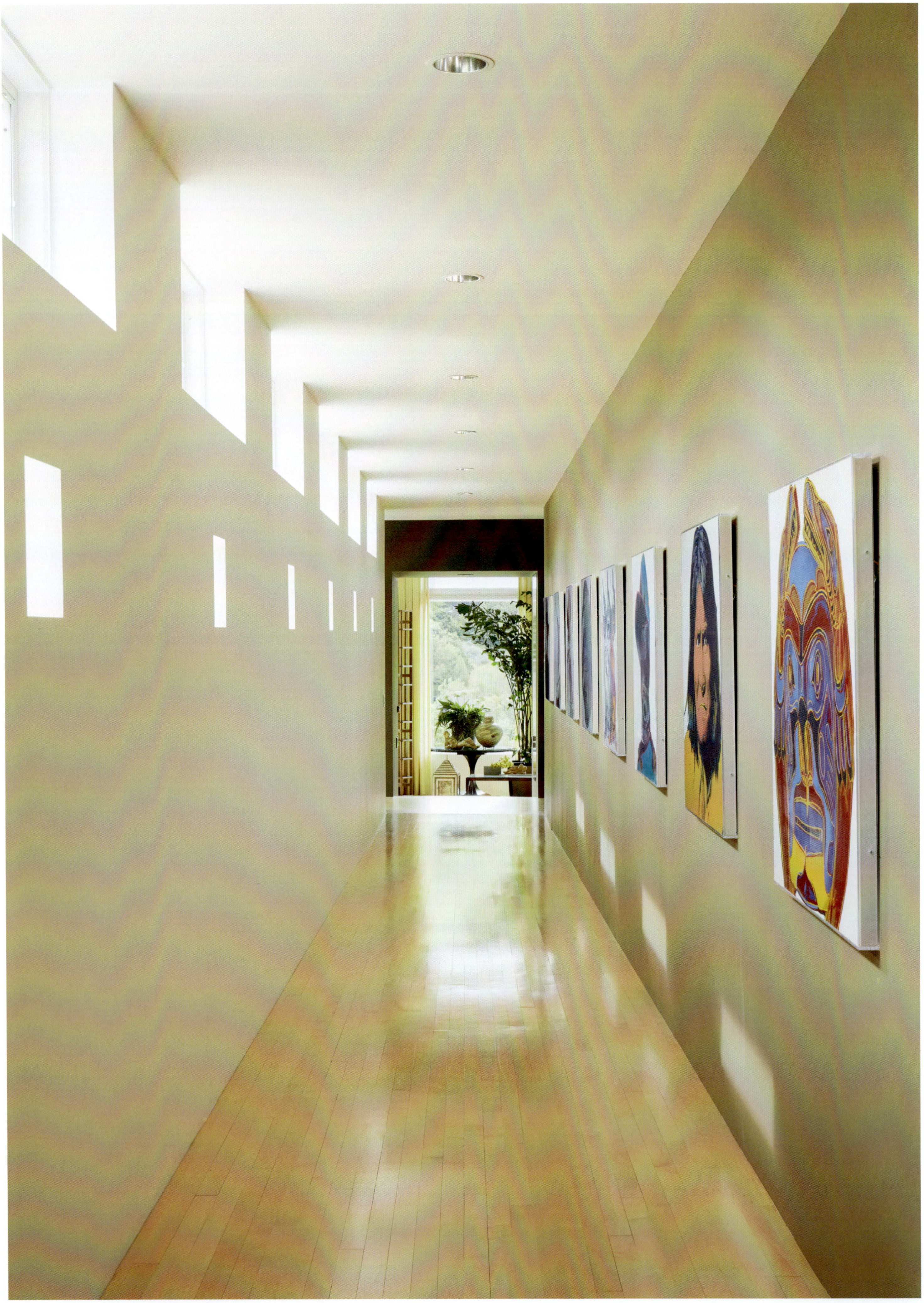

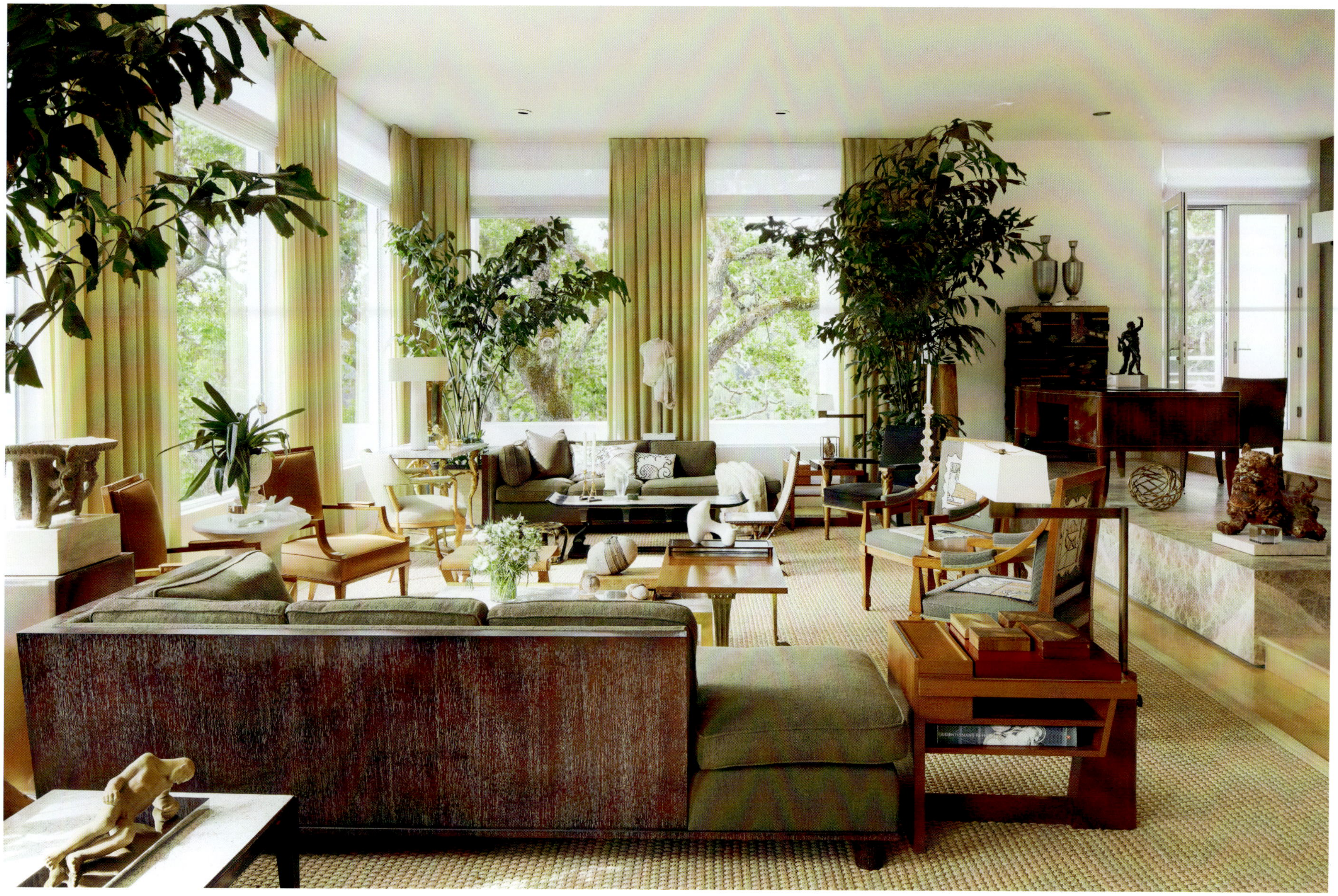

Lining the corridor to the living room is a set of artist's proofs for Andy Warhol's 1968 series *Cowboys and Indians*, which Thomas was instrumental in commissioning in partnership with art dealer and friend of Warhol's Edmond Gaultney.

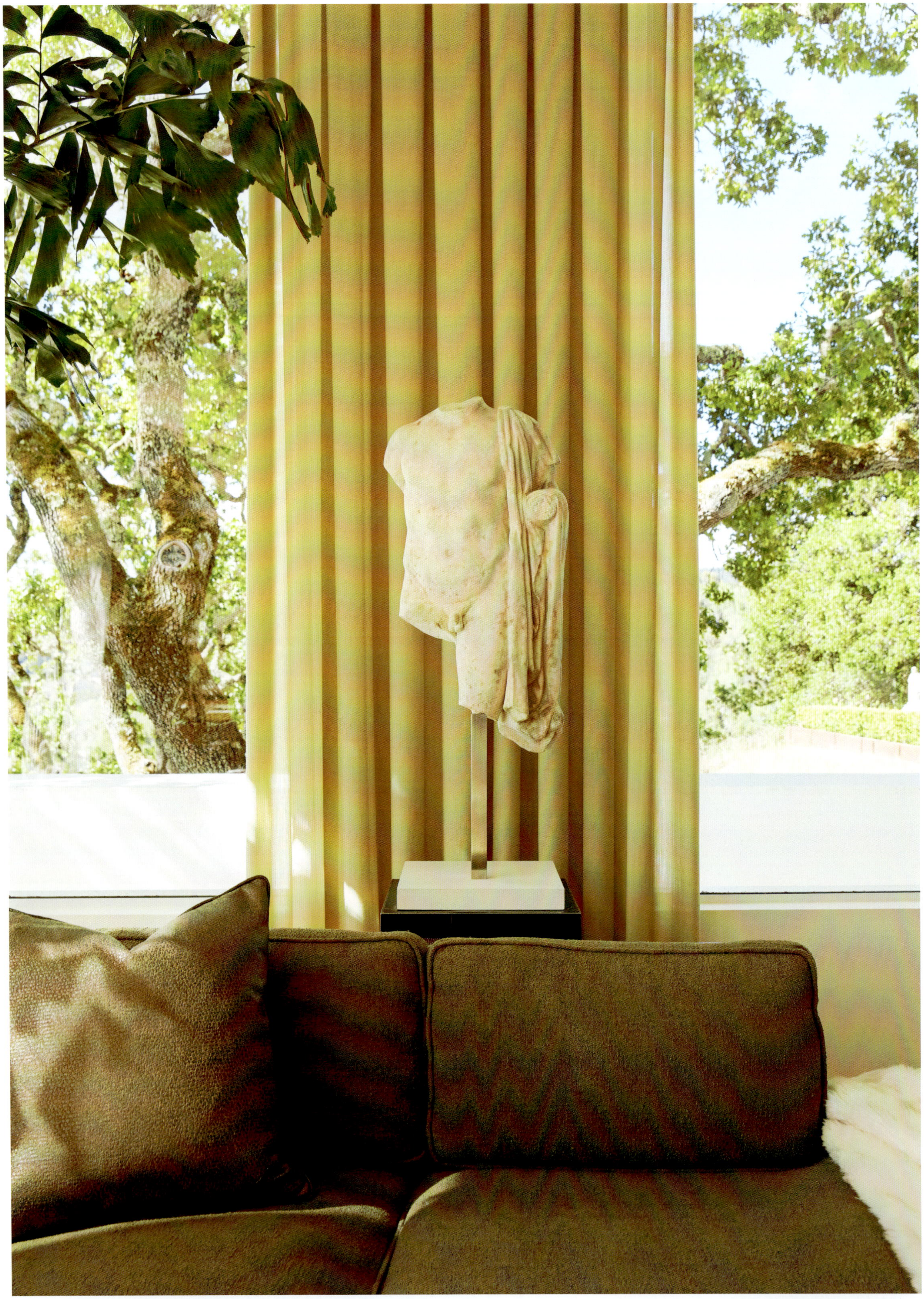

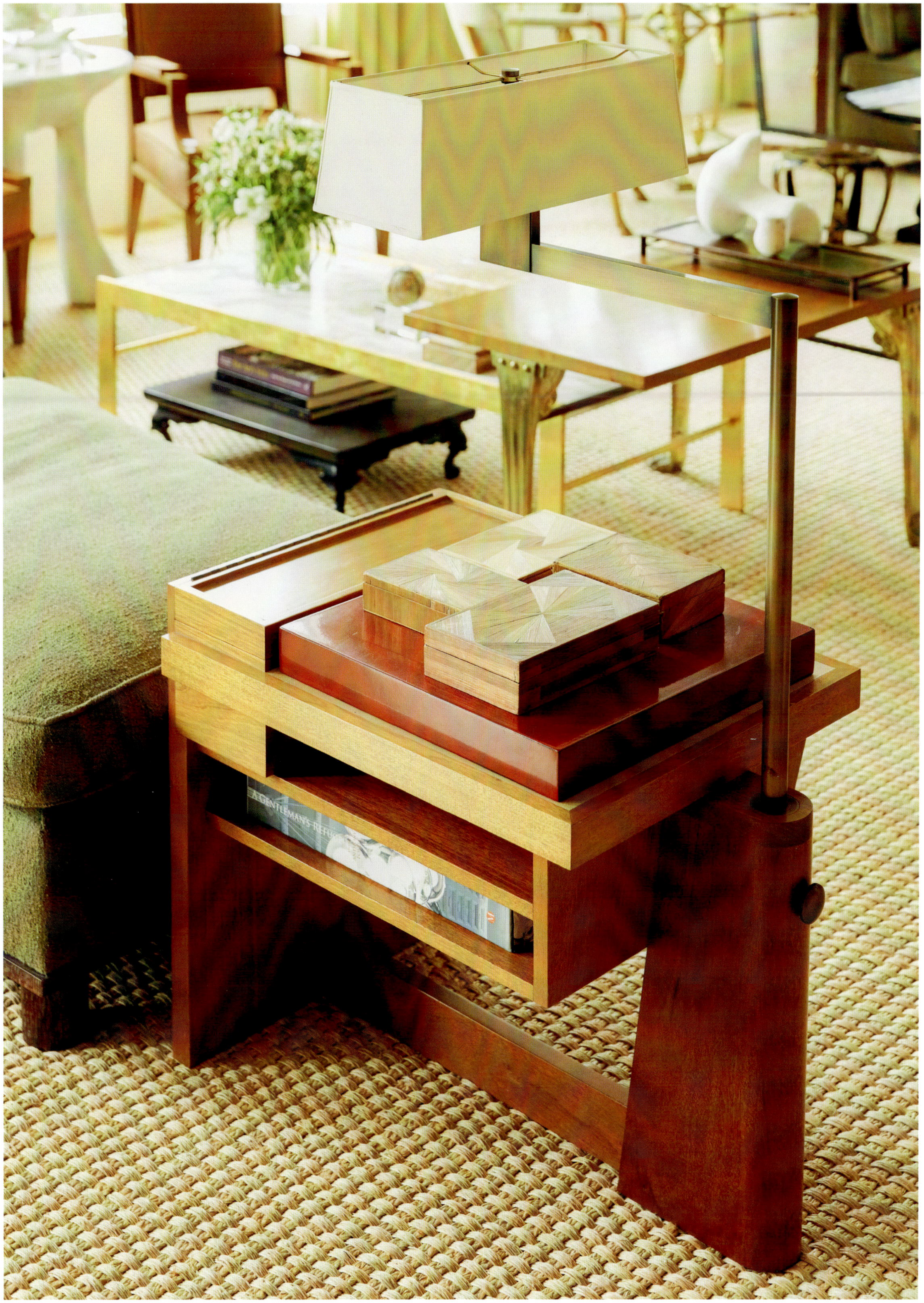
A GENTLEMAN'S

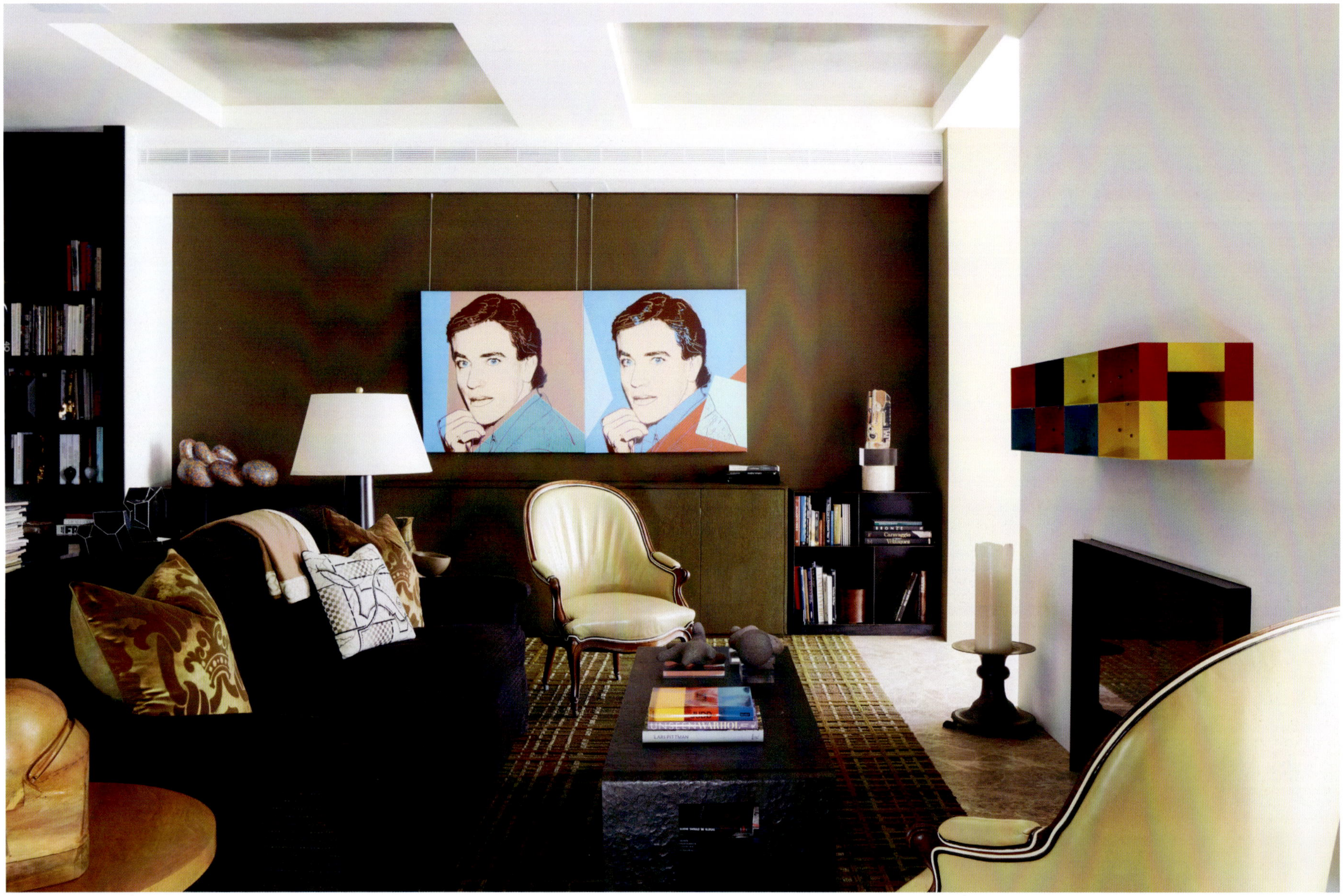

In the library, custom bookcases made of cold rolled steel with a bronze patina are so heavy, weighing in at about eight hundred pounds each, that an elaborate winch-and-sled system was developed by the contractor to hoist them into place. Tucked into a shelf is a photo of Warhol shooting the reference image of Thomas for a 1981 double-panel portrait that takes pride of place in the room, adjacent to a wall-mounted work by Donald Judd.

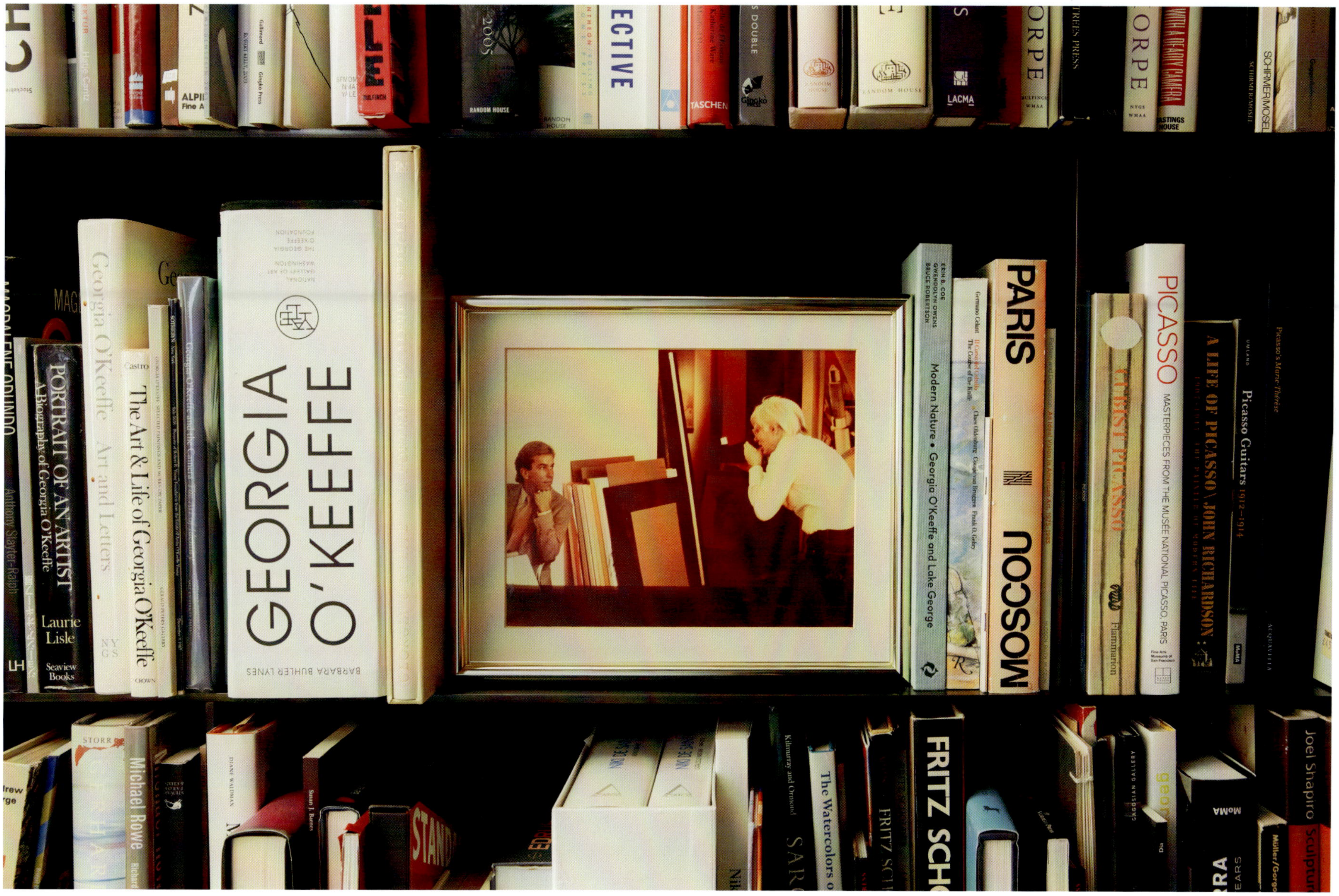
GEORGIA O'KEEFFE
BARBARA BUHLER LYNES
Georgia O'Keeffe Art and Letters
PORTRAIT OF AN ARTIST
A Biography of Georgia O'Keeffe
Laurie Lisle
Seaview Books
The Art & Life of Georgia O'Keeffe
Modern Nature • Georgia O'Keeffe and Lake George
PARIS
MOSCOU
PICASSO
MASTERPIECES FROM THE MUSÉE NATIONAL PICASSO, PARIS
A LIFE OF PICASSO
JOHN RICHARDSON
Picasso Guitars 1912–1914
Michael Rowe
Joel Shapiro
TASCHEN
RANDOM HOUSE
LACMA
MoMA

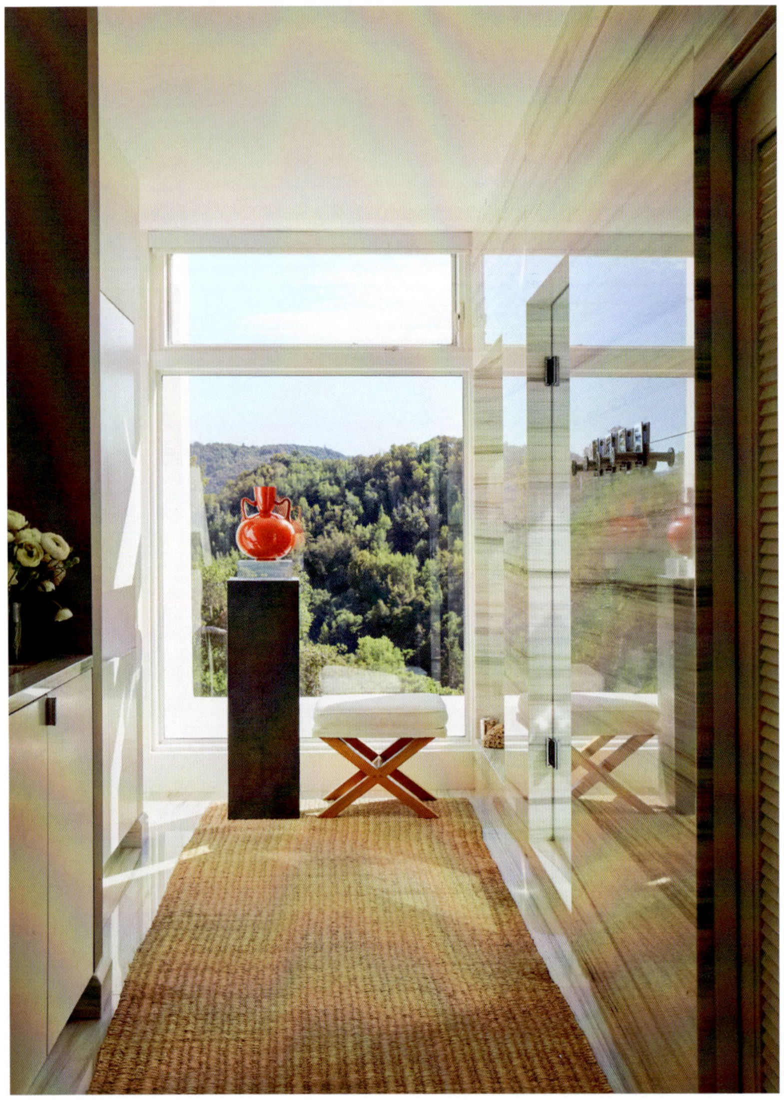

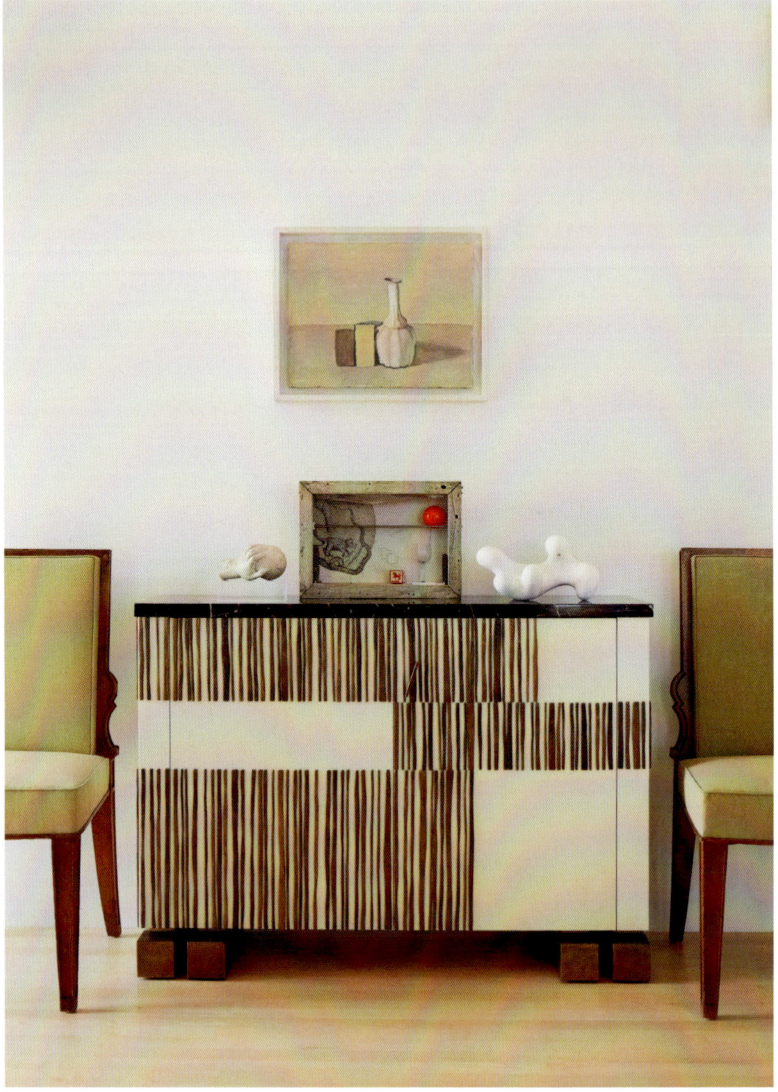

Thomas and Art Libera's collection is diverse but focused, mingling art from the 1970s to the present; twentieth-century decorative arts and furnishings, with an emphasis on French design of the 1920s and '30s; and art and artifacts from various periods, including an assemblage of San Sebastian figures from the sixteenth through the twentieth centuries. Case in point: the coral-red circa 1935 Murano glass vase, above left, created by Napoleone Martinuzzi and Francesco Zecchin, "my favorite of the many extraordinary talents working in Venetian glass between the wars," says Thomas.

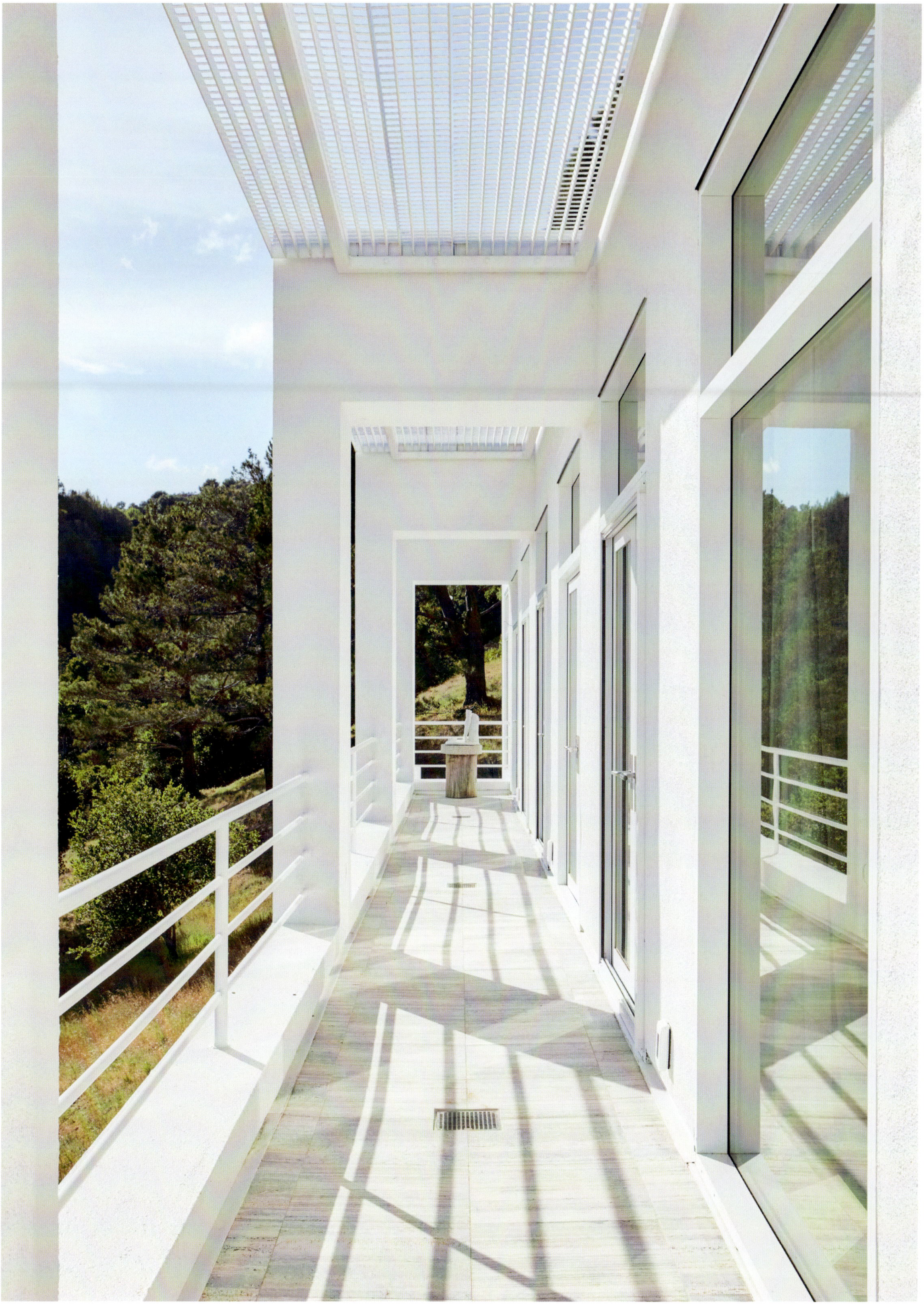

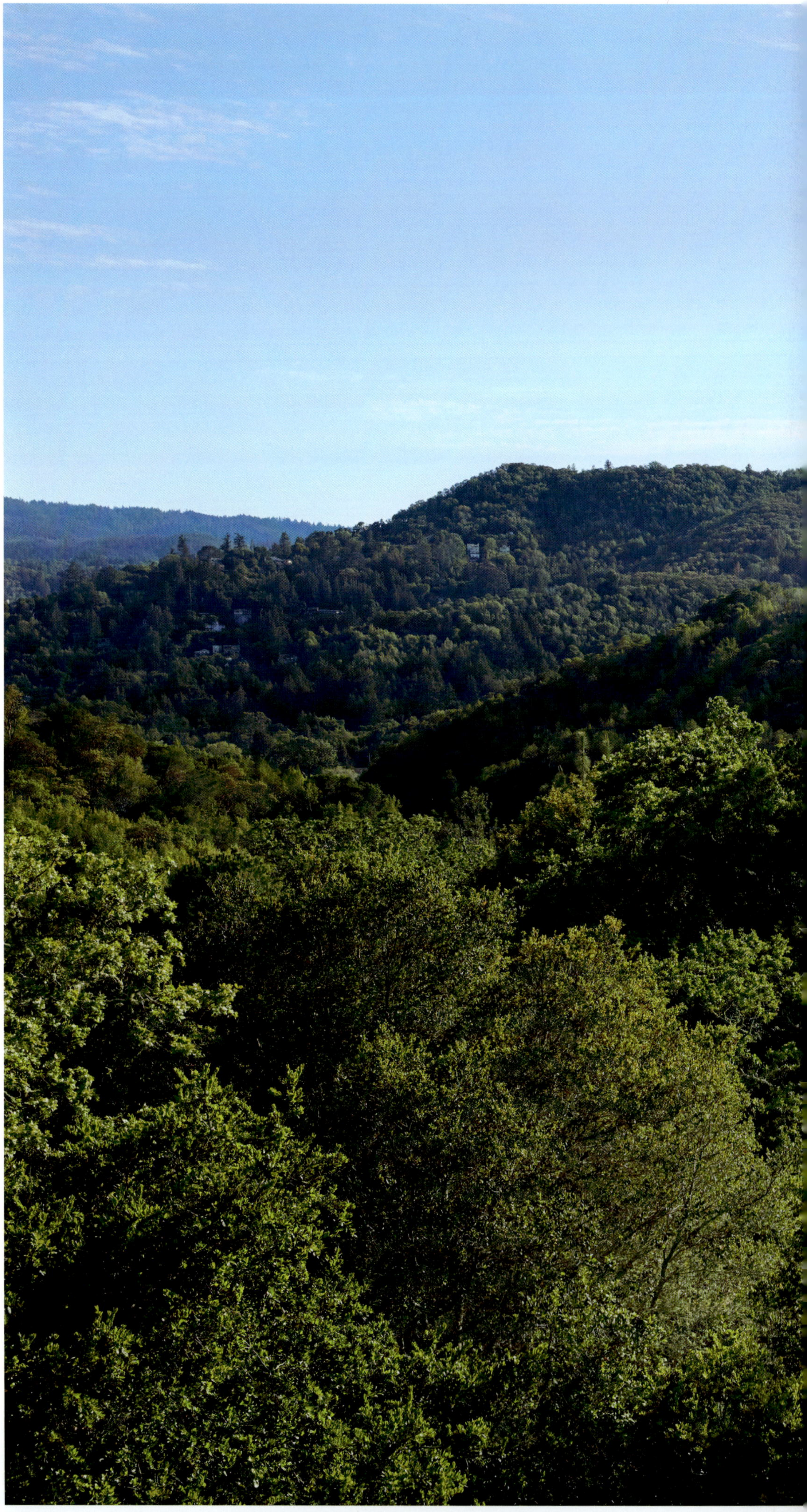

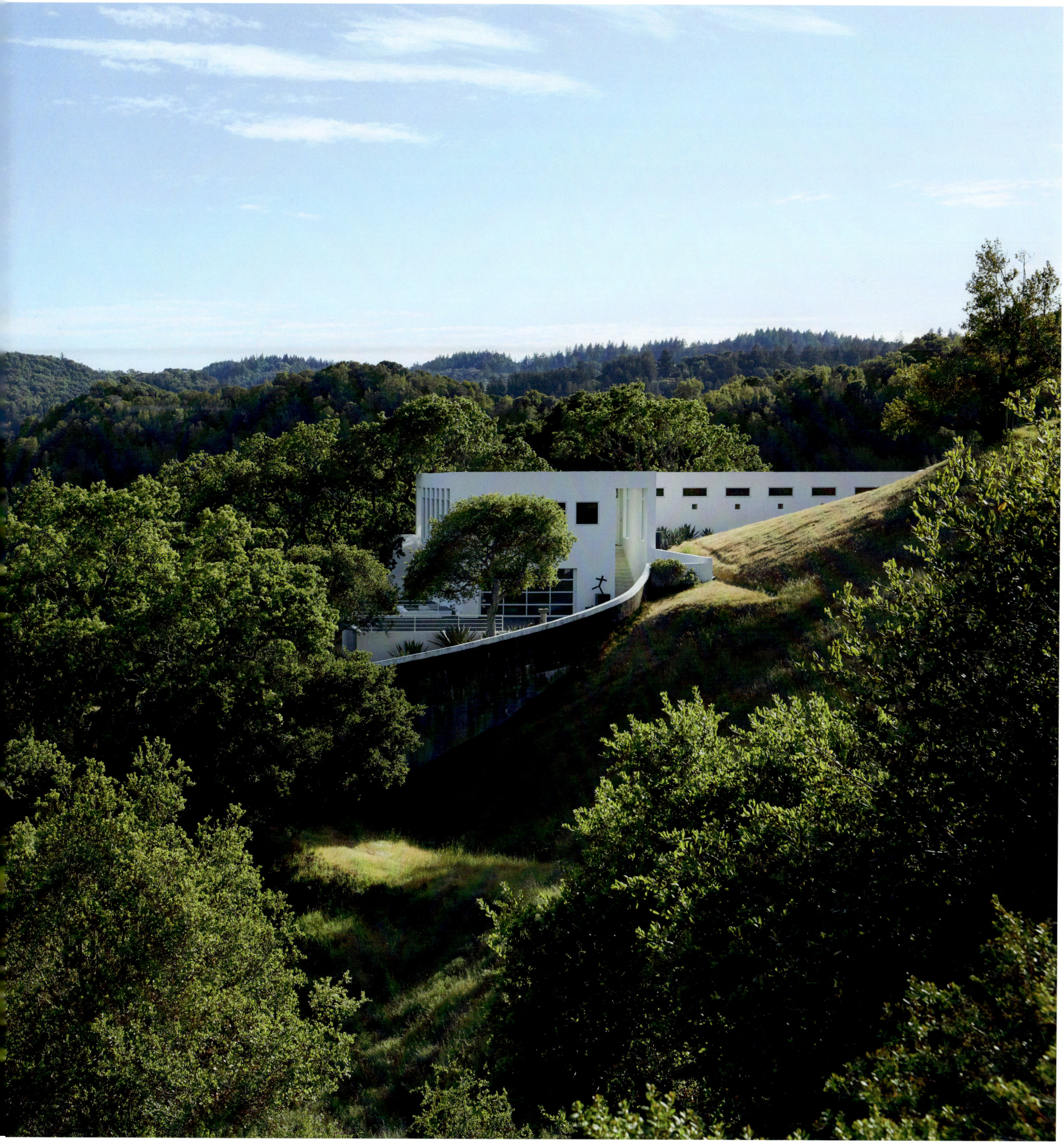

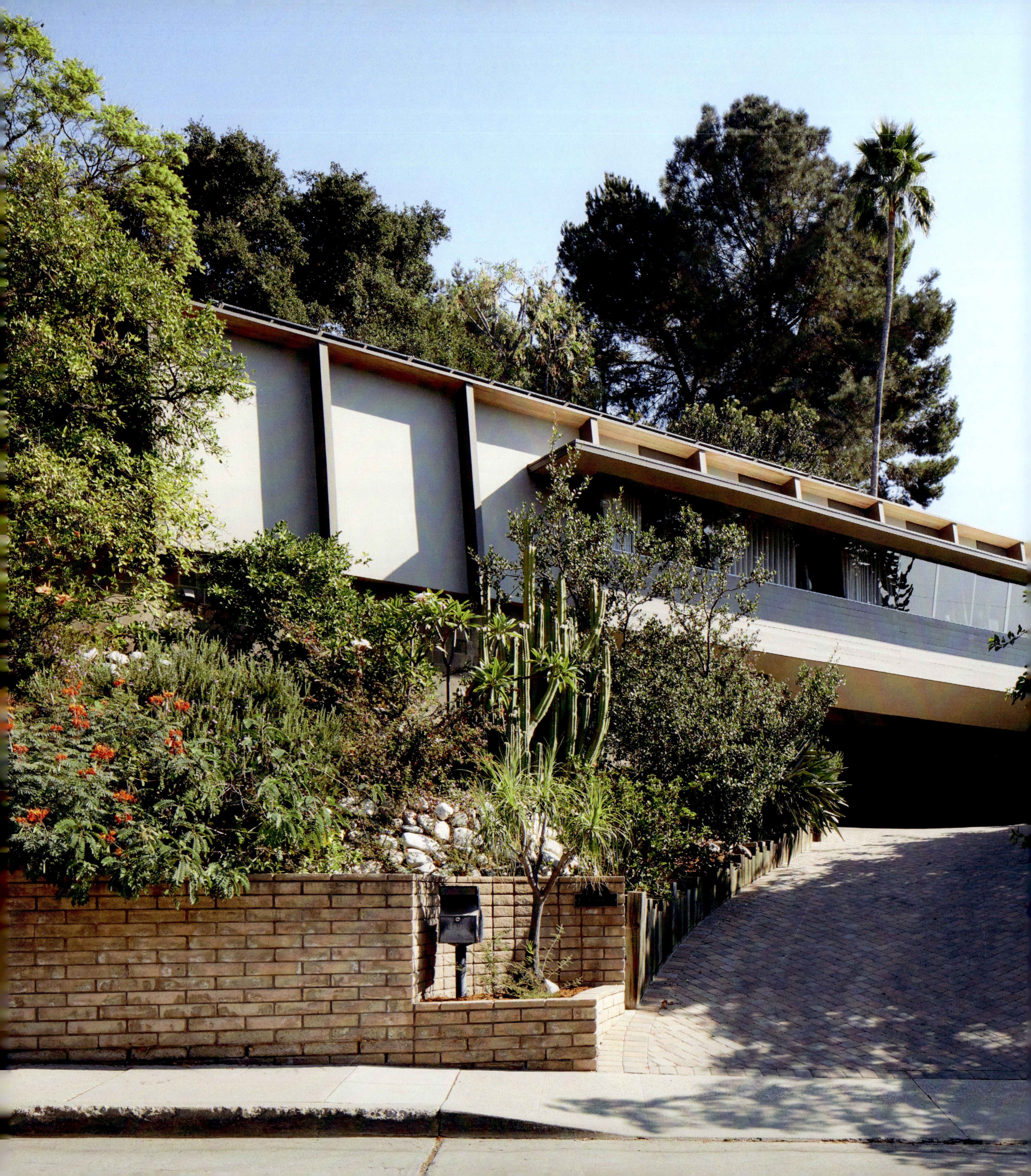

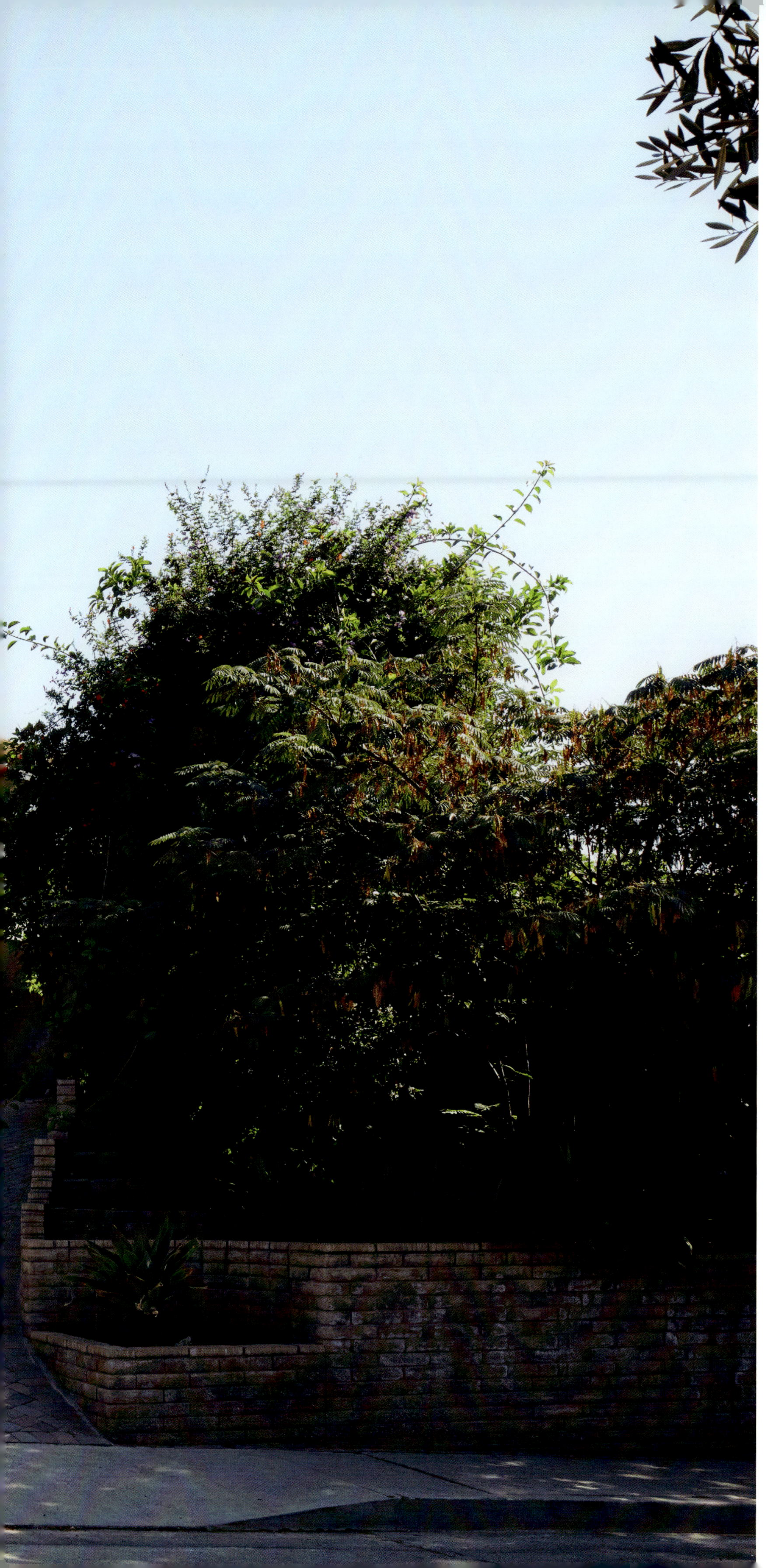

The Pilot House

Los Angeles

Architect

A. Quincy Jones
and Whitney R. Smith

Resident

Mary Weatherford

A day spent working with interior designer Oliver Furth is always a good day. The house is camera-ready, snacks are set out in the kitchen, there are white-glove movers on hand to help if help is needed (you try lifting a petrified wood side table), and while each space is different, every shoot with Oliver buzzes with creativity (he doesn't even mind the questionable music we play). Oliver's brain is a sponge, but mine, alas, is a sieve, and I only wish I could retain the stories he shares. His deep knowledge of design history paired with a willingness to experiment in his work makes each of his projects a joy to photograph. These qualities also made him eminently suited to returning this remarkable house to its original vision while expressing the voice of its artist owner.

The Pilot House, a designated Los Angeles Historical-Cultural Monument, sits on a curved road in a dense area of East Los Angeles, but the city seems to fall away the moment you walk through the gate and up the steps into the wild, private garden beyond. The views from inside the home are of treetops and hillsides.

When I first photographed this house, in 2019, it was completely empty, its unusual angles stripped to their bare bones. But even while so raw, it was glowing with the meticulous work undertaken to revitalize it. Designed in 1948 by A. Quincy Jones and Whitney R. Smith, the subsequent years had not been kind to the house. It took the attention of skilled craftspeople to complete the necessary but unsung nitty-gritty work required to refurbish so many of the storied houses in this book—in this case, updating the plumbing, the electric, and the cabinetry; stripping layers upon layers of white paint; and finally returning the plywood walls to the original milky-green, slightly pickled finish. In collaboration with the passionate homeowner, artist Mary Weatherford, and architects Frank Escher and Ravi GuneWardena, Furth helped restore this modern masterpiece.

When I returned to shoot the house a year later, it had truly become a home. The warm glow of sunshine permeated the space, and the smell of construction—concrete, paint stripper, plaster dust—had been replaced with the fresh air wafting in with the cross breeze. The house had taken new life with pops of color in rugs, fabrics, and tile work; favorite furnishings and artwork sang against the restored wood paneling and cinder block; and bees hovered and hummed in the garden. The creativity in every decision made by Furth and Weatherford is clear for all to see.

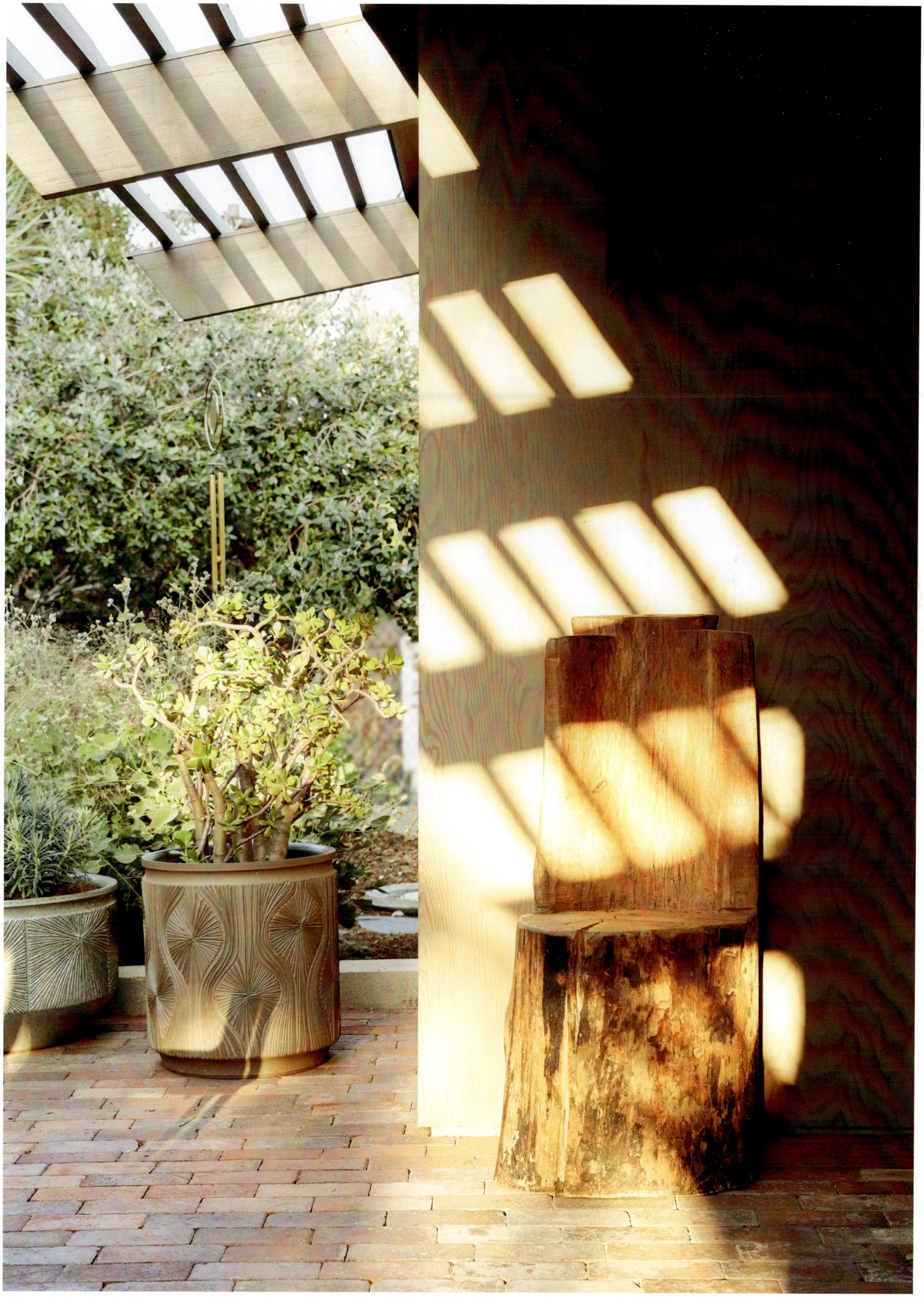

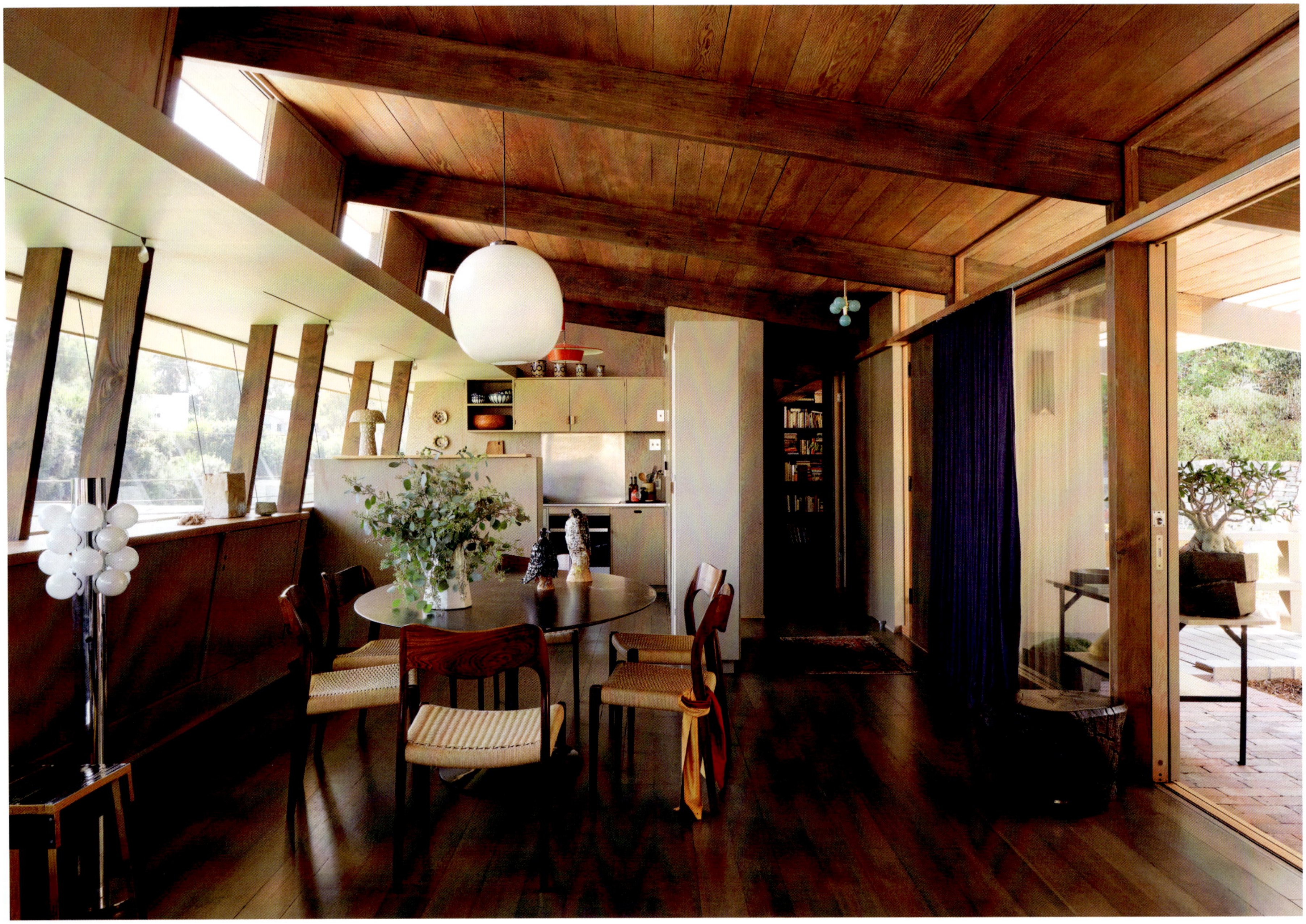

The kitchen is located at the center of the house, separating the living and dining rooms from the more private spaces. During the shoot, this became the hub for the crew as Mary graciously made everyone healthy green juices.

A significant component of the Pilot House's restoration involved stripping the plywood walls of layers of white paint and returning them to their original pickled finish, which Oliver Furth dubbed "Schindler green" in homage to architect A. Quincy Jones's predecessor Rudolph Schindler.

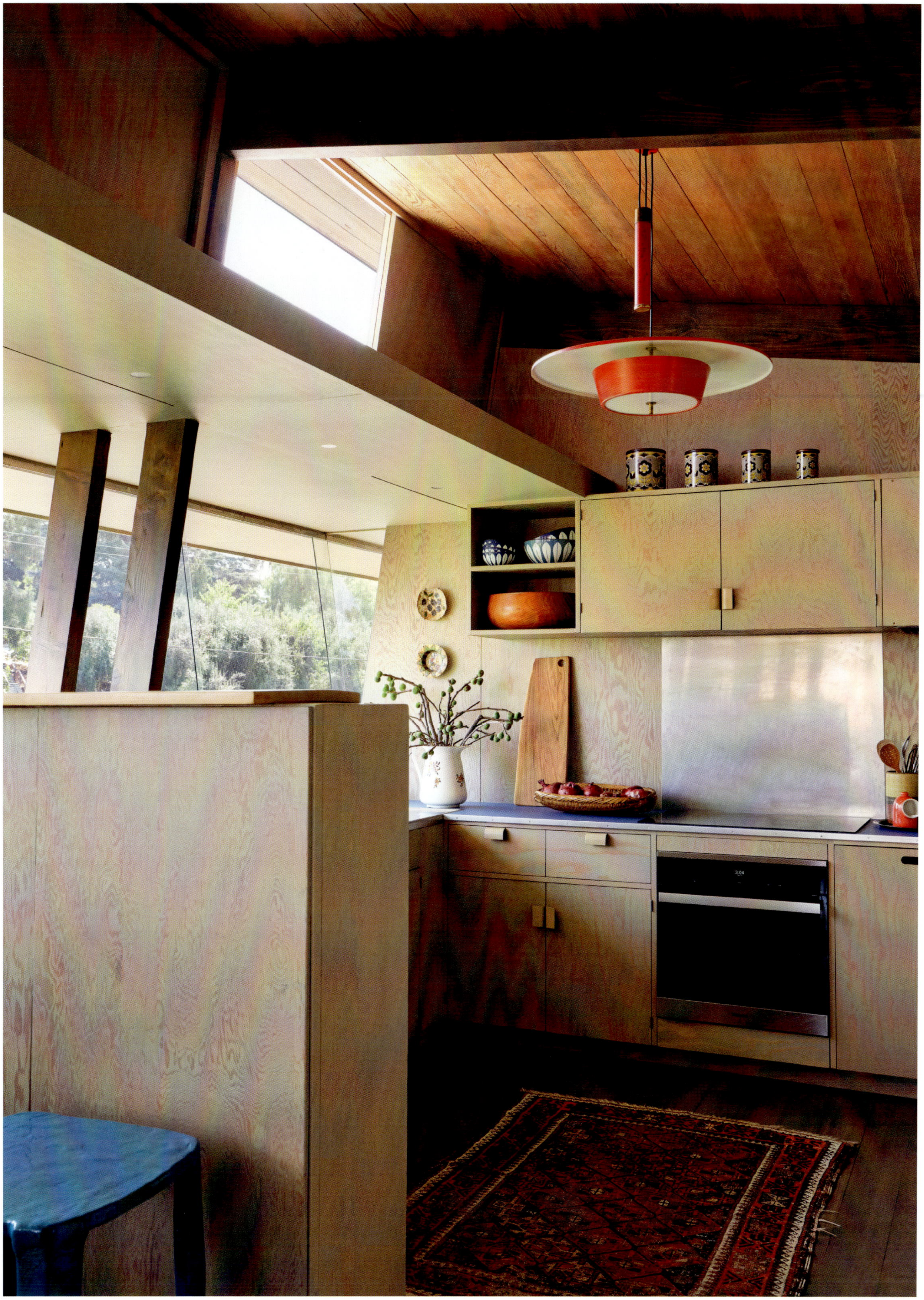

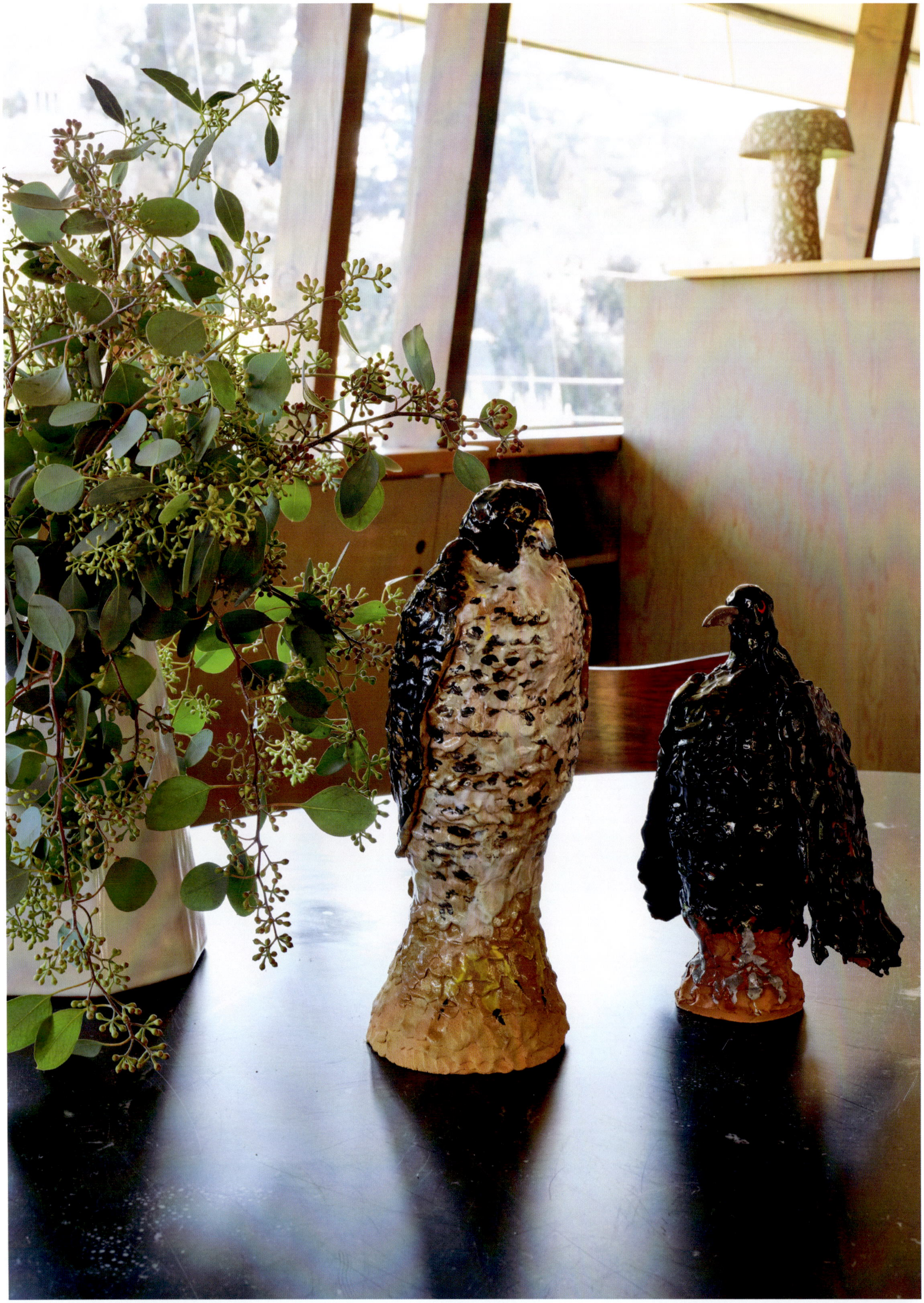

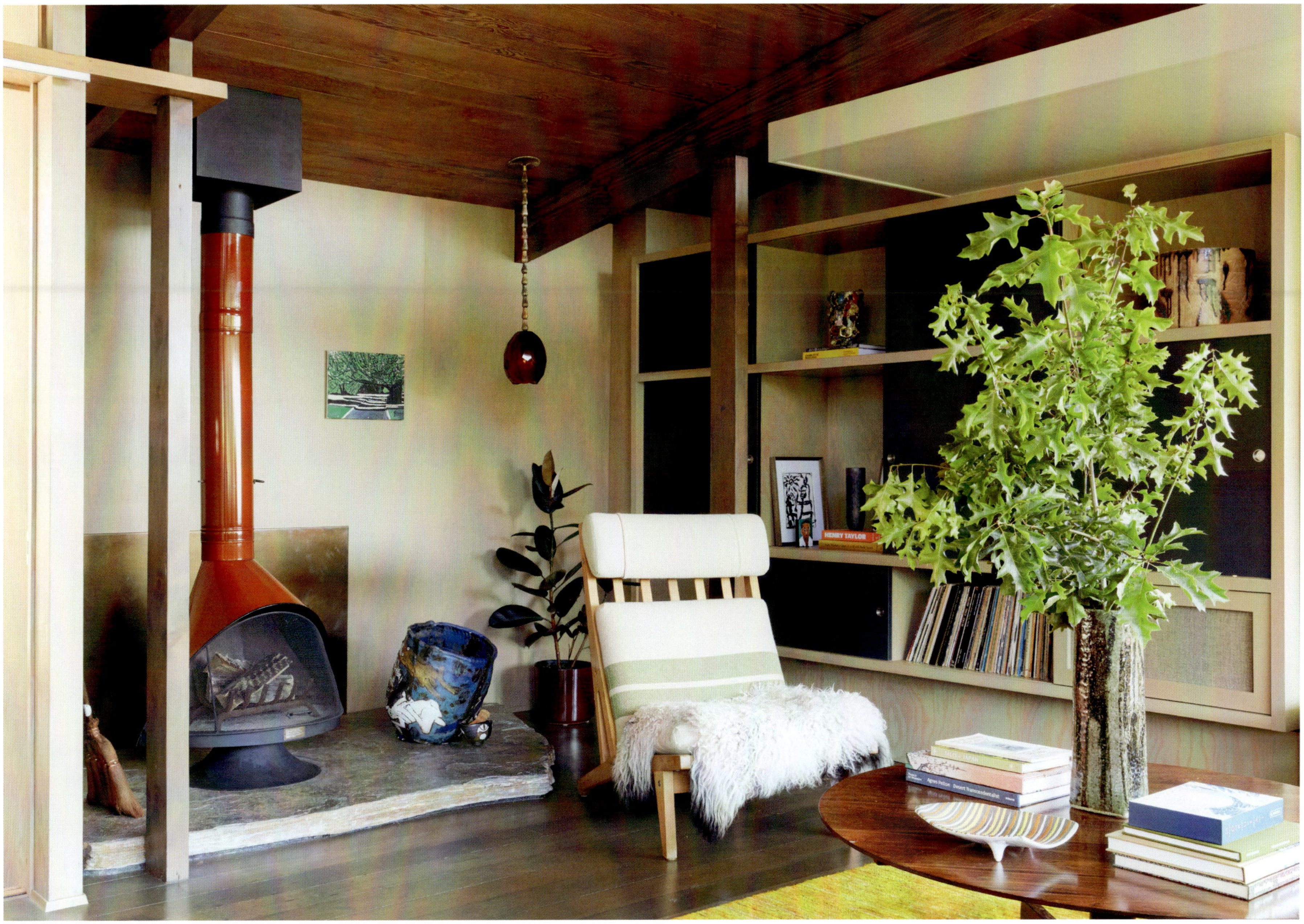
HENRY TAYLOR

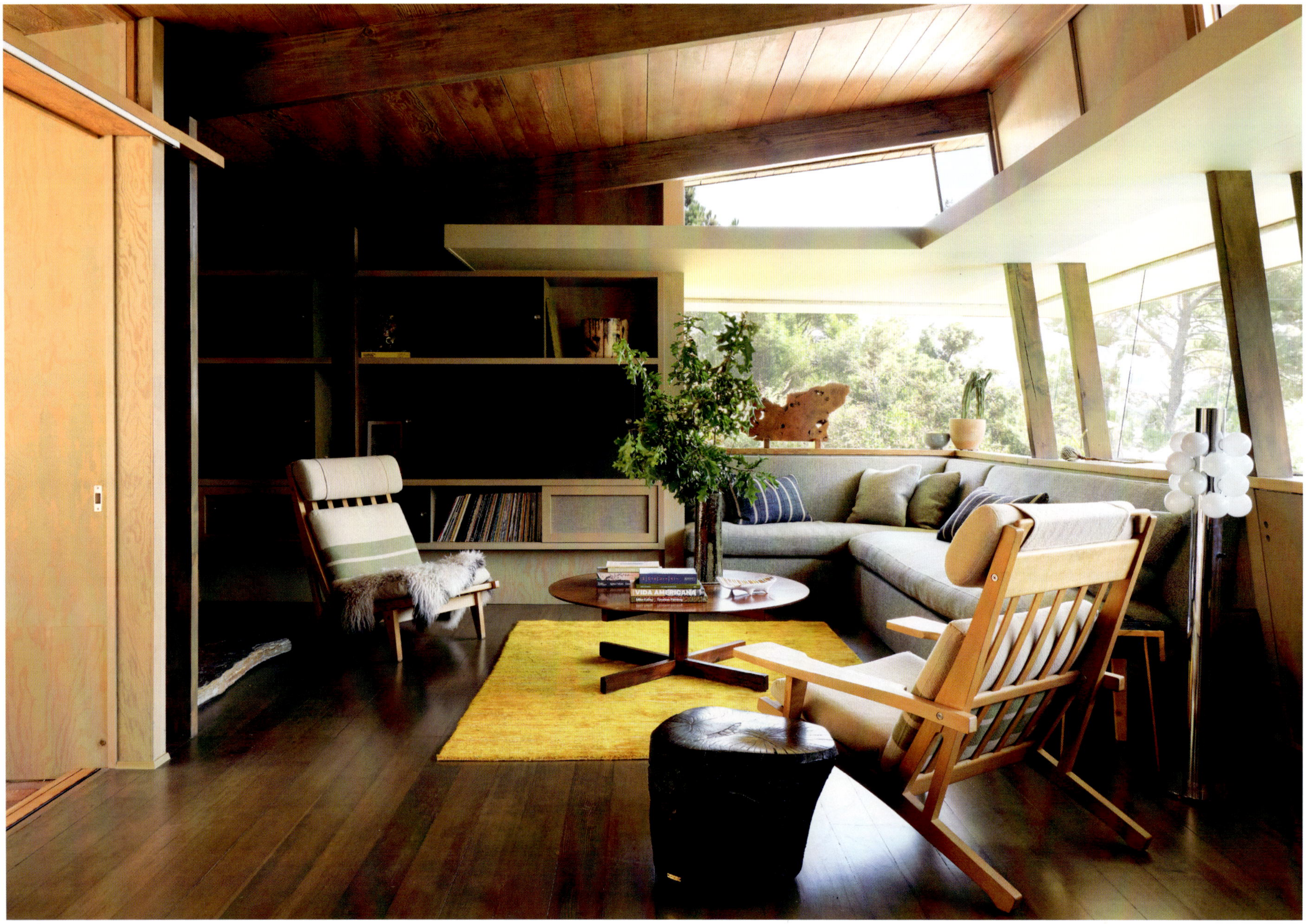

Classic midcentury modern designs by Hans Wegner, Eero Saarinen, and Serge Mouille sit alongside Los Angeles artists and makers—such as David Wiseman and Shin Okuda—whom Furth has long championed and sprinkles into all his projects.

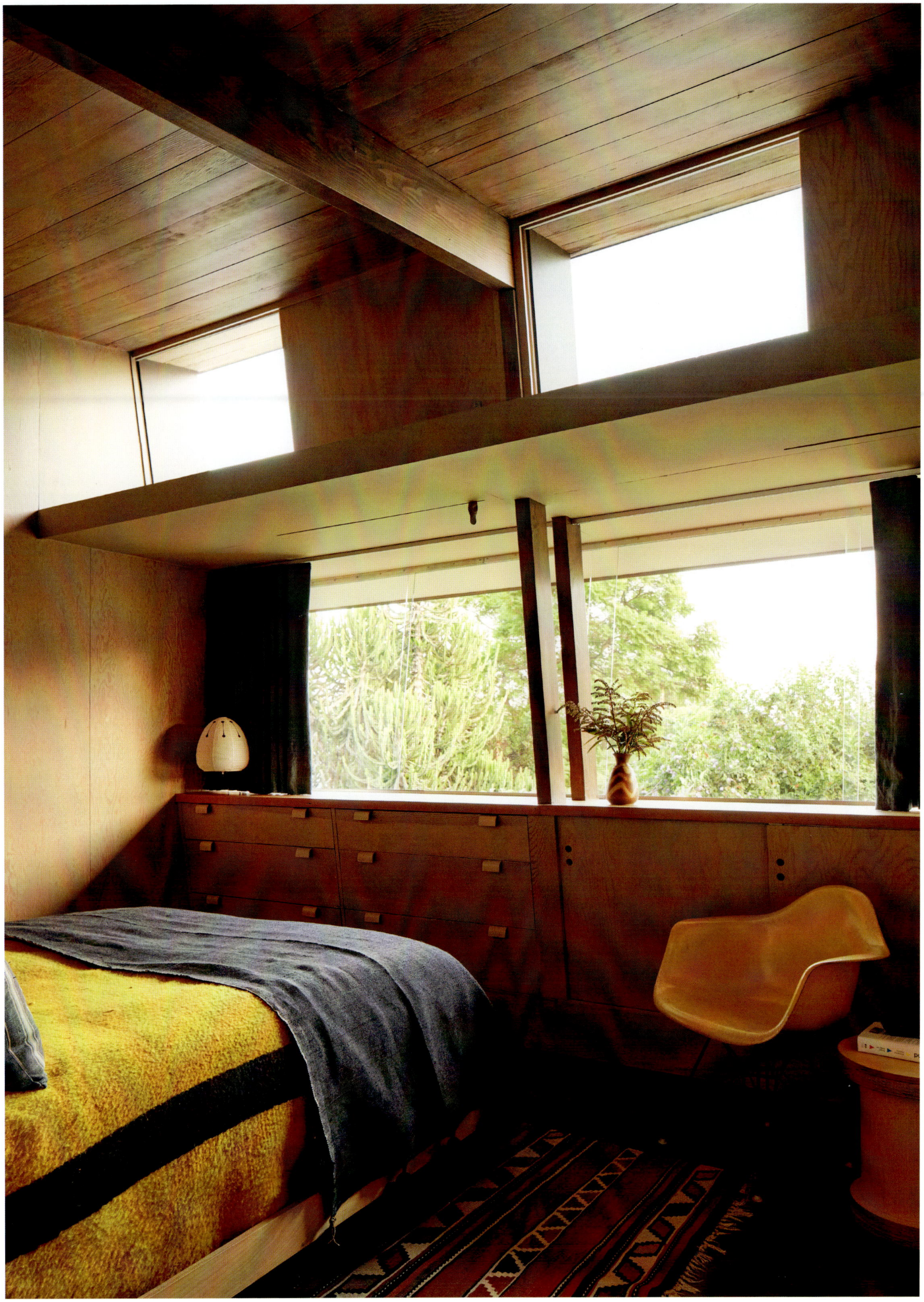

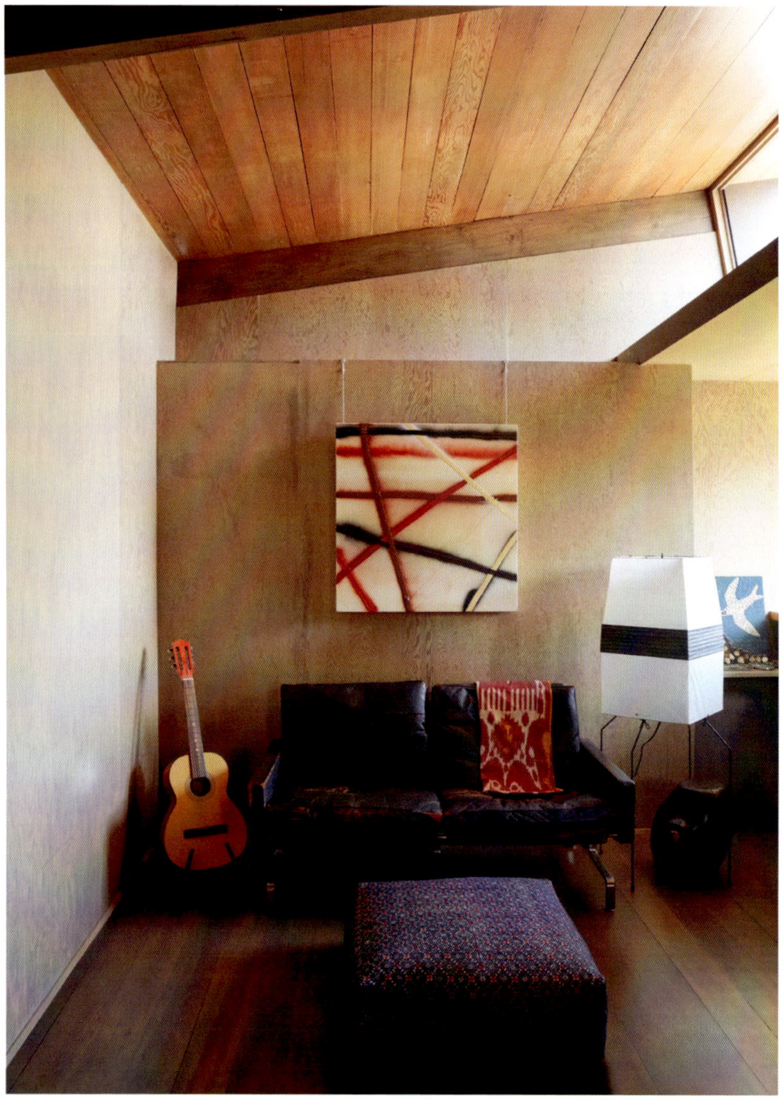

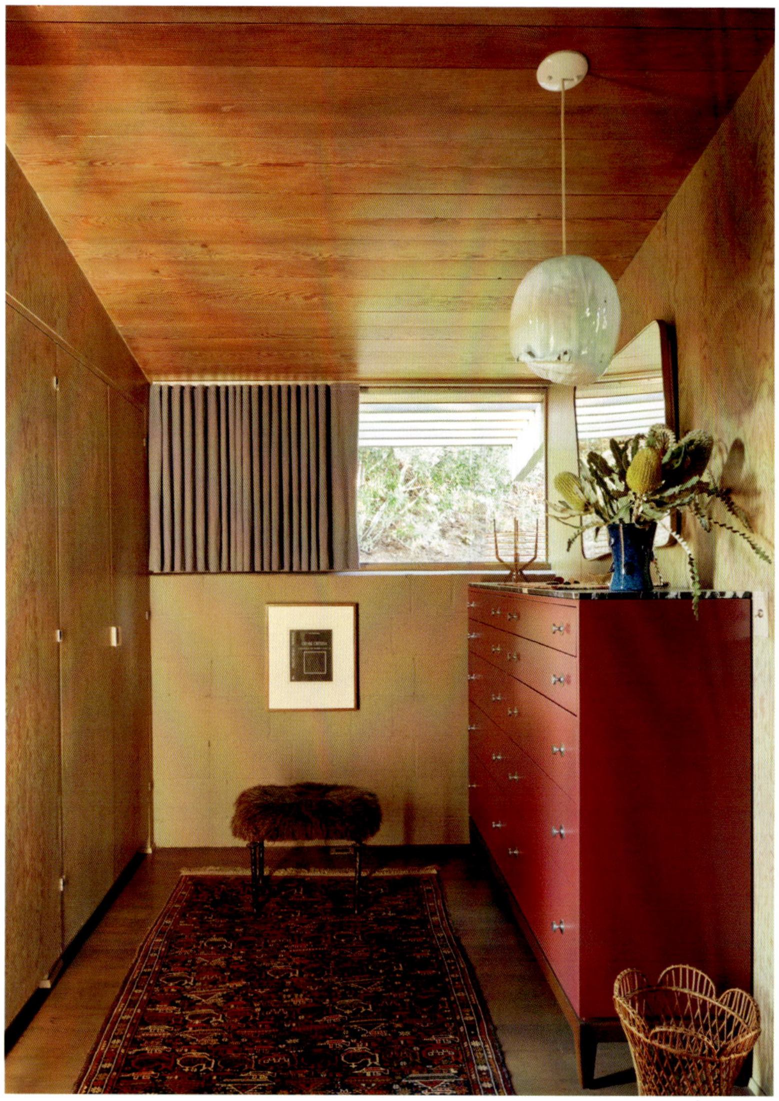

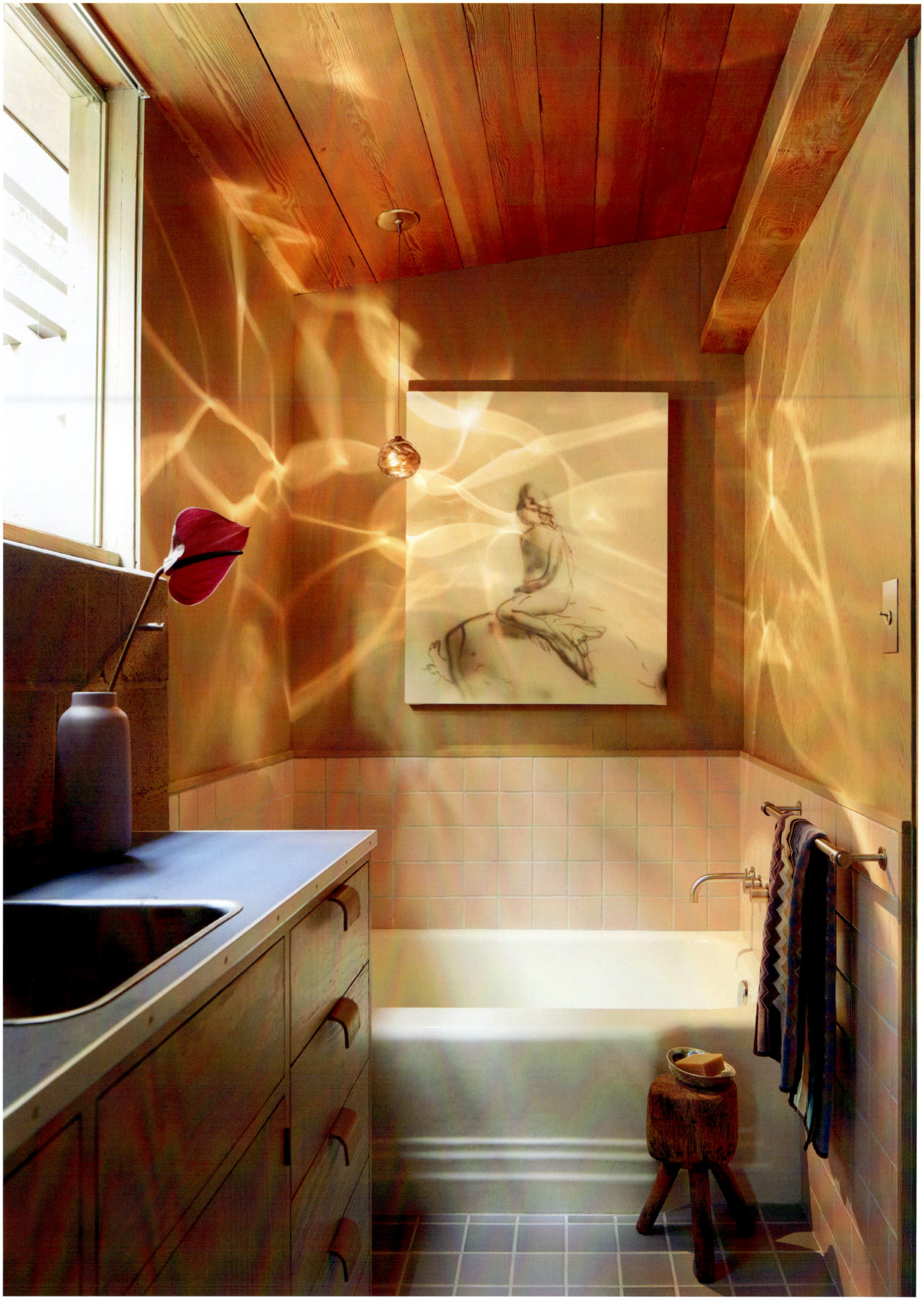

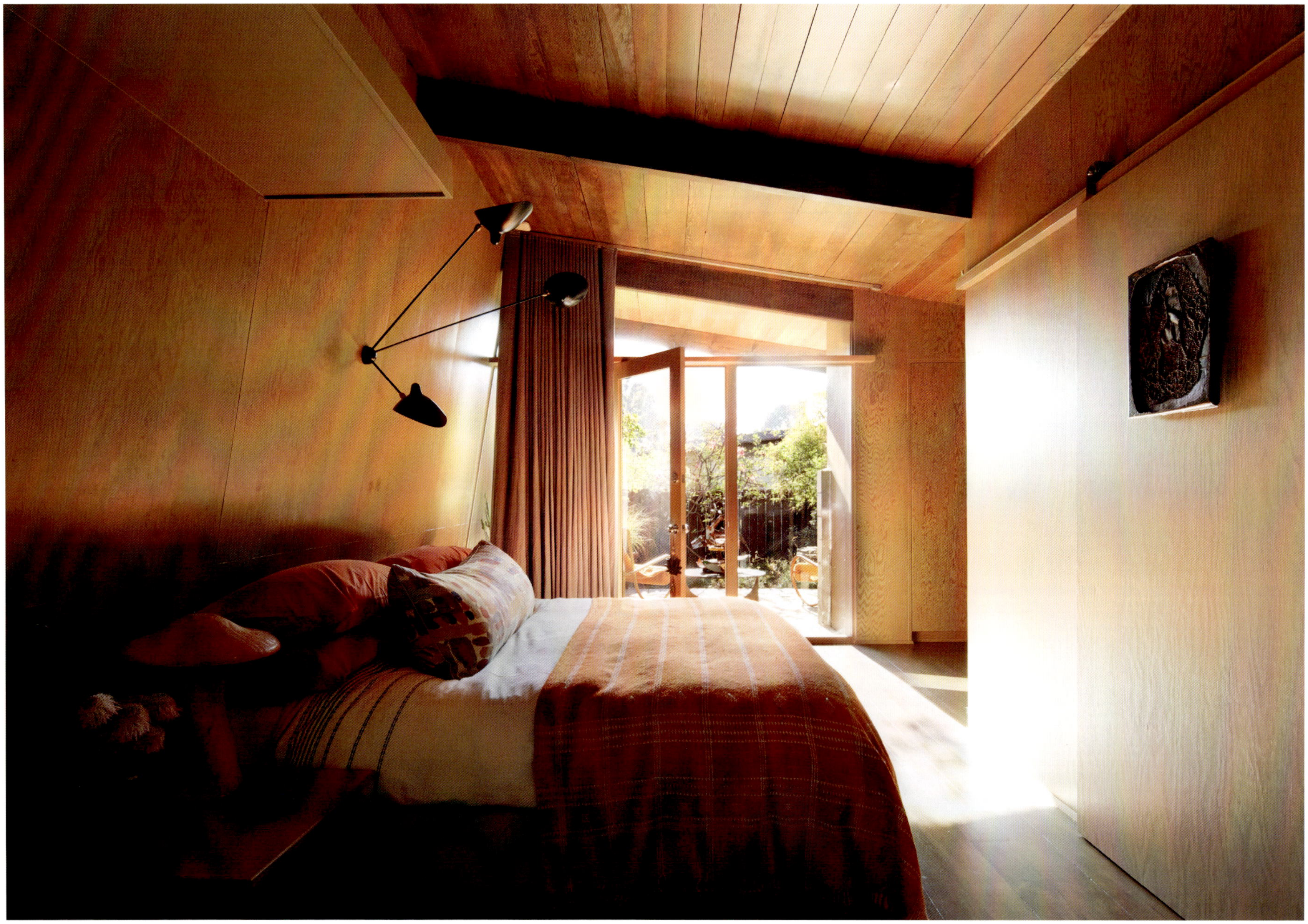

The lively house is full of work by other artists, including Ken Taylor, Karin Gulbran, Timo Fahler, Rebecca Morris, Mari Eastman, and Joey Kötting, among others.

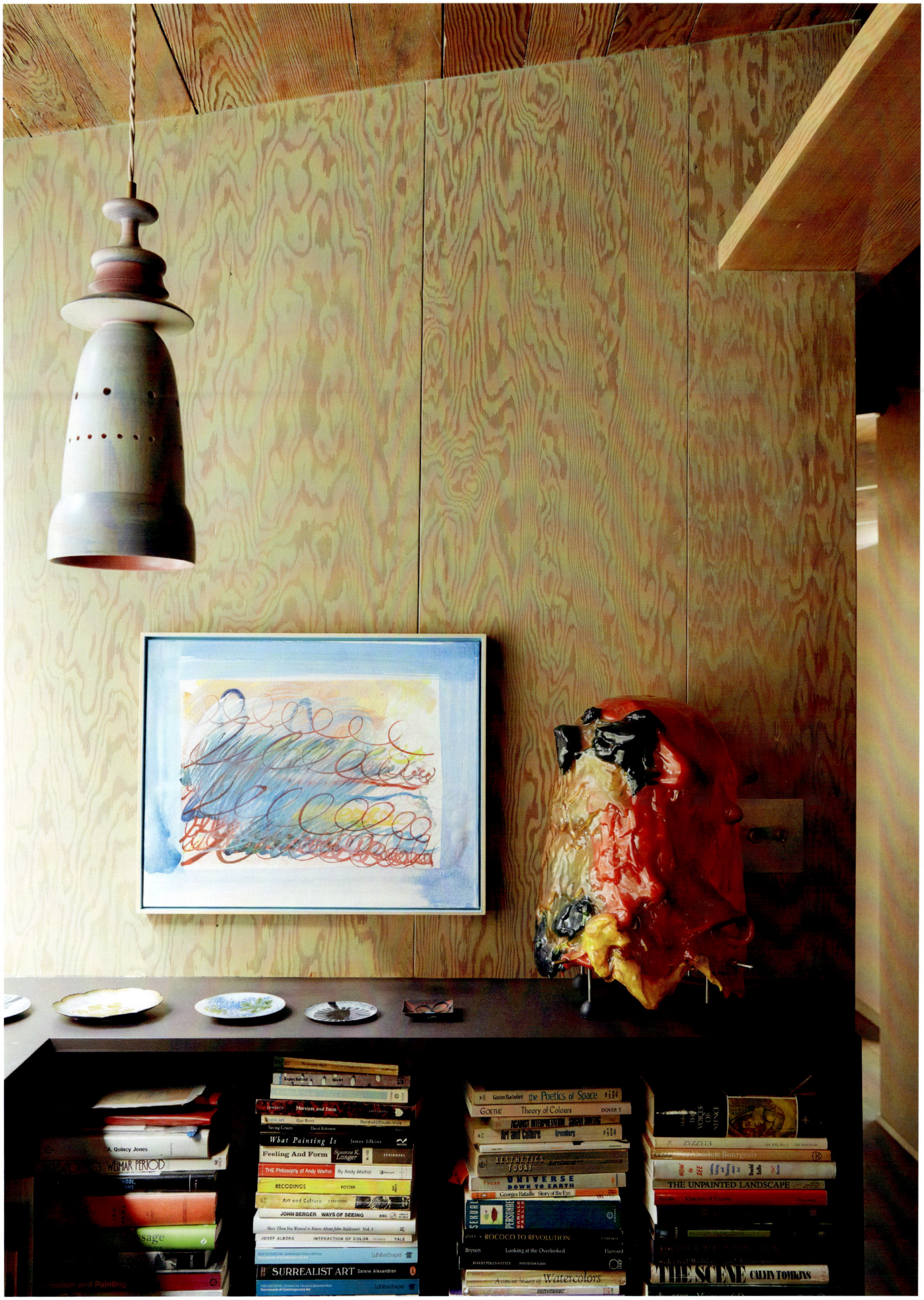
A. Quincy Jones
WEIMAR PERIOD
Marxism and Form
What Painting Is
James Elkins
Feeling And Form
Susanne K. Langer
THE Philosophy of Andy Warhol
Art and Culture
JOHN BERGER WAYS OF SEEING
JOSEF ALBERS INTERACTION OF COLOR
SURREALIST ART
Gaston Bachelard the Poetics of Space
GOETHE Theory of Colours
AESTHETICS TODAY
UNIVERSE DOWN TO EARTH
Georges Bataille Story of the Eye
ROCOCO TO REVOLUTION
Bryson Looking at the Overlooked
A concise history of Watercolors
THE UNPAINTED LANDSCAPE
THE SCENE CALVIN TOMKINS

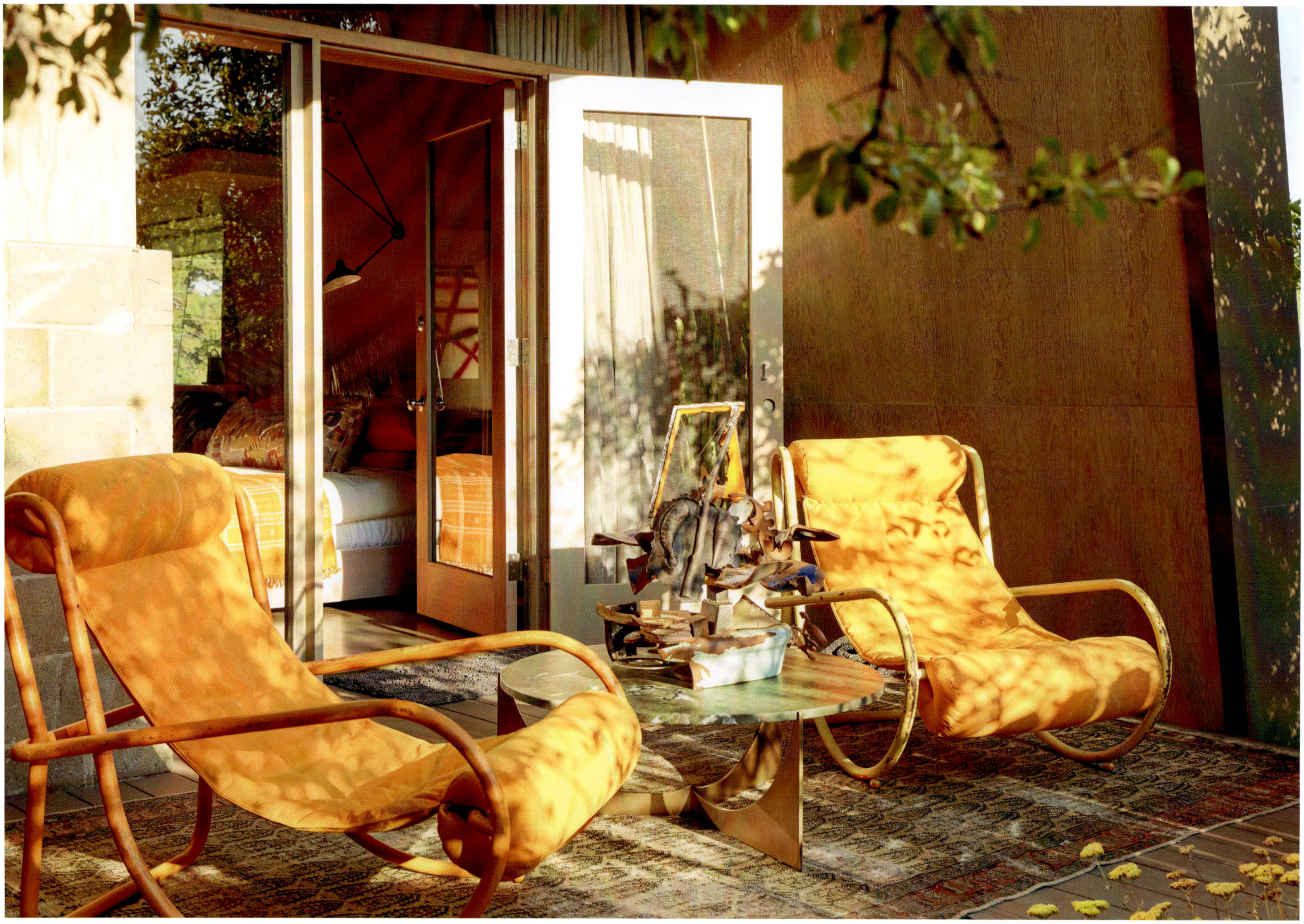

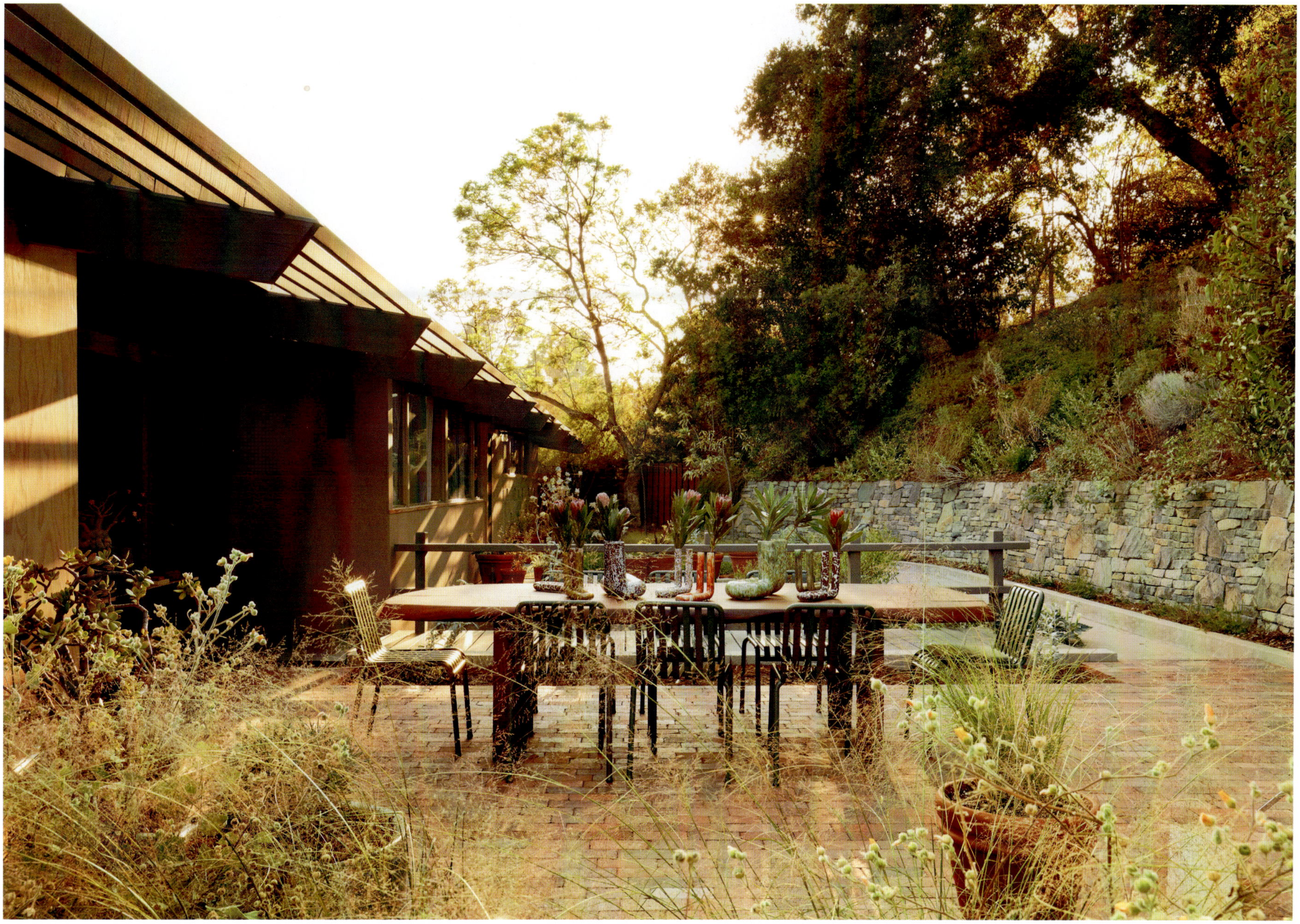

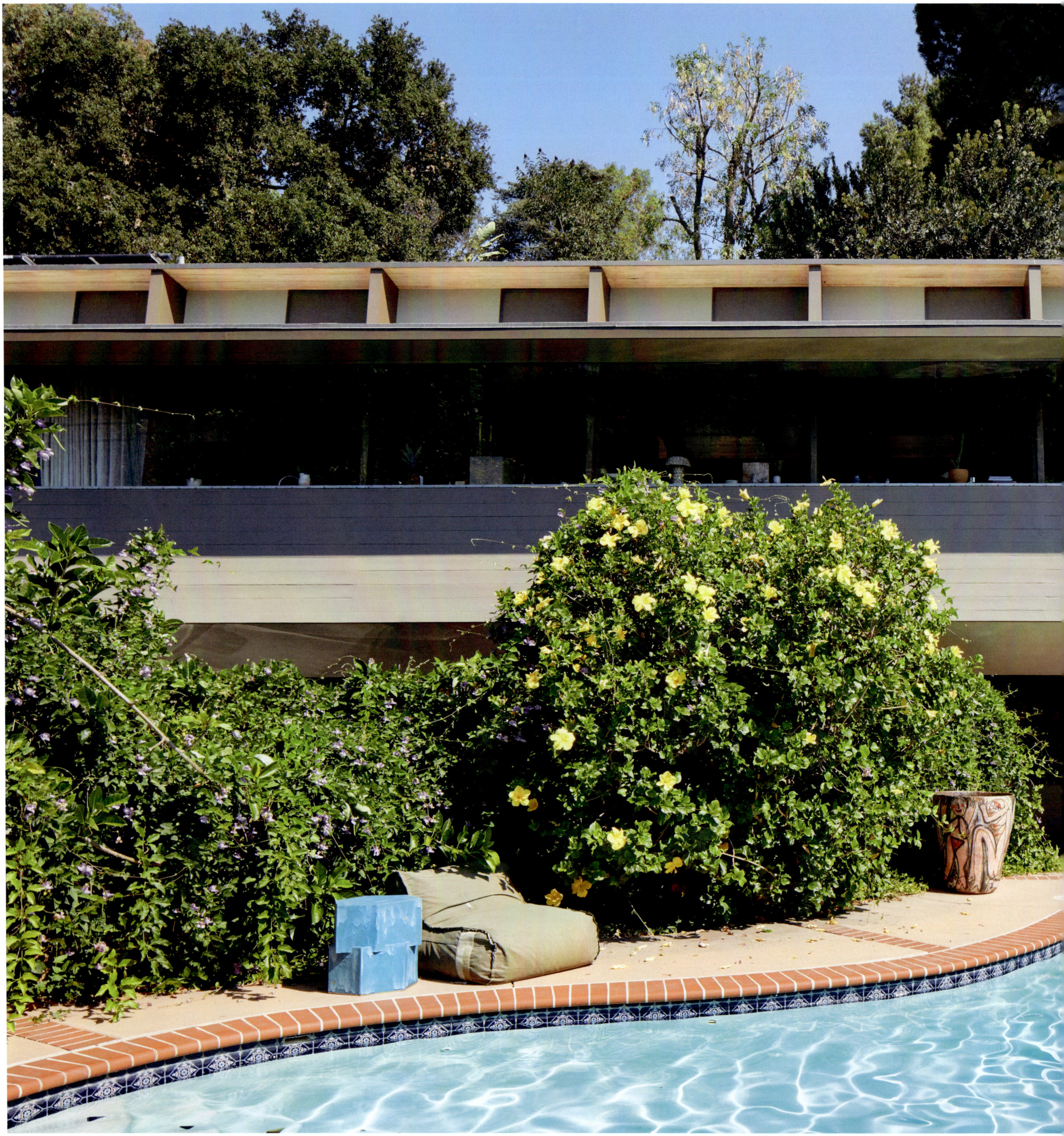

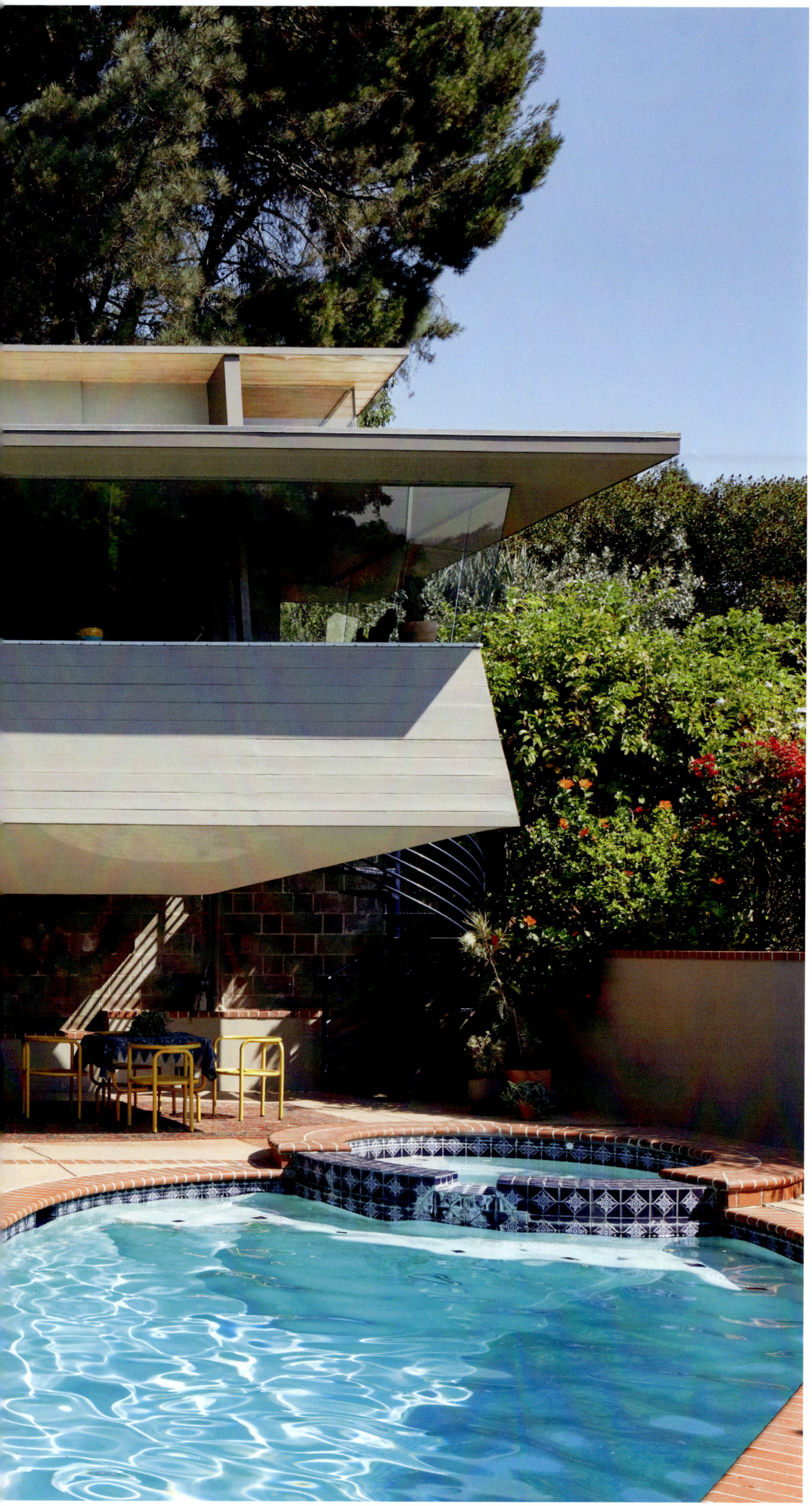

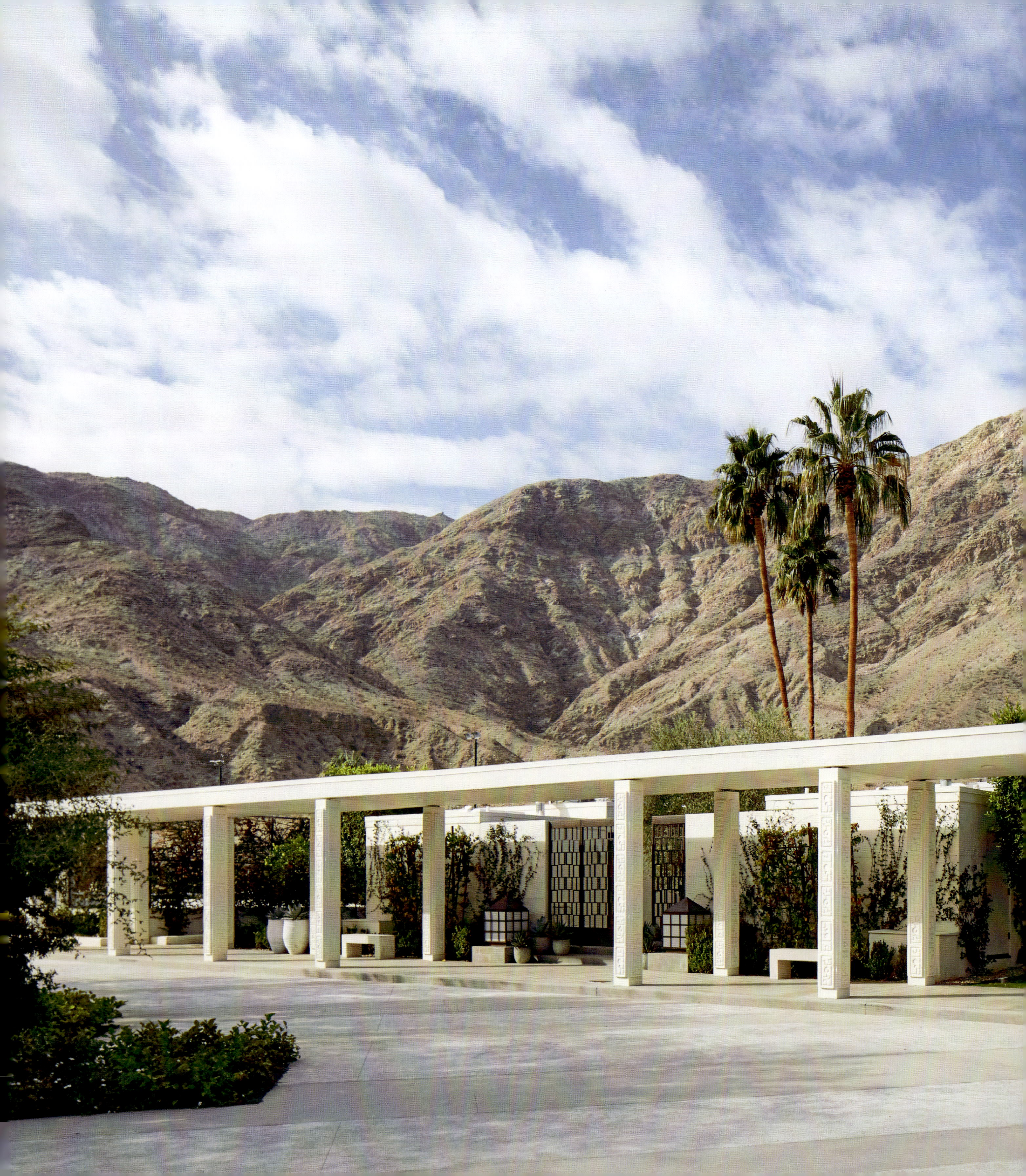

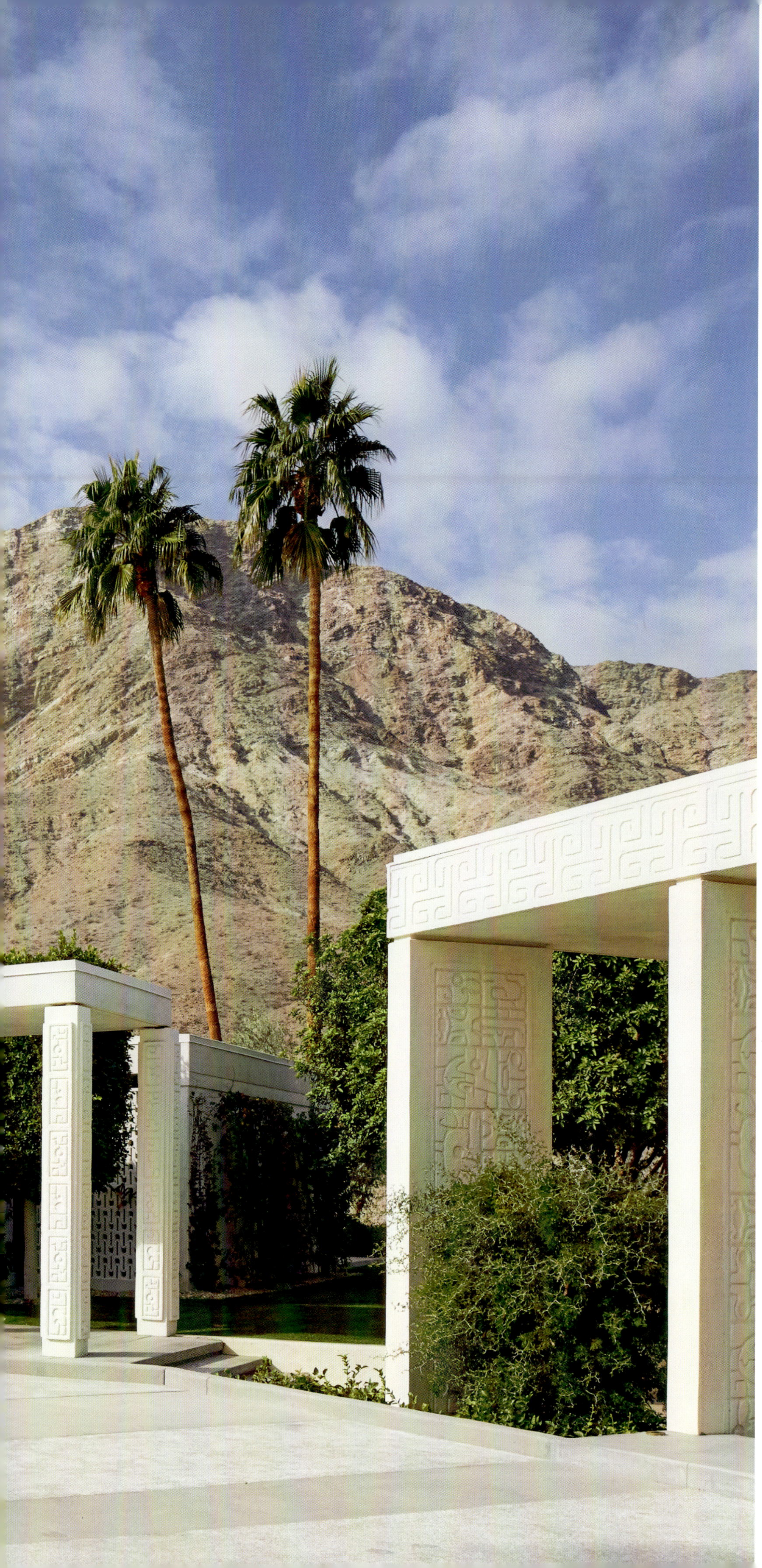

Ichpa Mayapan

Rancho Mirage

Architect

Howard Lapham

Residents

Michael Smith and James Costos

Many houses in this book are escapes for the homeowners and passion projects for the designers, and sometimes those are one and the same. This desert retreat, called Ichpa Mayapan, sits in the Thunderbird Heights area of Rancho Mirage and is a getaway for the acclaimed interior designer Michael Smith and his partner, former United States ambassador to Spain James Costos, who were dividing their time between Madrid and Los Angeles. Over the years I've tried to delicately extract some gossip about their guests and celebrity clients (think Cindy Crawford, Shonda Rhimes, and Michelle Pfeiffer), but my questions are politely deflected, as you would expect from a onetime ambassador and the man who designed the Obama White House.

Ichpa Mayapan, its exterior walls and columns carved with Mayan-inspired step-fret motifs, is unlike any other house. Designed in 1970 by architect Howard Lapham, its closest cousins are Frank Lloyd Wright's Hollyhock and Ennis Houses. After two years of renovation, Smith created a beautifully decorated but relaxed space, shying away from the midcentury modern aesthetic popular in the desert in favor of the 1970s glamour and elegance of a photograph by Slim Aarons (who once described his subjects as "attractive people doing attractive things in attractive places"). With lofty ceilings and a calm, white-and-green-dominated palette, the house is cool and airy during the day. At night, it is spectacular, with a panoramic view of the Coachella Valley.

This is a house built for entertaining, a sophisticated overlook where guests are welcomed with ease and style. Those guests have included the Obamas, who would stay at Ichpa Mayapan to escape the pressures of Washington. Here again, my questions went unanswered, but nestled high in the San Jacinto Mountains, the Secret Service could allegedly watch the mountain lions prowl at night, and that's all I was told.

This was a relaxed shoot with longtime assistant Albert Fu and editor Anita Sarsidi, all under the watchful eye of Smith and Costos's good friend—and former editor in chief of *Architectural Digest*—Margaret Russell. The sun sets early in the mountains, and much-appreciated drinks were enjoyed by all as the lights from the valley twinkled below.

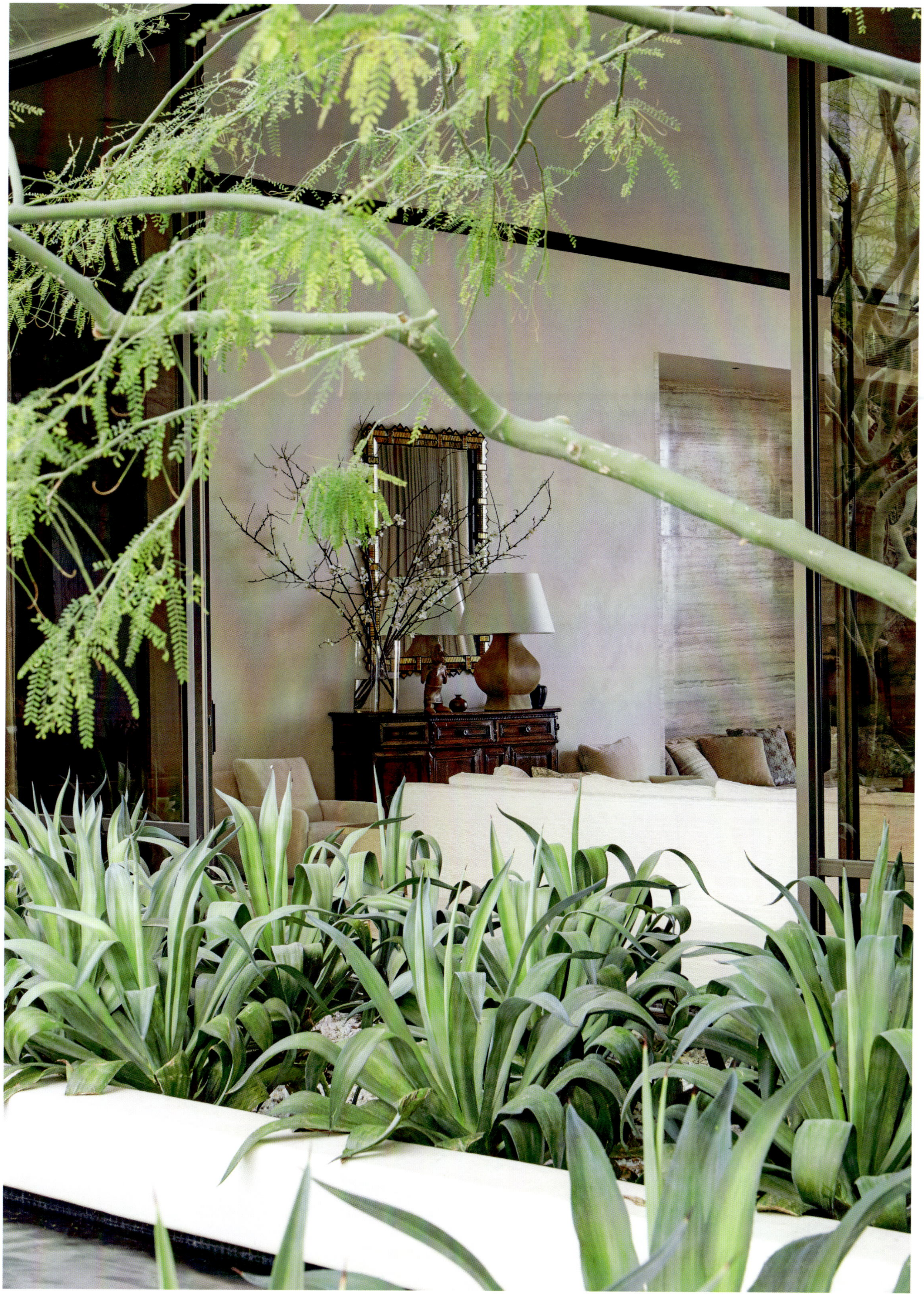

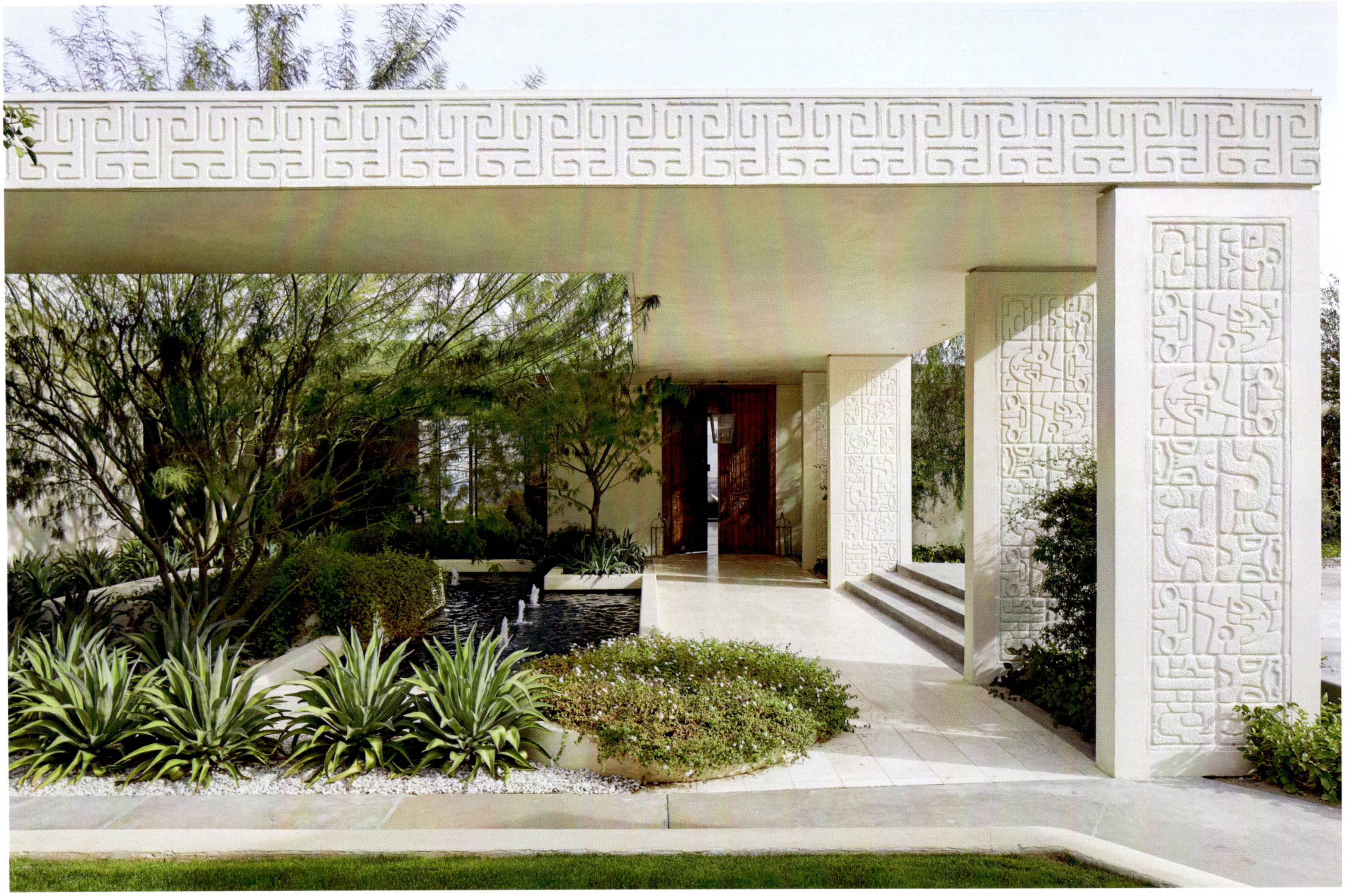

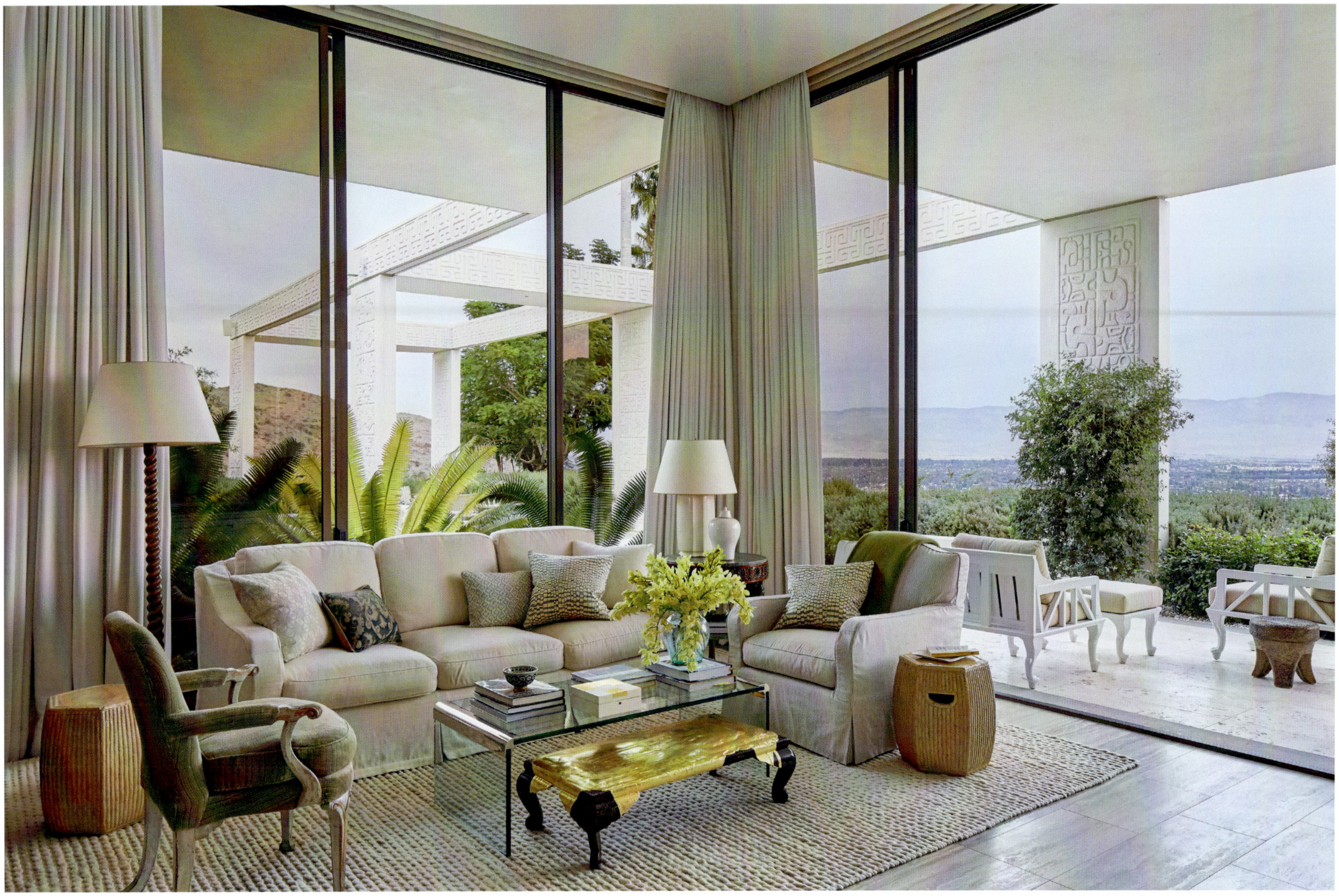

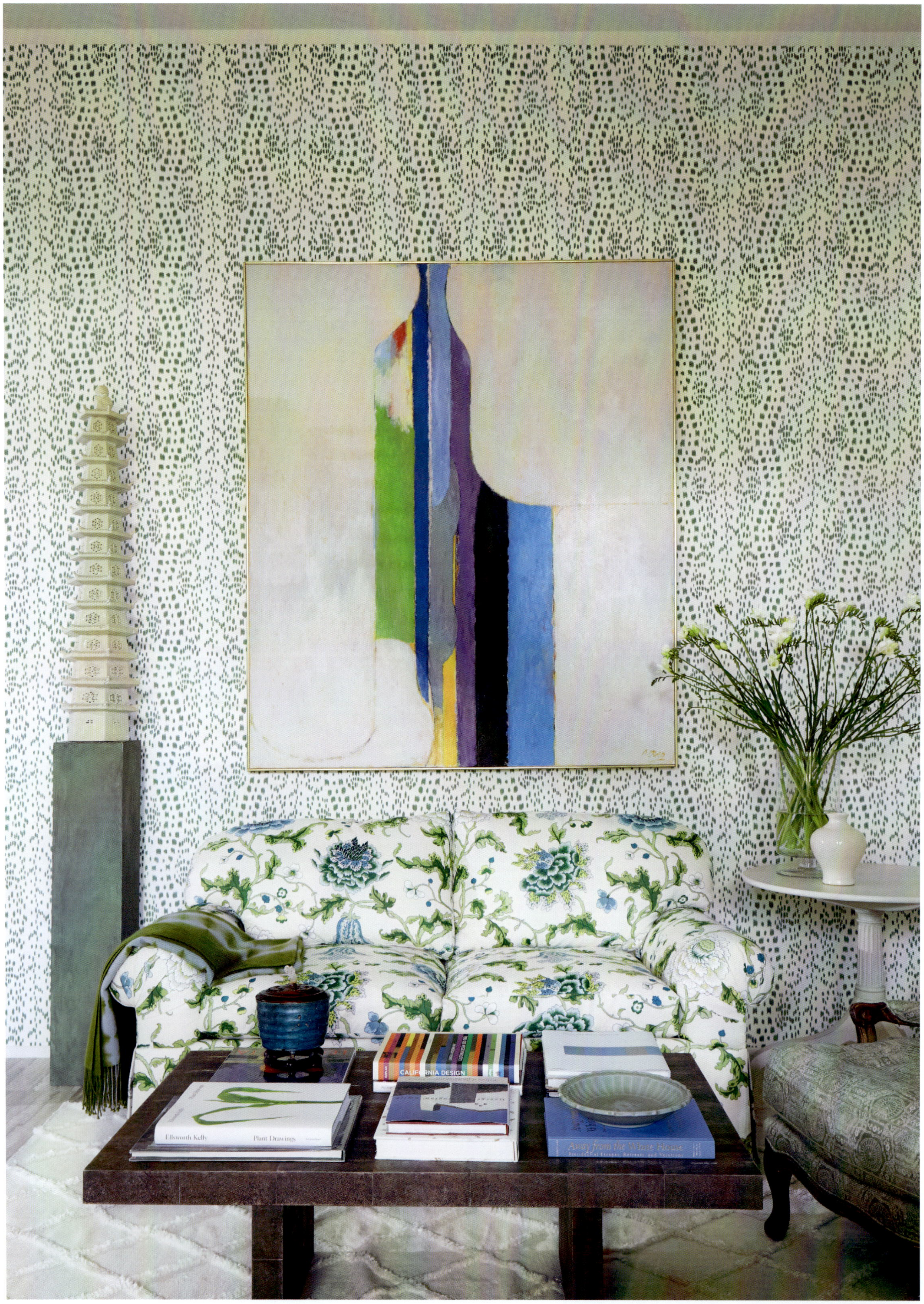
CALIFORNIA DESIGN
Ellsworth Kelly
Plant Drawings
Away from the White House
Presidential Escapes, Retreats and Vacations

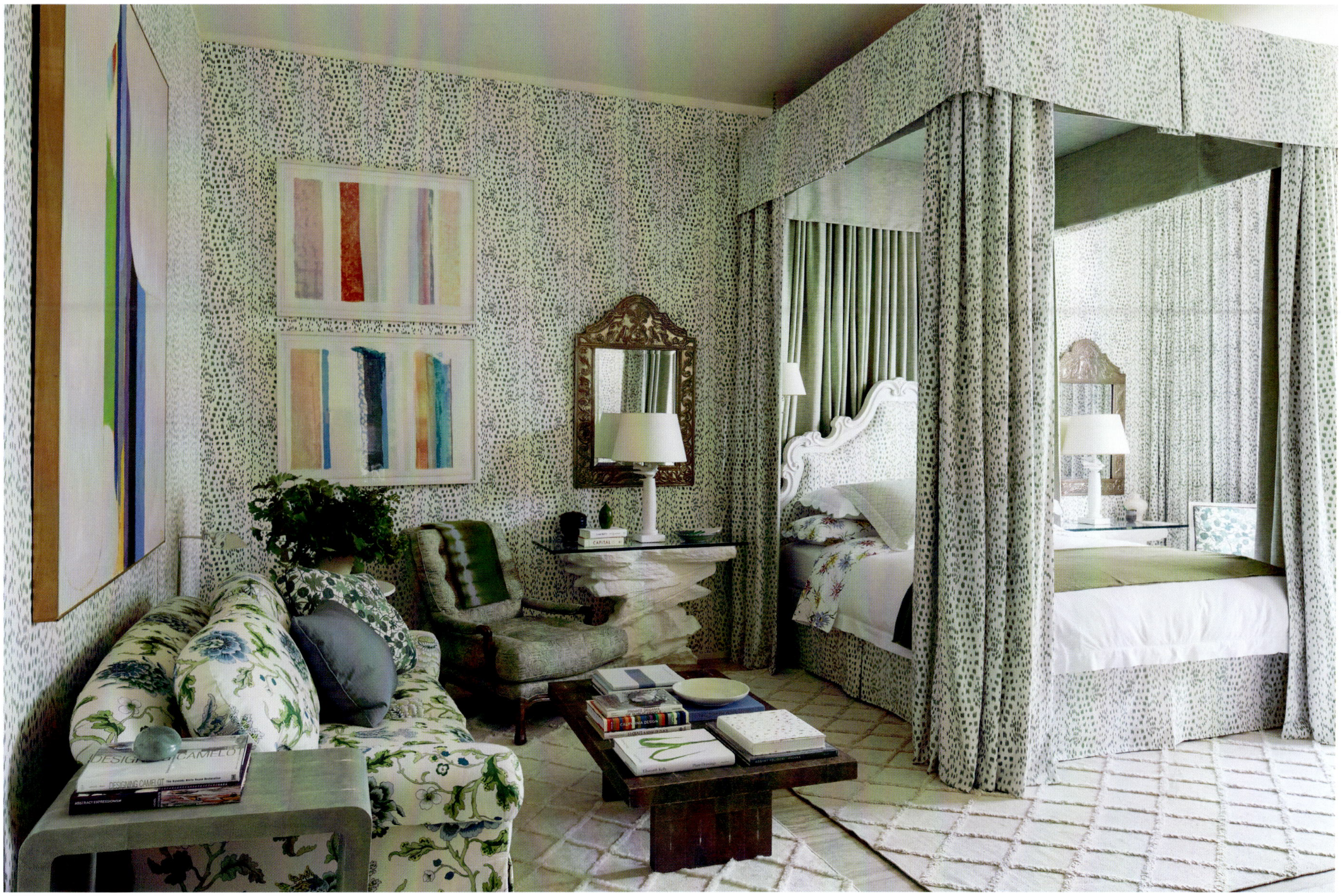

In a guest bedroom, which has hosted prominent visitors, an overall 1965 print by Brunschwig & Fils in a fresh green on white continues the Slim Aarons vibe. Tony Duquette, whose weekend home of several years is featured on pages 194–207, made the white pagoda.

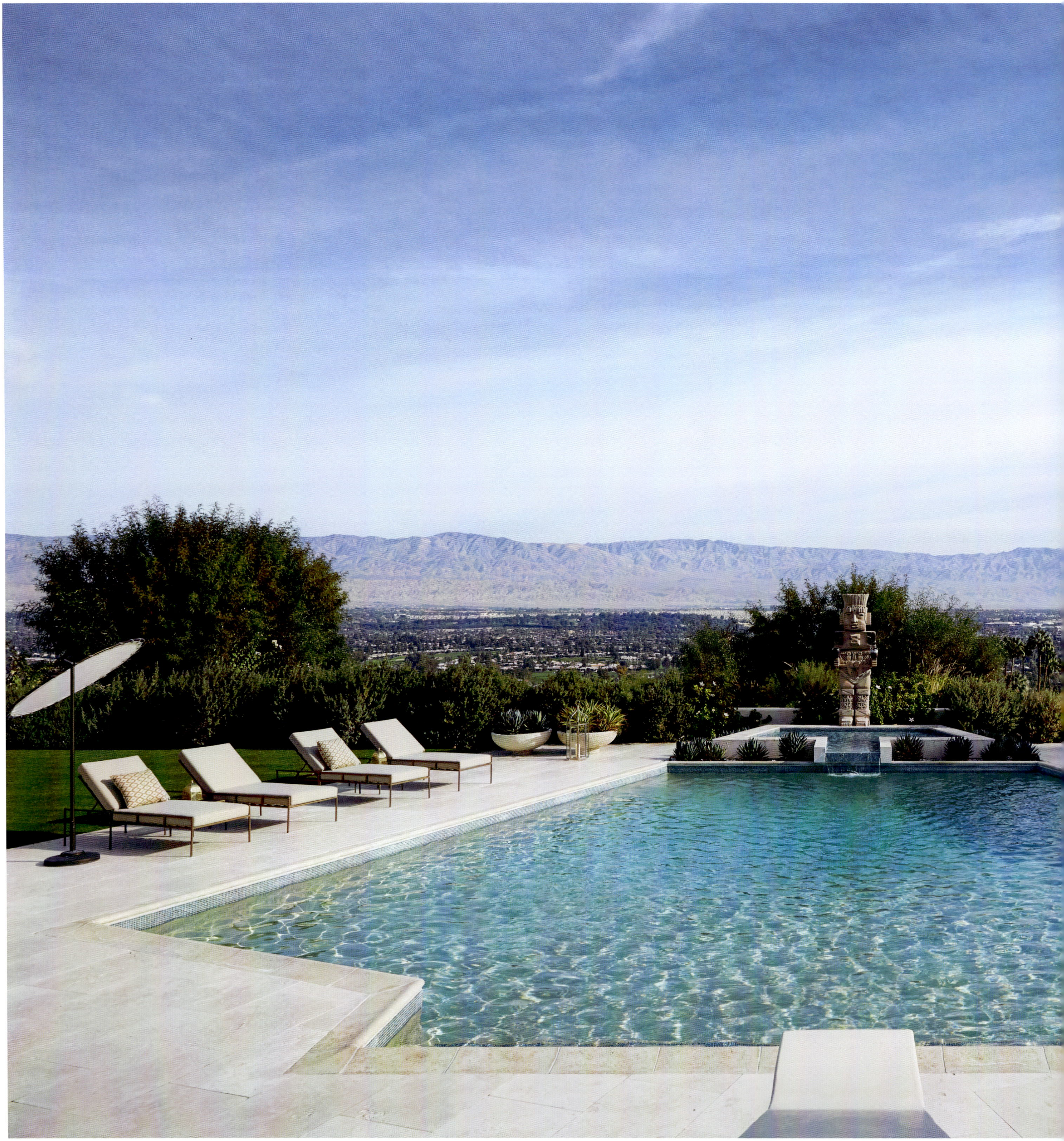

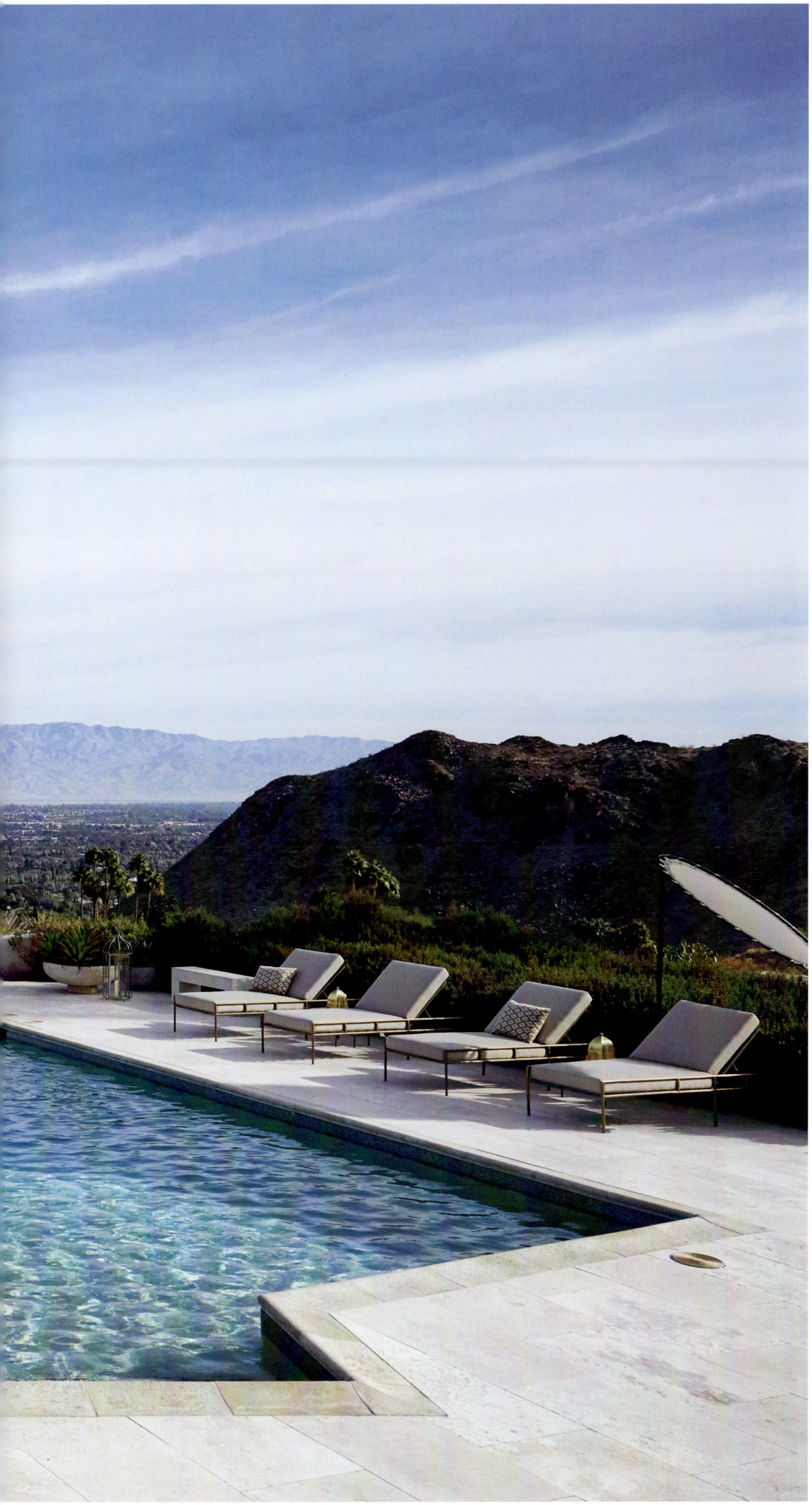

A Mayan-inspired figure sits at the end of the keystone-shaped swimming pool. At night, fire shoots from its torches.

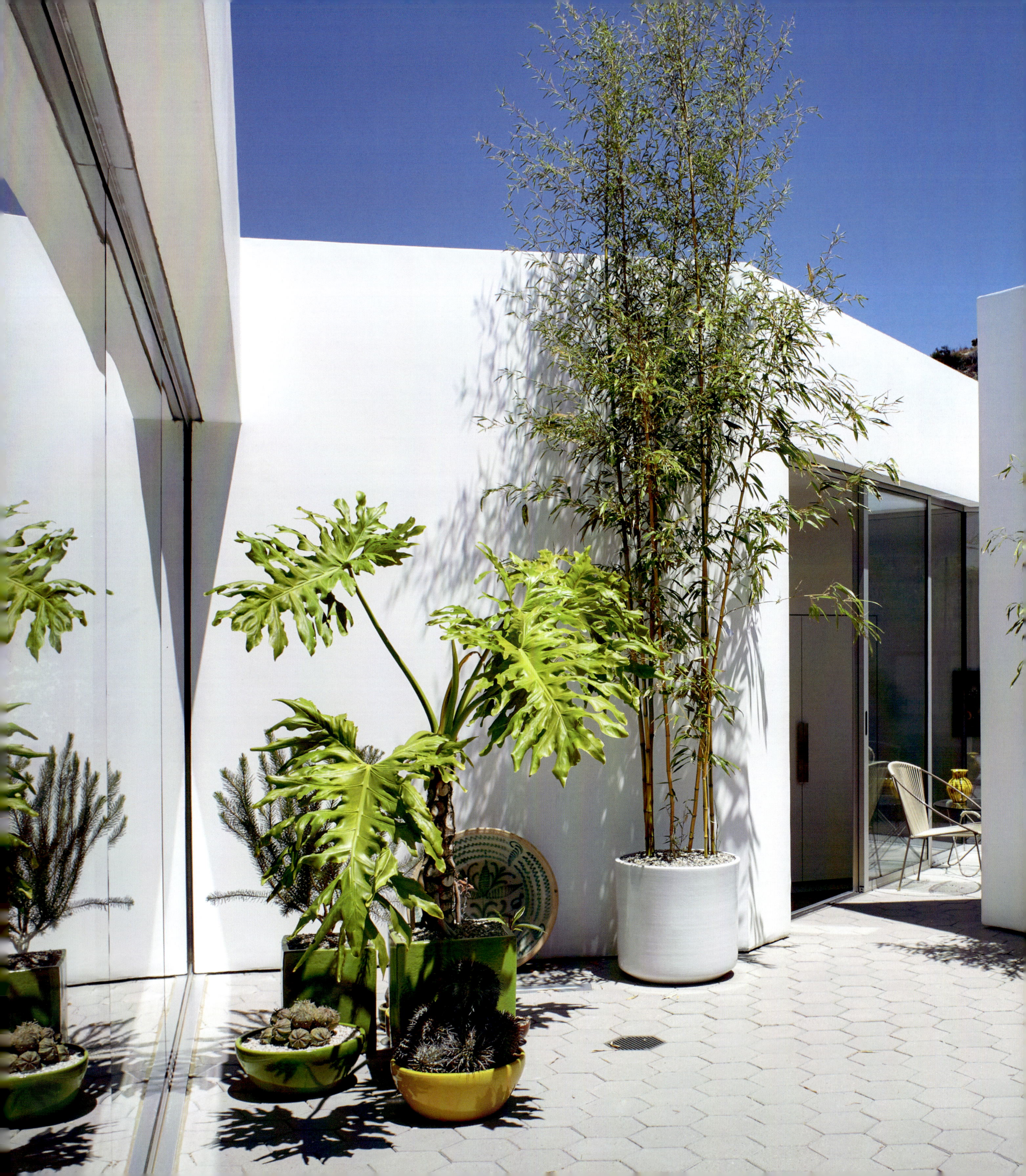

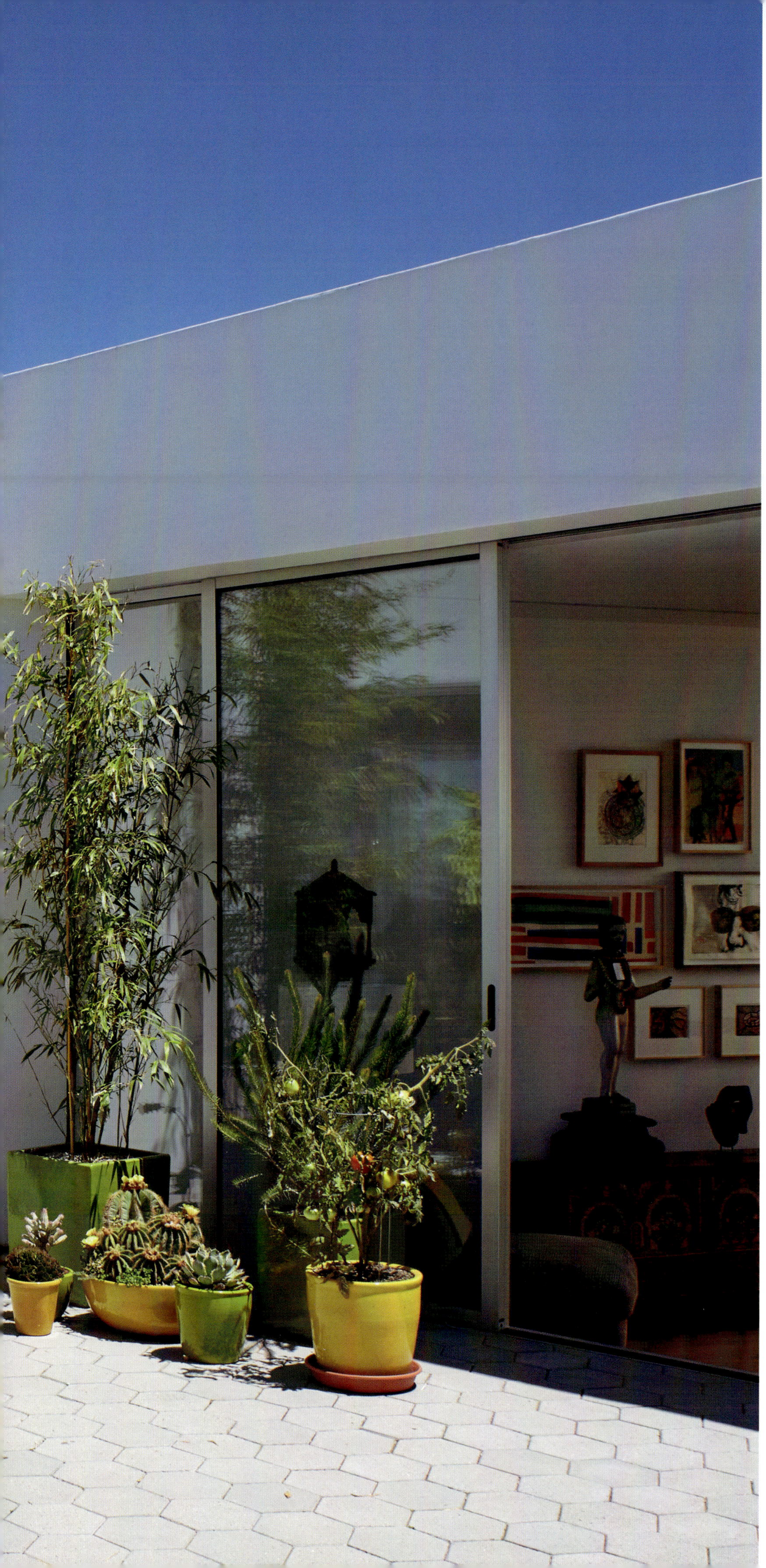

Pittman Dowell Residence and Serulnic House

La Crescenta

Architects

Michael Maltzan and Richard Neutra

Residents

Lari Pittman and Roy Dowell

Sometimes I'm told little about a commission. Before arriving at the home of artists Lari Pittman and Roy Dowell, I had been briefed that their house was remarkable, but that was all. The assignment proved to be almost too much for me.

I had long admired both of the artists' work, and the opportunity to photograph their home would have been enough in itself. They greeted me warmly at the entrance to a white spaceship overlooking what seemed to be the whole of California. I could quite happily have spent the day taking pictures of their carport, but as I toured the property, which sits on the edge of the Angeles National Forest, three distinct but interconnected areas revealed themselves, and each was extraordinary and entirely unique. In my excitement to get everything and more, I all but broke my nose on a sliding glass door. ("Walk, don't run" has been my motto ever since.)

Architect Richard Neutra had originally planned the six-acre hillside subdivision with pads for three houses. When Pittman and Dowell bought the entire six-acre property in 1998, some forty-six years later, only one residence had been built. The space I had arrived at was a heptagonal house designed for Pittman and Dowell in 2009 by architect Michael Maltzan. I had never seen anything like it; there were only two doors in the 3,500-square-foot house, with sight lines and privacy cleverly determined by the angles of the walls. The house was a wonder of thoughtful geometry.

Adjacent to the Maltzan house was an open-air pavilion surrounded by an extensive cactus garden that was more akin to the famed Huntington gardens in Pasadena than anything I had seen in a private residence. And finally, perched on the hillside above the garden, was the original house designed by Neutra in 1952 for George and Dorothy Serulnic (Dorothy was Neutra's longtime secretary). Restored to perfection and used by the couple as a guesthouse, it has welcomed visitors of all kinds. "I was walking through the house one day," says Dowell, "and discovered a three-foot rattlesnake stretched out sunning itself on the living room floor about two feet from our sleeping dog." Some guests are more welcome than others.

I worked my way around the site and squeezed all I could out of the time I had, knowing that I had been given a rare opportunity. Sometimes houses are saved through preservation, returning a space to the designer's original intent. Other times an artist's vision can move a project forward, respecting the past but adding new layers and making an environment that will be important for many years to come.

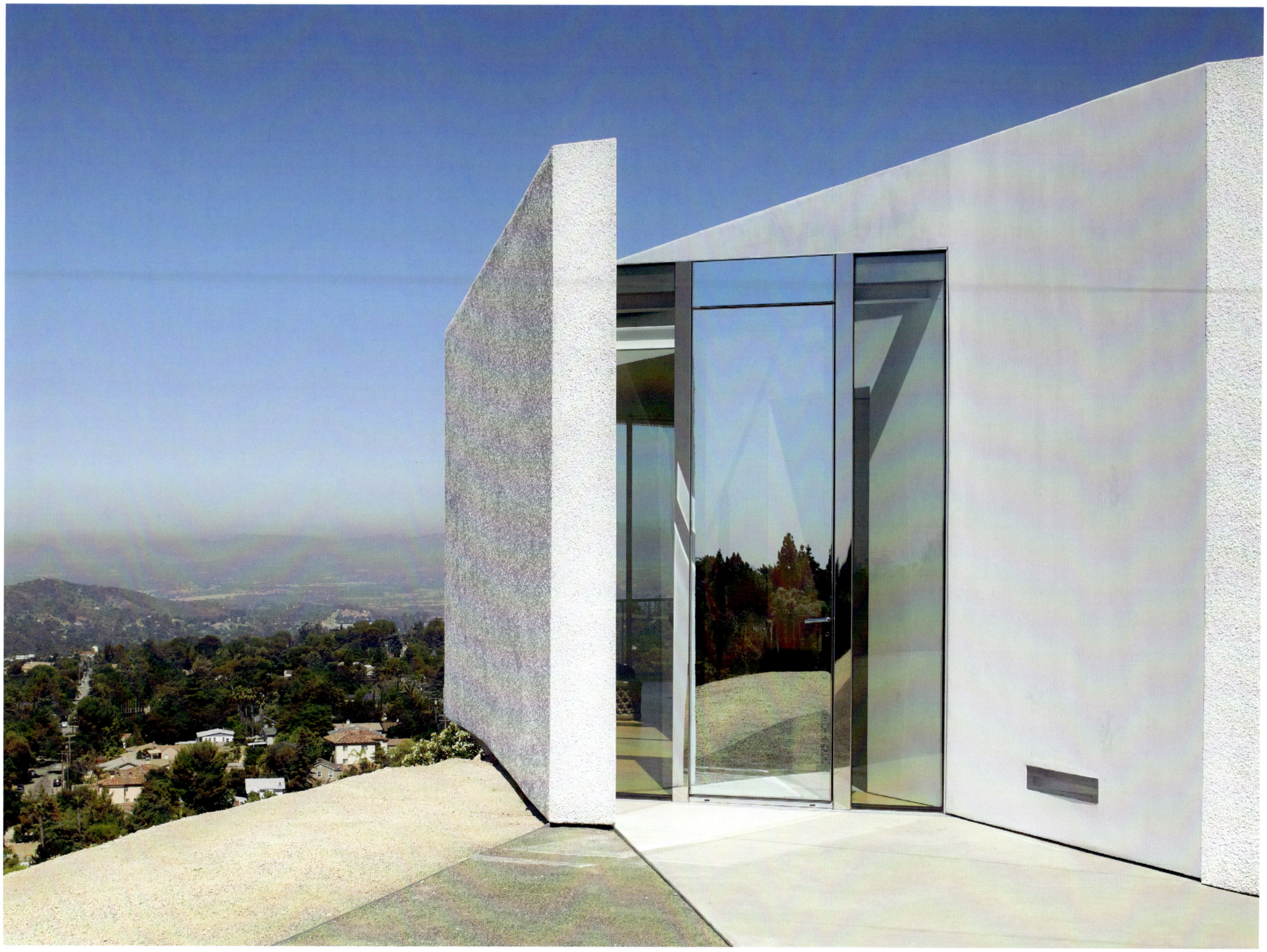

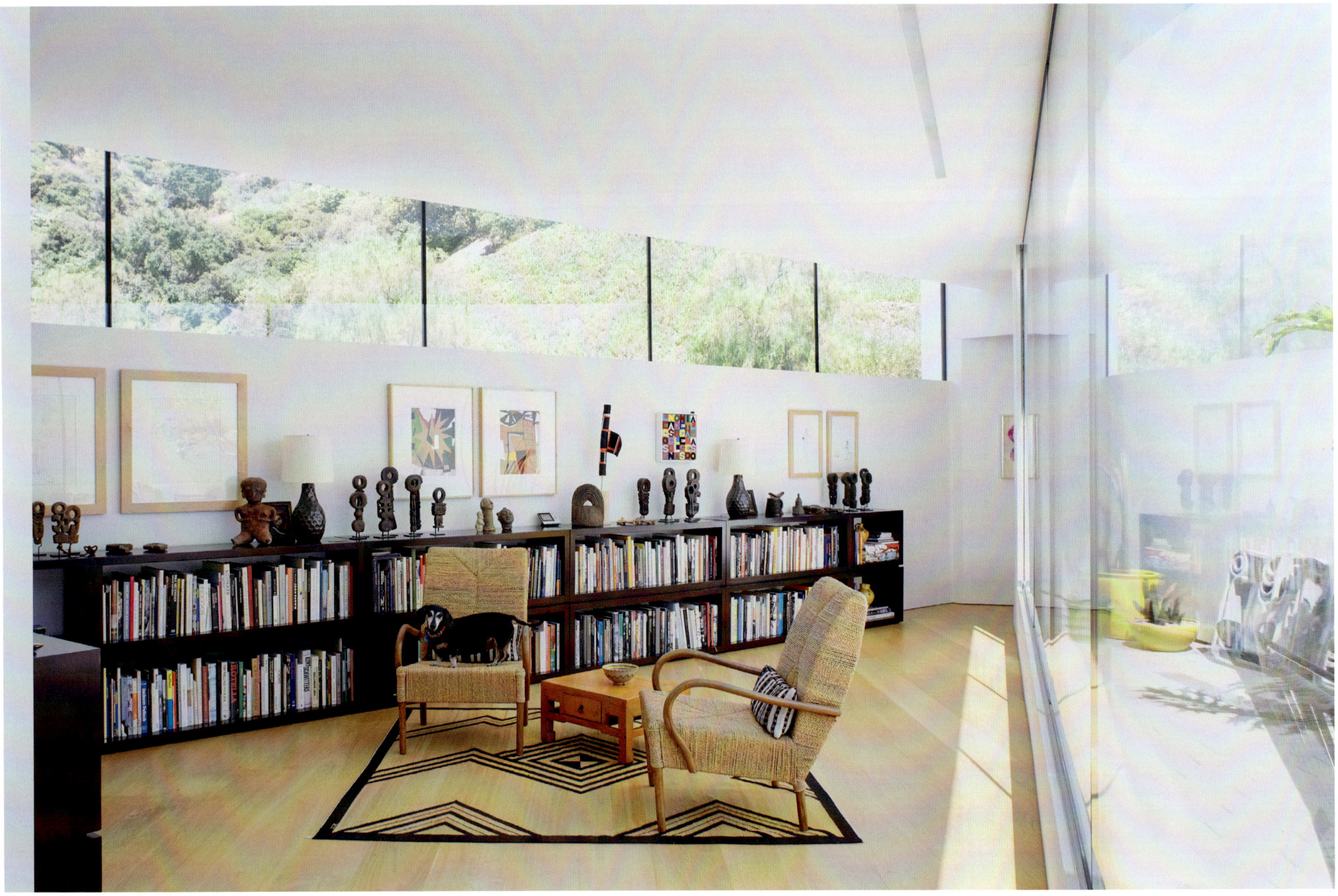

The buildings' proximity to the seven-hundred-thousand-acre Angeles National Forest means visits from wildlife other than Pittman and Dowell's dog, who itself had a close encounter with a sleeping rattlesnake.

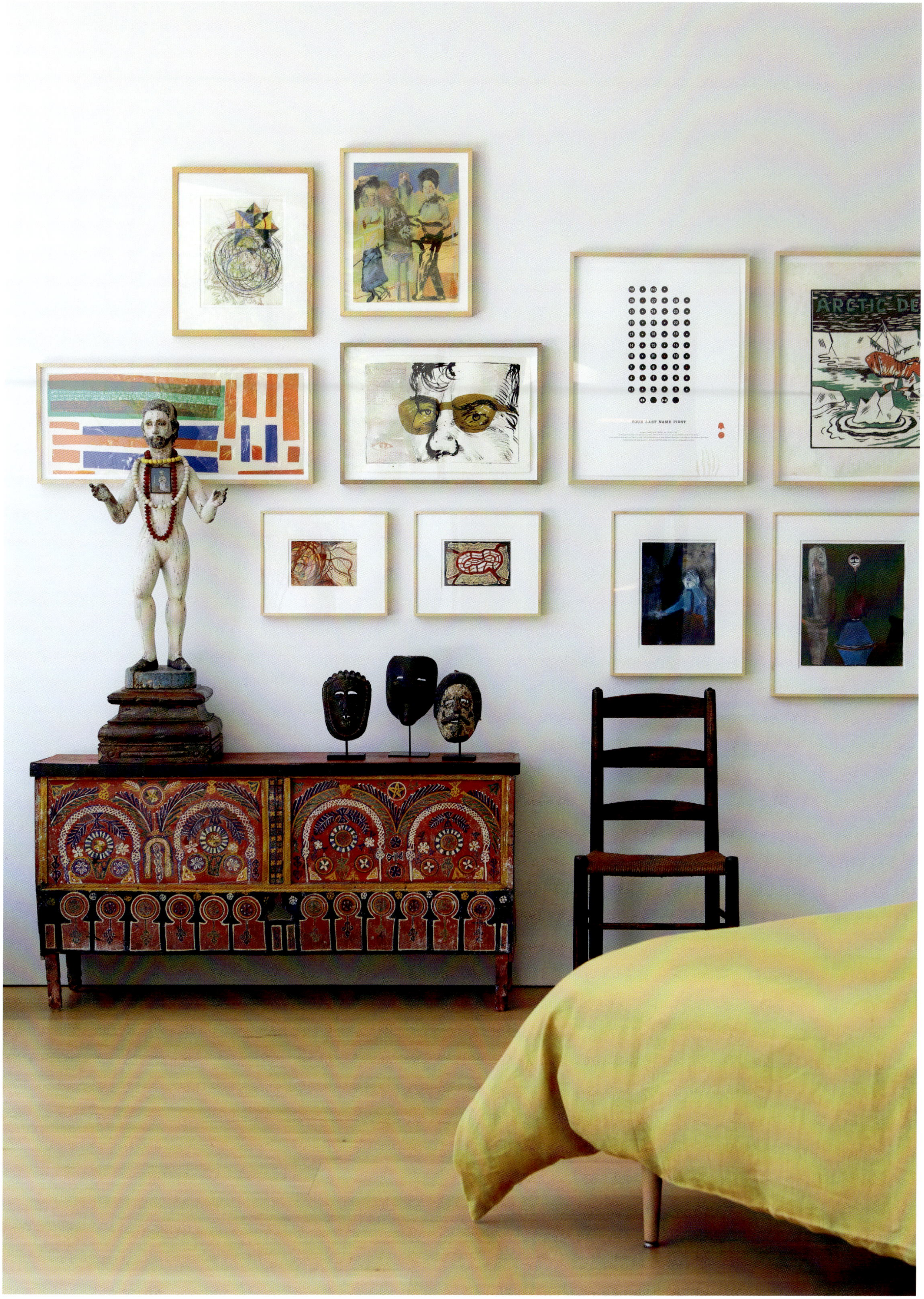
ARCTIC DE
YOUR LAST NAME FIRST

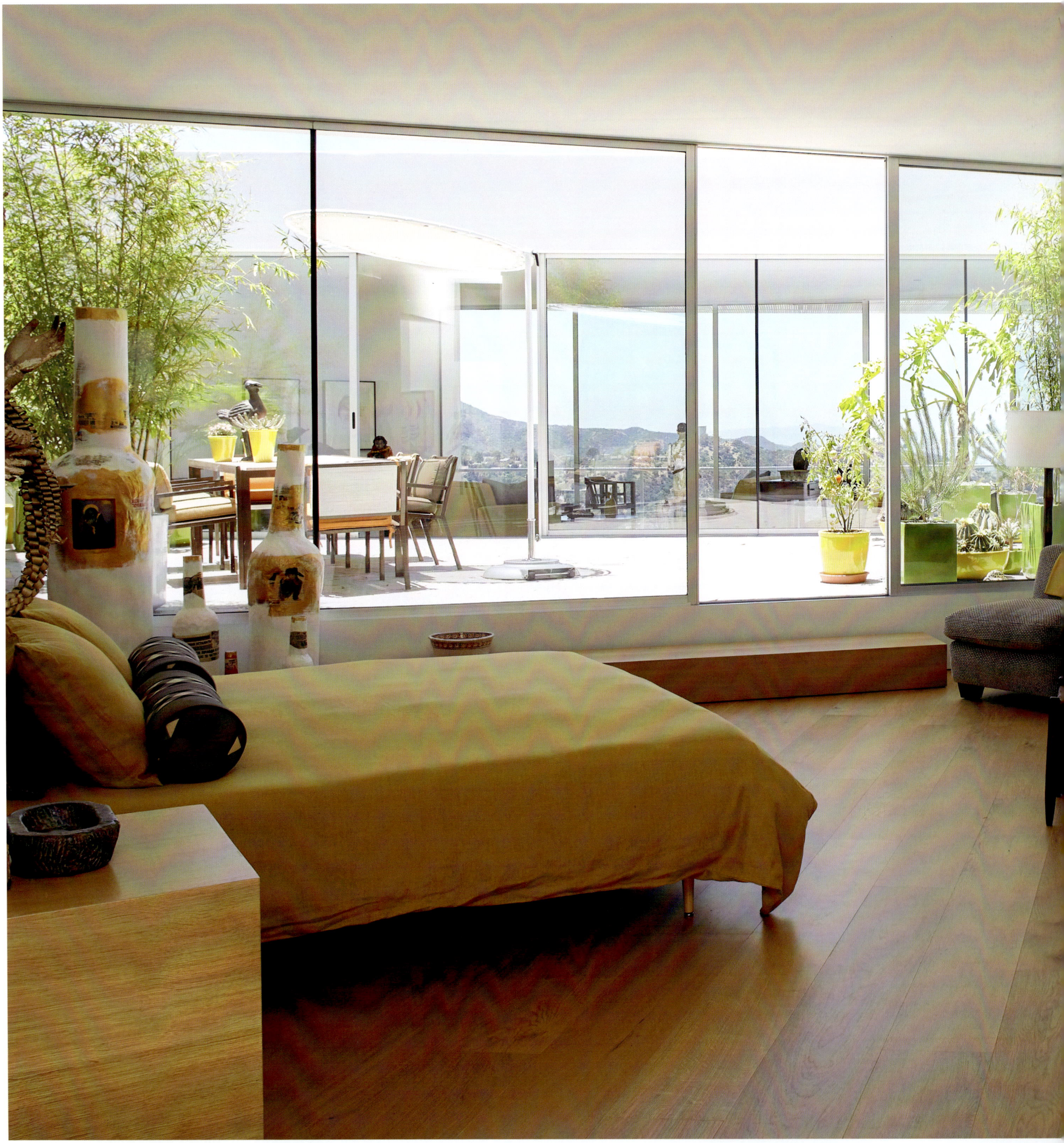

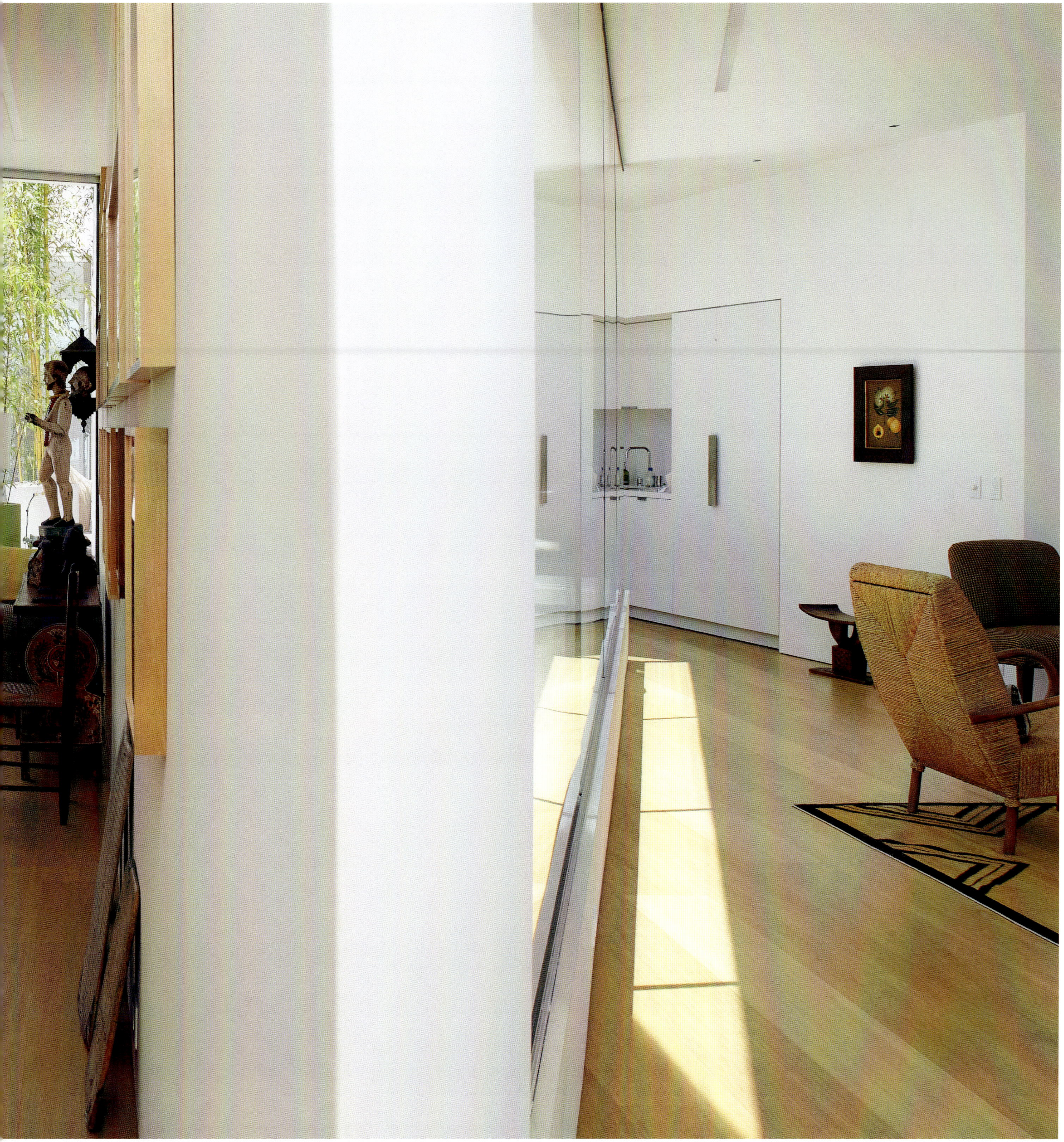

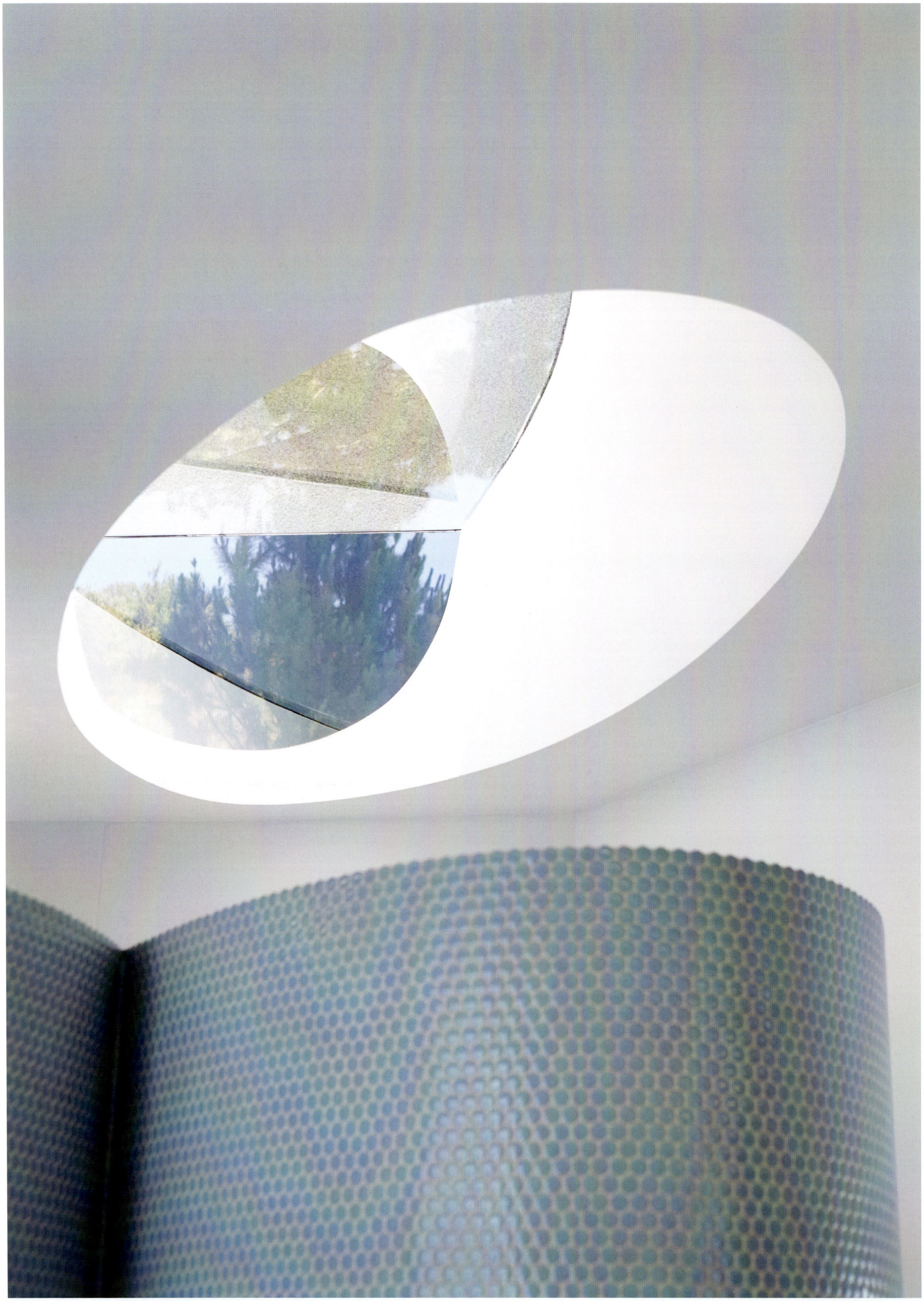

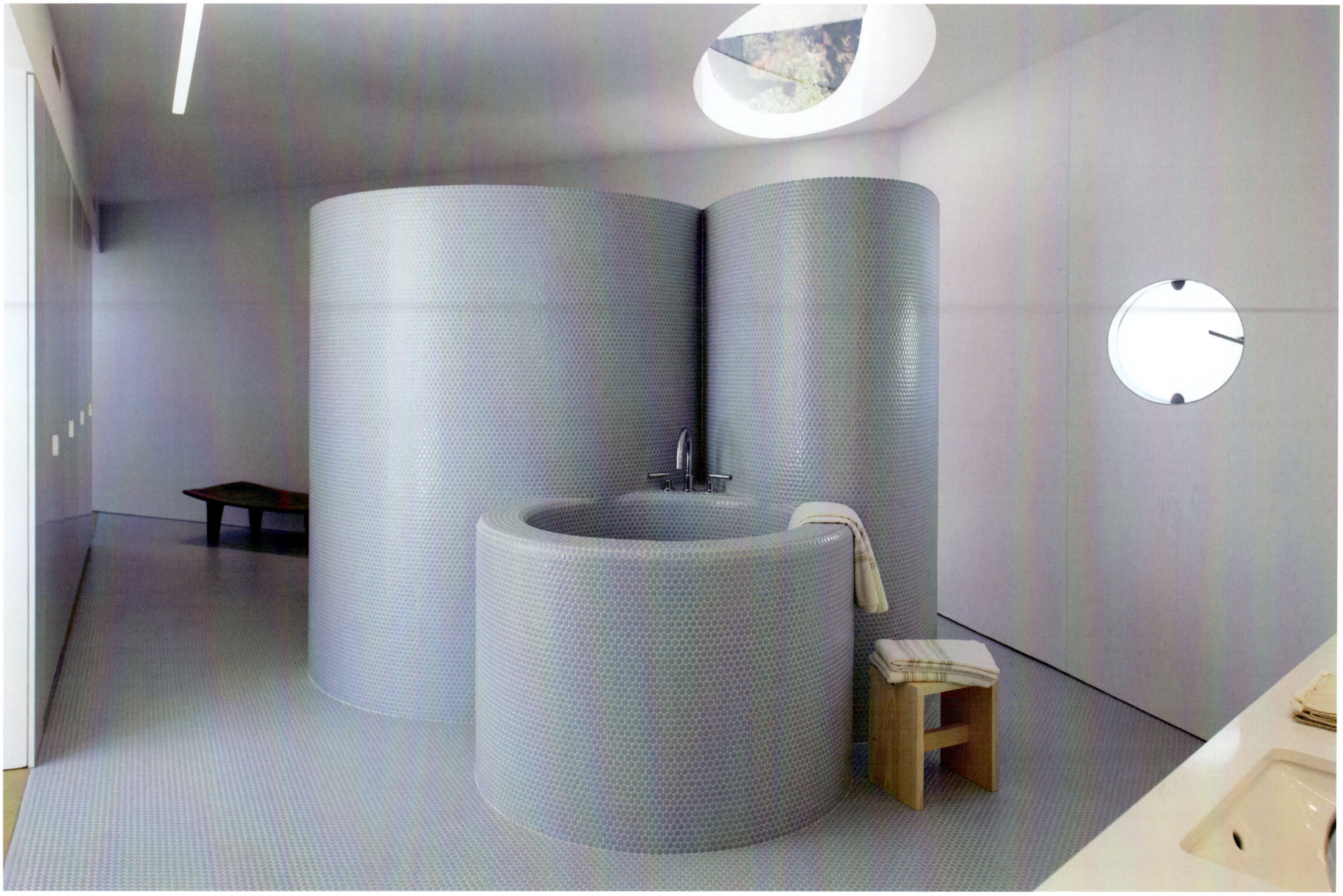

The only two doors inside the house close off a powder room and the laundry room. Privacy is otherwise ensured by the angles of the walls and, in the case of the shower and water closet, high tiled walls.

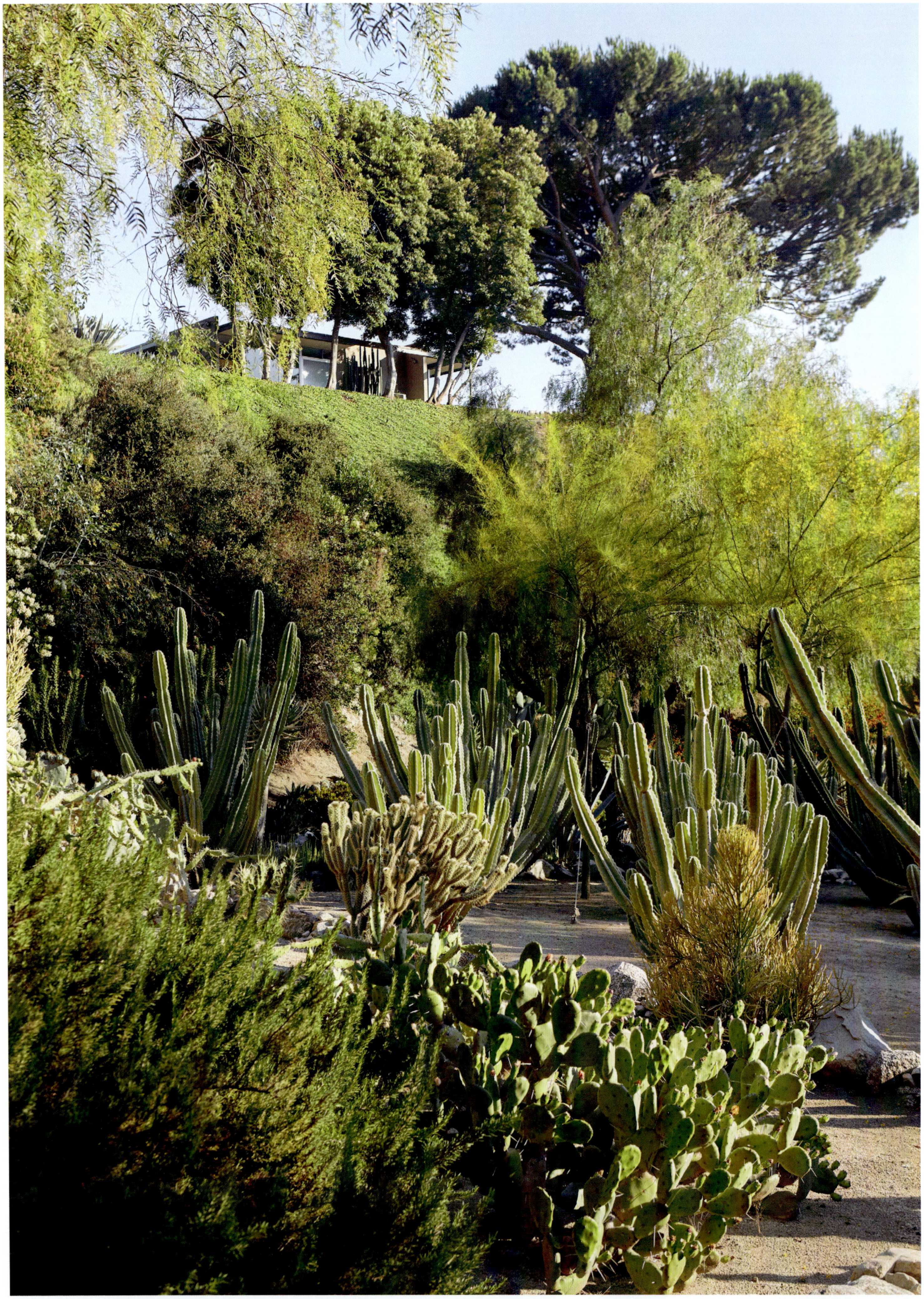

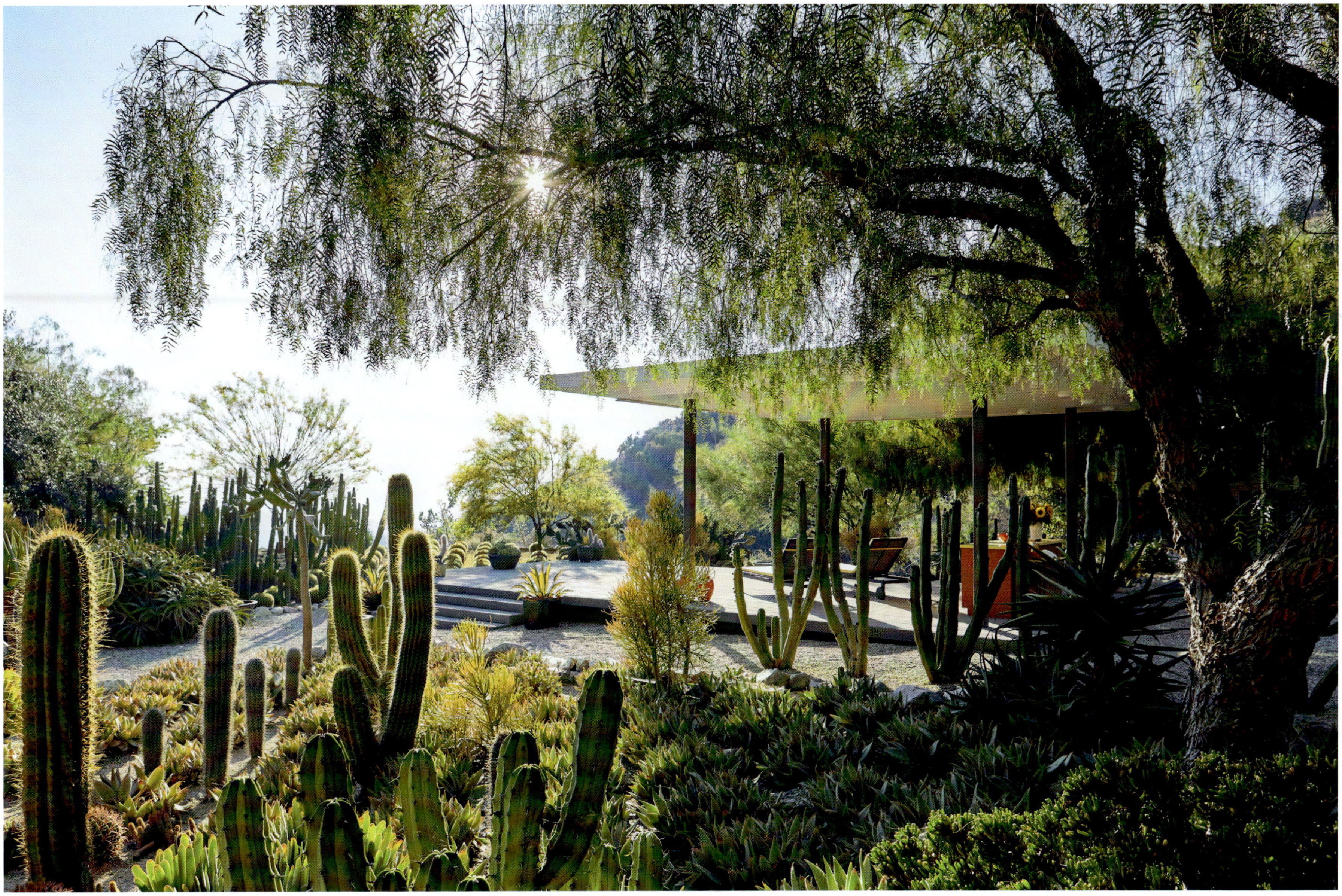

The original, Richard Neutra–designed residence on the property sits atop a hill overlooking a thriving cactus garden.

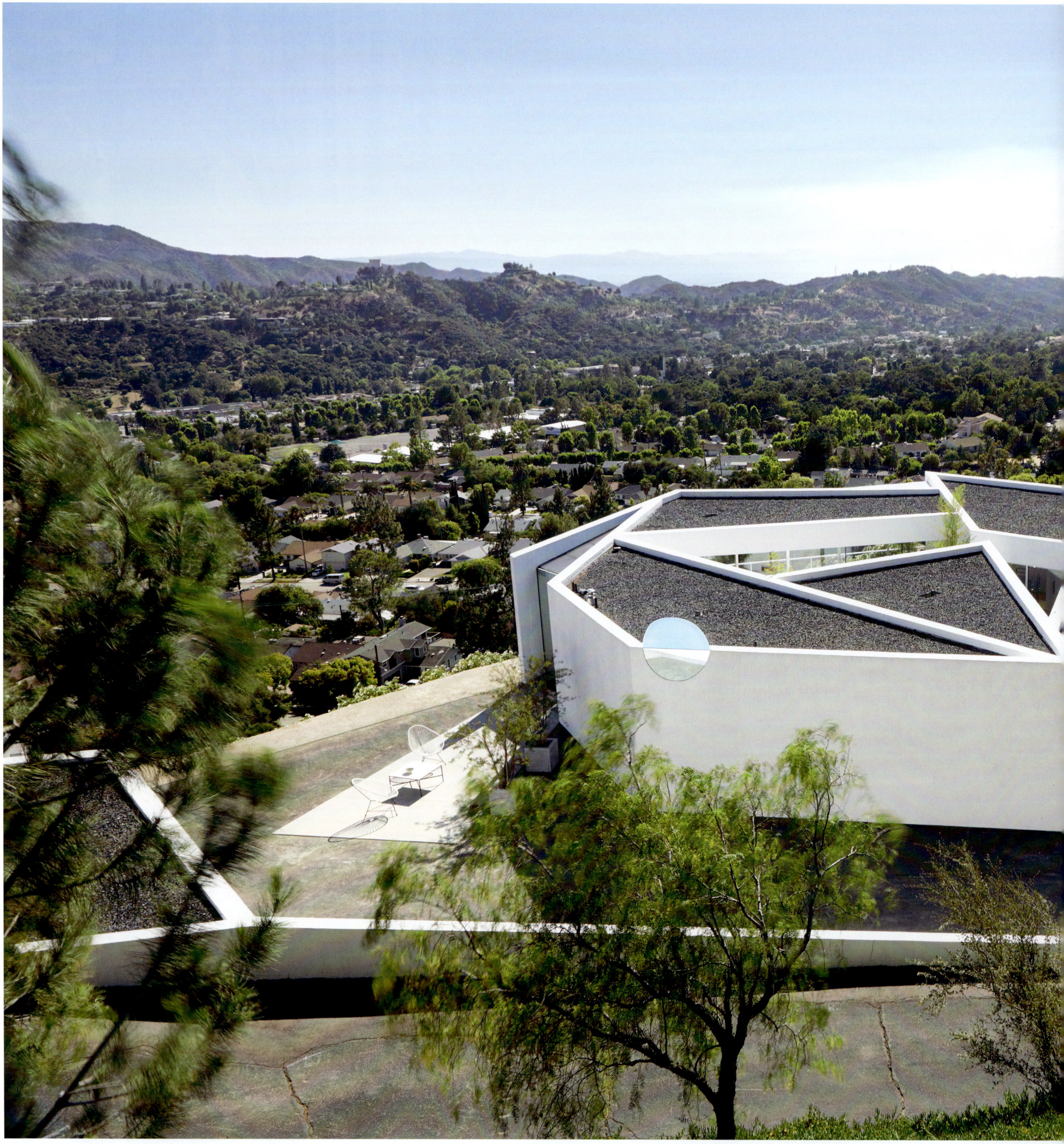

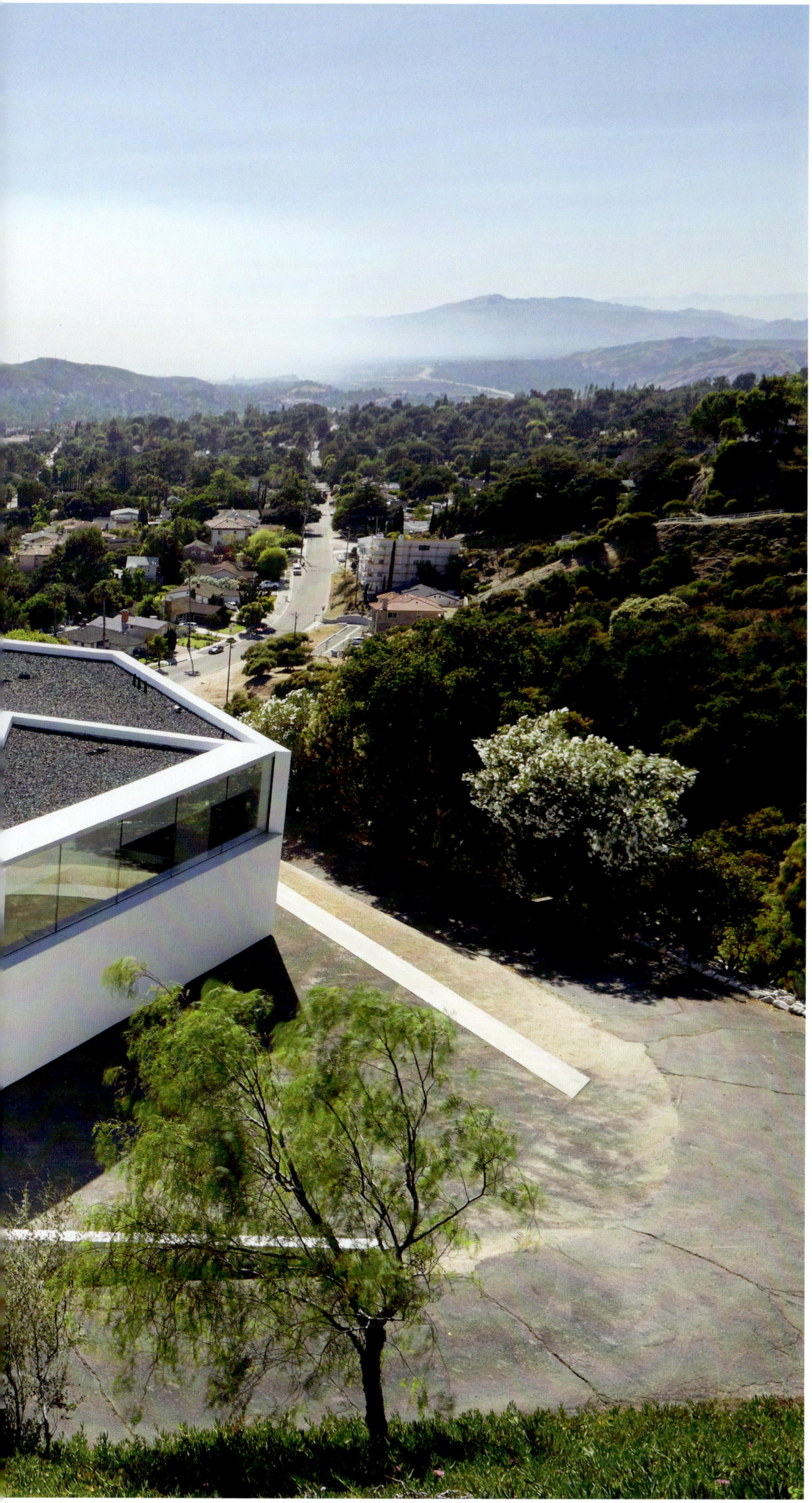

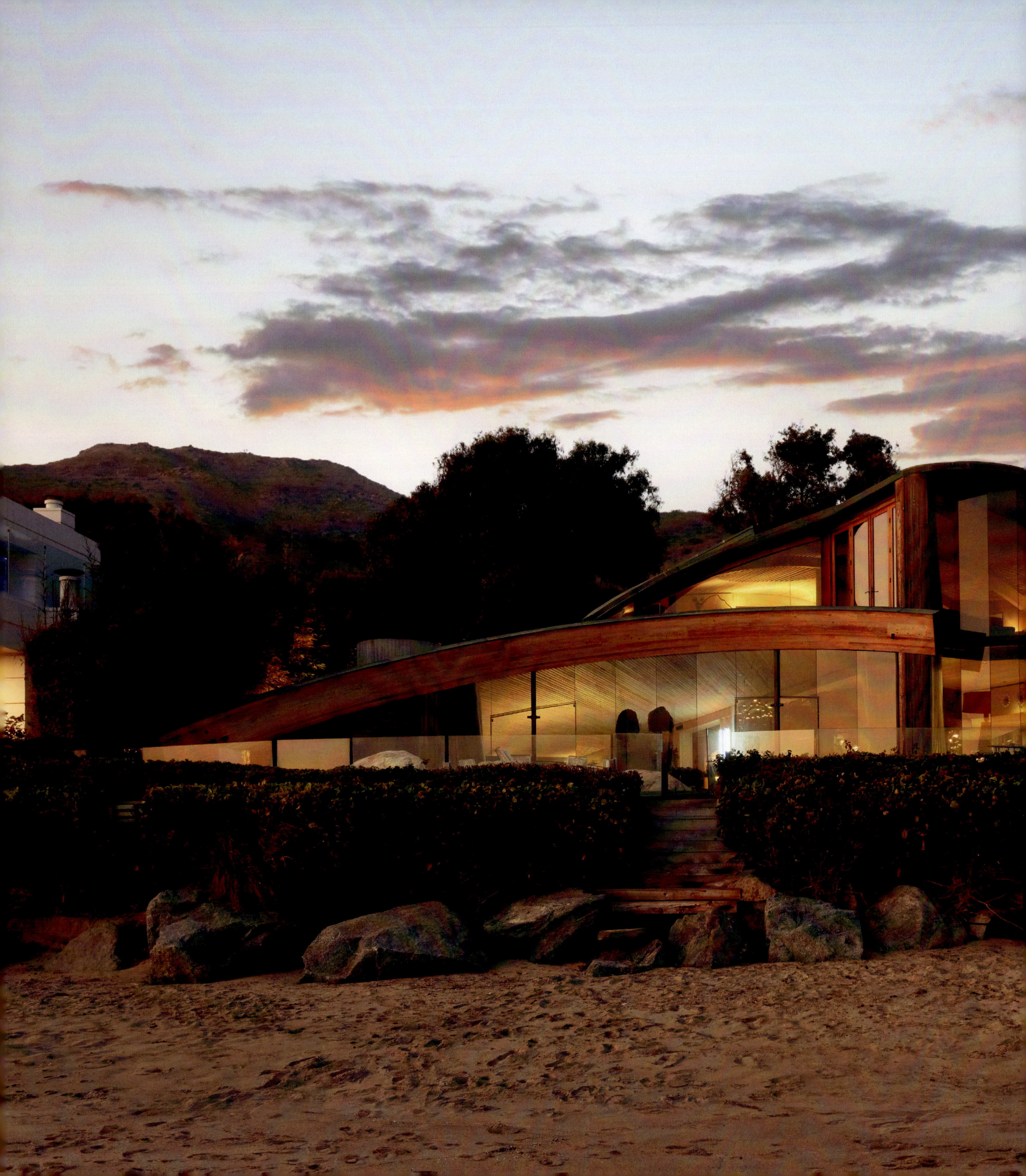

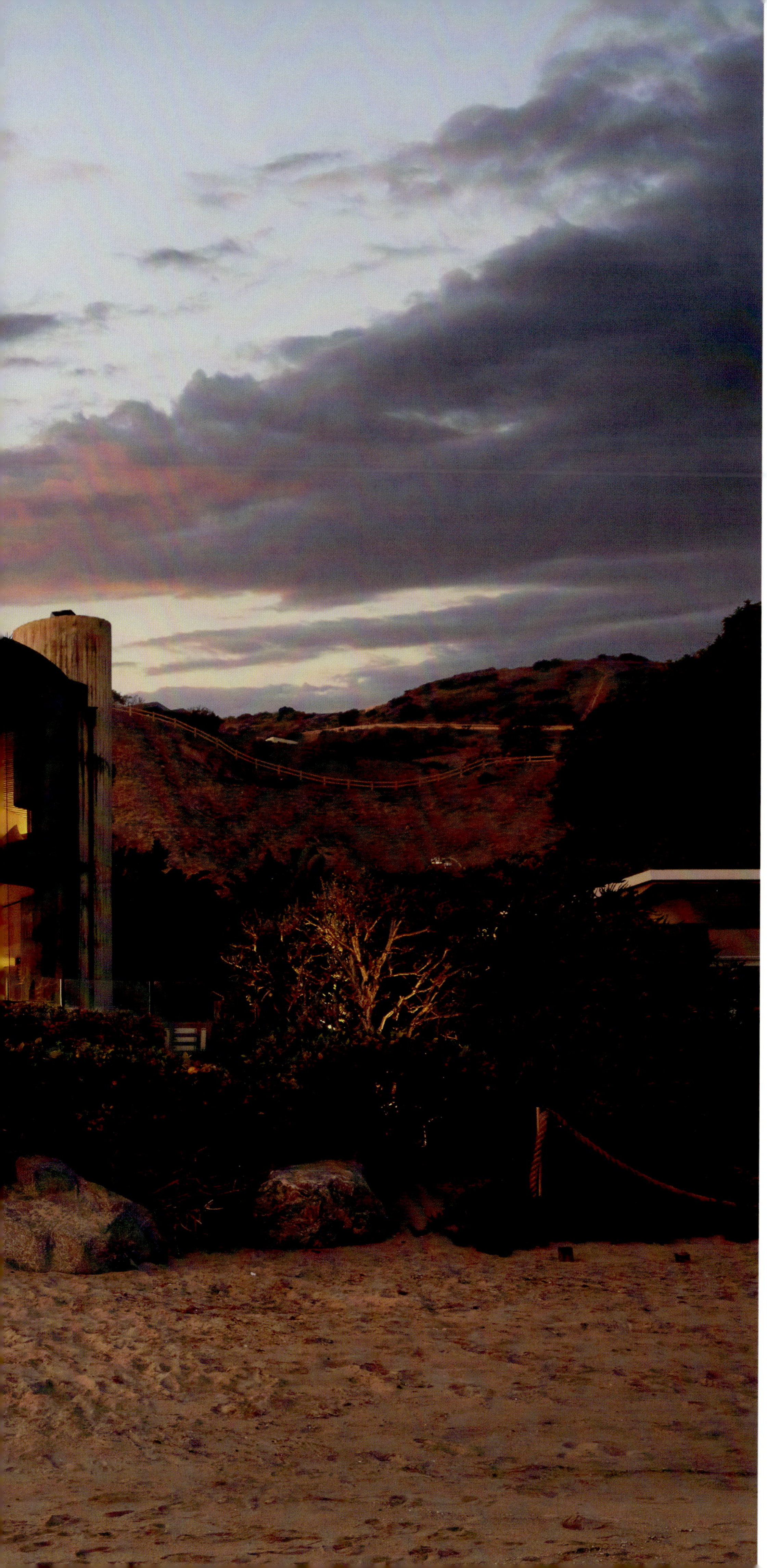

The Segel House
Malibu

Architect
John Lautner

Resident
Jamie McCourt

I'm incredibly grateful for the opportunities that magazines have given me over the years to photograph exceptional residences, and this John Lautner–designed house on Carbon Beach in Malibu, shot for *Architectural Digest*, was as good as it gets.

Commissioned by a dance therapist, Joann Segel, in 1979, the house originally included a dance studio on the upper level. Lautner considered this a breakthrough project for him, with its arcing, shell-like form producing a sense of refuge and its expanses of glass enhancing observation of the shoreline. With the beach just steps from the living room, the house is closely connected to the water, and I returned to reinforce this relationship with dusk shots (i.e., I should have done this more successfully the first time around).

Over the years the house had succumbed to a few unfortunate renovations but fell into good hands in 2006 when it was purchased by then CEO of the Los Angeles Dodgers Jamie McCourt, who later became the United States ambassador to France and Monaco. When I was arranging a second shoot with McCourt on a call from her residence in Paris, she said of the Segel House that she had tried to imagine how Lautner would have liked it.

Under the keen eye of architect Michael Kovac, McCourt managed an impeccable restoration that included removing an addition and adding a seamlessly integrated eighty-foot indoor lap pool separated from the iconic arched living room by only a sheet of glass. That's the sexy stuff, but passionate restoration goes deeper, and McCourt and Kovac started by getting down to the essentials—replacing glass, mechanical, electrical, and plumbing.

The house's wavelike curves are visually stunning but far from straightforward for a decorator, so McCourt hired the best—her friend and sometimes collaborator Los Angeles legend Waldo Fernandez. Fernandez placed furniture by French modernists Charlotte Perriand, Jean Royère, and Pierre Jeanneret alongside contemporary art by Doug Aitken, Jules de Balincourt, Robert Irwin, Jonas Wood, Iza Genzken, and others to create warm, intimate spaces within a rather sophisticated cave.

I get such a rush photographing any house by John Lautner, and after finishing the night shots from the beach with my assistant Huey (and losing another tripod to the sand and sea), I was filled with adrenaline driving home on the Pacific Coast Highway, watching the moon reflected in the crashing waves.

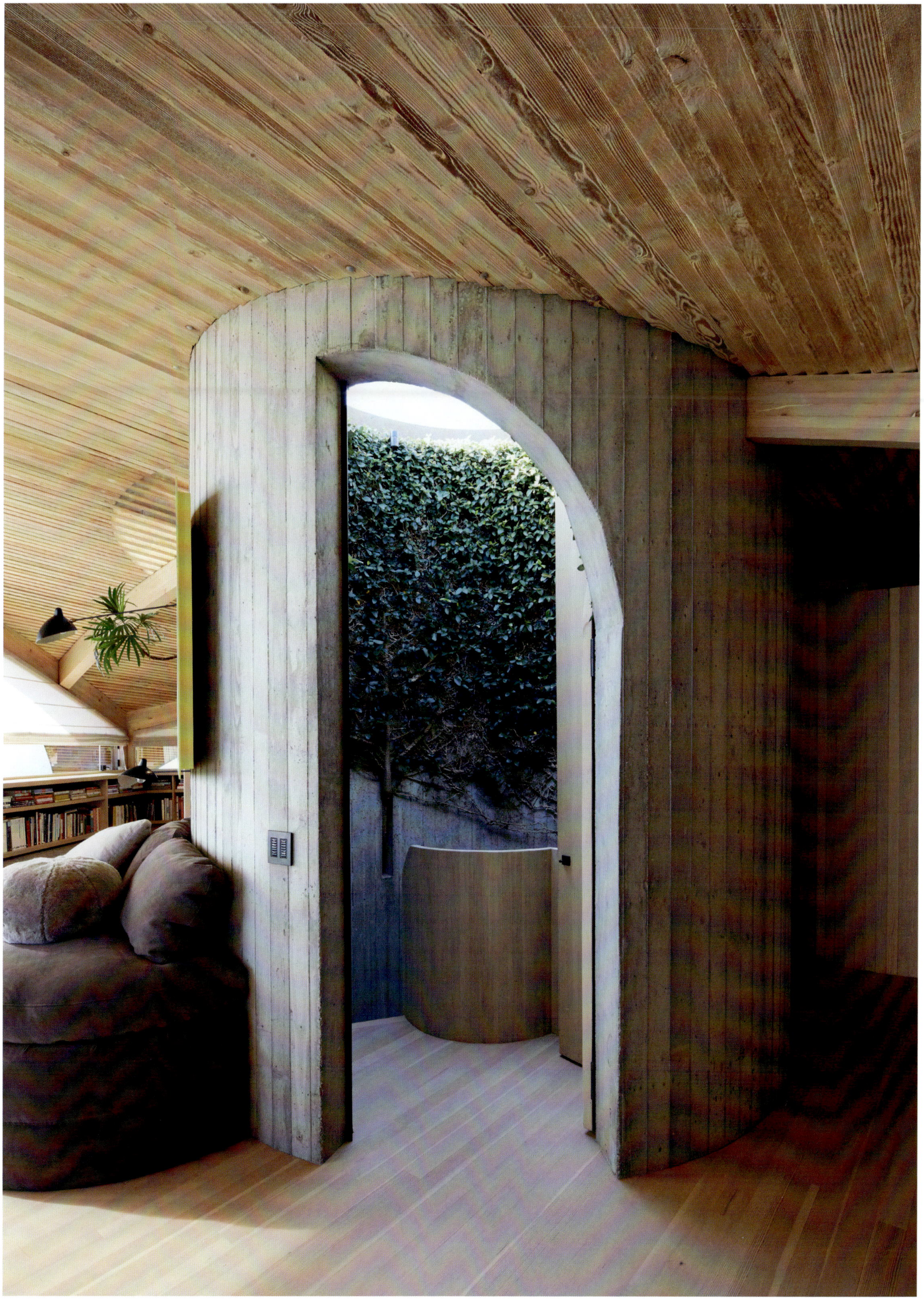

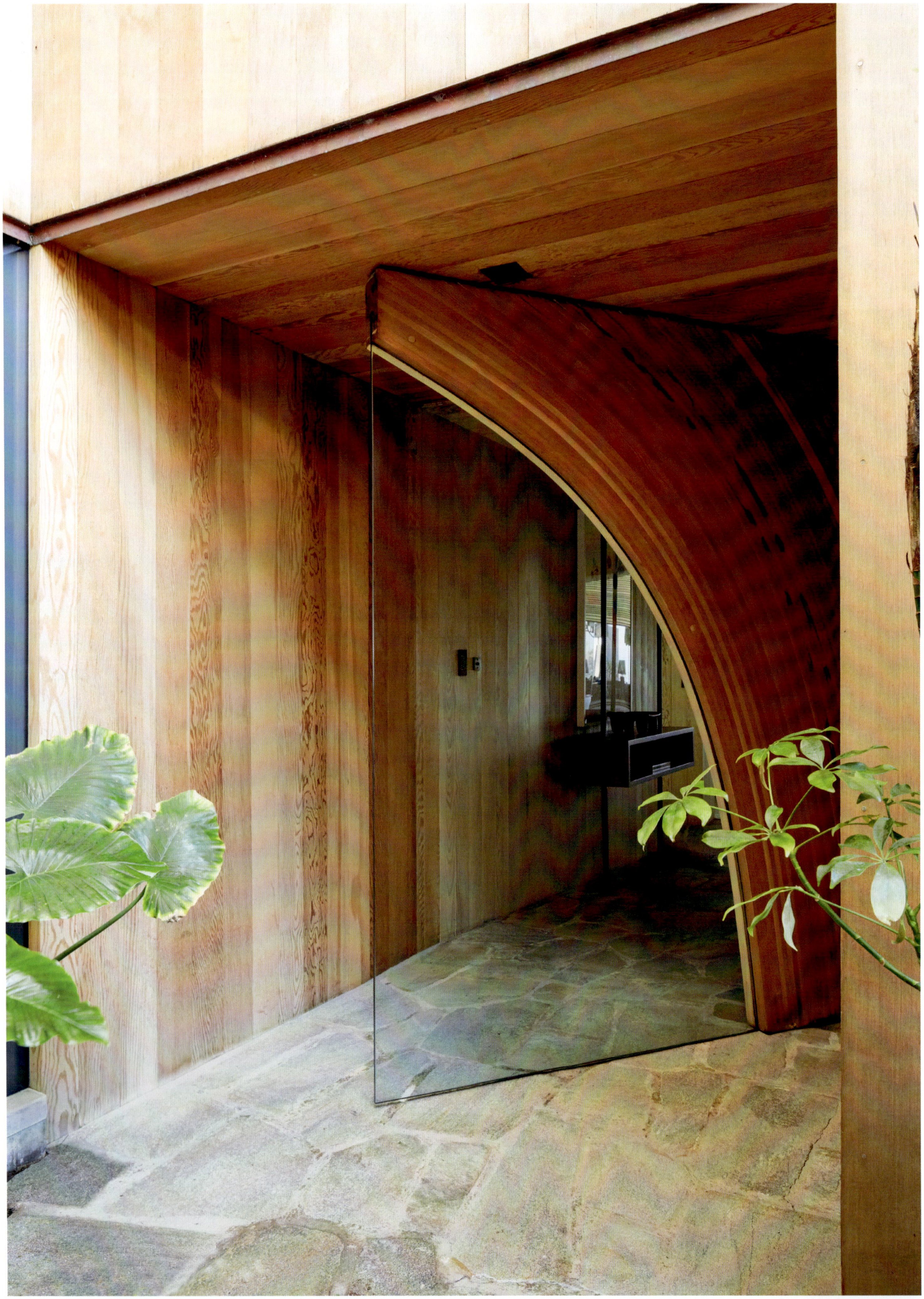

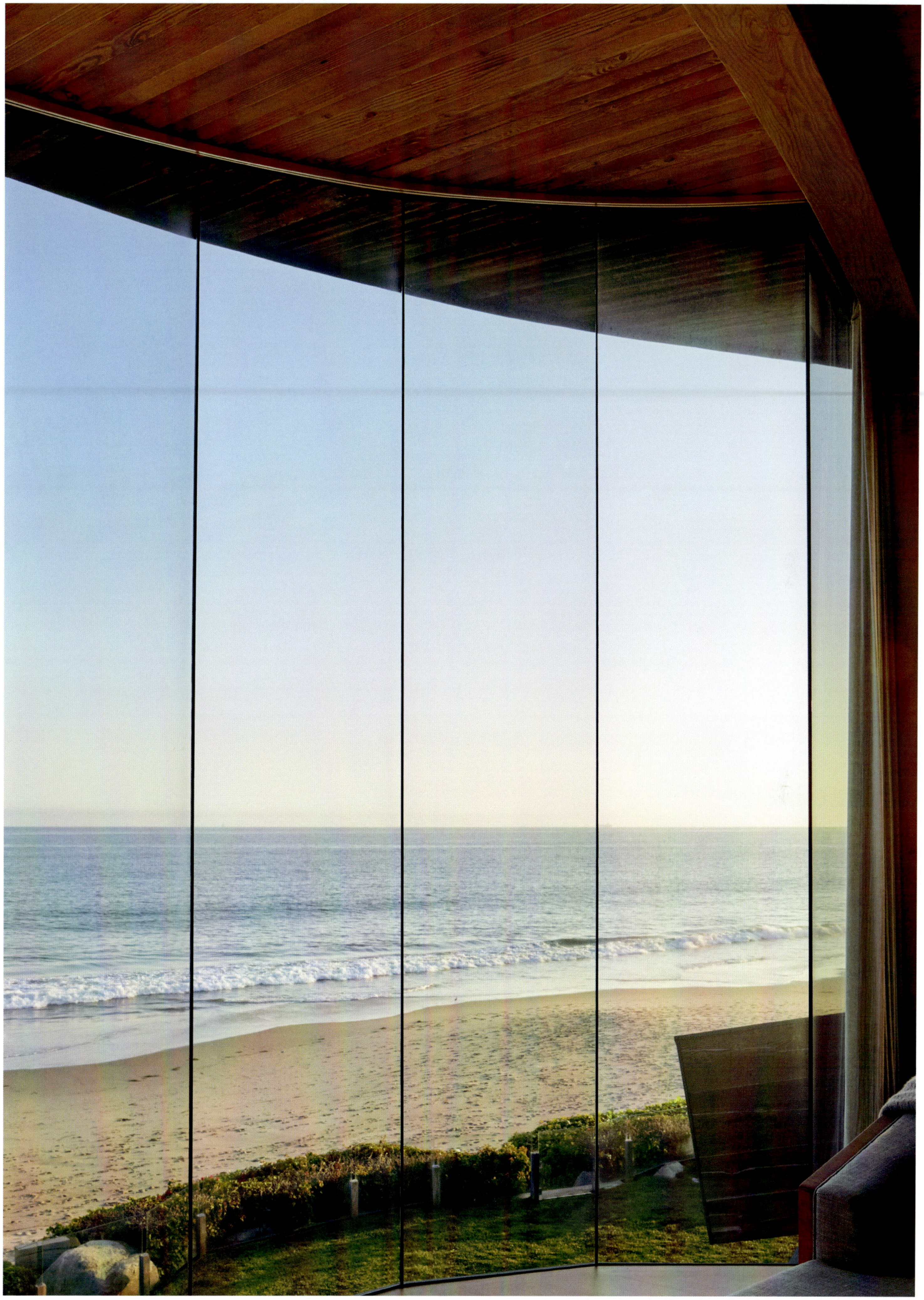

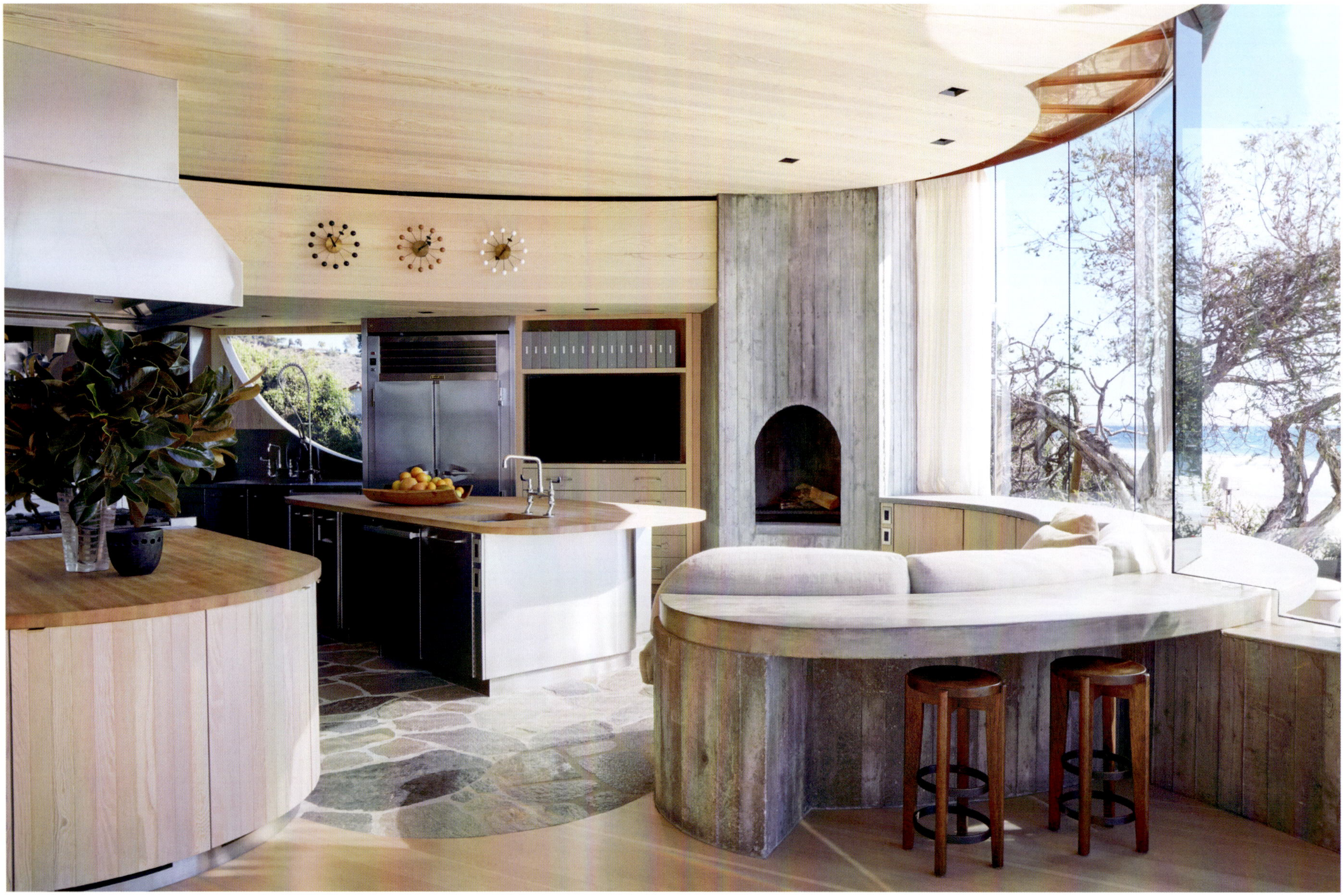

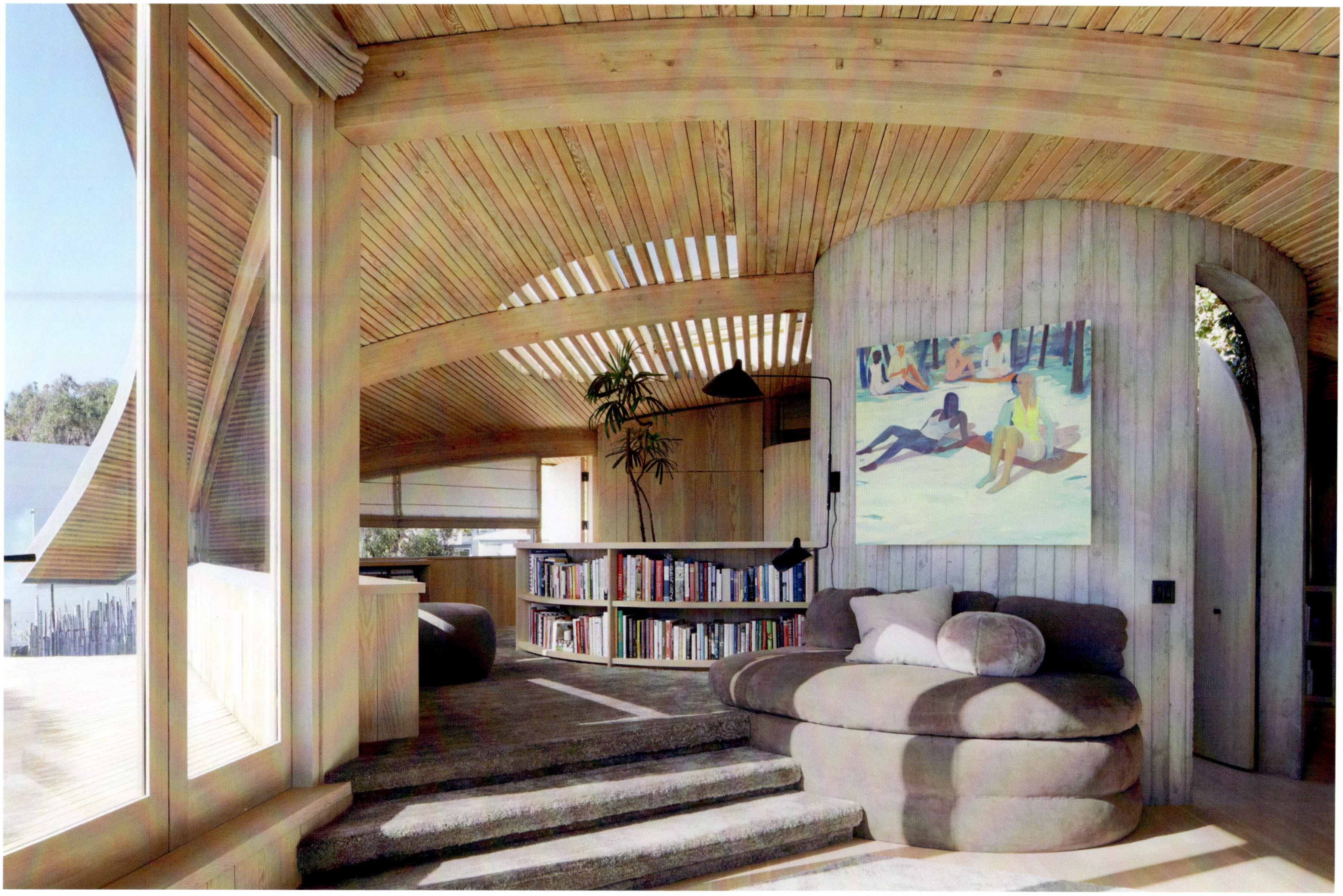

In designing the interiors of the house, Waldo Fernandez, like Jamie McCourt and Michael Kovac, respected John Lautner's original vision. "Architectural houses are always difficult to work with," says Fernandez. "They tell you, 'Don't screw around with me!' They demand to stay the same."

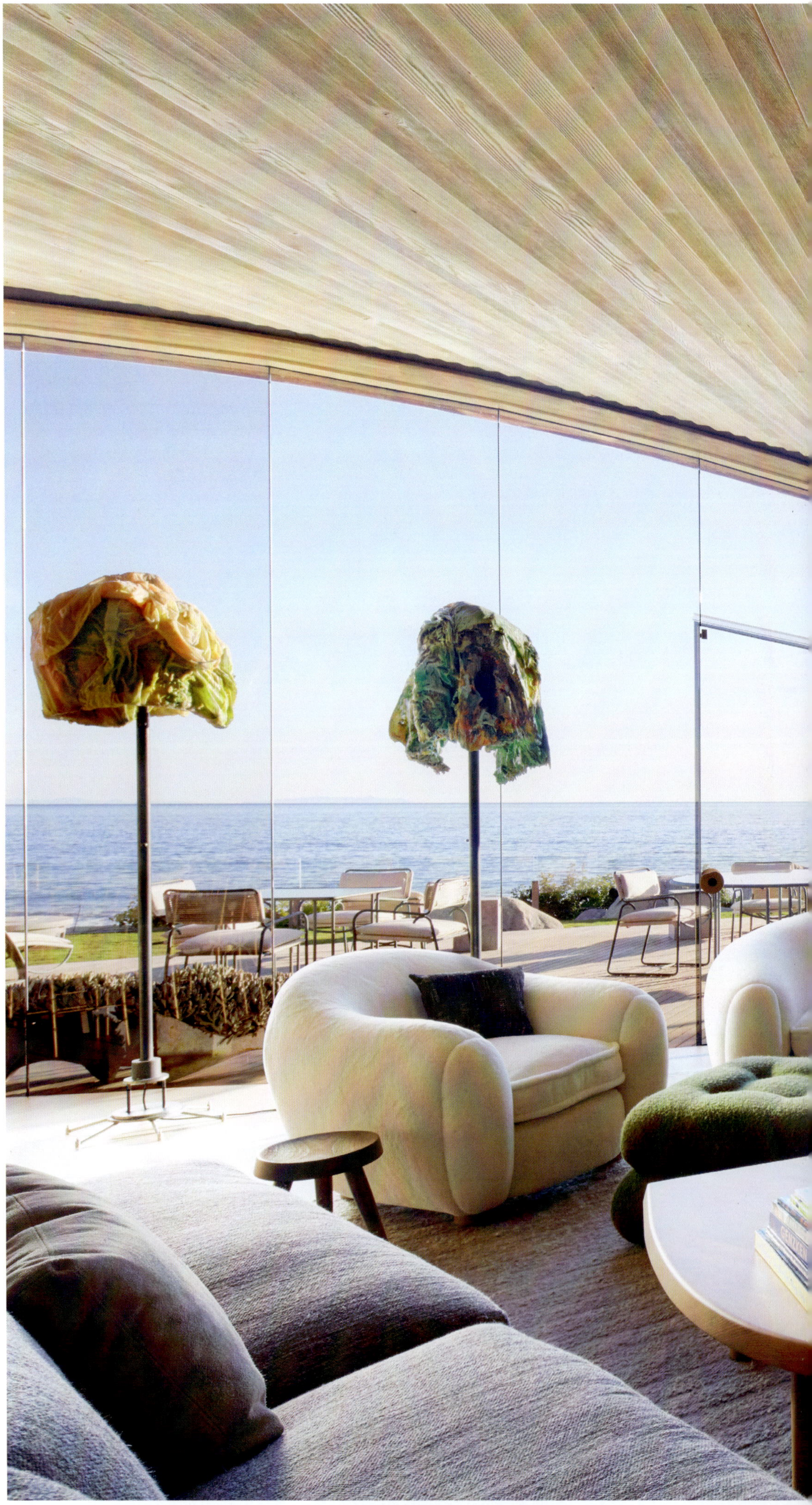

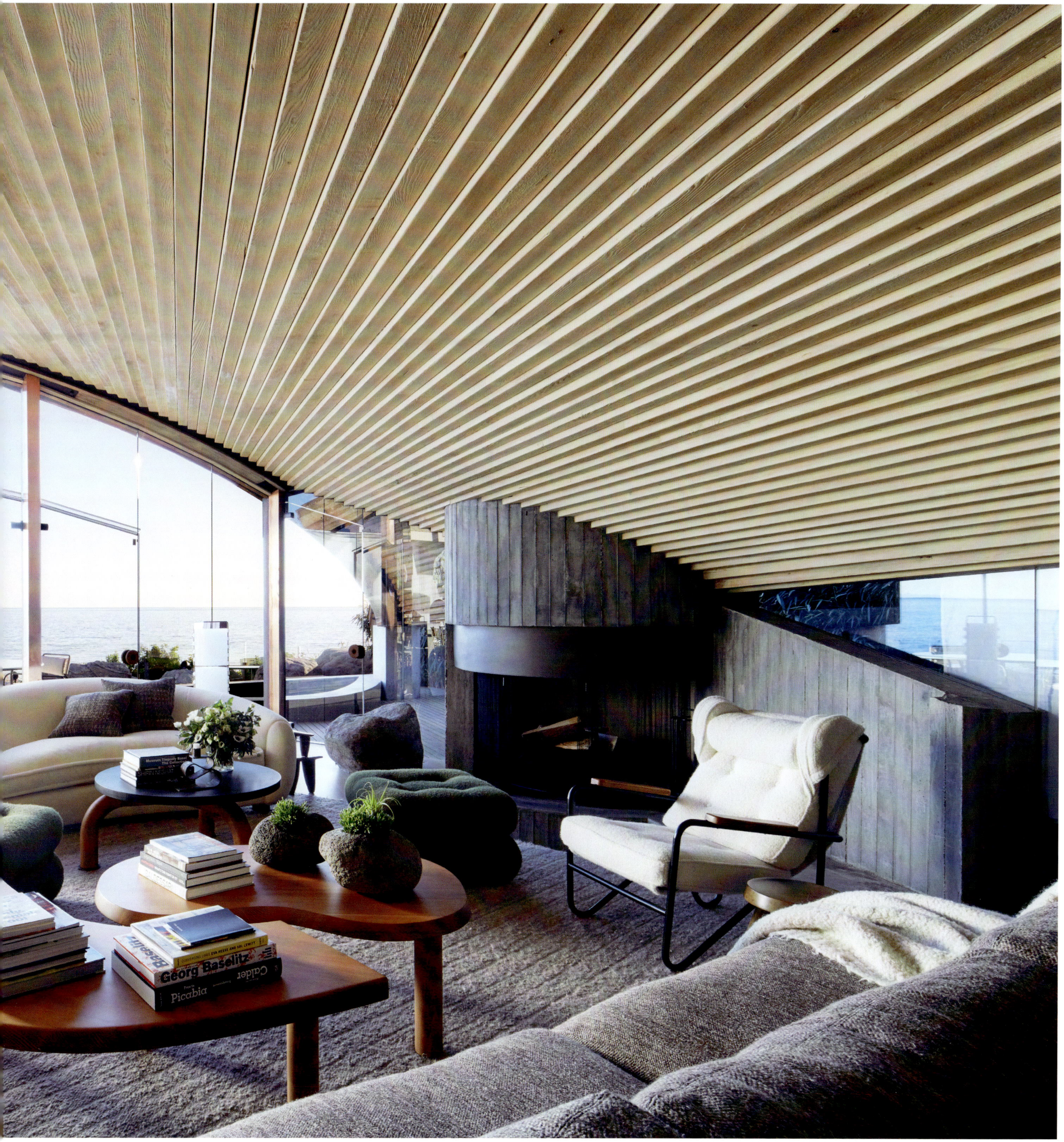
Georg Baselitz
Calder
Picabia

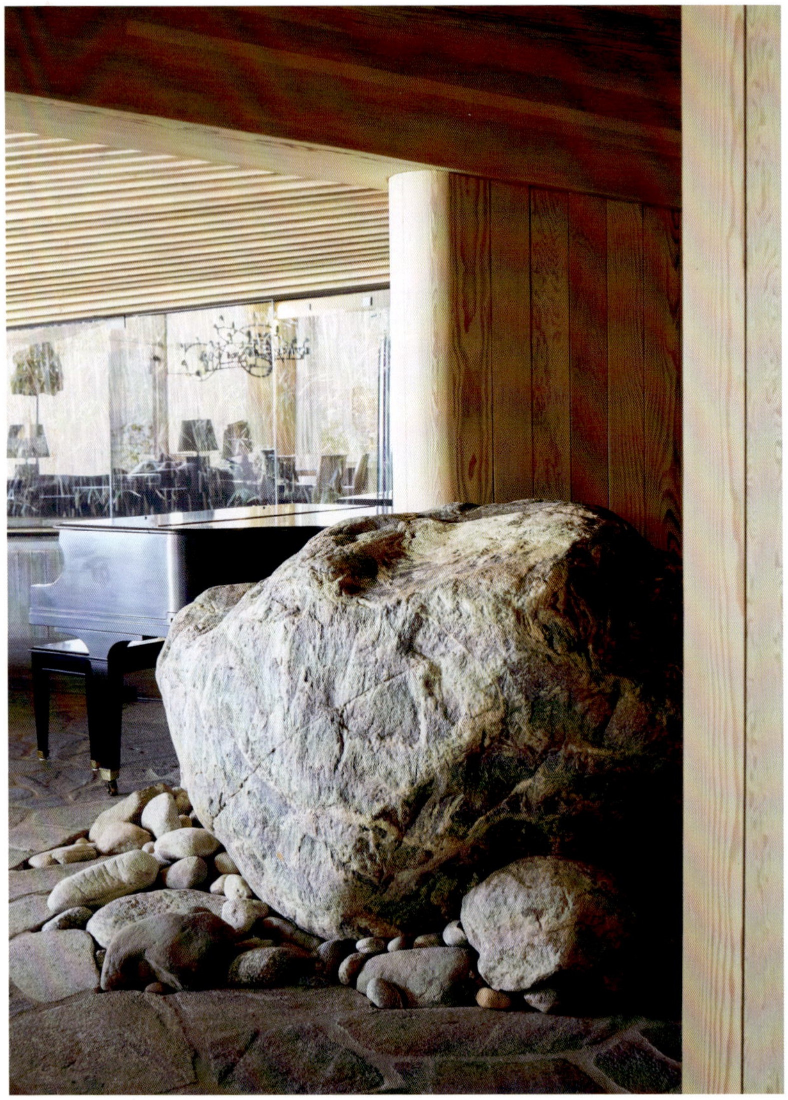

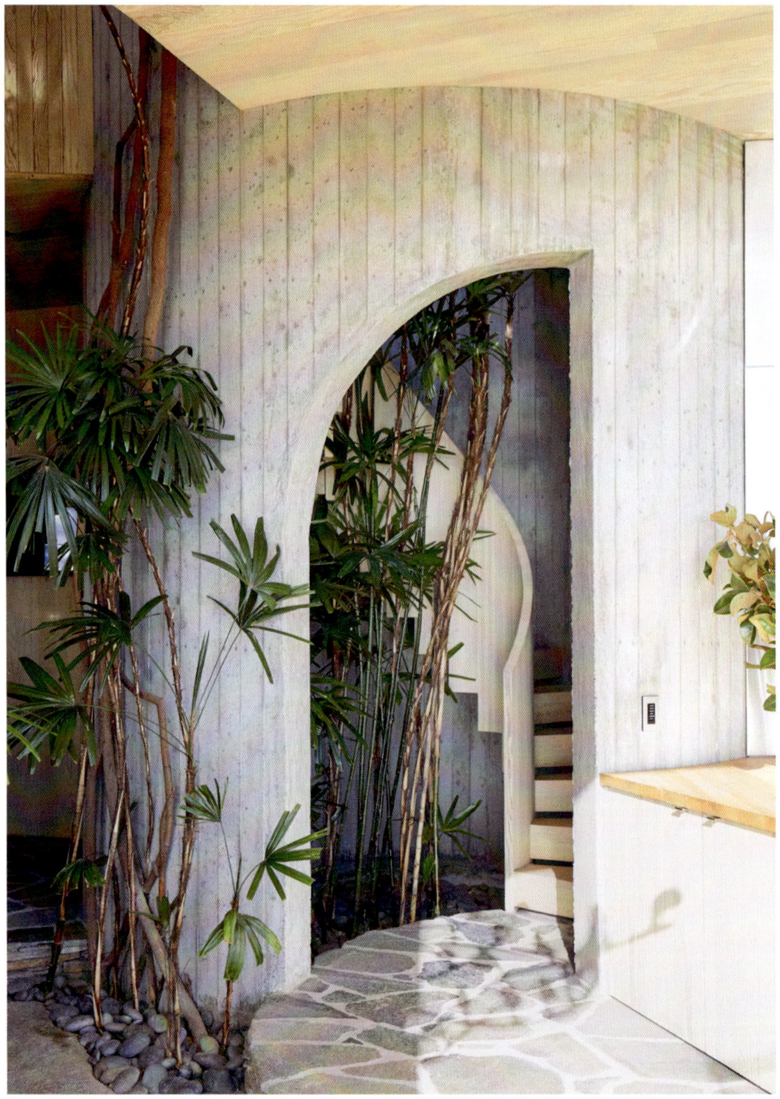

Nature absolutely permeates the cave- or shell-like residence: boulders seem to burst through interlocking stone floors; plants grow along board-formed, wood grain–imprinted walls; and sweeping windows bring in the ocean and sky.

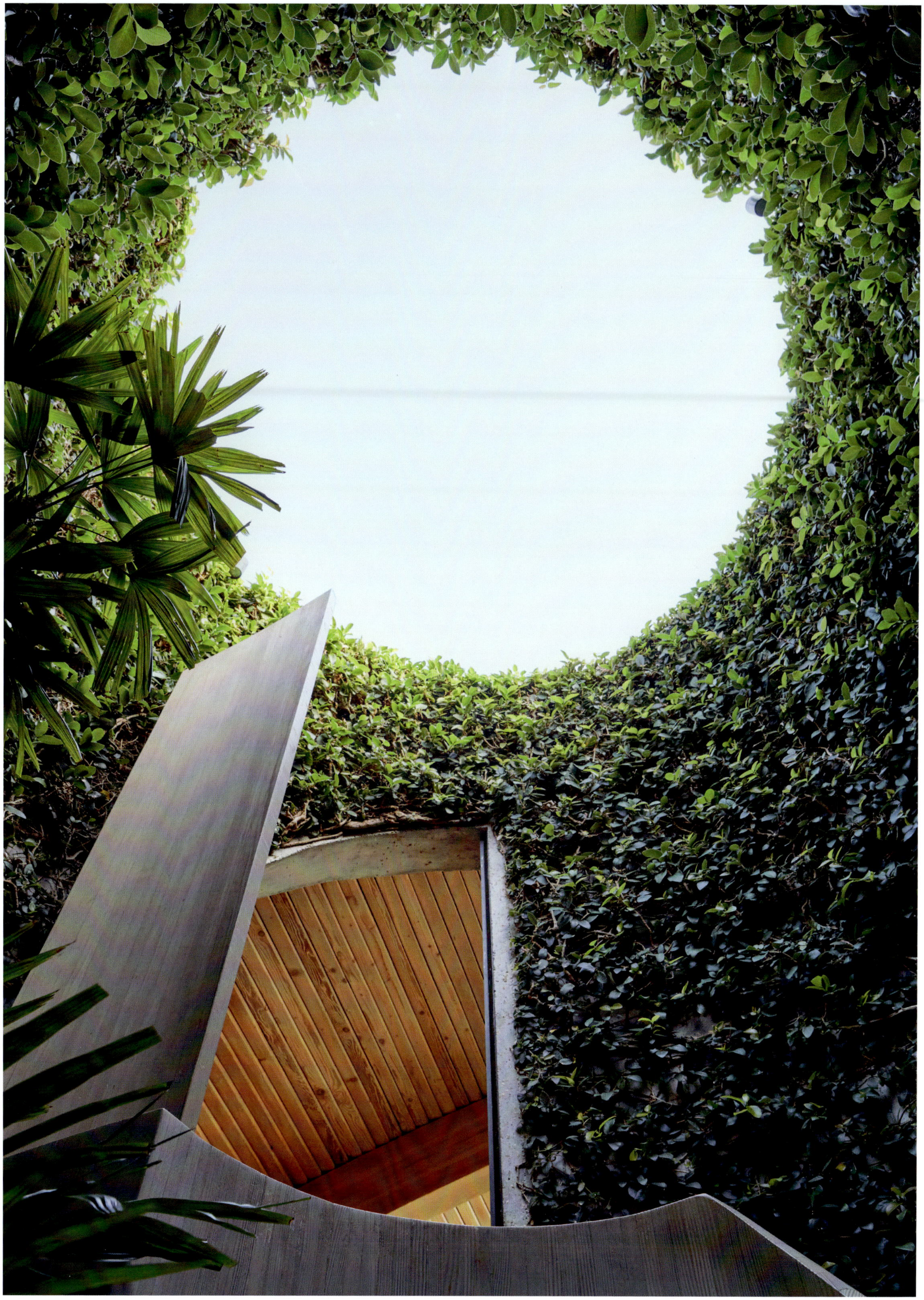

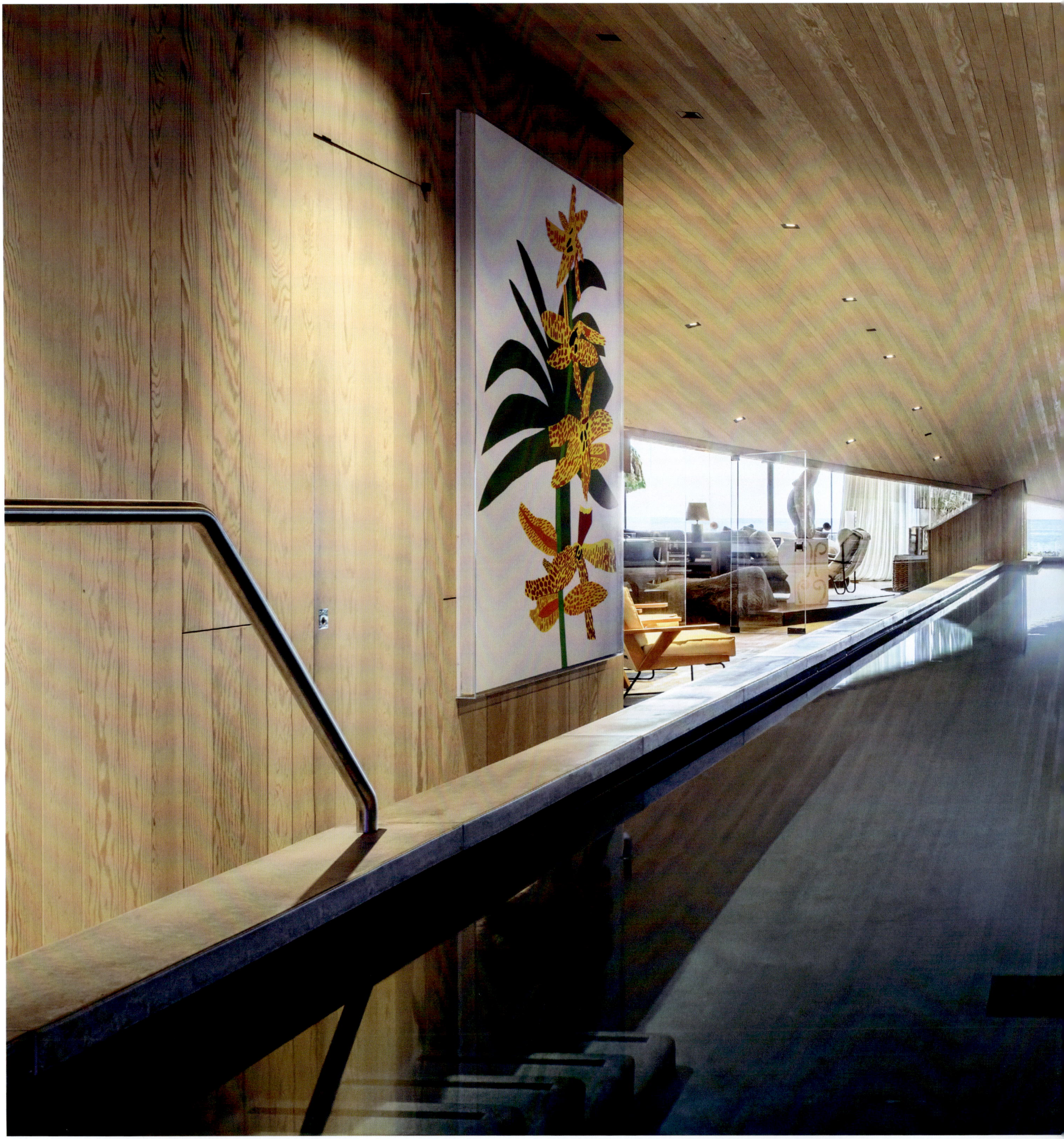

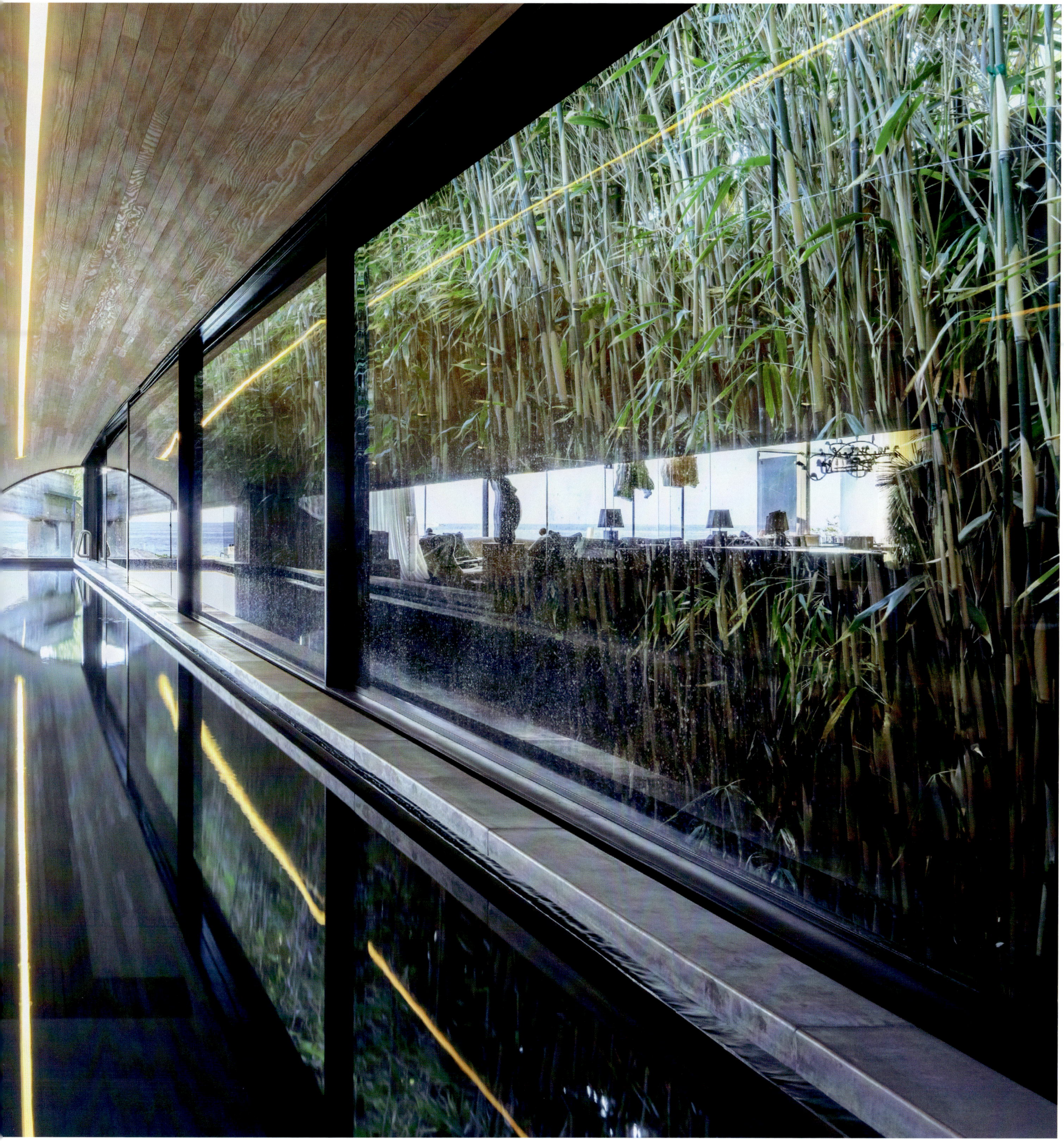

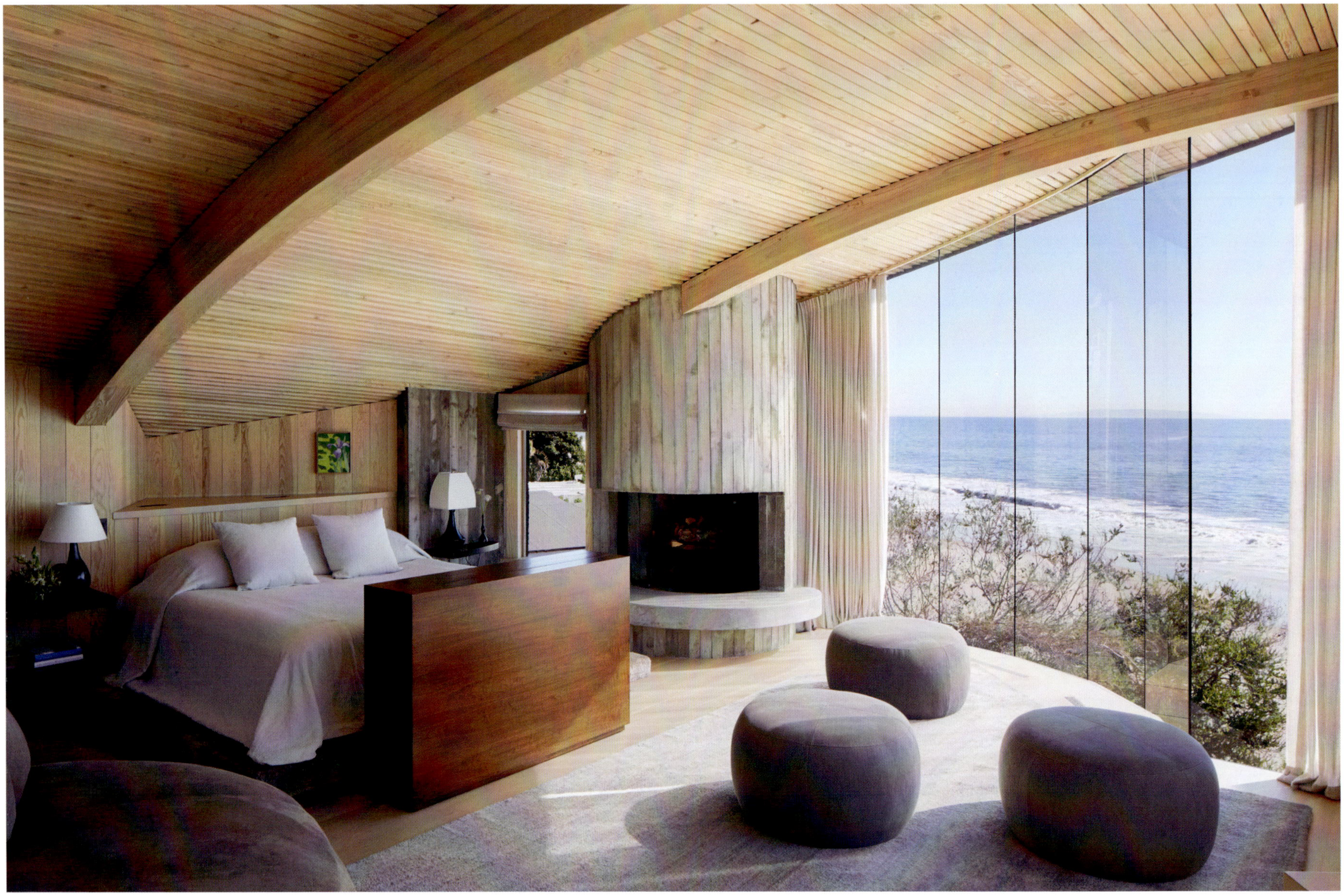

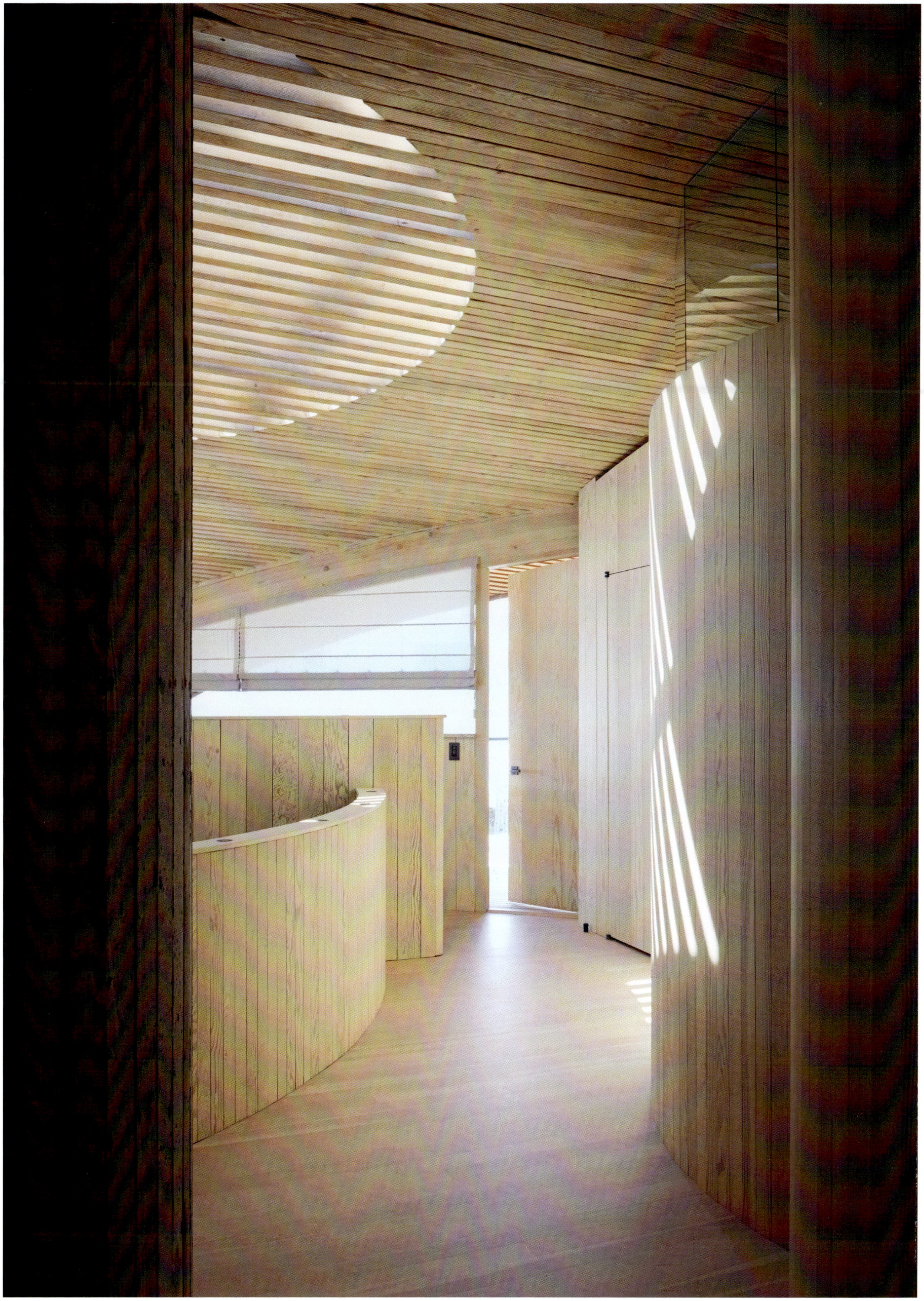

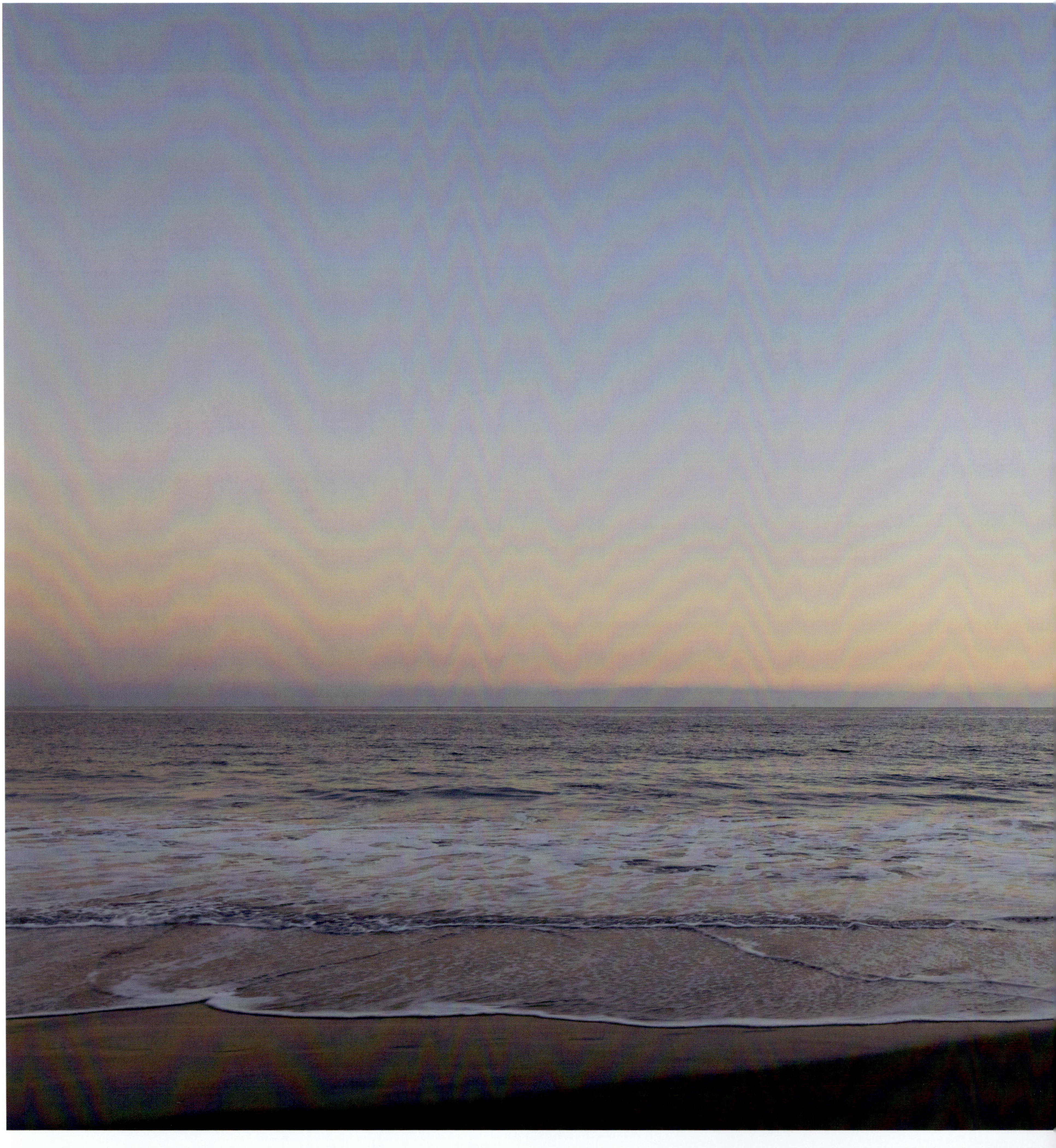

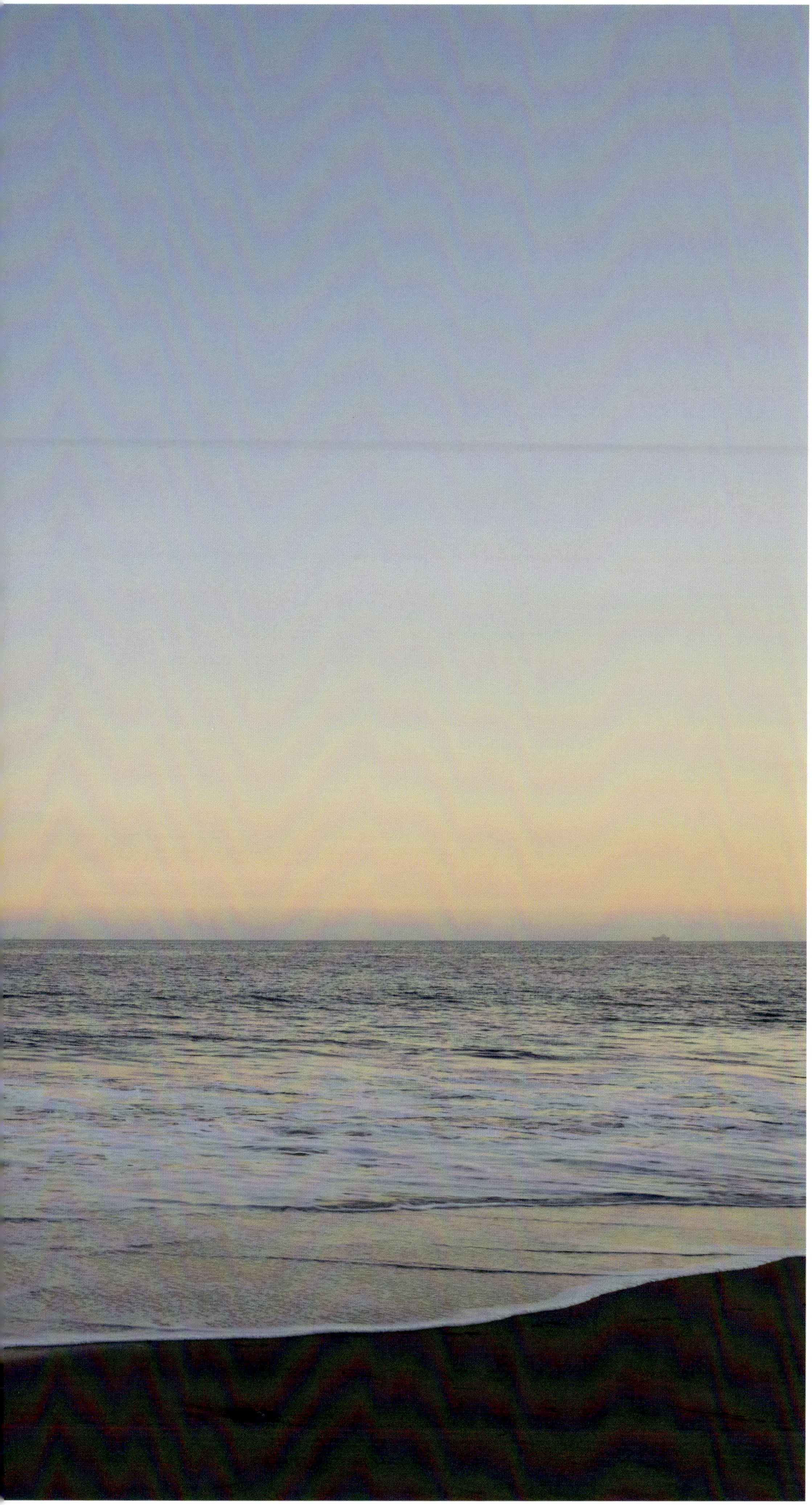

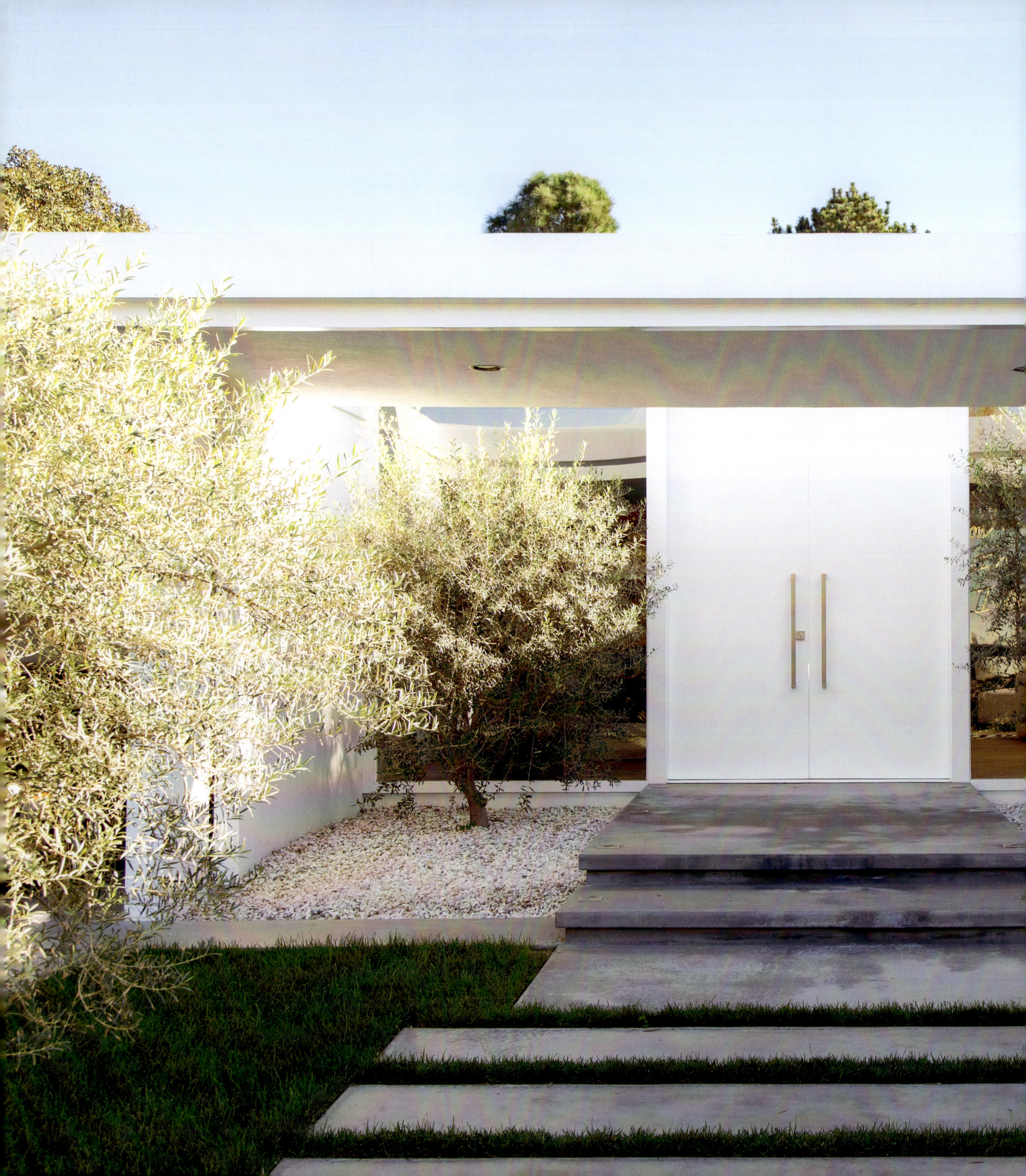

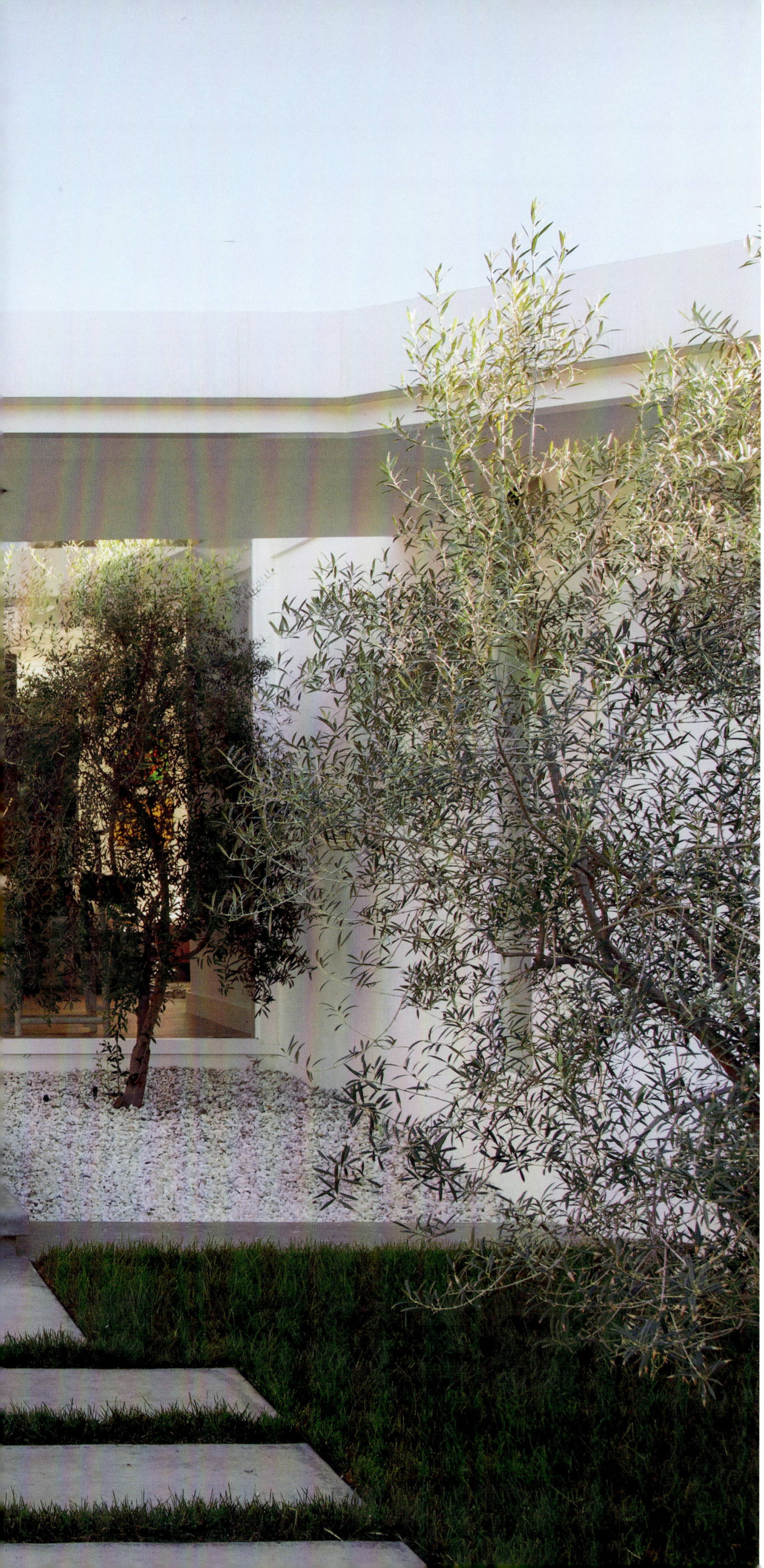

John Furnish Residence

Trousdale Estates

Residents

Elton John
and David Furnish

When my assistants and I arrived at the door of Sir Elton John and David Furnish, they quickly put us at ease with "I'm David" and "Just call me Elton." This down-to-earth approachability somehow typifies the five-thousand-square-foot Trousdale Estates home—downright humble by celebrity standards—despite the world-class collection of art and objects that fills every wall and surface. "The amazing thing about working with Elton and David," says interior designer Martyn Lawrence Bullard, "was the passion they both have for design, art, and the creation of a family sanctuary."

A photographer in Elton and David's house is like a kid in a candy store. As David graciously gave us a tour, my assistants and I got sidetracked by a grouping of spectacular William Egglestons (one of my all-time favorite photographers) amassed on a wall in the dining room. Two bedroom walls full of Robert Mapplethorpes had a similarly distracting effect. And these were truly the tip of the almighty iceberg of photographs that Elton, one of the world's foremost collectors of photography, has assembled and shared over the years, notably in the groundbreaking exhibition *The Radical Eye* at the Tate Modern.

The upward trajectory of Elton's career can almost be encapsulated by his collecting of photography: back in the 1960s, when he was in his twenties and living with his friend and collaborator Bernie Taupin in Pinner, England, Elton had a poster of Man Ray's seminal 1932 photograph *Glass Tears* on his wall. In 1993 he would set a new auction record for photography when he won the real thing at Sotheby's.

Though Elton began by collecting black-and-white prints exclusively—he has said he was once snobbish about color photography—his and David's house is evidence that he came around. Their home is as color-saturated as those Mapplethorpes and dye-transfer-printed Egglestons, bursting with vibrant hues that best show off their collections. "Never afraid of color, they allowed me to play with the spectrum and create a backdrop that makes their art the stars of the spaces," affirms Bullard. The result is a dramatic midcentury family home, thrilling to the eye and bursting with life.

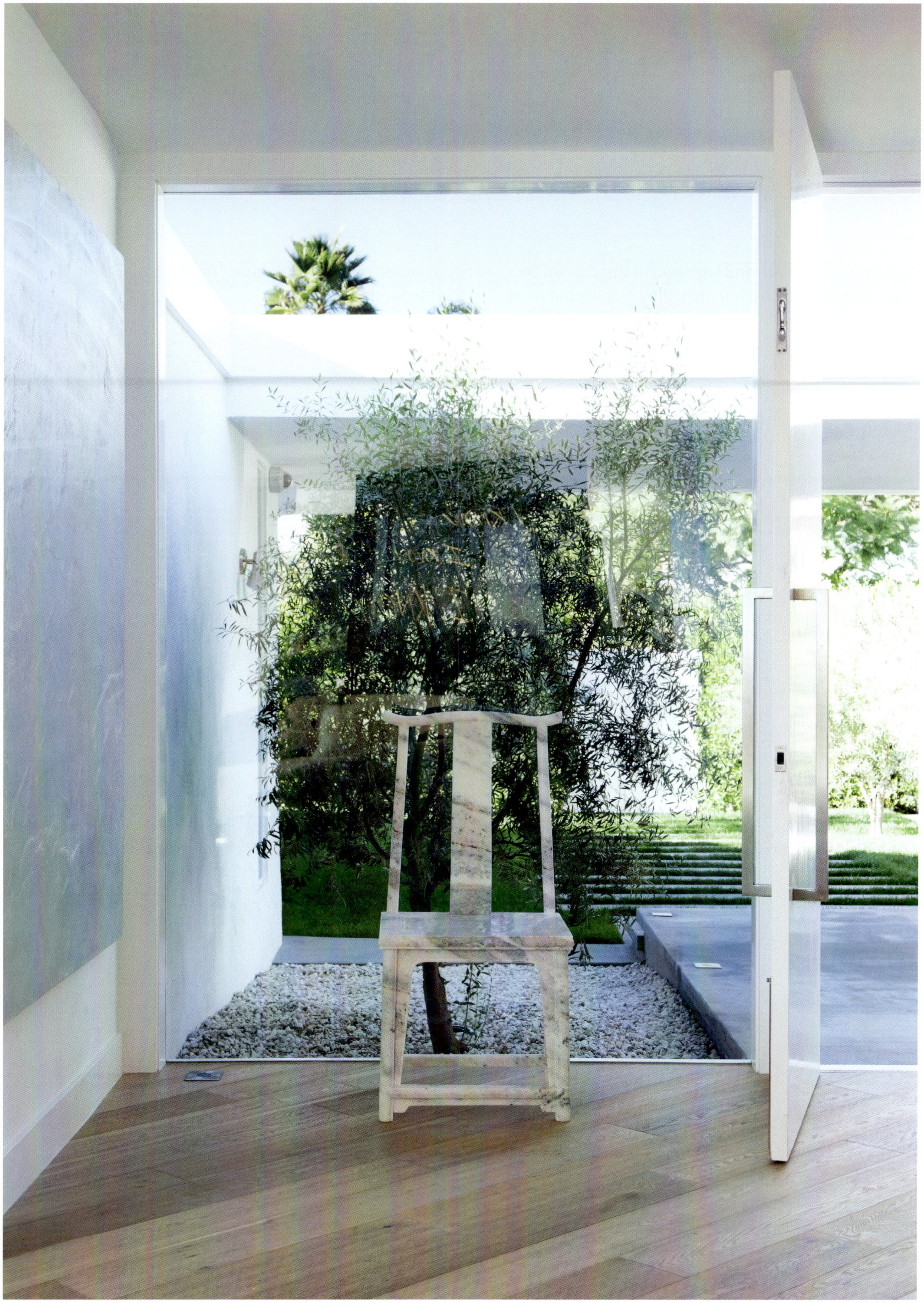

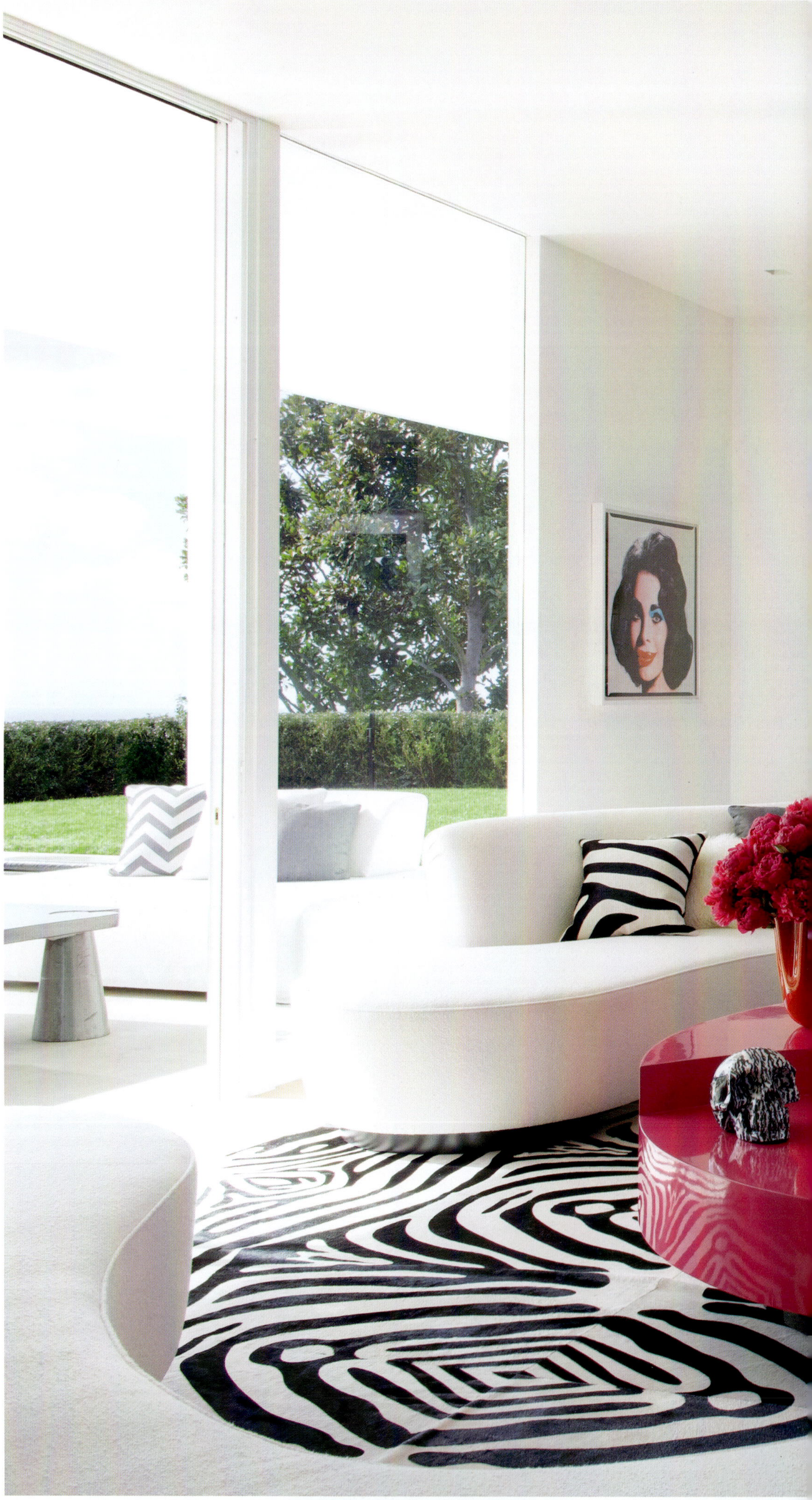

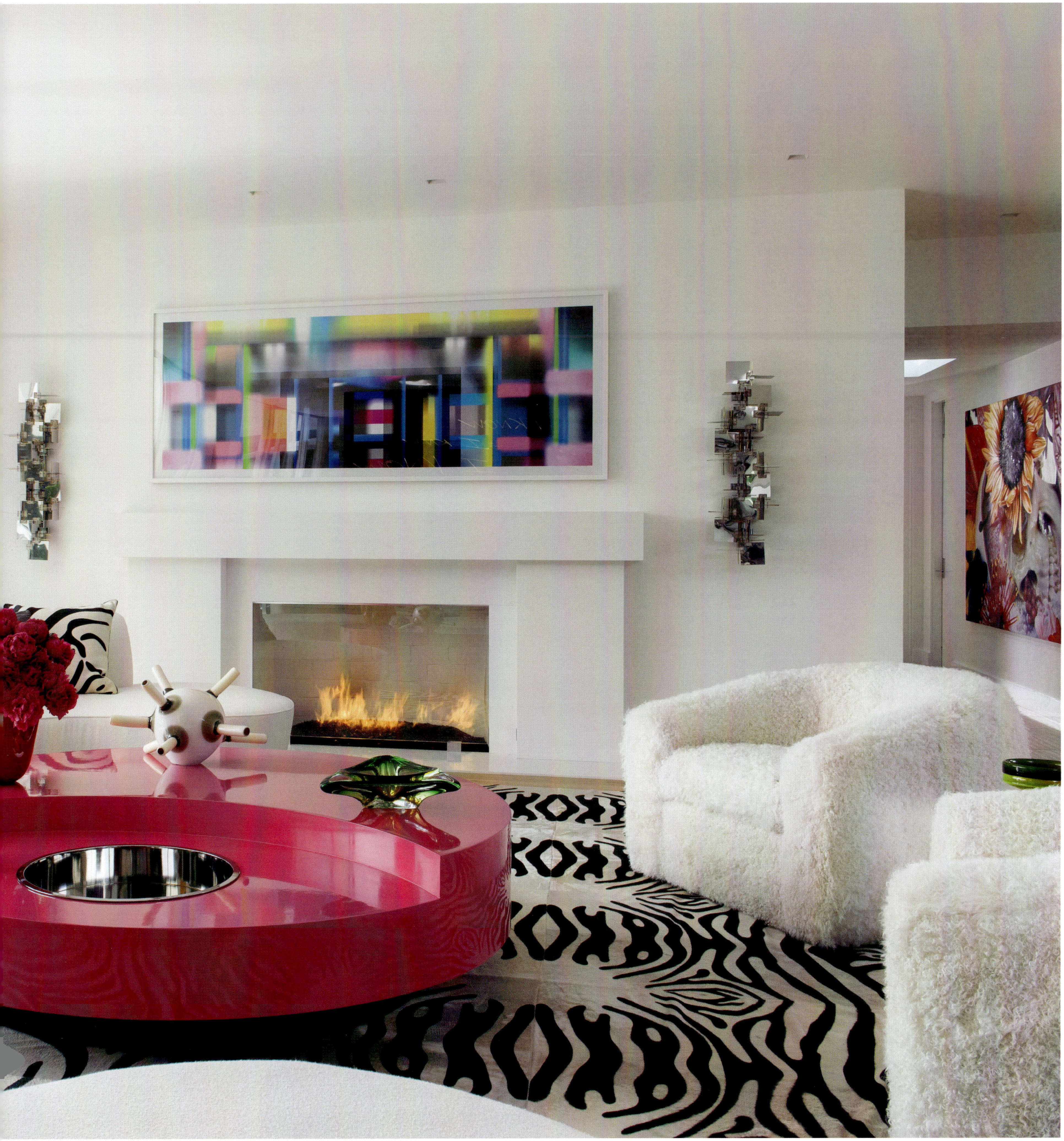

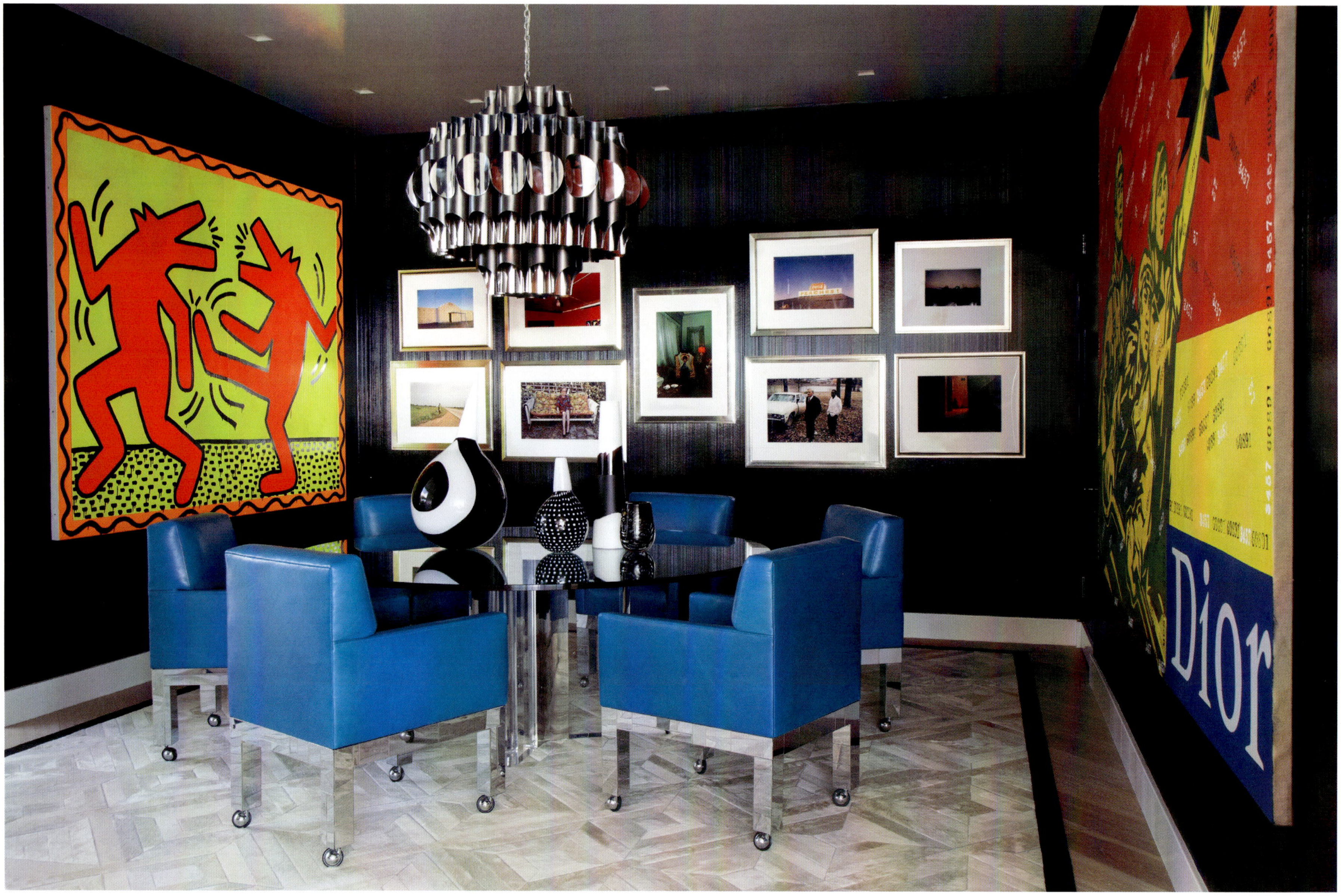

Of the house's interiors, Martyn Lawrence Bullard says "[They] burst with California style and capture the essence of midcentury architecture, blending comfort and form with an important and deeply personal art collection." Walls in dramatic black and clean white highlight the exceptional artwork.

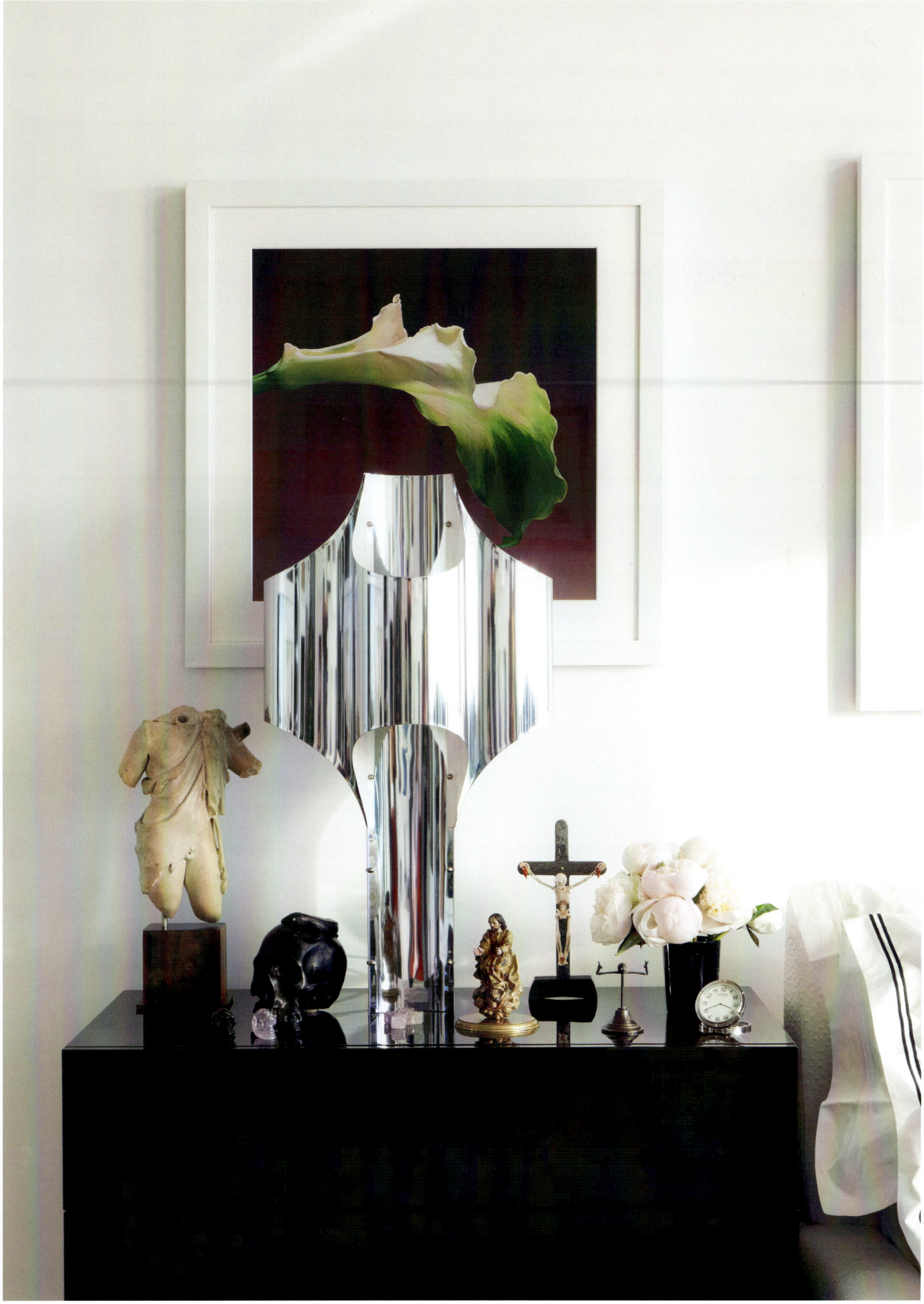

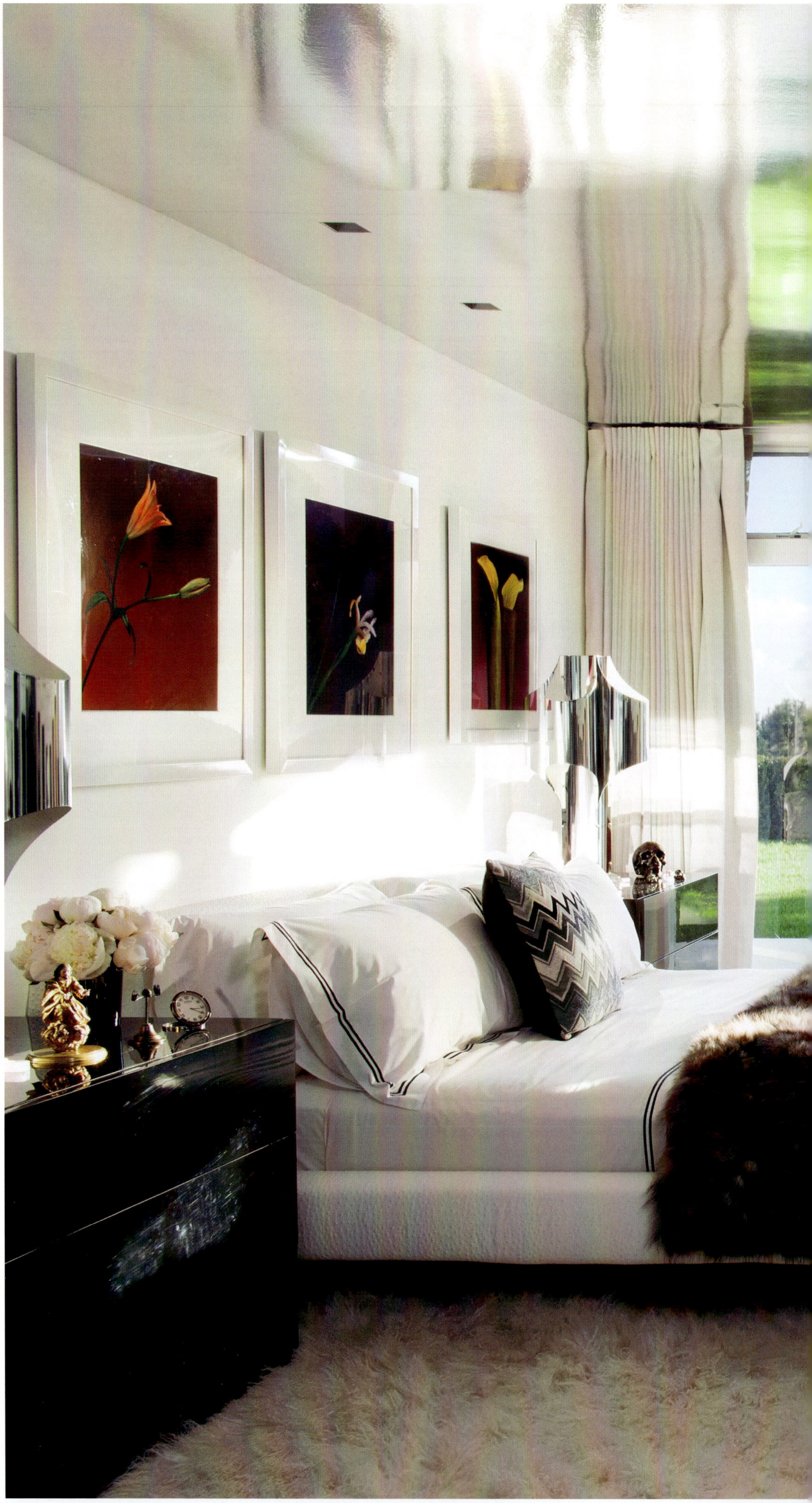

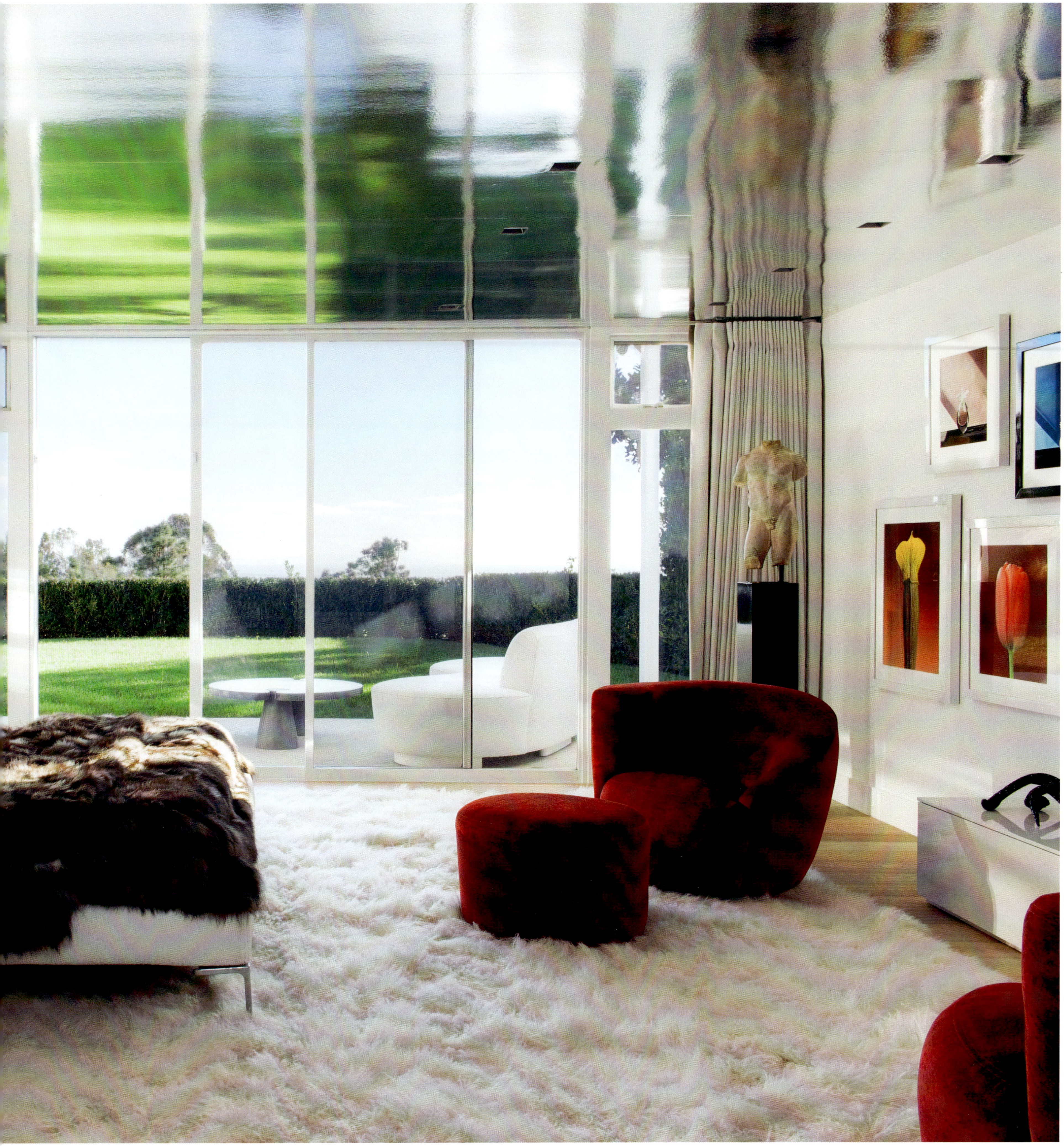

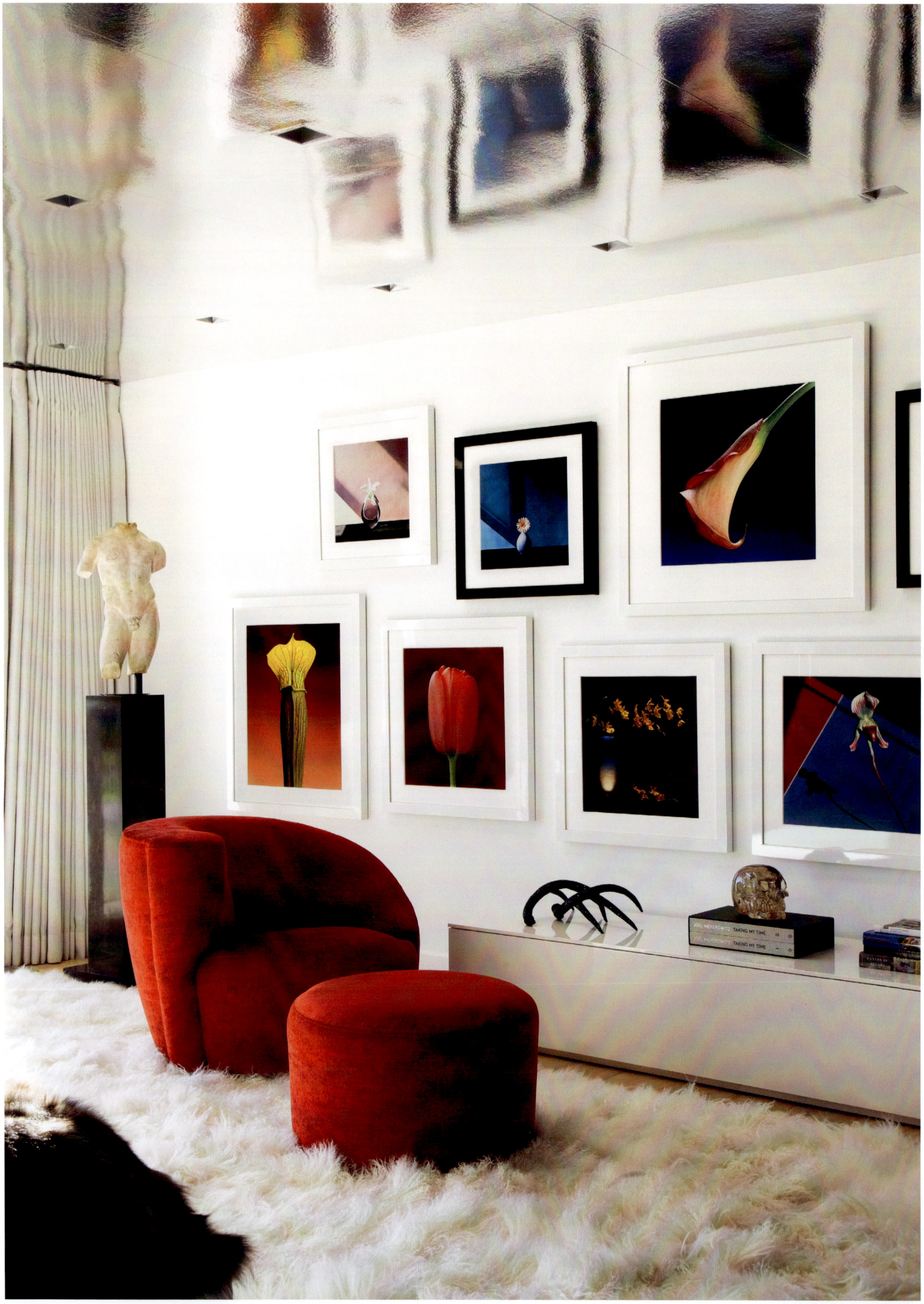
JOEL MEYEROWITZ TAKING MY TIME
TAKING MY TIME

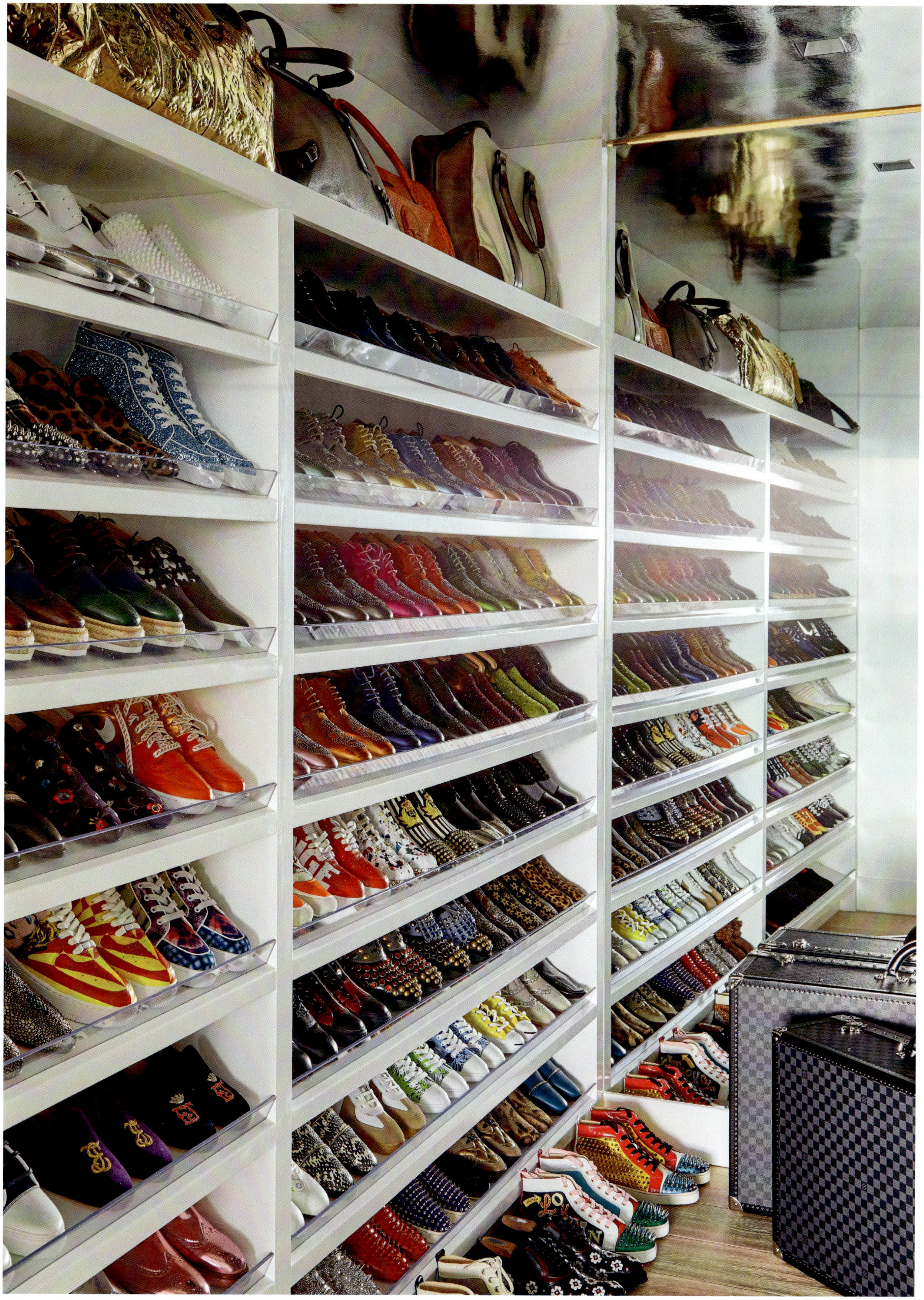

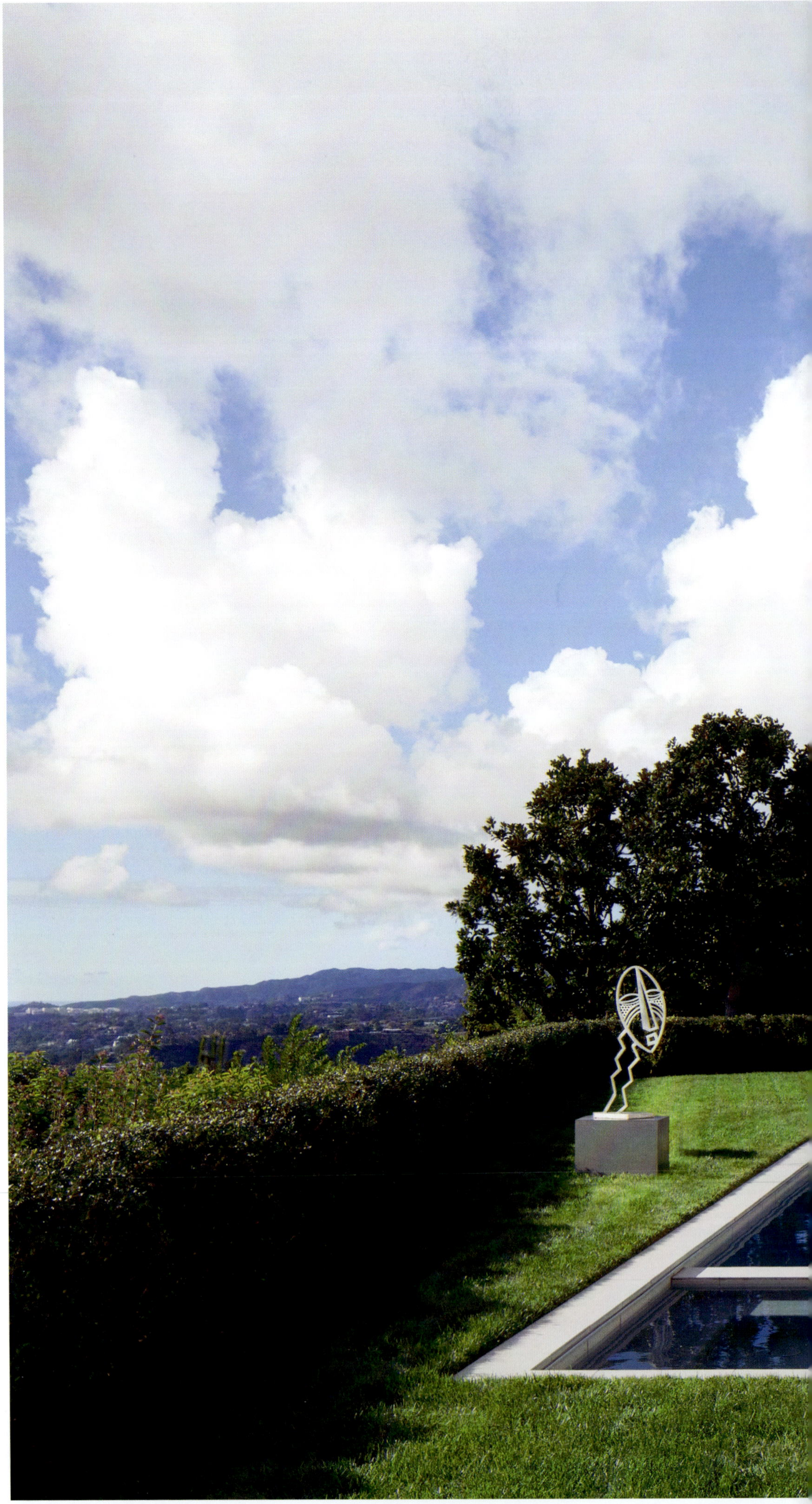

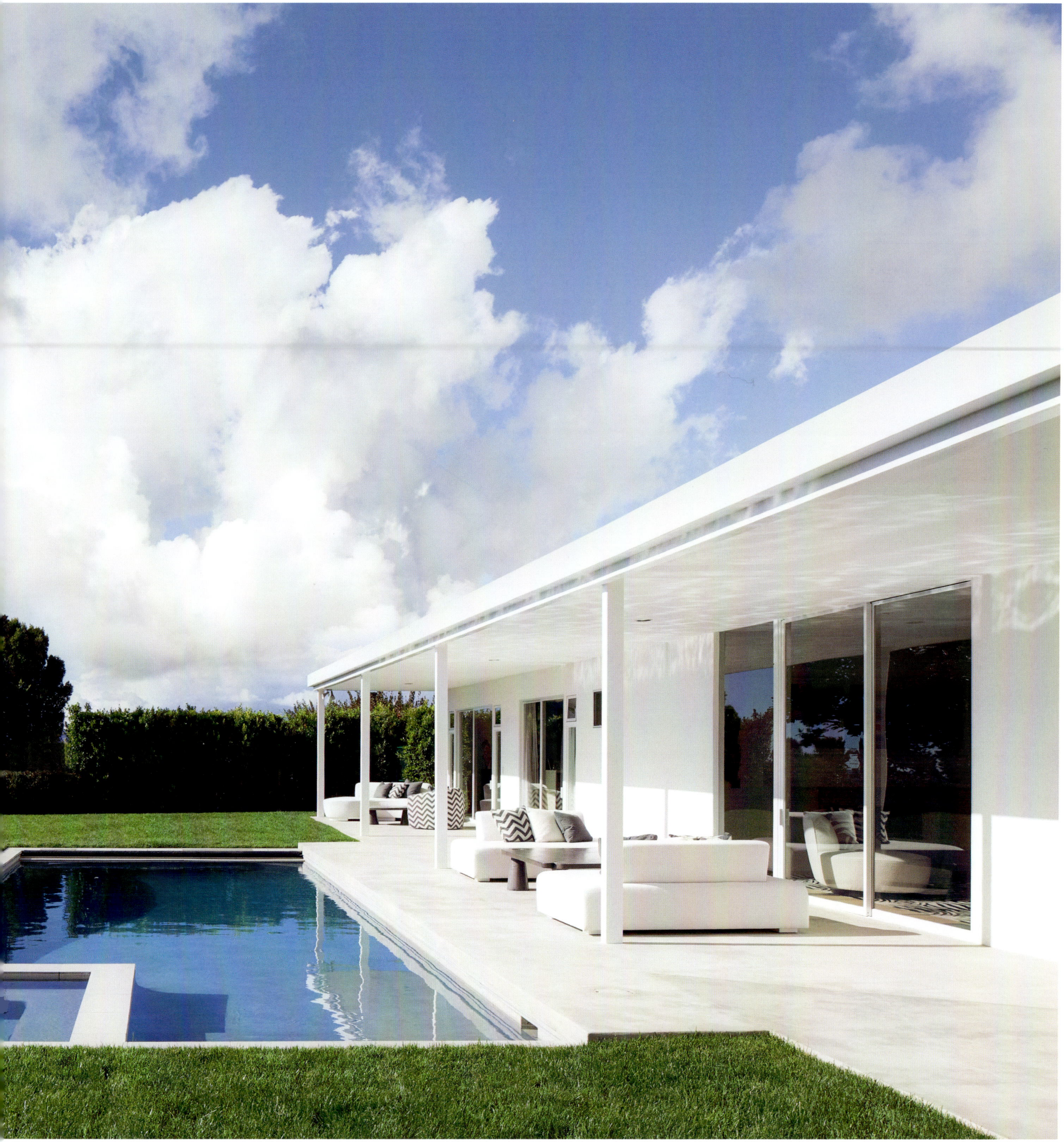

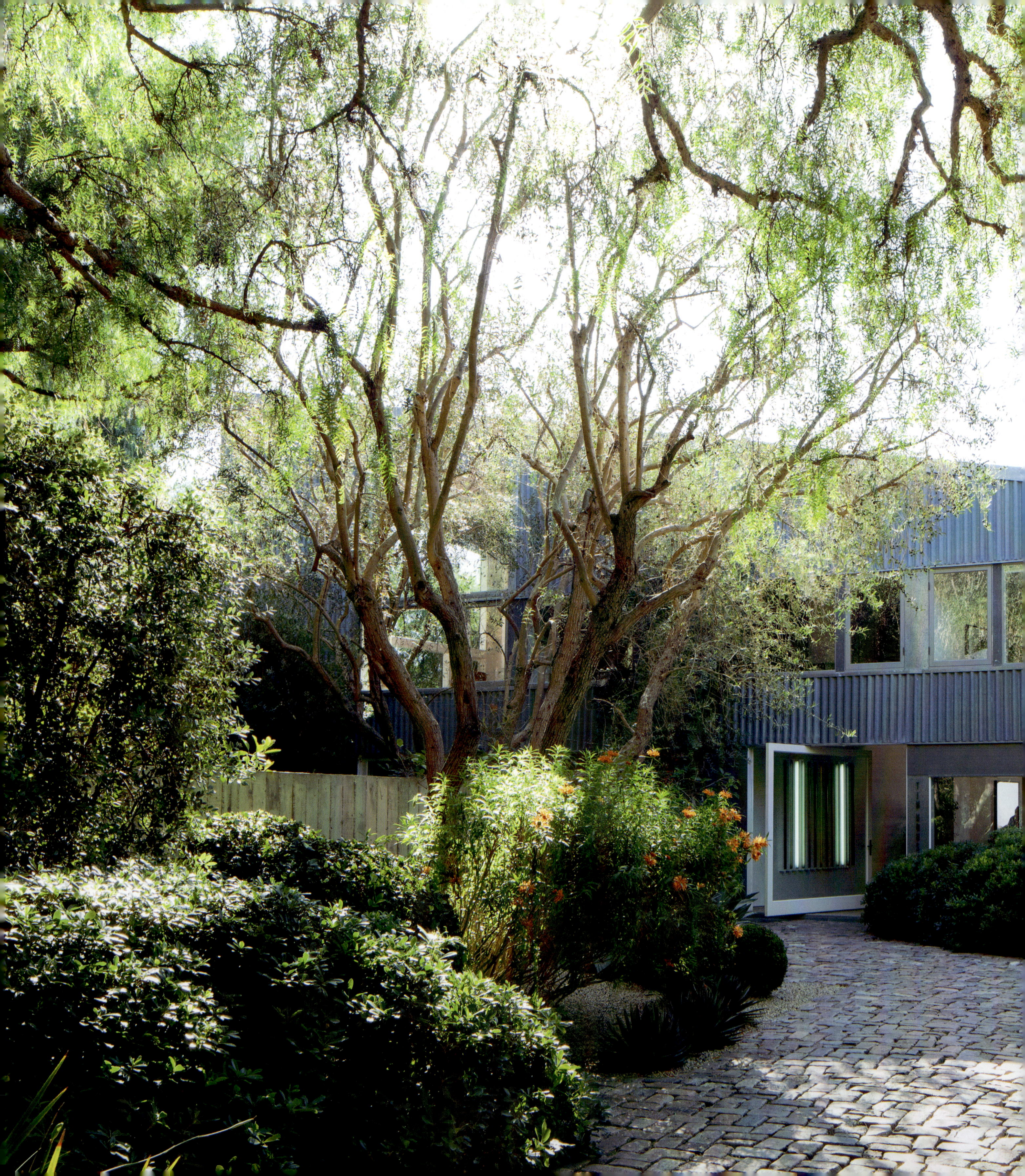

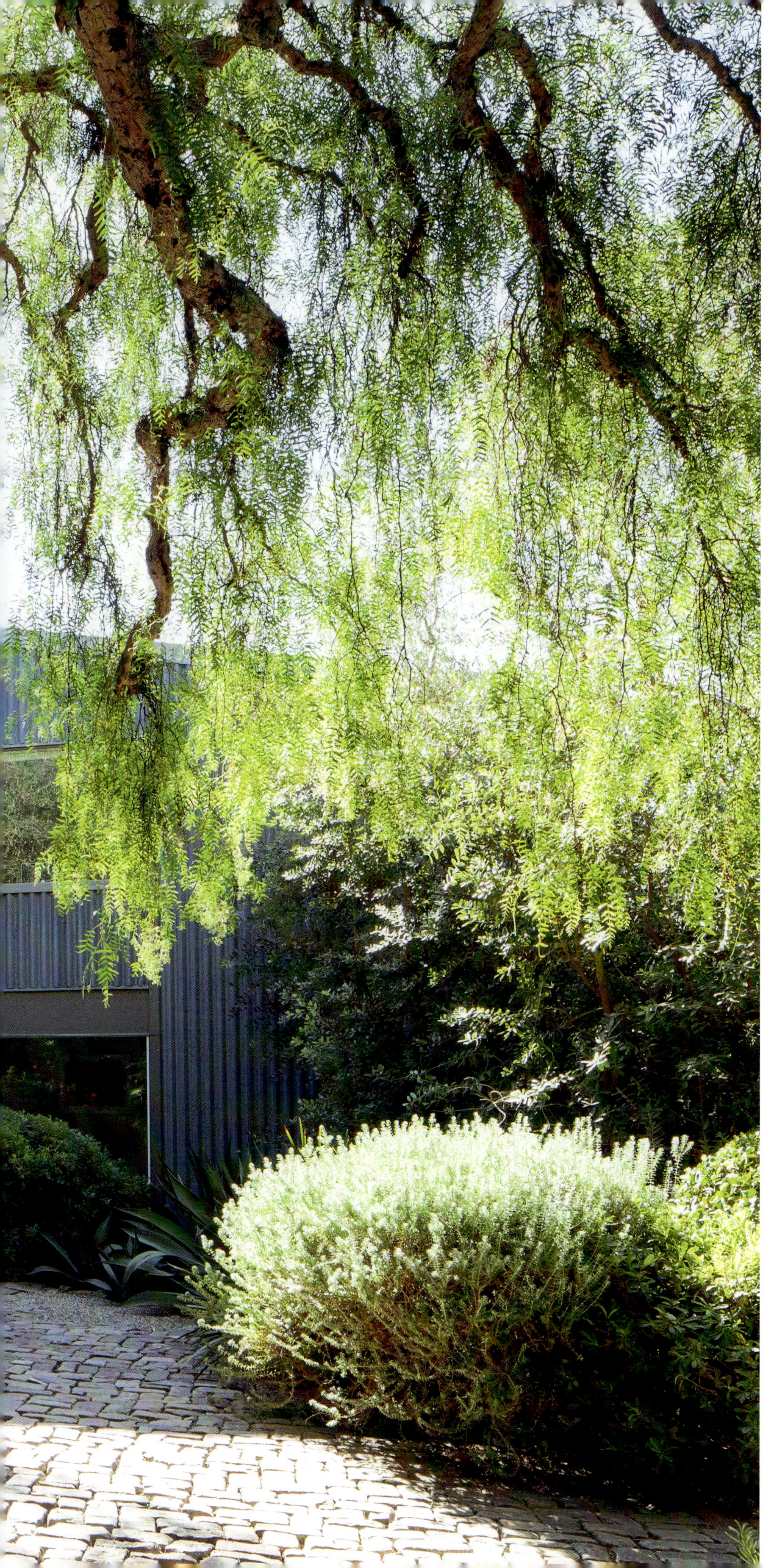

Tin House

Malibu

Architect

Frank Gehry

Residents

Patrick and Jillian Dempsey

Originally built as an artist loft for abstract painter Ronald Davis in 1972, this trapezoidal Frank Gehry–designed beauty in Malibu was the home of actor Patrick Dempsey and makeup artist Jillian Dempsey for seven years.

Still mostly open plan and clad in corrugated tin with multiple skylights and expansive windows, the house was lively and atmospheric and transformed as the light shifted throughout the course of the day. As the house was not originally designed as a family home, it was made inviting and comfortable by interior designer Estee Stanley, who added sound-dampening wood walls and carpeting to improve the acoustics. Landscape designer Scott Shrader had worked with the previous owners, but with the Dempseys he expanded the possibilities of the property for family life, with terracing, hidden walkways, an outdoor kitchen and dining pavilion, water features, vegetable and flower gardens, and more.

The Dempseys considered themselves stewards of Gehry's work and nodded to the artistic origins of the house with artwork from the Light and Space movement, which originated in Southern California in the late 1960s. Their passion for works by Light and Space artists John McCracken, Robert Irwin, and De Wain Valentine, and for the art of Ronald Davis, was intense. Some houses are all about the architecture; some are all about the art. This place was about the flawless merging of both.

When Los Angeles photo assistants and photographers are asked to recall their favorite shoots, the Dempseys invariably come up. Known for being completely lovely to cast and crew, it was icing on the cake that their home was so interesting. Sometimes on shoots we walk on eggshells, but not here; there was excitement and bustle, and the homeowners made us feel welcome, whipping up smoothies and driving us around the 3.3-acre spread on golf carts. Kids jumped in the pool, table tennis was played, donkeys brayed, chickens ran around, and sports cars purred. Patrick made pizzas for the crew in the garden oven while a game of soccer took off on the back lawn.

A few years after the Dempseys had moved out of this special house, sadly fire took it away. In 2018 the Woolsey Fire ripped through Malibu and destroyed it, along with four hundred other residences.

Guests were greeted at the front entrance with a work by Robert Irwin (and sometimes by the Dempseys' dog). The couple's collecting focuses on Light and Space art, a loose movement of Southern California artists defined by a seminal 1971 exhibition that included Irwin, among others.

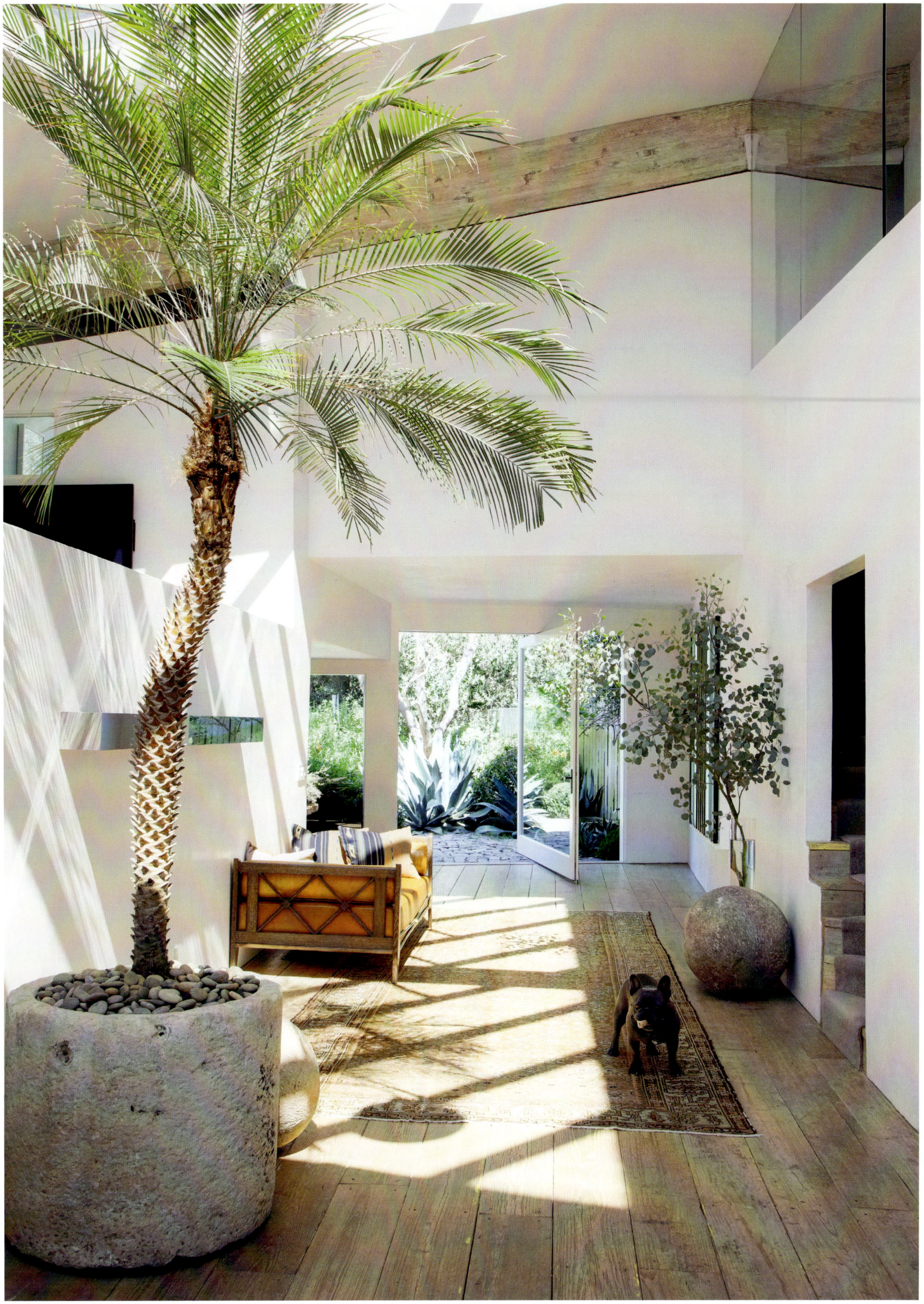

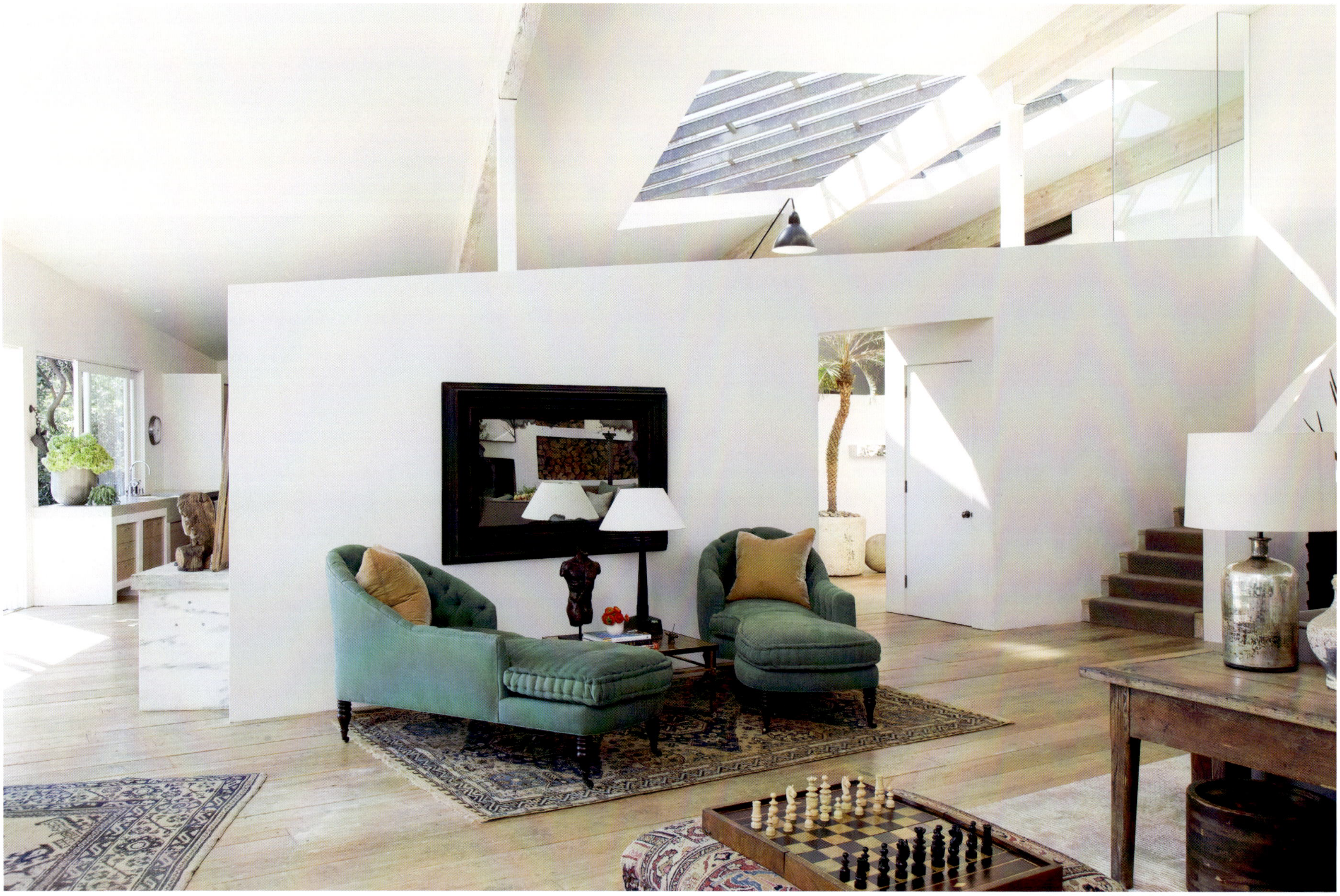

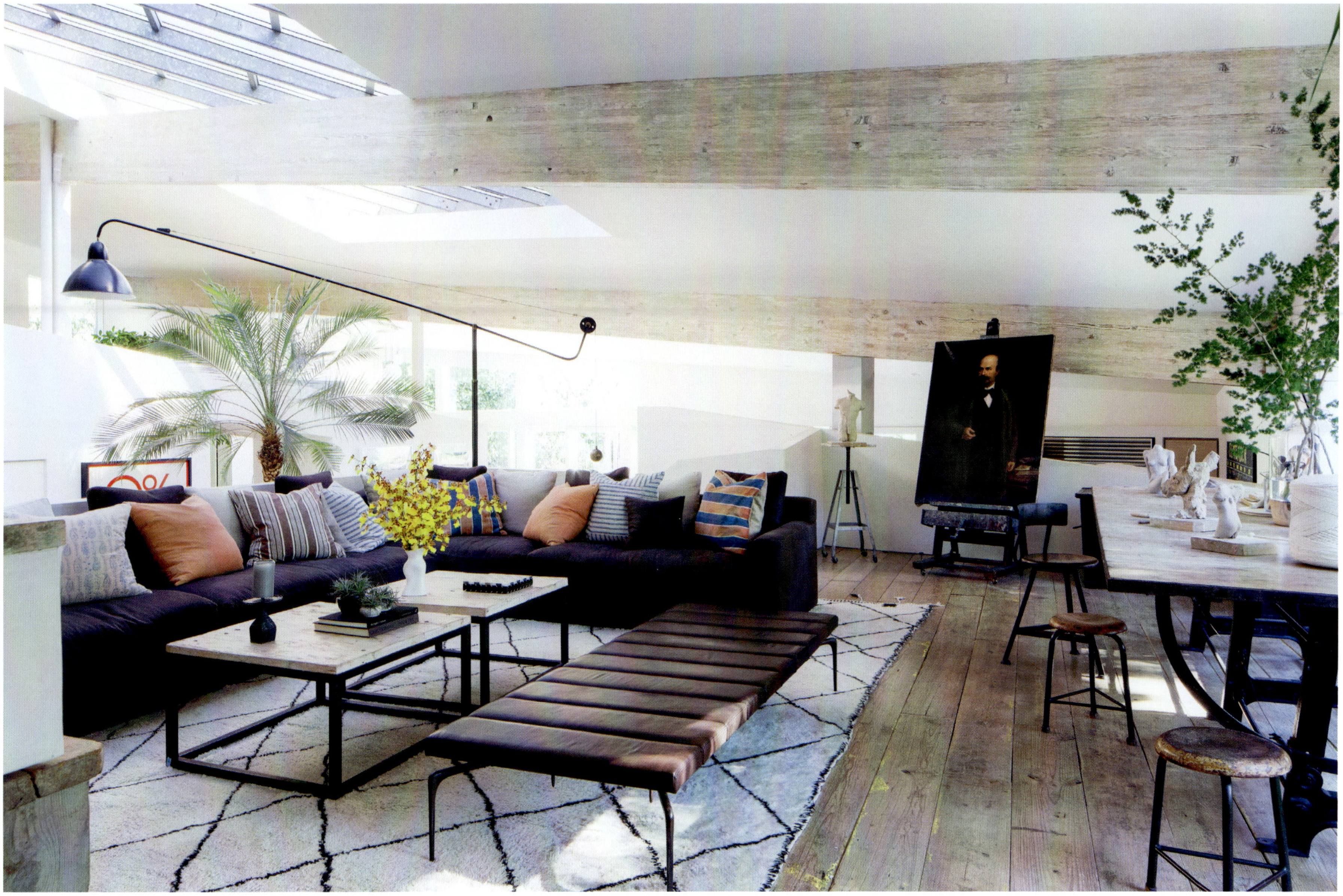

The mezzanine was used by Jillian Dempsey as a studio for her art and jewelry design. When Frank Gehry visited, he noted that this was his favorite space in the house.

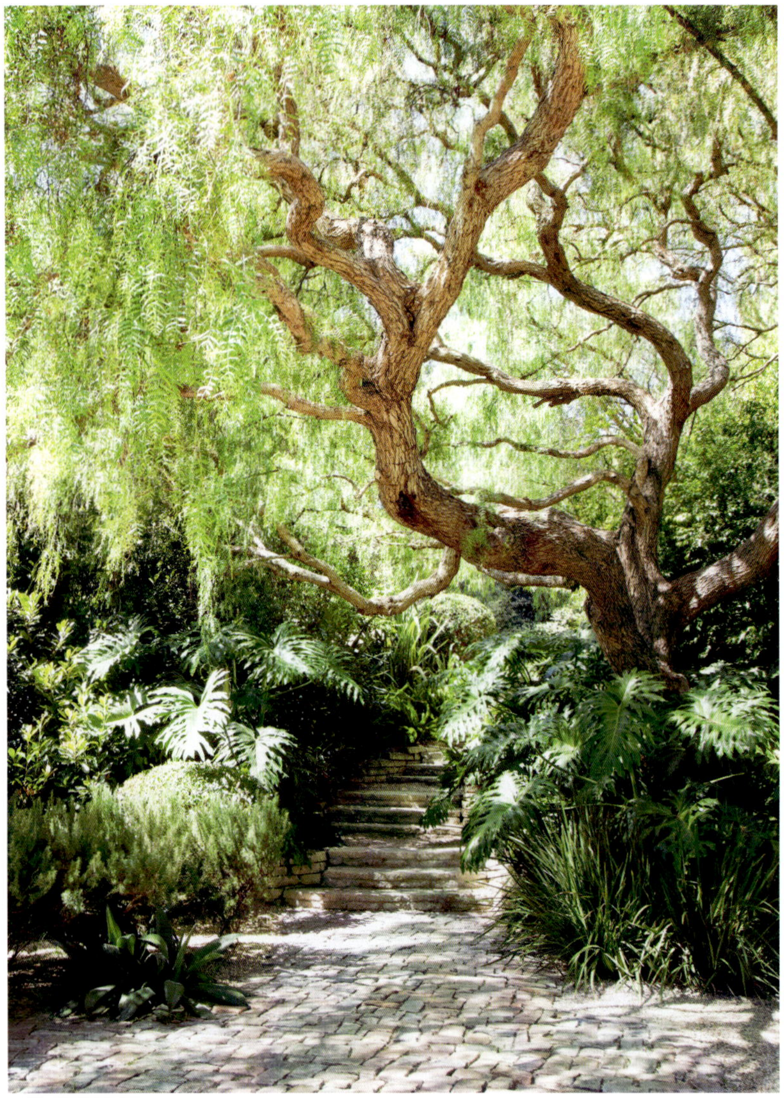

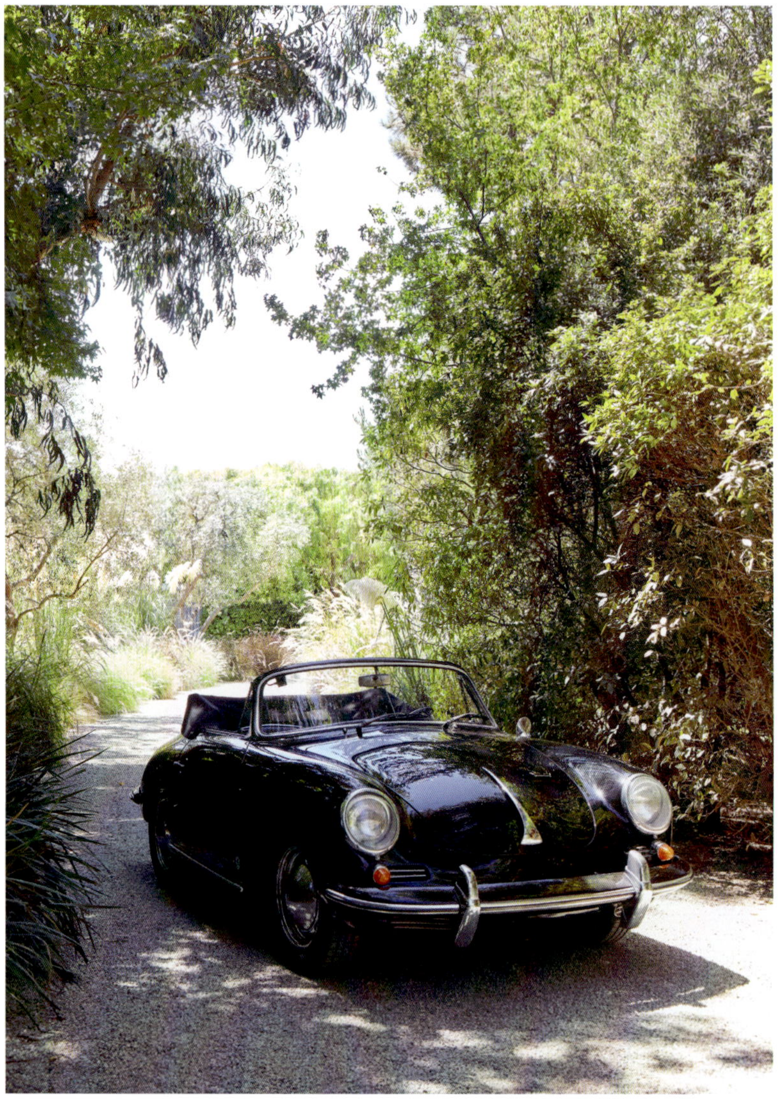

The Dempseys' extensive property featured sculpture by Craig Kauffman—another Light and Space artist—an Airstream trailer, a swimming pool, a pond, a pizza oven, a firepit, vegetable and flower gardens, and a menagerie that included four donkeys, two goats, two pigs, three dogs, chickens, and a turtle.

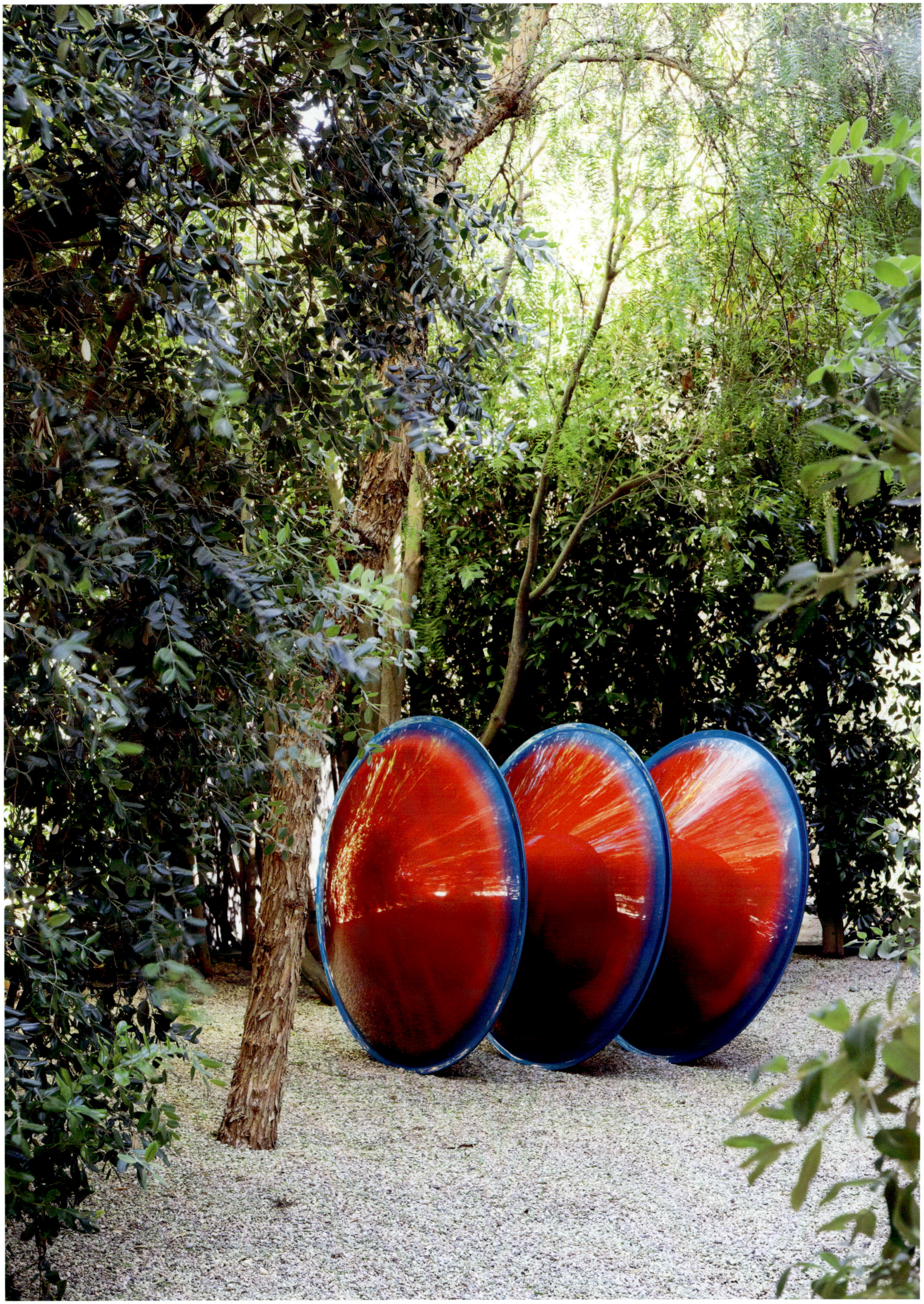

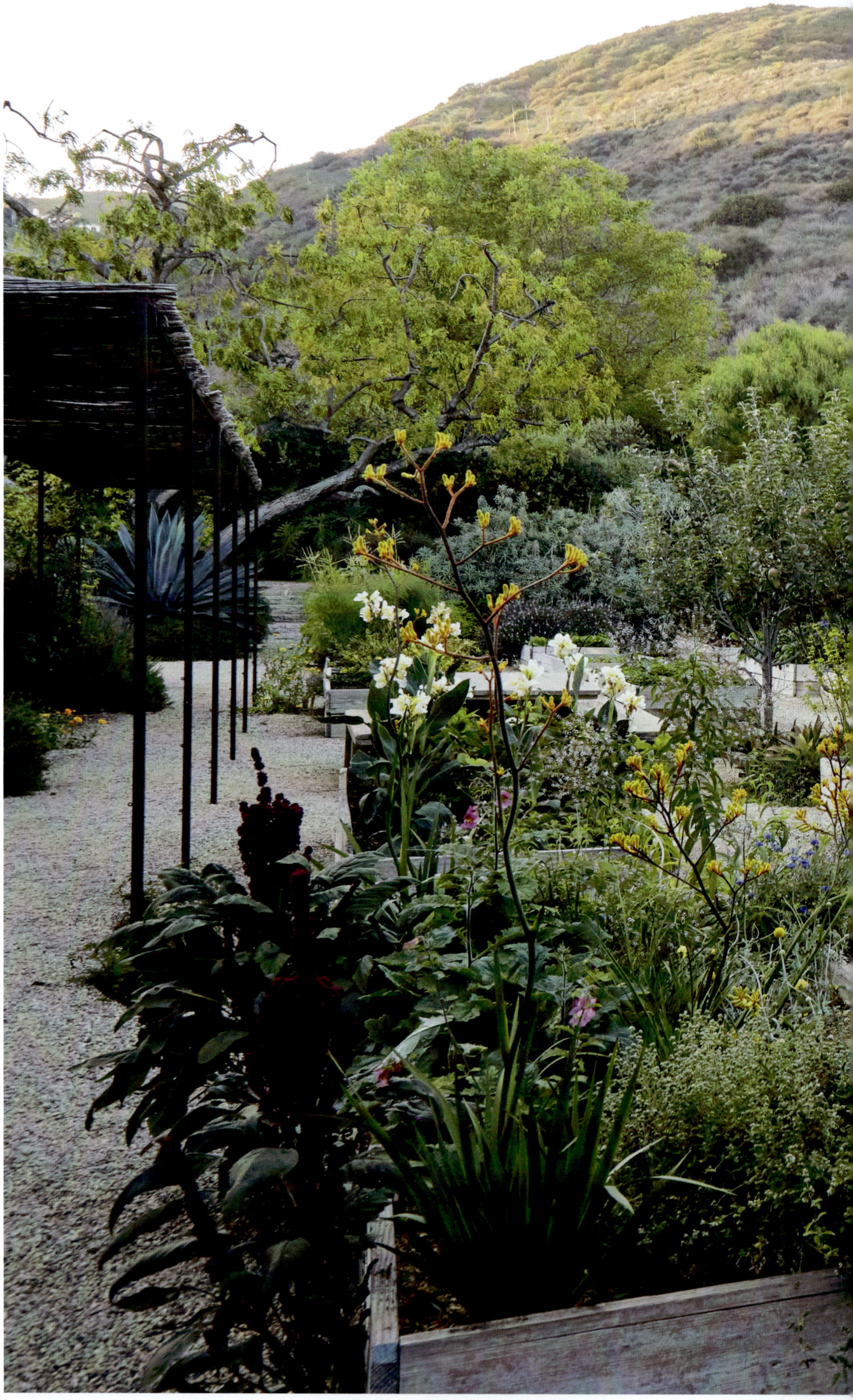

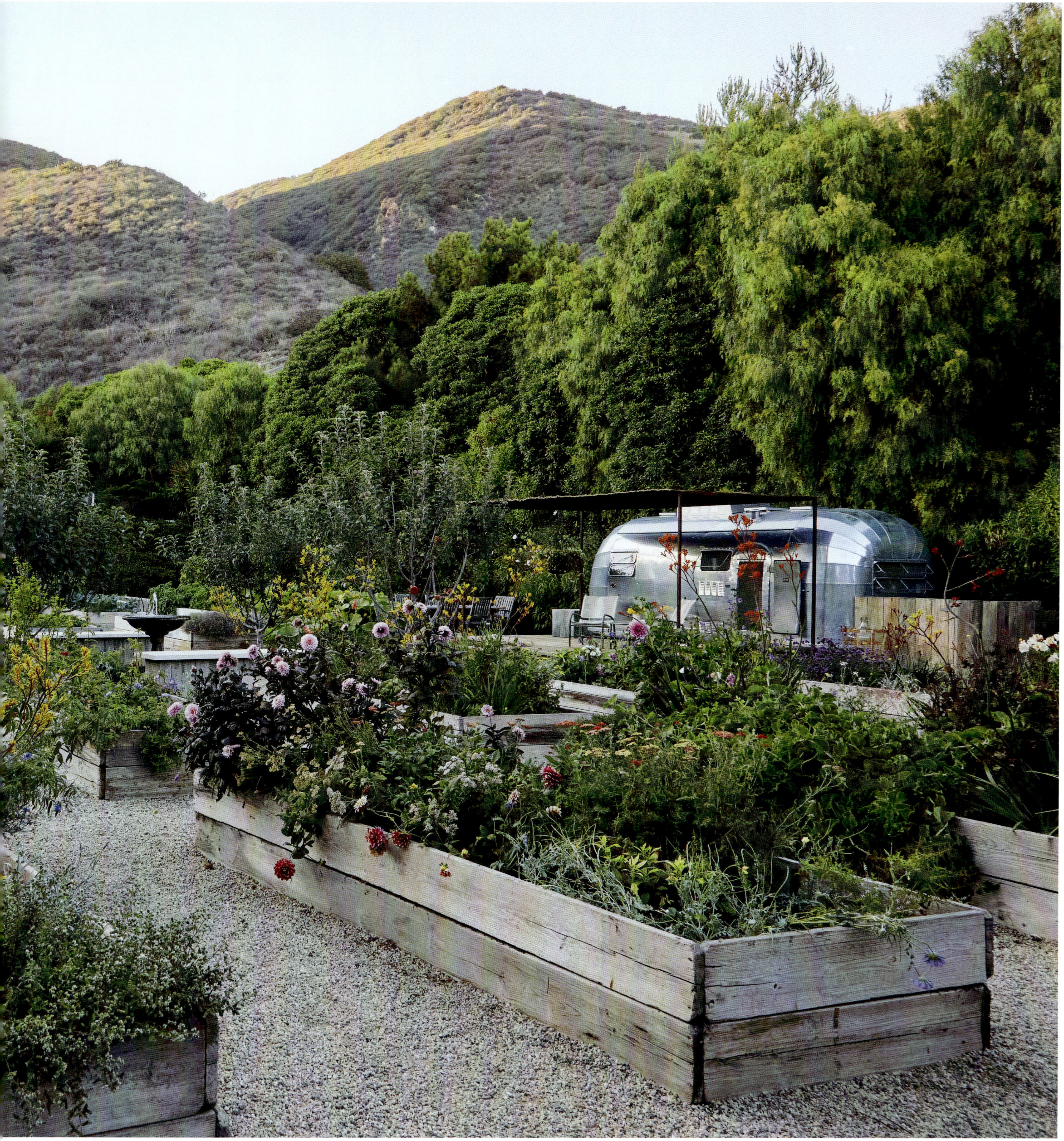

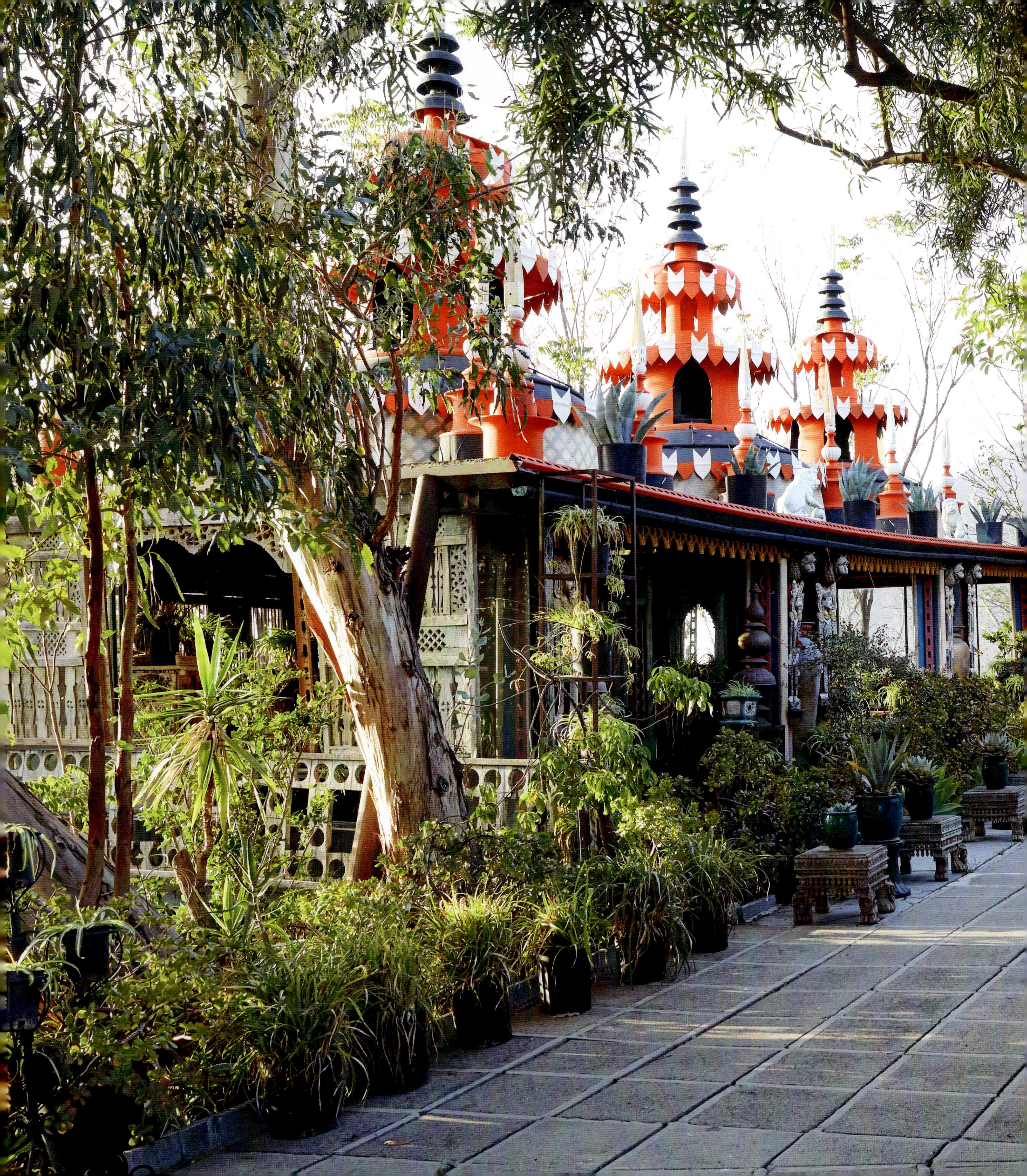

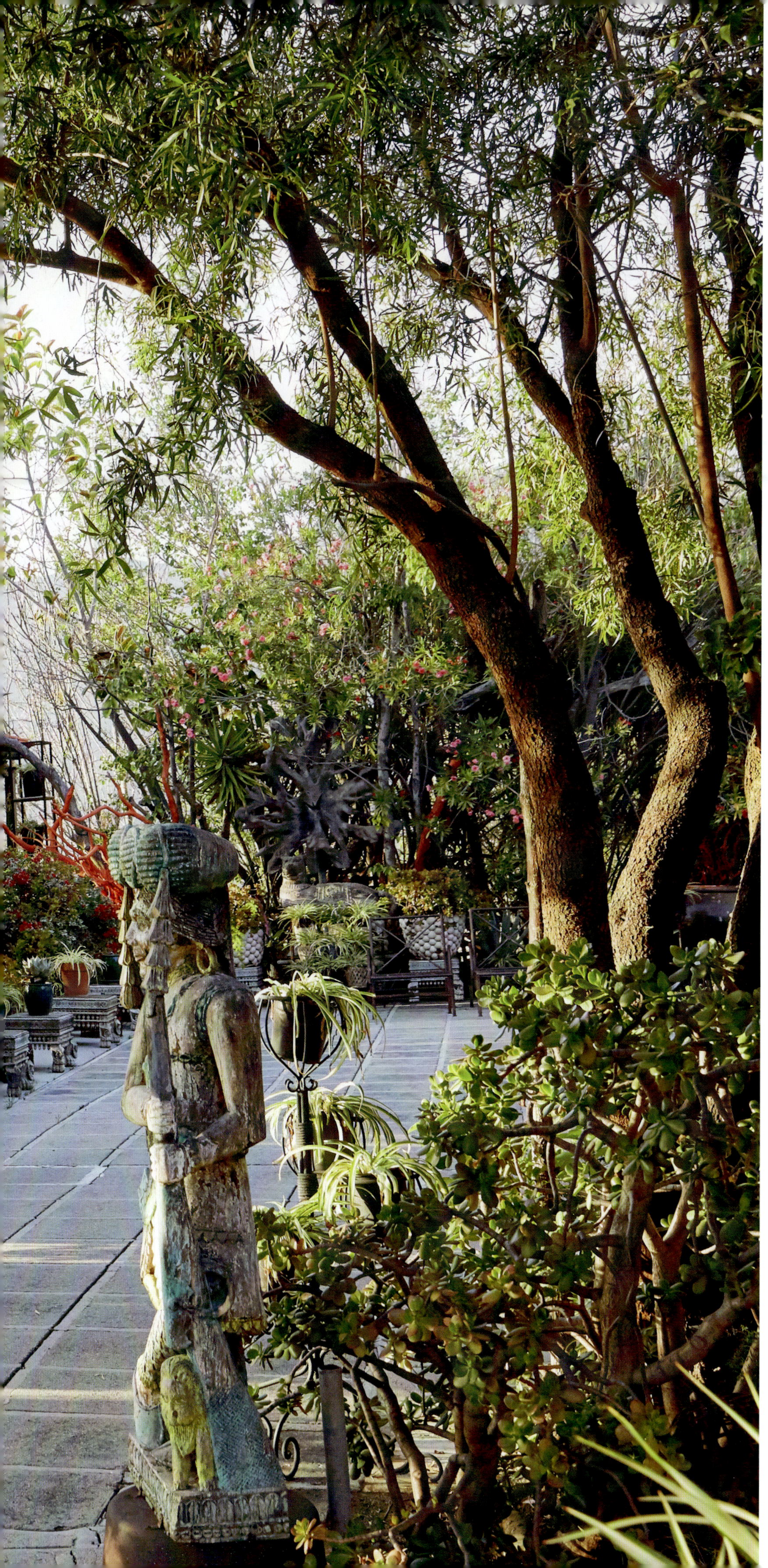

The Guest House

Malibu

Resident

Tony Duquette

Tony Duquette approached everything with unbridled creativity and unmatched flair, from his sets for theater, opera, and film to his legendary parties. He was synonymous with Hollywood glamour; attendees at the surprise reception following his wedding to Elizabeth "Beegle" Duquette—the couple's friends had been invited to a cocktail party—at Mary Pickford's Pickfair included celebrities Gloria Swanson, Fred Astaire, Vincente Minnelli, and Greta Garbo (Pickford was matron of honor).

After a 1988 fire destroyed the Duquette Pavilion in San Francisco, his self-made museum housing his life's work and collections, he resettled in the mountains of Malibu to create a Shangri-la he called Sortilegium. Shortly after Hutton Wilkinson, Duquette's longtime collaborator, and Hutton's wife, Ruth, purchased land abutting Sortilegium, Wilkinson received a $5,000 bill from a bulldozer company for a road Duquette had cut between the properties. "I called Tony and said, 'What the hell!' He said, 'I thought it would be nice to have a more direct route when I come over for lunch.'"

Disaster struck again when Sortilegium burned in the Green Meadow fires of 1993. As an act of deep generosity, the Wilkinsons offered Duquette and Beegle their guest house. And naturally Duquette set to work transforming it. "I said to him, 'Do anything you want to the inside of the house, but don't touch the exterior,'" says Wilkinson. "That was like telling a child not to eat the candy. We soon had gates and platforms and towers and outbuildings…"

Duquette spent every weekend for years at the Guest House, until his death in 1999. By then it was in need of a thorough refresh, and Wilkinson—being no slouch in the flair department himself—redecorated, adding his own theatrical elements.

Hutton and Ruth were the consummate hosts, warning the crew and me that the drive to the property was winding and difficult, and inviting us to stay the night. Having shot so many times in Malibu and preferring the comfort of my own bed, I politely declined. To this day I regret not taking the opportunity to stay in a living work of art.

I had been assigned to photograph Wilkinson's residence, but after touring Duquette's wildly imaginative "temporary" home over the course of the two-day shoot, I ran back and forth between the two, squeezing everything I could from both houses. Although this property was recently sold by the Wilkinsons, they still own and entertain in Duquette's fantastical, maximalist Beverly Hills home, Dawnridge, about which wonderful books have been written.

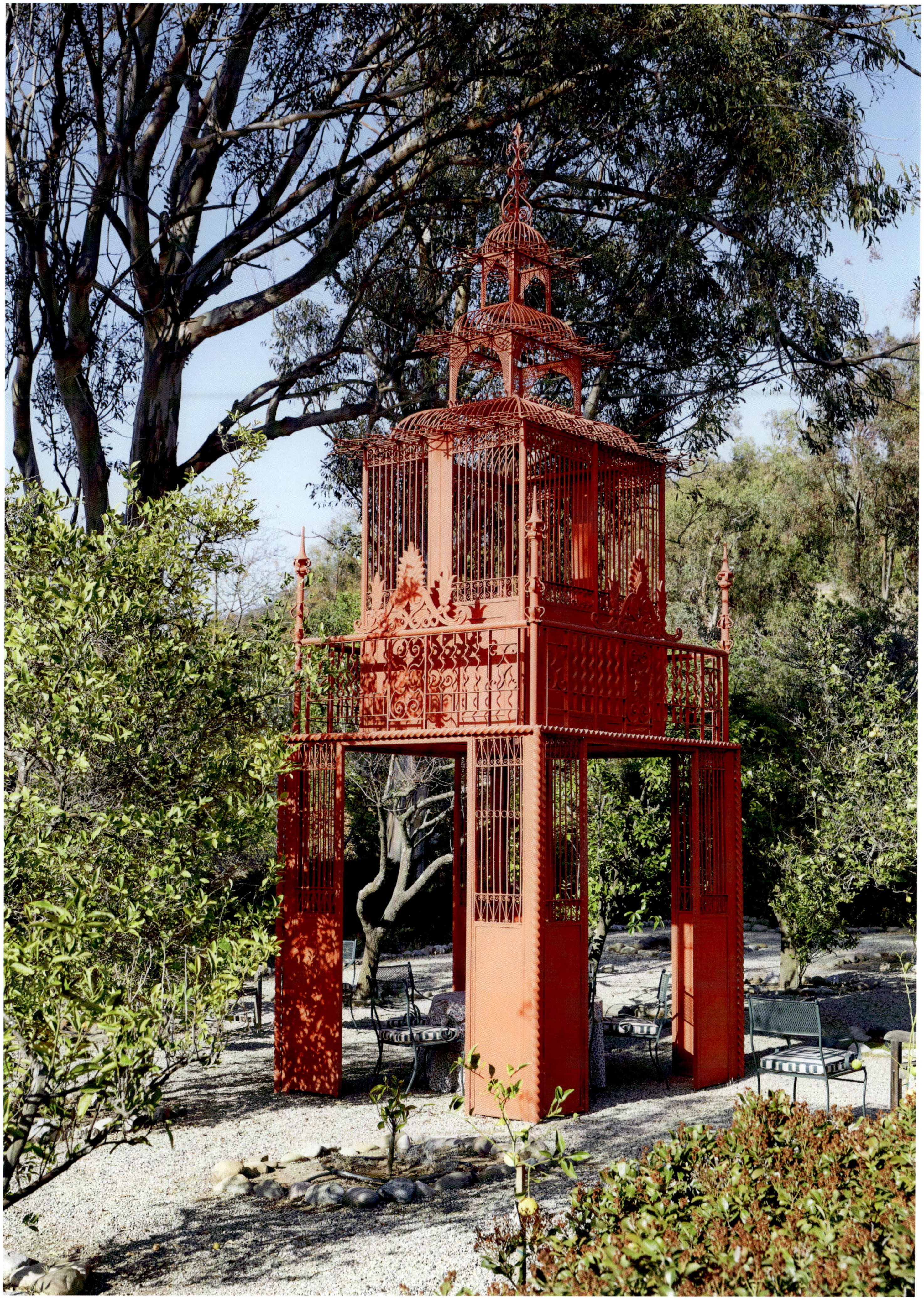

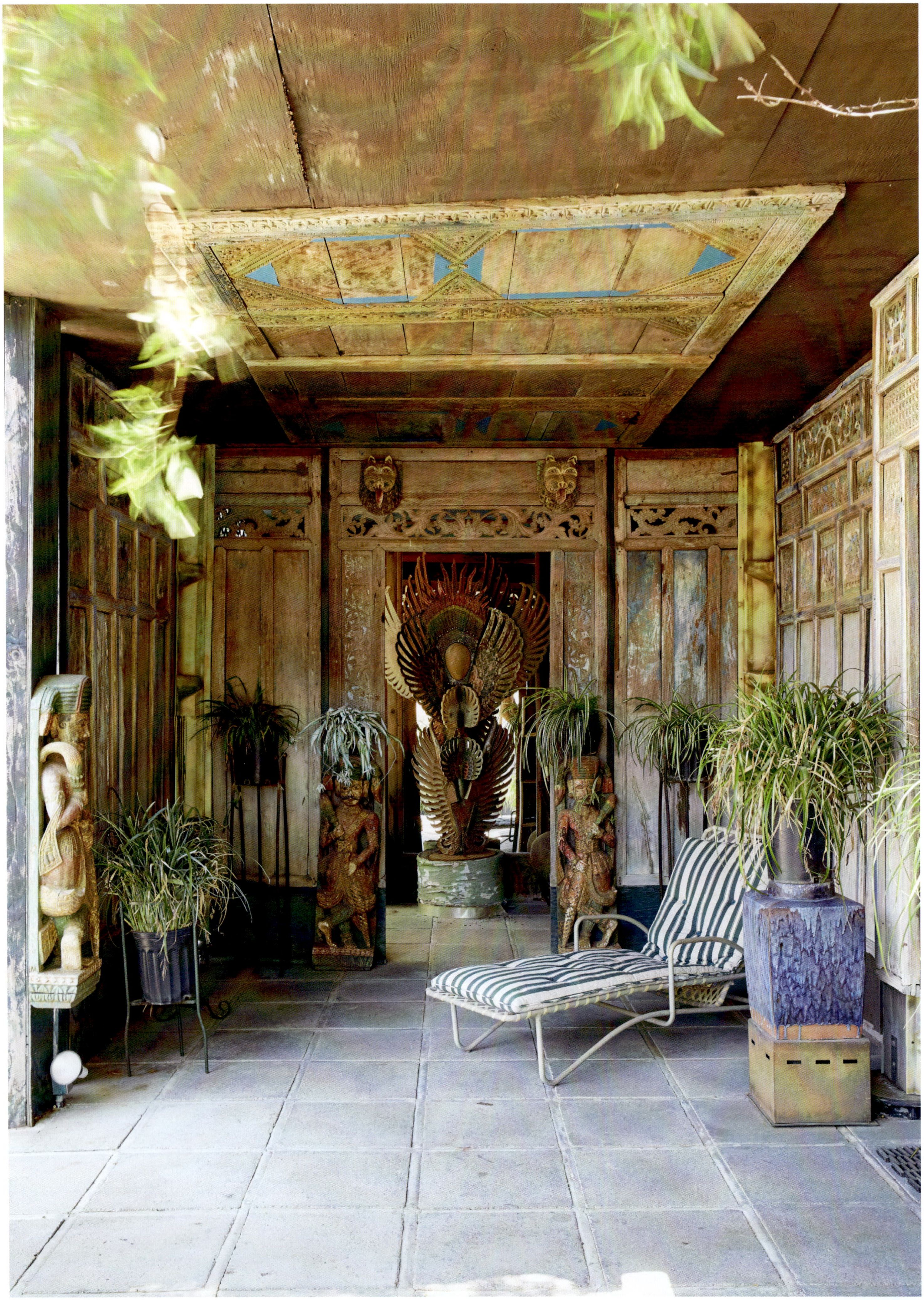

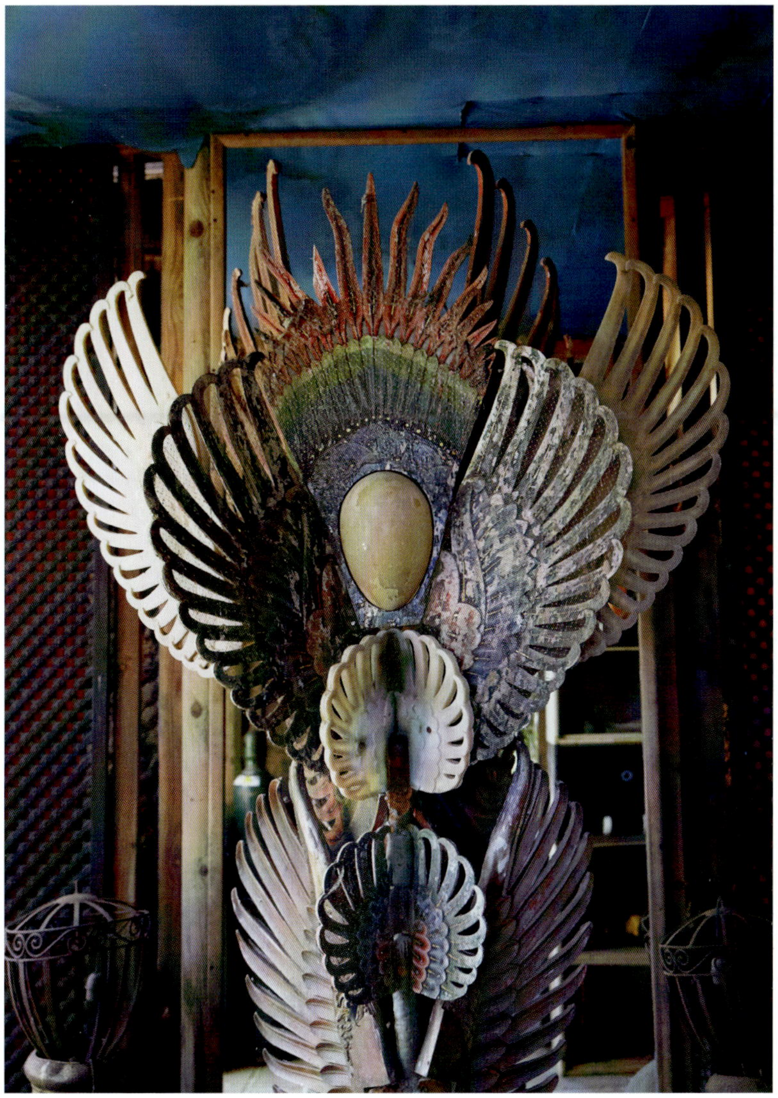

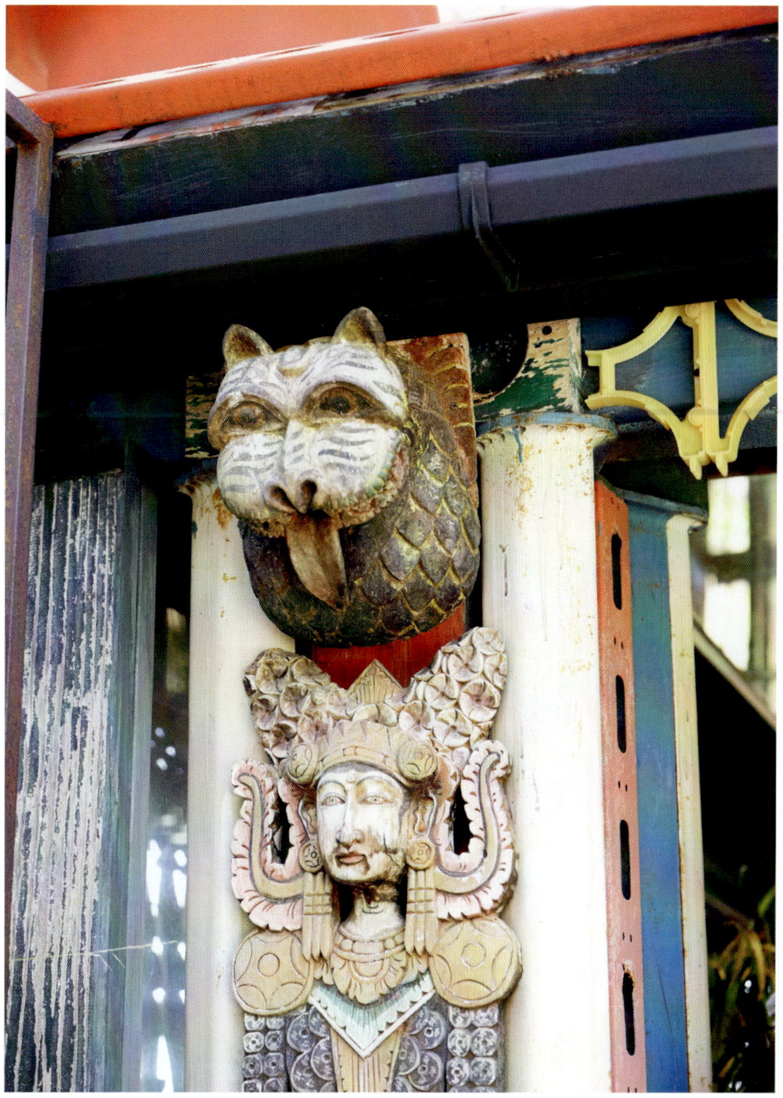

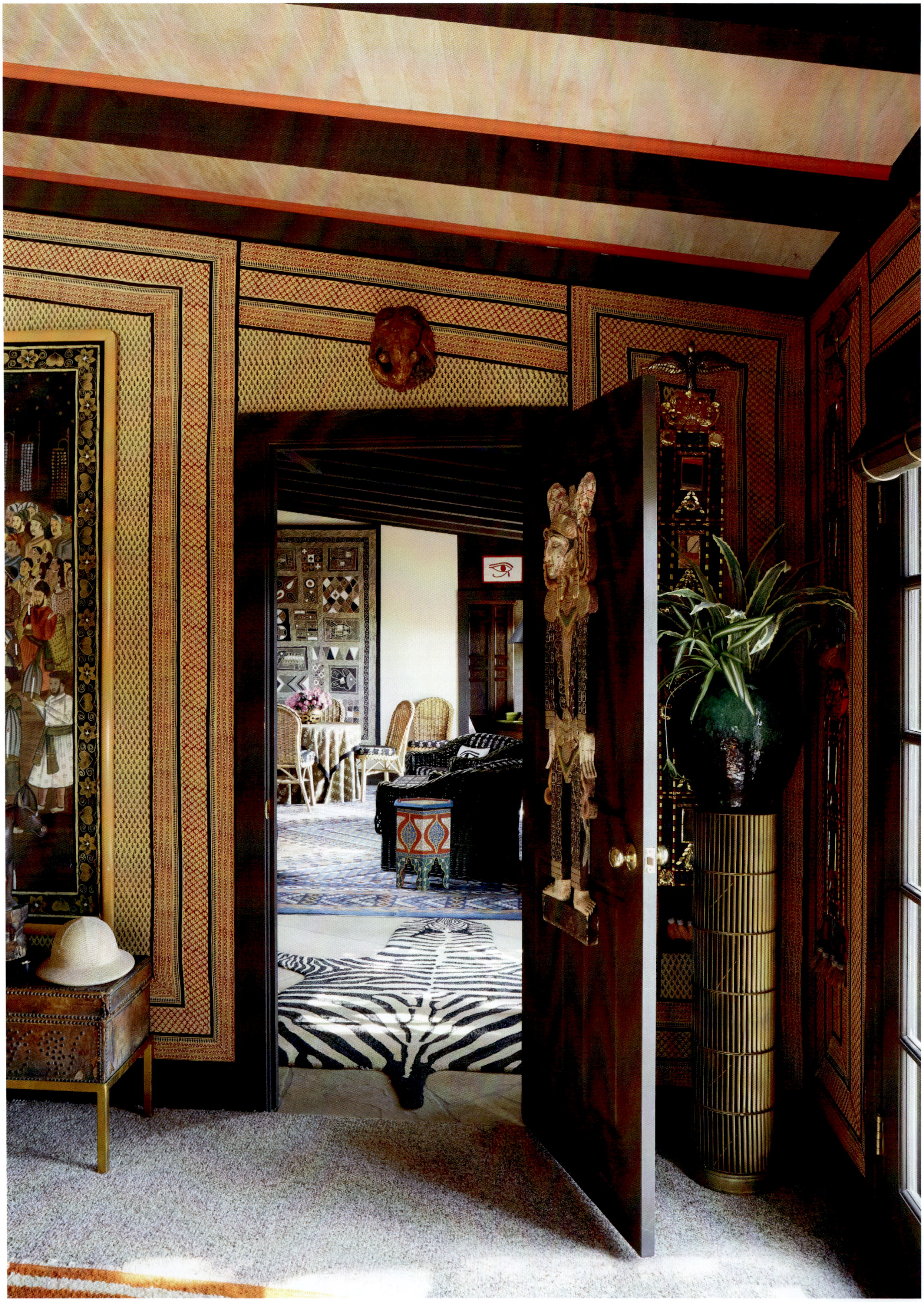

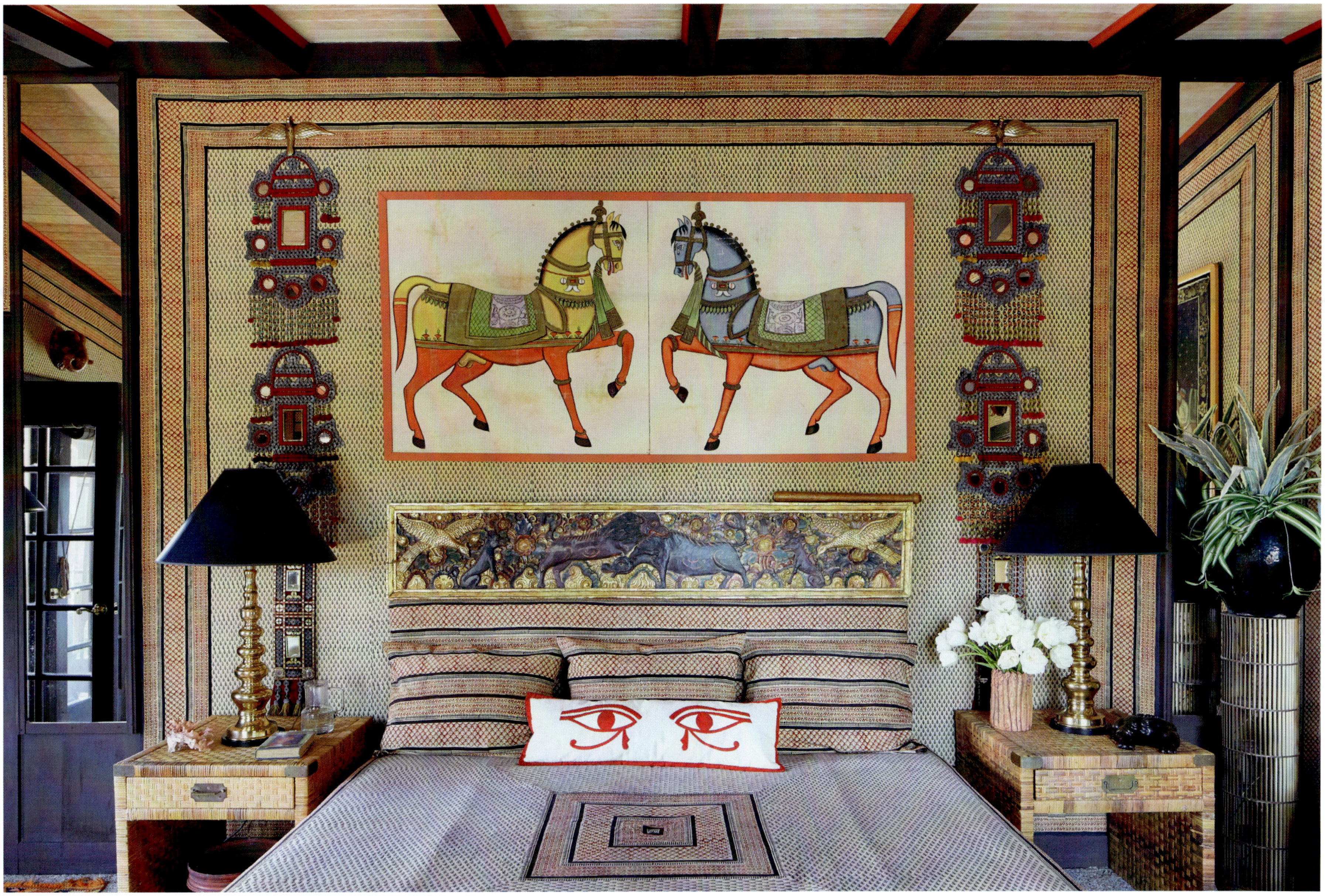

Both Duquette and Wilkinson were obsessed with the iconography of eyes, and the motif appears throughout the house, often in the form of the Egyptian Eye of Horus. The symbol of protection and healing is embroidered onto cushions and emblazoned over doorways.

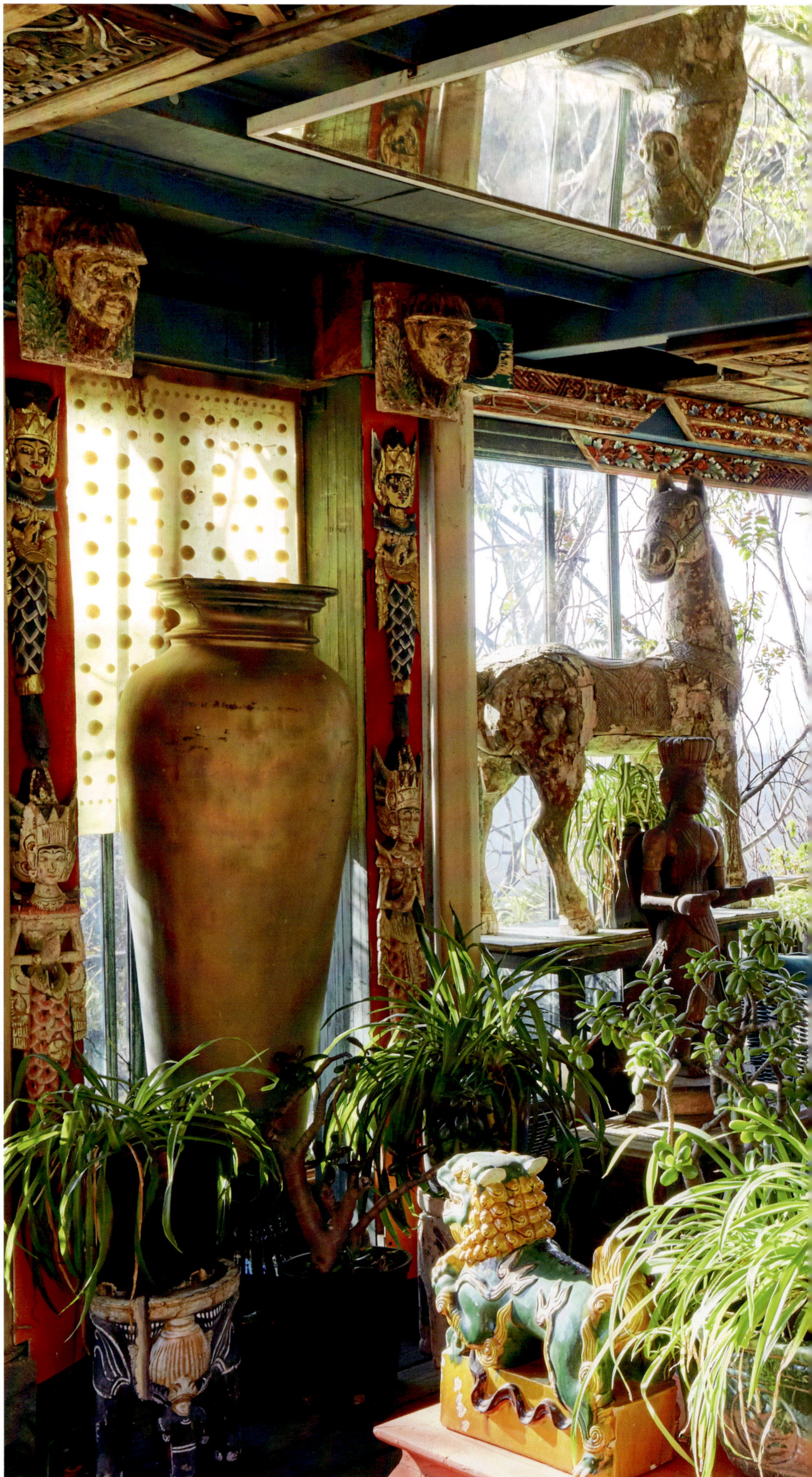

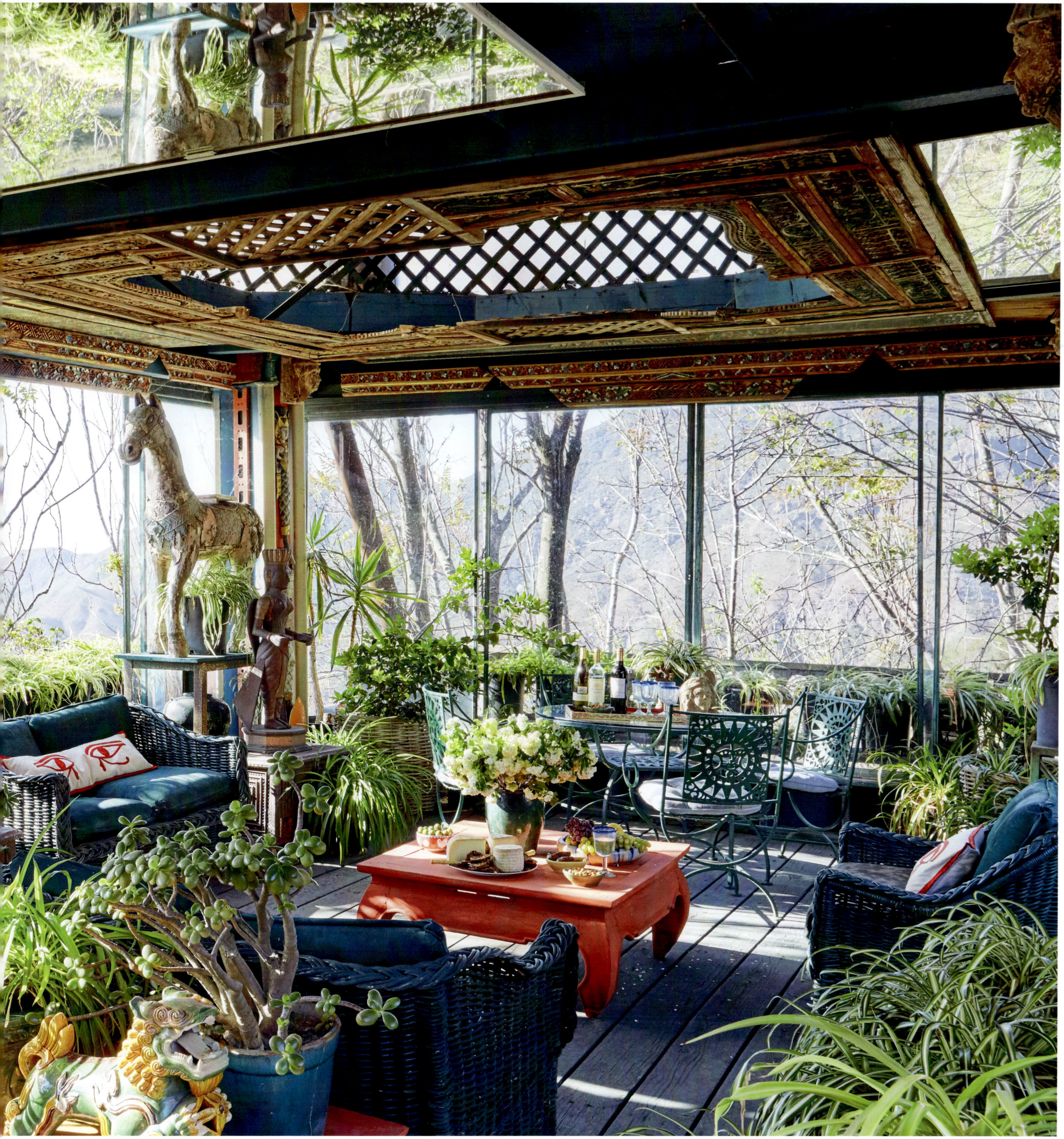

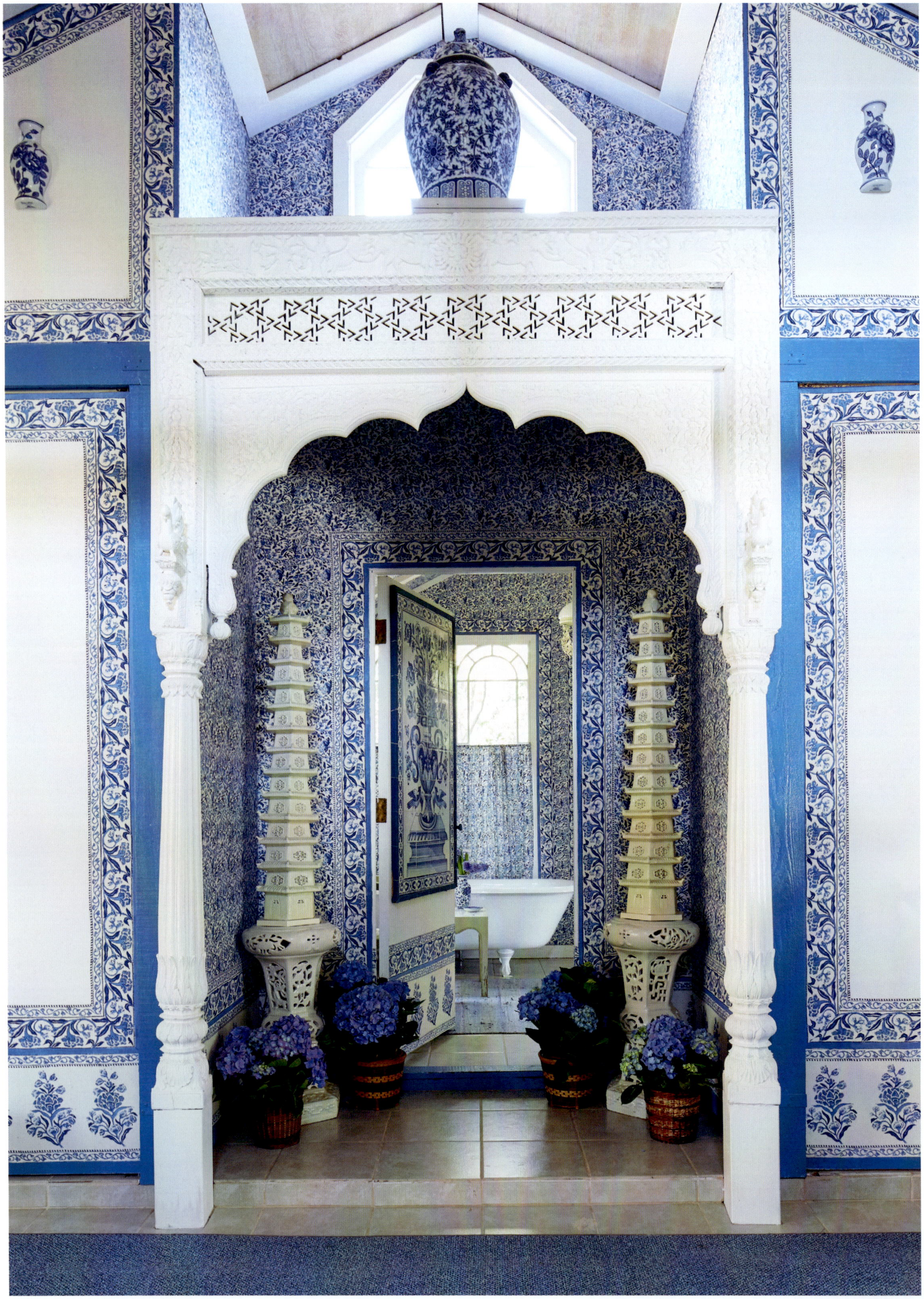

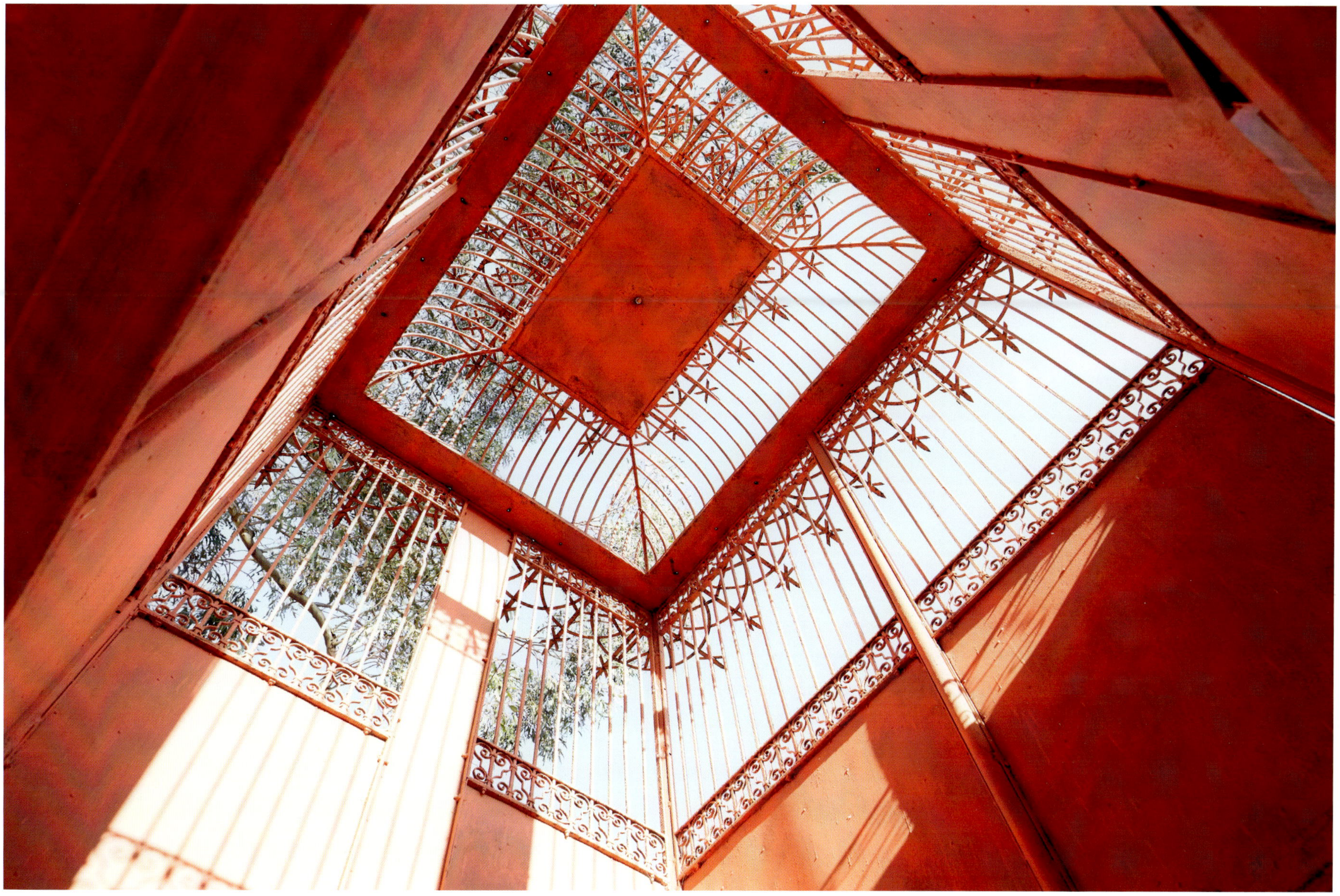

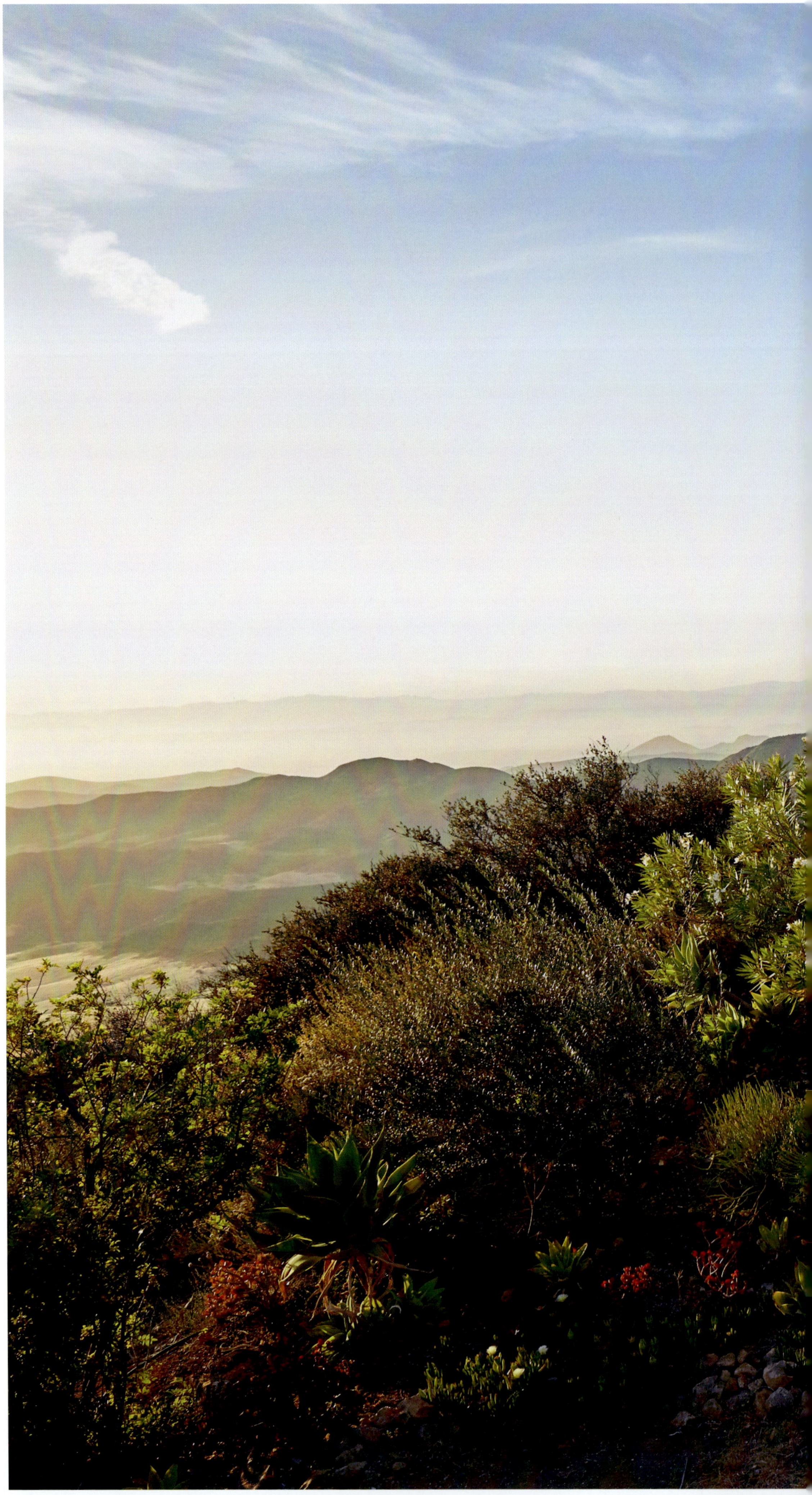

The dome of the gazebo overlooking the Santa Monica Mountains was part of the titular prop of the 1959 black comedy *The Gazebo*, starting Glenn Ford and Debbie Reynolds.

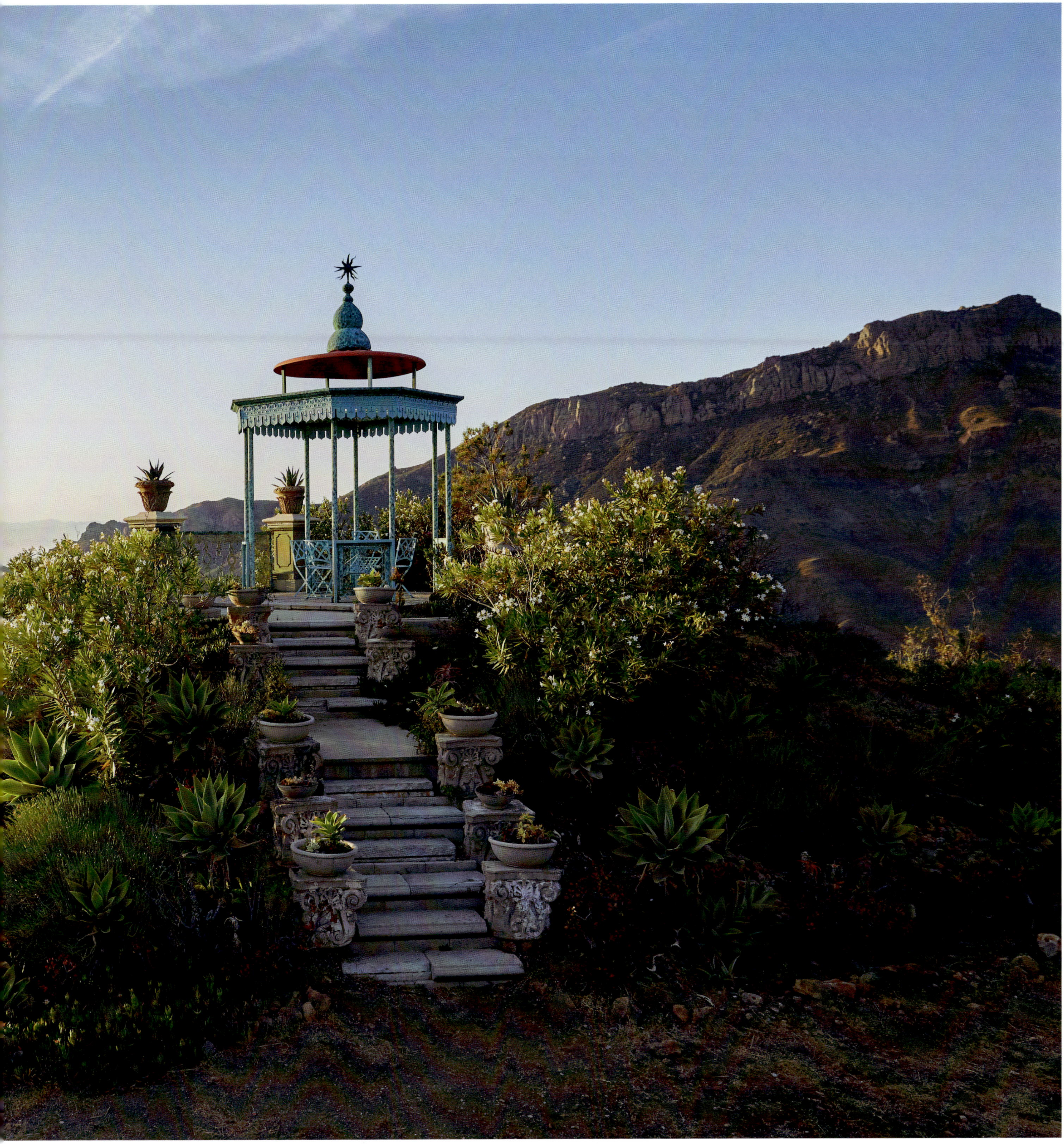

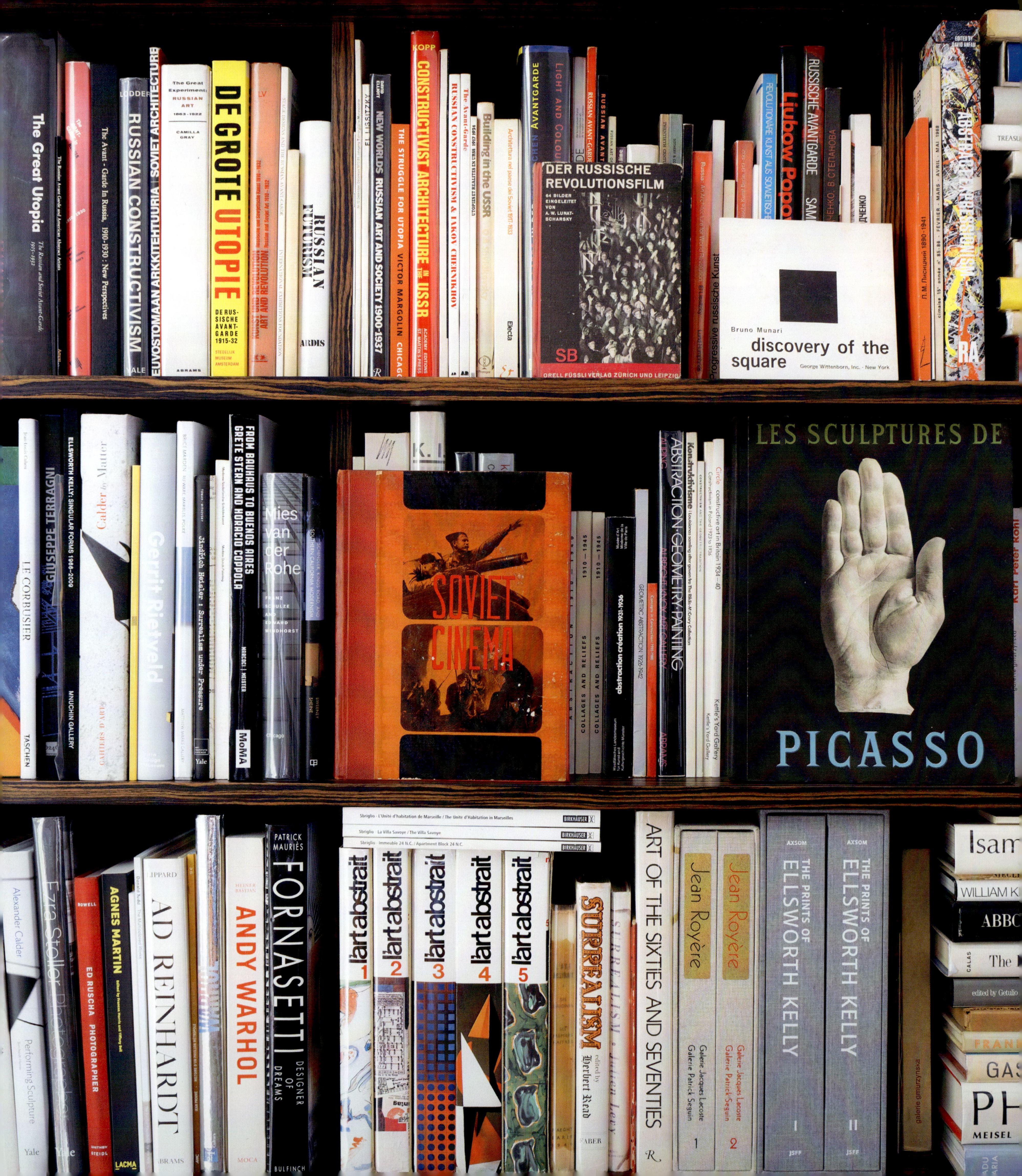
The Great Utopia
RUSSIAN CONSTRUCTIVISM
DE GROTE UTOPIE
RUSSIAN FUTURISM
NEW WORLDS RUSSIAN ART AND SOCIETY 1900-1937
THE STRUGGLE FOR UTOPIA VICTOR MARGOLIN
CONSTRUCTIVIST ARCHITECTURE IN THE USSR
Building in the USSR
AVANTGARDE
DER RUSSISCHE REVOLUTIONSFILM
ORELL FÜSSLI VERLAG ZÜRICH UND LEIPZIG
RUSSISCHE AVANTGARDE
Bruno Munari
discovery of the square
George Wittenborn, Inc. · New York
LE CORBUSIER
GIUSEPPE TERRAGNI
ELLSWORTH KELLY: SINGULAR FORMS 1966–2009
Gerrit Rietveld
FROM BAUHAUS TO BUENOS AIRES GRETE STERN AND HORACIO COPPOLA
Mies van der Rohe
SOVIET CINEMA
LES SCULPTURES DE PICASSO
ABSTRACTION GEOMETRY PAINTING
Ezra Stoller Photographer
ED RUSCHA PHOTOGRAPHER
AGNES MARTIN
AD REINHARDT
ANDY WARHOL
FORNASETTI DESIGNER OF DREAMS
l'art abstrait 1
l'art abstrait 2
l'art abstrait 3
l'art abstrait 4
l'art abstrait 5
SURREALISM
ART OF THE SIXTIES AND SEVENTIES
Jean Royère 1
Jean Royère 2
THE PRINTS OF ELLSWORTH KELLY I
THE PRINTS OF ELLSWORTH KELLY II

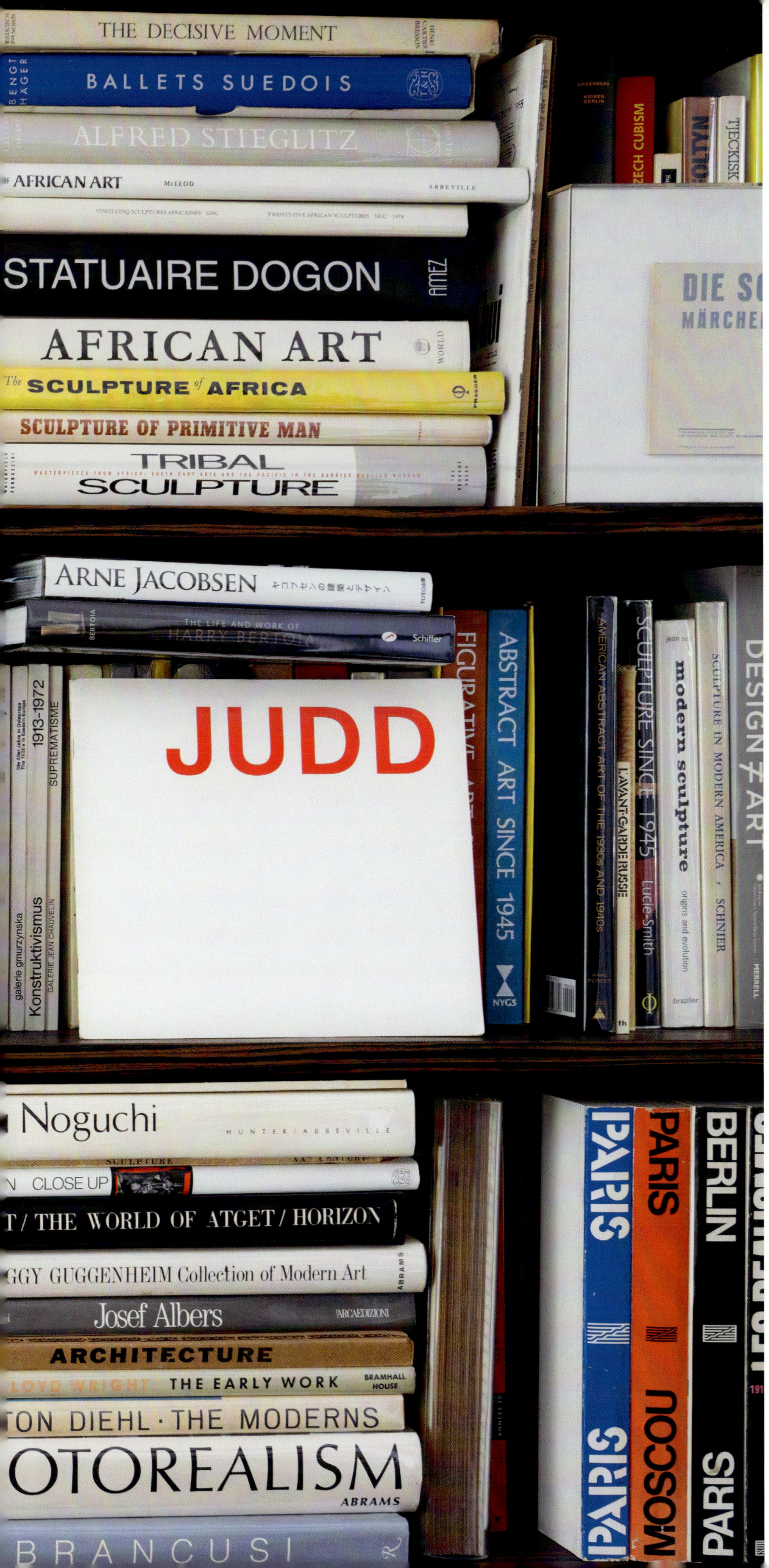

The Strick House

Santa Monica

Architect

Oscar Niemeyer

Residents

Michael and Gabrielle Boyd

Given an inch, every time I'll take a mile. I had been called to this house in Santa Monica to document an exceptional library, but homeowner Michael Boyd must have sensed my desperation and agreed to let me shoot more. He and Gabrielle Boyd were, after all, living in the only residence in North America by the legendary Brazilian architect Oscar Niemeyer.

Niemeyer designed the Strick House in 1963 for filmmaker Joseph Strick and his wife, Anne. The couple commissioned Niemeyer after seeing the architect's buildings in Brasília, the capital of Brazil. But because the architect was unable to enter the United States due to his vocal support of communism and Castro, the entire process was conducted by mail. The Stricks separated before the house was completed, but Anne lived there until it was time to sell nearly forty years later. In 2003, when developers who had bought the property applied for a demolition permit, the Landmarks Commission and preservationists intervened, and within a month the Boyds had stepped in.

In some circles, the Boyds need no introduction: they are celebrated collectors of twentieth-century design and prolific restorers of modern masterpieces, among them landmarked houses by Richard Neutra, John Lautner, and Craig Ellwood (including the Steinman House on pages 282–91). The house couldn't have fallen into better hands. In collaboration with Niemeyer's office in Brazil, they set about restoring the building with a deep sensitivity to the architect's original intent. They also relandscaped the property, which had been stripped by the developer, with a mother lode of tropical plants the Boyds had discovered in the back of an old auto repair shop in Altadena.

Pieces from Michael and Gabrielle Boyd's collections have appeared in many museum exhibitions over the years, and they have produced their own furniture and carpet designs as well. The Boyds truly live and breathe design, and the Strick House was bursting with their exquisitely curated collection of art, objects, furniture, and books. The only significant change the Boyds made to the house was converting the existing garage into the library, and what an Aladdin's cave it was. The bookcases were loaded with thousands of volumes, and around them were arranged vintage guitars, amps, motorbike helmets, rare furniture, sculptures, and a door by Charlotte Perriand (provenance: the Les Arcs ski resort in Savoie, France) that led to even more treasures.

The day of this shoot we were experiencing May Gray, a weather pattern feared by L.A. photographers (see also June Gloom). A fog settles in and then burns off in the afternoon, creating uneven light across the pictures taken over the course of the day. Luckily for us, this time the fog remained and we had consistent light and a break from the ever-present blue sky. Which reminds me of a time my mum visited from gray northern England and remarked disapprovingly on a beautiful Southern California day, "Ooh, it's pouring down with sun!"

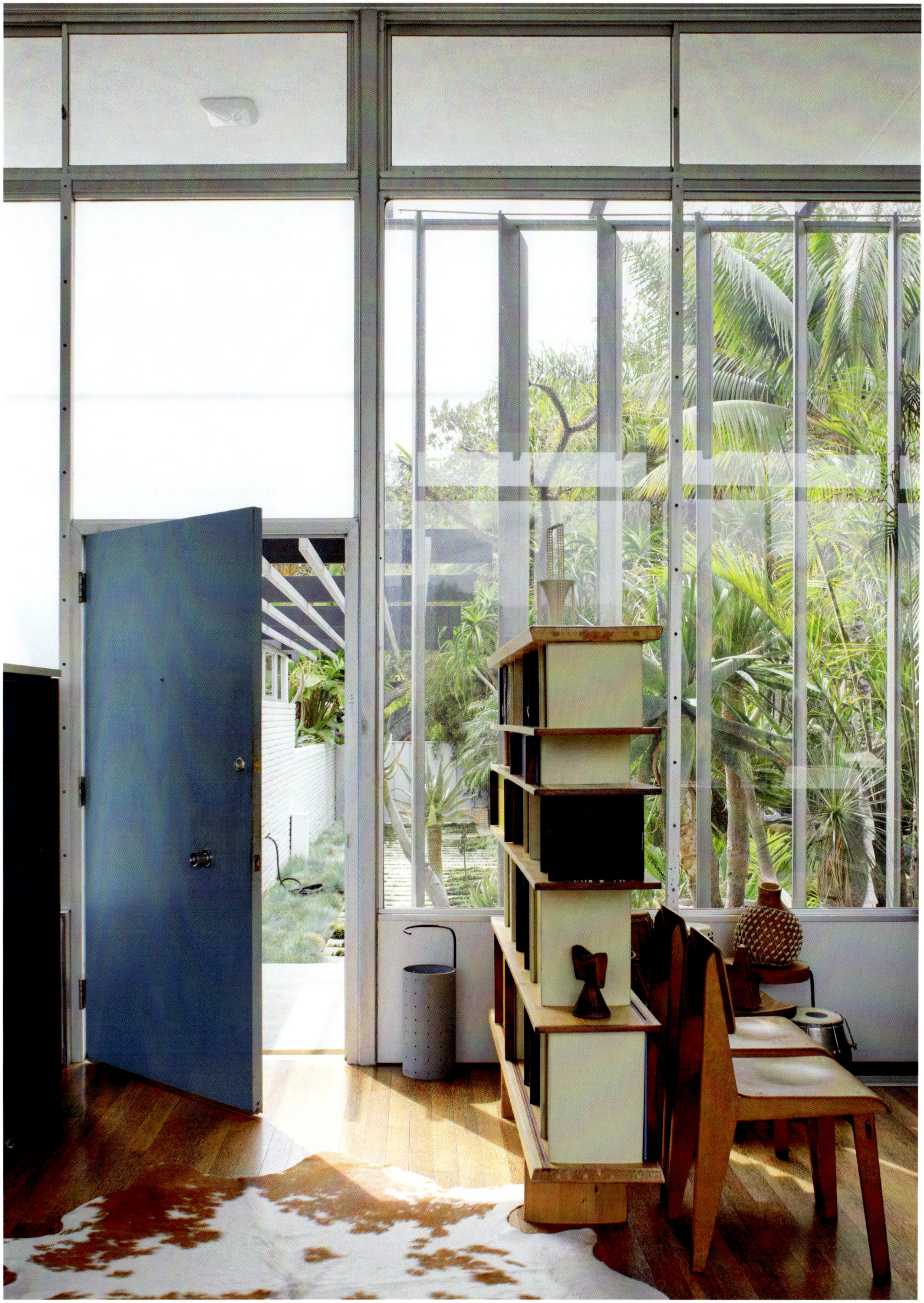

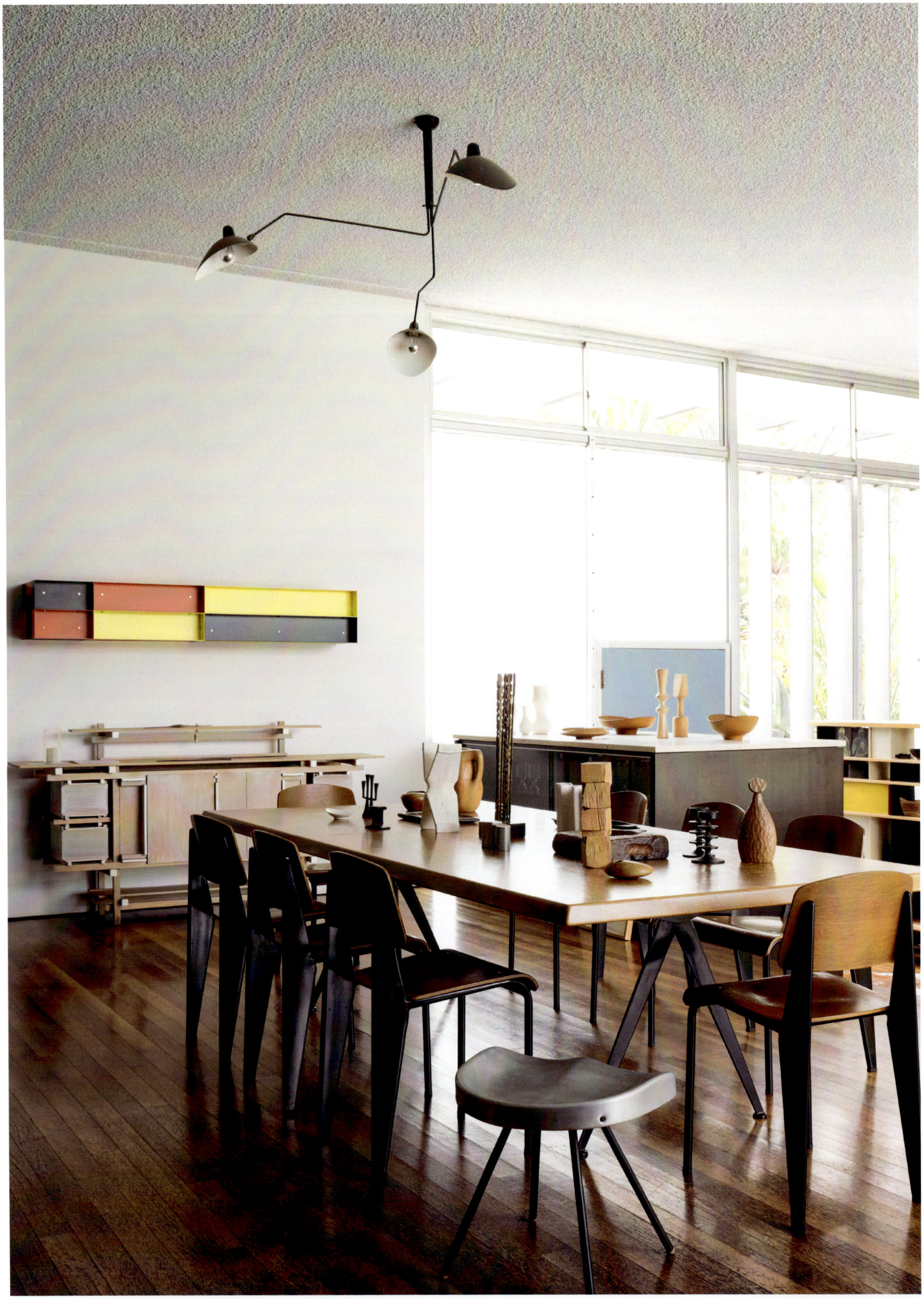

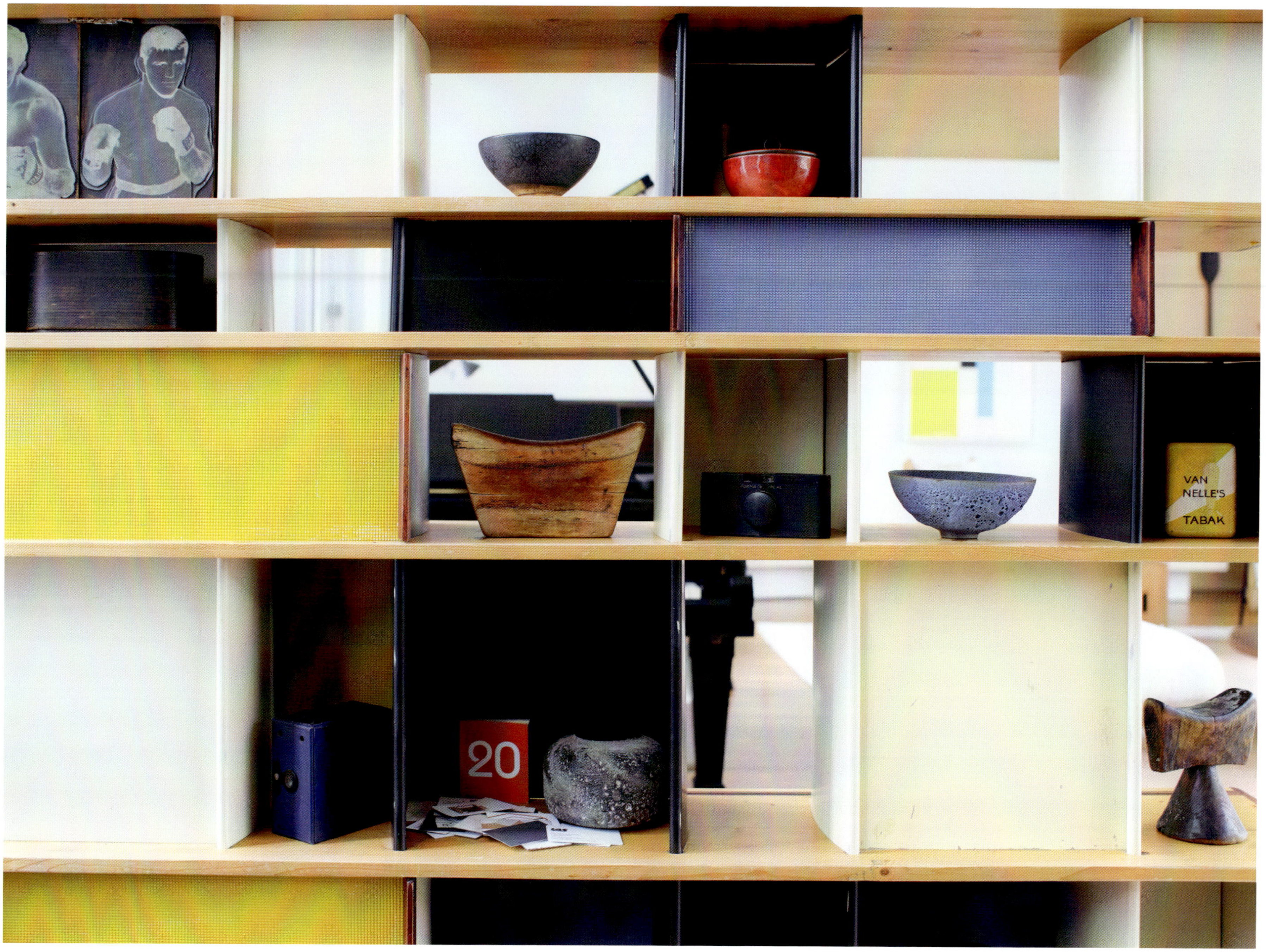

Michael Boyd consults on collecting art and design and restoring modernist architecture, so his home is, predictably, a treasure trove of incredible objects, among them a Charlotte Perriand shelving unit that separates the front entrance from the dining room, Jean Prouvé table and chairs, and a buffet designed by Gerrit Rietveld surmounted by a work by Donald Judd in the dining room.

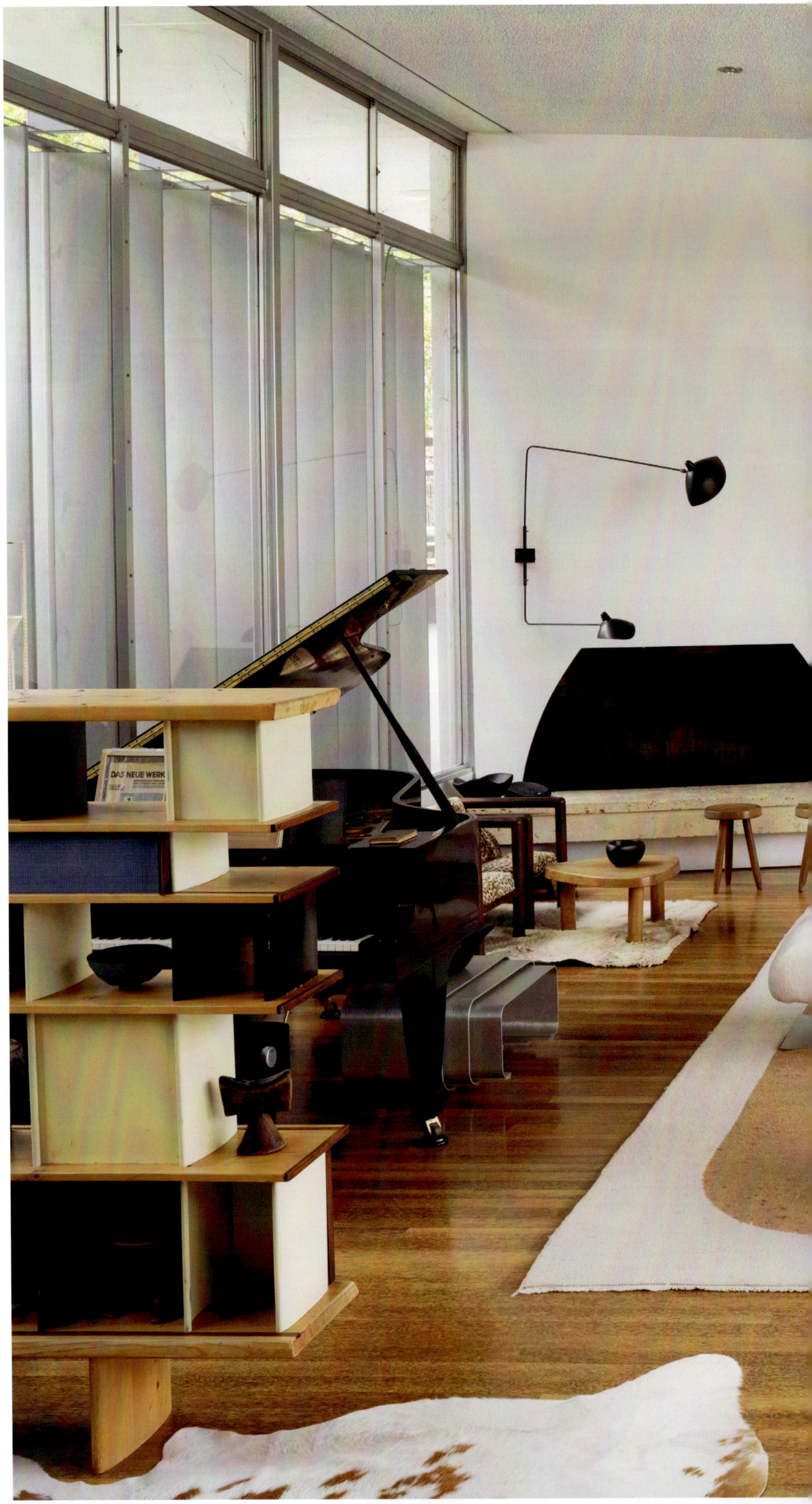
DAS NEUE WERK

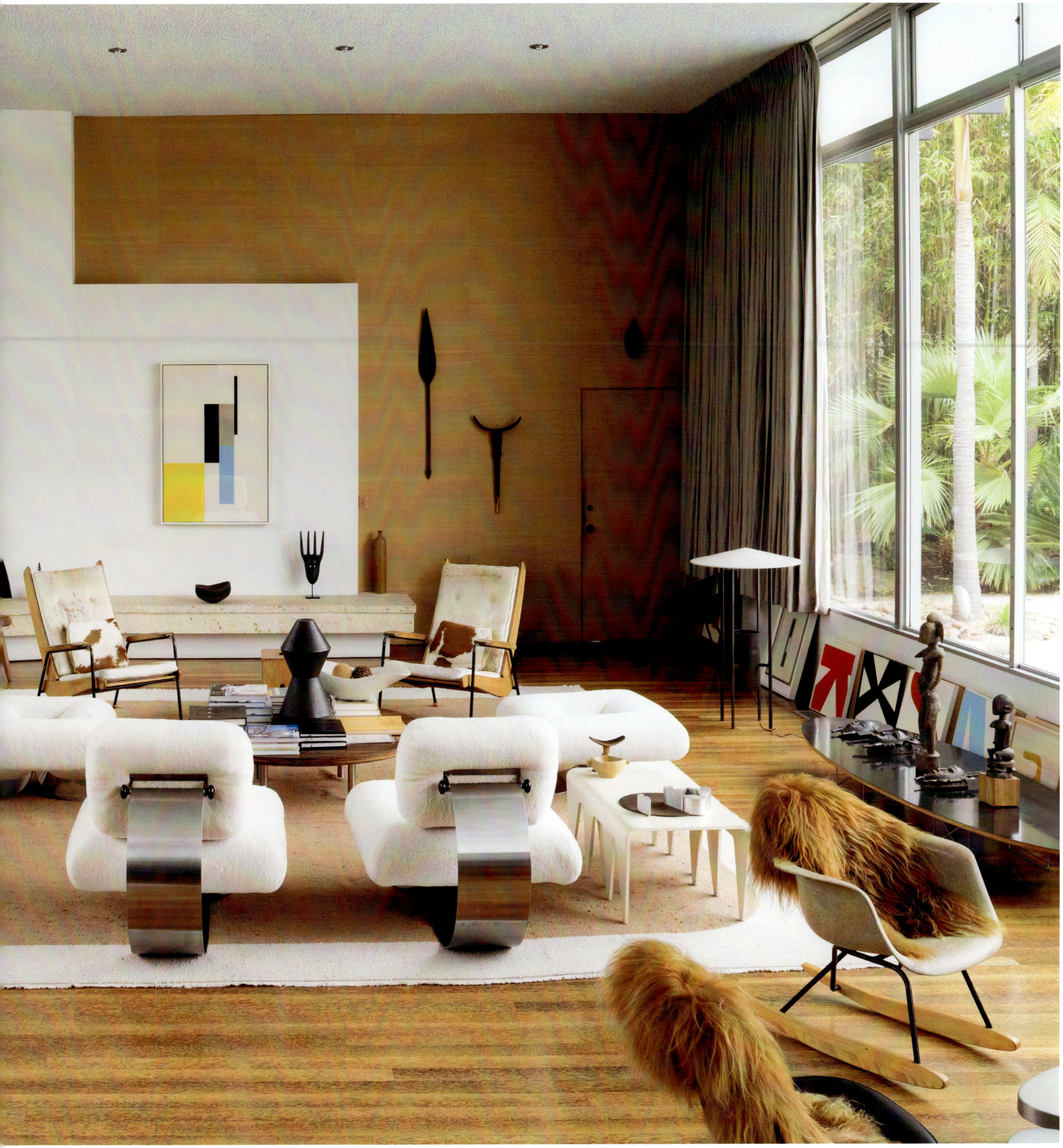

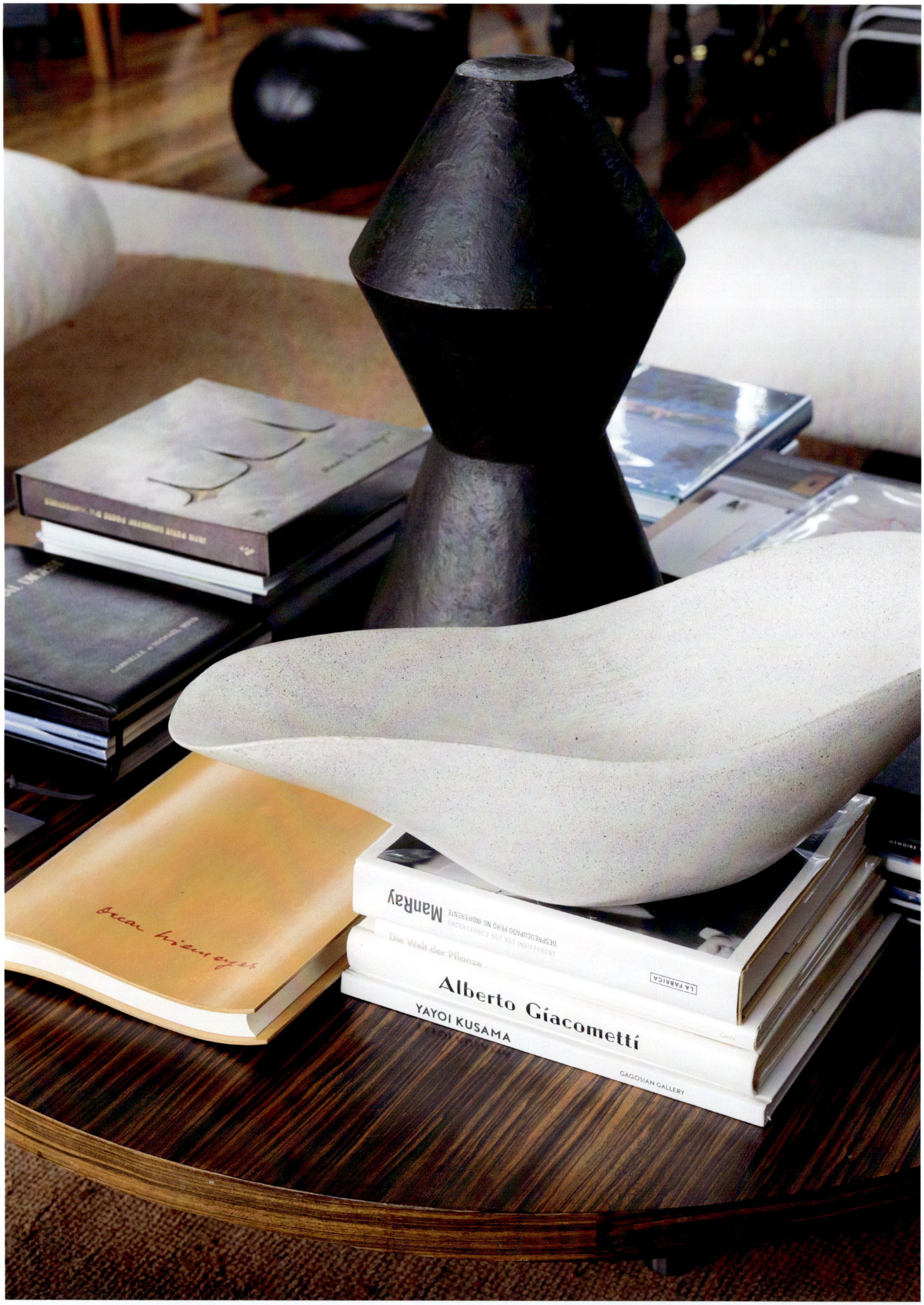
ManRay
DESPREOCUPADO PERO NO INDIFERENTE
UNCONCERNED BUT NOT INDIFFERENT
LA FABRICA
Die Welt der Pflanze
Alberto Giacometti
YAYOI KUSAMA
GAGOSIAN GALLERY

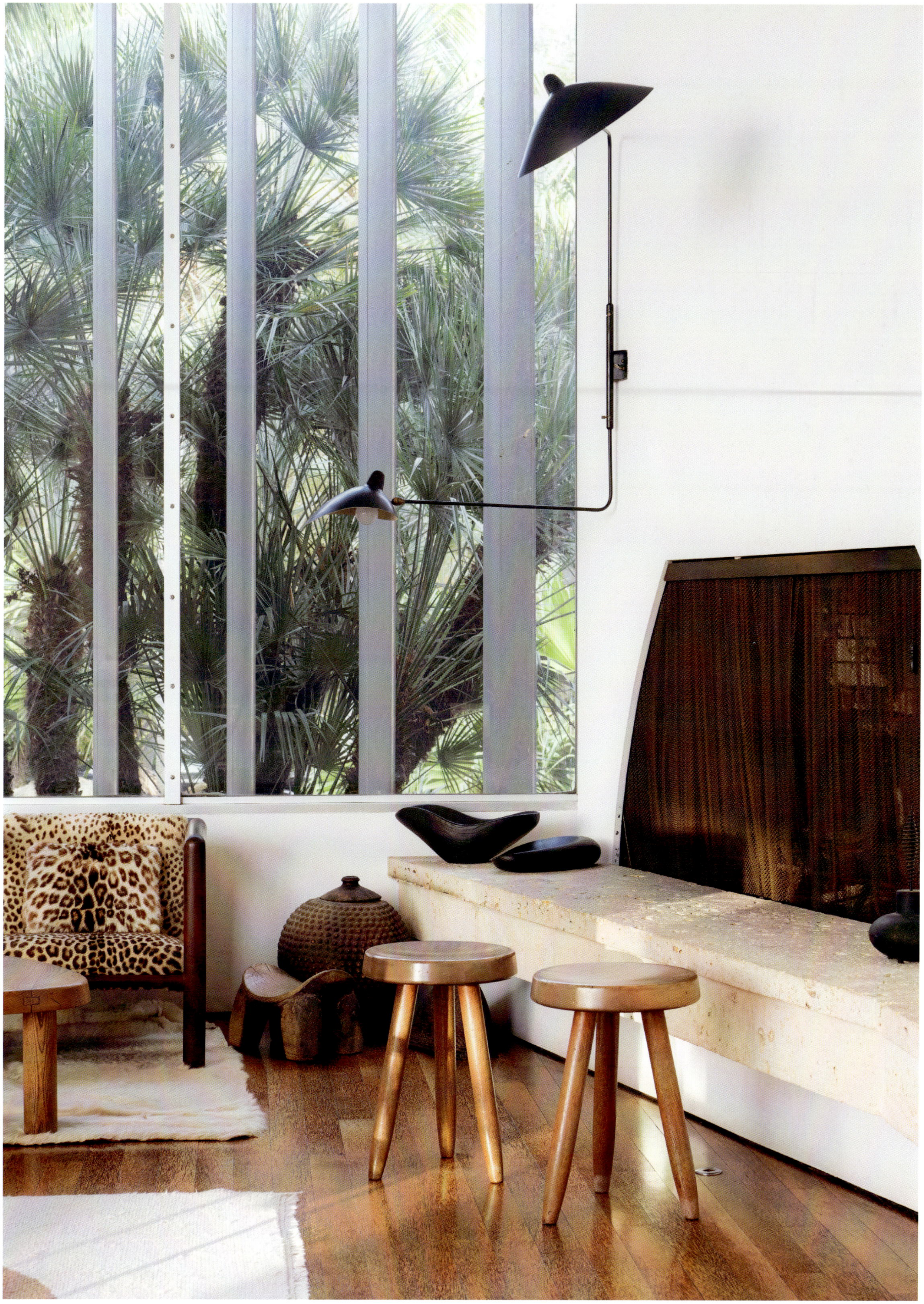

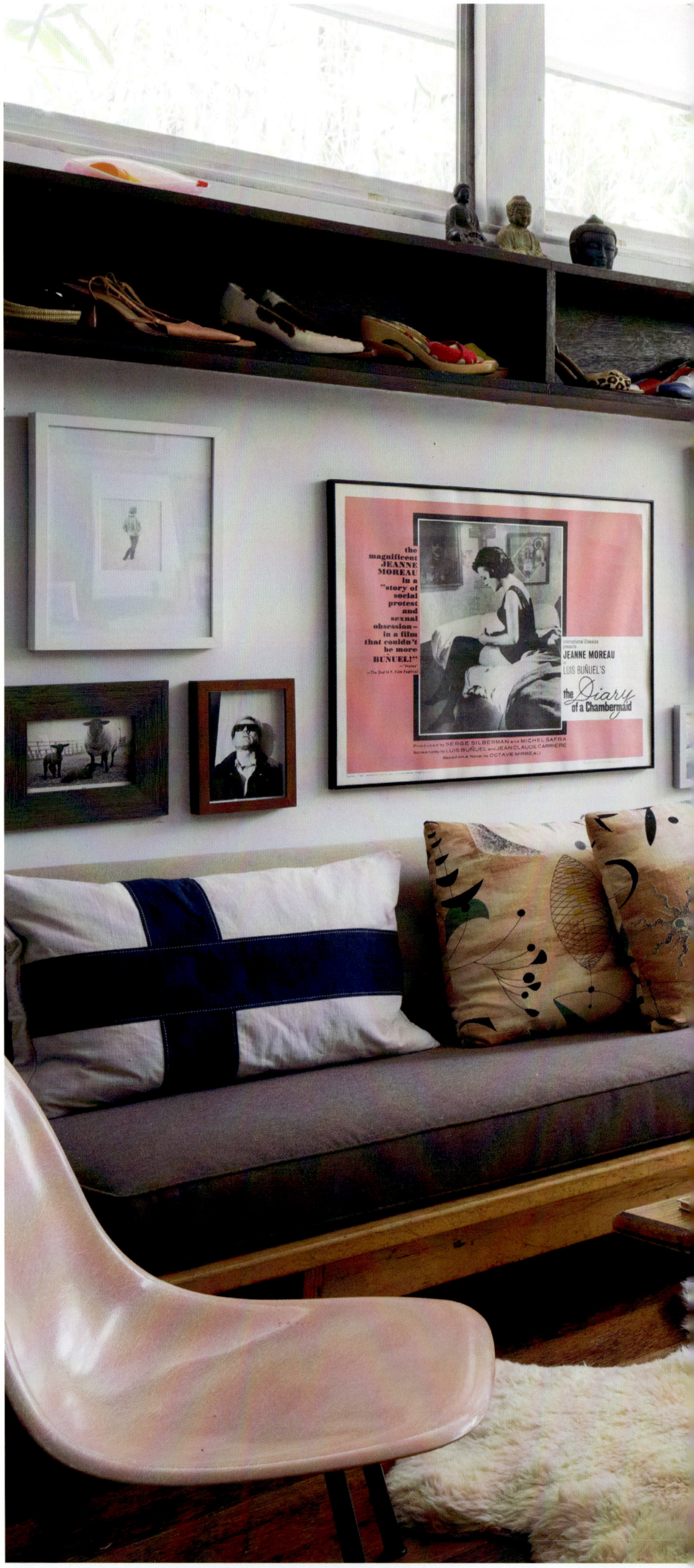

the magnificent JEANNE MOREAU in a "story of social protest and sexual obsession – in a film that couldn't be more BUÑUEL!"
International Classics presents
JEANNE MOREAU
LUIS BUÑUEL'S
the Diary of a Chambermaid
Produced by SERGE SILBERMAN and MICHEL SAFRA
Screenplay by LUIS BUÑUEL and JEAN CLAUDE CARRIERE
Based on a Novel by OCTAVE MIRBEAU

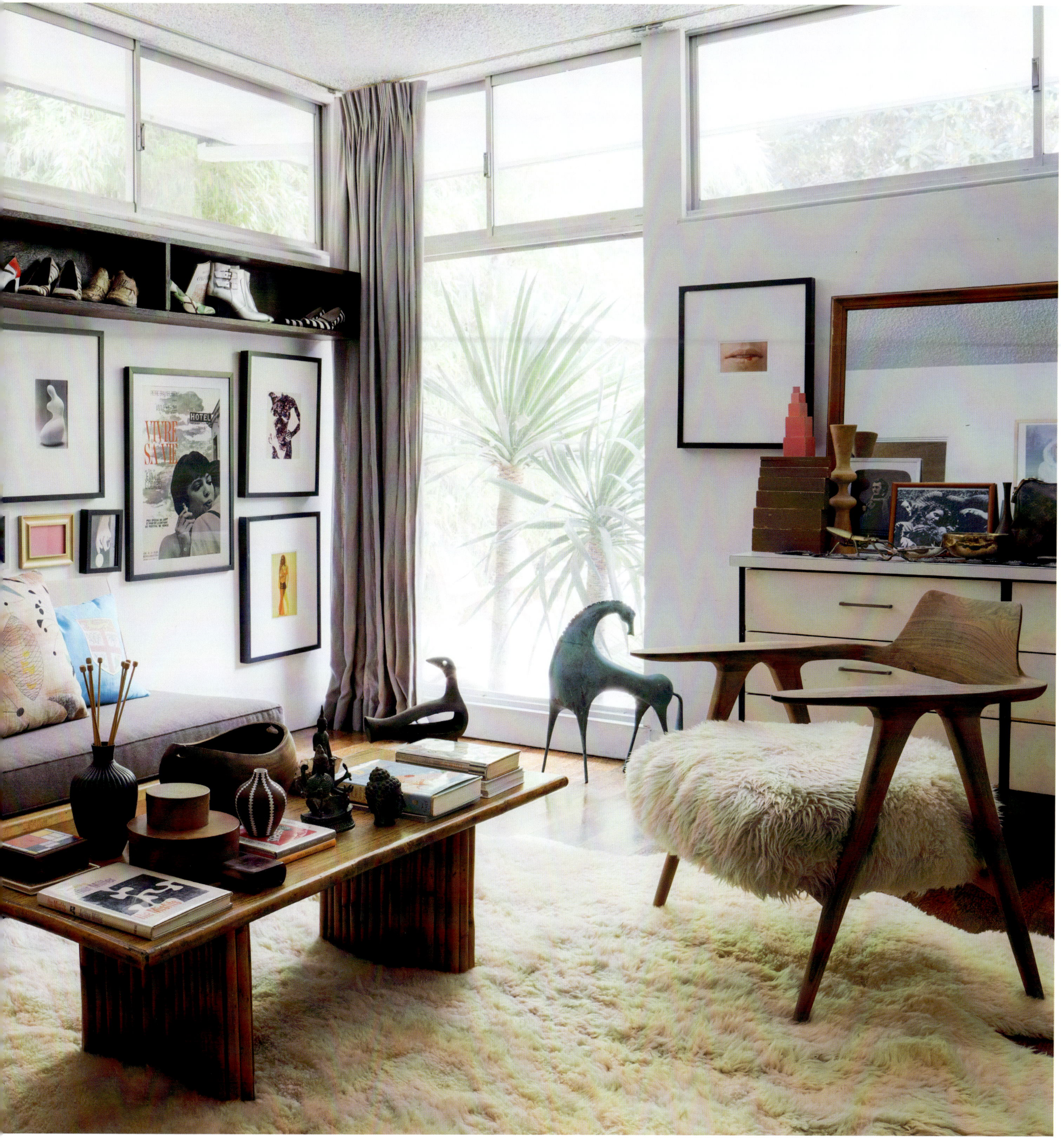
HOTEL
VIVRE SA VIE

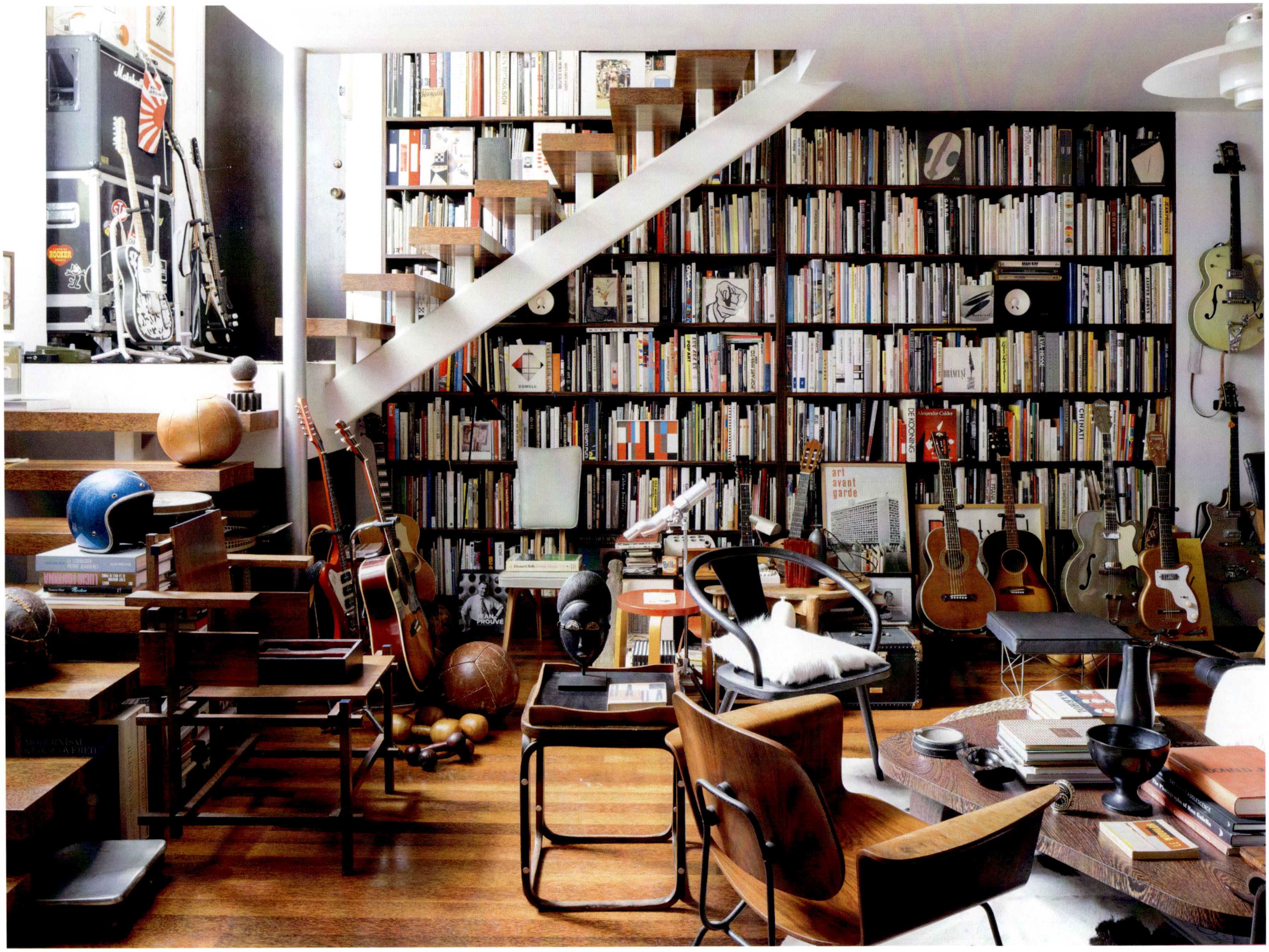

The Boyds' only architectural intervention was converting the former garage into a library. I had been commissioned to shoot this space only—and could have spent all day photographing its incredible contents—but the couple was kind enough to let me roam the rest of the house.

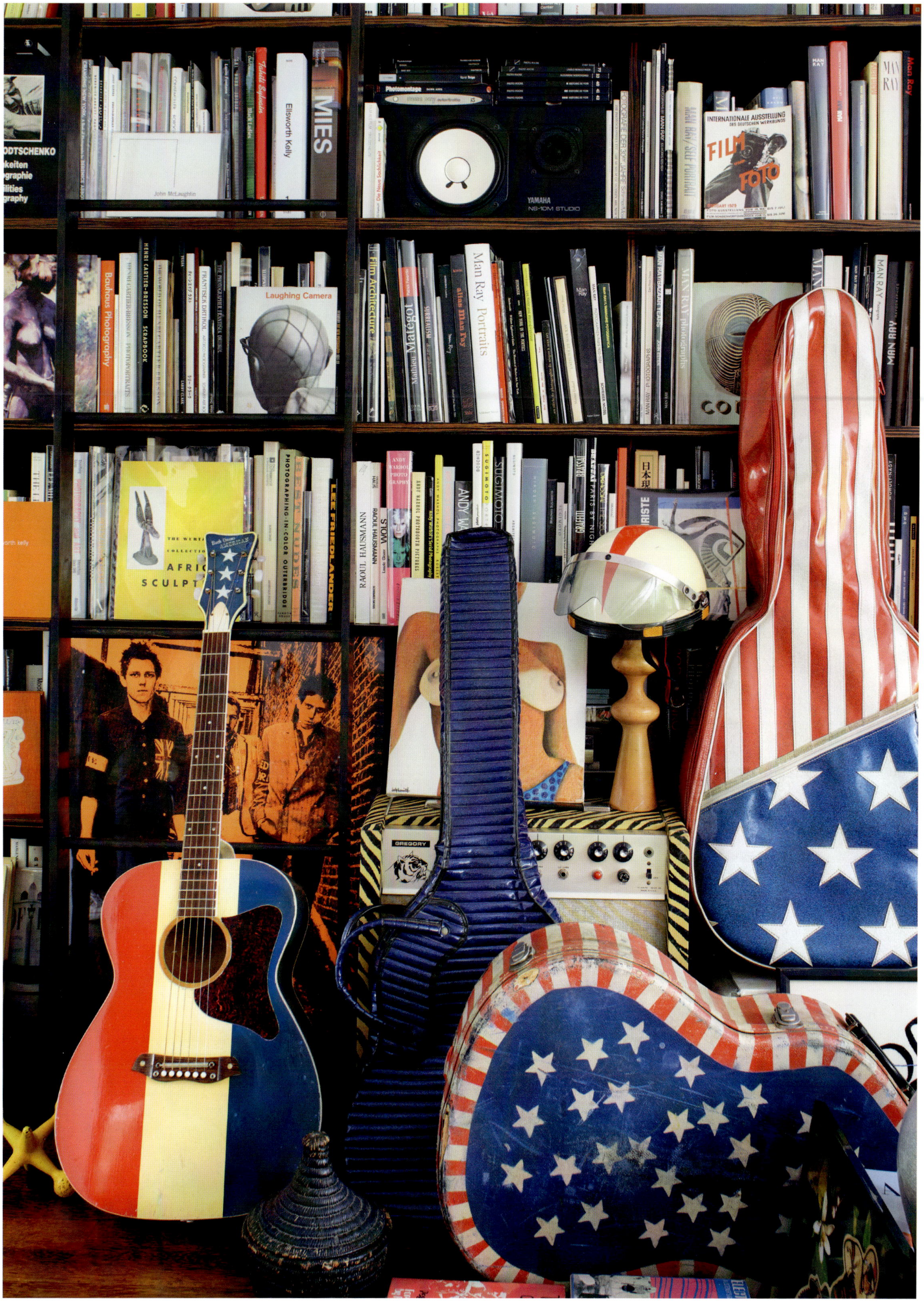
MIES
Ellsworth Kelly
John McLaughlin
Photomontage
YAMAHA
NS-10M STUDIO
INTERNATIONALE AUSSTELLUNG
DES DEUTSCHEN WERKBUNDS
FILM
FOTO
MAN RAY
Laughing Camera
Bauhaus Photography
HENRI CARTIER-BRESSON SCRAPBOOK
Film Architecture
Mathieu Matégot
Man Ray Portraits
MAN RAY photographs
PHOTOGRAPHING IN COLOR OUTERBRIDGE
LEE FRIEDLANDER
RAOUL HAUSMANN
SUGIMOTO
GREGORY

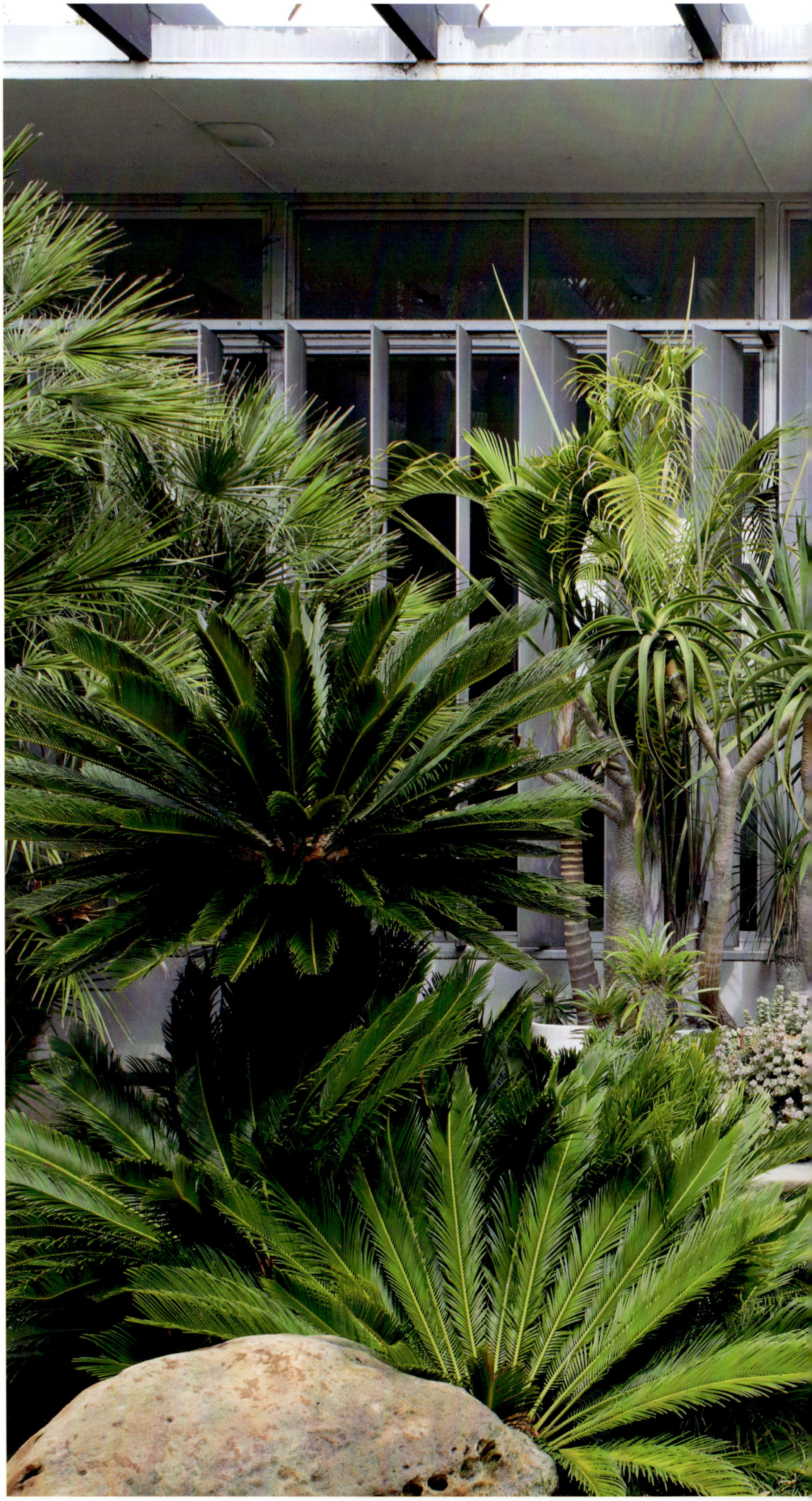

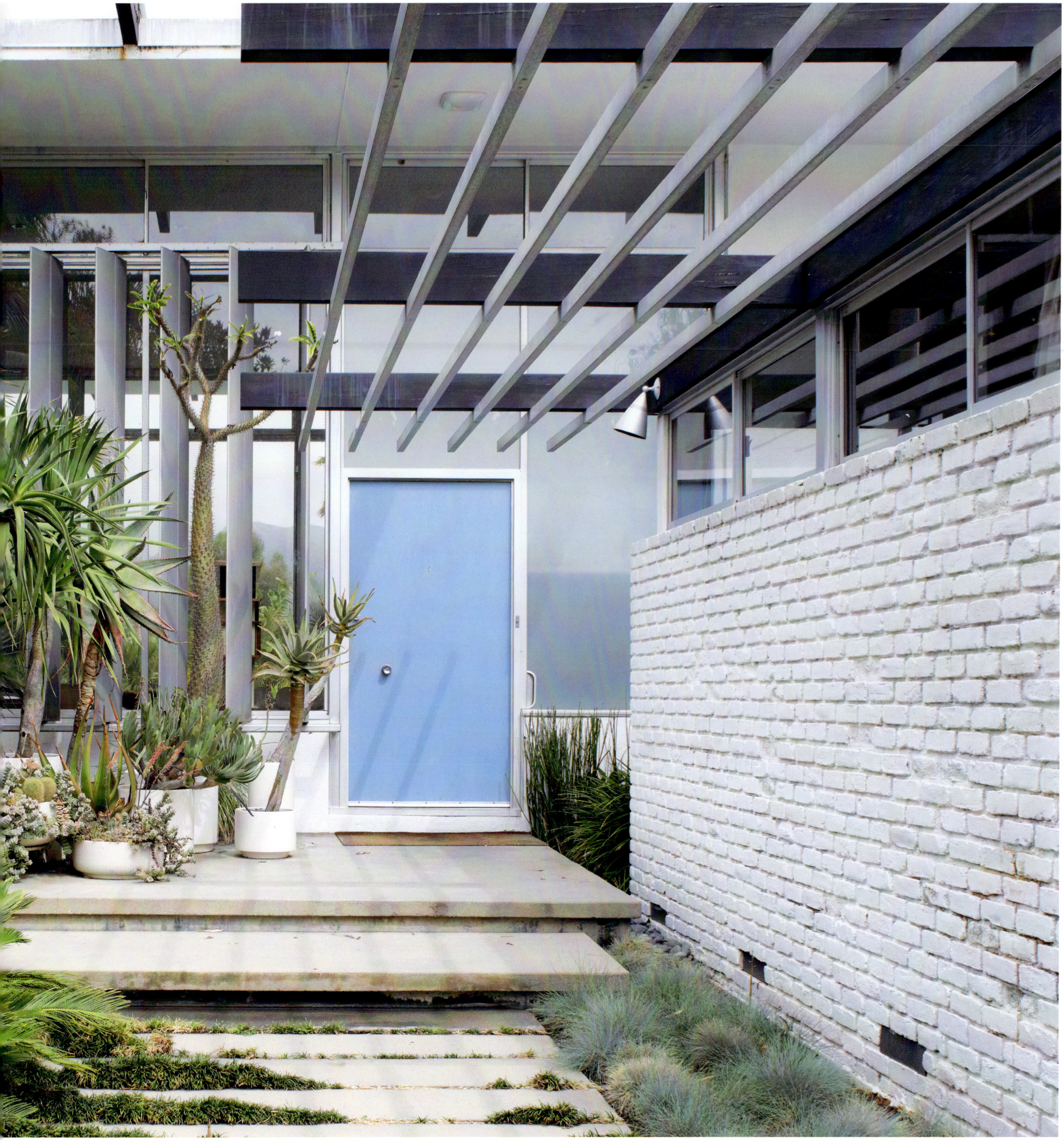

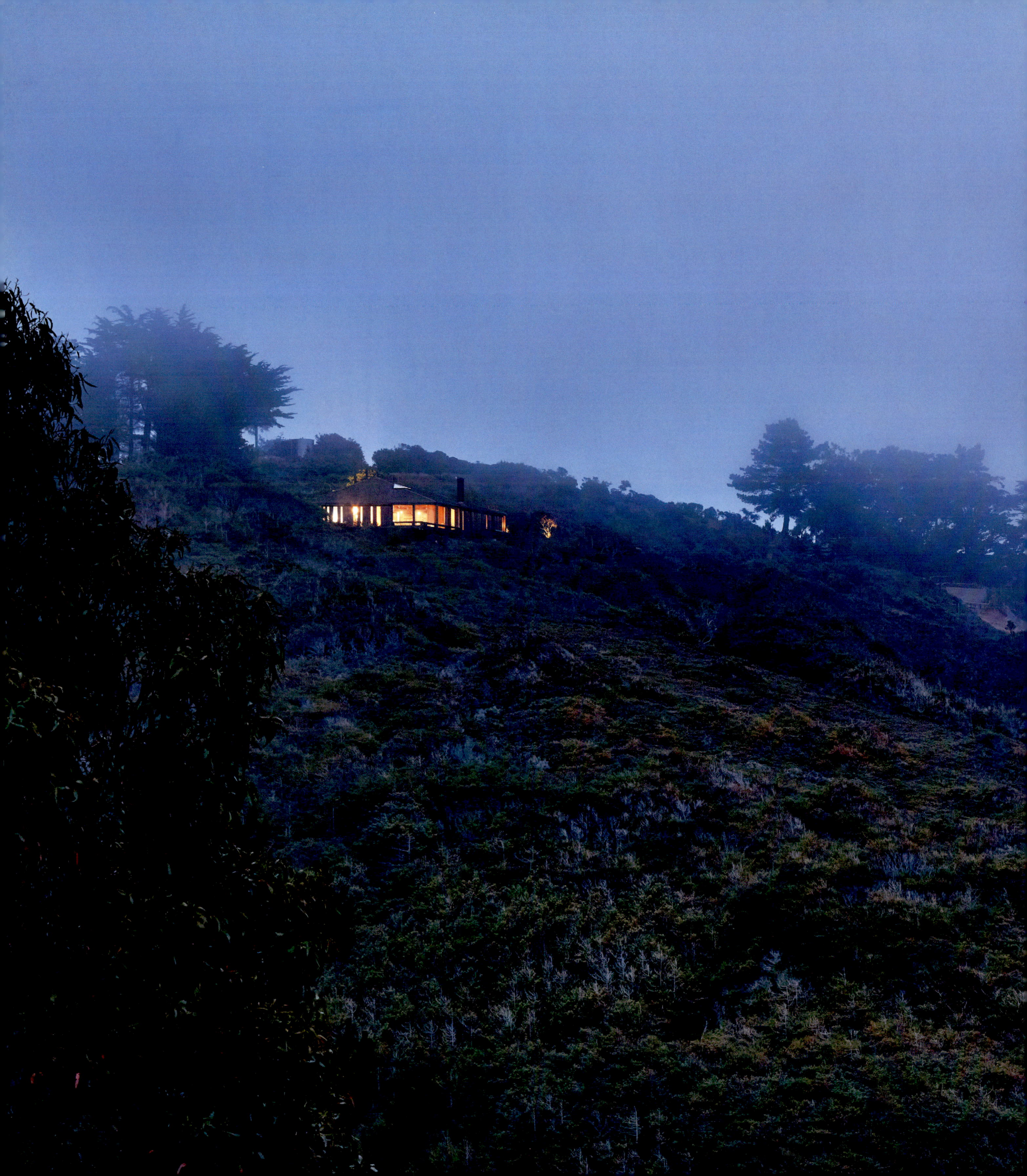

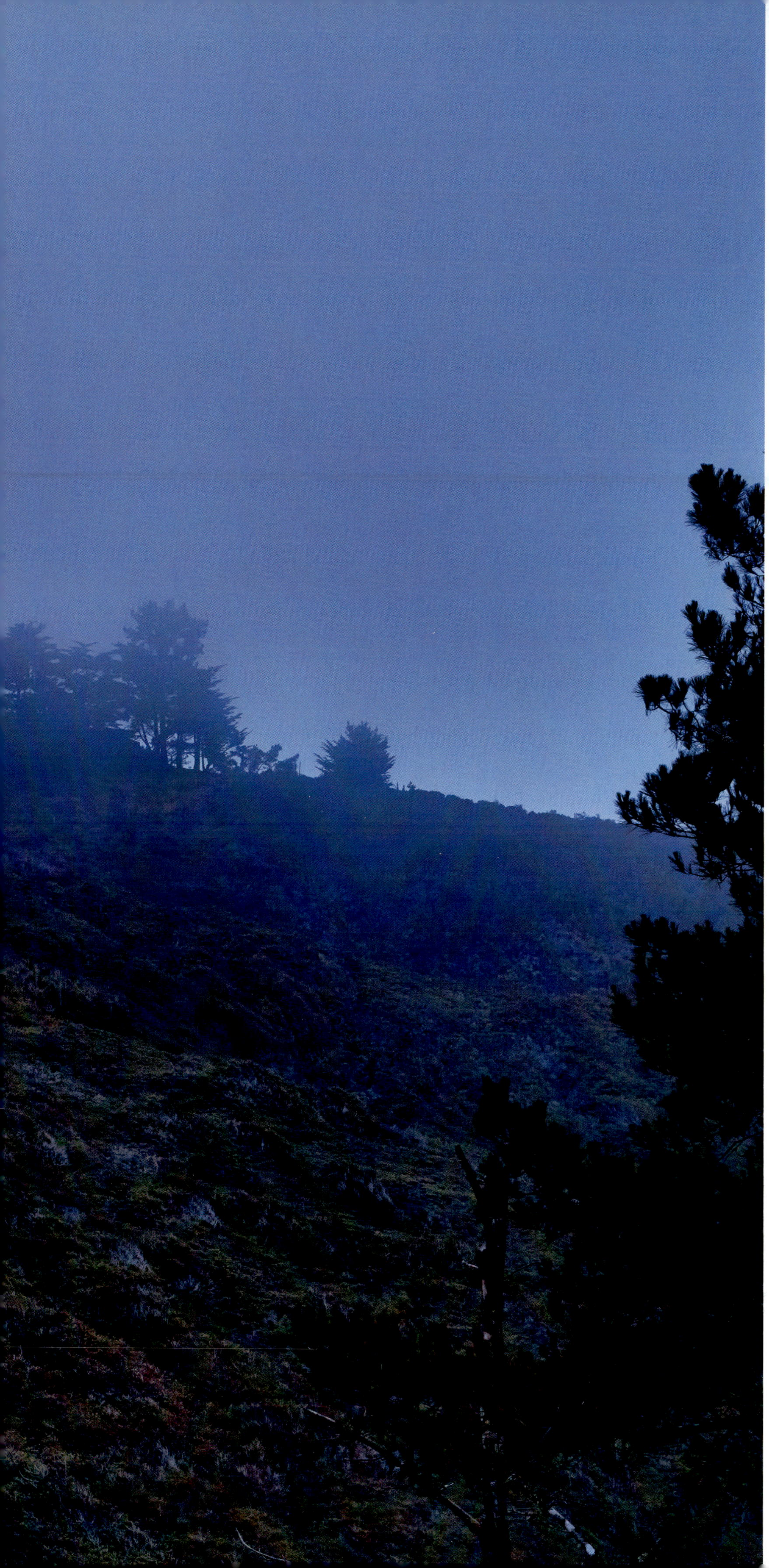

The Shaw House

Big Sur

Architect

Will Shaw

Resident

Mark Haddawy

Over the years I've photographed residences all over California, but while I've visited Big Sur with my wife annually for more than two decades, I had never shot there before 2021. Big Sur is where you would find me if I won the jackpot. To me, living there represents a perfect fantasy of raw nature and independent artistic freedom. This may not be the reality, but it keeps me coming back year after year (and buying lottery tickets).

Getting to Big Sur isn't easy, and that's kind of the point. The entire area can be cut off by fog, fires, or landslides, but when you're there, it's like traveling to another decade, another world. There's Deetjen's, the Henry Miller Memorial Library, Pfeiffer Beach, and the Esalen Institute. The air has a unique smell of woodsmoke and sage, the steep cliffs plunge into the sea, and there is a mystery to the half-seen houses that dot the cliffsides.

I met Mark Haddawy in 2011 while photographing a Los Angeles home that he had restored and designed. Haddawy co-owns Resurrection Vintage, which is widely known for some of the best collections of 1960s, '70s, and '80s couture and streetwear in the world. Haddawy restored and lives in John Lautner's Harpel House in the Hollywood Hills, and drives the most gorgeous cars. This is a man with seriously good taste.

In 2013, wanting a getaway from L.A., Haddawy bought the onetime home of Will Shaw, a California architect and advocate for the conservation of the Monterey Peninsula. The house had remained in the Shaw family, unaltered, since its completion in 1974. Apart from adding a carefully curated collection of art and objects—think Bertoia, Nakashima, pre-Columbian artifacts—Haddawy undertook a meticulous restoration, and the house looks much the same as when it was first built.

Shaw was an interesting character and did much to preserve the landscapes of Big Sur, Carmel, and Monterey. He sat on multiple boards and councils for urban planning and conservation, including one he formed in 1964 with photographer Ansel Adams called the Foundation for Environmental Design, which promoted the responsible integration of architecture into the environment. In 1967, after winning the prestigious Prix de Rome and spending a year abroad, Shaw returned to Big Sur to build a house for himself and his wife, Mary, using lumber reclaimed from the old Dolan Creek Bridge, which had been dismantled a few years prior.

The Shaw House is nestled into the hillside and shielded from the ocean winds, and like every house on the cliffs here, it has its own microclimate. Getting to the place is an adventure in itself, driving up and up along a series of one-lane switchbacks, through forests of redwoods reaching taller than two hundred feet, and finally down a winding lane. Then, as you approach, a curved path leads to a low front door, and it is only when stepping inside that the home opens up to a double-height ceiling and to panoramic views of the ocean. Despite the scale and the sublime scenery, there is a modesty and restraint to the architecture that exemplifies Shaw's principles: modernism tempered by an extreme sensitivity to the landscape and the region.

The sense of restraint in the building is carried through in Haddawy's consistent desire to pare design down to its essentials. Apparently one of Will Shaw's mottos to live by was to cultivate friendships with interesting people. I'm certain he and Haddawy would have been friends.

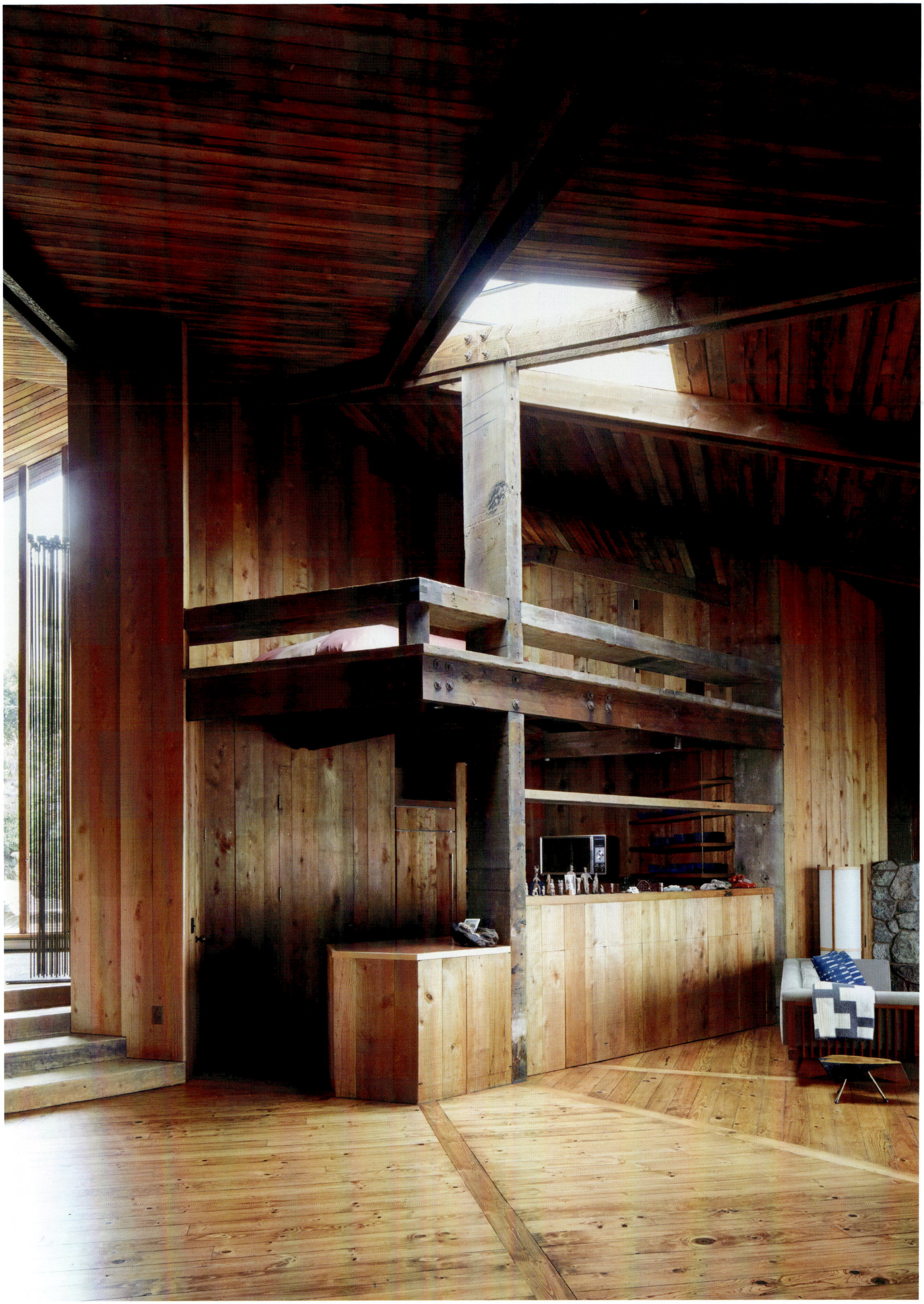

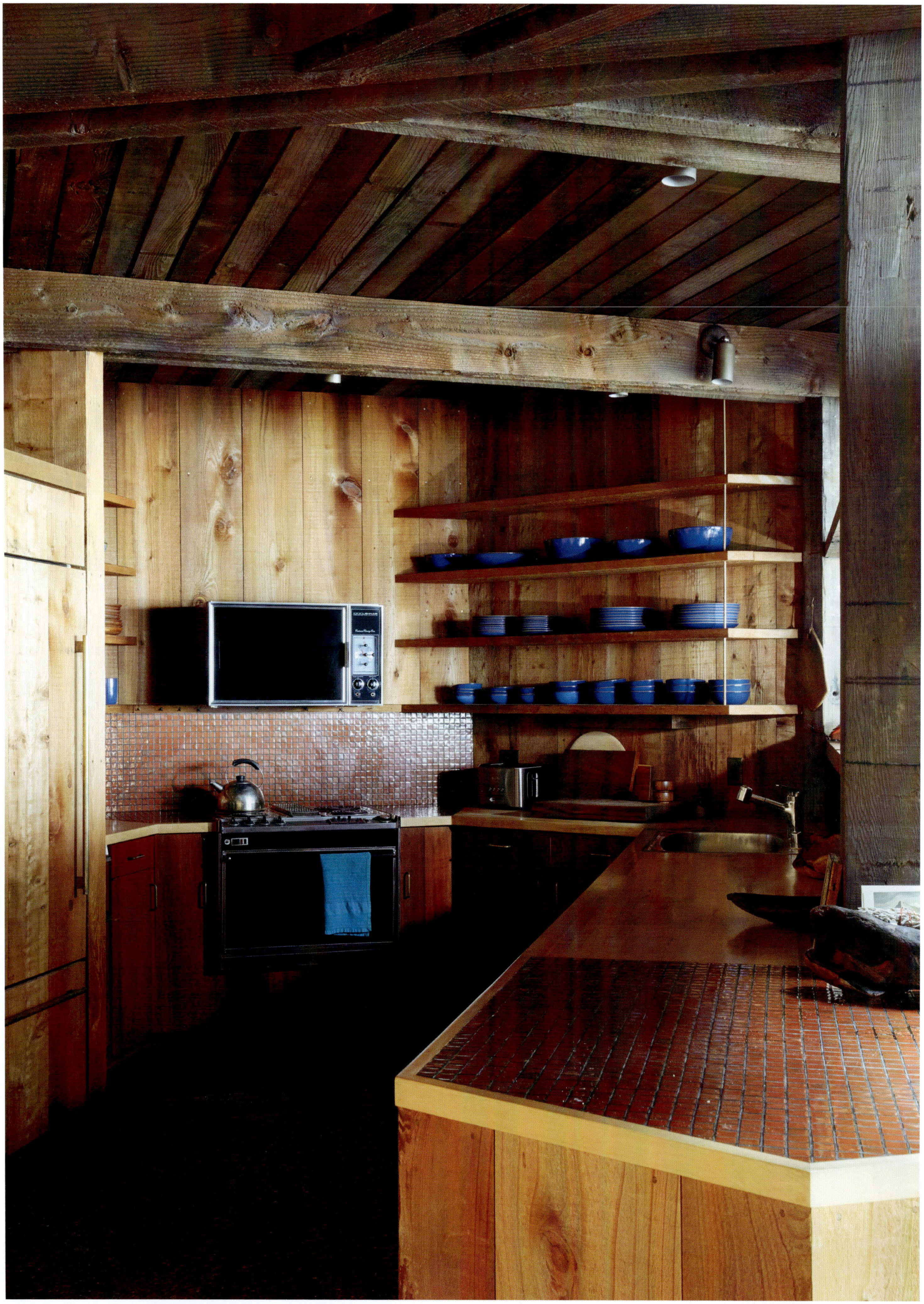

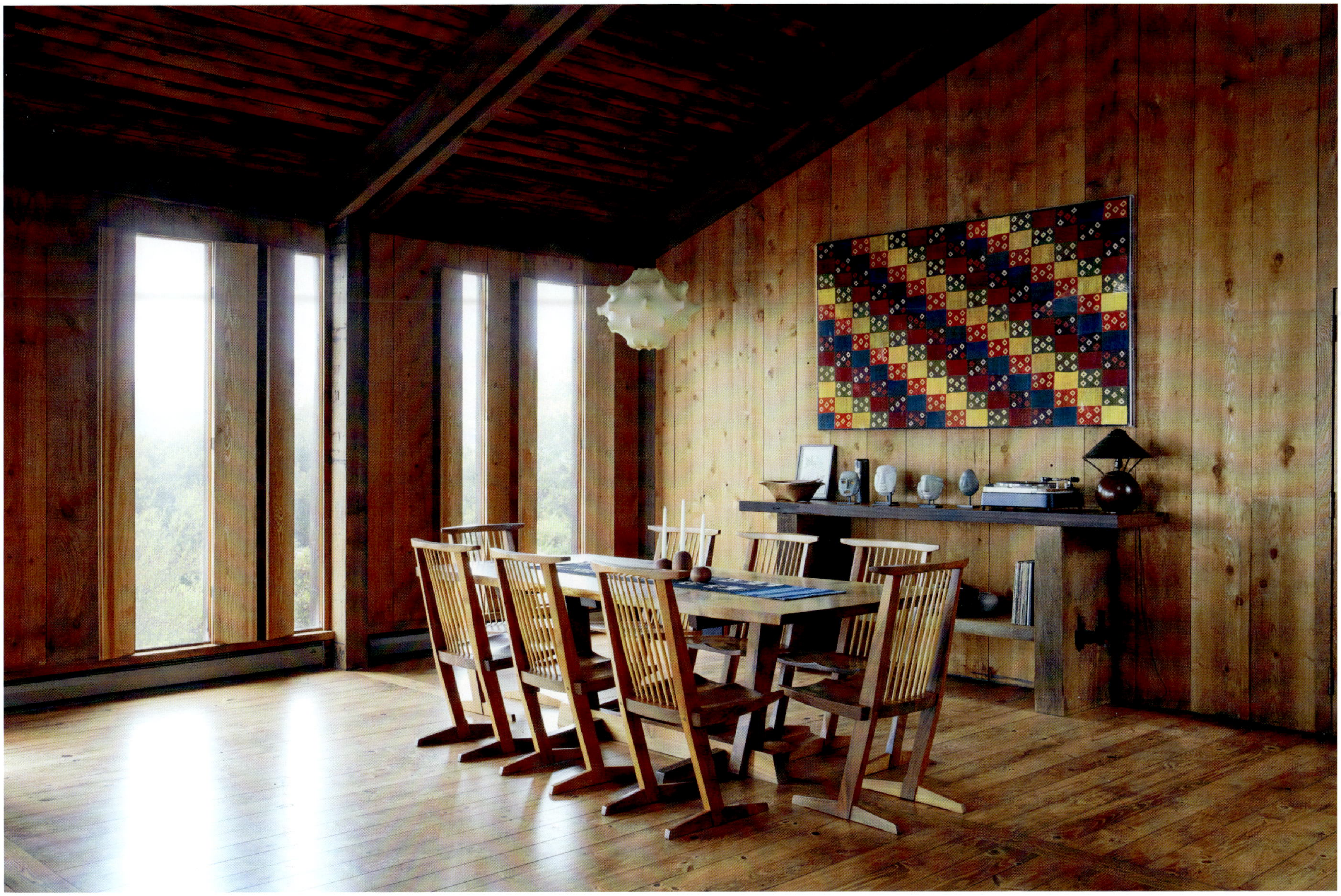

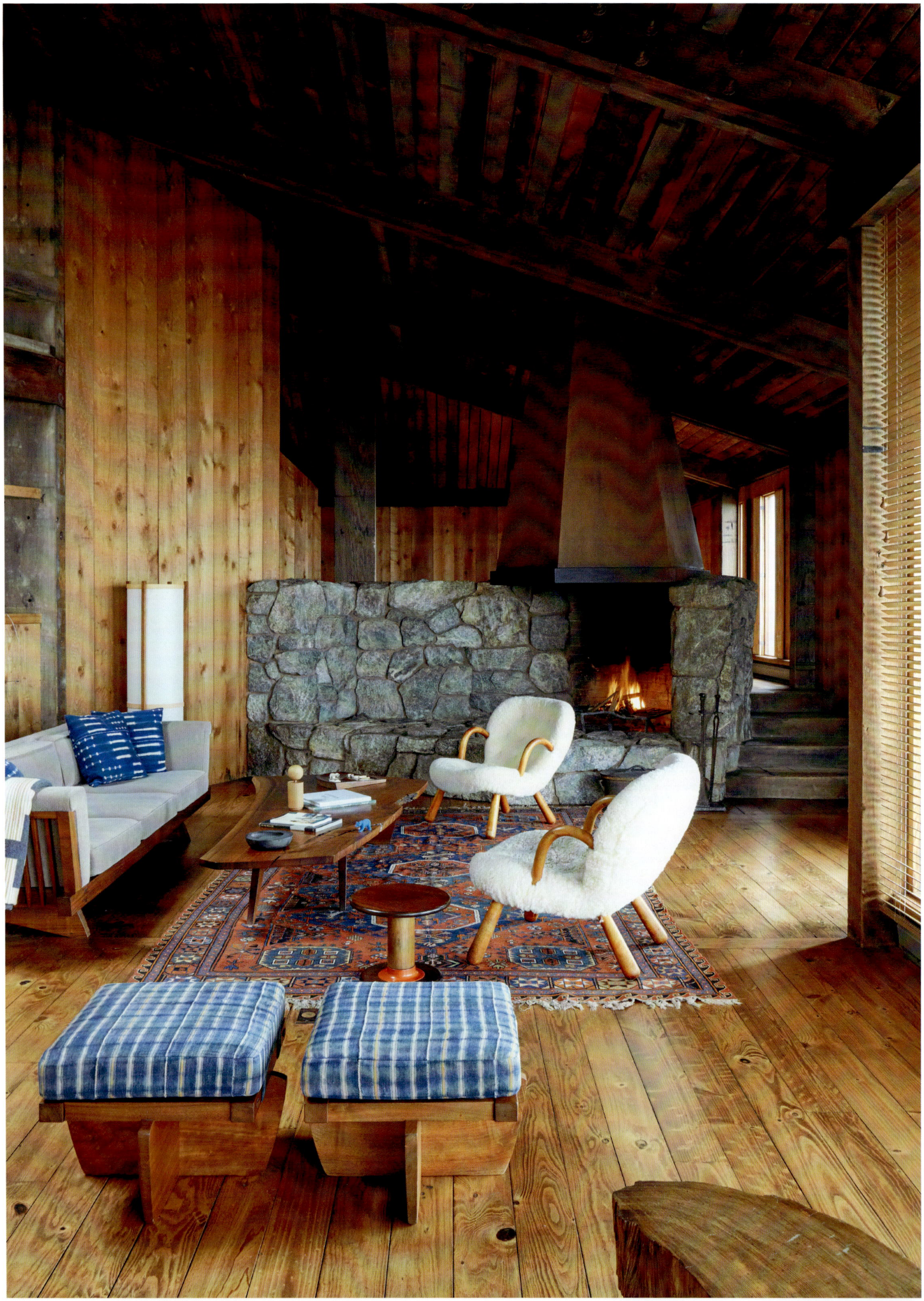

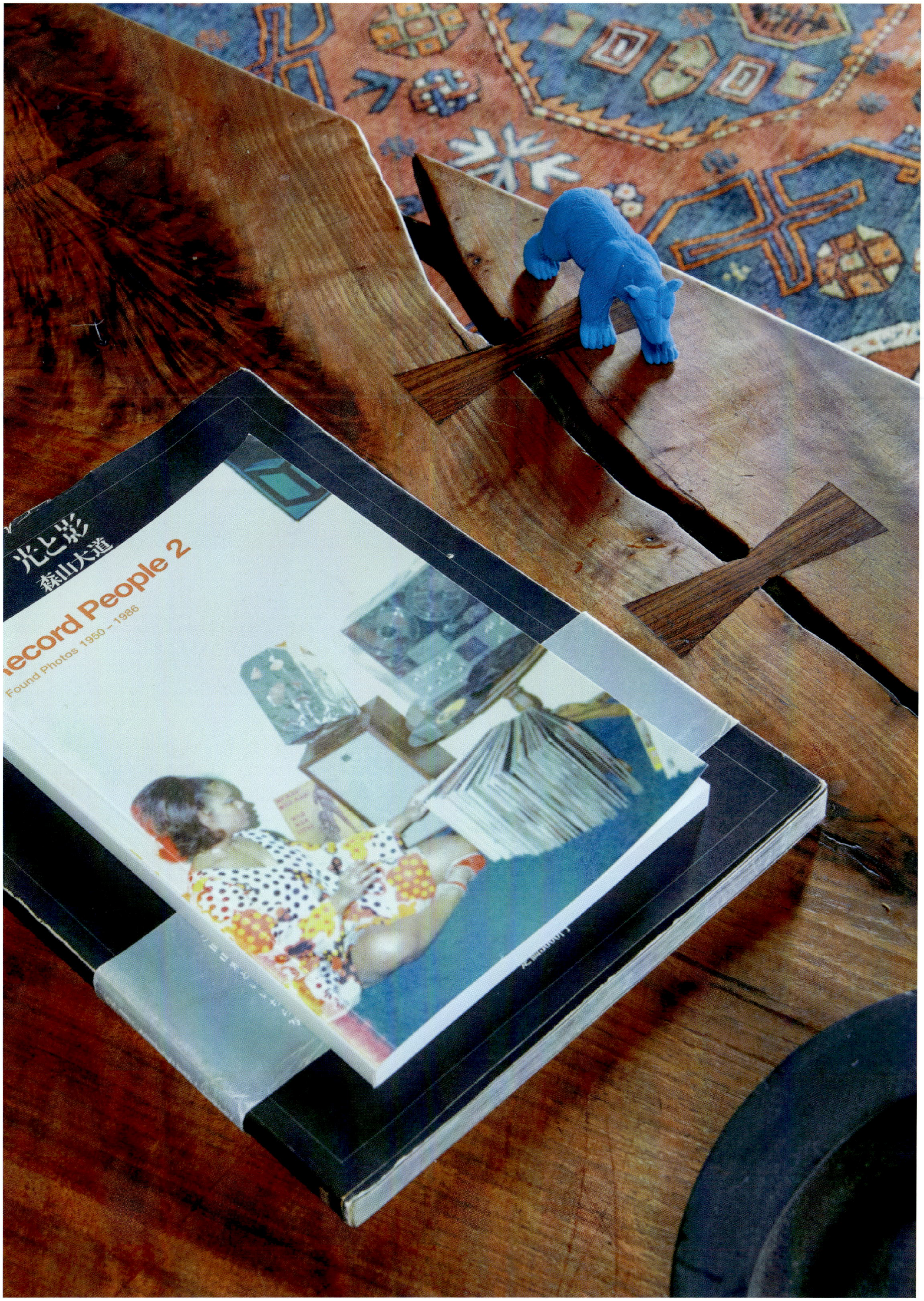
光と影
森山大道
Record People 2
Found Photos 1950 – 1986

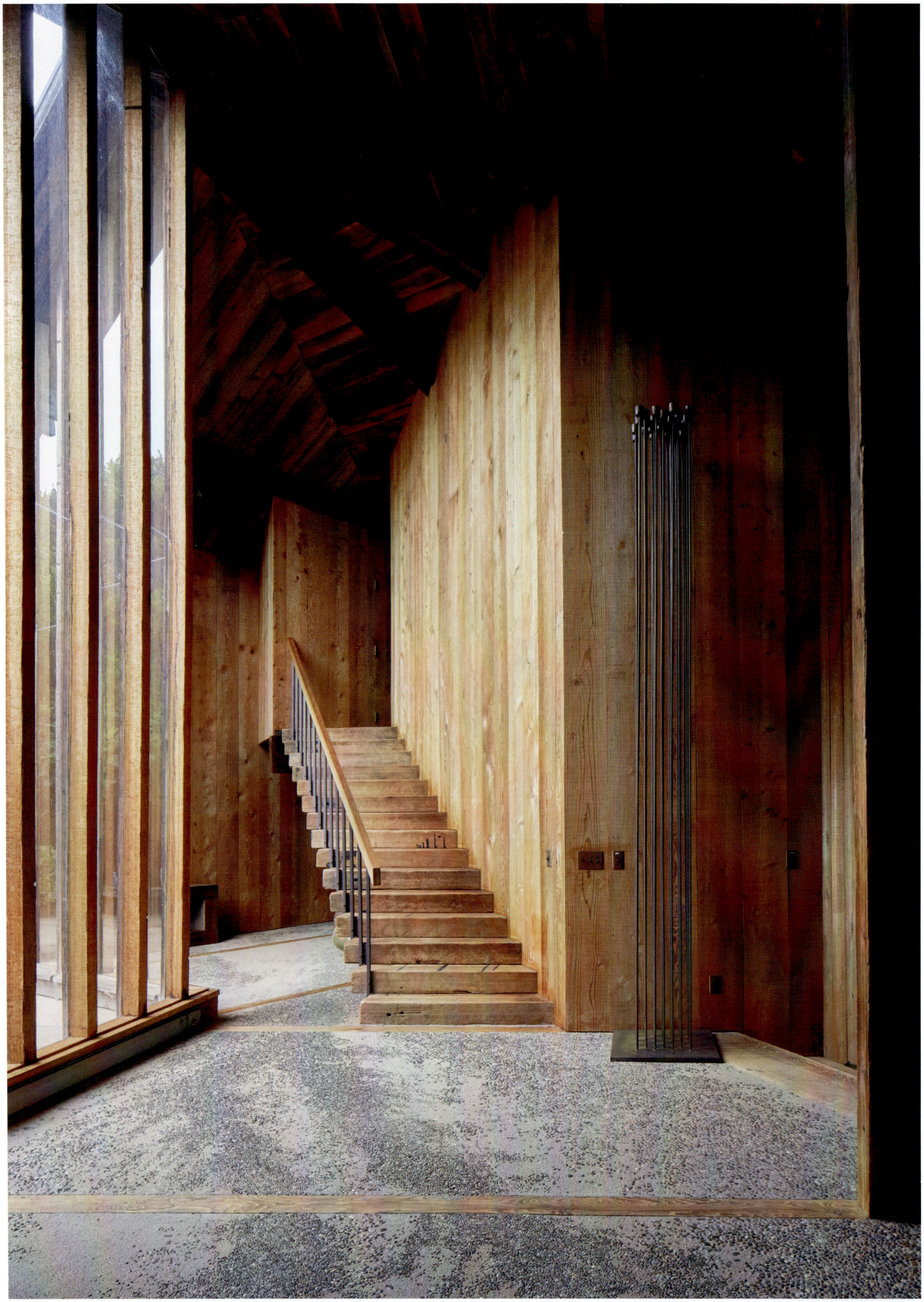

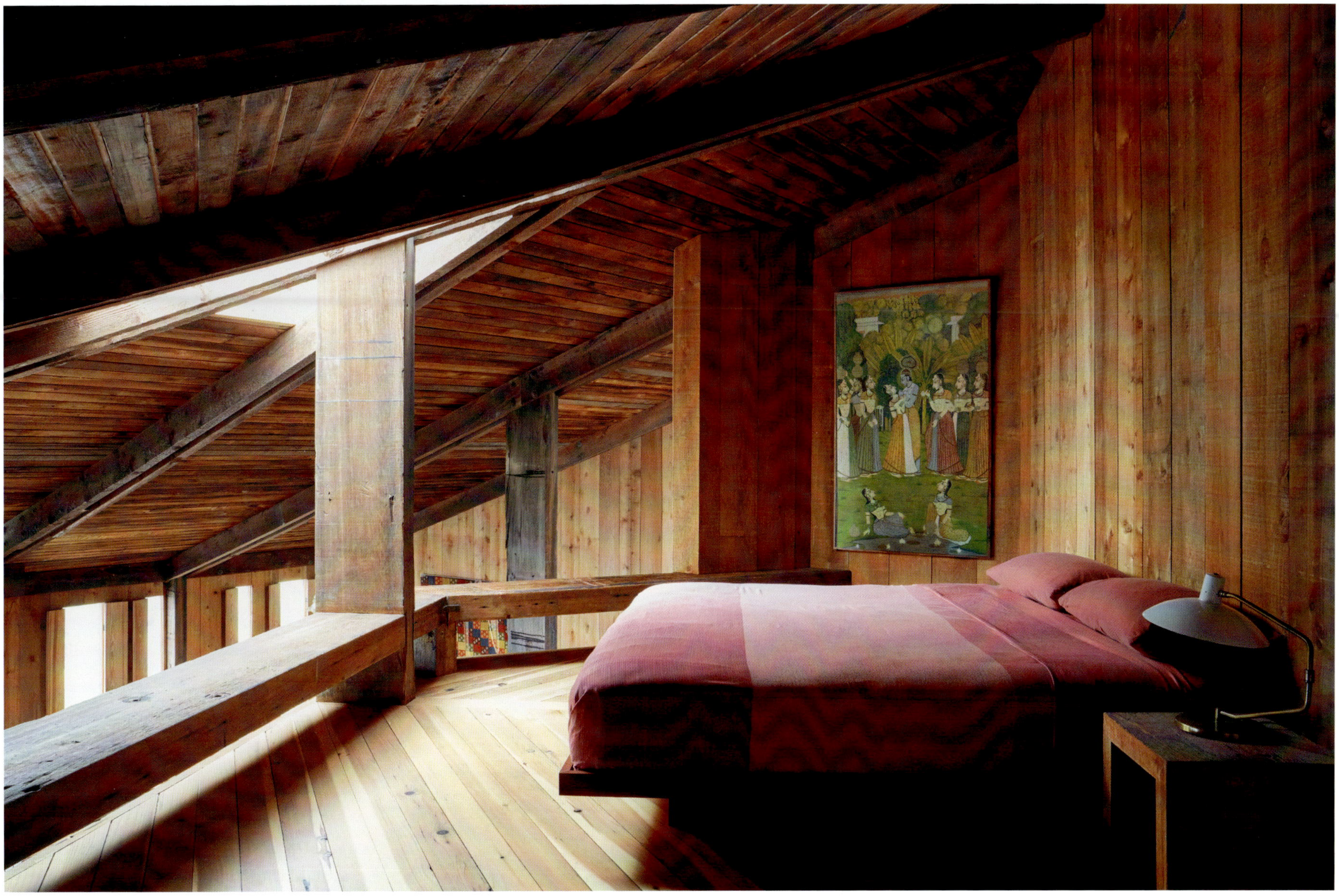

A twelve-foot-tall Harry Bertoia Sonambient sound sculpture is prominently displayed in the front entry hall. Just beyond, stairs lead to a sleeping loft. Will Shaw, the house's architect and original owner, purposefully preserved the bolt holes and stains on the redwood lumber that makes up the stairs, the sleeping loft, and the central beams, a reminder of its former life as the old Dolan Creek Bridge.

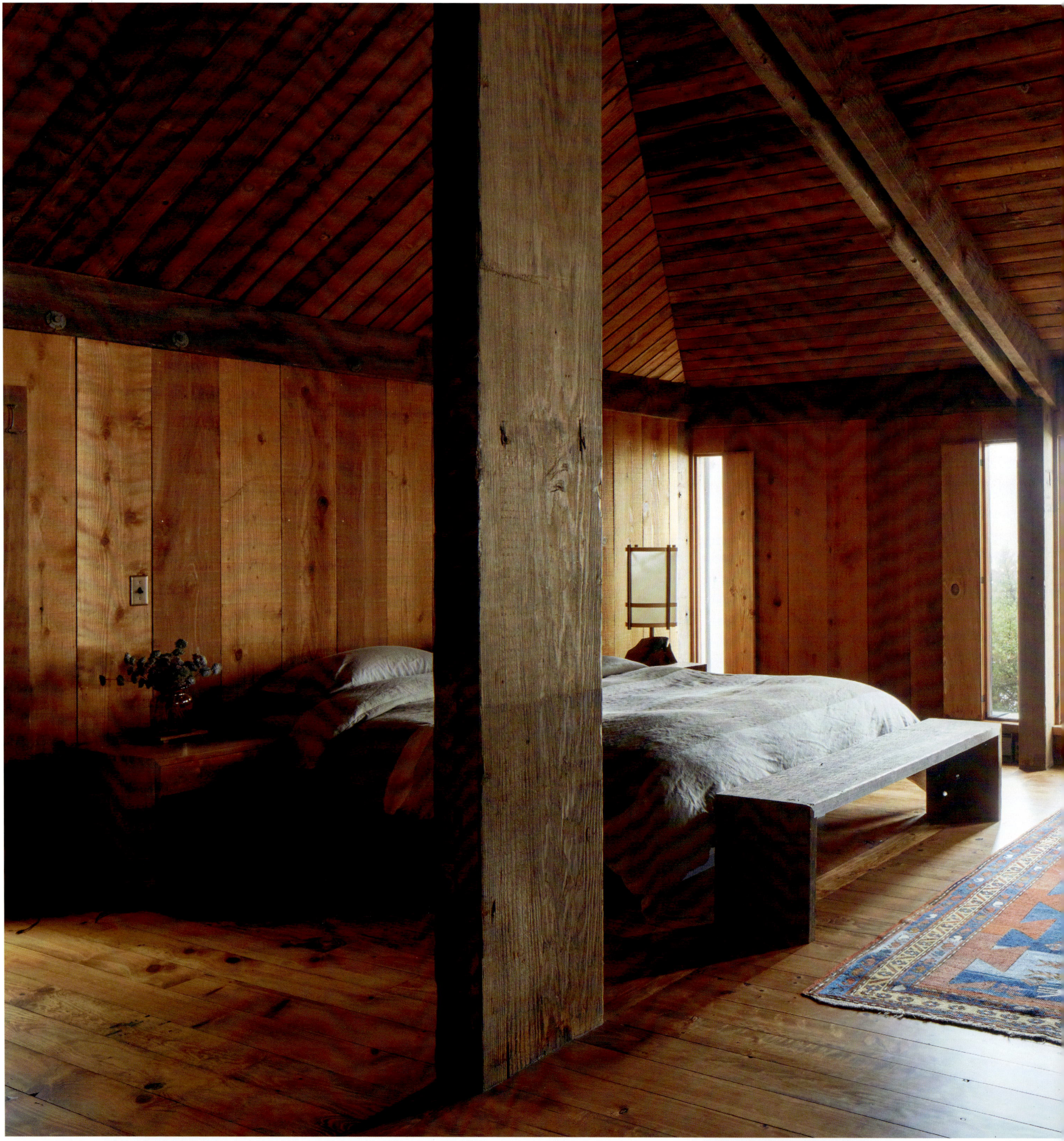

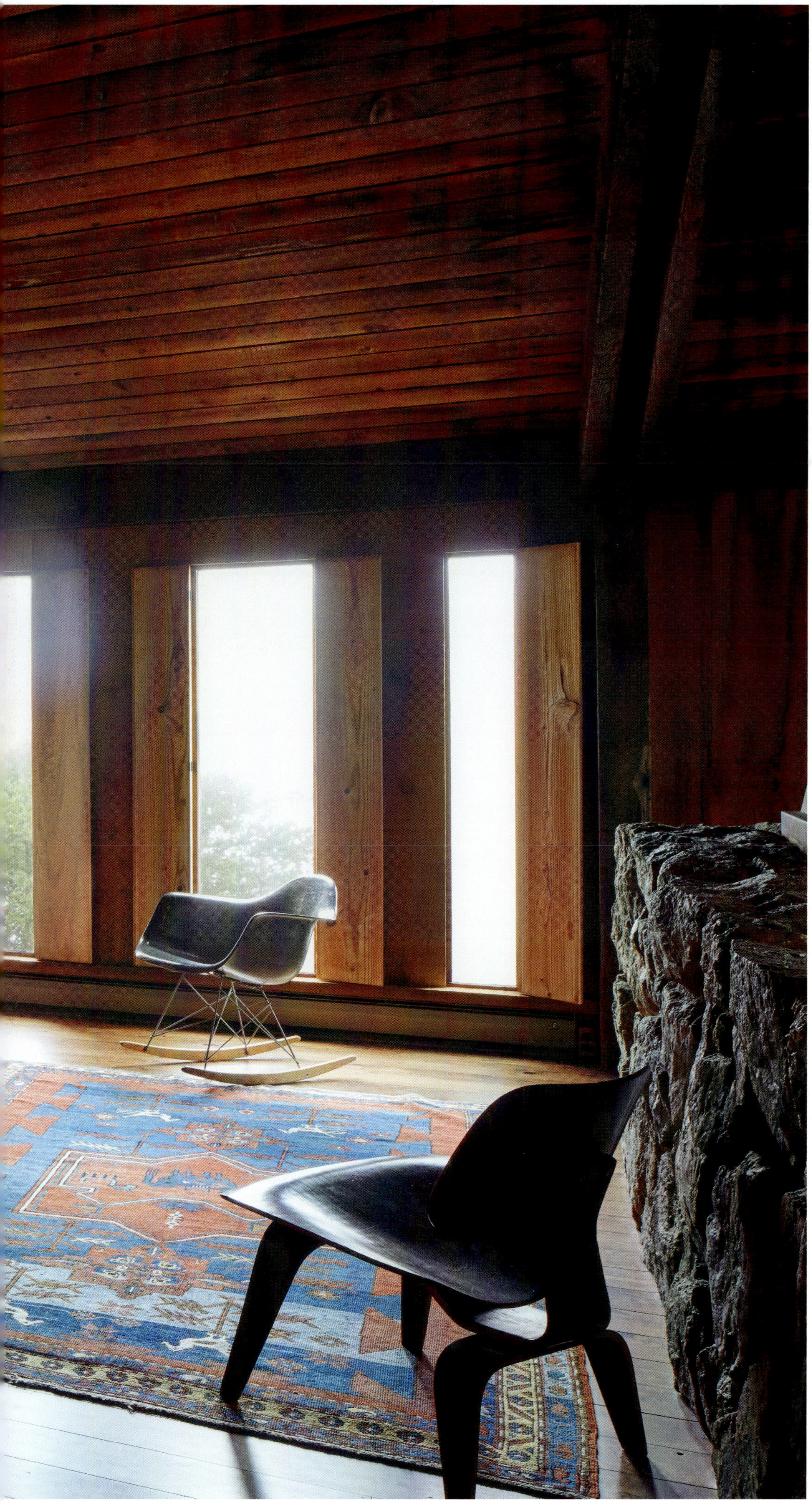

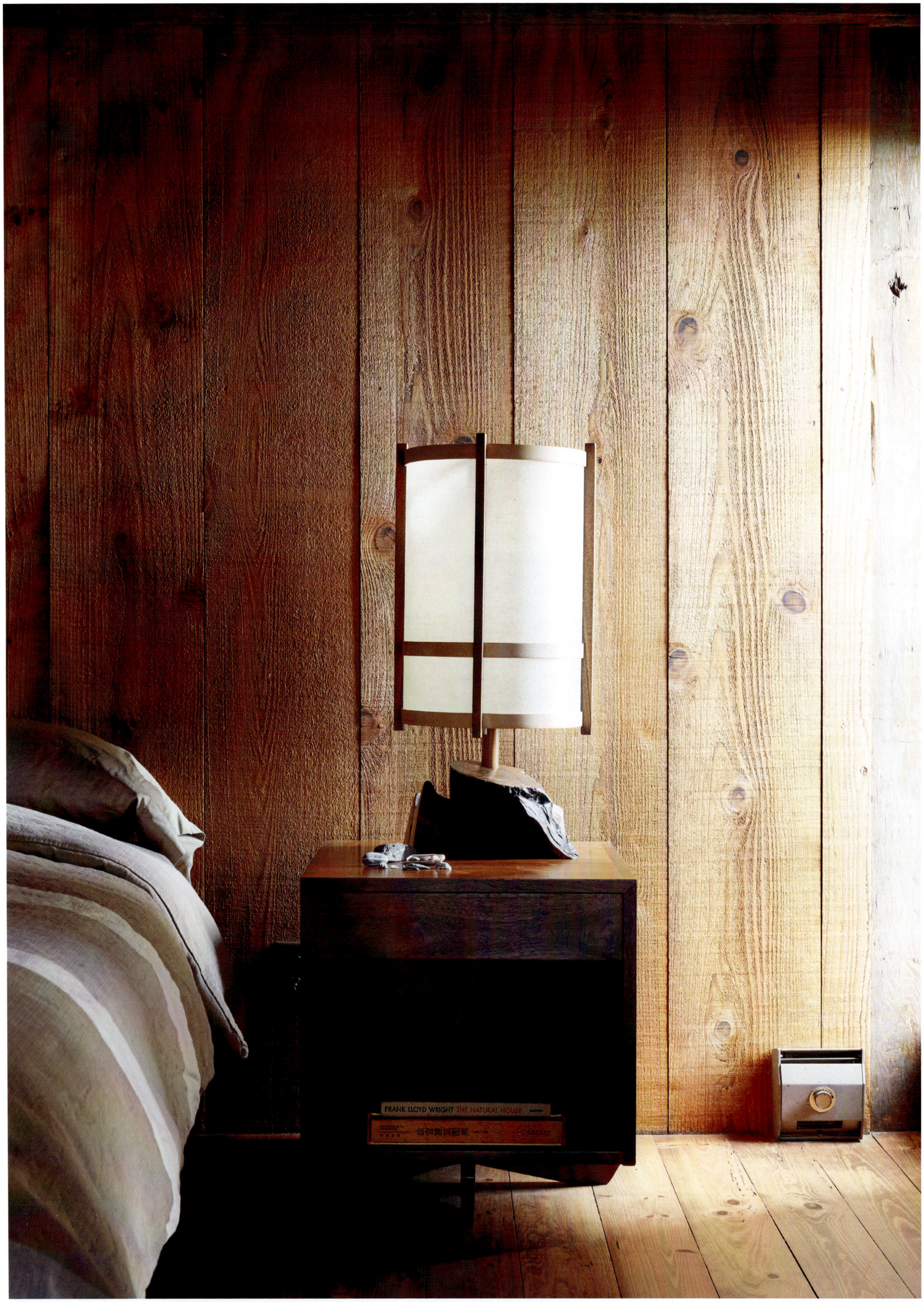
FRANK LLOYD WRIGHT THE NATURAL HOUSE

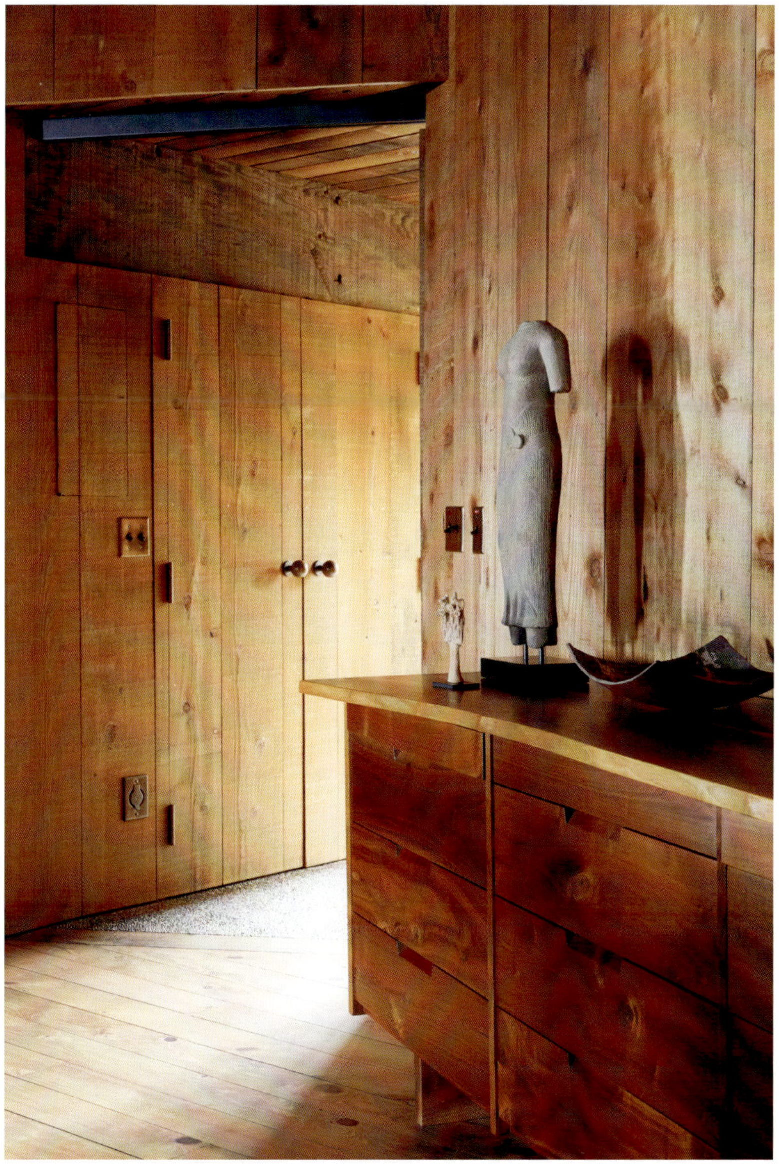

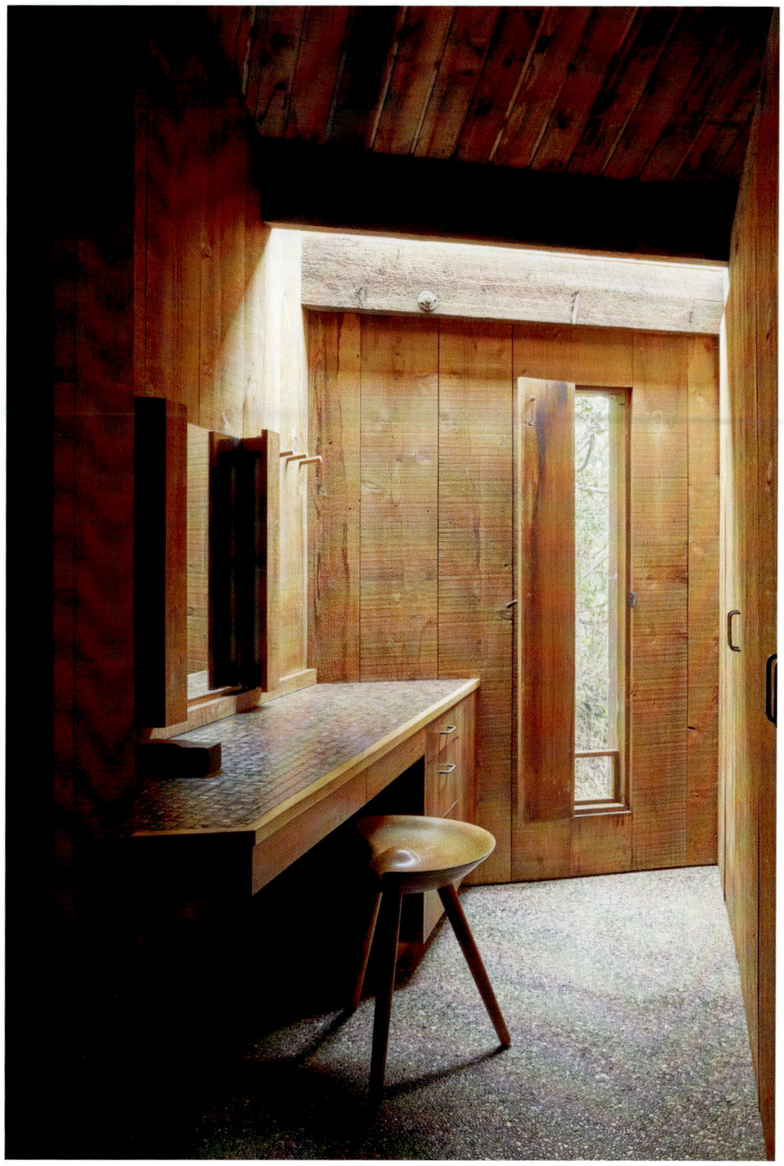

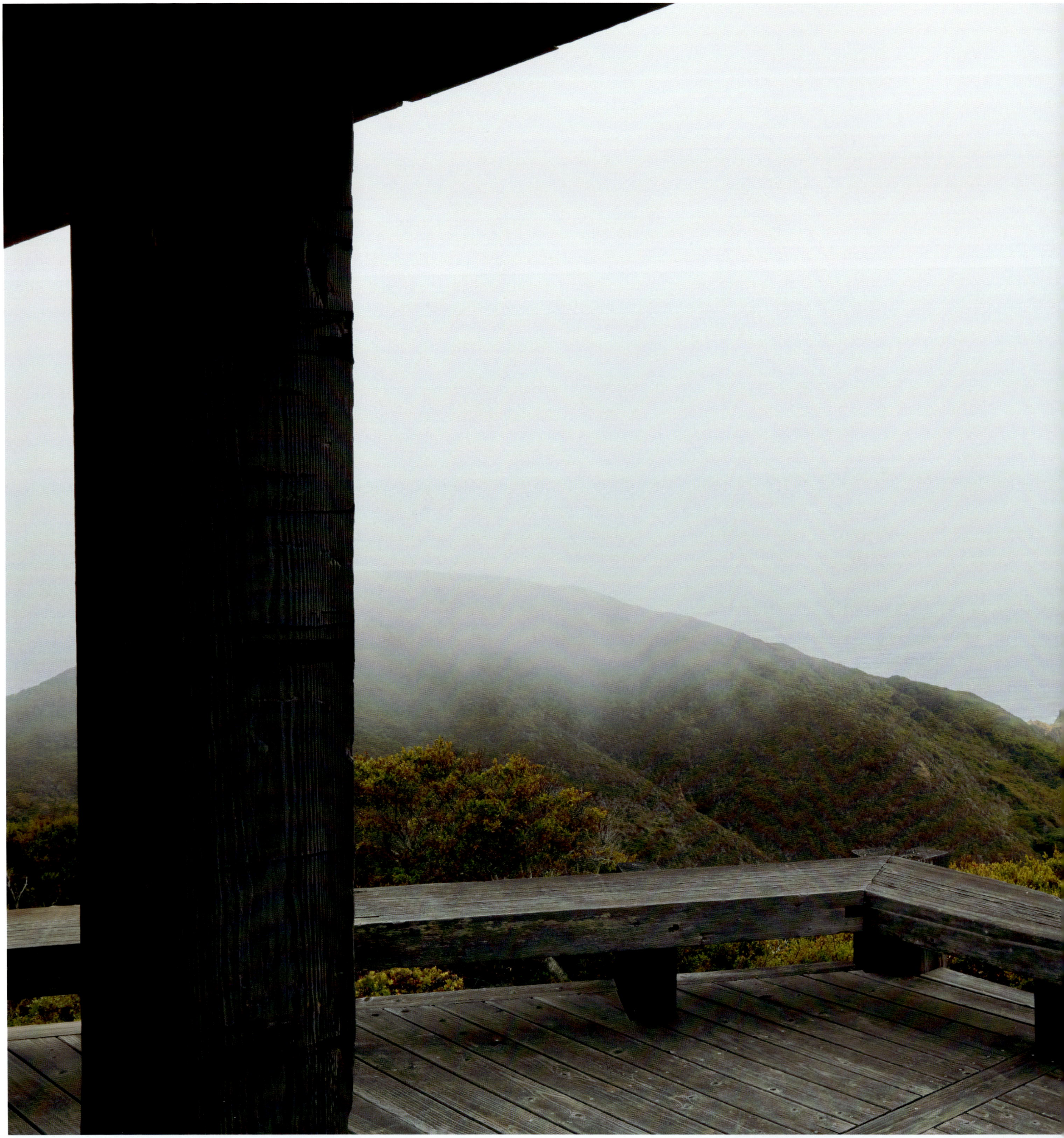

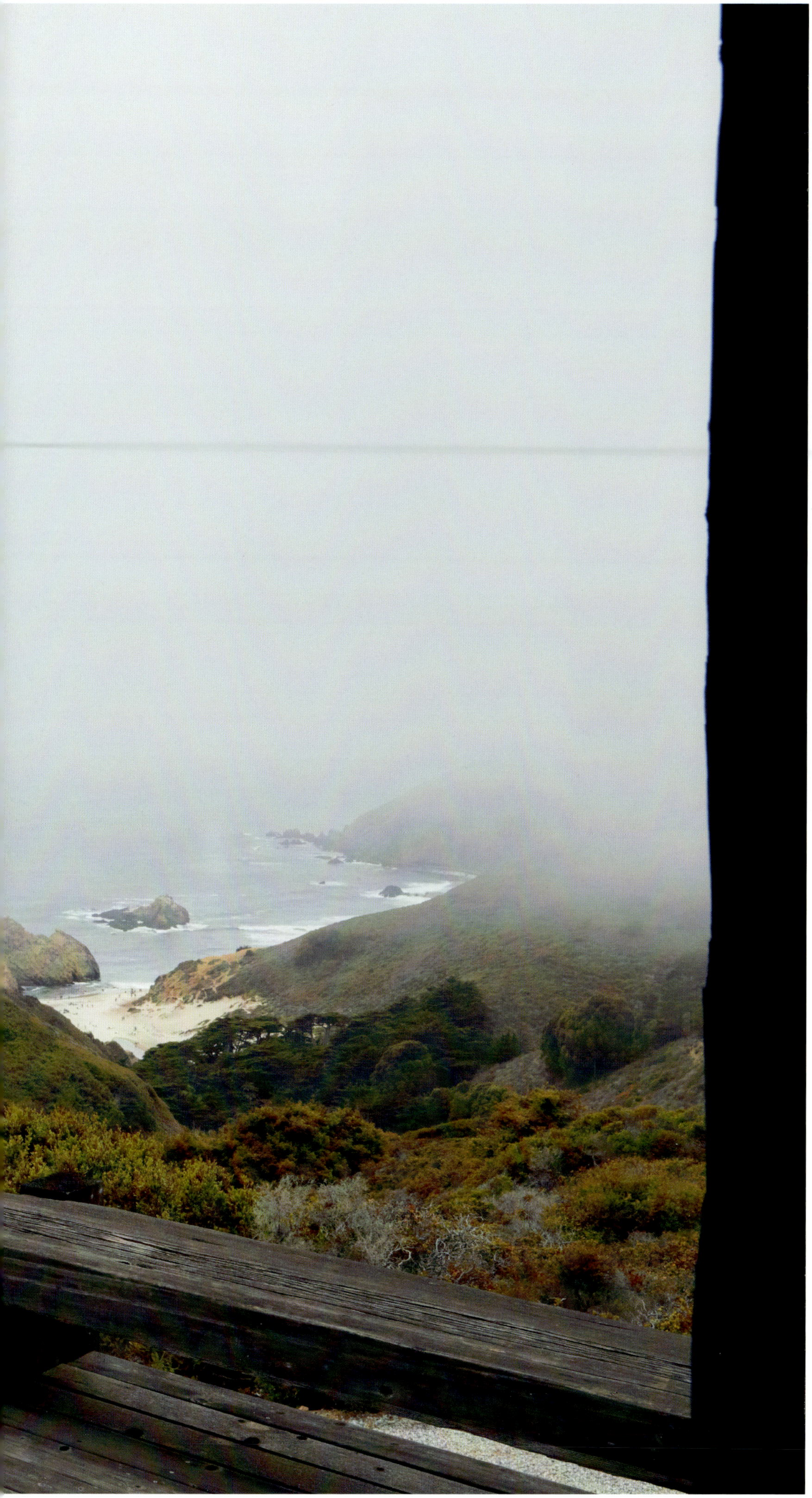

Big Sur feels primeval, ruled by the elements. The redwood trees on the hillside below the house are shaped by the wind, growing only ten to twenty feet tall but bearing downwind branches as long as sixty feet. During the summer months, and when the fog lifts, whales migrating from Mexico can be seen from the deck.

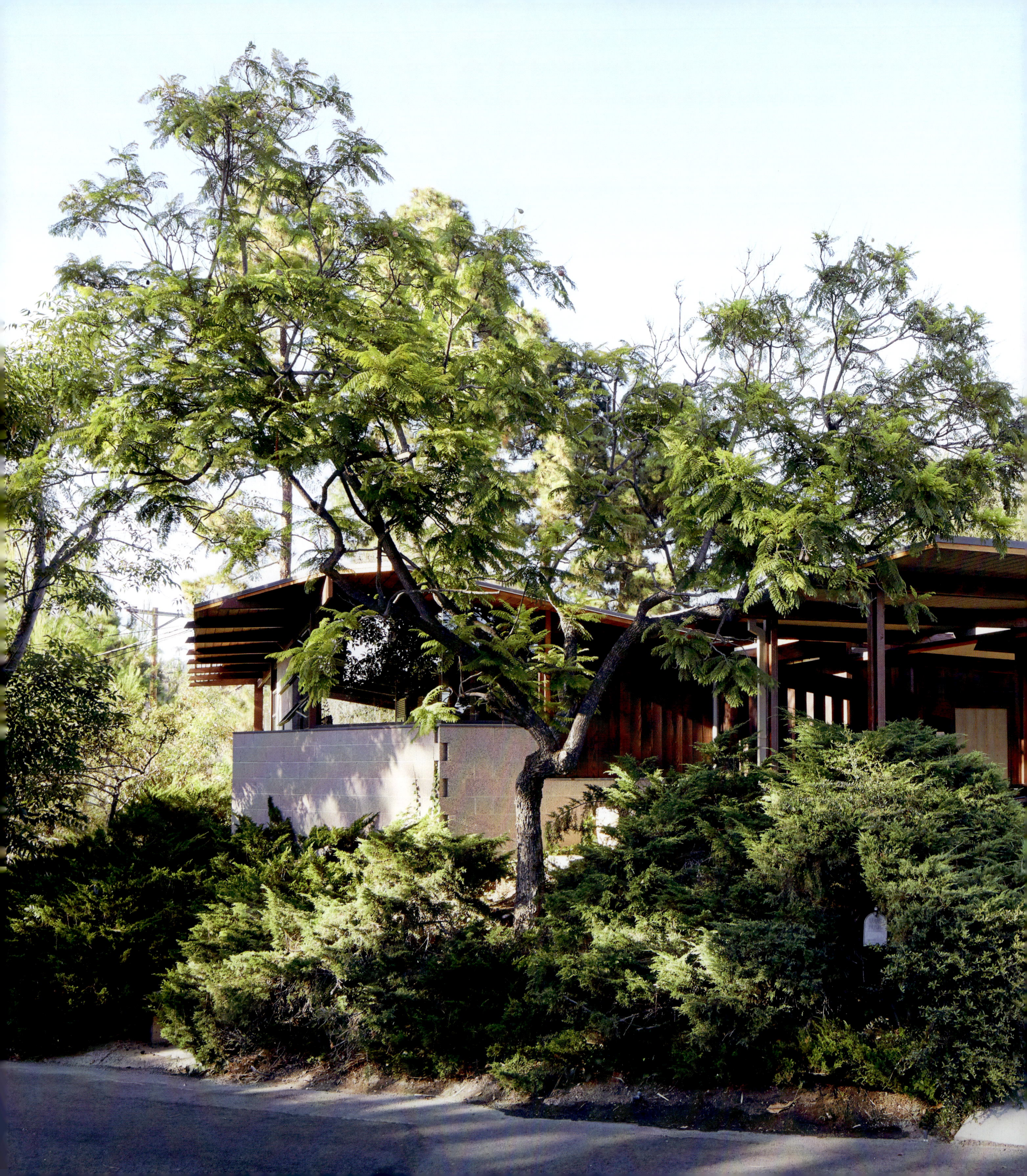

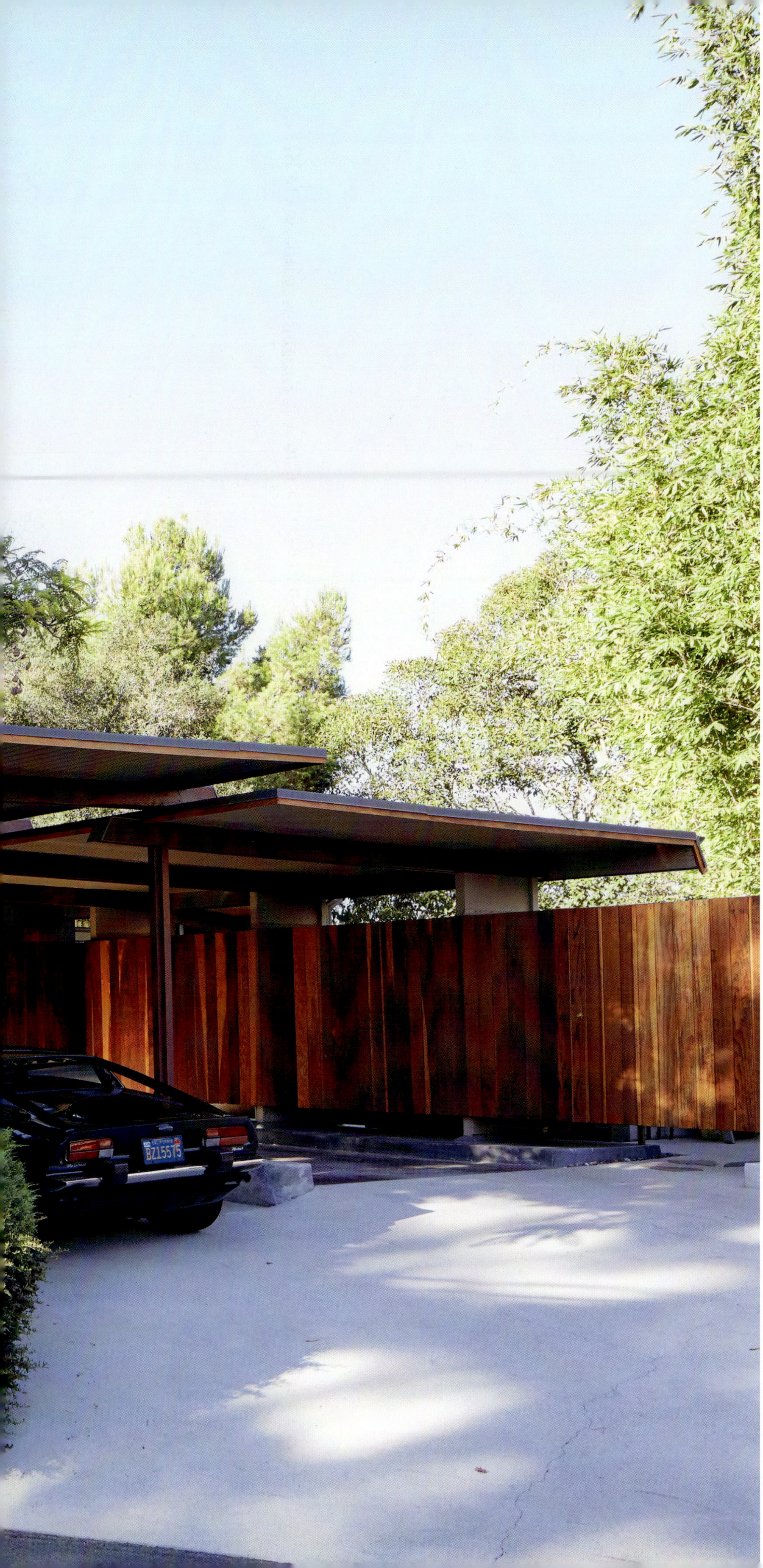

The Stein House

Crestwood Hills

Architect

A. Quincy Jones
and Whitney R. Smith

Residents

Adam and Kate Blackman

Tucked away within the Brentwood neighborhood of Los Angeles sits the small architecturally controlled community of Crestwood Hills, a cluster of midcentury jewel boxes by some of the leading proponents of postwar California modernism. For the last twenty-three years and counting, Adam and Kate Blackman have called one of these their home. The 1950 Stein House, designed by A. Quincy Jones and Whitney R. Smith for attorney Jay Stein and his wife, Lorayne, was built as part of the Mutual Housing Association, a cooperative established in 1946 to respond to the postwar housing crisis. The MHA would become a showcase of International Style residences by architects including Richard Neutra and Craig Ellwood, in addition to Jones and Smith.

Kate, a graphic designer, serves as the president of the Crestwood Hills Association, one of the last fully realized postwar cooperative housing projects in the country. Adam, with business partner David Cruz, runs Blackman Cruz, an influential antique and modern furniture and design showroom. I once stumbled on what I thought was a secret estate sale auction house in a dodgy part of downtown Los Angeles, only to see Adam's smiling face. I realized then that he has the inside track on everything.

Every few decades a fire rips through the neighborhood. The Bel Air Fire of 1961 wiped out nearly half of the MHA homes, and more recently the area was struck by the 2019 Getty Fire. Adam and Kate's house is a survivor, an architectural time capsule of the era in which it was built, in no small part due to the couple's efforts to restore the home's natural materials, and to fill it with furniture, art, and objects from the period. (This was a shoot that needed no styling. The house brims with curiosities, all reflecting the humor and quirkiness of the homeowners.)

Once they had finished their work on the house, the Blackmans determined to have it photographed by Julius Shulman, who had documented other Crestwood Hills homes decades earlier. "For six months, Adam called him practically weekly. Mr. Shulman answered his own phone every time, and every time Adam had to explain who he was, where we lived, and what we wanted," says Kate. The photographer was, after all, in his midnineties. To their delight, Shulman finally agreed. "He showed up with his crew and immediately was frantic about getting the first shot before the sun moved. He squeezed out the last shot of the day with the whisper of sunlight remaining, and we all celebrated with his favorite, single malt scotch."

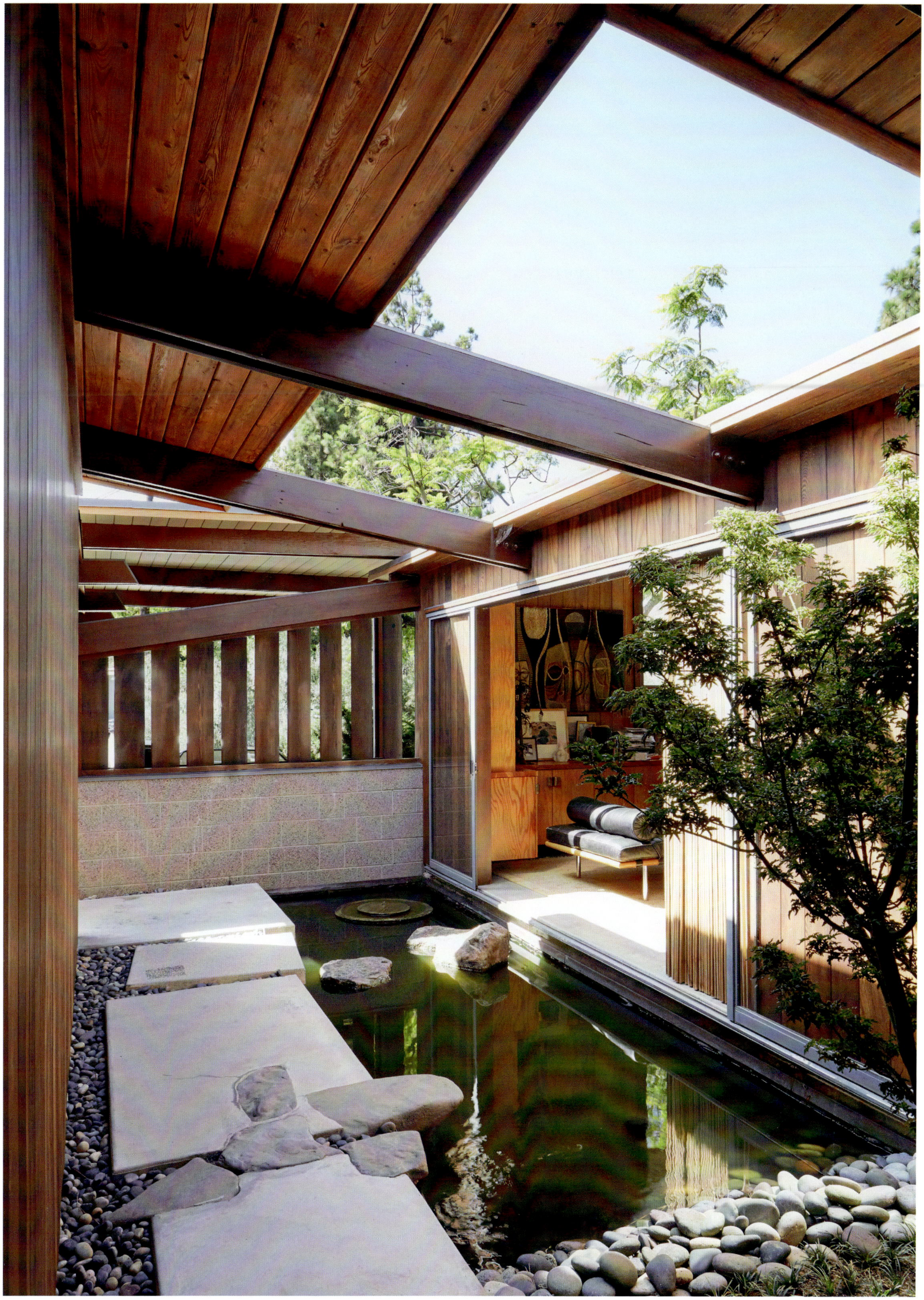

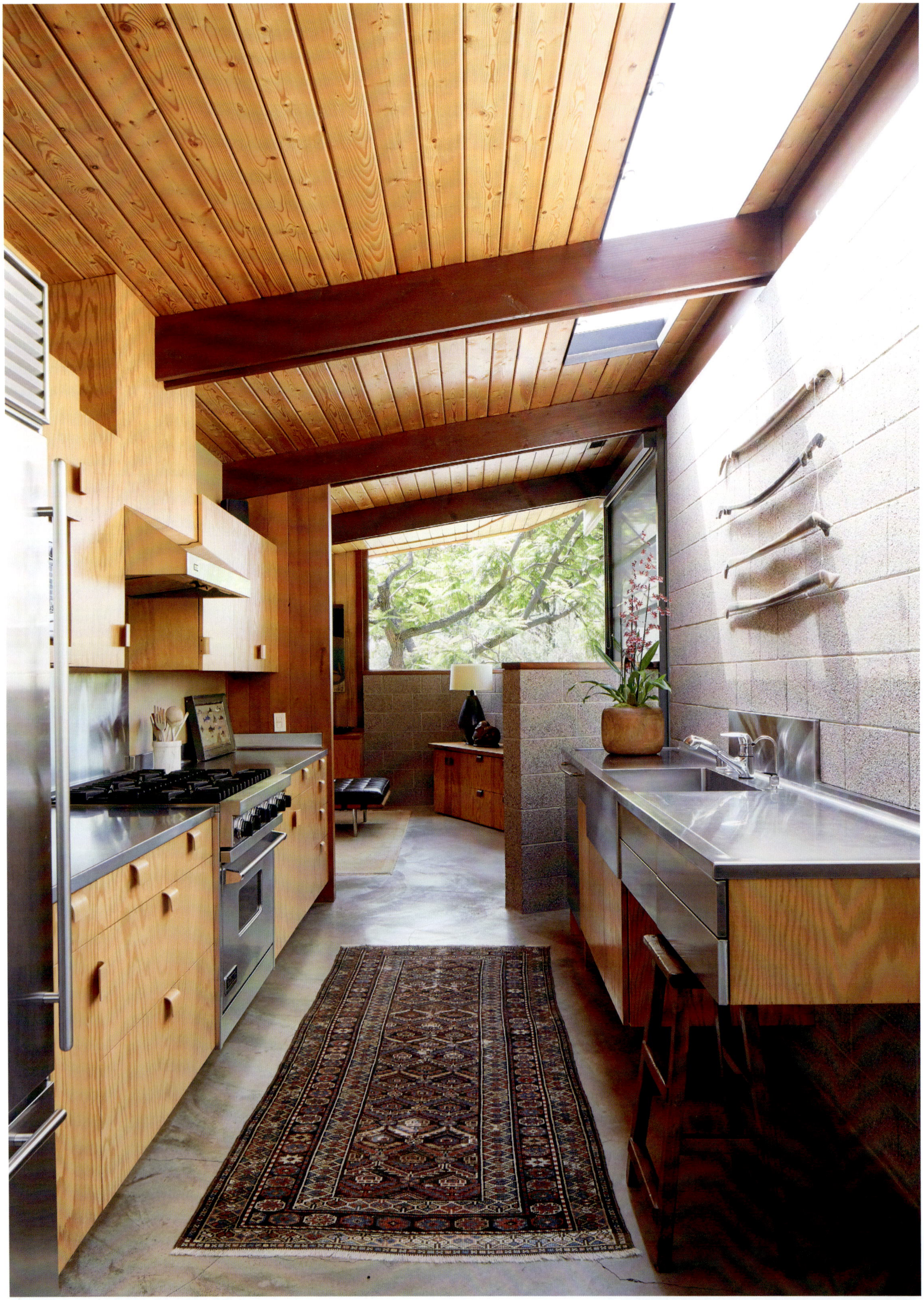

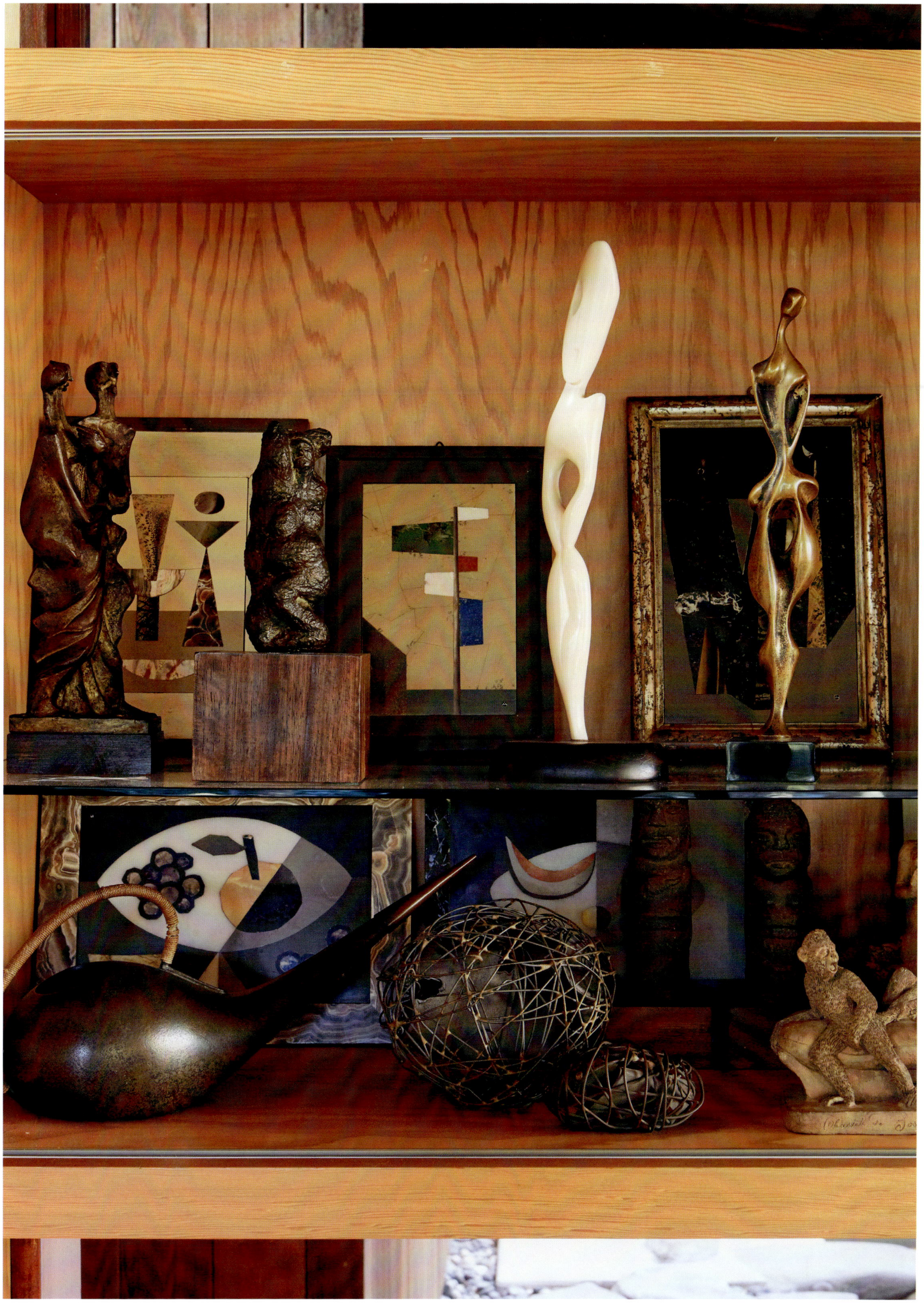

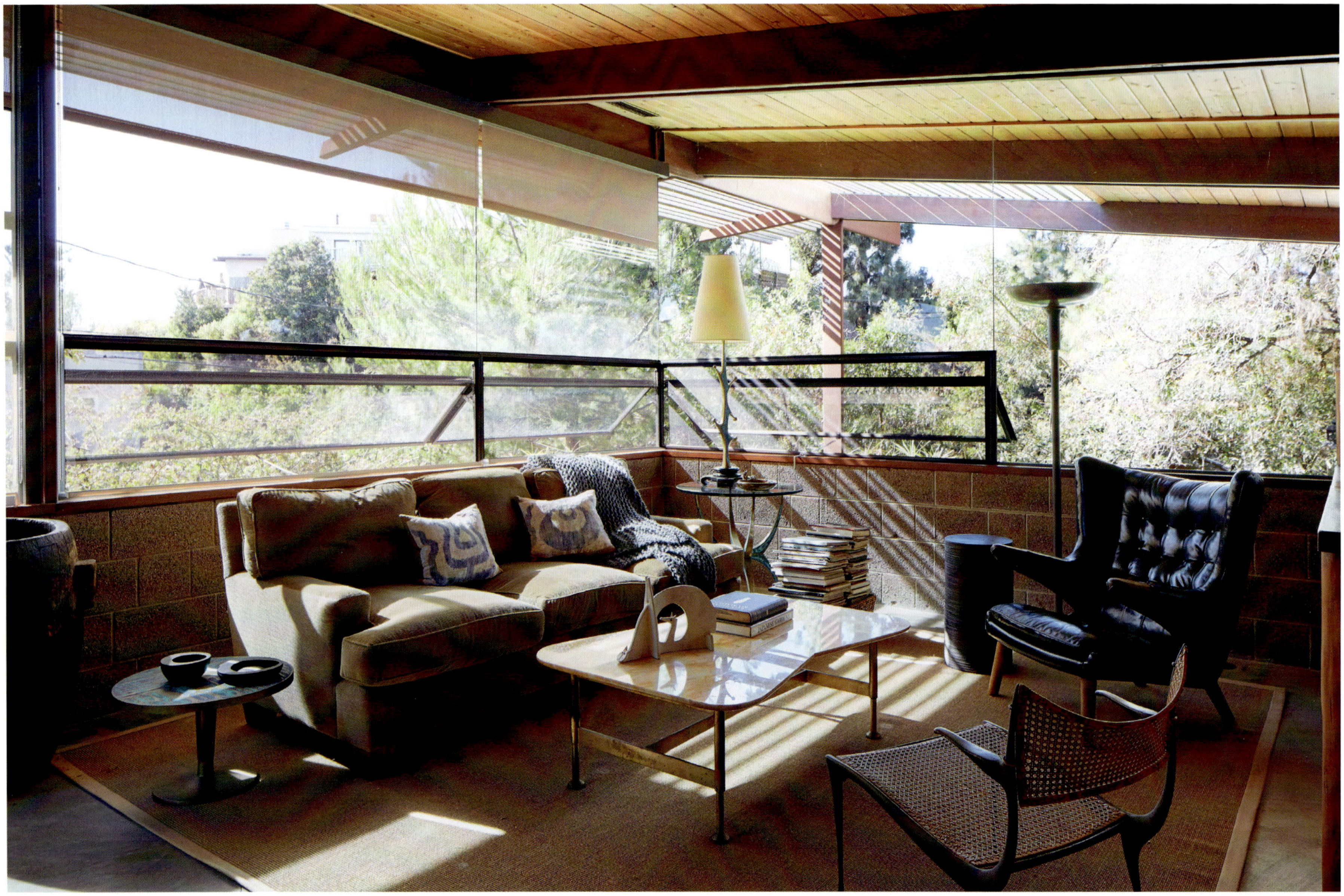

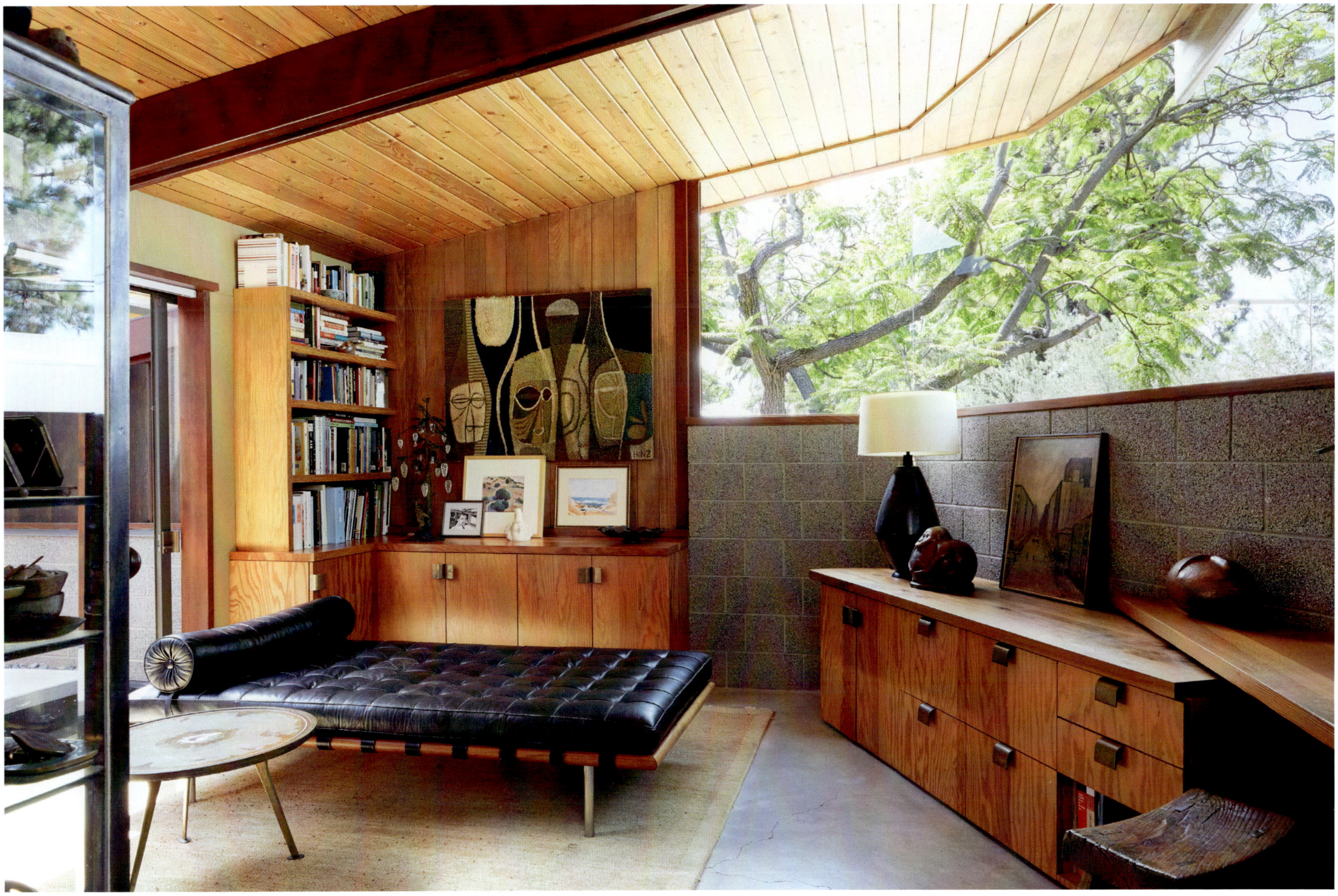

Some years ago the son of the original owner stopped by the house with his son and grandson. He pointed out details that only someone who had lived in the house would know, noted which trees he and his family had planted fifty years earlier, and mentioned that the roof had blown off when he was a child. After that, he recounted, heavy steel straps were bolted under the eaves to keep the roof in place.

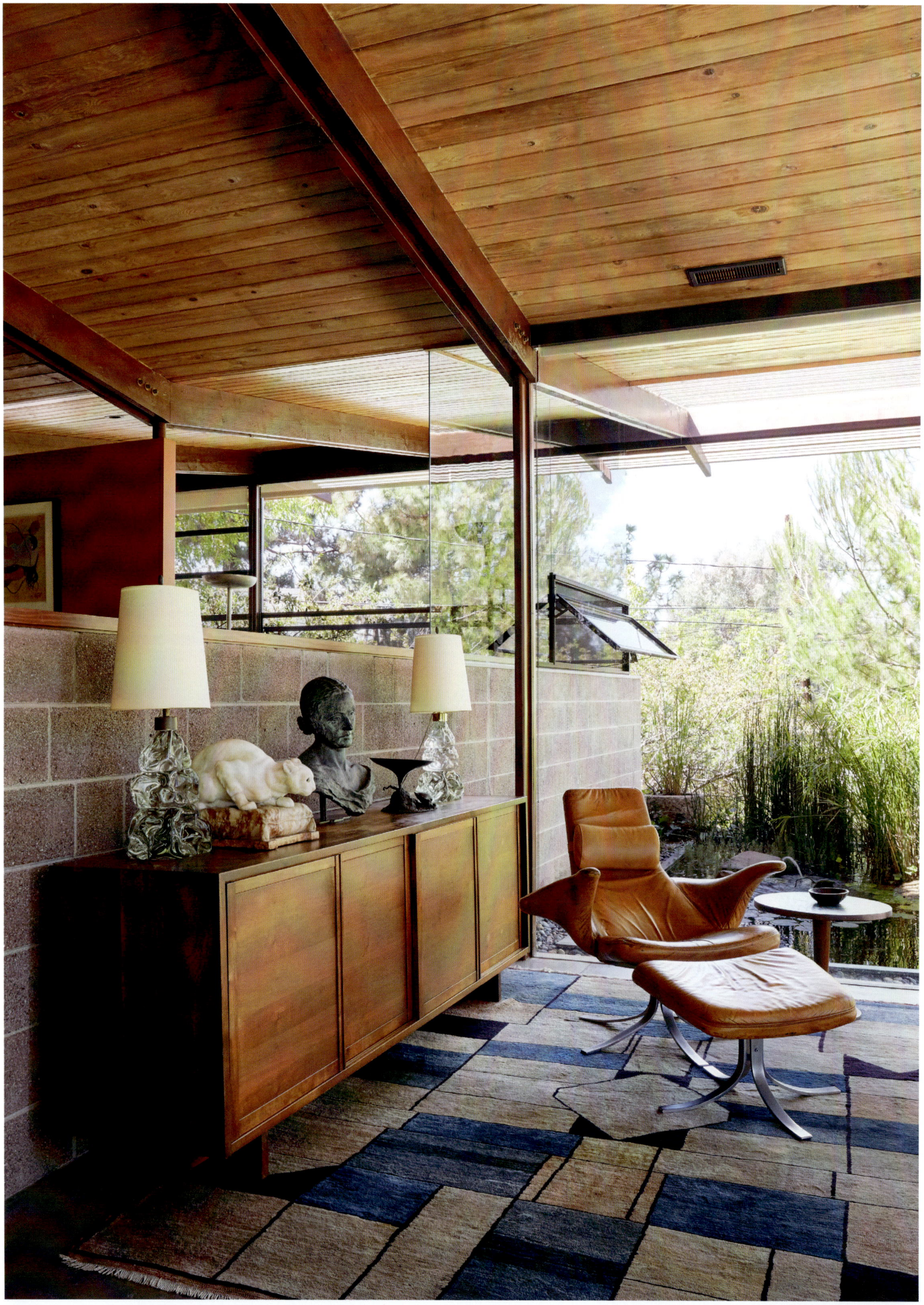

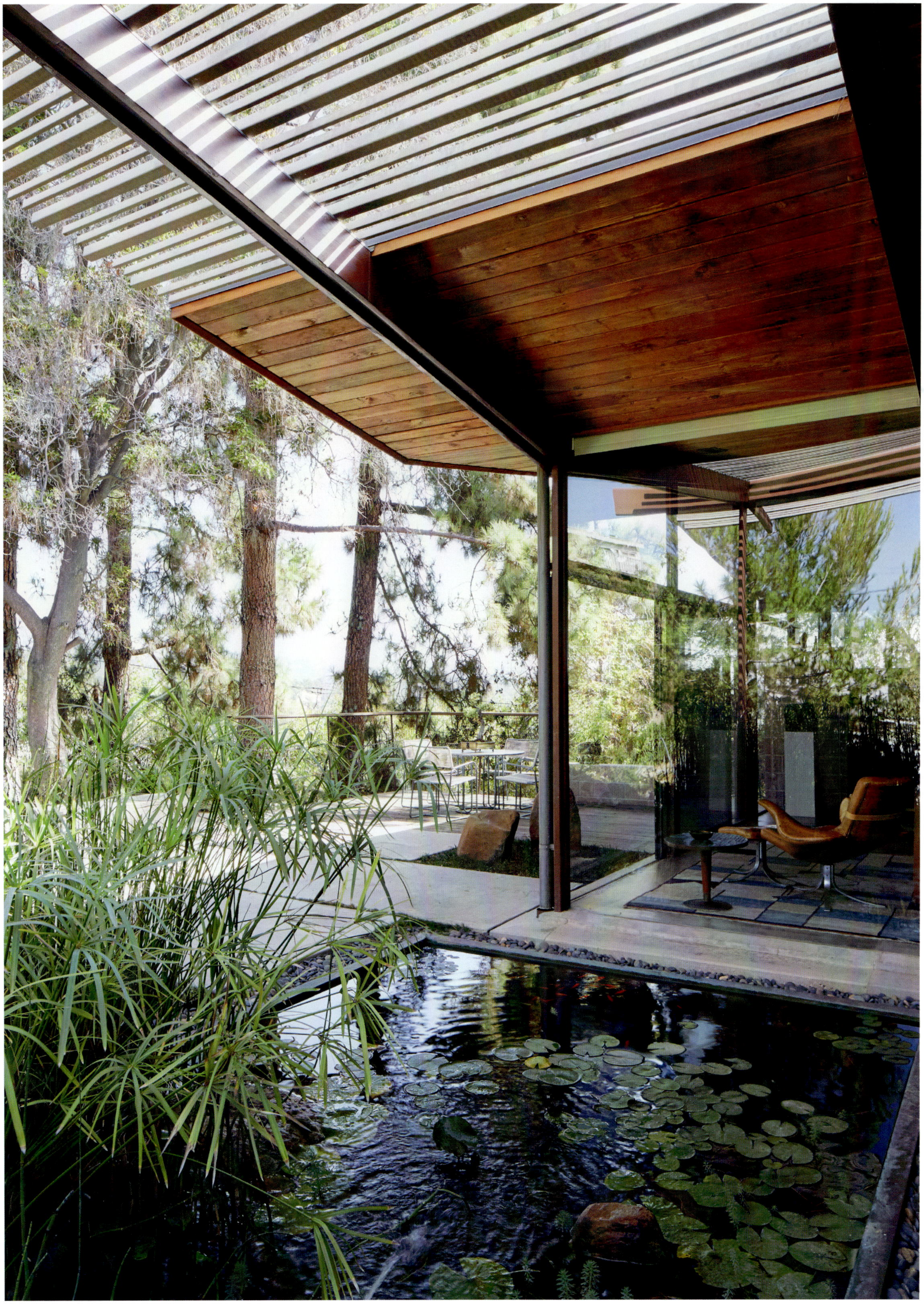

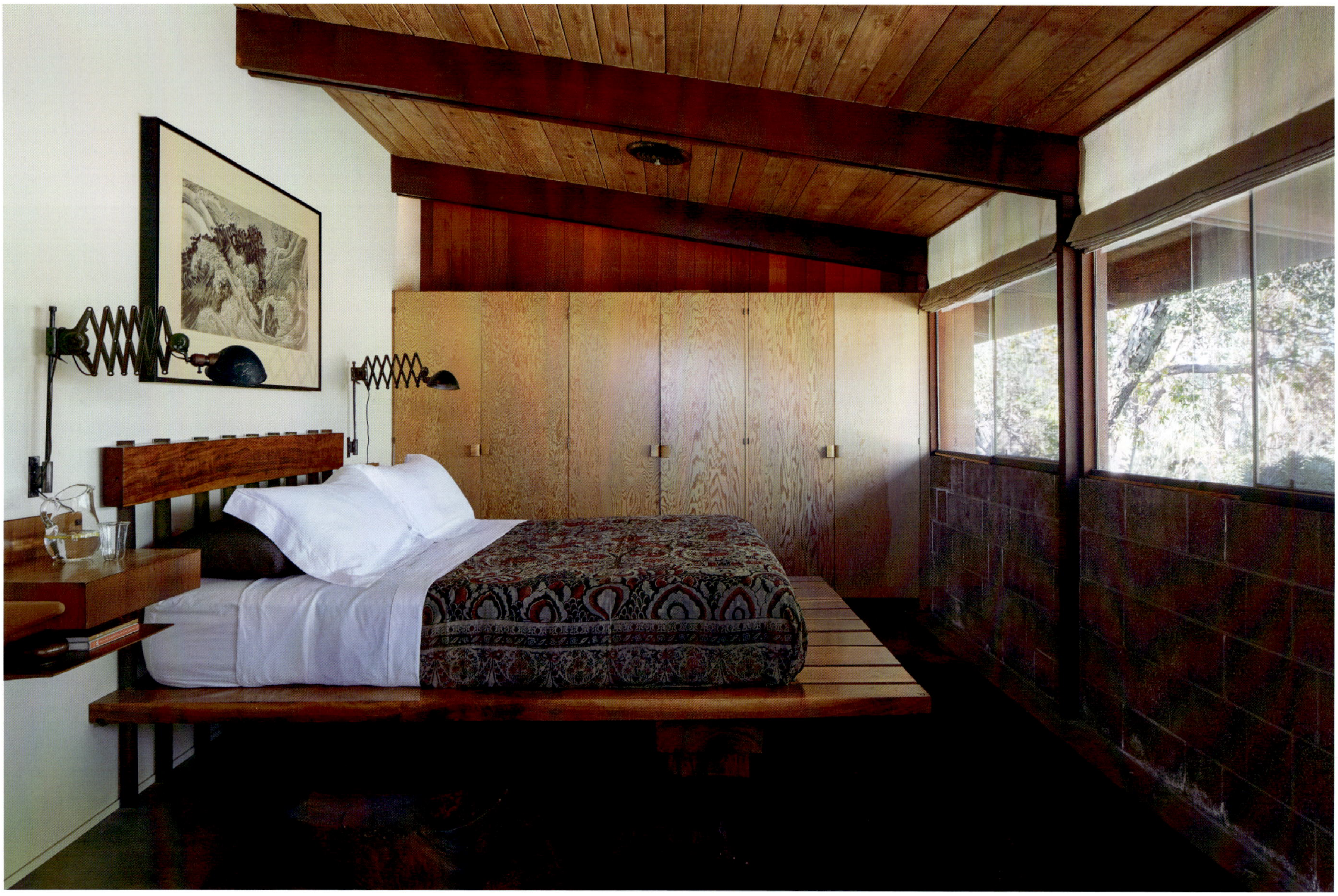

Previous: Despite the close positioning of the community's residences, once inside the house, the city melts away. An interior courtyard, mature garden, ponds, and glass walls expand the living spaces to the outdoors and welcome the landscape in.

When Kate and Adam Blackman purchased the house, the wood ceiling and cinderblocks had been painted white, and there was wall-to-wall white carpeting. The first thing they did was restore the interiors' natural materials, hand-stripping the ceilings, sandblasting the cinder block, and pulling up the carpet.

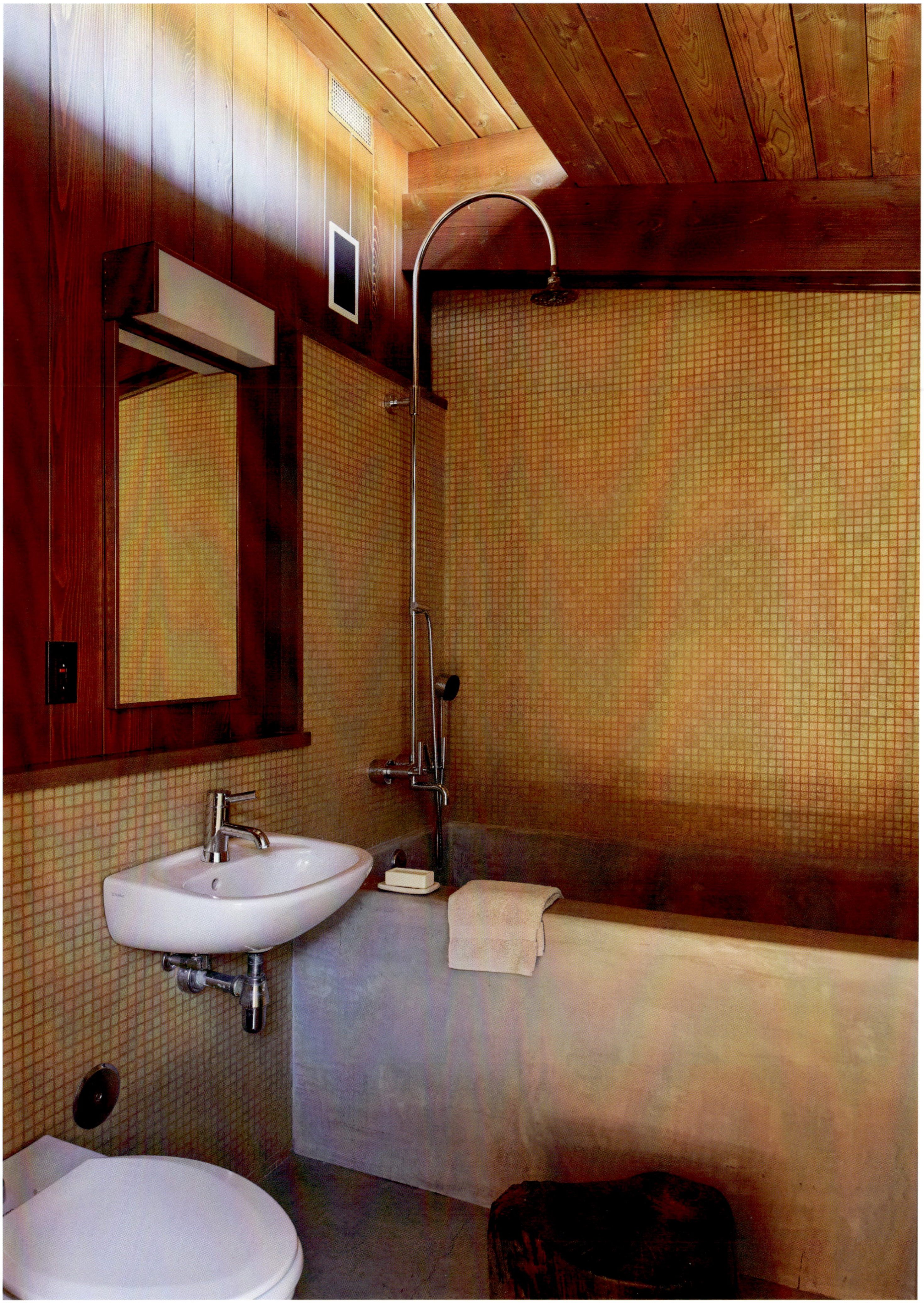

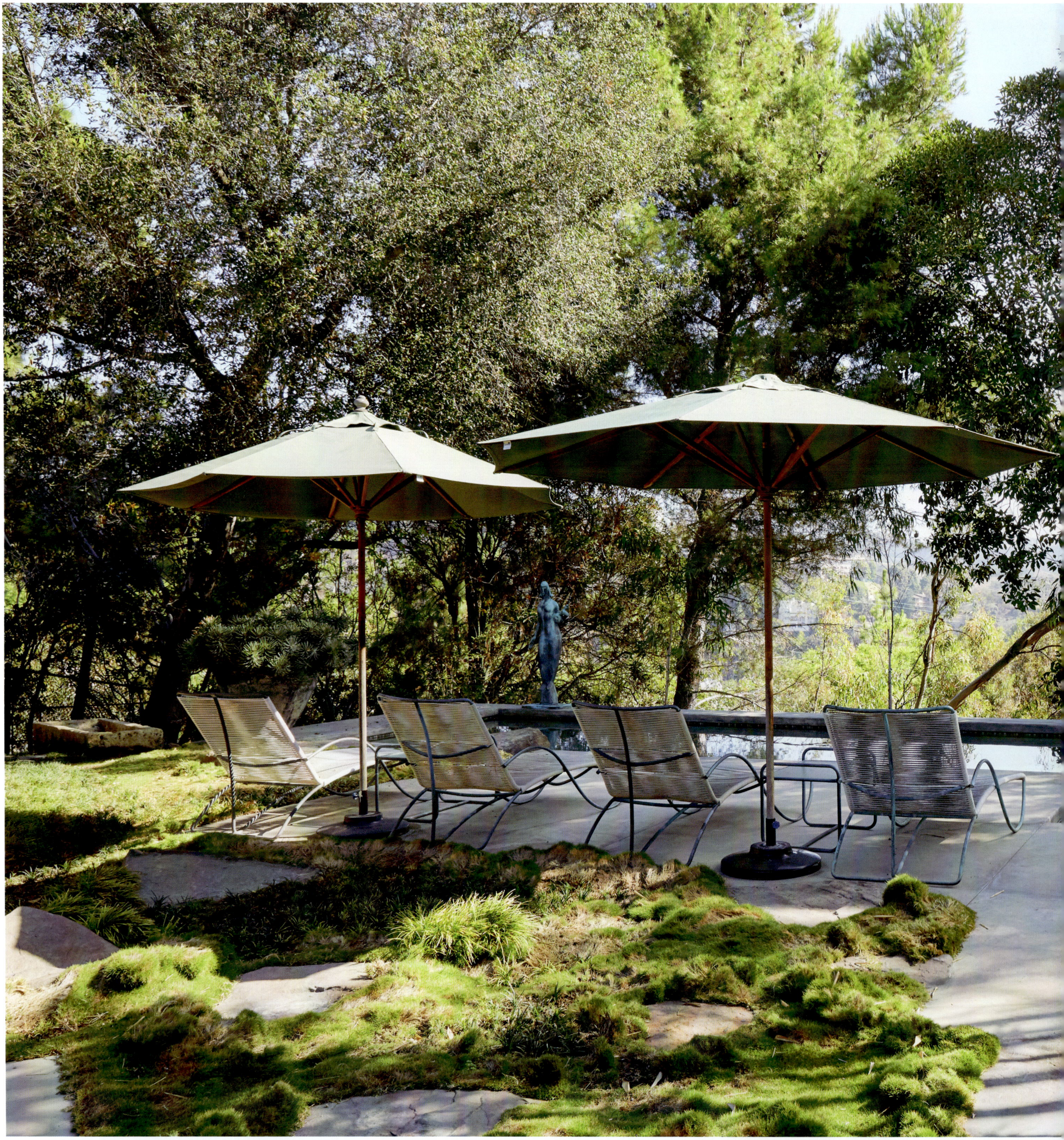

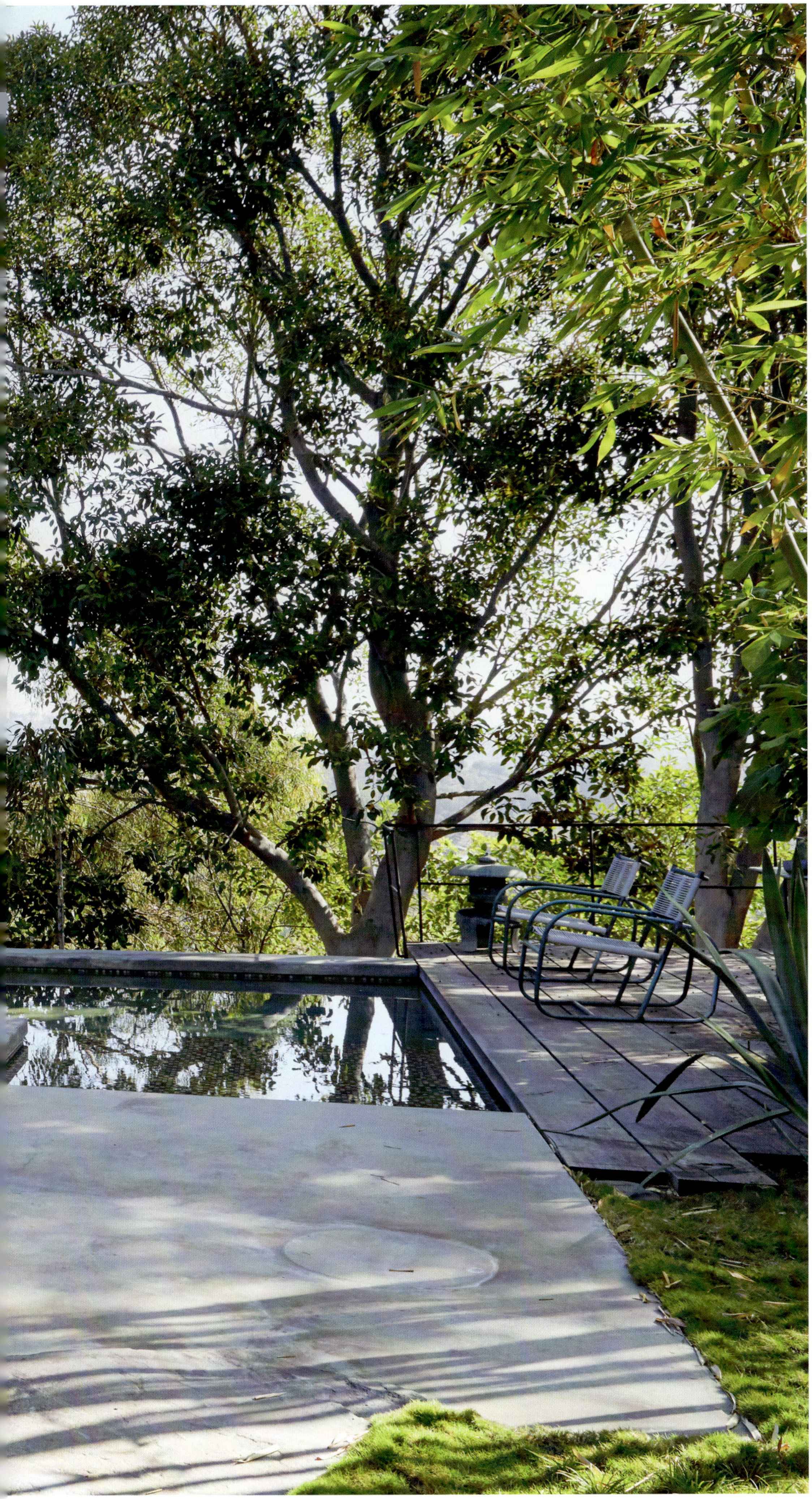

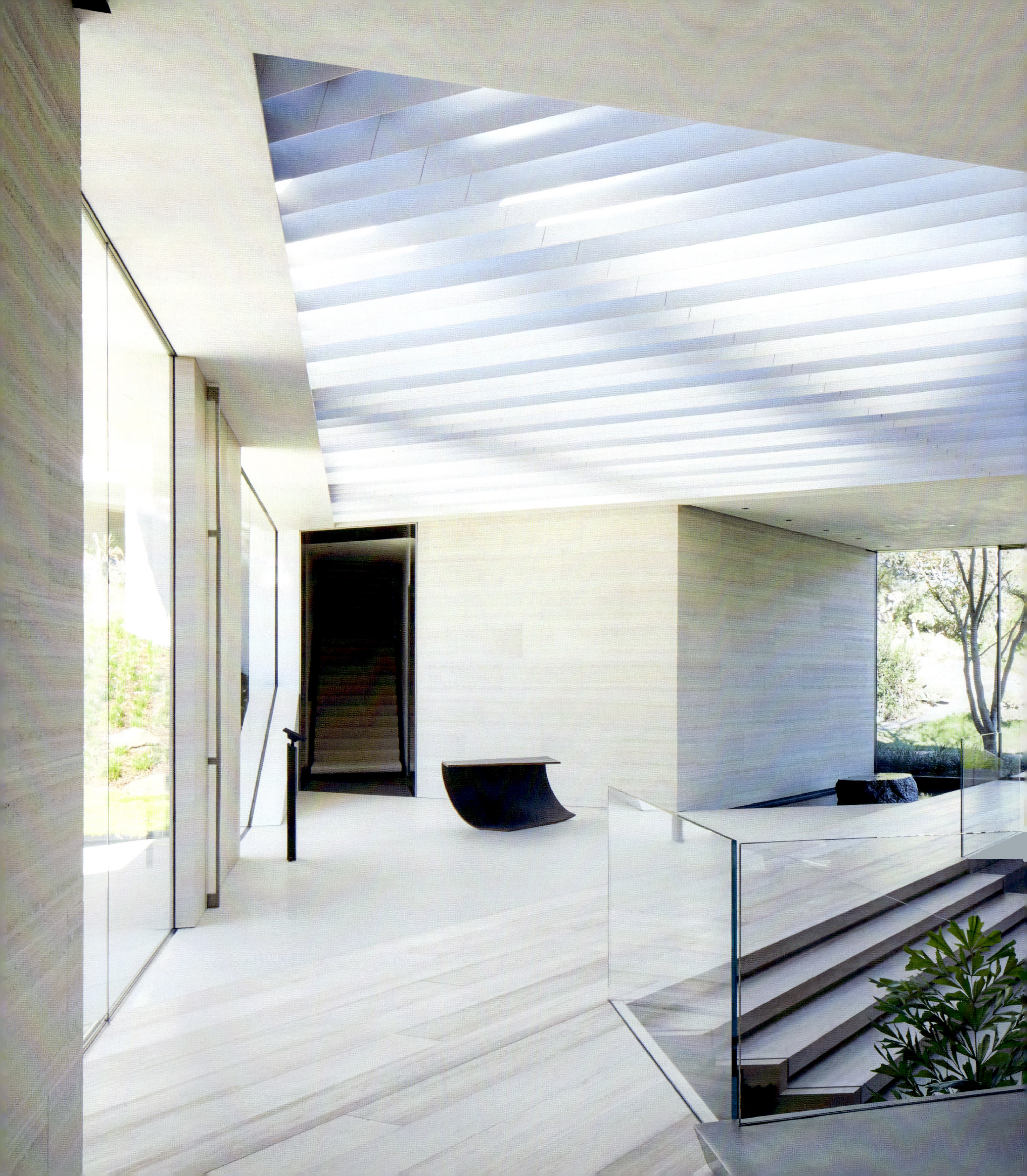

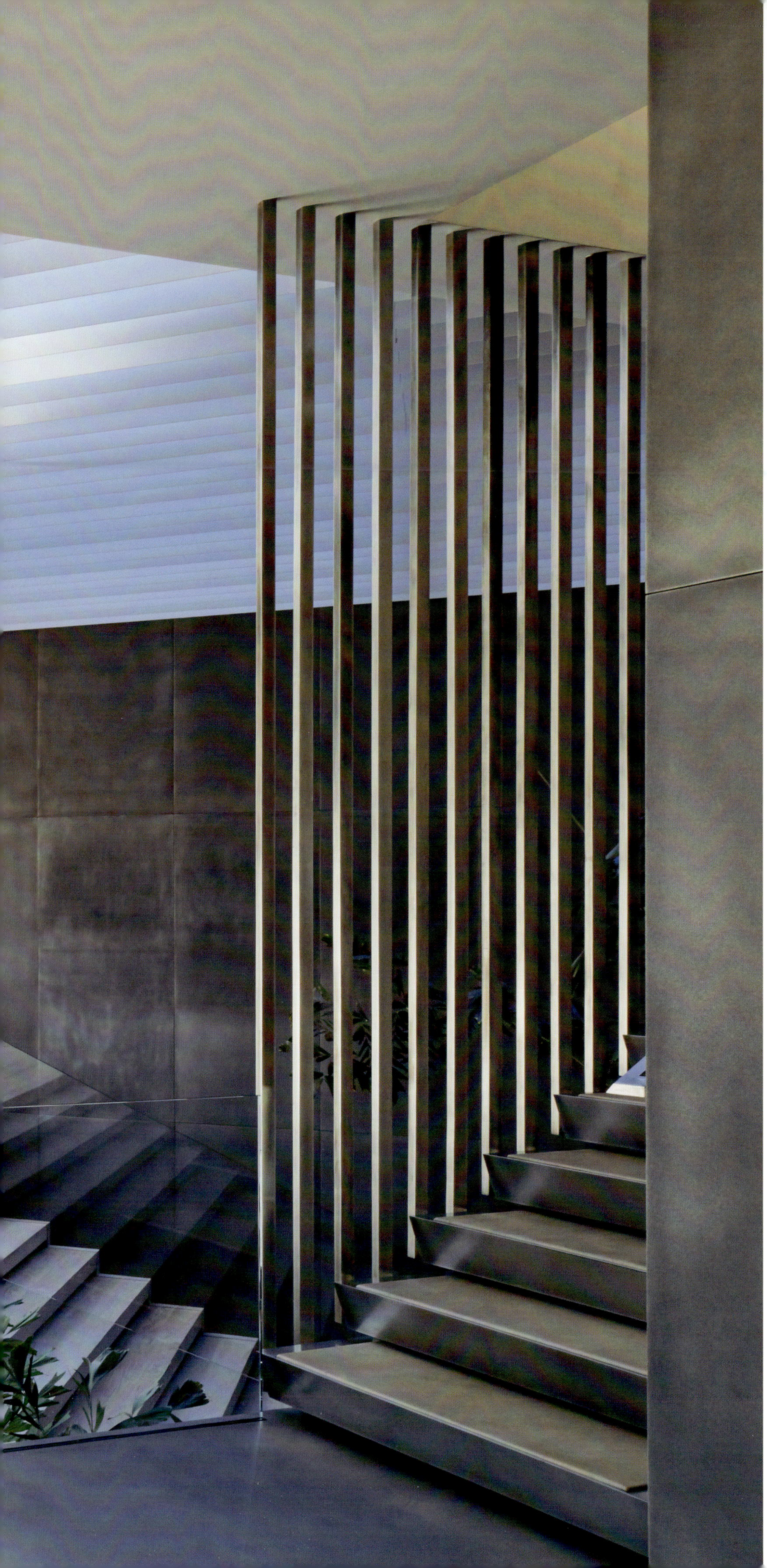

A Retreat in Bel Air

Bel Air

Architect

Chad Oppenheim

A successful film director has a unique artistic vision but has also mastered the complex choreography needed to achieve it, knowing when to delegate and to whom. This delegation is as true for Michael Bay's Bel Air property as it is for his films.

Armed with unlimited creative ambition, Bay and architect Chad Oppenheim have created an extraordinary vision, a serene retreat befitting an expert on action. Working with interior designers Lorraine Letendre and Lynda Murray, the caliber of every element unifies the project into a singular vision. With a sophisticated mix of art and furniture by Pierre Jeanneret, Axel Vervoordt, and Anish Kapoor, among others, the decor works seamlessly with the striking architecture. Often when I walk into a space, one or two ideal camera angles present themselves. In this property, where no room seems to have a right angle, I was like a kid in a candy store.

At one point on the shoot, I was balancing at the top of a tall ladder, leaning precariously over a hedge, attempting a shot with a long lens of the glass-sided swimming pool that overhangs the canyon below. A car pulled up and a paparazzo, who clearly thought I was one of his own, stuck his head out the window and shouted conspiratorially, "Who've you got? Can I come up and get a shot?"

Many houses I visit will have some level of technology built in, but none have been as advanced and seamlessly integrated as in Michael Bay's property. In the living room, a massive steel-and-glass wall outfitted with a hydraulic system rises to open the room to the landscape. There is also a three-hundred-foot infinity pool with a glass edge, a gym, a spa room with a hemlock-lined sauna, a cryo chamber (with snow!), and a state-of-the-art fifty-seat screening room. Part Zen retreat, part Bond lair.

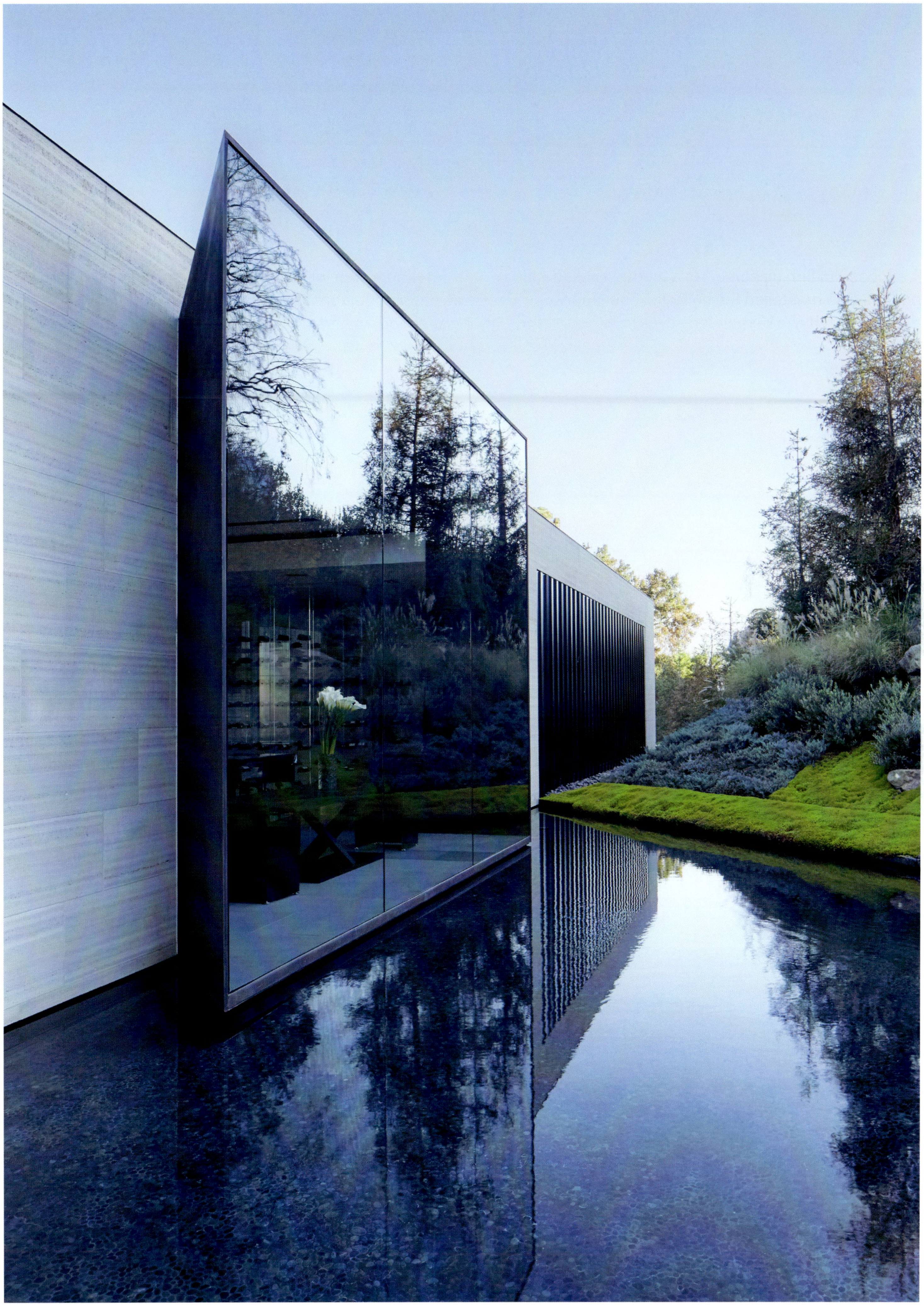

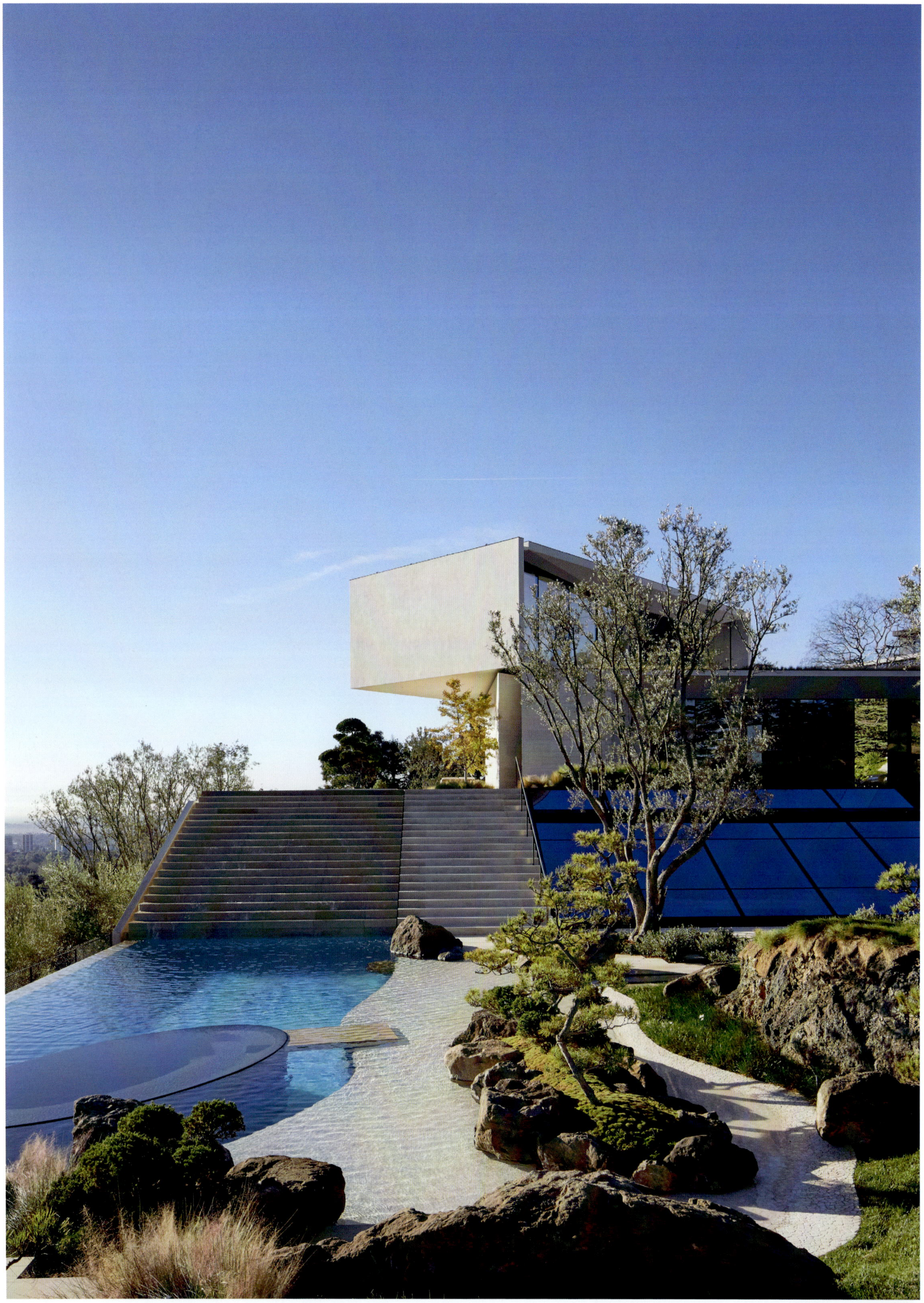

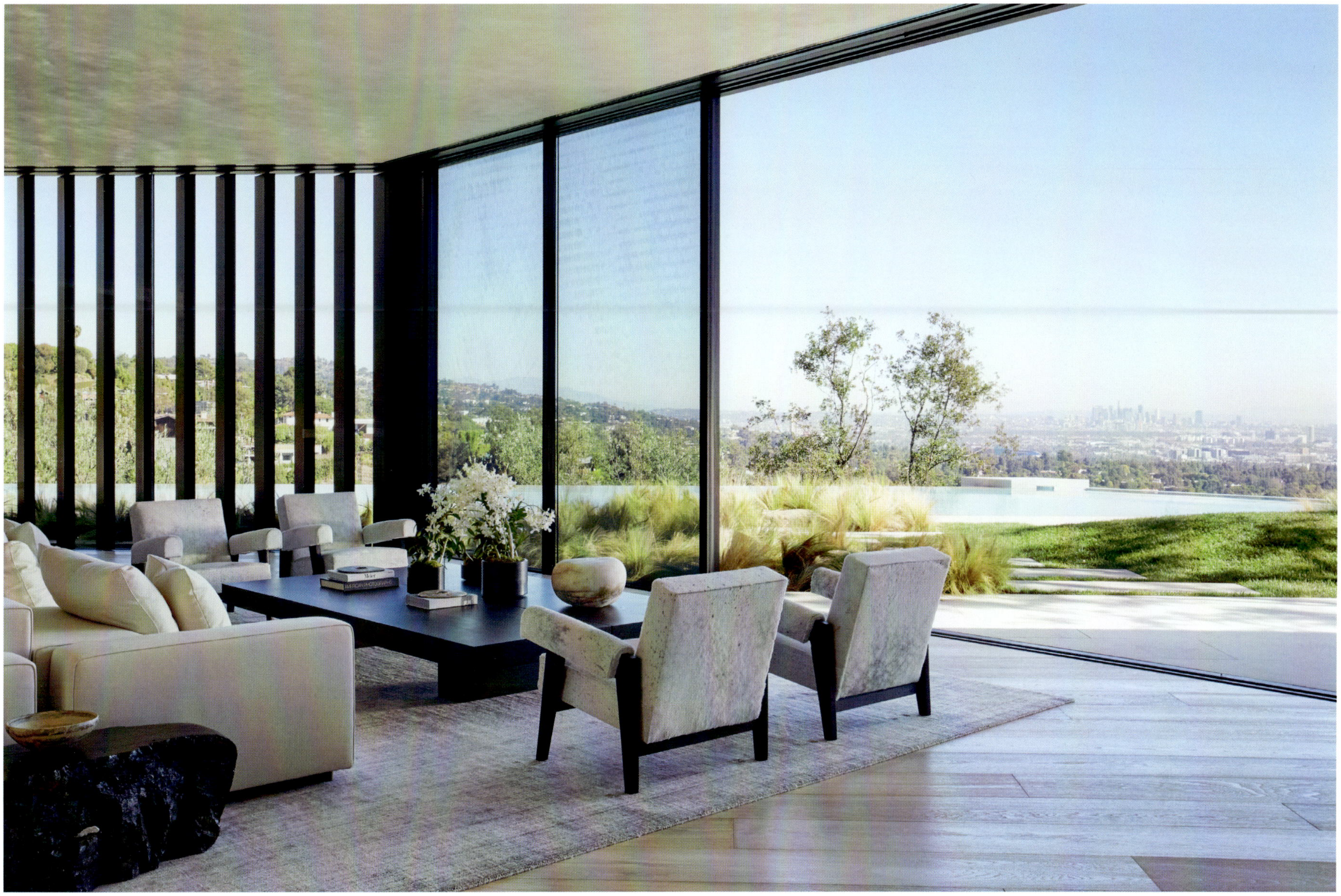

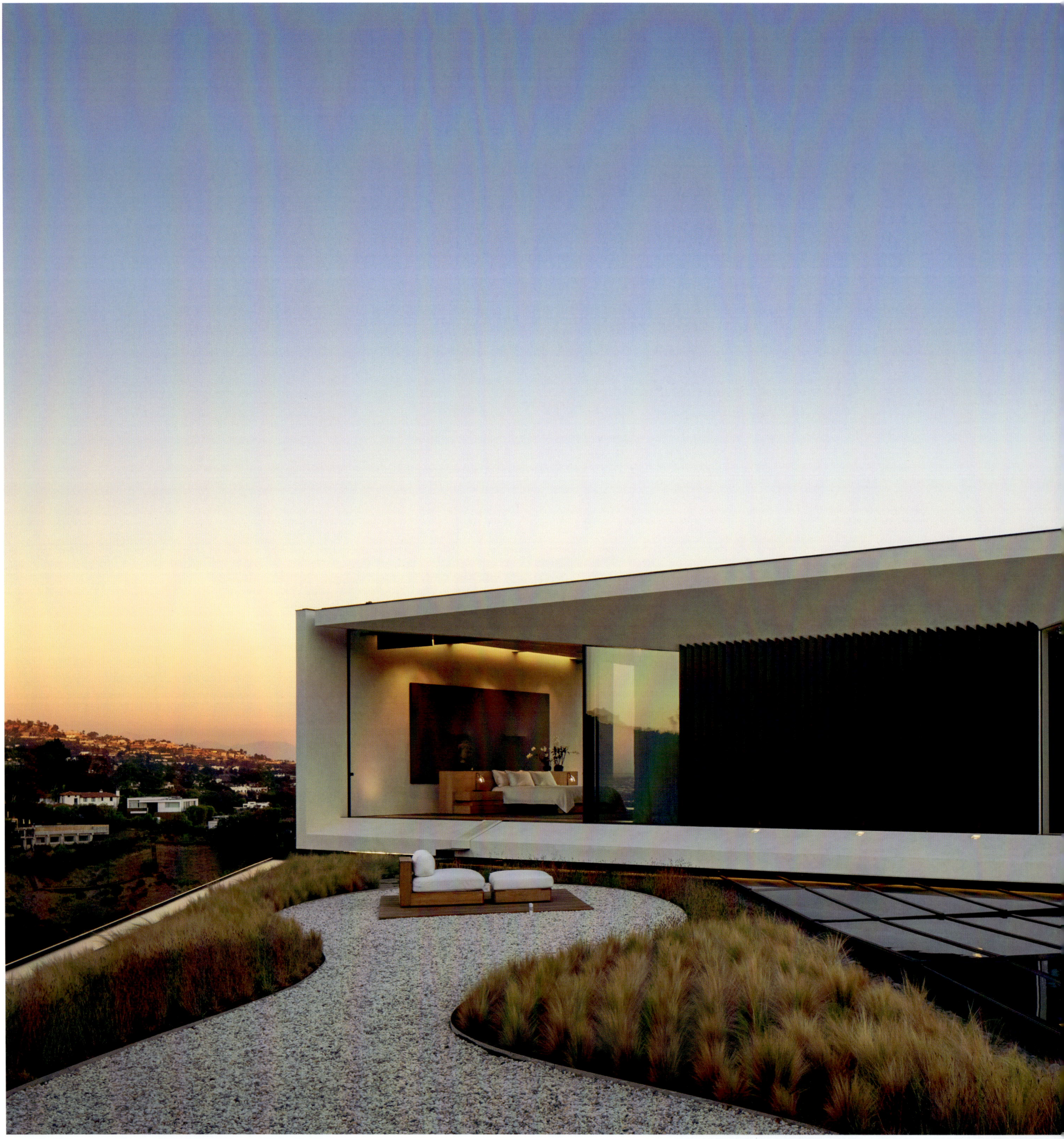

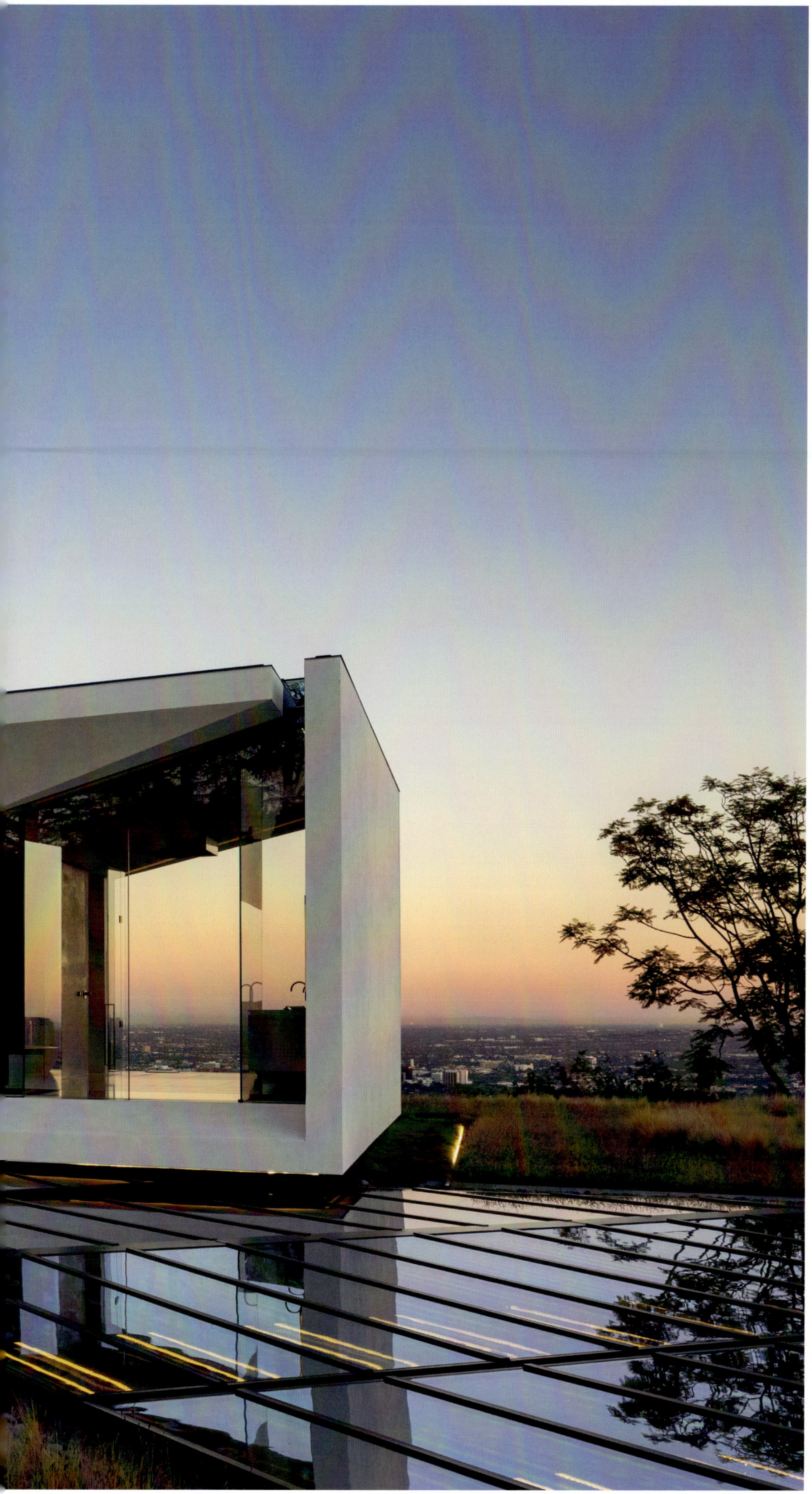

Built on a steep eight-acre lot in Bel Air, the thirty-thousand-square-foot property includes multiple swimming pools, a full spa with cryo chamber, a next-level screening room for fifty, and an eight-car garage. Bay's property is unlike any I've ever photographed.

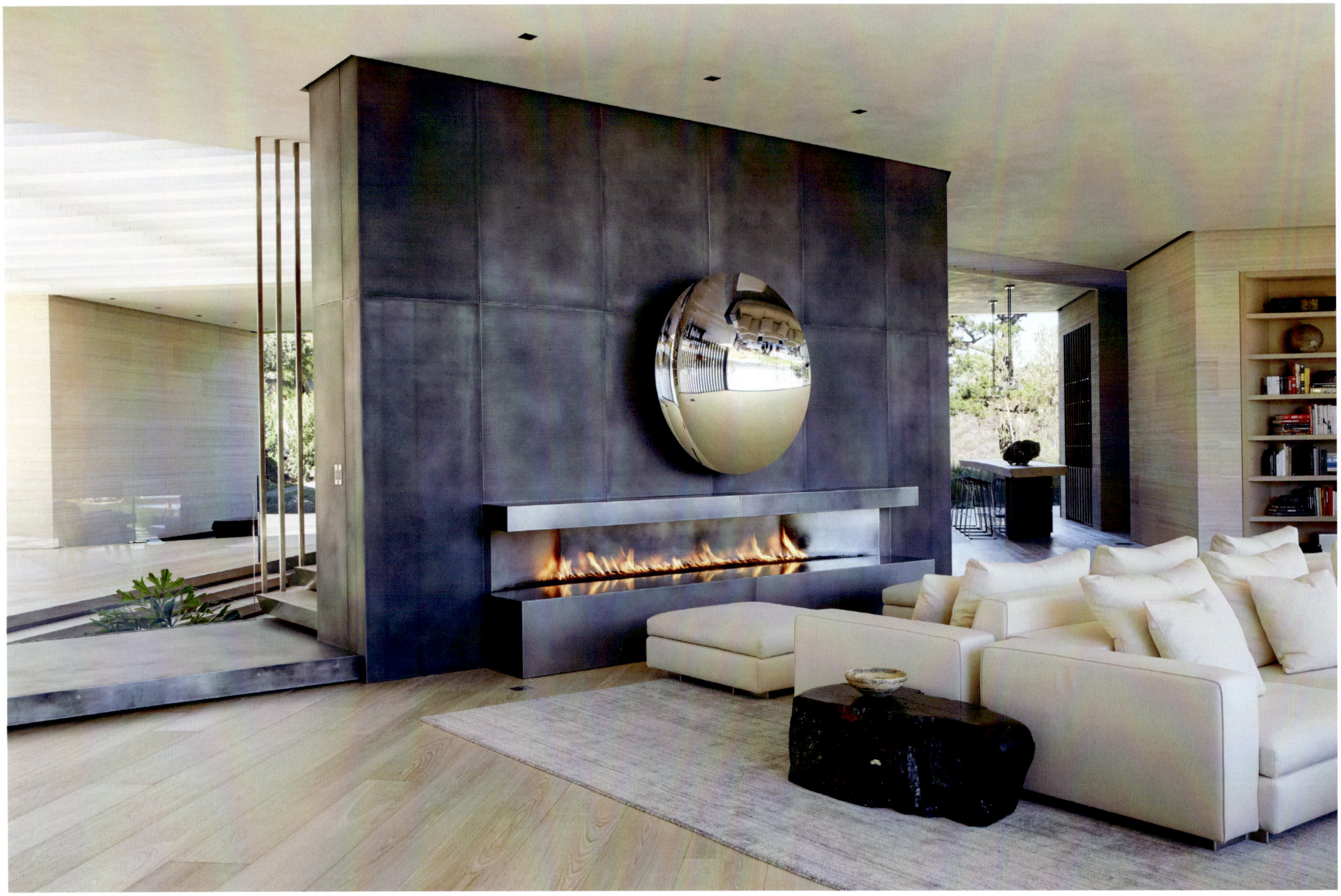

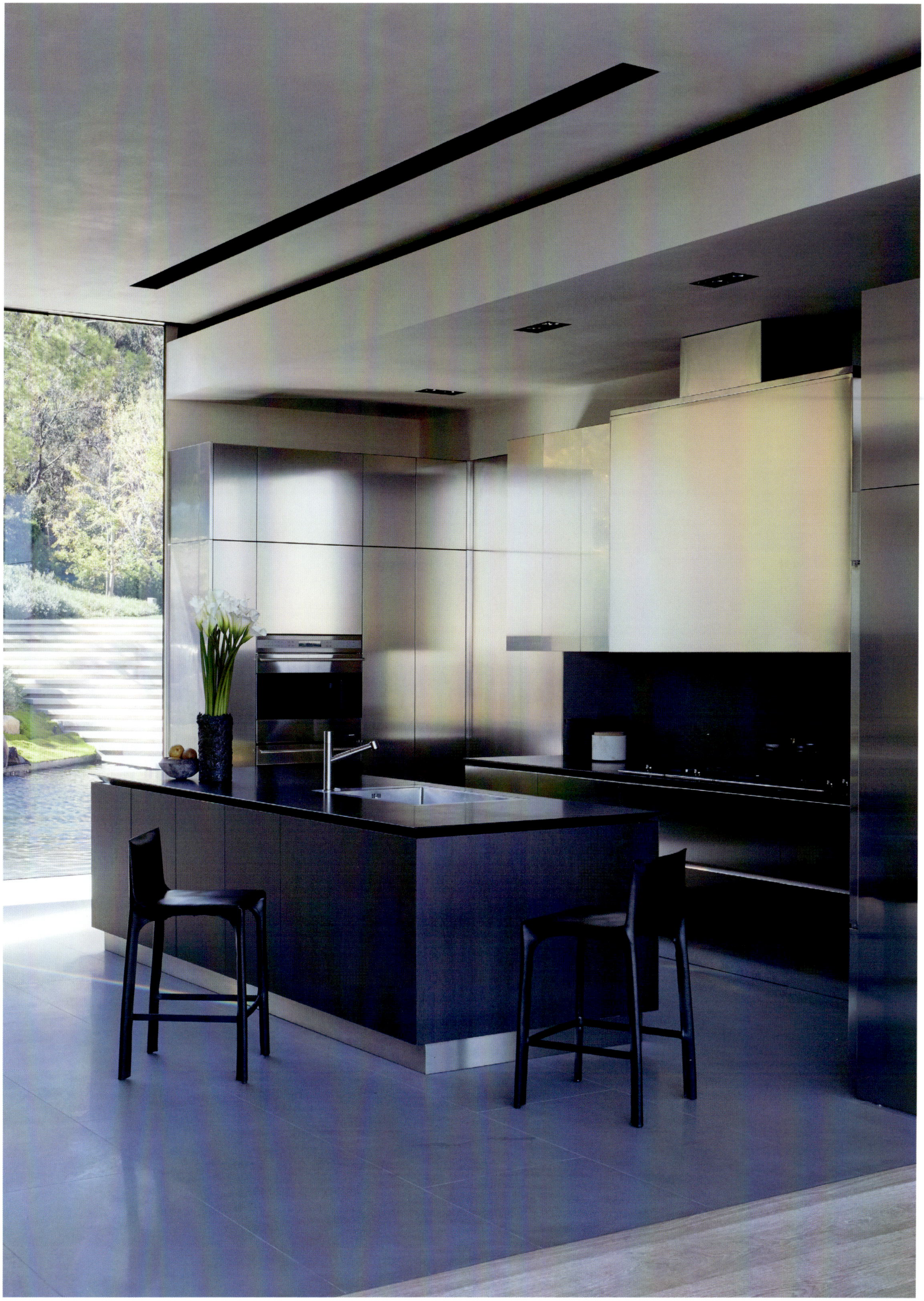

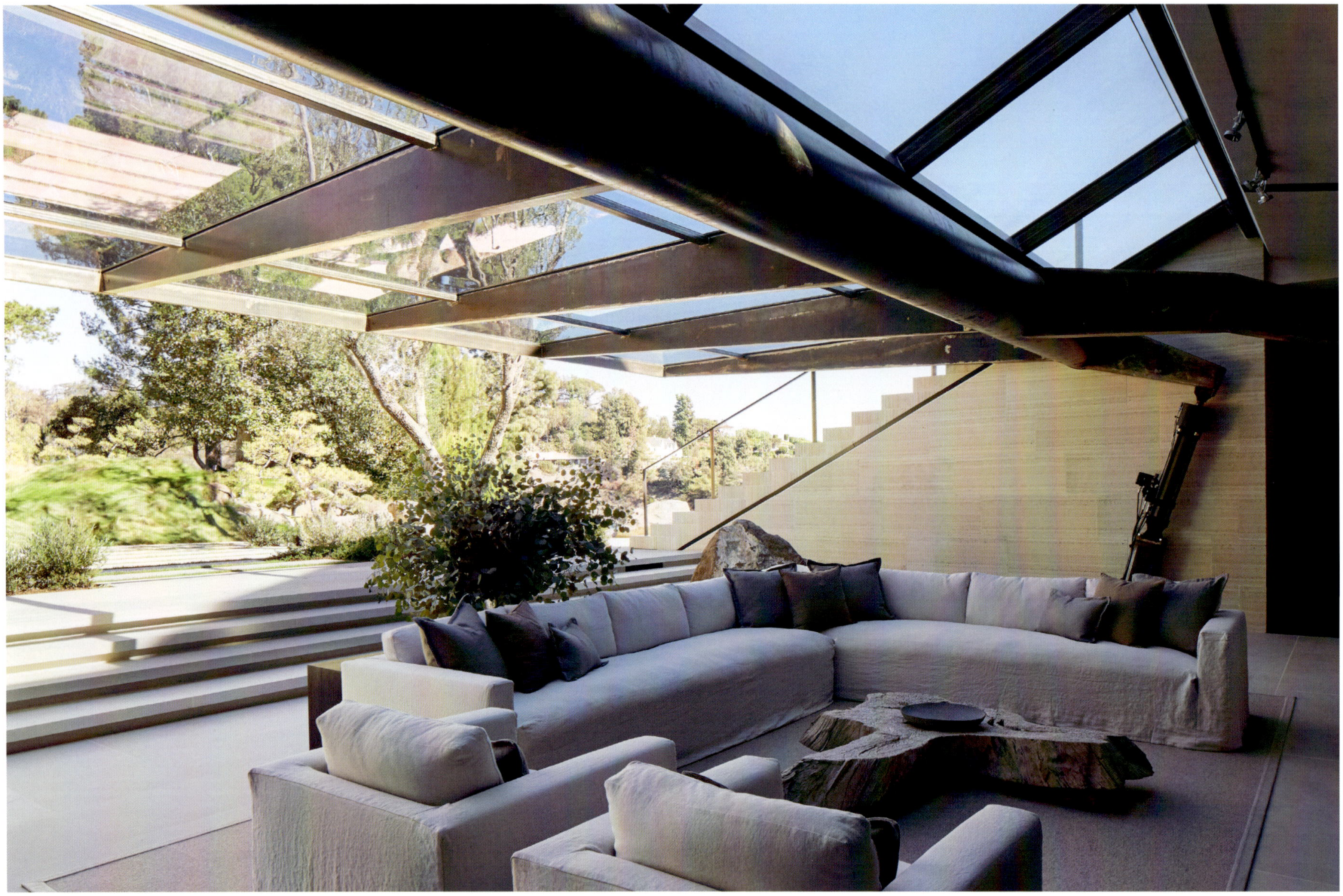

In the lounge, an entire windowed wall lifts to open the room to the landscape.

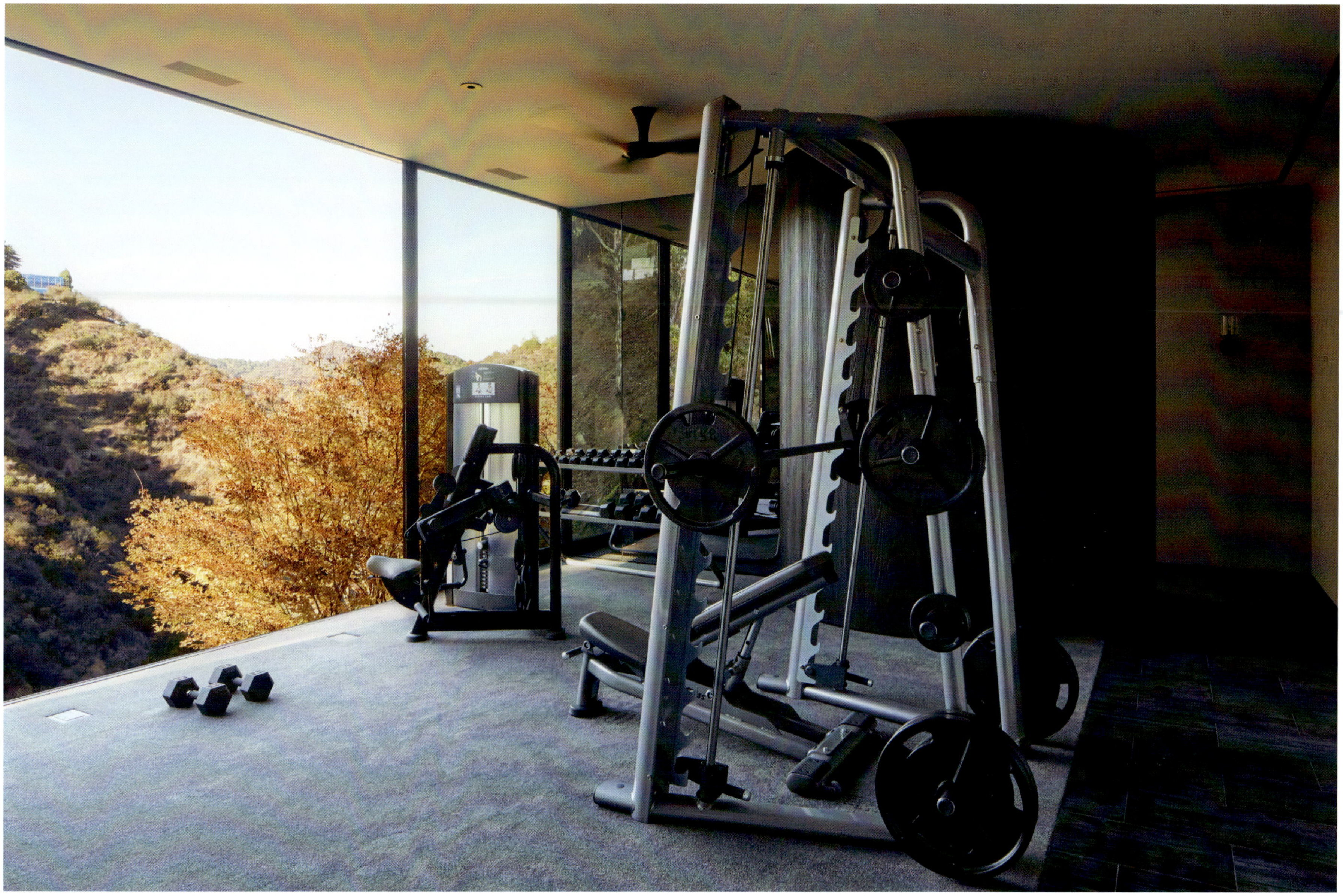

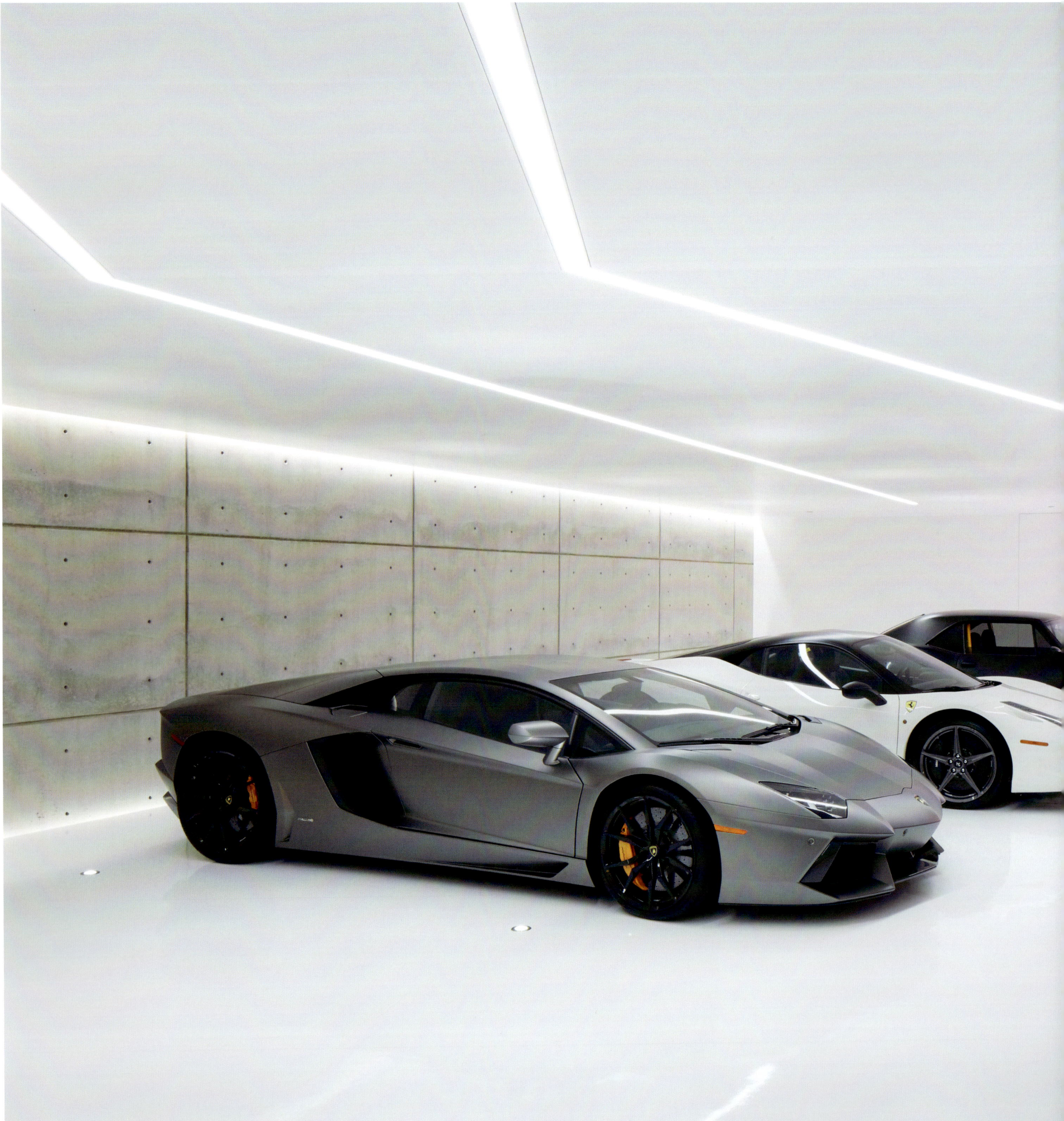

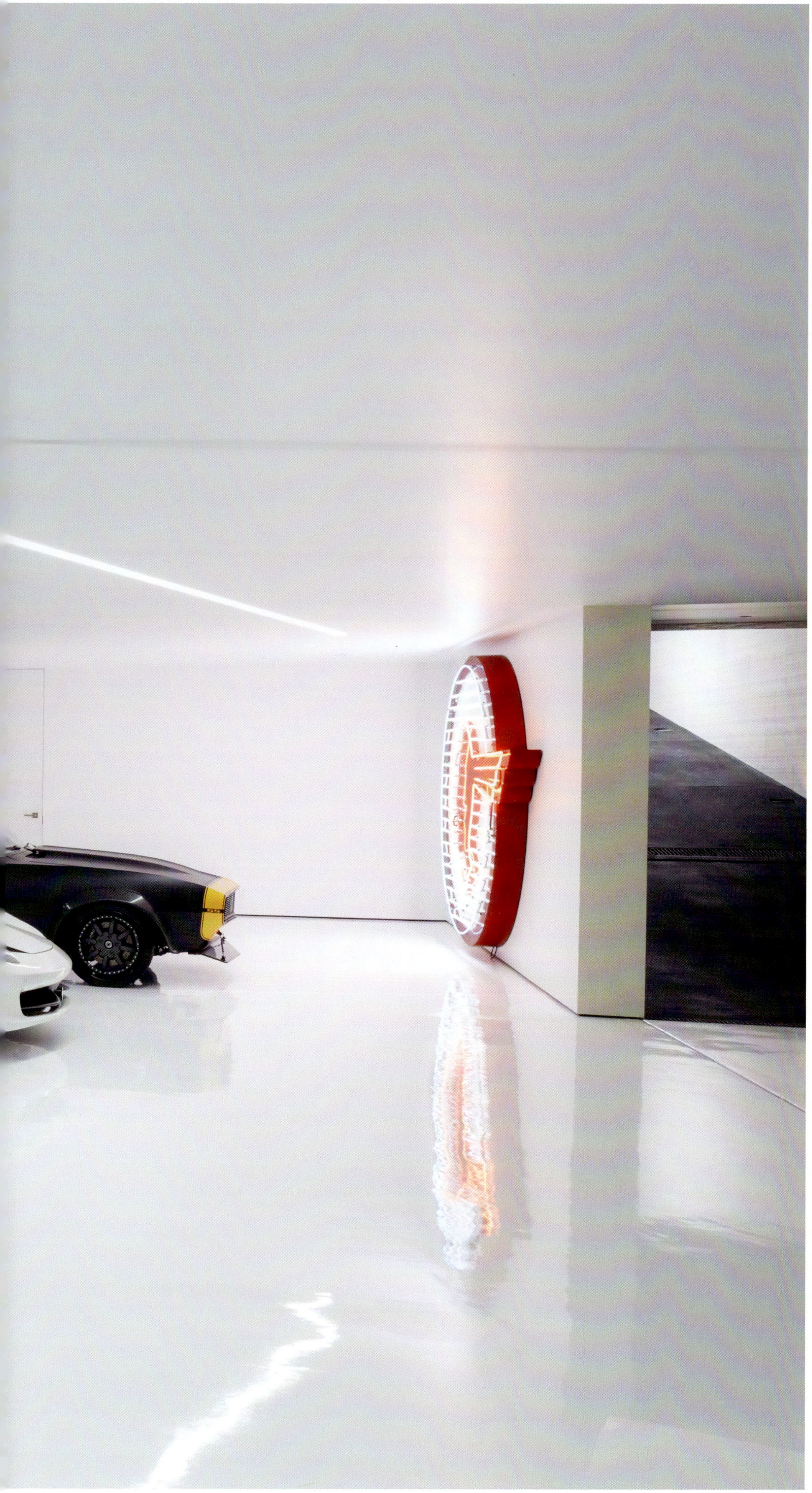

A collection of cars, including Lamborghini, Ferrari, and others, lives in an all-white, gallery-like garage. The lineup had my assistants and me drooling.

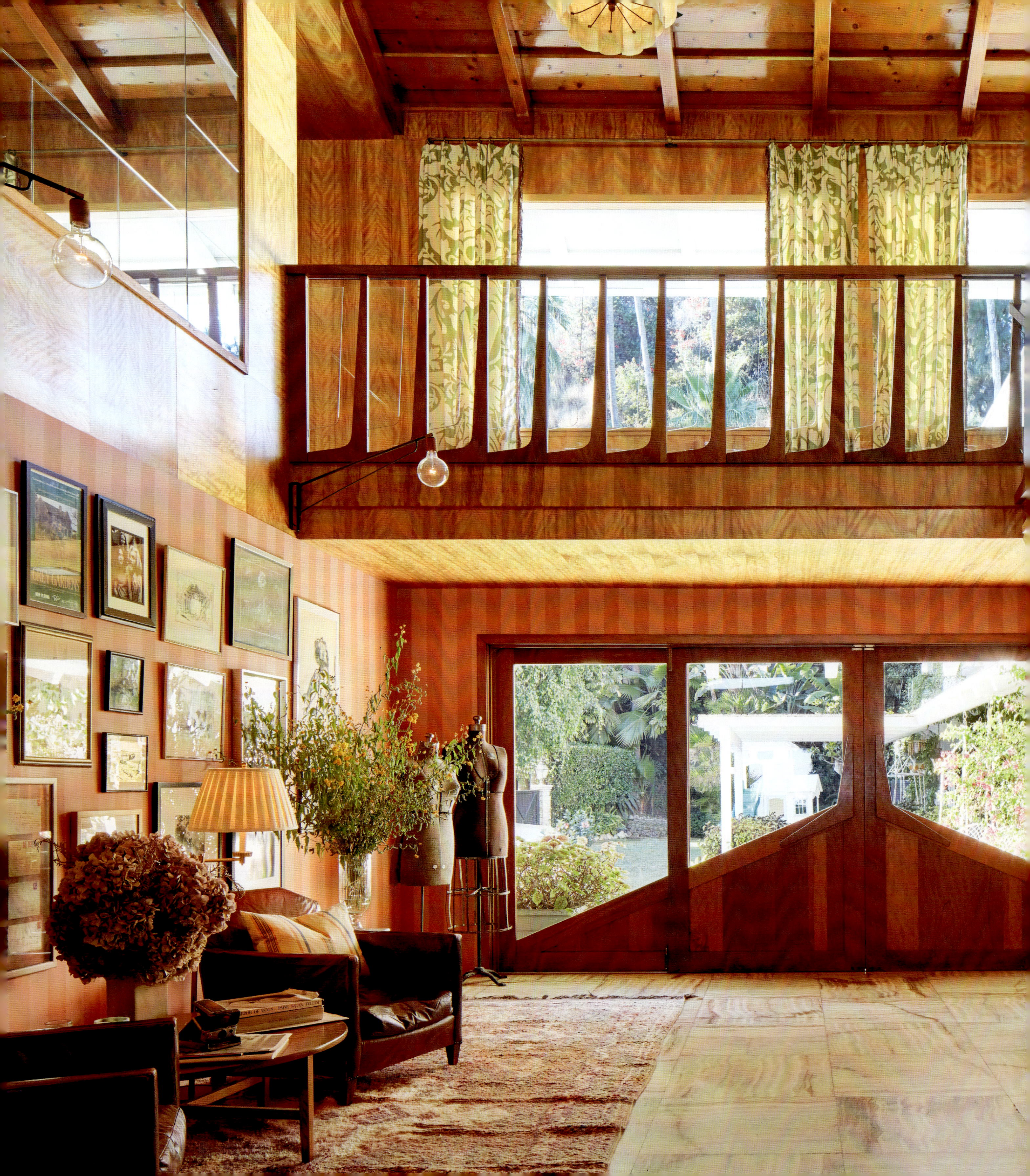
GREY GARDENS

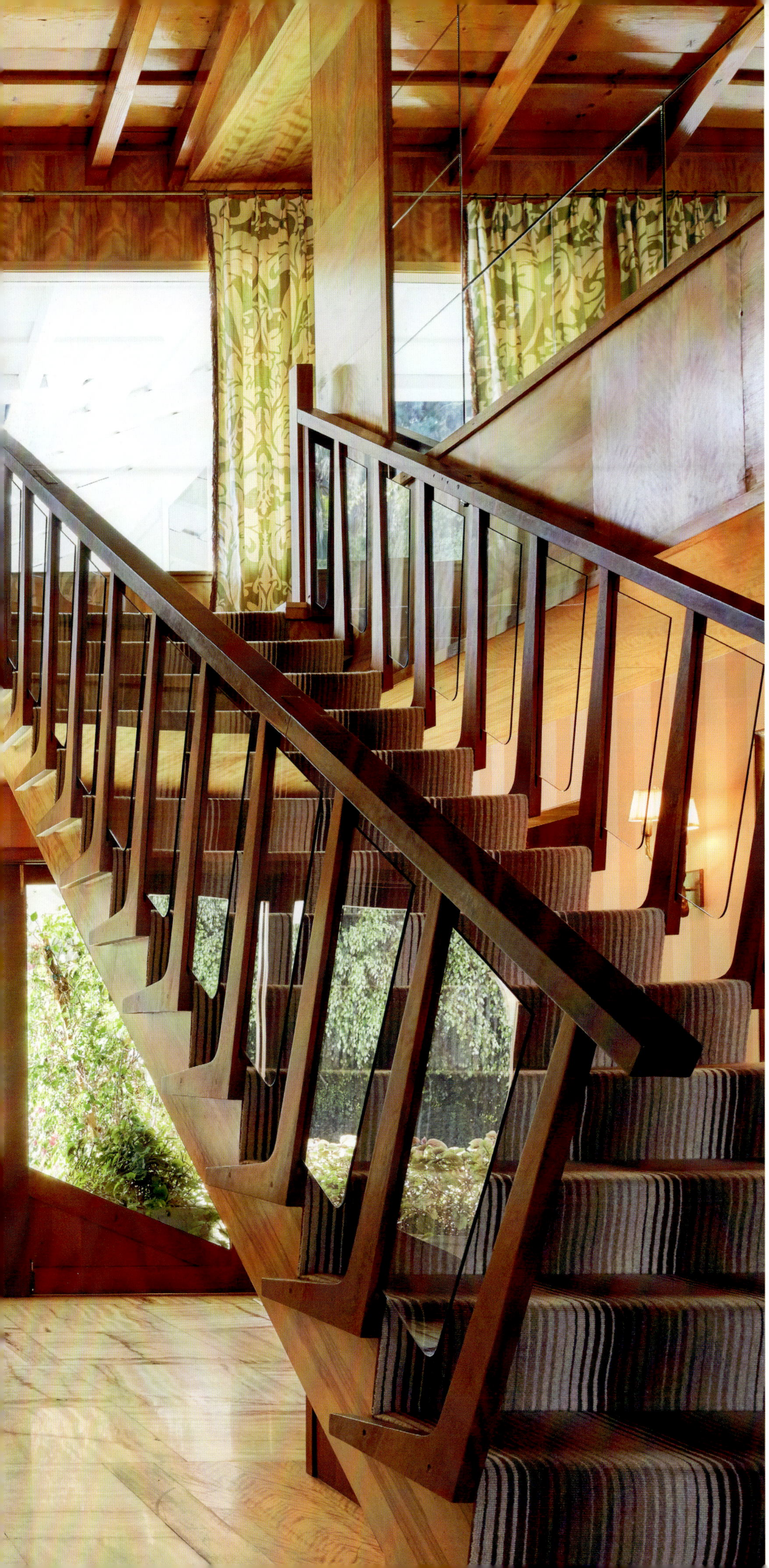

Barrymore Residence

Hollywood Hills

Resident

Drew Barrymore

Cool things have happened in this 1957 house in the Hollywood Hills: It was once the residence of Motown Records founder Berry Gordy. It's where the Beatles stayed while on tour in 1966 and where, a year later, John Boorman shot *Point Blank*, starring Lee Marvin and Angie Dickinson. Elvis Presley would drop by to fire guns in the brick-lined basement shooting range. And Drew Barrymore called it her home for more than twenty years.

While I photograph every house with the same creative intent, the images have different destinations. Sometimes they're shot for a book or a magazine, or sometimes for a lark. But the photographs for this house were taken as keepsakes for the owner, as a record of a home filled with history, stories, and love that she would empty and leave the next day.

On arriving, I was greeted by Drew with tears and a hug. It was my first time meeting her, but the emotions around leaving this beautiful home were raw and infectious. It was humbling to be invited in for this assignment, and in some ways it changed my thinking about the purpose of the images that I take as an interiors photographer.

It goes without saying, but Drew is well known as an actor, producer, writer, and director. Over the past few years, she's added TV host and designer to her résumé. Not as widely known is that she is also a photographer. Over two days and with direction from her and her lovely team, I documented familiar corners of her longtime home: the pencil marks on the wall recording her daughters' heights over the years; her beloved books, framed letters, and film posters; gallery walls full of art and photographs; her cats, dogs, and kids; her piano; and mementos of a family's history in Hollywood, both past and present, in order to preserve it all for the future.

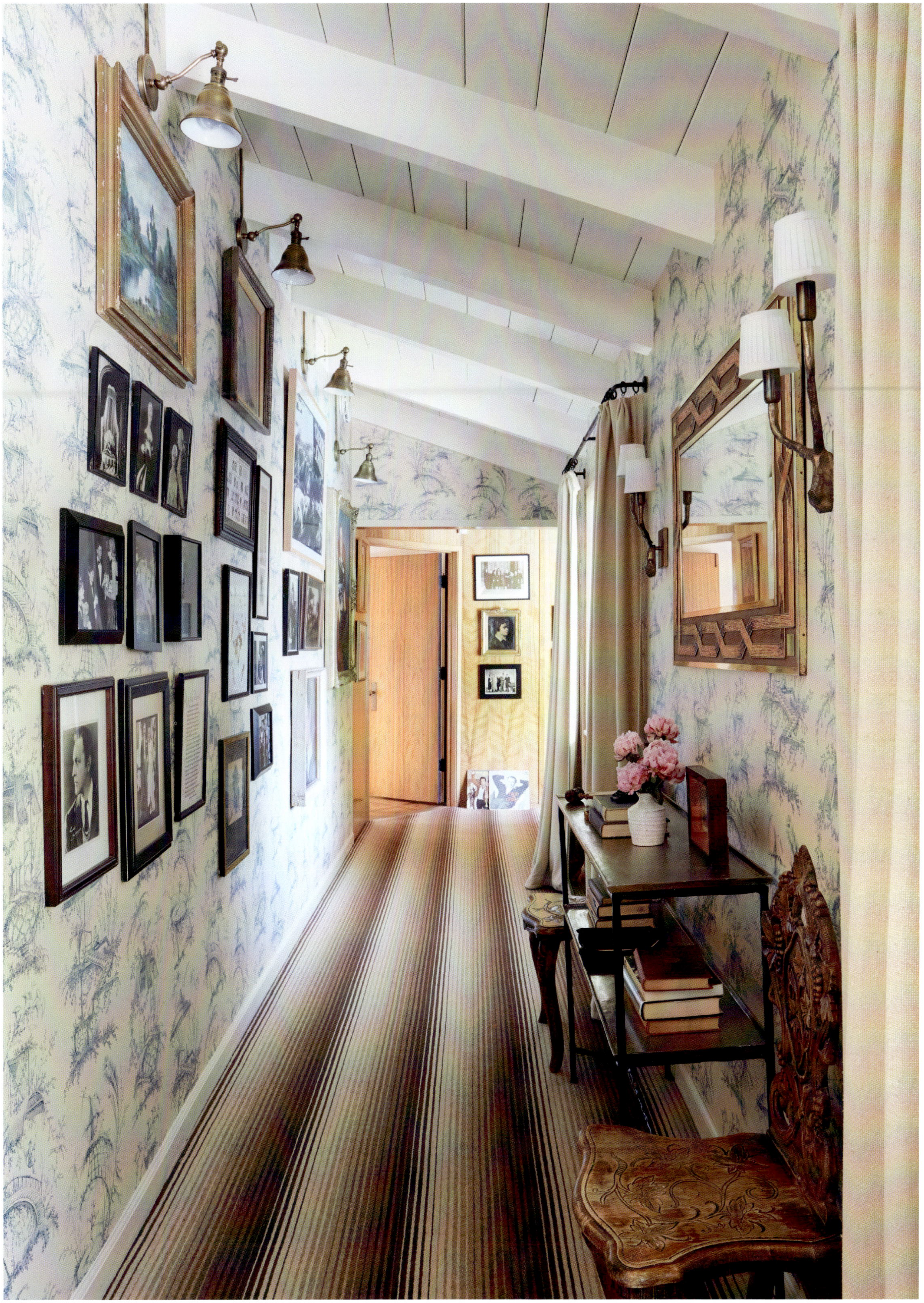

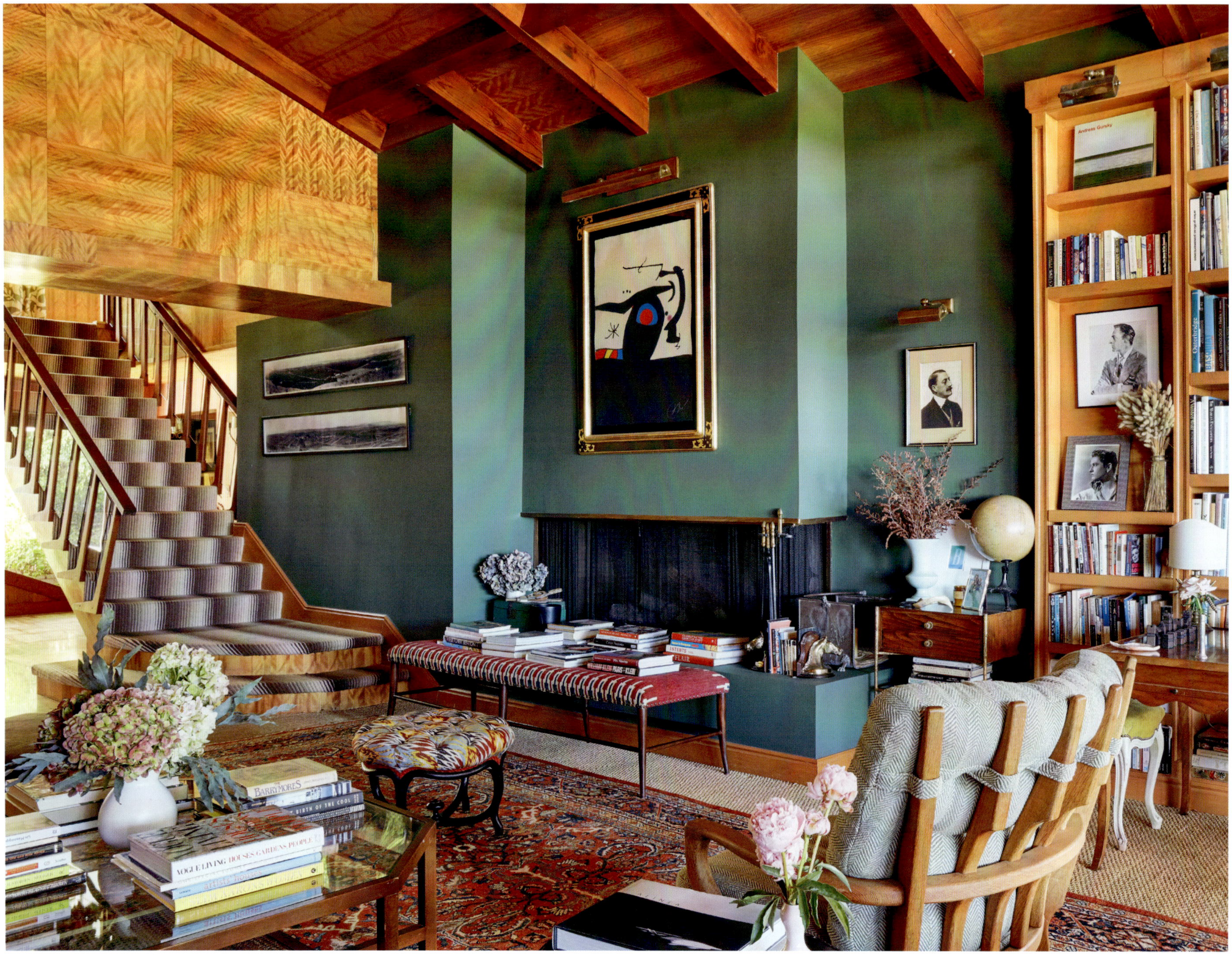
Andreas Gursky
BARRYMORES
VOGUE LIVING HOUSES GARDENS PEOPLE

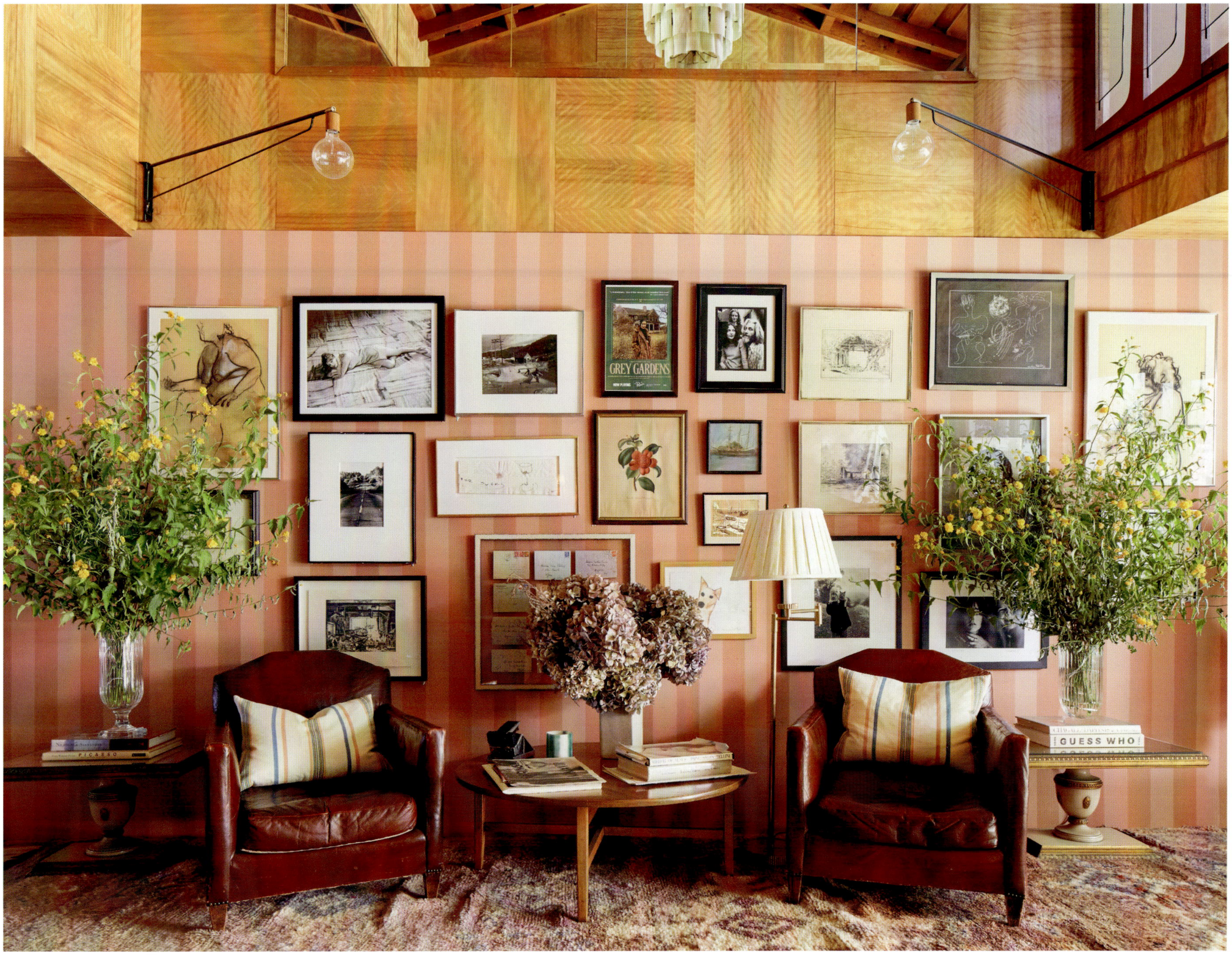

The walls and surfaces of Barrymore's home were happily chockablock with art and family photos, film ephemera, and framed letters—mementos of her celebrated career and the Barrymores' storied history in Hollywood. It was a true honor to make a record of her home of twenty years before she moved away.

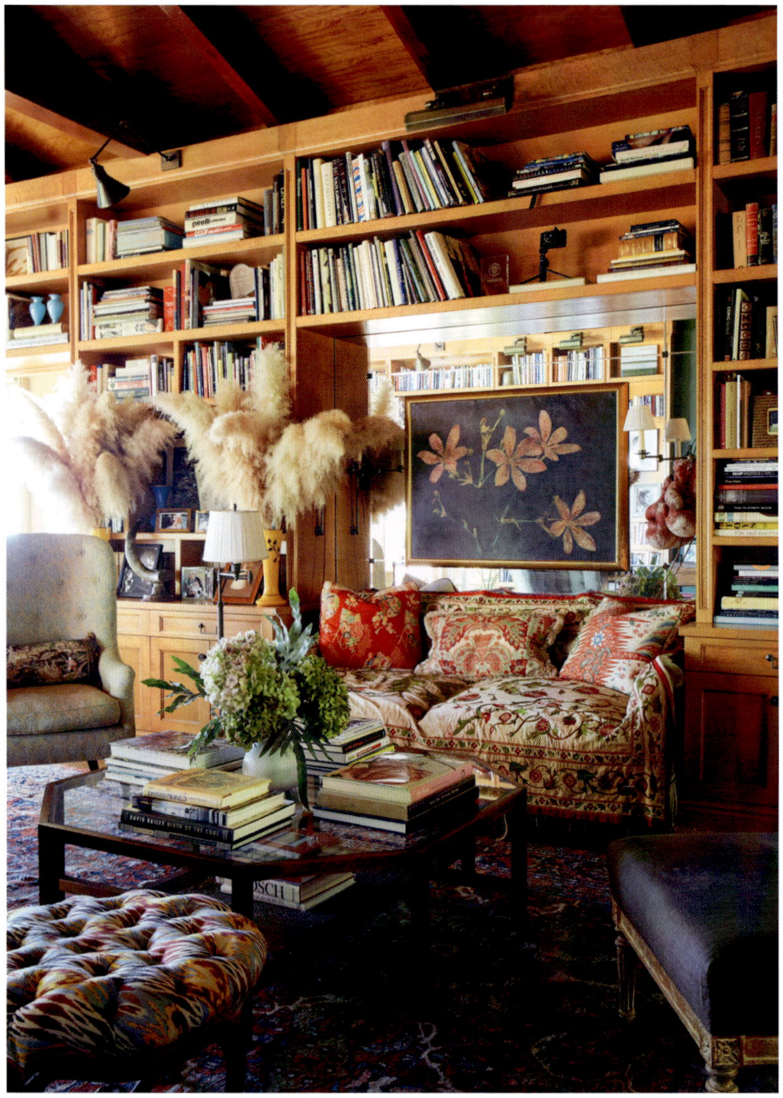

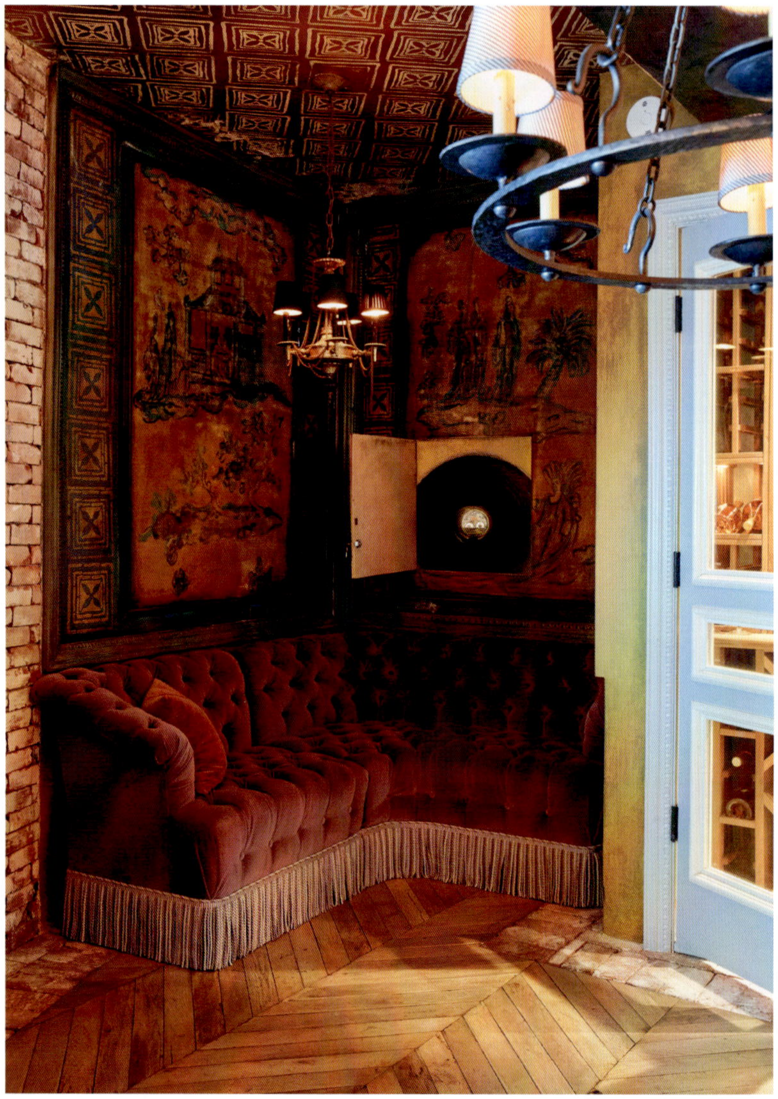

In the basement of Barrymore's Hollywood residence was an old fairground-style shooting range—rotating red ducks still visible at the far end—that Elvis would use for target practice. The seventy-foot concrete tunnel, which extends under the pool, was apparently one of the few private ranges in Los Angeles.

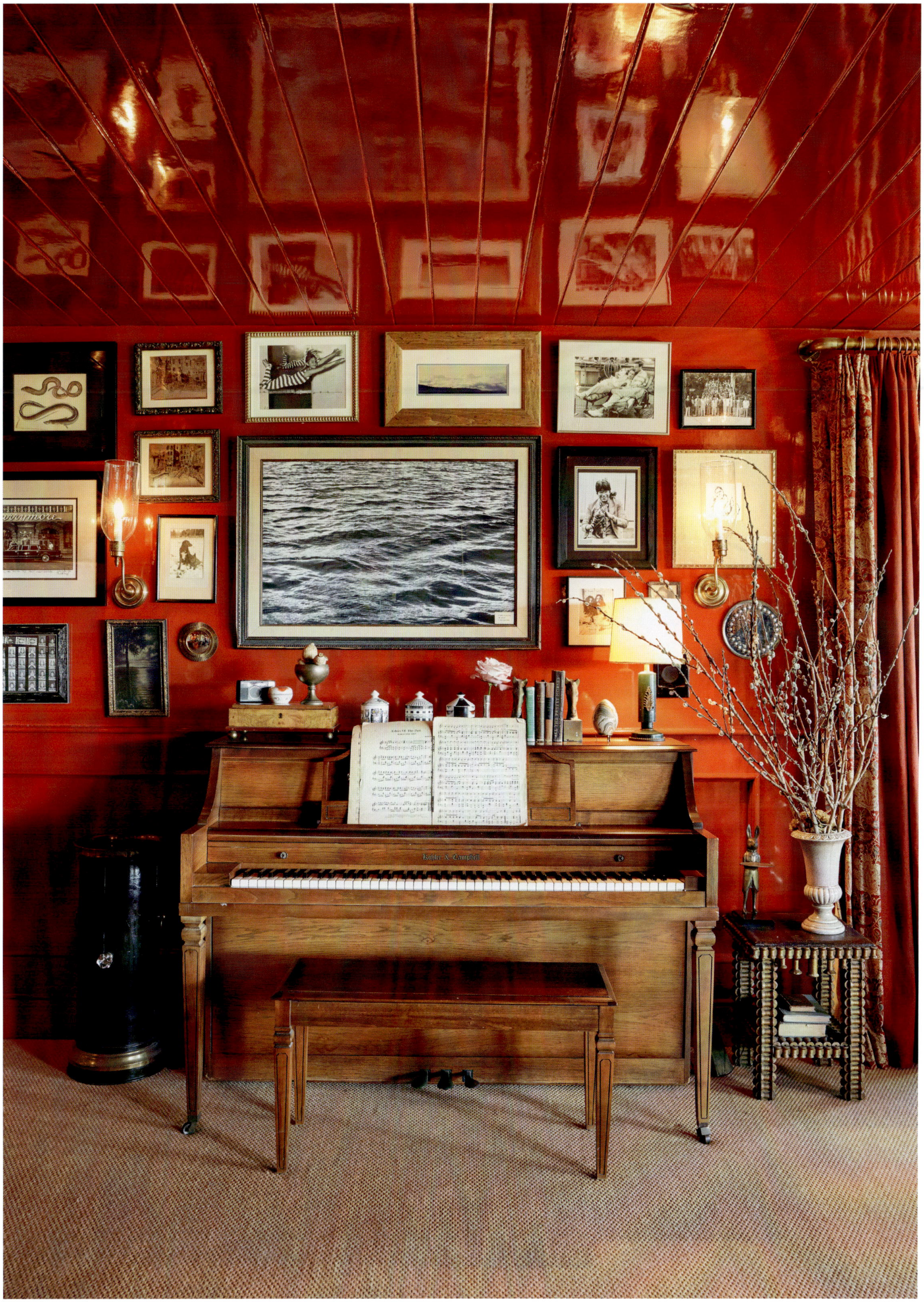

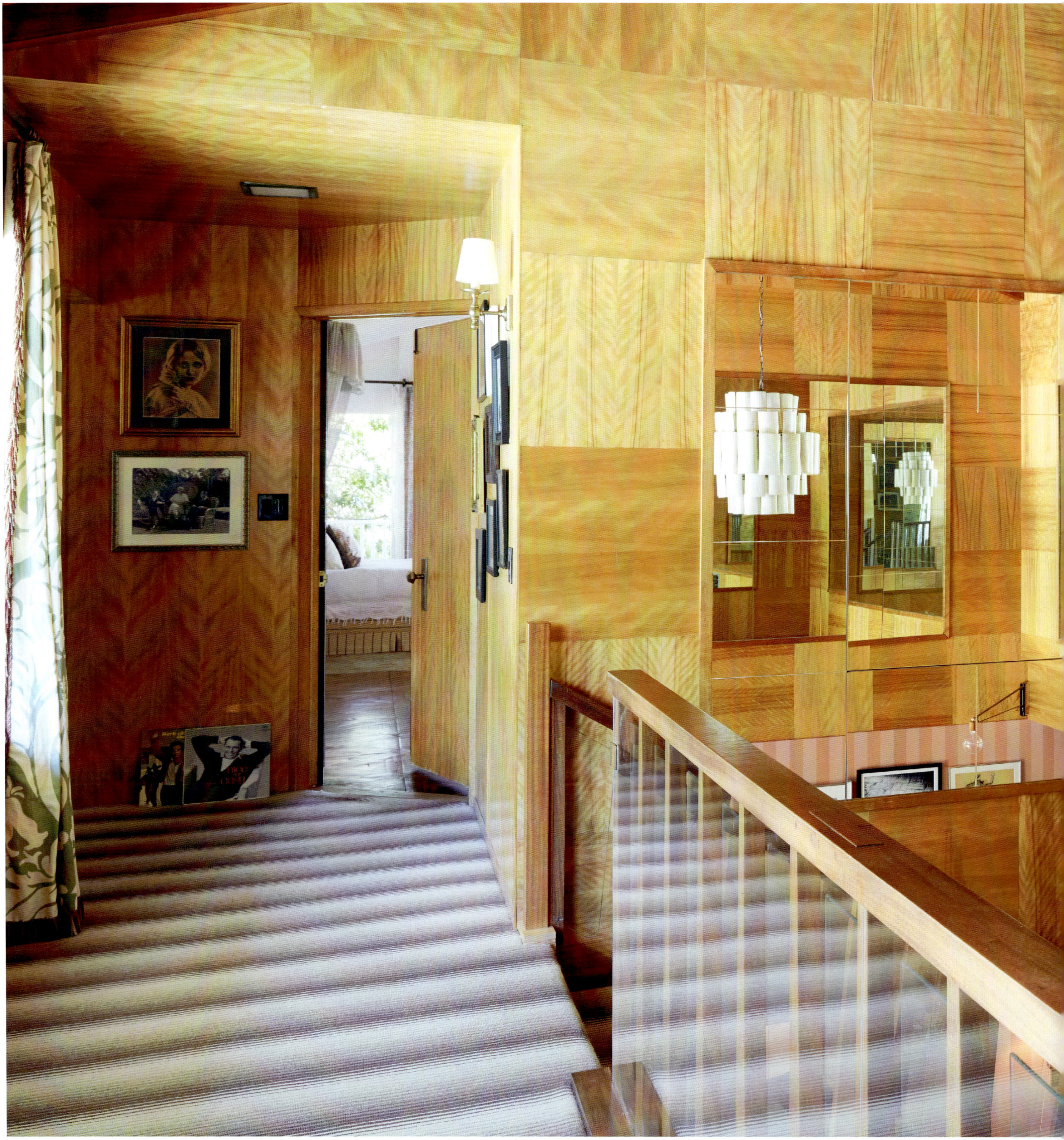

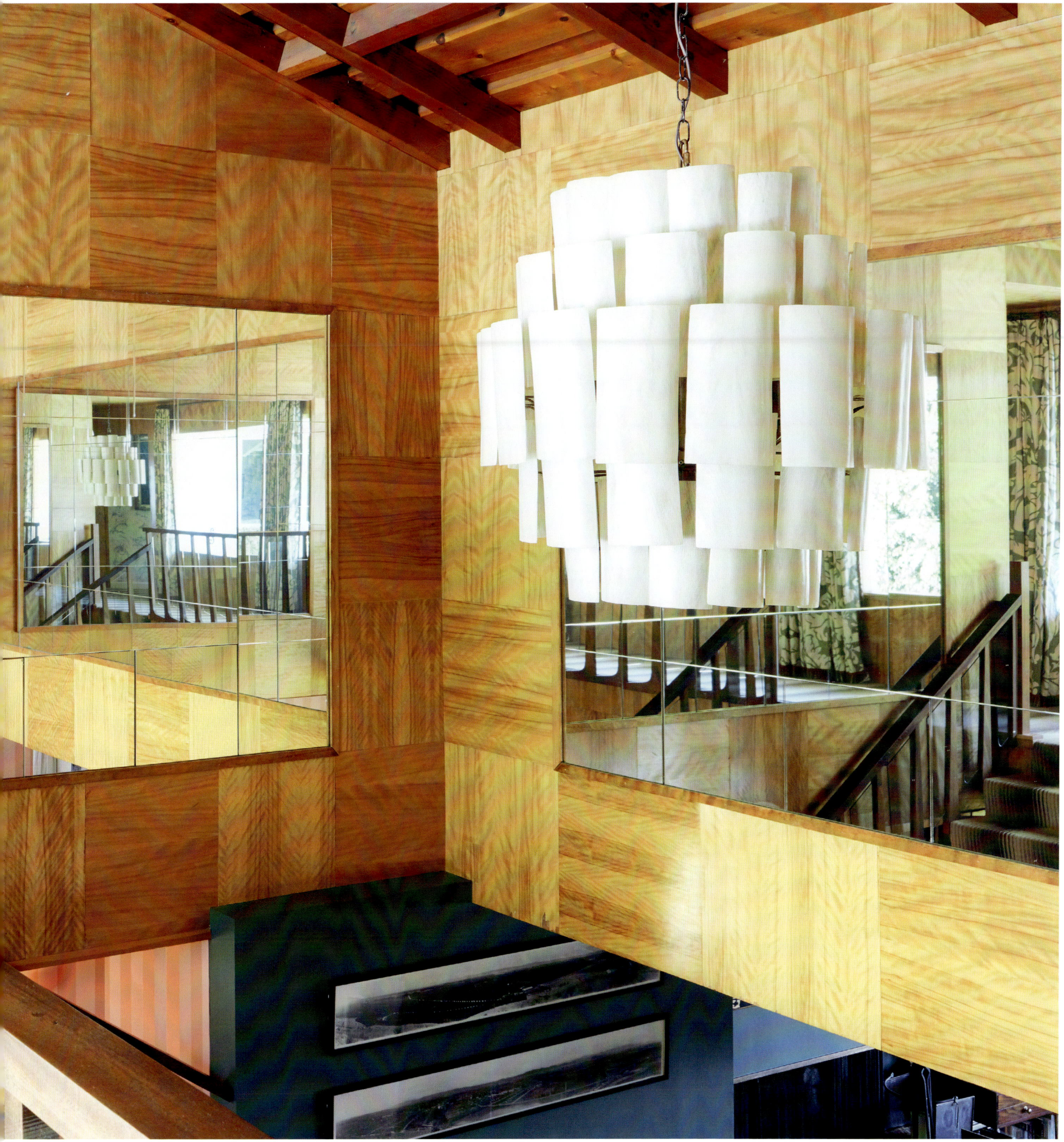

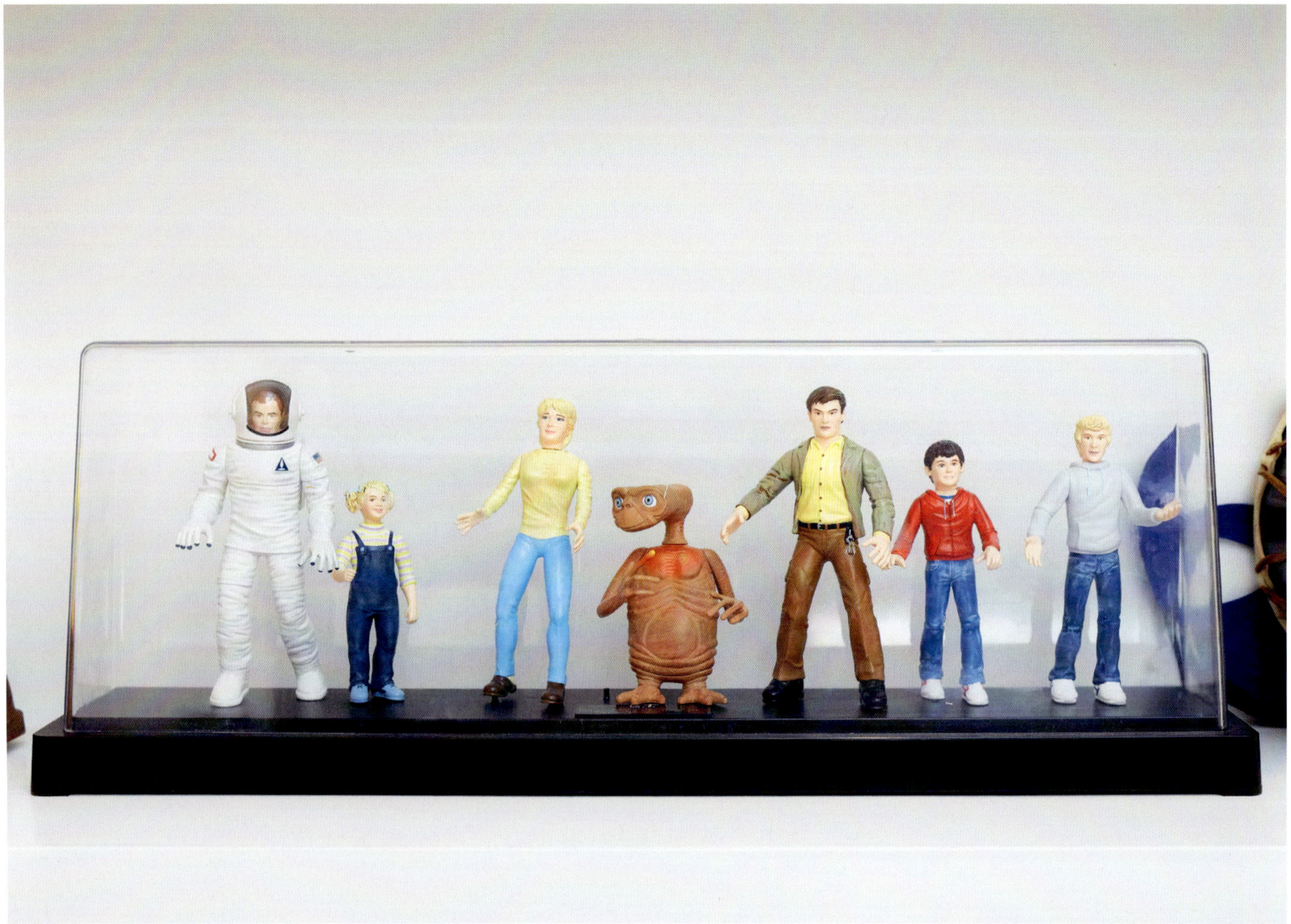

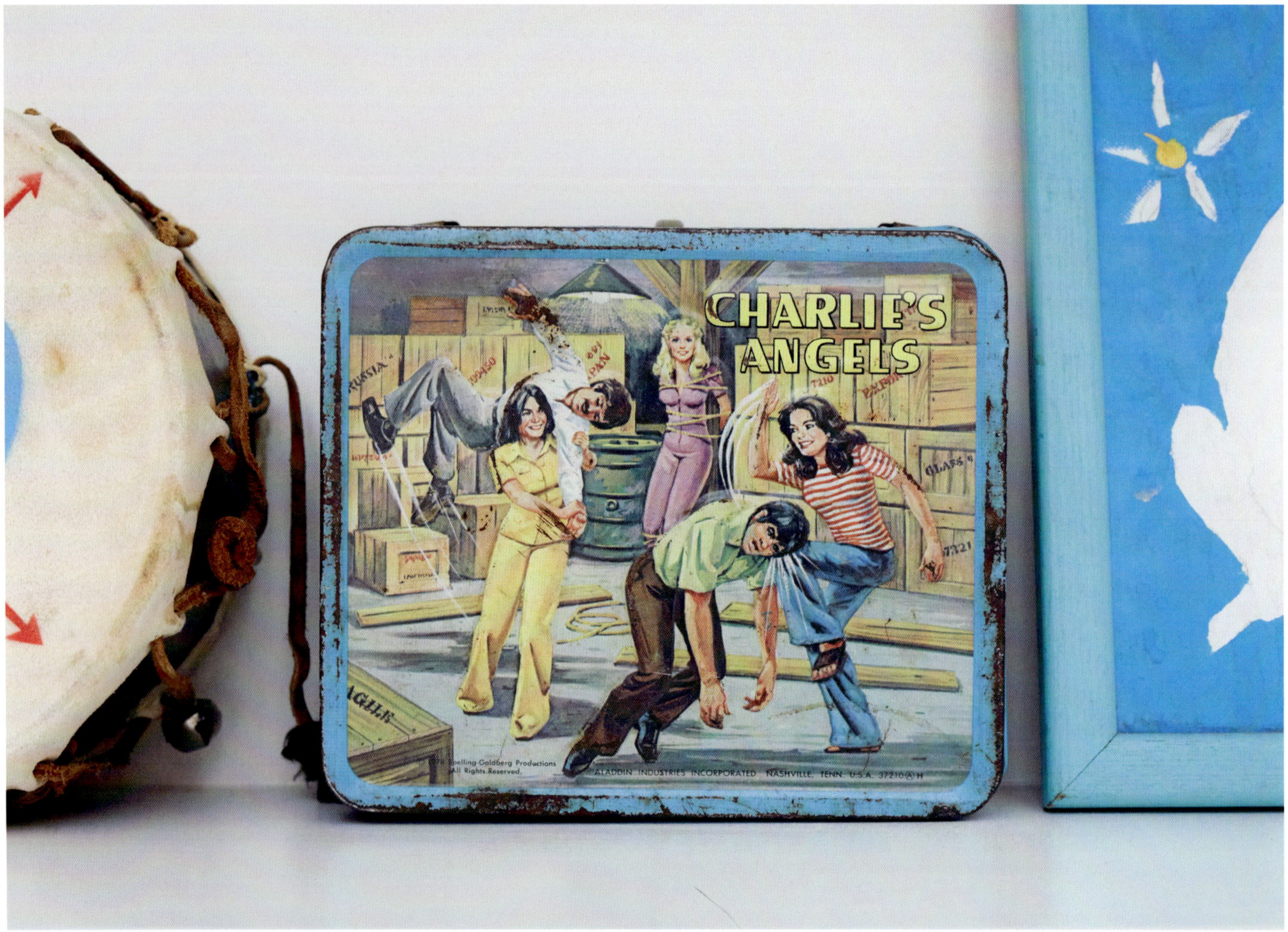
CHARLIE'S
ANGELS

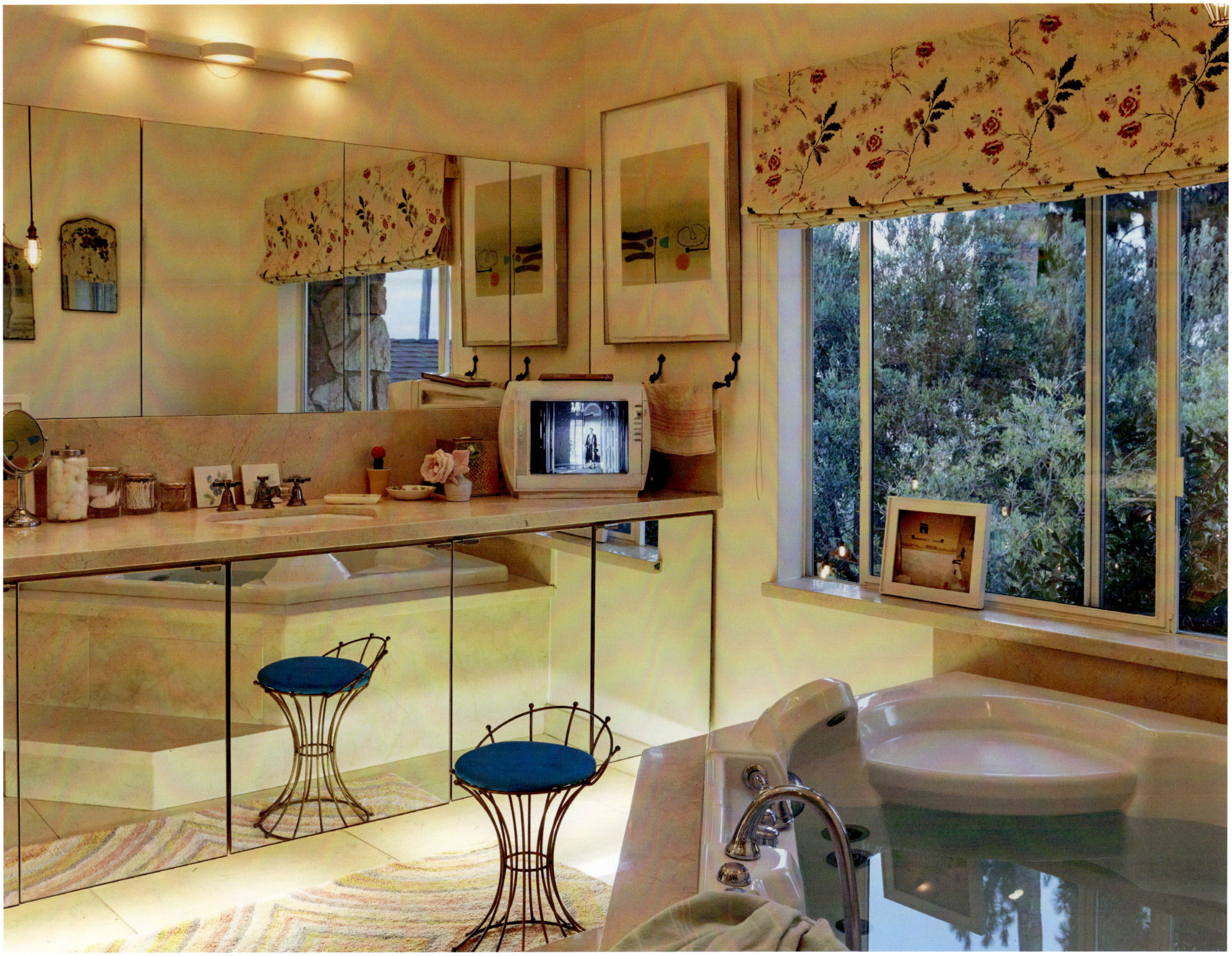

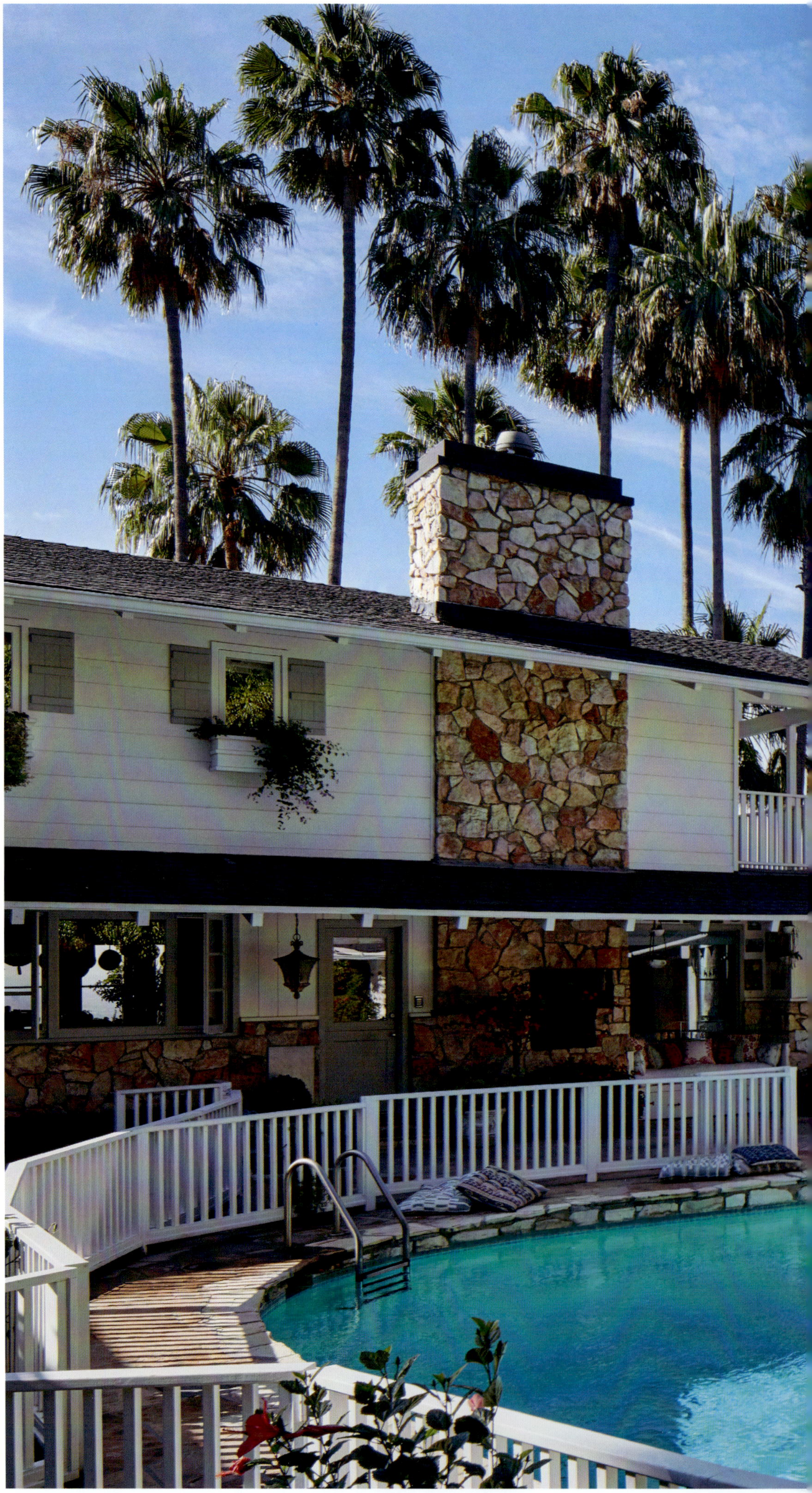

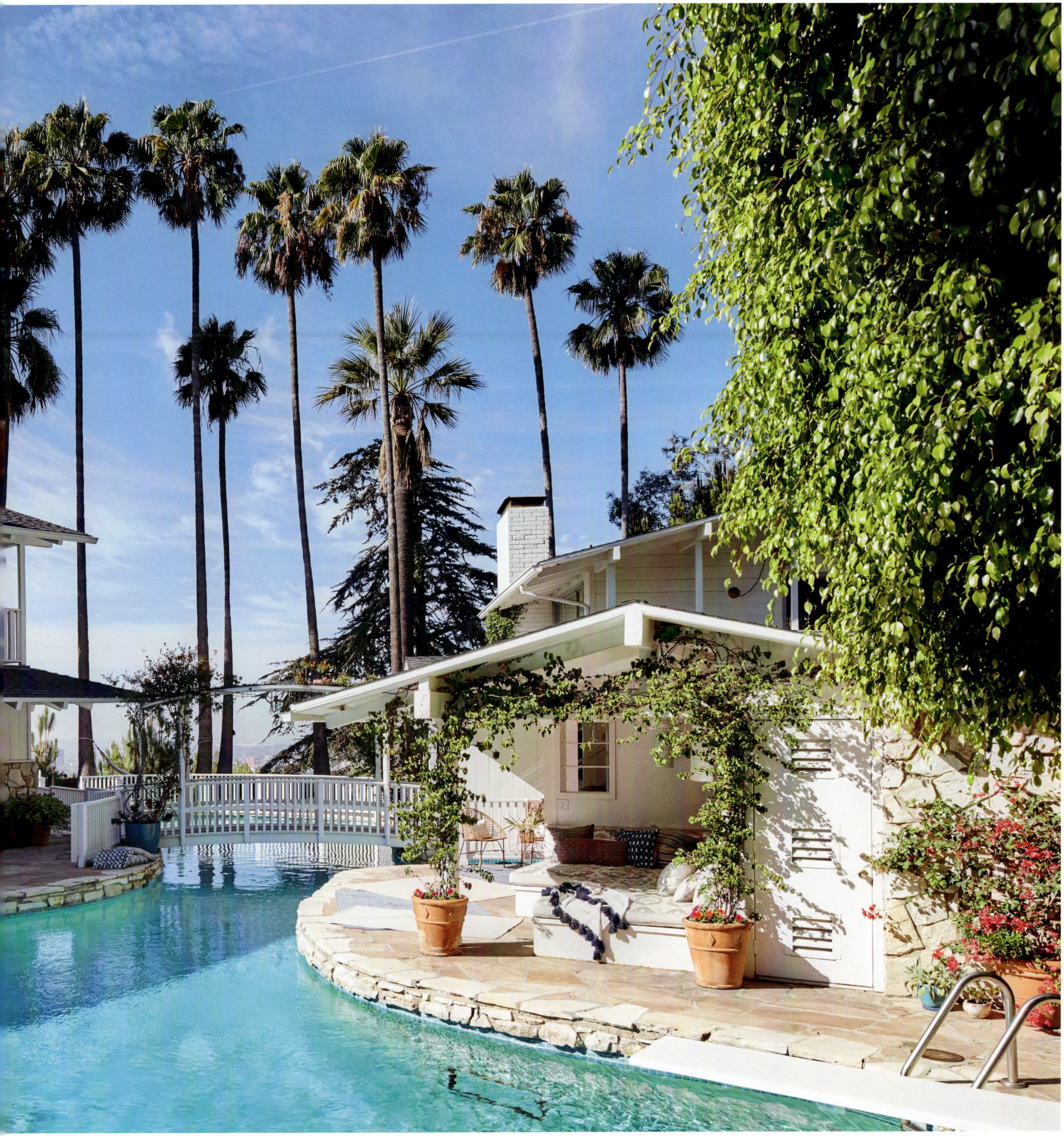

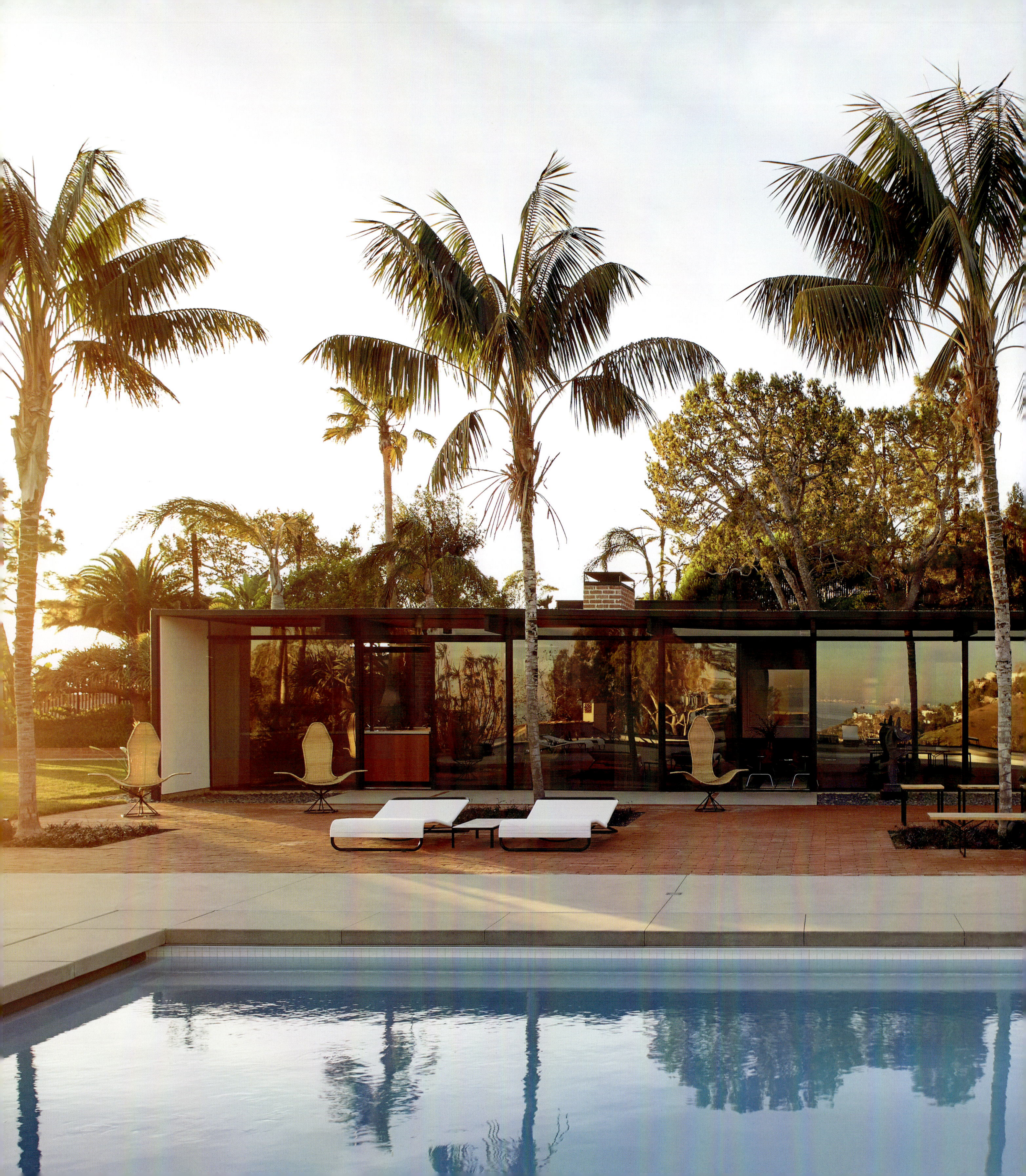

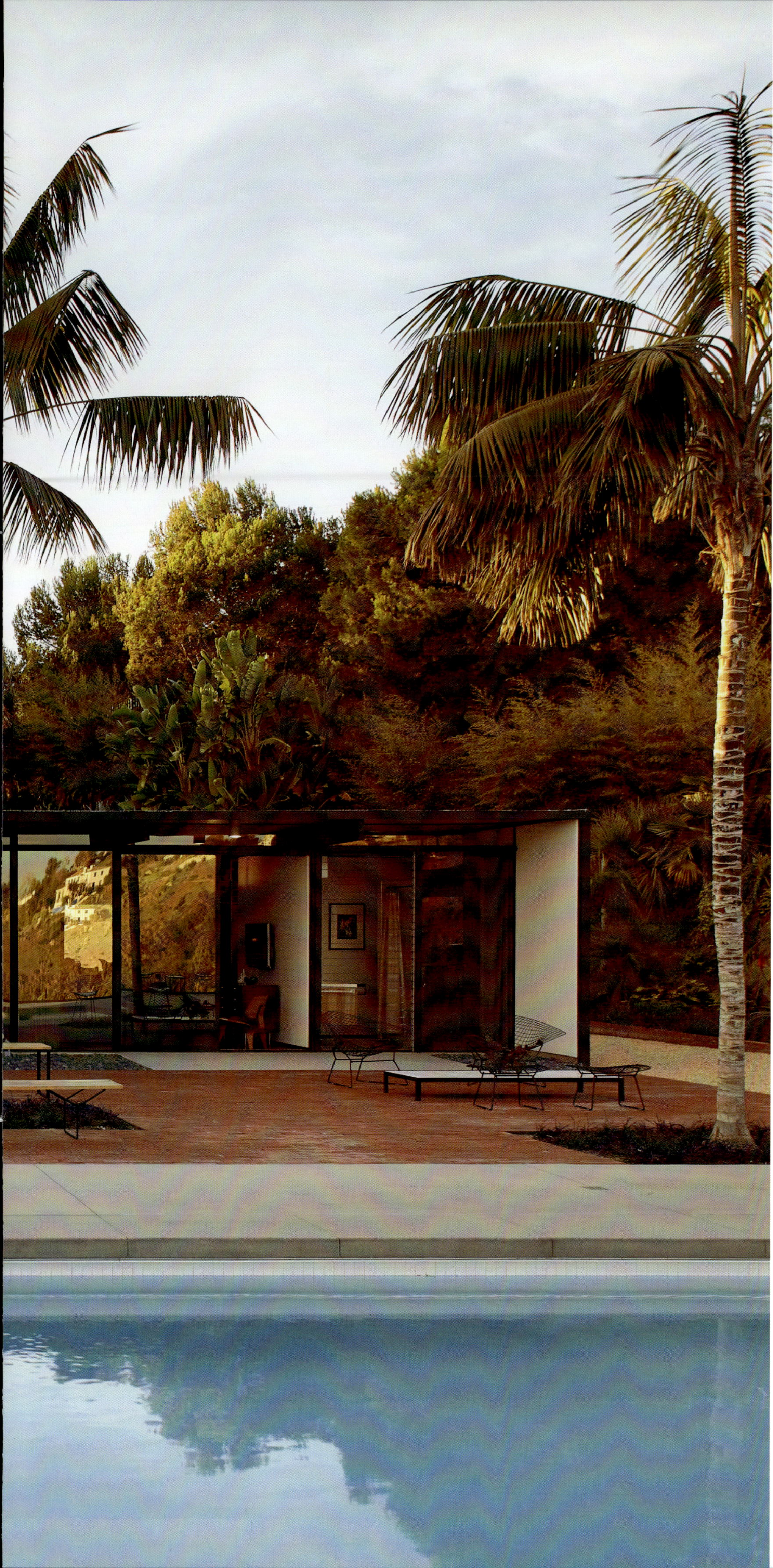

The Steinman House

Malibu

Architect

Craig Ellwood

Resident

Albert Baril

Driving through the hills of Malibu, with palm trees bending in the high winds, I arrived at a small, tidy midcentury home with a vintage Porsche in the carport. Perched high on a cliff overlooking the ocean, this 1956 International Style residence was designed by Craig Ellwood for a middle school principal who had been priced out of nearby Santa Monica into the bluffs of Malibu.

A Los Angeles star, Ellwood was known by some as the Cary Grant of architecture—he dated beautiful people, married a TV actress, and drove a Lamborghini with the license plate *VROOM*—and is today considered an icon of mid-twentieth-century California design. Ellwood's rise to success is a story fit for Hollywood: Born Jon Nelson Burke, on leaving the army he established an office in Los Angeles with his brother and two friends. As the story goes, he borrowed the name Ellwood for his firm from a nearby liquor store. (Burke later legally adopted the name himself.) Never professionally trained as an architect, he was nonetheless an impresario and a visionary, designing three of the influential Case Study Houses (nos. 16, 17, and 18) and working with partner Jerrold Lomax on the Steinman House, among other projects.

Thumbing through the *Los Angeles Times* real estate section on a lazy Saturday afternoon, art collectors Holly and Albert Baril came across a thumbnail ad for a midcentury modern house for sale in Malibu. It was a period of design they admittedly knew little about at the time, but they were intrigued. Before leaving the next day for a week-long trip, they drove by the property but couldn't see the house. The following week, they bought the place sight unseen. There ensued a moment when Holly, visiting the unrenovated and overgrown house while it was veiled in gloom and the ocean was hidden by the fog, thought they might have made a mistake. Only on returning in full sun and with the sight of the waves crashing below did they begin to see the house's true potential.

When it came to restoring and decorating the house, once again a fortuitous *L.A. Times* piece—a profile of designer and consultant Michael Boyd—led them in the right direction. A specialist on midcentury design and its preservation, Boyd helped bring new, period-perfect life to the entire house, from the furnishings and the garden right down to the knives and forks on the Van Keppel-Green kitchen table. In the mid-1950s, this was affordable living (with an ocean view), and if Ellwood himself was a showman, the Steinman House still epitomizes the stripped-back purity of his creative vision. Despite its relative modesty, it's a beauty.

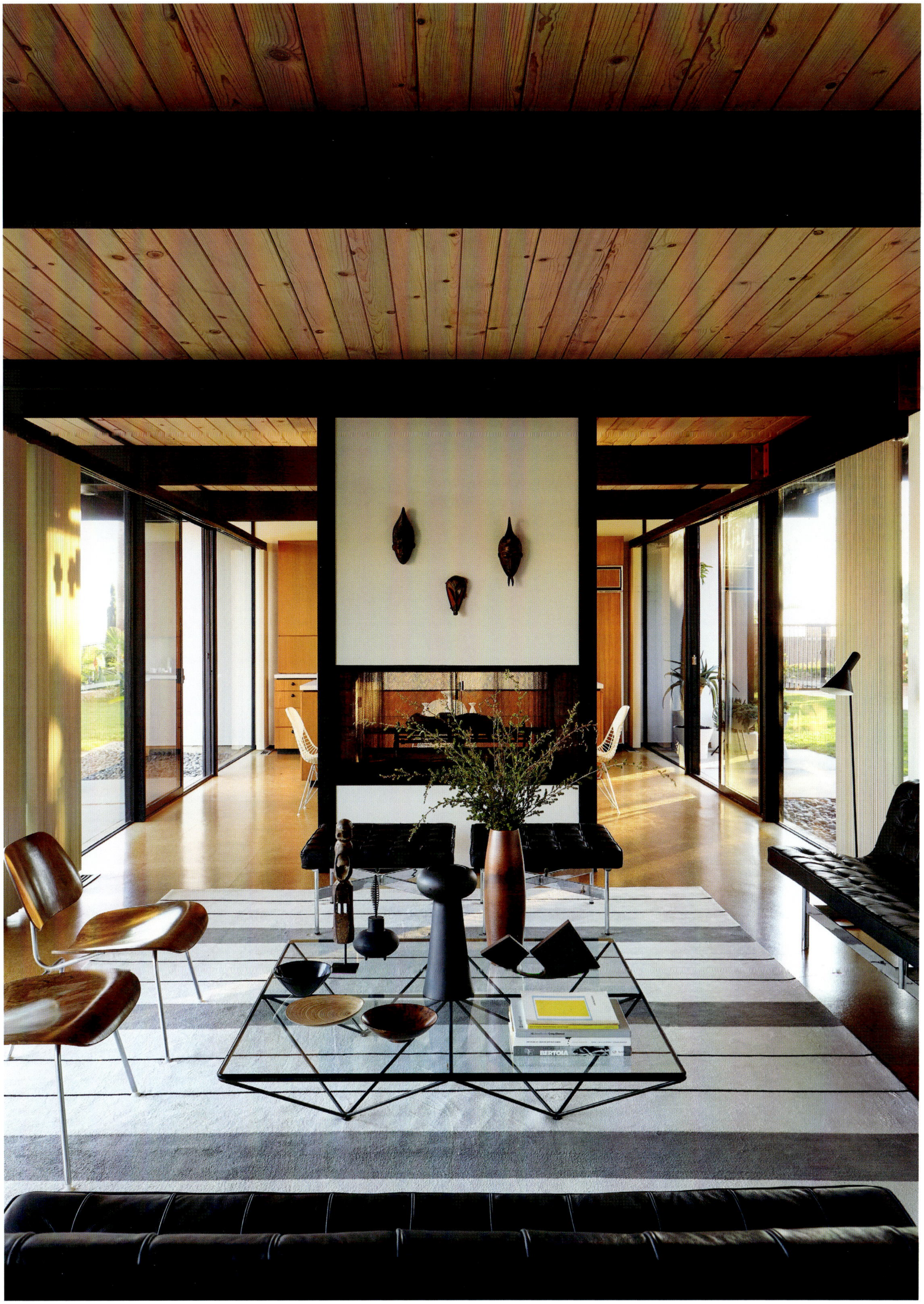
BERTOIA

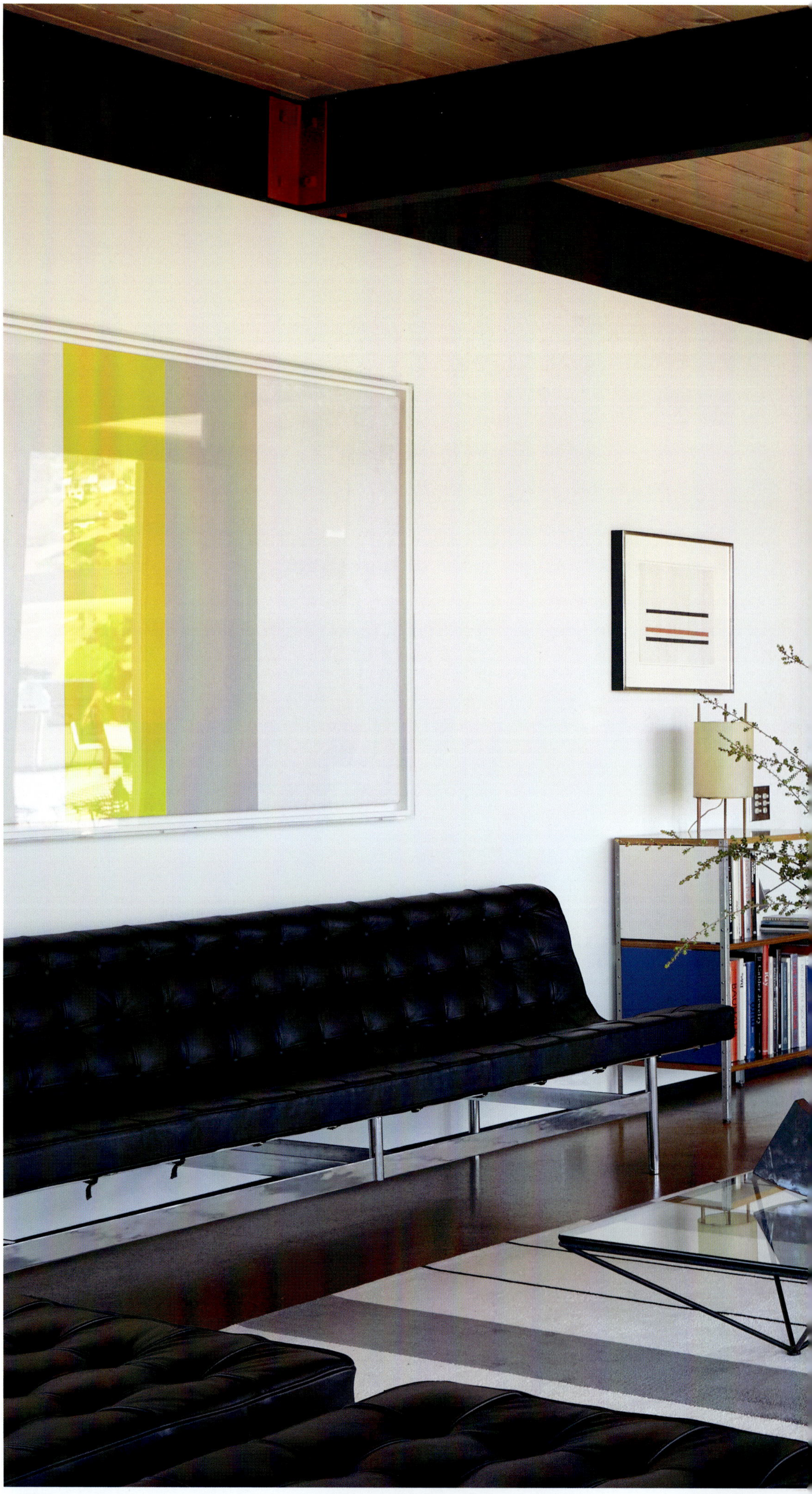

The Barils, already avid art collectors, purchased work by artists associated with the legendary midcentury Ferus Gallery to reflect the moment in which the house was built. The couple went in knowing little about modernist architecture and design. For them, living in the house and collaborating with Michael Boyd on the renovation and decoration was an incredible learning experience.

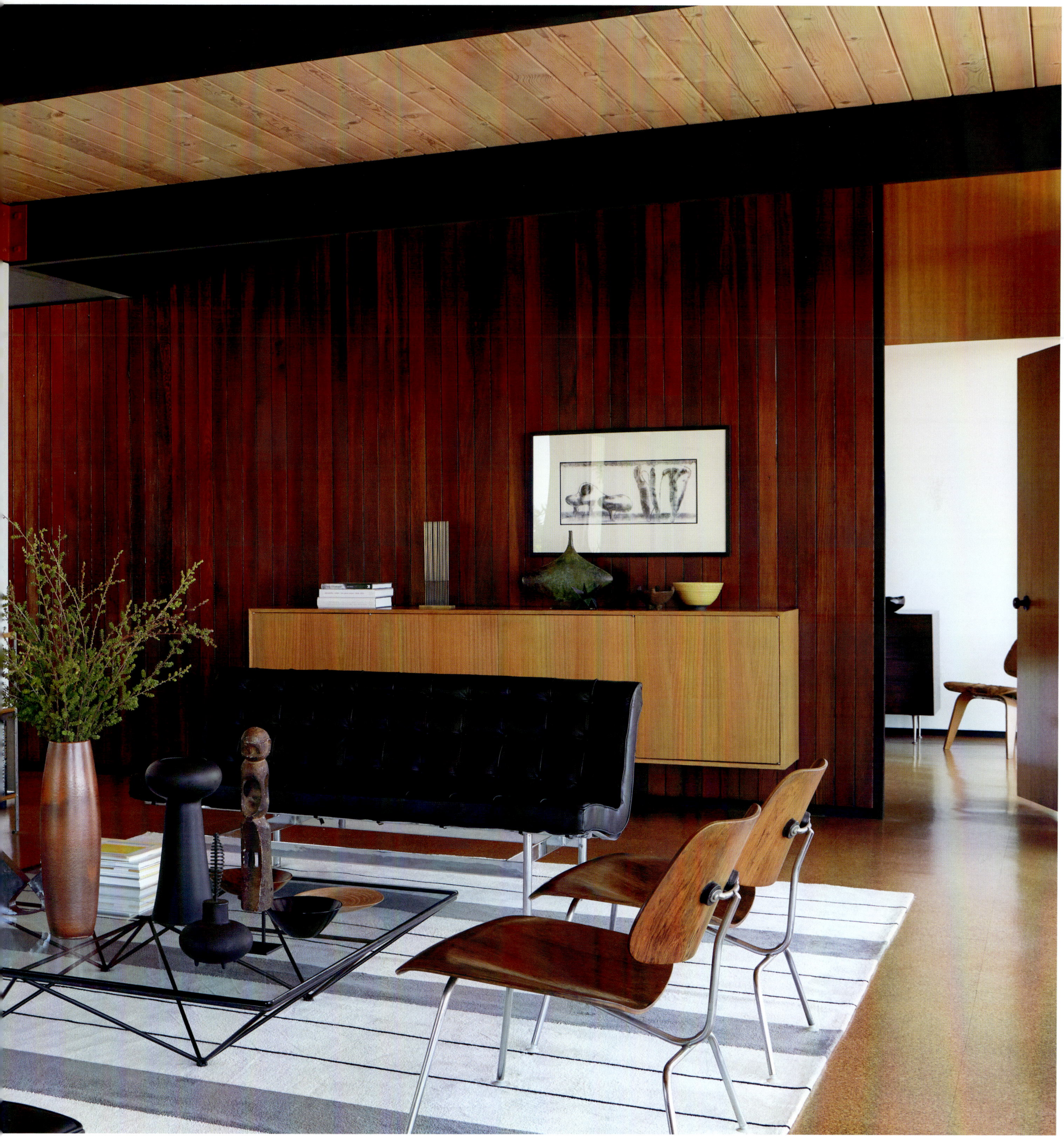

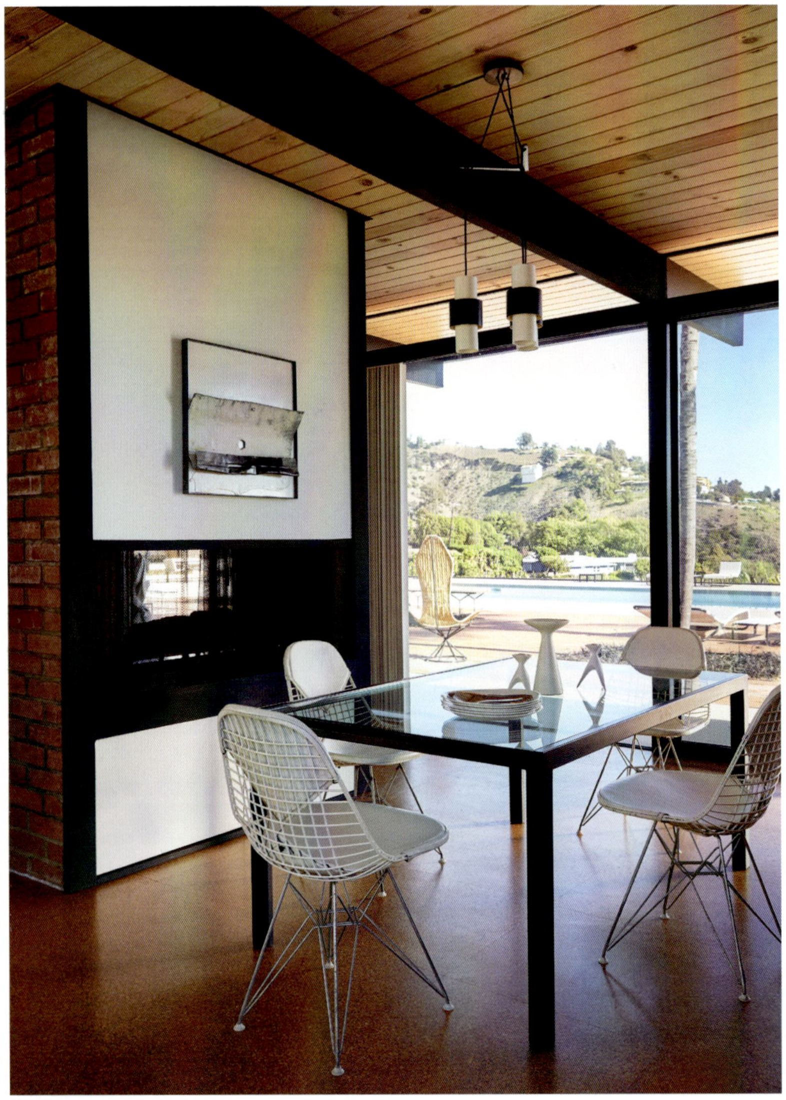

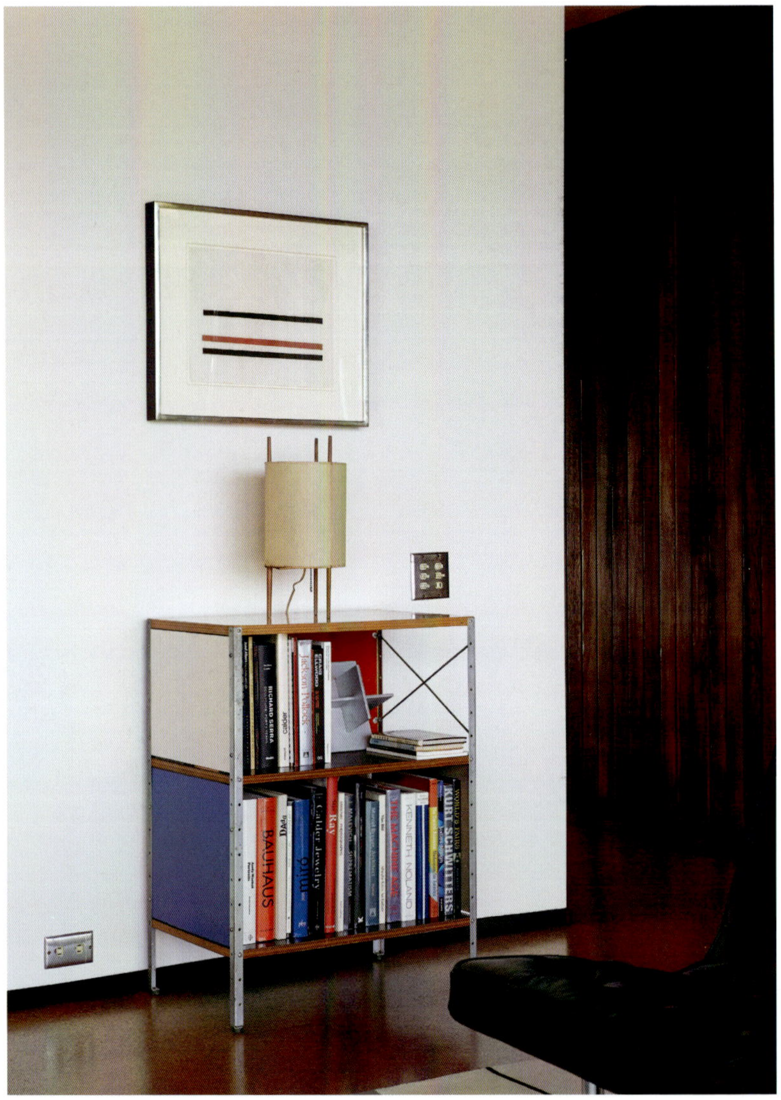

Five years after it was completed, the Steinman family had outgrown their little house, and in 1961 Ellwood returned to convert the garage into an additional room (presently the Barils' kids' room) and added a carport.

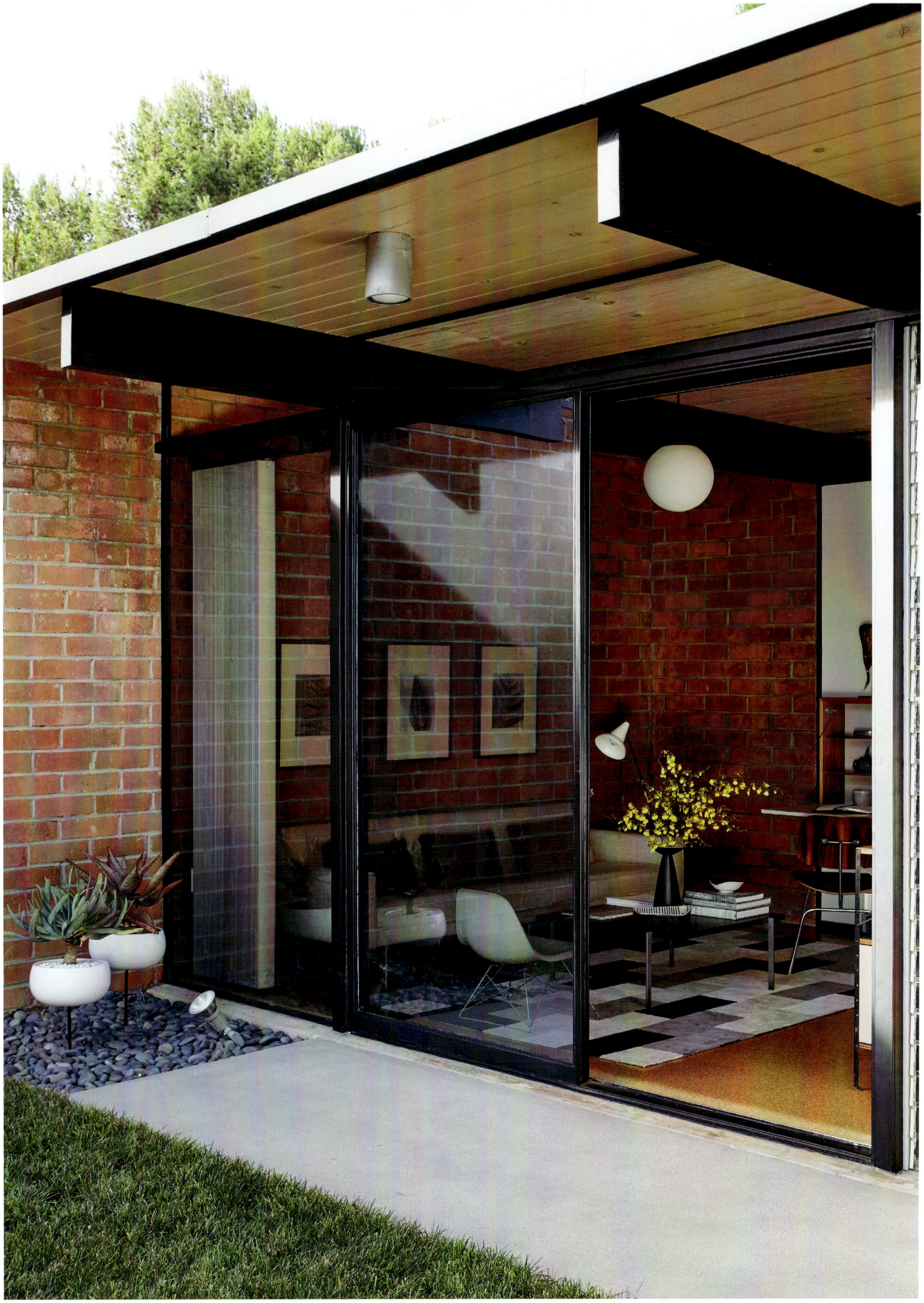

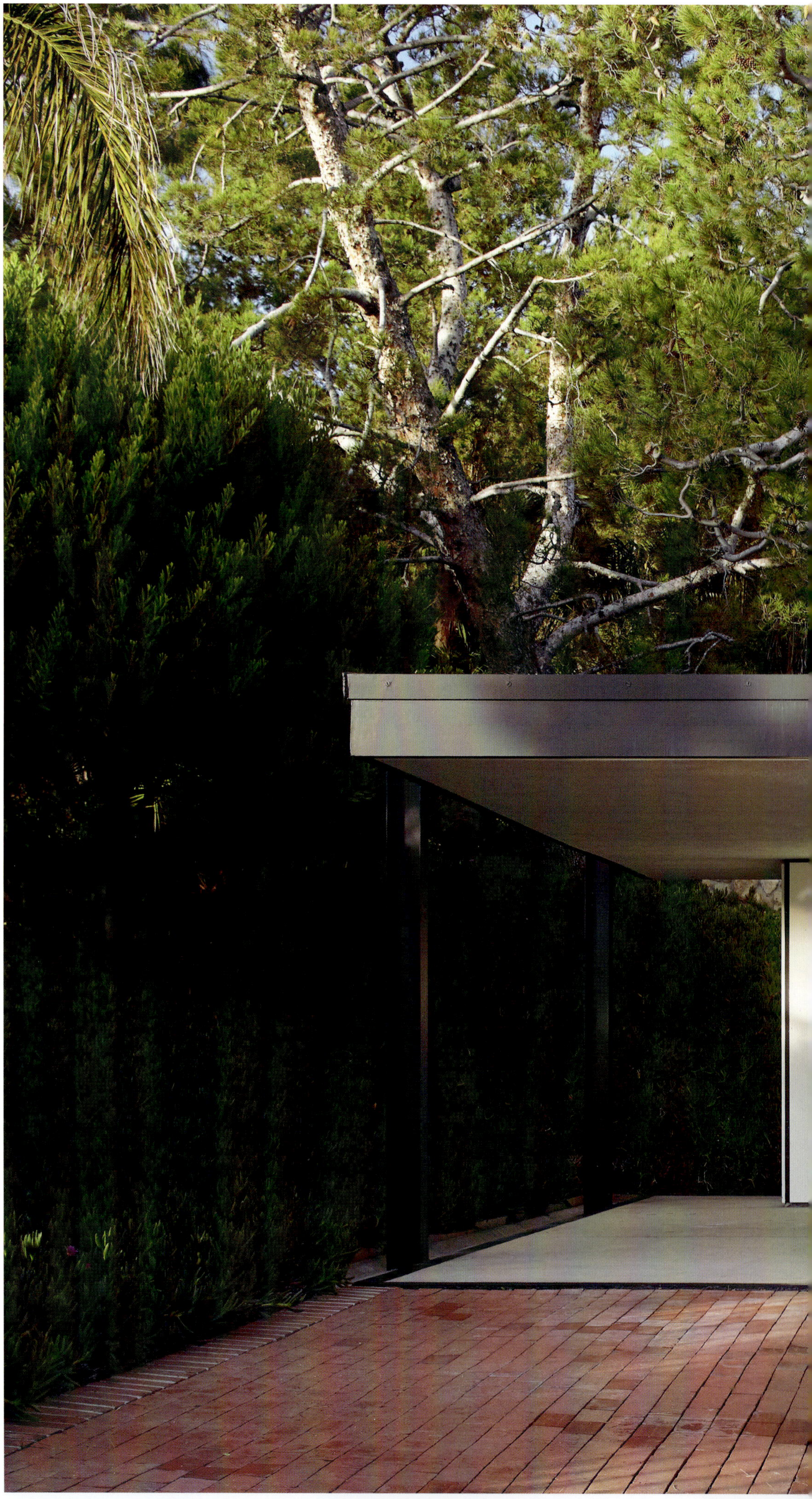

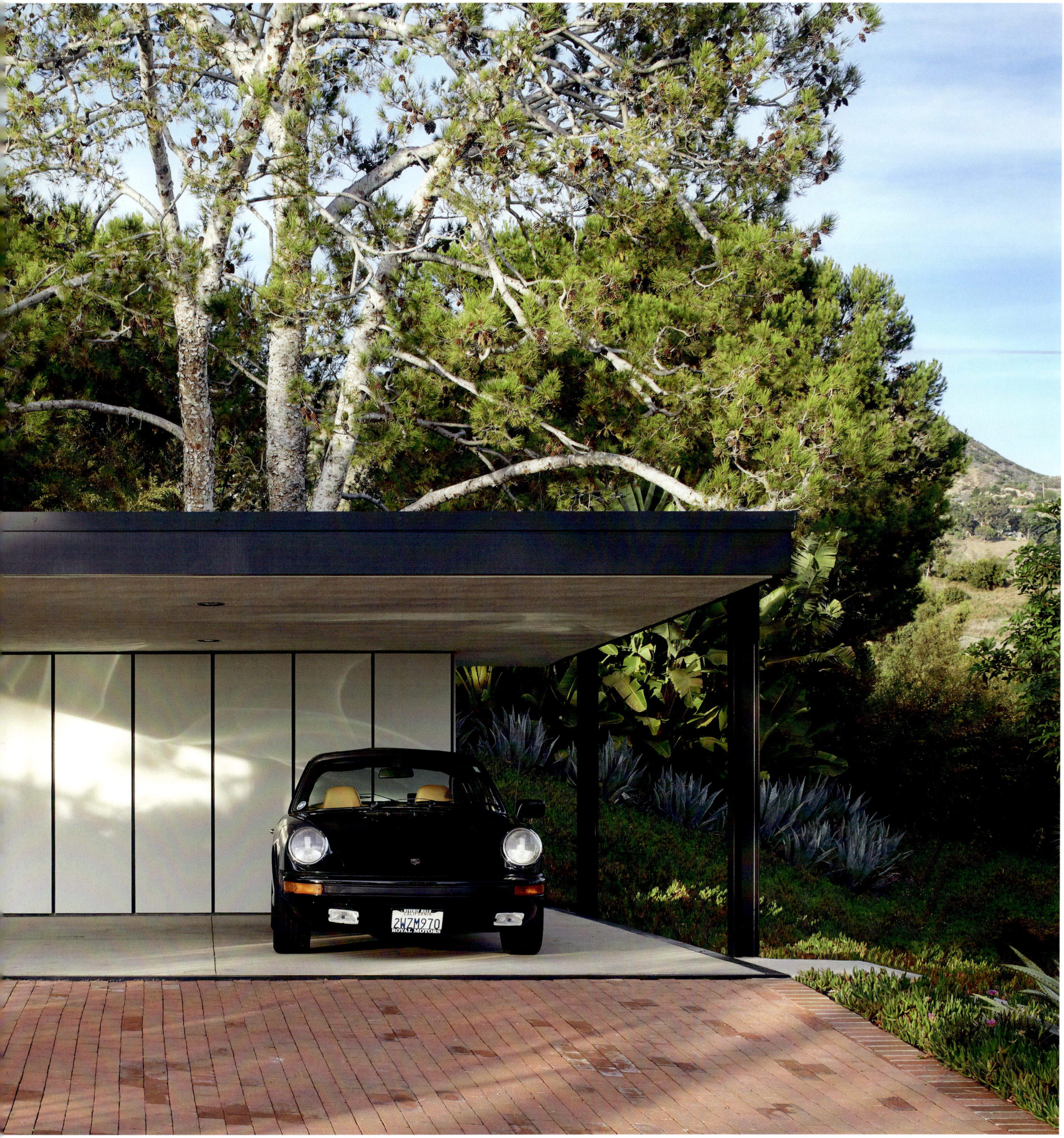
2WZM970
ROYAL MOTORS

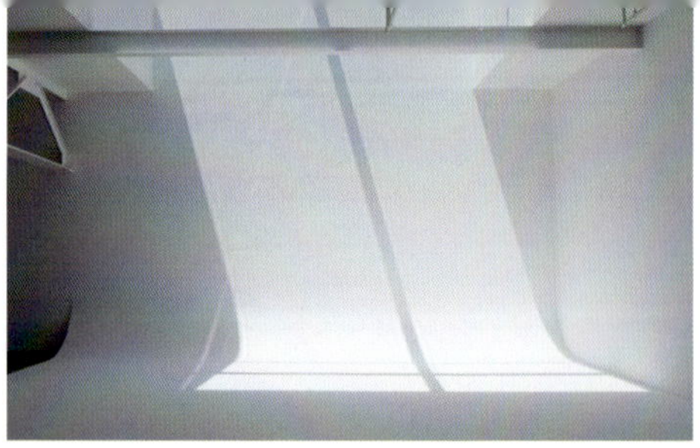

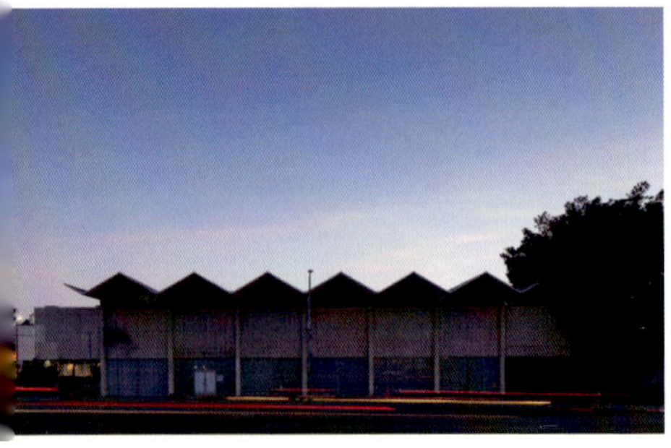

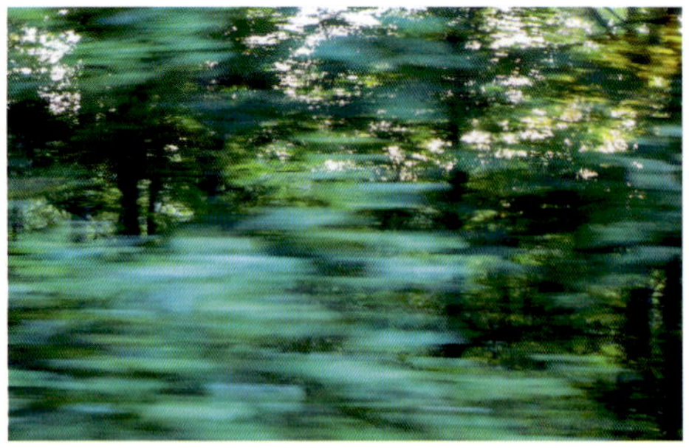

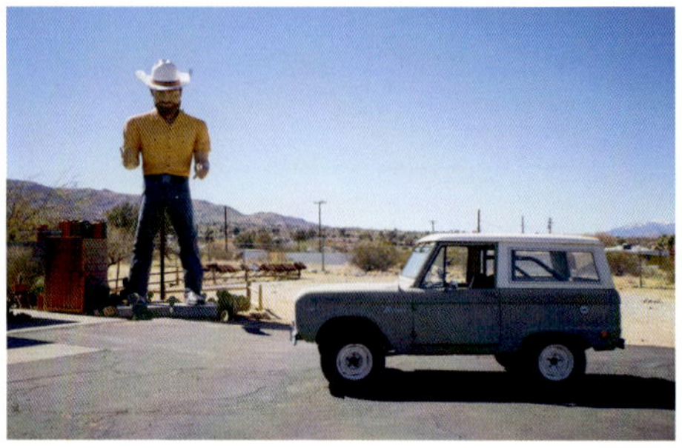

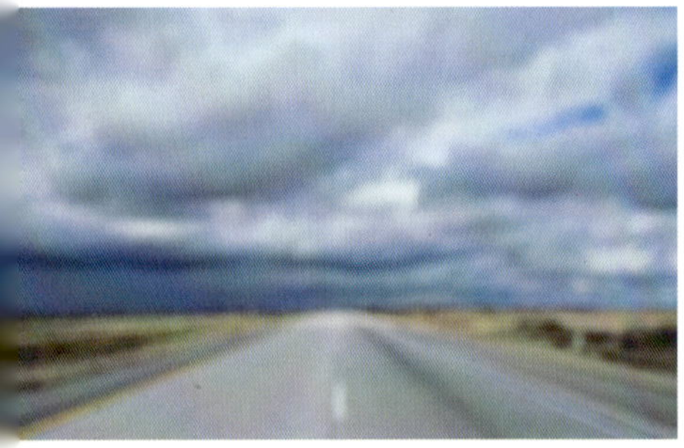

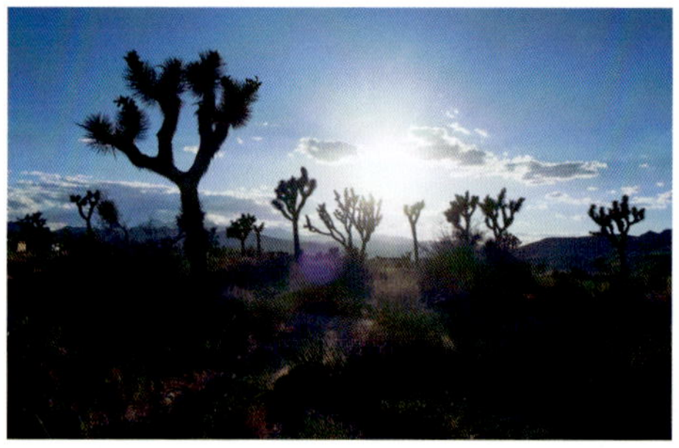

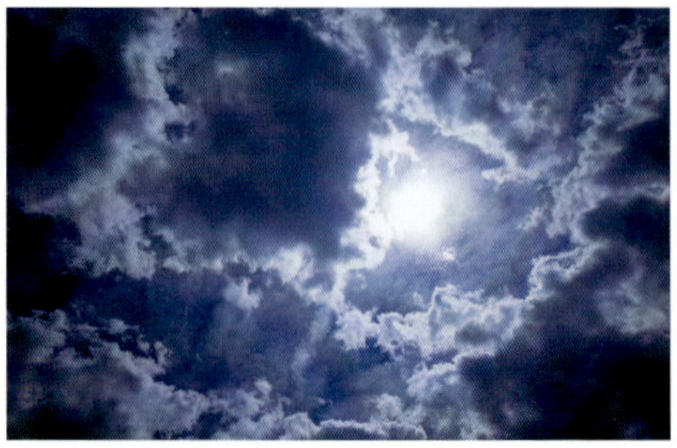

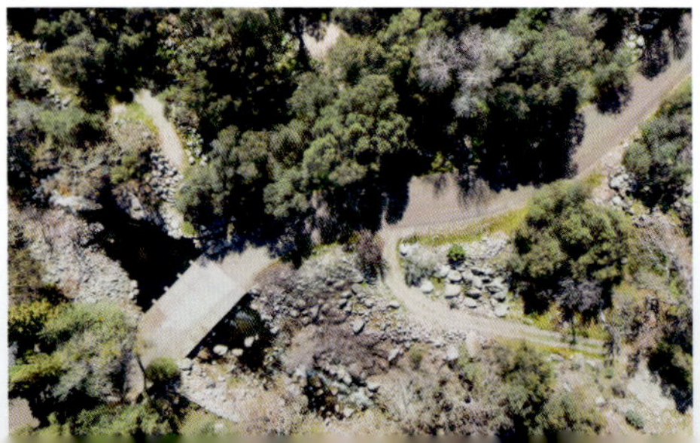

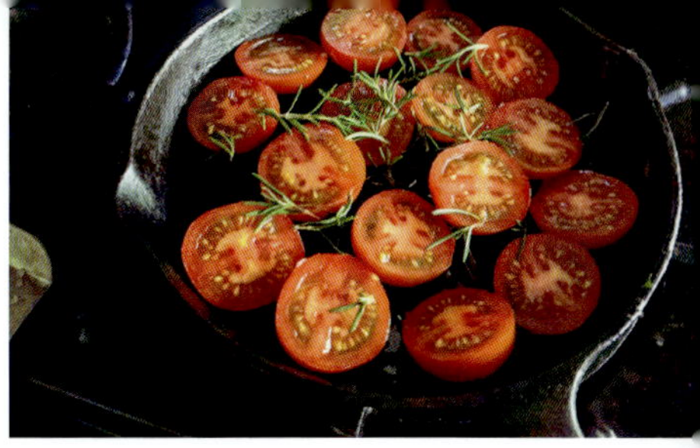

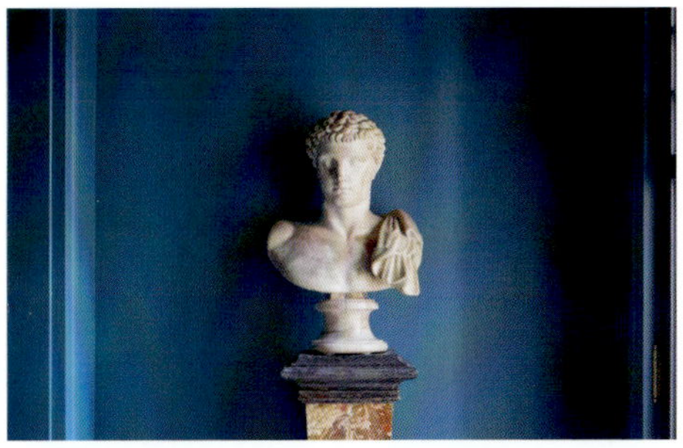

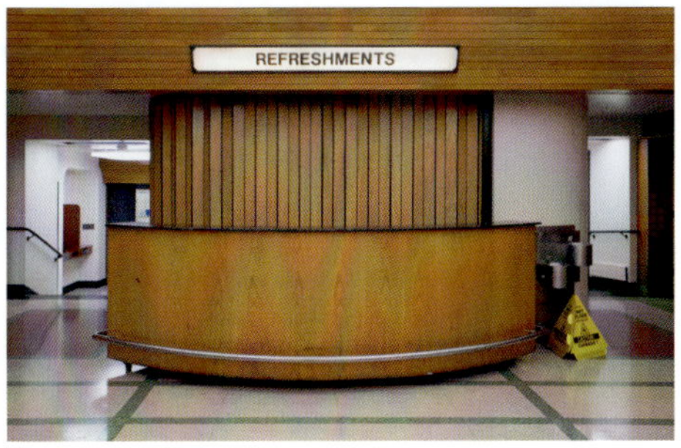
REFRESHMENTS

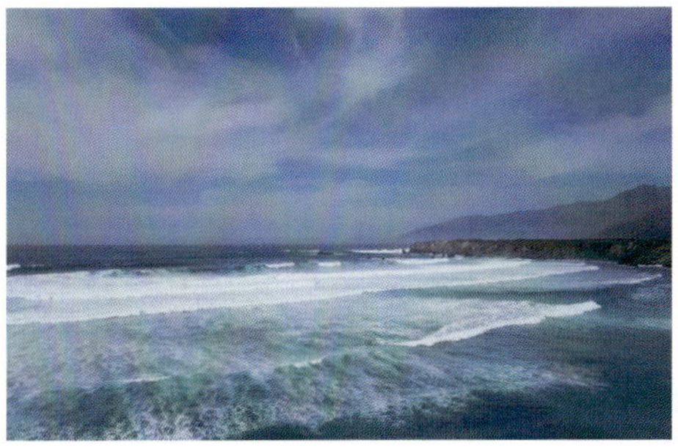

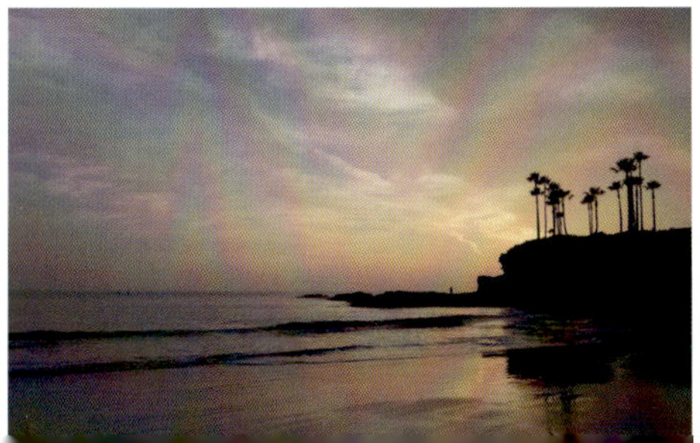

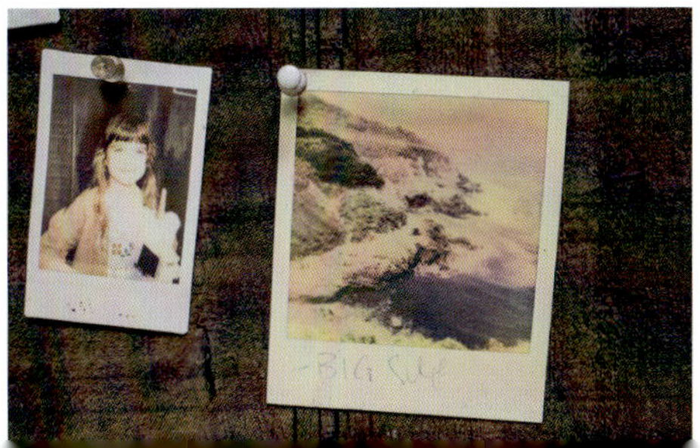
Big Sur

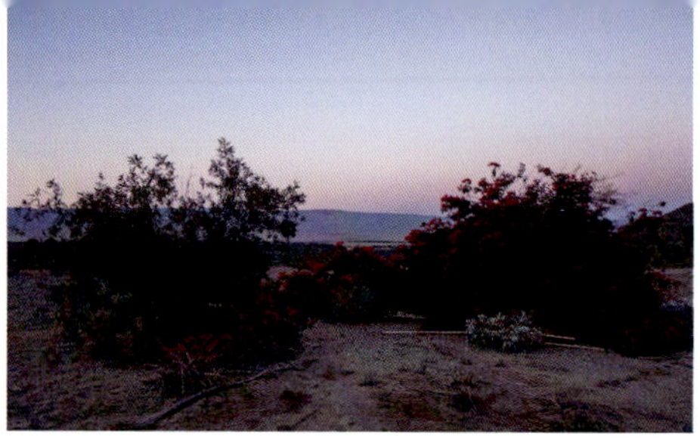

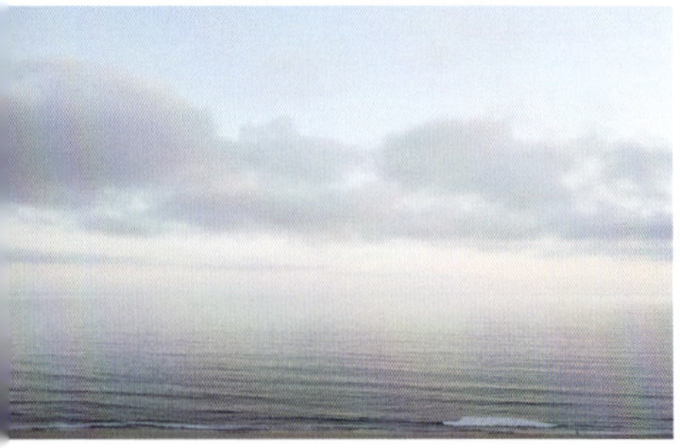

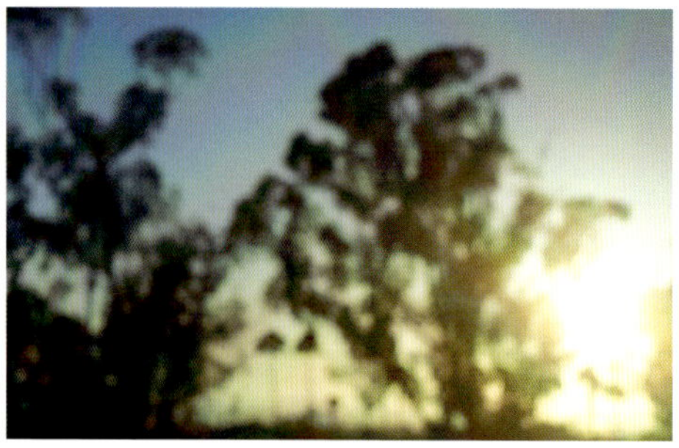

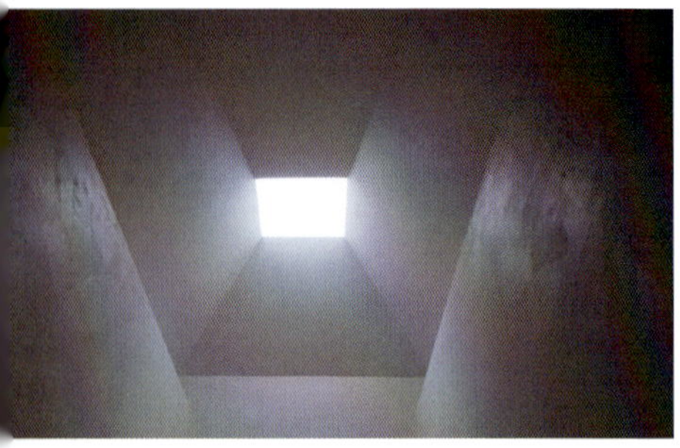

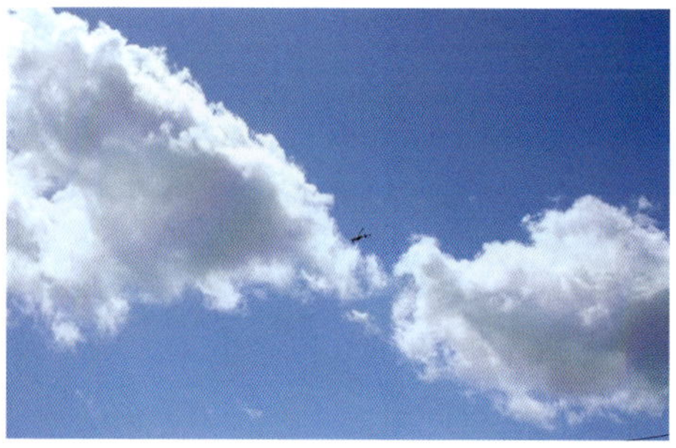

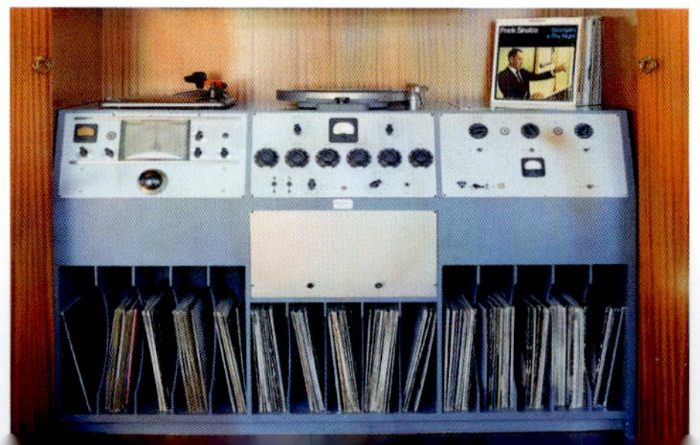

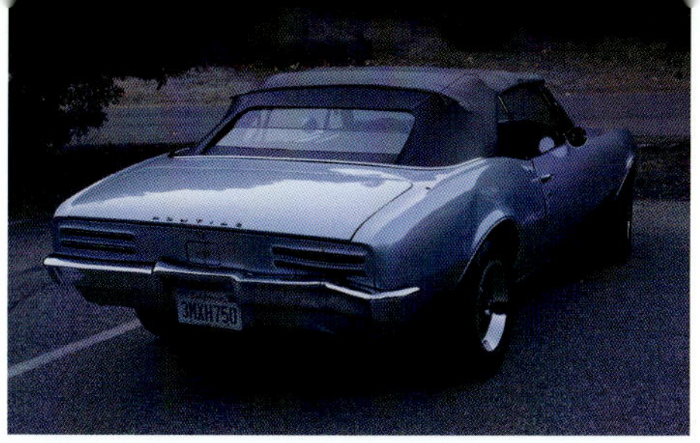

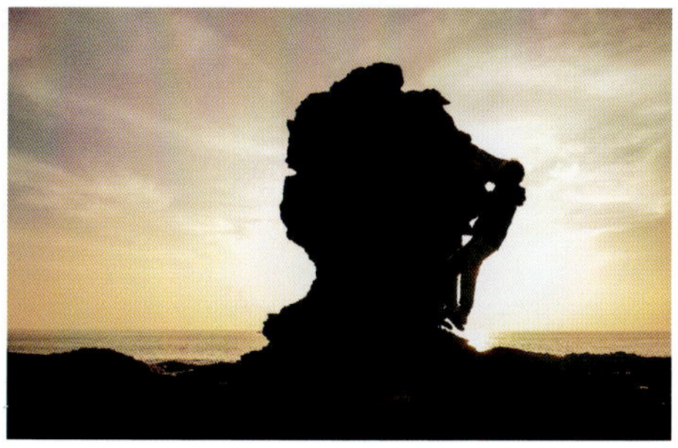

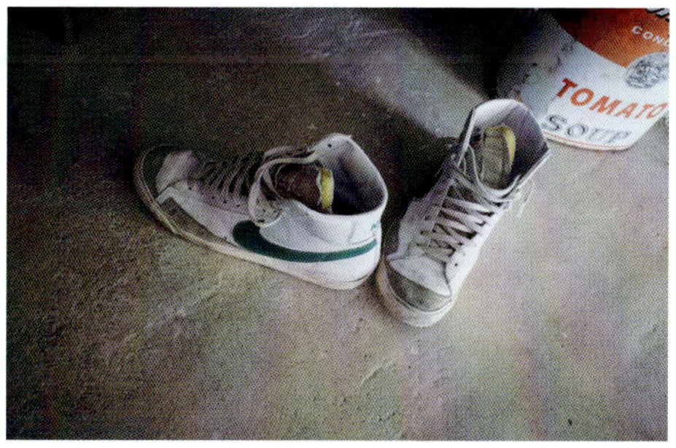

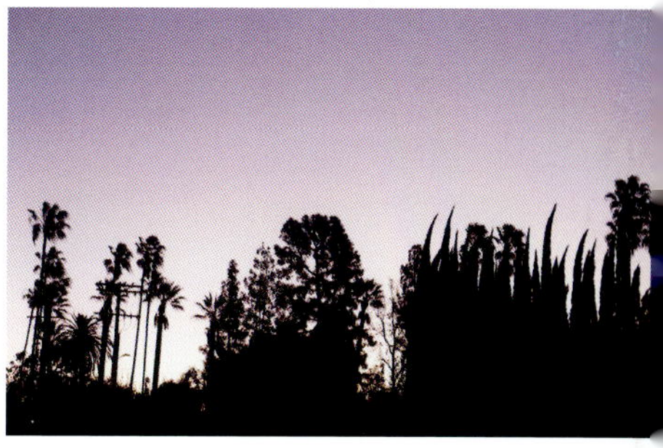

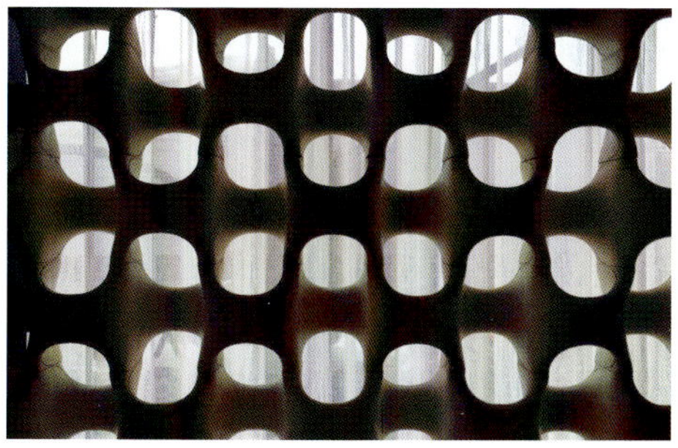

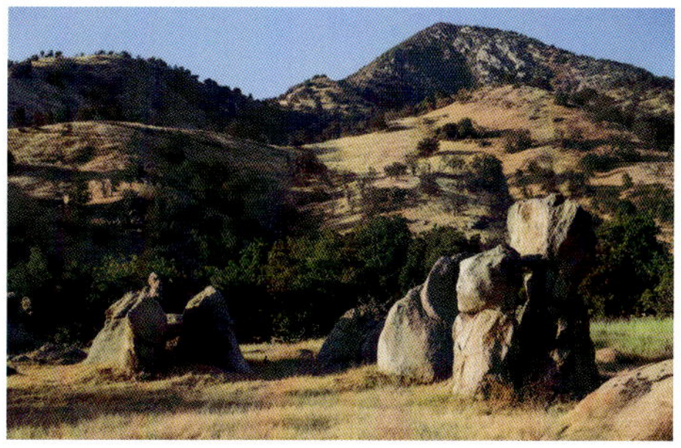

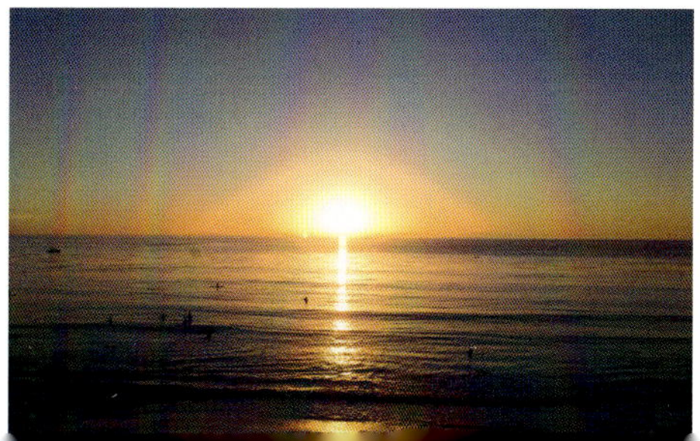

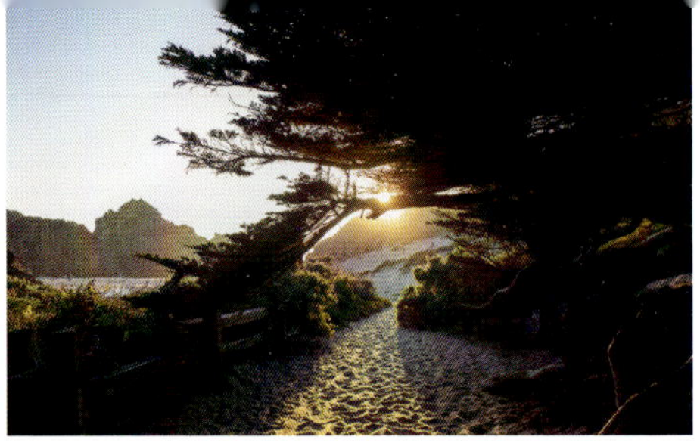

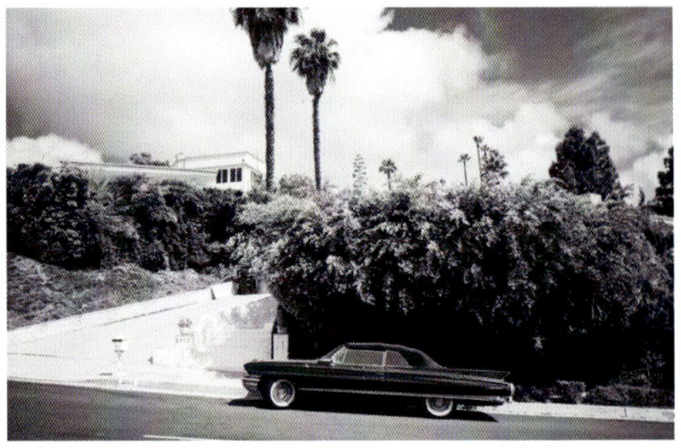

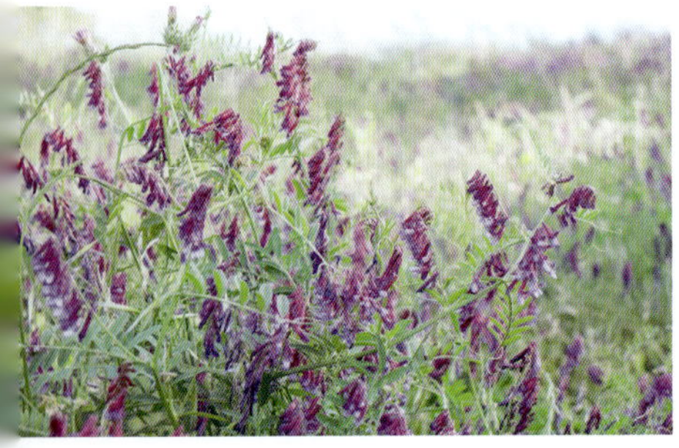

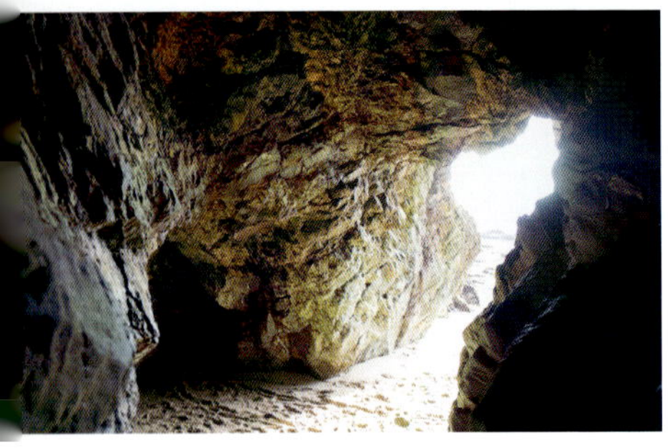

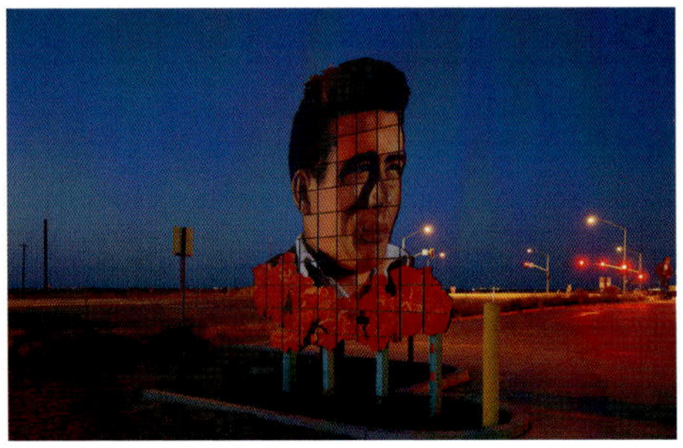

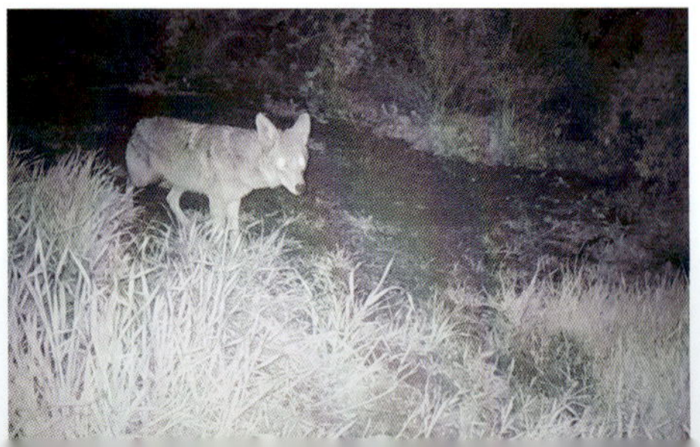

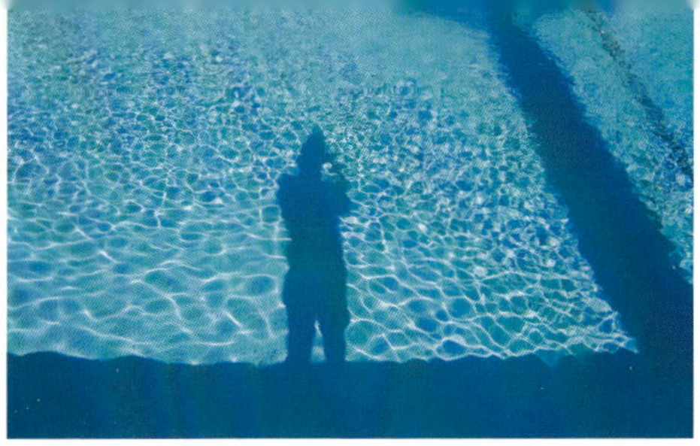
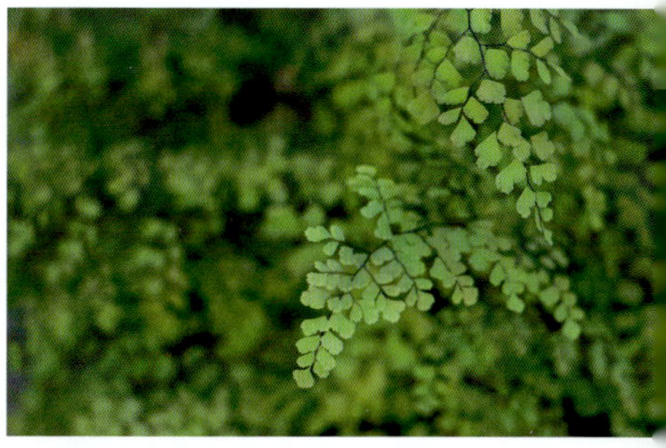
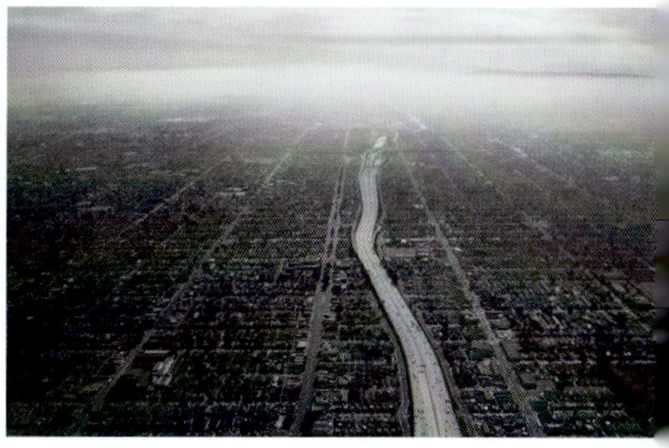
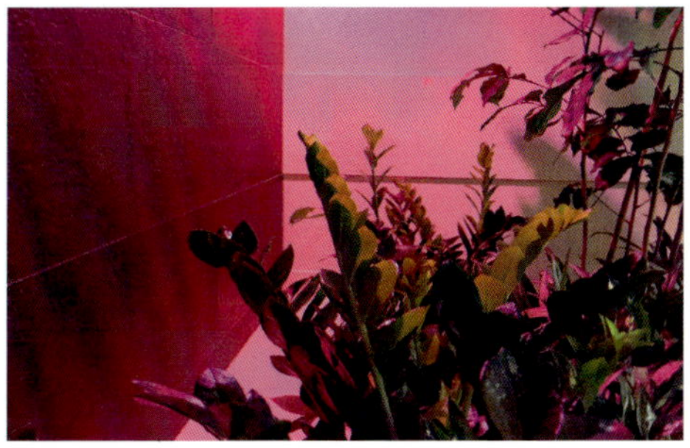
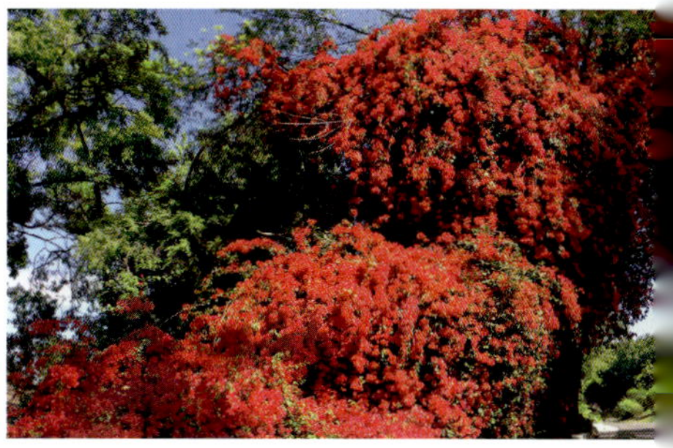
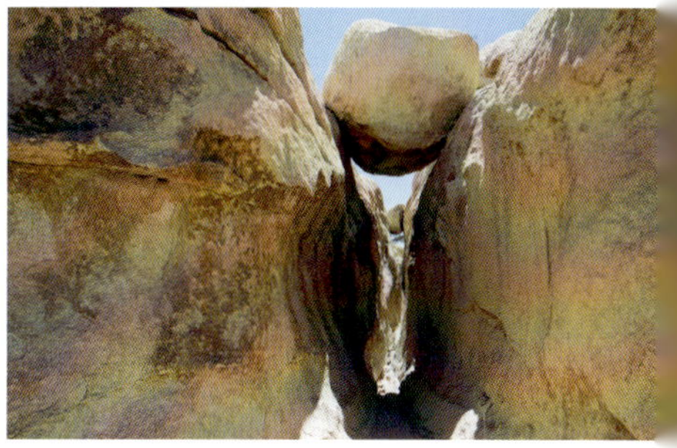
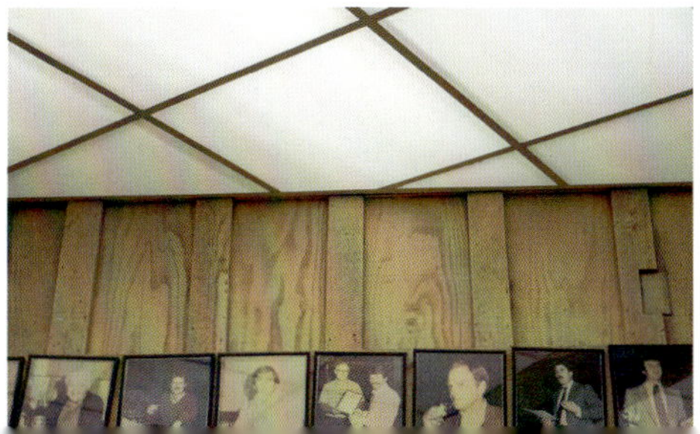

Credits

The Tree House
(1970)

Commission
Private, courtesy Bernard Judge and Blaine Mallory

Architect
Bernard Judge

Residents
Bernard Judge and Blaine Mallory

Photo Assistant
Albert Fu

A House in Malibu
(2013)

Commission
Private, courtesy homeowner

Architect
Tadao Ando

Architect of Record
Marmol Radziner

Photo Assistants
Jeff Gros, Justin Hollenkamp, Huey Tran, Chris Moore

Sheats-Goldstein Residence
(1963)

Commission
Vogue Russia

Architect
John Lautner

Resident
James Goldstein

Photo Assistants
Albert Fu, Kevin Gray

Broad Residence
(1994)

Commission
Architectural Digest

Architect
Frank Gehry

Residents
Eli and Edythe Broad

Interior Designer
Rose Tarlow

Landscape Architect
Rios Clementi Hale Studios

Producing Editor
Anita Sarsidi

Photo Assistants
Jeff Gros, Albert Fu, Tim Hirschmann, Brian Overend

The Garcia House
(1962)

Commission
Private, courtesy John McIlwee
and Bill Damaschke

Architect
John Lautner

Residents
John McIlwee and Bill Damaschke

Restoration
Marmol Radziner

Interior Designer
Darren Brown

Landscape Architect
Studio John Sharp

Prop Stylist
Blake Bachman

Photo Assistants
Huey Tran, Albert Fu

Drone Pilot
Justin Harrison

Ca Tana
(1992)

Commission
Private, courtesy Roger
Thomas and Art Libera

Architect
Daniel Solomon

Residents
Roger Thomas and Art Libera

Restoration
Kuth Ranieri Architects

Photo Assistant
Huey Tran

The Pilot House
(1948)

Commission
Private, courtesy Mary Weatherford
and Oliver M. Furth

Architects
A. Quincy Jones and Whitney R. Smith

Resident
Mary Weatherford

Restoration
Escher GuneWardena Architecture

Interior Designer
Oliver M. Furth

Landscape Architects
Native Sanctuary and
Tivoli Landscape Design

Photo Assistant
Huey Tran, Adam Matijasevic

Ichpa Mayapan
(1970)

Commission
Architectural Digest

Architect
Howard Lapham

Residents
Michael Smith and James Costos

Producing Editor
Anita Sarsidi

Photo Assistant
Albert Fu

Pittman Dowell Residence
(2009)
and Serulnic House
(1952)

Commission
Apollo

Architects
Michael Maltzan, Richard Neutra

Residents
Lari Pittman and Roy Dowell

Photo Assistant
Albert Fu

The Segel House
(1979)

Commission
Architectural Digest

Architect
John Lautner

Resident
Jamie McCourt

Restoration
Michael Kovac

Interior Designer
Waldo Fernandez

Producing Editor
Anita Sarsidi

Photo Assistants
Albert Fu, Huey Tran

John Furnish Residence
(1966)

Commission
Architectural Digest

Residents
Elton John and David Furnish

Interior Designer
Martyn Lawrence Bullard

Landscape Architect
Inner Gardens

Producing Editor
Carlos Mota

Photo Assistants
Albert Fu, Jeff Gros, Chris Moore

Tin House
(1972)

Commission
Architectural Digest

Architect
Frank Gehry

Residents
Jillian and Patrick Dempsey

Interior Designer
Estee Stanley

Landscape Architect
Scott Shrader

Producing Editor
Carlos Mota

Photo Assistants
Terrence Patrick, Harry Eelman

The Guest House
(1993)

Commission
Veranda

Residents
Tony Duquette, Hutton Wilkinson

Editor
Carolyn Englefield

Photo Assistants
Jeff Gros, Spencer Amonwatvorakul

The Strick House
(1963)

Commission
Private, courtesy Michael and Gabrielle Boyd, and Douglas Woods

Architect
Oscar Niemeyer

Residents
Michael and Gabrielle Boyd

Restoration
Michael and Gabrielle Boyd

Photo Assistant
Huey Tran

The Shaw House
(1974)

Commission
Private, courtesy Mark Haddawy

Architect
Will Shaw

Resident
Mark Haddawy

Restoration
Mark Haddawy

Photo Assistant
Huey Tran

The Stein House
(1949)

Commission
Private, courtesy Adam and
Kate Blackman, and Sean Yashar

Architects
A. Quincy Jones and Whitney R. Smith

Residents
Adam and Kate Blackman

Photo Assistant
Albert Fu

A Retreat in Bel Air
(2014)

Commission
Architectural Digest

Architect
Chad Oppenheim

Property Owner
Michael Bay

Interior Designers
Lorraine Letendre, Lynda Murray

Producing Editor
Michael Reynolds

Photo Assistants
Albert Fu, Henry Han

Barrymore Residence
(1957)

Commission
Private, courtesy Drew Barrymore

Resident
Drew Barrymore

Art Direction
Anna Golino, Francesca de la Fuente

Photo Assistants
Huey Tran, Jake Caminero

The Steinman House
(1956)

Commission
Architectural Digest

Architects
Craig Ellwood and Jerrold Lomax

Residents
Albert and Holly Baril

Restoration
Michael Boyd

Interior Design
Michael Boyd

Producing Editor
Robert Rufino

Photo Assistant
Albert Fu

Acknowledgments